IRELAND
A NEW ECONOMIC
1780–1939

IRELAND

A New Economic History

1780–1939

❧

CORMAC Ó GRÁDA

CLARENDON PRESS   OXFORD

Oxford University Press, Great Clarendon Street, Oxford OX2 6DP
Oxford New York
Athens Auckland Bangkok Bogota Bombay
Buenos Aires Calcutta Cape Town Dar es Salaam
Delhi Florence Hong Kong Istanbul Karachi
Kuala Lumpur Madras Madrid Melbourne
Mexico City Nairobi Paris Singapore
Taipei Tokyo Toronto
and associated companies in
Berlin Ibadan

Oxford is a trade mark of Oxford University Press

Published in the United States by
Oxford University Press Inc., New York

British Library Cataloguing in Publication Data
Data available

Library of Congress Cataloging in Publication Data
Ó Gráda, Cormac.
Ireland: a new economic history, 1780-1939 / Cormac Ó Gráda.
p. cm.
Includes bibliographical references and index.
1. Ireland—Economic conditions. I. Title. II. Title: Ireland,
a new economic history, 1780-1939.
HC260.5.O435 1994 330.9415—dc20 93-49444
ISBN 0-19-820598-8

3 5 7 9 10 8 6 4 2

Printed in Great Britain
on acid-free paper by
Bookcraft Ltd., Midsomer Norton, Avon

PREFACE

Despite considerable research activity in the field since the 1950s, general accounts of the Irish economy in the past are few. The present volume therefore seeks to fill a perceived gap. It combines the fruits of recent research by others, much of it in dissertations and the professional journals, and of new work of my own. The combination may suggest a textbook, though in truth a good deal of the material presented is too fresh for the usual textbook treatment. I hope that specialists will find something novel here. At the same time, I have tried hard to aim the volume also at a broader, non-specialist readership. The methodology is eclectic and inter-disciplinary. The 'new' in the subtitle acknowledges the book's cliometric debt, but only occasionally, when the topic really seems to require it, is the discussion technical.

In a general account such as this it is difficult to know when to begin and when to end. Economic epochs are loosely defined: historians disagree even about the timing of the Industrial Revolution in England. For Ireland the Act of Union in 1800 might seem an obvious starting-point. It certainly was a landmark in the political history of Ireland, but it had little immediate economic effect, and even its long-term economic impact has been exaggerated in the past. I open the account around 1780 because this coincides loosely with the beginnings of the Industrial Revolution in Ireland, and marks the publication of Arthur Young's famous *Tour*. The end-date, 1939, is also rather arbitrary. I rejected the good case for extending the story to the mid-1950s on the ground that I had already done enough work for one book: much about the period between the 1930s and the 1950s remains uncharted territory for the economic historian.

The sequence of the chapters is broadly chronological, though those expecting a blow-by-blow narrative will be disappointed. The Famine bisects the discussion of agriculture and population; the account of in-dustrialization (or the lack of it) in Chapters 12 and 13 straddles the Famine, and that of banking in Chapter 14 largely ignores the constitu-tional changes of 1920–1. The final section of the book (Chapters 15 to 17), which covers the post-1921 period, is inevitably more policy-oriented than the rest. While the focus throughout is usually on aggregates and averages, I often invoke stories and details of individual firms or agents, mostly taken from contemporary accounts and archives, both for their inherent interest and in order to illustrate particular points. The diagrams, cartoons, and photographs serve the same rhetorical function. Inevitably, the book contains its share of idiosyncracies and gaps. These reflect in part the current state of research in the field and the availability of sources, but also my own blind spots and preferences. In revising, I have attempted to be more comprehensive and to stamp out self-indulgence.

Some of the ideas and results reported here have already been aired in different form in the pages of the *Economic History Review*, the *Journal of Economic History*, *Demography*, the *Bulletin of Economic Research*, *Irish Economic and Social History*, the *Agricultural History Review*, *Irish Historical Studies*, *Studia Historica Finlandica*, the *New History of Ireland*, and in various conference volumes. I am grateful to the editors of these journals and books for allowing me to recycle and build on earlier work in this form. Some of the material on agricultural and demographic history presented in my *Ireland Before and After the Famine* (Manchester, 1988; revised edition, 1993) is summarized here in less technical form. Unless otherwise specified, references are to the revised edition.

Ron Weir, Peter Solar, and Joel Mokyr went to the trouble of reading virtually the whole book in draft for me, and produced—as always—pages of nearly always valuable and occasionally scathing suggestions. The same goes for OUP's readers. Several others kindly agreed to read sections in draft: they include Andy Bielenberg, Austin Bourke, Sean Boyle, Forrest Capie, Leslie Clarkson, Louis Cullen, Mary Daly, David Dickson, Joe Durkan, Stanley Engerman, David Fitzpatrick, Frank Geary, Tim Guinnane, Cathal Guiomard, Tim Hatton, Lynn Kiesling, Kieran Kennedy, Antoin Murphy, Diarmuid Ó Gráda, Kevin O'Rourke, Vivienne Pollock, Ron Rudin, Brendan Walsh, Kevin Whelan, and Jeff Williamson. I have done the same for some of them in the past; I hope I can repay the others in due course. Tony Morris of Oxford University Press was supportive throughout. Míle buíochas acu go léir: my thanks to them all.

I am grateful to the University College, Dublin's Committee for the Encouragement of Research for awarding me a Presidential Fellowship in 1991–2. The Fellowship allowed me to virtually finish this book. I am also grateful for research support from the Wellcome Foundation, the UCD Faculty of Arts Research Fund, and the US National Science Foundation. I also wish to thank the Rockefeller Foundation for awarding me a residency at its splendid Bellagio Center in April–May 1992 and my referees for persuading the Center that I was worth having there. Stephen Hannon of the Department of Geography, UCD, produced the maps, and Noel

Kissane, Éilís Ní Dhuibhne, Liz Kirwan, and Vivienne Pollock suggested some of the illustrations.

I wish to thank the following for permission to use material in their care: the National Library of Ireland, the National Archives, the Irish Banks Standing Committee, the Bank of Ireland, the Bank of England, the Royal Bank of Scotland, Allied Irish Banks, Cork Archives Council, UCD archives, the Rotunda Hospital, the Royal College of Physicians of Ireland, the Royal Bank of Scotland, the Royal Dublin Society, the Ontario Provincial Archives, and the Public Record Offices in London and Belfast. I wish also to record my thanks to the following archivists for their help and courtesy: Brian Donnelly, Lesley Hall, Ken Hannigan, Seamus Helferty, Tony Lambkin, Patricia McCarthy, Elizabeth Ogborn, and Sarah Ward-Perkins.

CORMAC Ó GRÁDA

Dublin
4 January 1993

CONTENTS

PART V   377

LIST OF PLATES

LIST OF FIGURES

KEY TO ARCHIVES CITED IN
THE TEXT

AIBA   Allied Irish Bank Archive
BofEA   Bank of England Archive
BofIA   Bank of Ireland Archive
IFC   Irish Folklore Commission
IBSCA   Irish Bank Standing Committee Archives
NA   National Archives
NBA   National Bank Archives
NLI   National Library of Ireland
PRO   Public Record Office (London)
PRONI   Public Record Office of Northern Ireland
RIA   Royal Irish Academy
RCPI   Royal College of Physicians of Ireland
TCD   Trinity College Dublin
UCDA   University College Dublin Archives

PART I

I

A False Dawn? Population and Living Standards, 1780–1815

Ireland's case affords so striking an illustration of the doctrine which
Mr Malthus has advanced in the late Essay on Population, that we are
surprised he did not enter into it more in detail.

ANON. (T. R. MALTHUS), 1808[1]

It may seem a matter of just surprize, that a country, fertile and well
situated, as this island, and which became a part of the British empire
at a very early period, should still betray so many symptoms of
poverty, rudeness, and ignorance.

HORATIO TOWNSEND, 1810[2]

This story begins, predictably enough, with population. Since the seventeenth century if not earlier, the Irish have been outliers in the demographic
history of Europe, attracting comments and analysis from observers far and
near. Both before and after the Great Famine of the 1840s, Ireland has
offered a particularly vivid case-study of the link between population and
economy. Before the Famine the fear was of population outstripping what
the soil could yield in food; later it was of the link between a declining
population and poor economic performance. Pre-Famine demographic
patterns seemed to imply that poverty prompted people to marry sooner,
but the popular historiographical image of the post-Famine Irish is of a
people traumatized into becoming the most marriage-shy in Europe.

The ideas of the great English economist Thomas Malthus have loomed
large both in contemporary controversy and in historiography. In 1796, in
an early formulation of his 'principle of population', Malthus denied the
conventional wisdom of his day that a country's happiness might be
measured by the size of its population. 'Increasing population is the most
certain possible sign of the happiness and prosperity of a state,' he declared,
'but the actual population may be only a sign of the happiness that is
past.'[3] By this criterion Irishmen and Irishwomen in the 1790s should have
been very happy people, since the population of Ireland was then growing

as fast as anywhere else in Europe.[4] Yet the few references to Ireland in
successive editions of Malthus's *Essay on the Principle of Population* are far
from supporting such a cheerful reading. In that famous work Malthus
blamed the endemic grinding poverty of the Irish, the famine of 1800–1
(which killed thousands of people),[5] and even the political unrest of the
1790s, on overpopulation. And still the poverty, if such there was, failed
to bring population growth to a halt, for on the eve of the Great Famine
(1846) Ireland contained 8.5 million people, against about 5 million in
1800.

Before jumping to the conclusion that Malthus misunderstood the connection between happiness and population growth, the effects of habit and
culture must be borne in mind—even when they cannot be measured.
Indeed Malthus made the point in his own Anglo-centric way: 'the cheapness of this nourishing root [the potato], joined with ignorance and
barbarity of the people, which have prompted [the Irish] to follow their
inclinations with no prospect than immediate bare subsistence, have encouraged marriage to such a degree that the population is pushed much
beyond the industry and present resources of the country.' Elsewhere,
showing more empathy, Malthus attributed the low living standards and
rapid population growth of the Irish Catholic masses to their lowly social
and political status. The lack of upward mobility and of a political voice
gave them little incentive to operate the 'preventive check'. This anticipates
the claim of modern sociologists that, given the right conditions, even the
poorest societies develop their own means of population control. The
lack or removal of a 'prestige structure' forces the breakdown of such a
homeostatic demographic regime.[6]

However, emphasis on another strain in Malthus's work leaves the way
open for population growth to occur while living standards are *declining*.
Suppose, to begin with, population is growing at a sustainable rate: this
rate could, of course, be zero. Consider now the effect of a medical
invention such as smallpox inoculation. Faster population growth should be
the immediate result, but in time this should cause the supply of labour to
outstrip the demand, putting downward pressure on wages. Eventually a
new equilibrium growth rate would be reached. In the meantime population
growth would be higher than previously, despite falling living standards.
In this scenario, the faster growth is a temporary, disequilibrium phenomenon.[7] Did such a scenario describe Ireland in the 1790s and 1800s?

Contemporary opinion in Ireland held that the last two or three decades
of the eighteenth century were, broadly speaking, decades of economic

progress. Agricultural output and rents undoubtedly rose, traditional industries such as provisioning, brewing, and distilling prospered, and the new techniques of the Industrial Revolution also made inroads. All sectors benefited from buoyant conditions in foreign, especially British, markets. The famine of 1800–1, noted by Malthus, was a reminder of the underlying inequalities, economic and political. Yet the economy continued to grow, spurred on by wartime demand, and the Irish share of British merchandise imports and exports managed to hold its own. The huge rise in property transactions bespoke a construction boom in the towns. However, a serious economic panic in 1810, followed by a decline in agricultural prices, and another subsistence crisis in 1817–19, augured in conditions that henceforth would be considered typical in Ireland. Soon both earlier progress and the harder times that were to follow would be put down to political factors.

1.1 Population Change

Ireland's first successful attempt at a census took place in 1821 (compared with 1801 in Britain, 1800 in France, 1790 in the USA, and 1750 in Sweden). 'Success' here is a relative matter; a previous attempt (1811–12) had been abandoned half-way, and historians deem none of the three completed pre-Famine censuses fully satisfactory. Even in 1841 the census allegedly 'inspired such feelings of alarm in the counties of Limerick and Clare, that the whole country was illuminated, hill and valley, with lighted firebrands. In the county of Westmeath there was scarcely a head of poultry left alive, an opinion having gone abroad that a tax or rate was to be levied on them.'[8] In this instance the reporter got quite carried away; for the record, over 200,000 hens and ducks survived the 'slaughter' of census night in Westmeath. Nevertheless, the 1821 and 1841 census returns are considered deficient, not only because some people were afraid or suspicious, but also because of the sloppiness or ignorance of enumerators. On the other hand, the 1831 figure may be inflated—or, ironically, nearer the truth—because the enumerators were paid (or assumed that they would be paid) on a piece-rate basis.[9]

The kind of alternative evidence used by historical demographers in other European countries to reconstruct the size and characteristics of pre-censal populations is sparse in Ireland. Because surviving Irish parish records were in general less scrupulously kept and carried less detail than, say, French or even English registers, they have less to reveal to historians. Unofficial local censuses are quite rare. Still, the outlines of demographic

Table   1.1. *Provincial   population   growth   rate*
estimates (% p.a.)

	1753-91	1791-1821	1821-41
Leinster	1.0 to 1.4	1.3	0.6
Munster	1.5 to 1.9	1.6	1.1
Ulster	1.8 to 2.2	1.1	0.9
Connacht	1.5 to 2.1	2.0	1.2
Ireland	1.4 to 1.9	1.4 (1.6)	0.9 (0.6)

Sources: Dickson, Ó Gráda and Daultrey, 'Hearth Tax,
Household Size and Irish Population Change'; Vaughan and
Fitzpatrick, *Irish Historical Statistics*, 3: 15-6. The bracketed
estimates for 1791-1821 and 1821-41 reflect Lee's suggested
correction of the 1821 estimate.

change before 1821 are plain enough, and an account of pre-censal population growth can be cobbled together from hearth-tax data, with some
help from other sources.[10] Current assessments show population rising from
2-2.5 million in the wake of the disastrous famine of 1740-1 to about 4
million in 1790, and 5 million in 1800. The 1821 census suggested a total
of 6.8 million. Population rose more slowly thereafter, to reach about 8.5
million on the eve of the Famine. The range of estimates just quoted
implies that Irish population growth was unusually fast by European
standards in the second half of the eighteenth century. After 1821 it was
less exceptional.

The regional pattern is described in Table 1.1. The surprise here is not
so much Connacht's headlong population growth, as the relatively slow
growth in Ulster after 1790, where modern industry was making greatest
headway. Within Ulster, hearth-tax data imply that population grew
fastest in the less developed west. Connacht's share of Irish population rose
from about 13 per cent in the 1740s to 16 per cent in 1815.[11]

Explanations of the Irish pre-Famine population explosion bring us back
to Malthus. Traditionally the age at marriage has been their chief focus.
Contemporaries who wrote on this subject almost invariably declared that
the Irish married early; with the spread of Malthusian thinking, this belief
was accompanied by reprimand. Indeed, in evidence before the Emigration
Commissioners of 1827, Malthus himself judged that Ireland's overpopulation problem was due to early marriage.[12]

The simplest Malthusian economic-demographic model consists of two basic relations. The first is technological; it states that the return to labour is a function of the land/labour ratio. The second states that population growth is a function of income; rising living standards prompt a decline in mortality and earlier and more frequent marriages. Together these two relations generate an equilibrium or sustainable population.[13] If population growth for some reason outstrips income, then a combination of 'positive' or 'preventive' checks must restore the balance. The positive checks—anything that conspires to increase the death-rate—are the nastier. Malthus objected to reductions in the birth rate—the preventive check—other than through sexual abstinence or 'moral restraint'.

Ireland on the eve of the Famine has been described as a 'case study in Ricardian and Malthusian economics'.[14] How does the label suit the period under review here? Curiously, some historians who accepted the first part of the Malthusian model—that Irish poverty stemmed from land hunger—added a new twist to the second part, by claiming that marriage in Ireland was an inferior good. 'The wretchedness of living conditions made marriage seem a welcome relief . . . the utter hopelessness with which [he] had to survey the future inclined [the Irishman] towards early marriage.'[15] If the implications of the original Malthusian model are bleak, those of the revised version implied here by Connell are apocalyptic. Now a *reduction* in living standards induces a *rise* in numbers; population is thus on a roller-coaster to disaster. There is no check, no equilibrating process. The minimum requirement for a convincing test of this neo-Malthusian model is some understanding of the trends in the age at marriage and living standards between 1780 and 1845. Comprehensive, definitive data on either, alas, are still unavailable. Let us take the age at marriage first.

The scarcity of statistical sources on marriage age and much else increases the temptation to invoke literary sources, whether fictional or documentary. Brian Merriman's *Cúirt an Mheánoíche* (Midnight Court), a tempting source for the demographic historian, highlights the pitfalls. The main theme of Merriman's rabelaisian poem, which was composed around 1780, is *gan fear in aghaidh triúr sa Mhumhain dá mná*, i.e. the reluctance of the menfolk of Munster to marry. The result was 'an empty Ireland whose fields had gone to seed, while its people grew old and grey'. Yet the implication that the people of Merriman's own County Clare married late or not at all is awkward, since in reality population growth in Clare was at an all-time high in Merriman's time. The example recalls Laslett's famous critique of those who invoked literary sources such as Shakespeare's *Romeo and Juliet* to argue for precocious marriage in early modern Europe.[16] Similarly,

Merriman alluded twice to contraception in *An Chúirt*. Contraception could
explain the low incidence of illegitimacy and premarital conception implied
by surviving pre-Famine Catholic parish registers; but surely it is more
plausible to argue that Merriman's central themes bore little relation to
either contemporary population trends or sexual mores.[17]

So what is the message of other literary evidence about the age at
marriage in Ireland in the late eighteenth century? Remember that it is
women's age at first marriage that is crucial for population growth.
Merriman's *Cúirt an Mheánoíche* apart, the qualitative, literary evidence on
this question is clear-cut: Irishwomen married young. The litany of quotations in Connell's classic study of pre-Famine Irish population is conclusive
enough. A fair inference is that the Irish married earlier than their British
contemporaries, though greater precision is impossible. Yet mean marriage
age was almost certainly never as low as Connell implied from the literary
sources. One reason for this, overlooked by Connell, is that qualitative
accounts usually reflect the typical or most common age at marriage rather
than the average, that is, they refer to the mode rather than the arithmetic
mean. A good example of the ensuing ambiguity is given by Henry Inglis,
who wrote of the Dingle area in west Kerry in 1834 that 'fourteen and
thirteen are common ages for the marriage of girls; fifteen is not considered
at all an early age for marriage; and there are even instances of their being
contracted at so early an age as twelve.' The census of 1841 hardly supports
Inglis, unless Dingle was very different from the rest of Kerry: it returns
99.5 per cent of Kerrywomen aged 13–16 years as single. Given the
skewness of the distribution of marriage ages, a modal age at marriage of
18 or 19 is entirely consistent with an average age at first marriage of 20–2
years.[18] Another caveat is that literary evidence usually referred to the
poor, who in pre-Famine Ireland tended to marry young.

There is, nevertheless, some statistical evidence in favour of the view
that marriage age was low in the early nineteenth century. For instance,
the medical registers of Dublin's Rotunda Lying-In Hospital imply that
working-class Dublinwomen married in their very early twenties in the
1810s. Pioneering studies of local sources in Ulster by Valerie Morgan and
William Macafee imply the same throughout much of that province. In the
south, data collected by a Limerick medical practitioner between 1822 and
1839 based on information gained from his working-class patients suggest
that the modal age of women's marriage was 20 years, and the mean age
22.1 years. Copies of the 1821 census lists from two parishes in south
Kilkenny and part of Waterford City again imply that women married

young. The evidence is in the gap between the ages of married women in their twenties and thirties and that of their eldest resident child. That gap was 22–4 years, which is consistent with an age at marriage of 21–2 years. While these snippets of data may fail to confirm the impressionistic evidence that most women married before they were 20 or 21, an average marriage age of 22 years is none the less low by contemporary European standards: it is at the lower bound of what statistician John Hajnal dubbed the 'European marriage pattern'.[19]

Connell's model of pre-Famine population growth is predicated on a decline in mean marriage age at some point before or around 1750. That decline cannot be documented. Indeed, Connell quotes William Petty's claim, made in the 1670s, that 'Irish women marry upon their first capacity'. Half a century earlier, the anonymous author of *Advertisements for Ireland* explained 'the increase in the numbers of the mere Irish' like this: 'they generally (be they never so poor) affect to marry timely . . . and take much felicity and content in their procreation and issue.' The literary evidence, in sum, cannot contradict the hypothesis that early marriage was the norm in Ireland long before Connell's period. Quantitative evidence on marriage age in the seventeenth and eighteenth centuries is sparse. Dickson's recent reworking of Cromwellian transplantation certificates—travel passes granted to families banished to Connacht in the wake of the wars of the 1640s and 1650s—belies Petty's impression that women married in their teens, but none the less indicates a low mean age at marriage, 22–3 years for women. Parish register data are few: one straw in the wind is the Church of Ireland register for Lisburn in County Armagh, an analysis of which implies a mean marriage age of 18–19 years for women in the late seventeenth and early eighteenth centuries.[20]

Historians have made much of the likelihood that the poor married earlier than the rich. Indeed Merriman's *Cúirt an Mheánoíche* has been interpreted as an attack on prosperous farmers for marrying late and cautiously. Labourers, by contrast, are supposed to have married young and for love.[21] Without denying the difference, Merriman should not be taken too literally in this case either, because popular ballads with a very different theme—farmers' sons eager to marry loved ones *gan bó, gan punt, gan ábhar spré* (without cow, pound, or dowry)—also abound. Perhaps the reality was less a case of Merriman's unwilling young men, than of parents who decided who married whom. The farmer's daughter, forced to marry the old man and forget the handsome *spailpín*, is the other side of that story: *'is mar gheall ar bhólacht a phóstar mná* (it is for the cows that women are

married).' The ballads suggest the operation of a strict marriage regime in
farming communities. But if marriages among the propertied classes put
economic considerations first, this does not mean that such marriages were
always loveless affairs. On the other hand, the free-wheeling romantic
element in labourers' marriages must not be exaggerated. The poor married
young, it is true, but also with an eye to security and mutual support.[22]

Does all this mean that marriage in Ireland was an inferior good, in the
economic sense that impoverishment increased nuptiality? Not necessarily
so, since the relative price of marriage and children differed across class. It
is more instructive, if less tidy, to think of different, culturally based
marriage regimes for rich and poor. This takes account of the paradox
highlighted in the research of Irish historical geographers, that pre-Famine
population growth was fastest in marginal upland areas.[23] For the settled
farming class living off the good land, the standard demographic regime
even before the Famine was late-arranged marriages, impartible inheritance,
and no subdivision. For the poor who eked out a living on the margins of
cultivation, such controls held little appeal. Holdings on the poorer land
were smaller, definitive celibacy rarer. Within each group, marriage was a
normal good, and a decline in living standards reduced its marriage rate.
But the effect on the overall average marriage age depended on trends in
income distribution and the relative size of both groups as well as on trends
in average incomes. A reduction in nuptiality among the poor, holding
income constant, required 'a better education and a deeper sense, not of
propriety alone, but of politeness and social decency'.[24]

Marital fertility was presumably high, though statistical corroboration
for this is scarce too. Family reconstitution, a technique which generates
past mortality, nuptiality, and fertility patterns from parish registers, and
has proved so revealing elsewhere, has attracted few Irish practitioners.[25] It
returns a perplexing result in one case, Valerie Morgan's pioneering analysis
of the Protestant (Anglican) population of Coleraine in County Derry.
Table 1.2, which reproduces family reconstitution data on the average
interval between births in a range of areas, puts the Coleraine study in
perspective. It implies that marital fertility was very low there in the
eighteenth and early nineteenth centuries. To reinforce the point, I have
included part of the poverty-stricken Ormansag region of Hungary, an area
where in the nineteenth century sexual abstinence was only the least brutal
of several means used to keep numbers down.[26] Note that the computed
mean birth interval in Coleraine rivalled that of the Hungarian parishes.
The irony is that the mean age at marriage of Coleraine Protestants was

Table 1.2. *Mean birth intervals* (in months)

Area	1st and 2nd children	2nd and 3rd children	3rd and 4th children	Remarks
Meulan	18.5	20.8	21.7	CF (1740–89)
Crulai (18C)	24.1	21.7	22.7	CF
Coleraine (1769–1847)	31.7	29.4	37.2	Excluding final births
Irish Quakers (1750–99)	20.5	20.5	22.4	Families with 4+ births
Colyton (1540–1769)	25.9	28.8	30.9	CF
French Canada (1700–30)	21.0	22.6	22.9	CF
Tourouvre (1781–1800)	20.9	24.0	24.8	Families of 6+ children
Vaszlo and Besence (1791–1820)	39.5	38.8	37.0	CF

Note: CF indicates complete families.

Sources: M. Lachiver, *La Population de Meulan* (Paris, 1969); H. Charbonneau, *Tourouvre-sur-Perche aux xviie et xviiie siècles* (Paris, 1970), 152; E. Gautier and L. Henry, *La Population de Crulai, paroisse normande* (Paris, 1958), 141; J. Henripin, *La Population canadienne au début du xviiie siècle* (Paris, 1954), 94; E. A. Wrigley, 'Family Limitation in Pre-Industrial England', *EHR*, 11 (1966); Morgan, 'The Church of Ireland Registers of St Patrick's Coleraine'; Vann and Eversley, *Friends in Life and Death*, 153; R. Andorka, 'Un exemple de faible fecondité légitime dans une region de la Hongrie', *Annales de démographie historique* (1972), 45.

very low, 22.3 years for women and 23.4 years for men. Such a low mean is not easily squared with the long birth intervals reported in the table. Gaps in the Coleraine register due to carelessness or the underreporting of infants who died very young probably explain the paradox.

Vann and Eversley's comparative study of the demography of Irish and English Quaker communities in the eighteenth and nineteenth centuries returns a more reassuring result. It shows that the marital fertility of Quaker Irishwomen was consistently higher than that of Quaker women in rural southern England. The Irish advantage (discussed more fully in Chapter 4) was substantial, strikingly so in the case of newly-wed women and those aged over 35. The Irish Quakers were mostly descendants of seventeenth-century immigrants from England. Though their interaction with the indigenous population was limited, their high fertility is probably a measure of their 'Irishness'.[27]

Mortality levels and trends in this period also remain almost a blank. With one important exception—inoculation against smallpox—medical innovations probably had little impact. Inoculation undoubtedly made its mark. In Dublin city, the only area where a comparison between two dates is possible, the change is striking. Smallpox accounted for one-fifth of all reported deaths in the capital between 1661 and 1745, but only 3 per cent in the 1830s. Admittedly Dublin's experience was not replicated elsewhere: during the 1830s smallpox was responsible for only 7 per cent of the reported deaths of children of 5 years and under in Dublin, but it accounted for 11 per cent nationally, 16 per cent in Limerick city, and 13 per cent in County Mayo. Moreover, the role of inoculation against smallpox in the pre-1770 population advance was probably small, so inoculation is best seen as contributing to the acceleration that occurred during the eighteenth century.[28]

It is tempting to base a Malthusian story about eighteenth- and early nineteenth-century population trends on the contrasting emphases of Thomas Newenham, who in 1805 posited a 'gap in famines' in Ireland after the famine of 1740–1, and William Wilde who, in the wake of the Great Famine, stressed the pervasiveness of subsistence crises in the immediate pre-Famine decades. However, evidence of considerable excess mortality in 1747–8, 1755, and 1766 has transformed Newenham's story of a 'gap in famines' into no more than a 'useful myth', and a closer examination of the later period shows Wilde's claims to have been exaggerated. Serious famines certainly occurred after 1800; famine-induced diseases killed thousands of people in 1800–1, and again in 1817–19. But mortality—40,000– 60,000 in each case—'would have been unremarkable by the standards of the 1750s',[29] and later subsistence crises, particularly those of 1822 and 1831, killed far fewer people. While the 'psycho-social perception of famine' was strong in such years, boosted no doubt by middle-class fears of disease, the toll in lives was small.[30] It would thus be wrong to build a case for a rising death rate in these years on an increase in the incidence of famine. Overall, while no firm data on mortality trends or indeed levels exist, some decline in mortality in the pre-Famine century is possible.

A little formal analysis may help at this stage. Analysing the Malthusian model in terms of elementary demand and supply schedules (Fig. 1.1), improvement in health will have shifted the population supply curve S_0S_0 outwards, to S_1S_1, i.e. it will have increased the supply associated with any given real wage. The demand for population, DD, is downward-sloping, reflecting the law of diminishing returns. The campaign against smallpox,

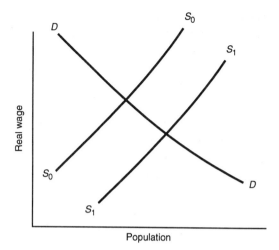

FIG. 1.1 Modelling population change

other things being equal, will thus on balance have reduced the equilibrium wage and living standards. Such a reduction will also have induced an increase in the age at marriage. Note too that only a once-off rise in population is indicated by these changes.

Clearly, there was more to it than this. If we allow also for a simultaneous, steady increase in the demand for labour, then sustained population growth at a constant real wage and age at marriage would have been possible. In such a scenario roughly constant nuptiality is a function of two countervailing forces: increases in both demand and supply. A nuptiality level previously associated with a steady population, is now, in the wake of medical improvements, associated with a rising population. Analogously, a rise in the demand for labour seems to nullify the effect of health improvement on the equilibrium birth- and death-rates.

1.2 Living Standards

Trends in living standards in late eighteenth and early nineteenth century Ireland remain elusive. Then as later, the country contained significant numbers both of urban professionals, traders, and manufacturers, and of comfortable rural farmers. An improvement in their lot in these decades is likely.[31] Numerically and historiographically more important are the landless and near-landless labourers and cottiers, and the following dis-

cussion refers mainly to them. The frequently cited impressions of two
celebrities, English agricultural writer Arthur Young and Scottish economist Adam Smith, both referring to the 1770s, deserve to be mentioned
here. Young, who toured Ireland in the mid-1770s, found the poor there
clothed 'very indifferently', and living in 'the most miserable looking
hovels that can well be conceived', but he was favourably impressed by the
diet dominated by potatoes and milk. For Young, the diet explained why
he found in Ireland poor people 'as athletic in their form, as robust, and as
capable of enduring labour as any upon earth'. In *The Wealth of Nations*
Adam Smith (who never visited Ireland) declared the Irish-born porters and
prostitutes of London 'the strongest men and the most beautiful women
perhaps in the British dominions' and put this down to the 'nourishing
quality' of their potato diet. Another basic, domestic fuel, was also widely
available in Young's time: he found the women 'roast[ing] their legs in
their cabbins till they are *fire* spotted'. Young's appraisal is a reminder of an
important point that remains valid up to the Famine: a wholesome diet and
plentiful, inexpensive domestic fuel in the form of turf compensated for the
tattered clothing and rudimentary housing of the Irish poor.[32] The low rate
of urbanization probably also helped, though even in the countryside the
widespread use of cast-off clothing, the damp climate, and the rudimentary
sanitary facilities and ubiquitous manure heaps cannot have improved the
state of people's health.[33]

   *Prátaí ar maidin, prátaí um nóin, is dá n-éireoinn meánoíche prátaí do
gheobhainn* (potatoes in the morning, potatoes at noon, and if I got up at
midnight, it would still be potatoes). The aphorism reflects the common
perception that the potato was the main food of the pre-Famine poor.
Bourke's ingenious political arithmetic confirms this, though the gargantuan
consumption implied by his findings—10–12 lb. (4–5 kilos) daily per
adult male—may seem astounding today. The following description of
poor people en route from north-west Cork to Canada in 1823 gives some
impression of how 'hooked' they were on the potato:[34]

It may be worth remarking as it is so characteristic of the fondness of the Irish for
potatoes, that the men preferred them to the cocoa, which they refused for several
days to taste till they saw the officers of the ship repeatedly breakfasting upon it.
The children during sickness called constantly for potatoes, refusing arrowroot or
any other aliment more congenial to their situation, and nothing could prevail on
man, woman, or child to eat plumb pudding which as is usual on ships board was
part of the Sunday's dinner. Few of them would eat the best English cheese and
when it was served out as part of their ration it was most commonly thrown
overboard.

A recent re-examination of data gathered by the 1836 Poor Inquiry provides a closer look at the diet of the bottom third or so of the population. It shows, not surprisingly, that the potato was universal in the 1830s. Milk was also common, though more likely to be skimmed; herrings and oatmeal featured too, though to a lesser extent, while butter and meat were rarities. The pattern was probably little different a generation earlier, though the quality of the potato and milk deteriorated in the interim. Not a very appealing diet, but a healthy one none the less: a recent comparison of Irish labourers' diets in 1839 and 1859 implies a marked deterioration in nutritional terms between those dates. Such detail on diet in the 1790s or 1800s is unavailable, though qualitative sources such as Young and Coquebert de Montbret indicate that the potato dominated. Even in Kilkenny, where beans, barley, and oaten bread had been common, labourers and their families had largely switched over to potatoes by 1800. The diffusion in the 1760s and 1770s of apple potatoes, 'not fit to eat before Christmas', meant that potatoes were available nearly all year long.[35] We return to the issue of pre-famine diet in Chapter 4.

Like turf and the potato, the widespread availability of a sustainable resource, seaweed, mitigated the poverty of those living along the southern and western coasts. A powerful booster of crop yields, seaweed entailed substituting labour for scarce land: gathering and hauling it inland were extremely labour-intensive tasks. In many places seaweed formed the main fertilizer for the potato crop, but sea sand and sea shells were also important. In the west Cork barony of Carbery in the early nineteenth century well over a thousand horse-cars were engaged in drawing sand distances of up to ten or twelve miles inland.[36]

Contemporary observers deemed the late eighteenth- and early nineteenth-century Irish very poor indeed. They noted that rudimentary comforts such as proper bedding and household furniture, a modicum of kitchen utensils, and decent clothing, items common or even taken for granted elsewhere, were rarely to be found in the cabins of the Irish. Wakefield, who spent much of 1808–10 in the country, declared in 1812 that 'an English, in comparison of an Irish labourer, knows not what poverty indicates'. In 1825 Quaker industrialist and philanthropist James Cropper reflected what he believed to be a consensus that the Irish poor were worse off than 'any other population in Europe'. Nor was poverty just a rural phenomenon: James Whitelaw's account of conditions in the poorer sections of Dublin in the 1790s is no more cheerful. Such snapshots are both evocative and telling, and a warning against complacency. Trends are more difficult to capture from travellers' impressions.[37]

In Britain (or England, at least) many contributions to the famous standard-of-living debate have focused on the trend in male workers' real wages. The limitations of this measure have also been stressed: its failure to take account of unemployment, its neglect of the labour of children, women, and the self-employed.[38] In Ireland, moreover, only a minority of workers were paid a money wage. Admittedly, in a well-integrated economy, the incomes of non-wage-earners would reflect those of workers directly involved in the labour-market. But even nominal wage series are scarce, and there is no comprehensive consumer price deflator for the period. Solar has improvised by proposing a series of cost-of-subsistence indices, based on weighted averages of oats, butter, and potato prices. These suggest a doubling in the cost of basic foods between the late 1770s and the early 1810s. The cost of clothing is likely to have fallen during this period, while information on housing is lacking. The Schumpeter–Gilboy English consumer price index virtually doubled between the late 1770s and the early 1810s, and the rise in the Irish cost of living cannot have been radically different.[39]

Arthur Young collected a good deal of information on nominal wages; his estimates of the wages paid to male agricultural labourers in the late 1770s average out at 6.7d. per day. Wakefield's quotations (c. 1810) are in the 10d. to 13d. range. In Dublin, building labourers' daily wages doubled between the 1780s and the early 1810s. Carpenters' daily wages in Cork rose from 18d. in 1771 to 24d. in 1780, 30d. in 1790, 39d. in 1795, and 52d. in 1815. The accounts of Bryan Bolger, a Dublin 'measurer' (or quantity surveyor), reveal the trends in the rates for a range of building trades (see Table 1.3).

The average rates paid rose in all the trades listed. Similar rises for plastering tasks and other carpentry work (e.g. roofing and ceiling joists) might be quoted. Unfortunately, these rises were largely wiped out by the rise in the cost of living. The daily rate paid to building workers fell back then from about 30d. around 1810 to 24d. by the 1820s.[40]

The contrast with the drop in the average weekly wages of Ulster cotton weavers from £2.33 in the 1790s to £1.58 in 1806–13 and £1.08 in 1813–20 is striking.[41] But the weavers—a privileged group at the outset— were under considerable pressure in these years. Their fortunes cannot be taken as an indication of general immiseration—any more than the plight of the British handloom weavers a few decades later reflects trends in British working-class standards generally. The most plausible inference to be drawn from Irish wage data between the 1780s and the early 1810s

Table 1.3. *Piece-rates in Dublin, c.1790–1810*

Period	No. of observations	Mean (pence)	Std. Deviation (pence)
Bricklaying and stonework (pence per perch)			
1789–1792	73	13.4	1.0
1793–1796	25	14.5	1.5
1797–1800	17	14.7	1.3
1801–1805	29	19.1	4.7
1806–1810	51	24.9	4.0
Roofing (pence per square)			
1789–1798	10	58.4	5.9
1803–1810	8	90.5	15.0
Slating (pence per square)			
1789–1801	8	80.1	28.6
1806–1810	10	135.5	25.3

Source: NA, Bolger Papers. All quotes are for workmanship only.

is a rise in nominal wages that just about kept pace with rising prices.

Another perspective is offered by quite a different source: historical data on the heights of population subsets such as military recruits or convicts. The starting-point is the observation that the average heights of well-fed Caucasian populations in Europe and North America today are almost identical. Thus the determinants of national and regional differences and trends in mean height are largely environmental, not genetic.[42] The connection between height, on the one hand, and nutritional status and even the standard of living, on the other, nowadays invoked by the World Health Organization and other international agencies as a measure of health and nutritional status in less developed countries, was noted by Malthus in the *Essay on Population*:[43]

The sons and daughters of peasants will not be found such rosy cherubs in real life as they are described to be in romances. It cannot be failed to be remarked by those who live much in the country that the sons of labourers are very apt to be stunted in their growth, and are a long while arriving at maturity. Boys that you would guess to be fourteen or fifteen are, upon inquiry, frequently found to be eighteen or nineteen. And the lads who drive plough, which must certainly be a healthy exercise, are very rarely seen with any appearance of calves to their legs: a circumstance which can only be attributed to a want either of proper or of sufficient nourishment.

Economic historians, frustrated in their quest for more direct evidence such as continuous real wage or consumption data, have increasingly invoked the link.

Armies have long relied on a minimum height requirement as a method of quality control. Height data may also help identify deserters. Military records are thus a rich source for historical heights data. Inferring the height of a population from a sample based on such data presents its own computational and interpretational difficulties, however. The frequency distributions of the heights of large randomly selected groups of people like those of, say, a series of observations on annual rainfall or crop yields, are bell-shaped or 'normal'. The heights of military recruits typically are not so distributed: smaller men are rejected, or are less likely to present themselves to the recruiting agent. The computational challenge has been met by the development of specially devised algorithms—one of the rare instances where economic historians have prompted the development of new statistical techniques. The Quantile Bend Estimator (QBE) generates a measure of the mean height of a population or sub-population from samples (such as our soldiers) subject to shortfall and truncation. So far, the analysis of historical heights data has yielded several surprising and some puzzling findings.[44]

The satirical seventeenth-century saga *Pairlimint Chloinne Tomáis* (The Parliament of Clan Thomas) provides an early Irish reference to the connection between diet and height at issue here. In the story the men of Meath, Fingal, and Kildare, bred on a diet of peas and oatmeal pottage, were *fearaibh gearra, bolgmhóra, tollreamhra, tábhachtachta* (short, pot-bellied, fat-arsed and important men). The men of Munster, even then potato-eaters, stood at a distance from them, *mar do bhádar 'na bhfearaibh boga arda* (being soft, tall men).[45] No firm Irish heights data for the seventeenth century survive to verify the *Pairlimint*'s claim, but, as in the case of many other European countries, a good deal survives from the eighteenth and nineteenth centuries. An appendix to Chapter 4 contains a fuller discussion of later data and of some of the limitations of the anthropometric approach. Here I focus on one source on the heights of the Irish during the decades under review.

In the economic history of late eighteenth-century Ireland, Robert Brooke is best remembered for founding and managing a giant cotton mill at Prosperous, County Kildare.[46] Before embarking on that venture in 1780, Brooke had spent many years in the service of the East India Company (EIC), most recently recruiting Irishmen for service in India. Some details about the men that Brooke enlisted in the late 1770s survive. Presumably from humble backgrounds, they were mostly labourers in their late teens and early twenties, recruited largely, but by no means exclusively, from Brooke's own stomping-ground of north Leinster. Here we consider one aspect of the surviving data, the men's reported height.

Applying the QBE method to the heights of Brooke's men, and comparing them to those obtained from a contemporary sample of English recruits, suggests that the Irish were considerably taller—65.7 inches versus 64.8 inches for men aged 22 years and over. Since armies typically enlisted poor men, the QBE's reflect the height of the poor. By modern standards, the implied height of men in both Ireland and England was very small indeed. That comes as no surprise, but what is rather remarkable is the inference that Irishmen of humble backgrounds born in the 1750s were nearly an inch taller than their English counterparts. Though the comparison is complicated by the operation of selection biases in recruitment—on which more below—the calculated difference in Irish and English heights seems too big to be purely the result of such bias. The results are tantalizing at least in their implications for the relative health and nutritional status—though hardly the economic welfare more broadly defined—of men born around the mid-eighteenth century. An analysis of a sample of men recruited by the American Revolutionary forces (1775–83) offers some corroborative evidence. Though this finds that foreign-born men were shorter than American-born, the gap between American- and Irish-born men was three-fifths of an inch less than that between American-born and English-born.[47]

The EIC's army, like the French Legion, offered a haven for hardened men, down on their luck or in trouble with the law. The Company tended to take on such men with no questions asked. The less desperate and the more risk-averse probably opted for His Majesty's forces. However, comparing the occupational breakdown of men joining 'John Company' and His Majesty's forces suggests that this had little bearing on the social background of recruits. In another respect, though, a career with the Company may have seemed less attractive: the life-span of the Company recruit was almost certainly shorter than that of the regular soldier in normal years. Tropical diseases and vast intakes of *arak* seem to have been mainly responsible. The gap must have been narrower in periods of all-out war such as 1790–1815, however.[48]

Over 5,000 Irishmen joined the EIC army between 1802 and 1814. In terms of regional origin and occupational background, they were more representative than Brooke's men. The Company's enlistment registers for the period include every county in Ireland and the Irish recruits extended over one hundred and fifty different occupations. Most numerous were labourers, servants, weavers, cordwainers, carpenters, tailors, masons, and smiths, but the lists also include gentlemen, miners, combers, dyers, miners from Kilkenny and Wicklow, Dublin stucco plasterers and dyers, a 21-year-old Kerry student, several tobacconists spread over ten counties, a fiddler and a letter-carrier from Fermanagh, and many more. The small number of farmers reflects the youth of the recruits: farmers' sons were likely to be returned as labourers. The regional and occupational distribution of the recruits is given in Table 1.4(*a*). The number of workers in occupations requiring literacy (6.5 per cent of the total), the overrepresentation of Dublin and the rest of Leinster, and the underrepresentation of East Ulster, hub of Ireland's industrial revolution, are noteworthy features.

An analysis of the heights of this much larger number of men (see Table 1.4(*b*)) again indicates that the Irish were drawn from a taller population, though the gap between Irish and English is now smaller (somewhat over one-third of an inch). In these years, the Company faced a serious shortage of recruits, and was forced to relax greatly its minimum height and age requirements. The results reported in Table 1.4(*b*) refer to adult men only. Evidently rurality and being a labourer had little influence on height in the Irish case, though country people were a little taller. Within Ireland, Munster and rural Leinster produced the tallest men, and Dubliners were about half an inch smaller than the national average. Weavers were typically short, while men declaring 'literate' occupations before joining the ranks were almost an inch above the mean. The comparison also suggests some reduction in Irish heights between the 1770s and the 1800s, and a rise in the English. These last results support the possibility raised above that the growth of Irish population in these years was a disequilibrium phenomenon. Though interesting, they must not be pressed too far, since as explained more fully in an appendix to Chapter 4, recruitment methods, catchment areas, and labour-market conditions differed across regions and over time. The low estimated heights in this period reflect the poverty of the reference sub-populations in both Ireland and Britain; at other times, when the Company could pick and choose its men, mean height rose significantly. Moreover, the Irish advantage in both periods may stem partly—and paradoxically—from the relative poverty of Ireland, since this would have induced a *relatively* better quality Irish recruit. Finally, relative impoverishment in England between the 1770s and the 1800s, by improving the quality of English relative to Irish recruits, might explain the contrasting patterns over time. While the Irish height advantage is striking and

Table 1.4(a). *Occupations and regional origins of EIC recruits, 1802–1814*

Occupational group	Region						
	EU	WU	W	D	EM	RL	Total
Labourers	179	489	533	336	637	891	3 059
Weaving	122	189	47	36	55	90	539
Clothing	33	68	76	147	129	158	611
Construction	9	16	26	67	45	81	244
Farming	1	5	7	9	4	17	43
Literate	13	40	60	110	39	103	365
Trade	10	18	19	35	23	52	157
Metal	17	16	17	43	37	42	172
Other	33	54	34	104	70	113	408
TOTAL	417	889	819	887	1 039	1 547	5 598

Note: EU = Antrim, Armagh, Down   WU = Rest of Ulster
       W = Connacht, Clare, Kerry   EM = East Munster
       D = Dublin   RL = Rest of Leinster.

Table 1.4(b). *QBE estimates of Irish and British heights, c.1800–1815*

Group	Sample size	Mean height
Irish	1 782	65.3
English and Welsh	1 390	64.9
Irish labourers	1 387	65.2
E and W labourers	560	64.6
Rural Irish	1 502	65.4
Rural E and W	1 046	64.9

Note: Only men aged 23 and above are included.

Source: Mokyr and Ó Gráda, 'The Heights of the British and the Irish c.1800–1815'. Only men aged 23 years and above are included.

probably genuine—it survives cross-tabulations by occupation and region, and I produce further evidence for it in Chapter 4—these limitations of inferences based on volunteer army data must be borne in mind.

Nevertheless, the Irish advantage is confirmed by two studies of the heights of convicts transported from Britain and Ireland to New South

Wales in this period. Separate studies on male and female convicts show those transported from Ireland between the 1780s and the 1810s to have been taller than their British peers. The urban–rural and skilled–unskilled differentials described earlier also hold in the case of the convicts. A convict-based study of female heights finds a modest increase in the heights of Irishwomen born between 1790 and 1820; and while rural Irish women convicts born at the beginning of the period were shorter than the English, those born towards its end were taller. Since the convict population was subject to different selection biases than the military, inferences based on convict data usefully supplement those based on soldiers or sailors.[49]

Related to health and nutrition is life expectancy, or how long the average person lived. A German visitor to east Galway in 1806–7, Johann Friedrich Hering, noted 'amidst all this wretchedness one still finds very old people, who not unfrequently reach 100 years'. The 1821 census counted 349 alleged centenarians, with Connacht (110) disproportionately represented.[50] One old woman from Knockane in Kerry was returned at 112 years! (In 1841 the total returned 'above 96' years was given as 1,696 but Connacht accounted for only 296 of these). Michael Dempsey who, it is claimed, was 115 years when he died in Longford in 1847, had been walking around without a stick two days before his death; the same report described a 103-year-old man from Loughgall, still able to walk the ten miles to Armagh, and back again. Other examples of Irish longevity might be cited, though historical demographers are suspicious of the reliability and representativeness of evidence unauthenticated by valid registration data. Still, life expectancy seems to have been relatively high in Ireland in this period. A recent attempt at gauging life expectancy at birth indirectly from age-distribution data in the 1821 and 1841 population censuses suggests a figure of 37–8 years. This may be low even by present-day Third World standards, but in the more appropriate league table of early nineteenth-century Europe it is not so bad: life expectancy has been estimated at 25 years for Hungary in 1830, 27.5 years for Spain in 1797, 38.1 years for France in the 1830s, 40 years for Denmark in 1787, and 40.5 years for England in the 1830s.[51] An Irish enthusiast for the potato, Samuel Hayes, noted in 1797 the practice of allowing children to help themselves at will to potatoes, roasted on a turf fire, and put the 'robust health' of the country people down to 'plenty of wholesome sustenance at this stage of life'.[52] Indeed, the key to the relative tallness and longevity of the Irish poor is probably that, thanks largely to the potato, they were relatively well fed. The higher marital fertility indicated above may also be a function of a healthy diet. Now, much more is known about potato consumption on the eve of the Famine than half a century earlier, so a detailed discussion of nutritional status is reserved for Chapter 4. Suffice it to state here that if recent assessments of the food of the Irish poor on the eve of the Famine also apply to the earlier period, then the Irish diet was adequate in calories and protein.

We conclude this chapter with two reservations to our claim that Irish poverty in the period surveyed here was mitigated by a plentiful supply of healthy food (potatoes) and fuel (turf). First, contemporary references to 'July of the cabbage', the 'meal months', or Amhlaoimh Ó Súileabháin's *buidhemis biaghann* (food-scarce July) suggest frequent seasonal shortages. These usually did not last long enough to affect overall health, but in the wake of a wet summer or a poor harvest, the ensuing fuel or food shortfall might well give rise to outbreaks of dysentery and typhus. To make matters worse, the lack of fuel sometimes forced people to eat their food raw and wear their clothes damp. It is in this sense that 'fever' was endemic in Ireland.[53] Secondly, the Irish poor would have gladly sacrificed some of their relative height and longevity in return for a more varied though less nutritious diet. In cross-section the 'inferior good' status of the potato in pre-Famine Ireland is also evident; Bourke has put consumption by the poor at a daily adult male equivalent of somewhat less than one stone, while his 'professional men and merchants' consumed at the rate of a still respectable 1 lb. daily.[54]

1.3 Conclusion

Historians and commentators who interpret the Great Famine as the culmination of a dynamic process driving Ireland inexorably towards disaster have painted a very bleak and doom-laden picture of the period described above—and of the decades that followed. The very occurrence of the Famine invites interpretations that make it seem more 'likely' over time. Without seeking to deny the misery and the problems, so often highlighted before, I have pointed to mitigating factors too. The Irish were better fed, better heated, healthier, and perhaps even happier, than such interpretations allow. I have also suggested that the great Irish population spurt of the late eighteenth and early nineteenth centuries—sensational by the standards of the day—may well have been a temporary disequilibrium phenomenon, already being righted long before 1845. The problem, then, was less the lack of demographic adjustment than its slow pace.

The Economy, 1780–1815

2.1 Agriculture

Sir William Petty (1623–87) is best remembered by Irish economic historians for his estimates of population and income and by geographers for his maps and surveys. In both fields he was a pioneer, and his work forms the starting-point for all subsequent inquiries. Petty also produced estimates of Irish agricultural productivity in the 1660s, presumably based on his own observations in the south. His measuring-rod was the ratio of output to seed planted, the crop yield ratio. Being a pure number, this ratio avoids problems stemming from variations in weights and measures, and that explains its appeal to agricultural historians. Petty's numbers, typically, are far from precise; the range for wheat is 4 to 9, that for oats 2.7 to 5.3. The lower-bound estimates seem positively medieval, but the upper-bounds are quite impressive, because in England a century later the yield ratios for wheat, oats, and barley were about 10, 8, and 9. In Ireland, such high yields, if at all common, must have reflected technology rather than intensive labour input, since the island was very sparsely populated in the seventeenth century. But Petty is a poor guide to average yields. Of course, seventeenth-century Irish farming was pastoral in orientation, and therefore reliable data on milk yields and carcass weights would have been more revealing.[1]

In terms of thoroughness, detail, and methodology, Arthur Young's *Tour in Ireland*, largely based (like most of Young's works) on notes taken on the spot, marks a giant leap forward over Petty. The *Tour* may be a hackneyed source, but it nevertheless remains our most comprehensive guide to late eighteenth-century Irish agriculture. Young, the champion of agricultural improvement, has always had his critics, and his methods failed to impress everyone in Ireland. The reaction of Irish politician and agricultural 'improver', John Foster of Collon, is worth noting:[2]

Young was at Collon, but there and everywhere he disappointed. He went with the rapidity of an express, asked for answers to a set of questions and seemed not to notice anything else; seemed, I hear, for I did not see him, very ignorant, not communicative, and to pay equal regard to the assertions of all persons. If so, his tour when published will be as bad as Twiss's. I had intended to have shown him all this country, to have given him all assistance into other countries, and as I was well acquainted with his writings, to have informed him of many points peculiar to this country in those objects he seemed to make the principal theme.

Young was also in a hurry in south County Wexford, to the chagrin of Robert Fraser, who later surveyed the county for the Dublin Society.[3] However, recent research suggests that Young was no charlatan, but a careful if opinionated scholar. Indeed, in an age when the use of statistical evidence was often cavalier, Young was a pioneer, who tried hard to distinguish the average state of affairs from best-practice. Moreover, by the time he travelled around Ireland he had already published studies based on three extensive English tours, as well as some other well-known works. Being somewhat of a celebrity, Irish gentlemen such as Foster vied for the privilege of entertaining him. Young naturally enthused about Irish 'improvers' such as Lord Bective or Lord Gosford, but he none the less saw his main mission as describing ordinary agriculture. The *Tour* is thus full of accounts of 'common' farming, statements such as 'they apply their grass chiefly to fattening cows', 'they plough five inches deep', 'their manures are marle, shells, sea-wrack', or 'they burn their mountain land'. 'They' and 'their' in such generalizations refer not to the wealthy improver, but to the typical tenant farmer holding twenty acres or more. The same goes for most of the statistics given in the *Tour* and in Young's other works.

Young deemed Irish agriculture very backward, which it undoubtedly was by 'best-practice' English standards. None the less, Young's own data reveal that Irish grain yields there were quite respectable by late-eighteenth century standards. Indeed, despite climatic disadvantages, they rivalled English levels, and easily surpassed the levels reported by Young on his French travels just over a decade later. Irish potato yields, of less interest to Young, were relatively high too, twice their contemporary French level. Placing his Irish data in the context of the huge inventory of European grain yields assembled by agricultural historians also reveals Ireland's relatively advanced position at this juncture. At least by this criterion, Irish agriculture did not deserve Young's opprobrium.[4]

Admittedly, corn output per acre is but one, imperfect gauge of agricultural productivity. Output per worker would be a better guide to what is at stake, the community's nutrition and well-being. Reliable estimates of either English or Irish aggregate output are simply unavailable for Young's period, though we may rest confident that English agriculture had a considerable advantage on this score. Moreover, one obvious reason for high Irish yields per acre was highly labour-intensive spade cultivation. Labour was cheap in Ireland in Young's time, and the spade prepared the ground for tillage better than the best-practice plough. But this is hardly the whole story, since ploughs were already the norm on larger farms and better land. The three-way comparison with England and France suggests that by Young's time Irish farmers had absorbed more of the creed of improvement than their French counterparts.

Moreover, it would have hardly made sense for Irish agriculturists to follow English techniques to the letter, as Young seemed to demand. Given a labour force subsisting largely, even in Young's time, on the potato, and the versatility of the same potato as both fodder crop and linchpin in a rotation involving a variety of grain crops, the advantages of the turnip were less striking for Ireland than for Britain. The benefits of artificial grasses in a country where a wide variety of clovers grew spontaneously were also less obvious than in Britain.[5]

Statistical evidence on the state of Irish agriculture in the late eighteenth and early nineteenth centuries is patchy. Young's achievement in the 1770s was emulated by Edward Wakefield, whose 1812 survey indicates improvement in the interim (see Table 2.1). Disappointingly, the series of statistical surveys sponsored by the Dublin Society, with government backing, between 1801 and 1832 contains very little time-series or even comparative data. Still, though quite variable in quality, they include a

Table 2.1. *Irish and English grain yields per acre, 1770s–1810s*

Source	Wheat	Barley	Oats
Ireland			
Young	21.2	34.7	34.7
Dublin Society	22.1	34.7	36.6
Wakefield	23.3	39.3	41.4
England			
Young	23.8	32.1	37.0
Typical c.1800	21.6	32.0	34.9
Board of Agriculture	22.6	32.6	36.1

Source: Allen and Ó Gráda, 'On the Road Again', 107.

great deal of useful impressionistic comment and *obiter dicta*. Their overall tenor suggests advances in agricultural techniques, animal breeds, farm implements, and, implicitly, in crop yields since Young's time. If in Monaghan the bulls were 'ill proportioned and misshapen', in Mayo 'cattle of every kind [were] in a high state of improvement', in Kilkenny 'the breed of sheep [was] rapidly improving', while in Clare 'as improvement takes place . . . the breed keeps pace with it'. In Cork, 'the general management has much improved', in Antrim 'varieties of wheat are every day appearing', in Tyrone 'every farmer of any note is possessed of [a wheel-car],' in Wexford clover and grass seeds were 'universal', and so on.[6]

Some of the Dubin Society surveys also convey a sense of how extraordinarily labour-intensive was Irish agriculture in the early nineteenth century. Lime and seaweed were carried great distances, and the high-yielding (if maligned) lazy-bed method of growing potatoes relied on laborious cultivation by specially adapted spades (*láí* or *rán*). The following passage from the Dublin Society's surveys of Wexford (1807) and Cork (1810), are evocative:

[I]n the more inland and westerly parts [of Wexford], there is also a degree of labour and industry that we have not observed to be equalled in the other adjacent districts of the island. In Shelmaliere, Bantry, and Scarewalsh, they manure with lime, which they procure with great expence and labour from the adjoining counties of Carlow and Kilkenny. The same also the farmers of Shelbourne are obliged to do. Those, however, on the parts adjacent to the Rivers Barrow and Suir procure from the beds of these rivers, at low water, a rich sediment of a marly nature, but which is very heavy, and cannot be brought to a distance from the river at a moderate expence; they, therefore, more internally are obliged to bring limestone from a greater distance.

Throughout the whole of this county, therefore, all is labour; whether employed in digging the marle from the pit, whether in drawing the limestone a vast length of often a miserable road, whether in dredging the wet and oozy mud from the beds of the rivers, whether, in the midst of wintry storms at the dead of night, dragging the uprooted sea-weed from the roaring surf, drenching them in its waves and threatening them with destruction! All is a constant round of industry almost unequalled, and strongly impressing on the admiring observer the ardent wish, that their labour may meet with its due reward. . . .[7]

During the winter months, they collect with unceasing diligence in all accessible places the weeds, which are torn from the rocks by the violence of the southern gales. When the storm subsides, the dissevered weeds float into the coves and the strands, some of which are so abundantly provided as to afford a very considerable profit to the proprietors of the ground . . . In addition to this supply, a great number of small boats are employed during spring, and the beginning of summer, in procuring the growing weeds. Each boat's crew consists of six men, provided with long light poles, furnished at one end with a sharp iron, bent in the form of a hook. With these they cut the weeds from the rocks . . . The labour of this service is often very severe. They frequently row from Timoleague to the old head of Kinsale, a distance of seven or eight miles, spend two or three hours in cutting and gathering the weeds, a fatiguing work, in which they are necessarily wet from head to foot, and return the same length of way without rest or refreshment. The tide, however, materially assists the process.[8]

Agricultural exports grew considerably during the Revolutionary and Napoleonic Wars. The share of grain crops in total exports rose from about one-tenth in the early 1780s to one-quarter by the end of the Wars. Local evidence also suggests a surge in tillage output: in Tullaroan (County Kilkenny) tillage had 'crept to the tops of the mountains' by the late 1810s, while in Aghadoe (near Killarney) tithe-book evidence suggests a doubling in the acreage under grain and potatoes between 1794 and 1812, a rise that occurred at the expense of livestock numbers.[9] This shift seems to have been more a response to the movement in input than in output prices: Solar's index of cereal prices rose by 92 per cent between 1780–4 and 1810–14, while his beef, mutton and butter price index rose 127 per cent. However, pasture-based products (beef, mutton, butter) continued to be more important than tillage items, accounting for three-quarters of food exports at the outset and one-half at the end.[10]

Farmers must have fared well in these years. This may be seen by comparing the change in the prices of their main inputs (land and labour) with that in output price. Estimates of average rent per statute acre by

Table 2.2. *Agricultural exports at constant prices, 1780s–1810s*

Date	Grain	Pasture	Pork
1780–4	100	100	100
1785–9	325	113	125
1790–4	340	107	156
1795–9	204	108	196
1800–4	194	104	149
1805–9	408	119	269
1810–14	745	155	369
1815–19	1 289	178	359

Source: Computed from Solar, 'Growth and Distribution', 252–3.

Arthur Young and Wakefield imply an increase from 9*s*. 7*d*. (47p) in the mid-1770s to 16*s*. (80p) in the late 1800s. The increase tallies well with Solar's estimate, which put the rise between the 1780s and the early 1810s at about 60 per cent.[11] These are averages; landlords not bound by leasehold agreements could increase rents by much more than this, and the price charged on new lettings over these same decades more than doubled. We have already seen that agricultural wages rose by 60 to 80 per cent over the same period. Land and labour constituted the two dominant inputs in farming. Since agricultural prices, as measured by Solar's output-weighted indices of southern prices,[12] roughly doubled, the average farmer was prospering.

2.2 Land Tenure

Popular accounts have long given landlords a prominent role in promoting or (more often) delaying agricultural change. Yet probably the best-known message of Irish agrarian historiography over the last few decades has been that 'the landlords are not central to Irish history'.[13] The message should not surprise the mainstream economist today, since in terms of efficiency, simple economic theory suggests that there is little to choose between a system of rent-paying tenants and one of peasant proprietorship: in either case the farmer retains the marginal return on extra effort. For this outcome to hold, however, landlords and tenants should be surplus maximizers in the following sense: the efficient landlord must eschew short-term predatory behaviour, while ready to evict the lazy and incompetent tenant, just as the lazy or incompetent owner-occupier must be willing to sell to his more energetic peer at a price reflecting the land's productive potential.[14] Some recent research into Irish landlord–tenant relations reaches conclusions that fit these theoretical presumptions more readily than the traditional landlord stereotype.

Still, the land market probably worked less smoothly than the model implies. Before the passage of the Encumbered Estates Act in 1849, the law made it difficult for creditors to relieve insolvent landlords of their properties. In the course of his travels Wakefield (1812) was told that only three large estates had been sold 'in recent years'. Yet examples of landlord extravagance and the ensuing arrears and insolvency were common. Thus when the second Duke of Leinster succeeded his father in 1773, he inherited debts of £148,000, exclusive of jointure demands on the part of his mother and grandmother. 'Big George', the third Earl of Kingston, ruined his north Cork estate by building a castle in anticipation of a royal visit which never materialized.[15] Lord Muskerry never quite completed the magnificent house he commissioned at Dromore; in 1810 not a stone of the building, which had cost £20,000, remained. Between 1806 and 1838 the arrears on another Cork estate, Lord Midleton's, rose by an enormous £70,000. By the time (in 1835) Lord Hartland of Strokestown, one of the largest proprietors in County Roscommon, had been declared insane and unfit to manage his affairs, he had allowed his estate to accumulate substantial debts. In west Clare, John Scott Vandeleur gambled away his modest estate in a Dublin club in 1833 and fled the country. The second Earl of Charleville, who had splurged vast sums on politics and high living for over two decades, was forced to retire abroad on £1,000 a year in 1844. Nor was Ulster immune. Successive owners of the Donegall estate in Antrim in the late eighteenth and early nineteenth centuries relied on a variety of strategems to avoid debts which were ultimately attributable to their efforts at aping or outspending other major Irish and British landlords. In the first half of the nineteenth century another major Ulster landowner, Lord Downshire, spent a quarter of his gross rental servicing debts incurred by his predecessor, and interest charges were his largest single expenditure outlay. Many other examples of improvidence might be given. Conspicuous consumption and generous settlements were an essential part of the game.[16] The law offered remedies to creditors, but these were cumbersome, time-consuming, and wasteful, so the ensuing uncertainties must have inhibited investment on affected estates.

'In Ireland', Wakefield noted in 1812, 'landlords never erect buildings on their property, or expend any thing in repairs, nor do leases in that country contain so many clauses as in England.' Dubourdieu, author of the Dublin Society survey of County Down, claimed that 'the management of estates is very simple; it consists in letting the different farms, receiving the rents, and in regulating the turf-bogs'. These statements do not exaggerate by much. Why did Irish landlords do so little? In part because they, unlike English landlords, were wholesalers rather than retailers in land, and therefore cared or knew little about the circumstances of individual farms or townlands. The very size of Irish estates partly explains this. In the late eighteenth century most tenants still rented from middlemen rather than directly from the head landlord. Yet if estates were too large for direct letting to those who cultivated the soil, a common theme is that most Irish farms were too small to warrant heavy capital outlays by landlords. This points to the importance of the substantial farmer (who

often doubled up as middleman) as agent of change. Many landlords
did, however, engage in infrastructural investment—in markets, roads,
and towns. When it came to farms, landlords let to middlemen.[17] Such
middlemen, head-tenants wedged between the proprietors and the farmers,
sometimes of minor gentry stock, sometimes descendants of the native Irish
and Old English aristocracy, were a natural response to conditions in
Ireland in the wake of the Cromwellian and Williamite confiscations.
Already under threat from head landlords in Young's day, they have often
been described as a parasitic excrescence (like their Scottish counterpart, the
tacksman), because they rarely provided the fixed capital in buildings,
walls, and drains that British landlords supplied.[18] None the less, the
stereotypical middleman behaviour highlighted by critics such as Young
is a caricature. Recent research instances many examples of 'improving'
middlemen: and in so far as the caricature rings true at all, it is because it
captures the rational response of a group about to be replaced. The inflation
of the war years and the relative buoyancy of food prices increased both the
money and real value of land, spurring head landlords into a more active
role. Long leases gradually began to give way to ones better geared to
inflation or to tenancies-at-will. The proprietor's change of role from agent
to principal has been equated with reduced security of tenure, but is better
seen mainly as the landlords' means of capturing more of the economic
rent.[19]

If the landlords' role was largely passive in this period, strong farmers (of
both Irish and English stock) partly substituted as improvers and in-
novators. Whelan has instanced the modernizing role in the south-east of
farming 'dynasties' such as the Scullys of Mantlehill and the Keatings
of Garranlea. The Keating enterprise was famed for the quality of its
livestock, and impressed Arthur Young. Padraig Ó Néill of Owning
in south Tipperary[20] is another good example. Nolan has given several
instances of middle tenants improving both country and village in the
north Kilkenny barony of Fassadinin. As these progressive farmers reinvested their profits in planting trees, improving breeds, and increasing
crop and milk yields, there is scattered evidence too of the spread further
down the line of new crops and new farm implements, though it is difficult
to chronicle precisely.[21]

In the history of land tenure in Ulster, the issue of 'tenant right' has
long had pride of place. Crawford has recently stressed the conflictual
aspect of this Ulster 'custom', charting its course over the eighteenth
century from merely a tenant's claim to priority when his lease came up for

renewal to a right to payment (in the words of one astonished observer) 'where no lease exists and where no improvement has been made'. Such a right can only have been gained at the expense, somewhere along the line, of the landlord's share in the economic rent. Nevertheless Ulster landlords ultimately acquiesced in tenant right, and even came to see advantages in it (see Chapter 5). Andrews has pointed to the humbler victories won by some squatters on the public commons, retelling with obvious relish the story of one John Doyle of Broadleas Common, a long-time squatter, whose registration as a freeholder was upheld in court on 1836. The shifts in property rights described by Crawford and Andrews occurred gradually, without bloodshed.[22]

Another common theme in the land tenure literature is that by the late eighteenth and early nineteenth centuries, when landed proprietors began to remove middlemen and take direct control of the running of their estates, the rural population was too great and holdings too small for direct management to have much effect. If the resettlement of smallholders was a precondition for improved, capital-intensive farming, many landowners were too heavily in debt to finance the added charge.[23]

2.3 Regional Dimensions

We must not leave the impression, as Malthus and many contemporary observers were wont to do, that Ireland was a homogeneous unit. The researches of Irish historical geographers highlight the importance of the regional dimension on several fronts:

1. In a recent study of eighteenth-century settlement and society, Kevin Whelan has identified four different Irish regional archetypes: the pastoral, the tillage, the small farm, and the proto-industrial.[24] Since this division applies equally to the pre-Famine decades, it is worth describing in some detail here. I will refer to these zones as A, B, C, and D. Whelan's pastoral Zone A of well-drained carboniferous limestone land had two cores.[25] The first was centred on north-east Leinster and east Connacht, but also included a marginal periphery encompassing much of Offaly, Longford, and Westmeath. The size of the periphery varied with corn prices. This was a region of substantial farms, large enclosed fields, good land, and low urbanization. Its main business was the fattening of cattle for the Dublin and English markets. Even in Young's time, the cattle trade was subject to a good deal of regional specialization. There were close spatial symmetries between poor land and breeding, on the one hand, and between good land

and finishing, on the other. Thus the substantial graziers of this eastern pastoral zone bought in young cattle from the west in October, fattening them on its rich limestone pastures before selling them off the following summer. Even within the pastoral zone, the best land was in the hands of graziers; a cluster of 'trifling farmers' was a sure sign of 'a bad vein of land'. The graziers of the east midlands, farming an average of a few hundred acres or more, were prosperous men; they rarely mixed with other farmers except for business reasons. In the 1770s in Meath fattening bullocks on winter fields required an acre and a half per beast, while on the famous plains of Boyle, Young noted, some of the land could carry a bullock and a wether per acre.[26] Settlement in Zone A was scattered and sparse, and important towns few.

The second part of Zone A specialized in dairying and butter production; it encompassed a lowland swathe of good land stretching from Kilkenny to west Limerick and north Kerry. Cattle density was also high in this area, but with cows dominating. Farms were somewhat smaller and employment higher than on the fattening lands. Calves were driven east. Whelan's Zone B, the tillage zone, was 'built out of the environmentally favoured Anglo-Norman coastlands', and fitted roughly within a triangle linking Cork, Dundalk, and Wexford. Soil and climatic conditions (low rainfall and plentiful sunshine) gave this zone a comparative advantage over Zone A in tillage. Here the social structure was more complex than in the grazing zone, with plenty of artisans gaining employment in ancillary trades such as coopering, milling, and brewing. A reluctance to negotiate leases and rent levels directly with hundreds of small tillage farmers made for a more passive landlordism. Resilient farmers and middlemen, rather than landlords, were therefore the vehicles of agricultural progress. There was a general air of prosperity. An account of 1814 refers to some farmers from the Wexford barony of Forth 'on farms of fifteen acres each [who] have lately ventured upon Government Debentures, and one of the party is sent up half-yearly in the mail-coach to the Treasury, to receive their interest, and to make further purchases'.[27] Unlike the towns of the pastoral zone, which came to life only on fair day, the towns of the tillage zone were busy, with farming creating forward linkages to flour mills, distilling, and brewing. Agriculture was much more labour-intensive than in the pastoral zone.

Thirdly, Whelan identifies a western and coastal small-farm Zone C, encompassing most of Connacht (though not parts of Roscommon and east Galway), west Munster and west Donegal. Zone C comes closest to following the 'peasant' model of rundale and 'clachan' proposed by historical geographer Estyn Evans and his followers. The rundale system, under which a single tenant's share of a lease might mean a few acres dispersed over a few dozen pieces of land, had something in common with the Russian *mir* and the European open-field system, and was subject to the same kind of criticisms: that it gave rise to constant friction about trespass and thieving, and contained an inbuilt bias against individual initiative and improvement. The system invariably meant clustered settlements (the *clachan* or *baile*) and communal decision-making, presided over by a *rí* or 'king'. The *baile* produced its own problems: according to Lord George Hill of Gaoth Dobhair, 'it tended to the spread of fever and other infectious diseases, in addition to which the women's life was taken up in wrangling and scolding, the packed state of the community affording copious sources of civil war; and, worse than all, the men were generally far away from their farms.'[28] It is in this zone of marginal land, where close-knit communities eked out a living on a combination of tillage, fishing, spinning and weaving, and seasonal migration, that population growth was fastest in the late eighteenth century, and where overpopulation would be most serious in a few decades. Some of the Zone C—such as the Kerry barony of Corca Dhuibhne—had been long settled, but much of it was also of relatively recent settlement.

Finally, there was the proto-industrial Zone D of the north and north-west, encompassing most of Ulster and parts of north Connacht, Louth, and pockets in Longford and Meath. In this area of poor land and small farms, the textile industry bulked large. Families alternated between farm and industrial work according to the season and relative prices. People married young, population density was high, and population mobile. In its economic organization, the region had more in common with areas such as the north of England and east Flanders than with the pastoral zone to the south of it.

The boundaries between these zones cannot be defined sharply like administrative boundaries. Nevertheless, Whelan rightly reminds us that 'given the enduring local bases of eighteenth century Irish life, the historiography is still haunted by these regional ghosts, which rise up to mock premature generalisations'.[29] Examples include the consequences of exogenous shocks such as agricultural protection under the Corn Laws or technical change in cotton textiles on the different areas. The first was most likely to benefit Zone B, while the second proved to have serious consequences for Zone C, whose rural textile workers were ill-geared to the new inventions in spinning and weaving. Though in the late eighteenth or mid-nineteenth centuries, differences in wage and rent payments could have had some influence on the patterns of specialization noted above, those differences were largely the product of differing endowments, and therefore survived any tendency towards factor price equalization. Indeed, improved communications probably accentuated some of the regional patterns outlined.

This schema provides an unexpected reminder of the recent emphasis in cliometric writing of the importance of 'small historical events'. Thus why much of Munster concentrated—and still concentrates—on dairying, while Kildare and Meath have concentrated on cattle-fattening, may have as much to do with differences in resource endowments as with tradition. Limerick's links to the eighteenth-century butter trade focused on the provisioning port of Cork, and the long-standing importance of the Dublin and British markets for livestock established enduring patterns of specialization. This explains why, although the spatial divisions outlined here refer to the eighteenth century, they are also clearly reflected in the official agricultural statistics compiled annually from 1847. The data in Table 2.3, though referring to the 1840s and 1850s, cast their shadow back further. They refer to eight baronies, chosen to describe the contrasts underlying Whelan's framework. In terms of their endowments of dry cattle, the two Meath baronies of Lower and Upper Deece stand out. The two Mayo

Table 2.3. *Selected agricultural data by barony, 1840s and 1850s*

Barony (County)	Holdings >50 acres (%)	Grass crop ratio	Dry cattle per stockholder	PLV per acre 1851 (£)	PLV per agr. family 1841 (£)
Deece, Lr. (Meath)	36.1	1.72	10.01	0.80	28.7
Deece, Upr. (do.)	37.5	2.71	19.75	0.99	40.0
Burrishoole (Mayo)	8.9	4.01	3.09	0.11	2.7
Erris (do.)	26.5	5.42	5.57	0.04	2.1
Armagh (Armagh)	2.8	0.54	1.58	1.42	16.7
Oneilland E. (do.)	1.6	0.35	0.79	1.33	38.8
Forth (Wexford)	9.4	0.85	2.98	1.19	21.5
Scarawalsh (do.)	25.6	1.15	2.58	0.46	11.3

Source: Based on data in *Returns of Agricultural Produce in Ireland in the Year 1854*, except for the last column, which used the number of families 'chiefly employed in agriculture' in 1841. The Poor Law Valuation (PLV) data refer to 1851, the agricultural data to 1854. 'Dry cattle' means total cattle less milch cows.

baronies were by far the poorest of those selected. The percentage of large
holdings in Erris is deceptive, since both it and the high ratio of grass to
tillage in Mayo reflected poor land quality. Holdings in the two Armagh
baronies (representing Zone D) were small and intensively farmed, but
according to an admittedly crude index of rural comfort—Poor Law valuation (in £) per agricultural family—living conditions were relatively good.
Finally, the Wexford baronies selected, though both part of Zone B, show
the scope for contrasts even within a single county. The data on one of the
Wexford baronies (Forth in the south of the county) reflect the relatively
snug conditions noted by Arthur Young and others, but in Scarawalsh in
the north of the county living standards were lower. On the eve of the
Famine, farmland per family 'chiefly employed in agriculture' ranged from
an average of 9 acres in Burrishoole and 11 acres in Armagh and Oneilland
baronies to nearly 40 acres of much better land in the baronies of Deece
Upper and Lower. A final comparison highlights the degree of specialization within Zone A. In the two Meath baronies of Upper and Lower Deece
cows accounted for less than one-tenth of all cattle in 1854, but in the
barony of Clanwilliam in south Tipperary, they accounted for well over
half.[30]

Figs. 2.1, 2.2, and 2.3, derived from the agricultural statistics of 1854,
are also instructive. Using the barony instead of the county as the unit of
measurement highlights the degree of variation within several counties.
Fig. 2.1, showing the ratio of milchcows to total cattle numbers by barony
in 1854, besides highlighting Zone A, also identifies the two main dairying
areas on the island. Then as later, dairying was more intense in the
southern than in the northern area. Fig. 2.2, describing the ratio of cattle
numbers to the acreage under crops, is a reminder of the share of marketed
output provided by cattle in the west, where the land was poor. Fig. 2.3,
describing the regional variation in poor law valuation per head, is striking
confirmation of the east–west gradient in living standards. Other maps,
such as those describing housing quality and literacy in the 1841 census,
produce broadly similar pictures. According to a recent study by Hochberg
and Miller, the east–west gradient reflects 'the process by which English
institutions were extended from the administrative centre of the medieval
colony, Dublin . . . differentiat[ing] Ireland as a whole into an eastern core
and a western periphery'.[31] Fig. 8.1 below describing the ratio of the
population resorting to the soup-kitchen during the Famine also replicates
the east–west pattern.

2. Jones Hughes's dot-map of farms valued at over £100 (representing

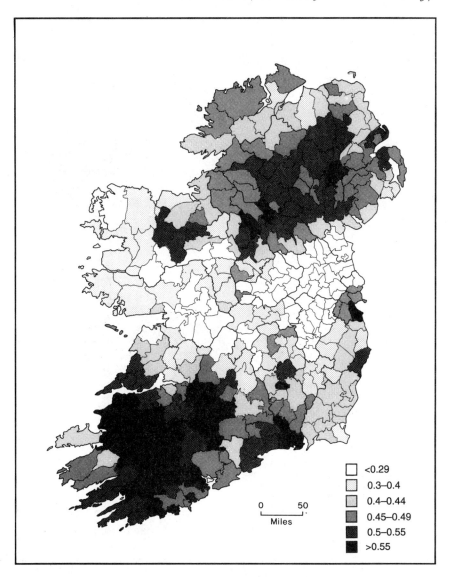

FIG. 2.1 Ratio of milch cows to cattle numbers, 1854

Source: *Agricultural Statistics, 1854*

an acreage of 100 acres or more), reproduced here as Fig. 2.4, refers to
1850, but its distribution of over 7,000 farms almost certainly also applies
to the period under review. The map reveals a remarkable regional concentration of large farms. Nearly half of the total were to be found in five

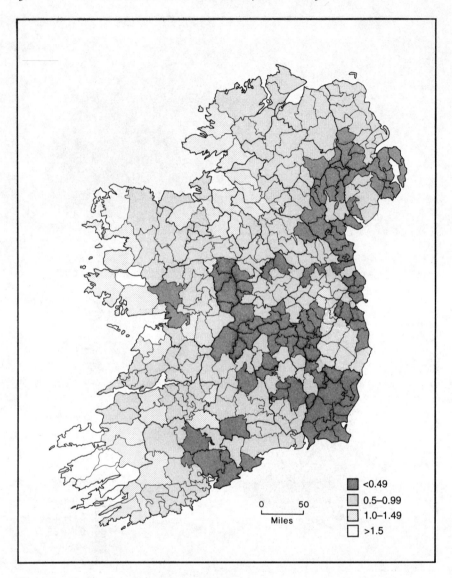

FIG. 2.2 Ratio of cattle numbers to acreage under crops, 1854

Source: Agricultural Statistics, 1854

north Leinster counties, and another quarter in east Munster. Jones Hughes
offers no simple explanation for the spatial spread of his large farms, but he
mentions 'landholding structures, settlement frameworks, the quality of
farmsteads and the ratio of planter to gael among their occupiers' as factors.

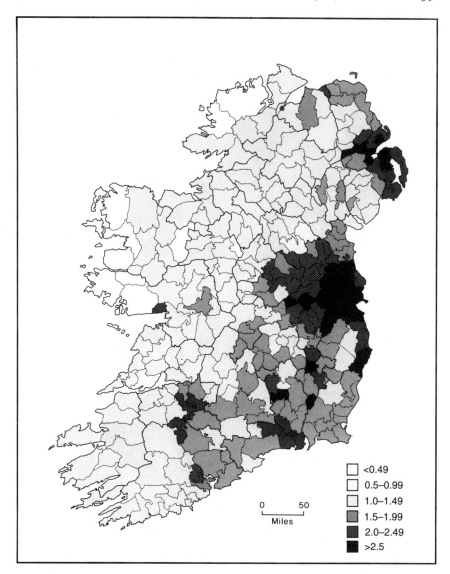

FIG. 2.3 Poor law valuation per head, *c*.1854

Source: *Census 1841* and *Agricultural Statistics, 1854*

By and large, communities of large farms were found where the land and
access to markets were good. A study of the farmers' surnames reveals traces
in east Munster and south Leinster of strong Catholic communities. Jones
Hughes has linked the resilience of the Irish language in this area well into

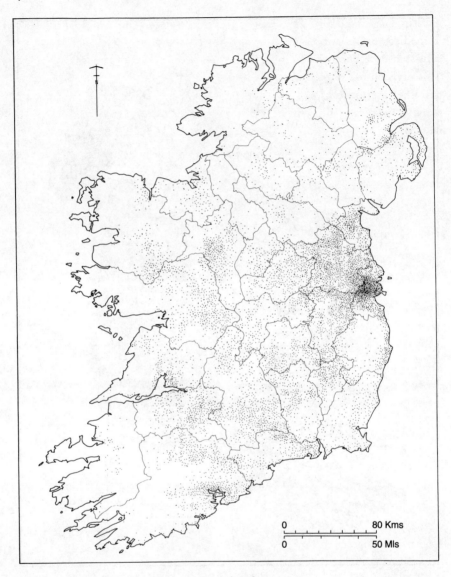

FIG. 2.4 Farms valued at £100 or more in 1850

the last century to the influence of a farm community that 'retained a greater than usual degree of self-respect and self-confidence'.[32]

3. Perhaps the most famous spatial division in the economic historiography of Ireland is that suggested over thirty years ago by two non-geographers, Patrick Lynch and John Vaizey, between a commercialized

maritime zone (comprising the coastal region from Belfast to Cork and the immediate hinterland of Galway and Limerick) and 'a rural, and mainly subsistence, economy which occupied the greater part of the country'.[33] This division has not survived detailed scrutiny. Lee and Mokyr have shown that the division between monetized and subsistence economies was more social than spatial. Rural labourers tended to be paid in kind (in land), and to pay off their rents in labour dues or, rarely, in produce. Instances of landlords being paid in kind may also be found, but in general landlords expected to be paid in money. Even in the remote barony of Erris in the 1780s it was said of the notorious land agent Eoghan Conway:[34]

> Ba ró-mhaith ag tógáil an chíosa é:
> ba bheag aige mí nó dhó
> go ndíolfaí an bhó ar an aonach
> nó an giota a bhíodh sa tseol.

Mokyr's assessment of the Lynch–Vaizey hypothesis, based on information about factor markets in the 1830s, found Connacht no less monetized than Munster, and Mayo no less so than Cork. Admittedly the degree of urbanization affected the proportion of people using money on a regular basis. But agriculture was highly commercialized, and rents (excluding most of those due on potato conacre) and taxes were paid in money. Moreover, seasonal migration from the 'subsistence' zone—both to other parts of Ireland and across the Irish Sea—was considerable and growing. These harvest workers (or *spailpíní*) were always paid mainly in money, most of which they brought home with them and spent at home.[35] Livestock fairs, another sure sign of commercialization, were ubiquitous by 1780, their number having grown from less than 700 in the 1660s to 3,000 in the 1770s. The network would grow further, to over 5,000 fairs spread over 1,000 sites, by 1845. Competition between buyers and fairs probably benefited the farmers in the long run. Increasing competition from other fairs, and the enterprise of English factors who saved western farmers the expense of sending their animals to Ballinasloe, explain the near-stagnation in cattle and sheep sales at the celebrated Ballinasloe October fair from the 1780s on. Significantly for the Lynch–Vaizey hypothesis, 'commercialized' Leinster's share of all Irish fairs fell more dramatically between the 1680s and the 1770s (from 43 to 27 per cent) than it would between the 1770s and the mid-1840s (from 27 to 23 per cent).[36]

Another sign of increasing commercialization was the tendency of the fairs to specialize by season and function. Early spring was the best time for horses, May for grazing cattle, and August for beef. Moreover, while the fairs had their origin in the trade for cattle and sheep, they gradually acquired a much wider economic and social function. In addition to its 5,000 fairs, the country had hundreds of active patented market-places in the mid-nineteenth century. Few parts of Ireland were more than 10–15 miles from a market centre, if the most isolated peninsulas on the western seaboard are excluded. Finally, millers, another proxy for commercialization, were to be found in even the most backward counties: Leitrim had fifty-nine in 1841 and Mayo 114.

3

Fiscal and Monetary Integration, 1790–1820

There is trade enough in the world for the industry both of Britain and Ireland.

ADAM SMITH (1779)

Irish economic history in the eighteenth century is a tale of ever-closer links with the British economy. Trade with the neighbouring island increased fourfold in real terms between 1700 and 1780, while trade with the rest of the world rose by less than half. By the latter date, Britain accounted for 74 per cent of Irish imports and 79 per cent of Irish exports. Meanwhile Ireland's share in British trade rose too, from 4 per cent in 1700 to an all-time peak of 15 per cent c.1780.[1] Commodity flows were complemented by factor flows; labour and capital moved in both directions almost without restriction. The Irish monetary system had strong ties with London. For some observers, economic and political integration was a natural progression, but history proved more complex. During the 1780s and 1790s an increasingly assertive Dublin Parliament sought to encourage native industry, promote tillage, and generally increase Irish economic autonomy. In the monetary field, the amalgamation of the Irish and English pounds was preceded by two decades of floating exchange rates between Dublin, London, and, for a time, Belfast. Similarly Britain's share in Irish foreign trade declined after 1780, though wartime conditions drove it to a new high by 1800. Full economic and monetary integration, then, followed some years of mild economic divergence. This chapter discusses some of the associated controversies.

3.1 Legislation

Economist Adam Smith, a fervent supporter of the Union between Scotland and England, also favoured a political union between Ireland and Great Britain. His reasons were not purely economic:[2]

By a union with Great Britain, Ireland would gain, besides the freedom of trade, other advantages more important, and which would more than compensate any increase in taxes that might accompany the union. . . . Without a union with Great Britain, the inhabitants of Ireland are not likely to consider themselves for many ages one people.

Legislative union was by no means a new idea in 1776, but it took a back seat in the 'patriotic' atmosphere associated with the Constitution of 1782. However, the United Irish Rising of 1798 and its savage suppression convinced the authorities in Westminster (and the Catholic Church in Ireland) of the need for a political union of Great Britain and Ireland. The details of the famous settlement of 1800 were largely the work of William Pitt, Lord Auckland, John Beresford, Irish Chief Secretary Lord Castlereagh, and Edward Cooke, a Dublin Castle administrator; Castlereagh assumed the responsibility for getting it carried.[3] Only Articles 6 and 7, which embodied the economic aspects, need concern us here.

Article 6 set out the the commercial arrangements, whereby an Anglo-Irish customs union would be created. It stipulated that 'all articles, the growth, produce, or manufacture of either country . . . shall thenceforth be imported into each country from the other, free from duty'. However, Castlereagh's wish that 'the counties of Ireland should be like so many English counties, and goods pass from the one to the other without interruption' could not be fulfilled overnight. Irish manufacturers sought a respite and, by and large, Article 6 was tailored to meet their demands.[4] Irritants such as British duties on coal and raw wool imports into Ireland, and on certain Irish exports, were removed, but the high Irish tariffs on cotton imports—50 per cent on calicoes, 35 per cent on muslins—were allowed to remain for seven years and then gradually to decline to 10 per cent, the rate granted other protected sectors such as silk, leather, haberdashery, and glass. All remaining protective duties were to go in 1821. These concessions failed to satisfy Dublin manufacturers, who were most vocal in their fear of free trade, and whose representatives in Parliament were to vote against the Union, broadly on economic grounds. The Cork cotton manufacturers, already under threat in any case, also protested the commercial clauses, though other Cork traders supported the Union. The opposition of Dublin artisans, Protestant and Catholic, would last into the 1820s and 1830s.[5]

The Irish national debt in 1800 was less than one-fifteenth of the British (£27 million against £420 million). A settlement that forced Irish taxpayers to pay for past British overspending would be patently 'unfair', so the financial terms of Article 7 of the Act of Union did not envisage immediate tax harmonization. Instead it fixed the Irish contribution to aggregate government revenue at two-seventeenths of the total. This ratio, due to Castlereagh, was bolstered by two other ratios: (*a*) that of Irish to British foreign trade, and (*b*) the relative value of the main 'enumerated' or dutiable goods—tea, sugar, malt, alcohol, tobacco—consumed in both countries. The proposed ratio of 1 to 7.5 lay close to the proportions given by either (*a*) or (*b*).[6] Of course, Castlereagh's 'tests of commerce and consumption' constituted a rather cavalier exercise in the economics of public finance. His ratio was intended to benefit Ireland, reflecting its smaller national debt. But how fair was it? The populations of Ireland and Great Britain at this time were about 5 million and 10.5 million, so the 2:15 ratio converts into 1:3.6 in per capita terms. At first glance this seems very generous, but that verdict is tempered by the presumably high income elasticity of demand of the dutiable items listed above. Assuming an arc elasticity of 1.0 for a bundle of the dutiable goods (*Q*), the implied income gap (*dY*) may be calculated as follows:

$$1.0 = (dQ/Q)/(dY/Y) = [(3.6 - 1)/0.5(3.6 + 1)]/(dY/Y),$$

whence $dY/Y = 1.13$. The implied income ratio is therefore $Y/(dY + Y)$ or 1:2.13. The higher the elasticity, the smaller the implied income gap: an elasticity of two would imply an income ratio of less than 1:1.6. No reliable standard-of-living comparison exists for the late eighteenth century, though the true gap may well have been wider than that implied by these calculations. If so, Castlereagh's formula—unintentionally, it must be said—'over-taxed' Ireland at the outset.

The early years of the Union, a time of all-out war, brought rising taxation to both Britain and Ireland. Between 1801 and 1816, in addition to £63 million of separate expenditure, Ireland's contribution to joint expenditure was £97 million. However, only about half of these sums was met by taxation and as a result the Irish national debt quadrupled from £27 million to £107 million, while the British debt less than doubled to £693 million. This left Ireland close to bankruptcy, and led to the amalgamation of the two national debts. The mounting deficits of 1801–17 sprung from a conviction that raising Irish excise taxes any faster would have diminished the aggregate yield; the alternative of imposing an income tax or land tax (as in Britain) was not attempted. The ensuing amalgamation of the British and Irish exchequers in 1817 did not result in immediate tax harmonization, however; additions to Irish taxation were small until the 1850s.[7]

Contrary to traditional Irish nationalist claims, the economic impact of the Act of Union in the short run was minor. Manufacturing output and trade continued to grow (see Chapter 12). Nor were fears of deindustrialization to the fore in the debate about the Union. In the event, even the removal of the Dublin Lords and Commons had little evident effect on the Dublin economy, partly because any resulting rise in gentry absenteeism was made good for a decade by an increasing military presence. The rise in the city's population from 180,000 in the late 1790s to 231,600 in 1821 was faster than during the 1780s and 1790s, usually deemed decades of prosperity and progress.[8] In the countryside, the high prices generated by war were a boon also to farmers and landlords. But the period was one in which lots of things were happening at once—Industrial Revolution, war, political change—making the analysis of any single factor's role almost impossible.

The economic gloom and famine conditions of the late 1810s made the pre-Union and war years seem like a golden economic age. Yet pre-1800 prosperity had little to do with legislative autonomy, and wartime gains were exaggerated. The wars benefited Ireland as an economy specializing in agriculture, but they also brought a vast increase in taxation and indebtedness. That the scale of government borrowing 'crowded out' some private capital expenditure seems likely. War, in addition, produced great instability, as indicated by the trend in bankruptcies (see Chapter 7). The net impact on aggregate welfare—gains from higher agricultural prices, losses ensuing from the destruction of capital and labour—remains unclear.

3.2 The Old Irish Pound

Until 1783 Ireland had a largely notional currency, the Irish pound, worth twelve-thirteenths of one pound sterling (£1 sterling = £Ir1.083). It was notional in the sense that there were no separate Irish gold coins, though coins such as Wood's controversial halfpence were denominated in Irish money. However, when the newly chartered Bank of Ireland, modelled on its sister bank in London, began to issue notes redeemable in specie in 1783, they had twelve-thirteenths of the specie value of the English pound, and Irish inland bills were also denominated in the Irish currency. Like Britain, Ireland had been on an informal gold standard since Isaac Newton's failed experiment in bimetallism. The rate of exchange implied by the discount rate on Irish bills in London never deviated far from par. However, with the suspension of gold payments in both Ireland and England in early 1797, the Irish paper pound was allowed to float against its English counterpart. For a time, though both currencies depreciated against third-country hard currencies, the London–Dublin exchange rate did not diverge much from its traditional level. The Irish pound began to lose value against the English in 1799–1800, however. In late 1803 the depreciation of the Irish pound relative to the English reached 10 per cent, and this led to considerable controversy, culminating in a parliamentary select committee.

The *Report of the Committee on the Circulating Paper, Specie and the Current Coin of Ireland*, which placed the blame for the depreciation squarely on excessive note issue, is a landmark in the history of monetary theory. Many reasons for the depreciation had been aired in the debates that preceded the Report; they included bad harvests, panic and speculation, the irresponsible behaviour of private bankers, an adverse balance of payments, and ministerial pressure on the Bank of Ireland for credit. The select committee, chaired by John Foster, last Speaker of the Irish House of Commons and now a rising political star in Westminster, took a firm 'bullionist' (in today's terms, a rigid monetarist) line in arguing that the faster growth in the money supply in Ireland relative to England fully explained the depreciation of the Irish currency in terms of the English. The Irish Currency Report put a virtual end to the controversy about the Anglo-Irish exchange, though it was invoked again five years later in a similar controversy about a fall in the specie value of the English pound. Meanwhile, it allegedly had the effect of convincing the Bank of Ireland to restrict its issues.[9]

The facts of the case are more complex. Though Irish circulation rose more than English after suspension, this was partly because Ireland relied less on paper money before the demise of gold. Besides, the Report's analysis was too quick to discount the potential impact of real factors such as severe harvest failure, rebellion and the fear of invasion, and massive military expenditure on the exchange rate. Pressure from hard-pressed ministers as a factor in note expansion was also ignored in the discussion. Critics of the Bank of Ireland simply assumed that it was eager to expand note issue in its quest for higher profits, but the minutes of the Bank's Court of Directors from 1797 on betray a marked ambivalence. Pleas and threats from the Lords of the Treasury rather than eagerness on the part of the Bank account best for the rise in circulation in these years.

Eighteenth-century Ireland had suffered from an endemic small change shortage. Mint issues of full-value silver had been virtually driven out of circulation after 1713, when Isaac Newton as Master of the Mint set the mint gold/silver ratio too high. The mint was also lax in its issues of low-denomination copper coins. The public therefore had to make do with a mix of coins consisting of gold (guineas, pistoles, Louis d'or, moidores), foreign silver (dollars), deteriorated silver and copper coins, and privately issued tokens and counterfeits. The incentive to export silver to Britain was strong, so that few full-value coins stayed in circulation for long, and gold was suitable for relatively large transactions only. The result was inconvenience and occasional confusion.[10]

In the wake of the Restriction of 1797 gold gave way to paper, except in the north of Ireland. Political uncertainty accentuated the shift, as people hoarded coin in panic. Silver, already scarce, became scarcer, though the Bank of Ireland's ploy in 1805 of importing silver dollars and allowing them to circulate at a realistic price helped. In 1806 an observer gave the following description of Ireland's circulating media:[11]

(1) a copious effusion of paper from a guinea note to several thousand pounds
(2) English guineas, seldom seen outside of the north of Ireland, worth £1. 2s. 9d. each
(3) dollars worth 5s. 5d. each
(4) silver bank tokens of 6s. Irish each
(5) silver bank tokens called 10d. and 5d. pieces and worth so much Irish each
(6) hogs or shillings, sometimes called thirteens, worth 13d. Irish pence each
(7) pigs or testers worth 7d. Irish each
(8) penny, halfpenny and farthing pieces.

The dollars mentioned above would have been minted in Mexico or Spain. The six-shilling bank tokens were also dollars, overstruck by the Bank of Ireland. Nor is the list above exhaustive; sometimes, more exotic foreign coins were employed, and copper tokens were issued locally, as by the mine-owners at Cronebane near Arklow. The ability of the public to master all this confusion should not be underestimated. Nevertheless, the profusion of denominations was a nuisance; the monied middle-class needed arithmetical tables to combine 'guineas and half notes, thirty shilling notes, six shilling tokens, and dollars' in the proper proportions, while the poor fell back on a combination of tokens, defective coins, and silver notes. The co-circulation of (1), (3), and (4) offers an interesting sidelight on Gresham's Law that 'bad money drives out good'. The point was not lost on the Irish Currency Committee, who remarked that 'the Dollar of the Bank of Ireland, if the Exchange were at par, would be nearly equal in value to

5*s*. 5*d*. Irish. The additional 7*d*. for which it is made to pass, is a further and nominal value, which it is obvious that it has been found necessary to give to it, in order thereby to secure the continuance of this circulation in Ireland.'[12]

3.3 Depreciation and the Bank of Ireland

The Bank of Ireland was already a powerful, self-confident institution by the late 1790s. The minutes of its Court of Directors bear out the role of politics in the rise in note-issue. On 31 March 1797 the Irish Treasury informed the Bank of 'their inability to discharge any part of the debt due to the Bank', and little more than a week later they were asking for more accommodation 'in the present exigency'. 'Exigencies' demanded another £Iro.1 million on 12 May, whereupon the Bank put its foot down, insisting that unless measures were taken 'to restore the circulation of specie it is the solemn opinion of the Governors and Directors that it will be impracticable in the present situation of credit to accommodate their Lordships with any further exchange of paper or securities.' The Bank also warned against the danger of excessive issues. Still, the Treasury persisted: £Iro.1 million was demanded, and granted, to relieve industrial distress, and another £Iro.15 million advanced on the security of British banknotes and specie. Evidently, the Bank still expected an early resumption of gold payments at this stage: the specie payments were at its request.

Thereafter the Bank of Ireland tried to link further advances to increases in its privileges and monopoly power. It demanded legislation preventing others from issuing low-denomination notes, and a guarantee from the Treasury that inward and outward payments be made in Bank of Ireland paper. These demands caused considerable resentment, and the Bank was eventually forced to back down. The Bank, of course, was caught in a dilemma. Patriotism and an eye to immediate profits dictated accommodating a series of insistent ministers, but the fear of resumption prompted caution. Asked by Chancellor of the Irish Exchequer, Isaac Corry, in May 1799 whether the Bank might advance another £Iro.5 million if required, the Governor replied that the Bank did not think it 'prudent in the present state of the circulation', but would 'think it their duty to his Excellency and the public to make such an advance should any emergency require it' Corry duly produced his emergency a week later, and the Bank agreed to £Iro.3 million repayable by mid-1801. Shortly after, another demand from Corry met a polite refusal. On the eve of the Irish exchange controversy,

Corry was at it again, pleading that since 'many late circumstances . . . rendered necessary that the expenditure of government for military purposes should become more extended and more immediate', the Bank should be prepared to advance a million on Treasury Bills. The Bank reiterated an earlier reply:

The Bank would be very happy to meet the wishes of Government by a further advance but after the most mature consideration on the former and present application they find they cannot without too far extending the circulation of their paper or contract the necessary aid to the public make any further advance.

Only a letter from the chief secretary, Wickham, on behalf of the Lord Lieutenant forced the Bank to relent. Soon Corry was seeking information from the Bank in connection with the exchange crisis. Part of the Bank's reply bears quoting:

[T]he Governors and Directors have been extremely cautious not to extend the issue of their paper beyond the demands absolutely necessary. And when it is borne in mind that the exigencies of the state required the Bank to advance a large sum (£1,200,000) on Treasury Bills, and that they supported the great commercial interests of Ireland, they are confident no ground whatever exists as a foundation to censure their conduct.

Before the restriction on payments in specie by the Bank, the circulating specie of Ireland was estimated at upwards of three million: Now as that circulating medium is by demands from England wholly withdrawn, no substitute can possibly remain to supply its place but paper, but it would be needless to observe to you that the encreased taxation and the encreased value of every article of consumption whether the produce of the country or foreign importation, must of necessity require an increased circulation to supply the demands that are in consequence created.

The first paragraph seems fair enough; part of the second articulates the famous 'real bills doctrine', the belief that short-term lending should be based on trade bills to solvent customers.[13] A final twist in the correspondence between the Bank and ministers is the Bank's reply on 19 June 1804 to Foster, lately appointed Chancellor of the Irish Exchequer. Foster was now pressing the Bank for accommodation: the Bank reminded him with obvious relish that this 'must evidently tend to increase the amount of the notes and post-bills of the Bank now in circulation'.

Economic theory today would lend more credence than did the Irish Currency Committee to the possibility that, in the short run, real factors can induce an adverse balance of payments leading to depreciation. The select committee scotched the possibility by producing new trade data suggesting a positive balance of payments in 1802; but their evidence was rough-and-ready and hardly conclusive. Besides, econometric testing suggests that the ratio of Irish to English note-issues alone cannot explain the course of the exchange rate.[14] Not even the return of the Irish pound to its old level after 1804 can be put down to the influence of the Report on the Bank; a 'stroke' by John Foster, appointed Chancellor of the Irish Exchequer in June 1804, was mainly responsible for this.[15] The Irish exchange showed further instability before the Bank of Ireland resumed gold payments in 1821, and the two pounds were amalgamated in 1826, but there was no further public controversy. None of this should be interpreted as a denial that changes in the money supply cause prices to rise and currencies to depreciate, but the kind of data invoked by Foster's committee could not prove this. Indeed, the necessary data for a full understanding—private banknote issue, balance of payments on current account, interest rates, debt transfers—are not available to today's historians either.

3.4 Private Banking before 1820

Ireland had made a precocious start in banking early in the eighteenth century, but this early promise was not sustained. At the outset Irish bankers, like English country bankers, tended to combine banking and commerce. Several banking failures in the mid-1750s, however, convinced Parliament that 'the publick credit of the kingdom . . . suffered from Bankers trading as merchants', and amending legislation prohibited merchants engaged in foreign trade from issuing notes. Banks were also prohibited from having more than six partners. Largely as a result of these well-intentioned regulations, between 1760 and 1797 only a handful of new banks were created in Ireland. Despite the creation of the Bank of Ireland in 1783, on the eve of the suspension of specie payments in 1797 Ireland was 'under-banked'.[16] The private banks that proliferated thereafter, like the increased circulation of the Bank of Ireland, were a direct consequence of the Restriction and ensuing legislation permitting the issue of small notes. With the virtual disappearance of bullion throughout most of the country, the public required a substitute 'money'. The result was a proliferation of suppliers of paper money in the towns of Leinster and Munster. Ulster was less affected, for reasons explained below; in remote areas where illiteracy was high, paper money made little headway either. Some of the new concerns were registered bankers, who issued stamped notes. However, most of the new 'banks' were small-scale local issuers of unstamped small-denomination notes. Typically, they were also traders and employers. The Report of 1804 condemned 'those numerous country shops throughout the South of Ireland (many of which can hardly be called Banks)'. The following passage from Foster reflects the Report's attitude to the trader-bankers:[17]

The enquiries of the Committee proved very unsatisfactory as to the number of private bankers in Ireland, the returns made to them being very incomplete; it would appear, however, from what they did collect, that, according to the system pursued in Ireland, the number of banks issuing notes ought to be in every place inversely as the extent of its commerce. London is supplied by one, Dublin by four; but less than twelve, it seems, are insufficient for Skibereen; and twenty-three are required to satisfy the demands of Youghal, a town in which it may well be doubted whether there are twenty-three persons who follow any other trade. So extensive indeed seems the demand for labourers in this department, that female bankers appear to be not uncommon. It would be easy to dilate upon this system, but it is unnecessary to pursue the disgusting topic.

In the same scathing vein, Foster accused issuers of notes 'for crowns, half-crowns, shillings, and sixpences, promising to pay the same in Bank of Ireland notes whenever a sufficient sum should be tendered', of tricking the public by choosing denominations that were not aliquot parts of a pound.[18]

During the Restriction Period Irish private banks were often accused of fuelling inflation. More generally—and this is a separate point—they were blamed for increasing economic instability.[19] In England, where each crisis produced its crop of bank failures and stoppages, the same charges were often laid against the country banks. The ensuing further disruptions of economic activity, even though short-lived, were much commented on. And though the Bullion committee exonerated the country banks, un-fettered provincial banking was often blamed for the inflation of the period.[20] Over 300 English banks failed between 1790 and 1826. Statistics highlight the bunching during economic slumps: 42 of the failures occurred in 1810–12, 76 in 1814–16, 63 in 1825. This convinced the author of the classic study of English country banks that the 'strong suggestion of underlying structural weakness in the steady trickle of failures' must not 'obscure the cyclical pattern [and that] other than institutional factors must be sought as causes of economic fluctuations'.[21]

The Restriction period had some of the features of what is known in monetary history as 'free banking'. The 'banks' of the period were par-ticularly 'free' in the sense that many never registered as bankers, and were under no obligation to purchase and deposit bonds as reserves (as in nineteenth-century America), or to pay specie on demand (as from 1821 on). However, most accounts of Irish private banks in this era are negative, echoing criticisms made of country banks in England and in the USA. According to Collins, 'a History of the Rise and Fall of Irish Country Banks at this period would be a continuous record of note-issues, panics, failures, and bankruptcies'. And undoubtedly there were fly-by-night 'cowboys'. Waterford banker John O'Neill, who 'after a hectic career of little more than eighteen months', went under in 1801, with £160,000 of his 'worthless' notes in circulation, is a notorious example. Williams and Finn of Kilkenny may have been two more: Sir John Newport claimed that when they failed with a note circulation of between £200,000 and £300,000 outstanding, 'it was perfectly known afterwards that the partners had never been possessed of £1,000'. John Carr met a militia bandsman in 1805, a former banker who claimed to have *failed for five pounds!*'[22] Some such opportunistic behaviour is to be expected. But the spate of recent research into the history of free banking elsewhere suggests that such 'wildcat' bankers were atypical, on the argument that the market forced profit-seeking banks to behave responsibly. This research is motivated by the premiss that endemic opportunism on the part of private bankers implies an implausible degree of credulity on the part of the public. Where does it leave Irish banking?[23]

The Irish private banks were probably not quite as bad as they were painted. They were largely innocent of the charge of fuelling inflation. One reason for this is that instead of holding their reserves in bullion, they tended to hold them in Bank of Ireland paper. But since this meant that they could not expand their note-issue without a prior injection of Bank paper, they were hardly responsible for the depreciation:[24]

The paper of the Bank of Ireland was the stock upon which all the private banks in the kingdom traded; and, in proportion to the quantity of the national bank paper the private banker was able to get into possession, he was enabled to issue his own paper which he was bound to pay in national bank paper to a much more considerable amount; according to the principle of banking stated by some writers, in the ratio of three pounds for one.

This statement by Foster anticipated the famous verdict of the Bullion Report that 'the whole paper of the Country Bankers is a super-structure raised upon the foundation of the paper of the Bank of England'.[25] Alas, no private bank records survive to test the proposition rigorously in the Irish case, but the paper notes of several banks at least bore the promise to pay on demand in Bank of Ireland notes.[26] A corollary of the criticism that private banks over-issued was spelt out by Lord King:[27]

It may be safely asserted as a general rule upon the subject of paper credit, that the circulation of all banks is limited by the extent of their capital, and the public demand for their notes. They can in no case transgress these limits without considerable danger. The contrary supposition will be found to involve the greatest absurdities. If country banks really possessed this power, it must necessarily follow that there would be great partial depreciations; and that the value of the currency would vary according to the different degrees in which the due quantity of notes for circulation was exceeded by the bankers of different districts. But no such irregularities are, in fact, ever experienced.

Lord King's point is that the banking public force banks who over-issue to pay a price. In early nineteenth-century Ireland, the panic-proneness of holders of small-denomination notes was a particular consideration. Newport, former Chancellor of the Irish exchequer, and member of a well-known Waterford banking family, recalled in 1826 that 'so much inconvenience has been experienced by the private bankers themselves, and so much distress from the sudden calls on them that it has ceased to be an object with men who have any real or permanent property to rely on, to become issuers of paper in general circulation'.[28] Plainly the safest option for a bank was to keep adequate reserves of Bank of Ireland notes.

The defence of private banks against the charge of causing inflation need not rest on a priori reasoning alone, however, since there is evidence at least in the case of registered banks that the expansion in the note supply was modest. By law, registered bankers' notes under three guineas bore a 1.5d. stamp, while three- and four-penny stamps were paid on notes under £10 and £50, respectively. The disproportionate rise in the number of low-denomination notes between 1800 and 1804 is telling (see Table 3.1).

An overall rise in note-issue of no more than 20–30 per cent in 1800–4 is indicated, and this was mainly accounted for by the rise in small-note issues. As for the numerous banker-traders, the aggregate value of their 'silver notes', largely in smaller denominations still, was small. In 1804, Jeremiah D'Olier, an experienced Director of the Bank of Ireland, thought that £400,000–£500,000 in silver coins and £100,000 in copper would be enough to drive out the 'silver notes'.[29] In sum, it is unlikely that the Irish private banks, registered or unregistered, could independently have forced a sustained rise in prices during the Restriction.

Conclusive tests of opportunistic, wildcat behaviour on the part of Irish banks during the Restriction period are elusive, but there are some pointers

Table 3.1. *Stamped notes issued, 1800–1804*

Year ending 25 March	Duty paid		
	1.5*d.*	3*d.*	4*d.*
1800	148 112	198 361	104 248
1801	242 673	147 211	65 201
1802	941 894	196 108	95 600
1803	823 673	204 940	67 594
1804	1 110 217	256 801	90 265

Source: Fetter, *Irish Pound*, 73.

against it. First, given the undeveloped state of banking in Ireland before the Restriction, failures among the '1797–9 generation' are only to be expected. Wakefield claims that of the fifty bankers registered in 1804 only nineteen remained in 1812. Though Wakefield blamed the high attrition rate on mismanagement, he conceded that there was a learning aspect to this:[30]

[T]he practice of their forcing paper into circulation, by attending at fairs like a company of hucksters, is an evil that will in time cure itself.

Second, the clustering of failures in crisis years such as 1814–16 and 1820 is significant, because it links them to declines in the assets held by the banking system generally. The downturn in agricultural prices in 1814 led to a fall in business confidence and to a flurry of rumour and counter-rumour. The suspension of payments by Ffrench's Bank of Dublin and Tuam in late June was accompanied by reassurances, relayed by the Dublin *Evening Post*, that 'there is ample property to cover all demands'. The *Southern Reporter* denied a lack of confidence in Cork; the *Limerick Gazette* scotched a rumour in the *Dublin Evening Post* of 'a great stoppage in Limerick'; the *Belfast Newsletter* confessed gratification that 'this town appears fully to retain its usual credit'. But some of this was mere wishful thinking. Soon after the failure of Ffrench's, another Galway bank, John Joyce & Co., was forced to close its doors. In Dublin the smaller firm of John Malone succumbed on 12 July with debts of about £50,000, though notes, mainly in small denominations, constituted only two-ninths of the total. The Nenagh Bank failed in December 1815. Six months later it was the turn of Anderson's in Fermoy; whether this should be linked to the others remains unclear. The Newry Bank also failed in 1816.[31]

Table 3.2. *Agricultural prices, 1810–1824*

Year	(1)	(2)	(3)	(4)	(5)	(6)
1810	17.72	8.09	111.78	390	110.1	131.7
1811	16.79	7.78	119.73	377	110.8	124.0
1812	23.73	12.14	116.24	390	127.4	151.7
1813	18.88	11.24	115.51	439	131.9	150.1
1814	12.21	7.20	120.89	358	120.8	150.2
1815	12.05	5.95	116.70	272	97.4	91.9
1816	16.10	7.15	92.20	264	90.3	91.2
1817	16.65	10.59	99.58	303	106.3	138.7
1818	16.50	10.13	124.30	288	125.2	144.3
1819	14.34	7.98	99.61	307	104.7	126.6
1820	11.71	6.02	85.04	(262)	87.0	90.8
1821	9.90	5.18	85.68	(318)	76.8	65.1
1822	7.14	4.99	76.76	261	66.8	64.9
1823	9.65	5.84	80.88	281	74.6	67.7
1824	12.13	7.32	91.34	(255)	93.4	105.0

Notes: (1) Waterford wheat prices (s/cwt.)
(2) Waterford oats prices (s/cwt.)
(3) Waterford butter prices (s/cwt.)
(4) Average sale prices of cattle (Townley Hall/Mountainstown)
(5) Irish agricultural prices, export-weighted index of southern prices
(6) Potatoes/pork southern index

Source: Solar, 'Growth and Distribution', ch. 2.

During the American free banking period (*c.* 1836–60), banks typically were required by law to deposit a stipulated number of bonds with a public official as security for notes issued. Declines in the value of these bonds were linked to bank failures; 'free banks failed when economic times turned bad and the value of their portfolios declined'.[32] The balance-sheet of Ffrench's Bank at the time of bankruptcy illustrates the similar predicament faced by many Irish banks in 1814–15: drained of specie or Bank of Ireland notes, they were left with debt balances and overdue bills, mostly illiquid and often likely to turn out worthless.

Solar's price data (Table 3.2) indicate another serious fall in agricultural prices in 1819–20. The persistence of low prices gave rise to doubts about the ability of some small banks to meet their obligations. On 25 May 1820, Roches' Bank in Cork, 'victims of the combined effects of good nature and bad times', stopped payments, followed by a neighbour, Leslie's, a few hours later. Runs ensued and several other closures. Two days later a bank in Limerick closed its doors, and yet another two days later. Having failed to relieve the pressure on several southern banks, Quaker business-men Joshua and Joseph Pim approached the Bank of Ireland for assistance, and the Bank honoured £40,000 of their London bills and allowed them another £15,000 on the security of government bills. Pleas on behalf of Shaw's, Latouche's, Ball's, Finlay & Co., and the Charleville bank followed. This did not prevent Loughnan's in Kilkenny, Newport's in Waterford, and Riall's in Clonmel from having to close their doors. Others were forced to close too, at least temporarily. Indeed, it seems that the only Munster bank to remain open for business throughout the crisis was Roches' in Limerick. Commercial activity was strongly affected for some weeks by the want of a medium of exchange, and there were urgent deputations to Dublin Castle.[33]

The *Dublin Gazette* provides an alternative measure of bank failures over a longer period, and a means of relating them to trends in Irish business generally. Bankruptcy is a legal condition, and firms declared bankrupt constituted only a fraction of all business failures. Private agreements between an embarrassed firm and its creditors were often preferred. Still, the award of a commission of bankrupt to creditors—followed by the 'gazetting' of the bankrupt's failure—is nevertheless a good measure of the movement in business failure. It is a surer measure than the more frequent announcements and reports in the *Gazette* of the proceedings of commis-sions of bankrupt. Even awards involve the danger of double-counting, since separate commissions of bankruptcy were sometimes issued against individual partners. Thus during our period, two commissions were awarded in 1820 against those involved in Anderson's Bank, and the three awards in the same week in 1791 against three 'merchants, dealers and chapmen' in Strabane more than likely referred to a single business.[34] Tables 3.A1 and 3.A2 at the end of this chapter report the total number of awards by year and region, and those for banks and other financial institutions. The bulk of the awards referred to Dublin concerns. Throughout, most of the awards were directed at traders rather than manufacturers. However, they included a wide range of businesses, including bankers and related financial oc-cupations such as 'dealers in exchange'.

Though preferable to the punishment meted out to some medieval bankers who failed to meet their obligations—public execution in front of their establishments—a commission of bankruptcy was no pleasing prospect for a debtor. When an offer to surrender all his landed property was not enough to save the lordly owner of Ffrench's Bank in Tuam and

Dublin from one in 1814, he was driven to suicide. The same fate befell Samuel Newport in 1820. On the failure of his bank in the same year, Sir William Alexander sold the family estate at Belcamp in a (successful) attempt at avoiding litigation.[35]

The failure of a bank gave rise to considerable disruption. The multiple failures of 1820 virtually put an end to market activity for some weeks. In Ennis, the notes of Roches' of Limerick were accepted, but only against goods of equal or greater value. More generally, fairs and markets could not function for the want of an agreed medium of exchange. 'What a state the country must have been in these few days past', wrote the *Freeman's Journal* correspondent in Carlow, 'when the butcher, baker, grocer and even the huxter would take the word of an honest customer, sooner than of any provincial banker in Ireland'.[36] It should be added, however, that a timely ministerial instruction to the Bank of Ireland to freely discount bills in the affected areas put an end to the disruption within weeks. Bank of Ireland note circulation rose from £2.6 million in March 1820 to £3.3 million in June, and reached a new high of nearly £3.5 million by the end of the year.

The economic disruption caused by the bank closures of 1820 bears comparison to the minimal effects of the extended bank closure in Ireland in 1972. In the latter case, the willingness of many people, notably shopkeepers and publicans, to cash cheques for customers meant that the closure had very little impact on the level of prices or economic activity. Of course the crucial difference between the two episodes is that nobody expected the Irish banks to remain closed indefinitely in 1972, while people were justifiably wary of the solvency of the Munster banks in 1820. When the banks reopened for business again in 1972 it was found that only a tiny proportion of the cheques cashed 'bounced'.[37]

As in contemporary England, Irish bank failures peaked in periods when the total number of bankruptcies was highest.[38] An informal approach to the issue of causation corroborates this finding. Regressing the total number of commissions of bankrupt granted (*Total*) *less* those in banking (*Banks*) and exchange-dealing (*Dealers*) on *Banks* and *Dealers* and a time-trend (*T*) for 1790–1817 shows this:

$$(Total - Dealers - Banks) = \underset{(18.12)}{32.91} + \underset{(8.60)}{18.03 Banks}$$

$$+ \underset{(3.10)}{6.90 Dealers} + \underset{(1.02)}{3.14 T}$$

$$N = 28; \; F(3, 24) = 9.38; \text{ s.e.'s in parentheses}; \; R^2 = .54$$

However, lest this be invoked as evidence that the failures of financial houses 'caused' the others, note that treating millers analogously yields:

$$(Total - Millers) = 55.99 + 17.08Millers + 2.13T$$
$$(10.46) \quad (3.54) \quad (1.05)$$

$$N = 28; F(2, 25) = 15.70; \text{s.e.'s in parentheses}; R^2 = .56$$

Overall, the number of bankruptcy awards against banks after 1797 was not large—an average of less than one per year during the Restriction Period. The best way of squaring this number against Wakefield's is to surmise that most of those who failed did so without incurring large losses, and were able to persuade creditors to avoid litigation.

True, bankruptcies were more frequent during the reign of the private banks than either before or after. Here the best defence of the banks is the point that war and the ensuing inflation and policy shocks induced instability. No formal test of this is offered here, but in England, variations in government expenditure, blockades, and panics meant that economic growth was slower and economic activity subject to greater fluctuations than later;[39] presumably the same held for Ireland.

Because paper money was easier to counterfeit than gold or silver coins, the Restriction proved a boom for counterfeiters. In January 1816 the *Freeman's Journal* reported the death of one Robert James, a notorious forger, '[s]o extensive was his practice and so numerous were his agents, that it might be truly said he had been the cause of bringing 100 poor wretches to the gallows and contributed more towards peopling Botany Bay than all the other forgers of Ireland put together'.[40] Perhaps the banks were at fault for not taking adequate precautions with their notes, though fundamentally the problem here lay with technology and with the government for not stopping the forgers.

One final point about the private banks. If this was indeed a period of growth in the number of quasi-banks, then the bankruptcy *rate* among our best proxy for these—dealers in exchange—was *lower* during the Restriction than earlier. The share of exchange dealers in the total number of awards granted fell from 4.2 per cent in 1780–96 to 2.3 per cent in 1797–1820.

The rising dominance of the Bank of Ireland rules out this period as a 'clean' case-study of the virtues of free banking. Indeed the precocious transformation of the Bank of Ireland into a quasi-central bank fits rather well the model of central bank evolution proposed by Goodhart.[41] As we have seen, the economic problems which forced the Restriction were also making the Bank of Ireland the Government's bank. The experience of the Bank also highlights the conflicts of interest attendant on a private bank playing the dual role of profit-seeking and public bank. Thus the Bank used the demands being made upon it by hard-pressed ministers as a means of increasing its monopoly privileges. In order to guarantee its circulation, it demanded that all payments in and out of official coffers be in Bank paper. Less successfully, it sought legislation to restrict the note-issuing powers of its less powerful rivals. Similarly, in 1804 the Bank shirked the task of looking after the exchange, pleading a conflict of interest. Too many of its directors, it claimed, had much to gain or lose by fluctuations in the exchange: exchange rate management should therefore rest with the Treasury or some other body. However, as early as 1799, the Bank could be seen performing another classic central banking function, that of providing credit to a solvent but potentially illiquid bank: it bailed out the Dublin private bank of Beresford and Co., under threat because of the withdrawal of a major partner.[42]

3.5 The Short Reign of the Ulster Pound, c.1797–1810

The Irish Currency Report dwelt gleefully on the anomalous monetary situation in the north of Ireland, where Bank of Ireland notes did not circulate, and landlords and linen factors insisted on payment in specie. This had some curious consequences. Jebb's contemporary account is worth quoting at some length:[43]

The state of silver currency in Ireland agrees entirely with theory. In Dublin and those places where there are no guineas in circulation, and no paper notes, the silver coin is of a much worse kind than in England or in the north of Ireland, where there is still some gold. As you approach the north, the difference in coin is palpable, and is very accurately understood there. If you offer Dublin shillings in change in Drogheda, there is some degree of scruple, but still they are taken; in Dundalk there is still more difficulty; in Newry, and so on to Derry, they will not be taken on any terms, they have no currency. In Dublin, those very counters pass in the shops with scarcely any examination; in the public offices, as the post office, &c. there is some difficulty; in the bank their value is well known, but still as they are paid there, their value cannot be refused . . . The shopkeepers, either following the example of the bankers, as to get off their base coin, in which many of them traffic, use every endeavour to substitute silver change for notes, and it is now become very common for them to solicit persons to whom they make payments, to accept silver instead of notes; which indeed is a proof that the trade of the retailer in base coin has considerably increased, and the coin has sunk very much below its relative value in bank notes.

'Silver notes' penetrated rather further north than this account allows: they were being issued in the Ulster 'border' towns of Cavan, Monaghan, Newry, Enniskillen, and Aughnacloy in the early 1800s. Moreover, notes and bills on Dublin continued to find a limited market.[44] Yet the continued rule of specie in the heartland of the province is clear from, for example, the Dublin Society surveys for Ulster counties. This gave rise to another much-noted consequence of the Restriction, the emergence of separate Dublin–Belfast and London–Belfast rates of exchange: 'The real exchange, that is where the Bills of Exchange are paid for in Specie, as in Belfast, hav[e] been in favour of Ireland during the whole of the year ending 5th January 1803.' This was deemed further evidence in favour of a bullionist explanation of the depreciation.[45] However, differences between the Northern and Southern economies and their susceptibilities to real shocks, should not be ruled out as a factor. In particular, that the agricultural crisis of 1800–1 had a disproportionate effect on the South is strongly implied by trade data. While linen exports—mainly from Ulster—were no lower in 1799–1801 than they had been since the mid-1790s, agricultural exports—mainly from the South—were 30 per cent lower by volume and 10 per cent lower by value.

Curiously, though Ulster bankers in the 1820s claimed that the reintroduction of gold payments then would be deflationary, they denied that the effect in 1797–1808/9 had been to depress the northern economy relative to the southern. 'By no means', claimed a director of the Belfast Bank, 'because we had enough at that time to circulate for the limited trade we then had; but at present the trade is so much extended that I should imagine we could not procure a sufficient quantity of gold to circulate in lieu of notes.'[46] This neutrality of money in the 1800s is asserted, not proved. The paucity of regional data makes it difficult to test. One indirect and modest check is to compare the share of all bankruptcies occurring in Ulster before, during, and after the Ulster pound. These are 13.4 per cent (1792–6), 14.9 per cent (1797–1807), and 16.3 per cent (1808–23). No evidence here of an 'Ulster pound effect'.

Why, when banknotes quickly replaced specie in the south after 1797, did guineas remain the predominant medium of exchange in the north? The Irish Currency Report, by implication, lauds the northern refusal to have any truck with depreciated paper. However, Cullen has recently stressed a more negative reason: the 'archaic' insistence by a conservative northern gentry on payment in guineas reflected the backward social and economic state of the north—outside the Belfast–Lurgan–Dungannon 'linen triangle'—in 1797. Unlike their southern peers, the northern landed classes showed little interest in industry or commerce—or in banking. The banks established in eastern Ulster in 1808–9 were not gentry affairs; they were mercantile banks, reflecting a yearning on the part of local business-men to be independent of Dublin. The Belfast Discount Company, a predecessor of those banks, had been established in 1793 and survived twenty years or so. By eschewing note-issue, its fifteen partners could fulfil the standard banking functions of discounting bills and accepting deposits without contravening the Bank Act of 1755. The Discount Company paid 5 per cent on deposits and got around the usury laws (which imposed a maximum of 6 per cent on loans) by charging administrative fees; in 1806 it discounted bills worth £300,000. A surviving balance-sheet for 1800 reveals a cash balance of less than £200,000, probably the product of both a determination to economize and the shortage of specie.[47]

Ironically, the situation which attracted such wonderment in the *Report* and elsewhere proved short-lived. By August 1805 an Armagh medical practitioner noted:[48]

Paper currency is making its way rapidly into this quarter of the kingdom, and into the North at large. Some still maintain that there is abundance of gold and silver for all the purposes of inland trade and navigation, but that those who have it won't bring it forward in consequence of the introduction of paper money—and, in case of any disturbance or convulsion in the country, the gold and silver will bring its value, but that the paper would be cried down and depreciated. But the great majority seem to think that the kingdom is drained of specie, and that enough cannot be procured to answer the purposes of a medium of currency. Why or how this has happened I don't pretend to determine . . . I am told, a man's note will be more readily discounted now than heretofore provided he take small paper money.

The notes of the three banks established in Belfast and Lurgan in or around 1808 successfully superseded specie, much as southern banknotes had done in the south a decade previously. A law passed in 1812 made Bank of Ireland notes legal tender, and in May of that year the *Belfast Monthly Register* could 'quote no price for the discount of banknotes. Since the passing of the late act, all transactions for the buying and selling of guineas must surely be clandestine.'[49]

Commissions of Bankrupt in Ireland, 1788–1826

Table 3.A1. *Commissions of Bankrupt awarded in Ireland, 1788–1825*

Year	Total	Dublin	Munster	Ulster
1776	25	14	2	7
1777	62	36	3	4
1778	79	52	2	8
1779	60	46	4	5
1780	33	19	6	4
1781	22	13	3	3
1782	40	19	7	9
1783	35	22	3	6
1784	49	19	12	11
1785	46	26	7	8
1786	61	40	10	7
1787	57	43	5	4
1788	112	45	25	26
1789	—	—	—	—
1790	56	33	11	7
1791	73	46	12	6
1792	77	46	11	5
1793	142	91	12	23
1794	76	51	6	10
1795	57	41	4	6
1796	65	42	6	9
1797	108	66	15	9
1798	53	31	4	11
1799	32	13	5	7
1800	55	34	8	9
1801	174	97	32	24
1802	102	57	12	18
1803	120	61	22	24
1804	130	57	25	20
1805	82	45	16	7
1806	141	77	18	19
2807	117	67	16	18
1808	122	71	21	12
1809	108	61	23	12
1810	269	135	62	41

Table 3.A1. *Continued*

Year	Total	Dublin	Munster	Ulster
1811	130	61	25	21
1812	94	46	9	21
1813	138	84	19	16
1814	193	110	22	33
1815	197	92	42	32
1816	205	93	36	39
1817	111	51	16	23
1818	62	32	11	11
1819	73	35	16	12
1820	112	61	18	19
1821	52	24	13	8
1822	35	15	8	9
1823	40	22	6	7

Source: *Dublin Gazette*. The 1799 and 1800 data are incomplete, those for 1789 so far unobtainable.

Table 3.A2. *Commissions of bankrupt awarded against Irish bankers and dealers in exchange, 1788–1826*

Year	Banks			Dealers in exchange, brokers, notaries public, and scriveners
	Munster	Dublin	Total	
1776	—	—	—	—
1777	—	—	—	—
1778	—	1	1	4
1779	—	—	—	3
1780	—	—	—	2
1781	—	—	—	1
1782	—	—	—	1
1783	—	—	—	1
1784	—	—	—	—
1785	—	—	—	1
1786	—	—	—	2
1787	—	—	—	2
1788	—	—	—	8
1789	*	*	*	*
1790	—	—	—	—
1791	—	—	—	1

Table 3.A2. *Continued*

Year	Banks			Dealers in exchange, brokers, notaries public, and scriveners
	Munster	Dublin	Total	
1792	—	—	—	4
1793	—	—	—	7
1794	—	—	—	5
1795	—	—	—	3
1796	—	—	—	4
1797	—	—	—	10
1798	—	—	—	3
1799	—	—	—	—
1800	—	—	—	—
1801	1	—	1	4
1802	—	—	1	5
1803	—	—	—	5
1804	—	—	—	5
1805	—	—	—	2
1806	—	2	3	1
1807	—	1	1	4
1808	—	—	—	—
1809	—	—	—	2
1810	1	—	1	3
1811	2	1	3	2
1812	—	—	1	—
1813	—	—	—	5
1814	—	3	3	1
1815	—	—	—	6
1816	—	1	2	5
1817	—	—	—	5
1818	—	—	—	1
1819	1	—	1	—
1820	3	—	4	2
1821	—	1	1	—
1822	—	—	—	—
1823	—	—	—	—

Source: *Dublin Gazette*. The 1799 and 1800 data are incomplete.

PART II

4

Population and Poverty, 1815−1845: From one Waterloo to Another

> The destiny of Ireland in the early nineteenth century was very largely moulded by the ideas of two great economists, Adam Smith and Malthus, and of the two the latter was probably the more influential.
>
> GEORGE O'BRIEN (1921)

> At least as far as prefamine Ireland is concerned, [Malthusian] models seem to have little explanatory power.
>
> JOEL MOKYR (1983)

4.1 Population Change

Textbook discussions of this period, not without reason, often bear titles such as 'Rural Crisis', 'Years of Crisis', or 'Malthus Vindicated'. The conventional wisdom of steady impoverishment produced by the law of diminishing returns and ever-worsening subsistence crises, culminating in the Great Famine, has the ring of plausibility to it. Yet as we shall see in this and following chapters, the full story is more complex. In its almost unrelieved gloom-and-doom, the traditional historiography has left signs of adjustment and improvement before the Famine unnoticed, and conceded the game to fatalism and Malthusian determinism.

The preoccupation with population growth is pervasive, and understandably so. Numbers continued to rise, from 5 million in 1800 to about 7 million in 1821 and 8.5 million in 1845, but the increase was less rapid after 1821 than before, and closer to the European norm. By the 1820s the rate of increase was declining even in areas of fastest growth within Ireland. The extent of this pre-Famine demographic adjustment is highlighted by comparing estimated population growth in 1790−1821 (1.4 to 1.6 per cent), in the 1820s (0.9 per cent), and in 1830−45 (0.5 to 0.6 per cent). Taking Ireland as a whole, these numbers point to important differences in the demographic regimes operating in the late eighteenth century and on the eve of the Great Famine. Was the adjustment merely the product of emigration, or did movements in fertility and mortality play a part? A recent simulation exercise puts the decline in the birth-rate in the 1820s and 1830s at about one-tenth,[1] but direct evidence on trends in celibacy, mean age at marriage, marital fertility, and life expectancy in this period is scarce. Mokyr's estimates of age-specific marital fertility, the most comprehensive available, are census-derived, but rest on a series of assumptions about age-heaping, underrecording and infant mortality, including the crucial assumption that the number of children 'aged 1 month' in the 1841 census referred instead to children aged 30 days or less. Mokyr's estimate of the Coale−Henry index of marital fertility I_g for Ireland in the early 1840s is 0.80 to 0.84. This puts Ireland well ahead of England (with an I_g of 0.65 c.1851), France (0.53 in 1845), and Denmark (0.67 in 1851), and on a par with The Netherlands (0.82 in 1859). Such a lead is by no means implausible, though Mokyr's provincial rankings, which put marital fertility in Connacht (estimated at 0.75 to 0.80) last of the four provinces, and urban Ulster (0.90 to 0.91) first, are somewhat baffling. By 1881 these rankings would be radically reversed (see Chapter 9 below).[2]

Eversley's demographic study of Ireland's Quaker community is one remarkable piece of direct evidence on pre-Famine marital fertility (see Table 4.1). That community was always small, numbering less than 2,500 on the eve of the Famine, mainly urban, upper middle-class, and very rich: only in Ulster were the Quakers represented among the numerically-dominant small farmers. If the close-knit Irish Quaker community was '*in*

Table 4.1. *Fertility rates at different ages of the mother: Irish and English Quakers (1750−1799 and 1800−1849) and Hutterites*

Age-band	Ireland		England		Hutterites
	1750−99	1800−49	1750−99	1800−49	
<20	410	—	282	—	—
20−4	598	514	450	393	550
25−9	502	445	425	418	502
30−4	470	437	367	387	447
35−9	426	366	264	306	406

Note: The numbers refer to the number of births annually per thousand married women in the different age-bands.

Sources: Eversley, 'Irish Quakers', 67; Coale and Treadway, 'Summary', 154.

Ireland, but scarcely *of* it', its demography had traits commonly associated with the pre-Famine Irish masses. The fertility of Irish Quaker women was astounding. Not only did it exceed that of English Quakers: in the later eighteenth century it surpassed even that of the benchmark population of historical demographers, America's twentieth-century Hutterite community.[3]

Delayed marriage and definitive celibacy also played a part in demographic trends. In 1840 Robert Hammond, a young but destitute Derry weaver, admitted to an official inquiry into the plight of handloom weavers in the United Kingdom:[4]

I am a single man still. I could have made a good match since I came to this town but my sweetheart found out that I was a weaver and would not have me. They know the weavers have not the means of keeping a wife and family, and no prudent wife would have one at all.

Though it is reassuring to find Derrywomen exercising the Malthusian prudential check, again firm statistical evidence is preferable to anecdotal accounts. The hard evidence for some decline in nuptiality in the pre-Famine half-century is thin. It is tempting to juxtapose the statement of Thomas Newenham, usually a reliable source, who in 1805 dwelt at length on the 'extraordinary frequency of marriage' in Ireland, and the finding of the 1841 census that over 12 per cent of women aged 46 years or more had never married, and nearly 10 per cent of the men. On the eve of the Famine the Irish propensity to marry was not high by European standards. The value of I_m, the Princeton index of nuptiality used by Mokyr, was 0.446 in Ireland *c.*1841. This is less than England and Wales's 0.483 in 1851, France's 0.516 in 1841, or Italy's 0.56 in 1864. Among west Europeans, only the Danes (with an I_m of 0.436 in 1852), the Dutch (0.406 in 1859), the Swiss (0.38 in 1860), and the Belgians (0.375 in 1846) were slower to marry than the Irish. Indeed, such was the Irish reluctance to marry that it swamped any advantage gained from a high marital fertility rate. Mokyr's estimates mean that I_f (the product of I_g and I_m), a commonly used index of overall fertility, was 0.36 to 0.37 in Ireland in the early 1840s. This compares with 0.35 for England and Wales *c.*1851, 0.39 for Germany *c.*1875, or 0.4 for Italy *c.*1865.[5]

Direct evidence on the trend in marriage age is scarce. The 1841 census invites calculation of the median marriage ages of couples who had married during the 1830s. The result (see Table 4.2) supports the contention that marriage age was rising, though modestly, in that decade. Note that since

Table 4.2. *Median marriage age in Ireland in the 1830s*

Date	Ireland (women)	Ireland (men)	Rural Connacht (women)	Rural Leinster (women)	Cork City (women)	Civic Ulster (women)
1830	22.7	27.1	21.9	23.6	22.6	22.0
1831	22.5	27.1	21.6	23.5	22.7	21.2
1832	23.6	27.9	23.2	24.3	23.2	22.6
1833	23.4	27.5	23.0	24.2	22.7	22.6
1834	23.4	27.1	23.0	24.1	23.0	22.7
1835	23.4	27.1	22.9	24.1	23.3	22.8
1836	23.4	26.7	23.1	23.9	23.3	23.1
1837	24.2	28.2	23.6	24.8	24.4	23.4
1838	24.1	27.9	23.6	24.7	23.6	23.4
1839	24.2	27.9	23.7	25.1	24.0	23.4
1840	24.0	27.8	23.4	24.9	23.9	23.4
1830–4	23.1	27.3	22.5	23.9	22.8	22.2
1835–40	23.9	27.6	23.4	24.6	23.8	23.0

Source: Derived from *1841 Census*, lxvi. Of course, these 'medians' are based on projections using 5-year age-bands of somewhat doubtful accuracy.

the data are 'retrospective' and exclude some who died in the interim, they are subject to a downward bias in the calculated median age, a bias that increases the further back one retreats from 1841. It would be foolish therefore to make too much of these numbers. Still, suppose that the 600,000 or so women who married during the 1830s did so on average half a year later than their sisters one decade earlier. This would have resulted in an annual 10,000 to 20,000 averted births. In the absence of the modest 'moral restraint' implied by this calculation, population growth during the 1830s would have been, say, about 5 per cent higher. The implied adjustment is doubly interesting in view of the pervasive notions that (*a*) the Irish were feckless and oblivious to hardship in their marriage strategies, and therefore (*b*) Ireland was sitting on a 'population bomb'.

Since the distribution of marriage ages is typically skewed to the right, the mean age at marriage exceeds the median marriage age. Assuming that the shape of the distribution in pre-Famine Ireland mirrored that found elsewhere, we may infer women's mean age at marriage on the eve of the Famine by adding one year or so to the median age in Table 4.2. The result is an average marriage age about the same as contemporary England's.[6]

Some firmer evidence of a rise in marriage age is available. In the parish of Killyman, at the western end of the Ulster's 'linen triangle', Macafee has shown that the female mean marriage age in the Church of Ireland community rose from 21.8 years in 1771–1800 to 23.6 years in 1811–45. In a much larger County Antrim sample encompassing all communions Morgan and Macafee find that women's average marriage age also rose during this period, though less impressively. Turning to Dublin city, an analysis of the Rotunda Lying-In Hospital registers and ward-books suggests a rise in the average marrying age of Dublin working-class women from about 21 years in the early 1810s to 23 years in the 1840s. The trend in the percentage age-distribution of first-time Rotunda mothers is corroborative[7] (Table 4.3). In sum, while we wait in hope for more family reconstitution studies, we cannot dismiss the likelihood of some rise in Irish mean age at marriage before the Famine, even though Malthus was quick to do so in parliamentary evidence in 1827. And even if the age-specific marital fertility of the mass of Irishwomen in general did not change, the effect of even a seemingly modest rise in mean marriage age would have been substantial. Finally, there is Eversley's conclusion, based on an analysis of Ireland's Quaker communities, that 'some sort of peak of fertility, whatever the age of marriage, occurred some time between 1775 and 1825'.[8]

As noted in Chapter 1, the evidence on mortality trends is almost a blank. Against the strong Malthusian presumption for higher mortality, there is the likelihood of reductions in deaths from smallpox and subsistence crises. The demographic crises of 1800–1 and 1817–19 resulted in a considerable number of excess deaths—40,000–60,000 in each case—but the administrative lessons learned then kept deaths to a minimum in the wake of poor harvests in 1822 and 1831.[9] Again, in the admittedly atypical setting of the Dublin slums, the records of the Rotunda Hospital imply some reduction in child mortality between the 1820s and the 1840s.

Table 4.3. *Ages of first-time Rotunda mothers, 1813–1846 (%)*

Age-group	1813	1835	1845–6
15–19	14.1	14.1	11.4
20–4	57.9	53.9	47.1
25–9	21.5	24.3	30.1
30–4	5.0	5.9	9.0
35+	0.8	1.7	2.2

Source: Rotunda Hospital ward-books.

Perhaps, despite the increasing precautions taken against contagion, poverty increased the incidence of fever: the evidence is lacking.[10] Overall, the role of emigration in demographic adjustment in the pre-Famine period was much more important than the trends in the birth- or death-rates.

4.2 'The Wandering Irishman'

Mass emigration from Ireland predates the Famine. After 1815 the outflow was huge by contemporary European standards, and rising over time. Between Waterloo and the Great Famine, about 1.5 million left, emigration to Britain accounting for about one-third of the total. Those who crossed the 'briny ocean' to north America split roughly half-and-half between the USA and Canada. The analysis of surviving passenger lists has provided us with a profile of those who crossed the Atlantic. Pre-Famine emigrants to north America were more likely to be male and members of a family group travelling together than post-Famine emigrants; they were more likely to hail from Ulster or Leinster. Most of them were labourers, though the emigrant ships contained a sprinkling of highly skilled workers too.

The earliest detailed passenger data available refer to emigration to the USA between 1803 and 1805. They suggest that Ulster emigration still dominated, with counties Tyrone and Donegal to the fore. Of the first 1,500 or so whose county of origin can be traced, almost four-fifths were from Ulster, and another 15 per cent from Leinster. Only Sligo of the Munster or Connacht counties supplied an appreciable number of emigrants. Arthur Young had already noted in the late 1770s that 'the spirit of emigrating in Ireland appeared to be confined to two circumstances, the Presbyterian religion and the linen manufacture. The Catholics never went; they seem not only tied to the country, but almost to the parish in which their ancestors lived.'[11] This may exaggerate, but there are several plausible reasons for the preponderant role of northern counties in the migration of 1803–5 and before. Most obvious is that the northerners who left were themselves often the children and grandchildren of immigrants, and for that very reason were more likely to be mobile. A second factor is that they tended to be more literate than the southerners, and exclusively English-speaking besides, features which added to their mobility. When in 1718 over 300 Ulster immigrants petitioned the Puritan colony of Massachussets for admission, it is reported that all but thirteen of them signed the petition 'in fair and vigorous autography'. A historian of the Scottish-Irish in America commented with pride: 'thirteen only or four per cent made their mark on the parchment. It may well be questioned whether in any other part of the United Kingdom [*sic*] at that time . . . so large a proportion as ninety-six per cent of promiscuous householders in the common walks of life could have written in their own names.'[12] Thirdly, though by no means rich, these northerners were less likely to have been caught in the poverty trap which during the eighteenth century may have prevented others from wanting or being able to leave. Even when short of passage money, it seems to have been easier for them to travel as indentured servants or redemptioners, and they were more highly valued in America than their southern compatriots.[13] It is surely significant that while a temporary crisis in the linen industry and the prospect of higher rents could drive thousands of Ulster folk to the colonies in the early 1770s, a massive famine in the south in the early 1740s produced hardly a ripple in the emigrant flow. A final reason for the greater mobility of the northerners may have been conditions in the American colonies themselves: anti-Catholic bigotry was strong in several of them.

One southern migration, that from the south-east (Wexford, Kilkenny, Waterford) to Newfoundland, caught the attention of Arthur Young in 1780.[14] The Irish name for Newfoundland is *Talamh an Éisc* (the Land of the Fish), and the migration had its origins in people wintering there from the 1750s for the cod-fishing season. In 1795 over two-thirds of the population of St John's, Newfoundland's largest town, were Irish. In contrast to Ulster emigrants who tended to travel in family units, these southern emigrants were mostly unmarried males. The outflow is consistent with the form of property transmission (a single son inheriting the property intact) and of demographic control usually associated with the post-Famine period. The area supplying these emigrants also had a tradition of recruitment in Jacobite armies.[15]

The 1803 passenger lists also provide some useful insights into the previous occupations of transatlantic emigrants. Of those who supplied the information, labourers (42.5 per cent) and farmers (30 per cent) provided the lion's share. One-seventh were described as 'spinsters', and the rest included a sprinkling of clerks, merchants, gentlemen and ladies, surgeons, servants, and dealers. Other features of these early data are common to pre-Famine emigration as a whole. In 1803–5, for instance, male emigrants outnumbered female by over two to one. Later pre-Famine passenger lists and the 'memoirs' collected by the first ordnance surveyors in Antrim and Derry parishes in the 1830s indicated a somewhat lower ratio, but among unaccompanied emigrants it was much higher. Later in the nineteenth century (see Chapter 9), women would sometimes be in the majority.

The Ordnance Survey Memoir lists throw some light on another issue on which most other sources are silent, the religious affiliations of the Ulster emigrants. The lists indicate that only Presbyterians and other dissenters left in greater numbers than their share in the population would predict. Whether this was because dissenters were more responsive to any expected income differential than the rest, as suggested above for an earlier period, or because the decline in rural industry affected them disproportionately, is an unresolved issue. A more detailed look at the Cumber–Faughanvale area in north-west Derry suggests that there it was the textile-weaving townlands that lost population most heavily, townlands which were heavily Presbyterian. A further point arising out of the Ordnance Survey Memoir data concerns the destinations of emigrants by religion. This is an interesting issue since a common pattern might be taken as evidence that all people from a given area used the same information network about opportunities in the New World. This is not borne out by the data, however (see Table 4.4). Recent micro-studies of migration to Canada in the pre-Famine era by Elliott and by Houston and Smyth, based

Table 4.4. *Destinations of Derry emigrants in the 1830s* (%)

Destination	Dissenters	Catholics	EC
West Derry			
New York	19.3	28.3	14.3
Philadelphia	43.7	16.2	9.5
Quebec	25.3	40.3	47.6
St Johns	11.7	14.9	28.6
South Derry			Other
New York		45.8	20.4
Philadelpia		14.7	18.3
Quebec		32.4	45.5
Other		7.1	15.8
East Derry			
New York		15.6	11.0
Philadelphia		7.8	27.0
Quebec		55.8	51.6
Other		20.8	10.4

Source: Derived from the Ordnance Survey Memoirs.

on detailed studies of censal and genealogical data, highlight the importance of community informational networks and chain migration. Thus most of Elliott's north Tipperary Protestant emigrants headed for settlements in London, Ontario or the Ottawa Valley, where they linked up with other Protestant Irish immigrants to form a distinct Protestant-Irish community. Catholic immigrants bound for Canada forged their own networks and settlements.[16]

The Ordnance Survey Memoirs also highlight the importance of Canada in pre-Famine emigration. Of the 1800 or so Derry emigrants whose destinations are given, nearly half wound up in Quebec. In the post-Famine emigration, Canada took a back seat, but Irish-born people still probably formed a higher proportion of the Canadian population than the American throughout the nineteenth century. In 1871, the Irish-born accounted for 6 per cent of people living in Canada (220,000 of a total of 3.5 million), whereas in the USA their share was 4 per cent.

The regional and socio-economic origins of pre-Famine migrants to Britain have been less studied, but a variety of sources suggests that the emigrants were more likely to hail from the west and south. Thus details on the county origins of nearly 3,000 migrants deported from London and home county parishes under the Vagrancy Act in 1824–5 indicate the predominant importance of County Cork. Of 2,737 vagrants processed through Colnebrook for Maidenhead, nearly three-quarters had come from Cork, and another 10 per cent from Limerick, with Kerry and Tipperary accounting for most of the remainder.[17]

The economics of emigration remains an abiding issue for Ireland.[18] Even before the Famine economists argued the case for and against. The case for emigration held that both those who left and those who stayed gained: the typical emigrant revealed his preference by remaining abroad, while those who remained benefited from the resulting tighter labour-market. In pre-Famine Ireland, with the law of diminishing returns undoubtedly a threat, any tightening of the labour supply must have helped. In a world of efficiency wages (see below), where some emigrants might have been underemployed and underfed, the same holds. In this sense, the nineteenth-century Irish, unlike the poor of most Third World countries today, were fortunate in that at least some of them could seek work and—sometimes—land in any of several destinations from Bolton to Boston. Emigration reduced population pressure; the areas least affected by the Great Famine (Ulster, south Leinster) had long been attuned to emigration. Even if pre-Famine emigration tended to relieve population pressure least where this was most needed, nevertheless this safety-valve aspect was very important.

The worry was that 'through Cork harbour the life blood of the nation flowed away'. The case against emigration emphasizes the brain- and skill-drains that allegedly follow. Though a brain drain is intuitively plausible—the bright and resourceful 'get up and go'—it is difficult to test. The outcome of one recent search for a 'brain drain' in the passenger lists of ships bound for North America returns a verdict of 'not proven'. Admittedly, the clues provided by the passenger lists—occupational breakdowns, and age data that yield a rough-and-ready proxy for numeracy—were rather weak ones. Nicholas and Shergold have proposed an ingenious new test of the 'brain drain' hypothesis from an unlikely source, using the records of Irish-born convicts transported to New South Wales in the early nineteenth century. These records contain information on the age, literacy, and occupation of the convicts, both those sent for crimes committed in Ireland and those born in Ireland but sent from Britain for crimes committed there. The issue is whether those transported from Britain were 'different'; the 'brain drain' hypothesis implies that they should have been. And, indeed, Nicholas and Shergold find that the emigrants were more likely to be literate and to report skilled occupations than those sent directly from Ireland. Some 'skill drain' among emigrants to Britain is thus indicated. Note, however, that if the reported skills had been employed on doomed industries in Ireland—such as weaving in Bandon or Drogheda—the 'loss' to Ireland was not commensurate. Thus Nicholas and Shergold classified weavers, bootmakers and—most implausibly—soldiers as 'skilled'; reclassifying them as unskilled would have increased the proportion of unskilled among the Irish emigrants from half to over two-thirds.[19]

A further potential source of loss stems from the age-profile of the emigrants, or the life-cycle effect. The argument is that Ireland incurred the cost of rearing and schooling the emigrants, but the dividends were reaped elsewhere. Since most of those who emigrated were in their late teens or early twenties, they emigrated when the present value of their lifetime earnings was close to its peak. One estimate of the ensuing loss to those who stayed puts it at 1–3 per cent of GNP. In the pre-Famine era, emigrant remittances were by no means enough to match this.[20]

It can be shown that any emigration that disturbs the existing ratio of labour to other inputs must make those who stay behind worse off on average. The 'brain drain' argument is one side of this. But the removal of unskilled workers inflicts losses on owners of complementary factors (land

and capital) that outweigh the gains to remaining workers. This is easily seen from Fig. 4.1, where N_0 and N_1 represent the working population before and after a labour outflow, and ABC the marginal product of labour. Clearly the loss to the owners of complementary factors, BCD, is greater than the gain to the remaining labourers, $EBFD$. In a loose welfare sense the gains of the landless poor—the majority of the people—outweighed the losses of landlords and capitalists. Paradoxically, the Great Famine may well have produced such an effect in the short run, reducing the average living standards of those who survived it, but remained on in Ireland.[21]

Emigration has also elicited a long and largely inconclusive debate about the relative power of 'pull' and 'push' factors in influencing the outflow. A more detailed analysis of this issue is taken up in Chapter 8. Here, it seems safe to argue that 'push' factors dominated before the Famine. Deindustrialization played a role in many areas, and there was downward pressure on workers' living standards generally (see below).

Seasonal migration within Ireland and between Ireland and Britain was also an important feature of rural life in the pre-Famine decades. Areas of poor land such as north Connacht, west Ulster, and west Munster were the main sources of supply; they fitted well Braudel's characterization of mountainous regions throughout early modern Europe as *fabriques d'hommes à l'usage d'autrui* (factories producing men for the use of others). Seasonal migration from Ireland had been noted by Berkeley in *The Querist* (1731); literary references in Irish to internal migration may be found around this

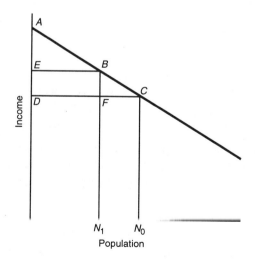

FIG. 4.1 The brain drain

time in poems by Mac Cuarta (c.1650–1733) and Ó Neachtain (c.1650–1728). The size of the annual migrant flow cannot be ascertained with any accuracy, though its total easily exceeded 100,000 on the eve of the Famine. The more important routes may be retraced through the use of both printed and folklore sources. In Ireland as elsewhere, the areas supplying seasonal migrants were places of rapid population growth and early marriage. In the short run at least, the demographic influence of seasonal migration was conservative, in the sense that it acted as a substitute for permanent emigration and rapid population adjustment. Those Connacht migrants who made the yearly journey across Ireland to Dublin and Drogheda *could* have remained on in Britain, but most of them used their harvest wages to supplement what they earned at home from conacre, fishing, and domestic industry. Their determination not to leave Ireland explains why their annual contacts with 'lowland' English-speaking regions did not force the seasonal migrants to forsake the Irish language: on the contrary, most places supplying seasonal migrants remained overwhelmingly Irish-speaking.[22] Migration also fulfilled a transitional role, however, preparing people in backward regions for eventual emigration. Seasonal migration is discussed in greater detail in Chapter 9.[23]

4.3 Living Standards before the Famine

> Never believe them that would make you think that we'd eat *wet lumpers* if we could get good bread.
>
> GALWAY LABOURER, 1835[24]

> Pádraig Ó Dálaigh 's mála mine aige
> Dhá chéad práta sáite sa tine aige
> Práta ina láimh aige 's práta á ithe aige
> 'Gus thabharfadh sé an leabhar go n-íosfadh sé
>   tuilleadh acu.
>
> EAST CORK VERSE[25]

> There were plenty of beggars, no doubt . . . but it never struck me that there was much distress in those days. The earth gave forth its potatoes freely, and neither man nor pig wanted more.
>
> ANTHONY TROLLOPE[26]

As far as living standards are concerned, the decades between Waterloo and the Great Famine are much better documented than the pre-1815 period. Among official sources, the Poor Inquiry of 1835–6 is particularly useful.

This ambitious and well-designed survey provides a great deal of information on the conditions endured by the bottom third or so of the population on the eve of the Famine. An index of impoverishment derived by Mokyr from hundreds of replies to one of the Inquiry's questions[27] implies widespread immiseration throughout Ireland before the mid-1830s among those designated 'poor' by the Commissioners. The informants—mainly magistrates and clergymen—were merely asked to report their impressions, but they were well informed, sympathetic, and probably truthful witnesses. Only in one county of the thirty-two—Wexford—did their replies indicate improvement. Mokyr's index has the advantage of bearing on an issue broached in Chapter 1—living standards depend not merely upon consumption levels but upon the perceptions of those concerned. The impression of pervasive abject poverty, if not impoverishment too, is corroborated in the accounts of well-known contemporary observers such as Wakefield (1812), Bicheno (1831), Inglis (1834), de Tocqueville (1837), de Beaumont (1839), Thackeray (1843), and Kohl (1844).

Curiously, other scraps of evidence imply some amelioration. The trend in literacy is one example, even though it is based on a comparison of patchy records (Table 4.5). In pre-Famine Ireland education was rarely entirely free, though 'free' education was becoming more common; even when no fees were charged, the opportunity cost of their children's time presumably weighed with parents. Certainly, evidence based on anthropometric data supports the claim that the demand for schooling was income-elastic: in pre-Famine Ireland, adults professing literacy were on average half an inch to an inch (or 1.2–2.5 cm.) taller than those without it. A rise in school enrolments might therefore be seen as due to increased purchasing power.[28] The first aggregate schooling return (1808) is little more than a

Table 4.5. *School attendance before the Famine*

Year	At school	Population (millions)
1808	over 200 000	c.5.0
1821	394 813	7.0
1824	568 964	7.2
1834	633 946	8.0
1841	c.700 000	8.3

Note: The 502,950 at school on census day in 1841 are assumed to represent 70 per cent of those on the books.

guess, and the second (1821), though census-based, is also clearly defective: it records no scholars in many parishes in which schools are known to have existed in 1821, and returns implausibly low numbers for some counties (e.g. Derry and Cavan). Only one small school was returned for the barony of Demifore in Westmeath, and three all-male schools for nearly 8,000 school-age children in the barony of Tyrkeeran in Derry. Yet almost two-thirds of the people of Tyrkeeran and over two-fifths of those of Demifore claimed that they could at least read in 1841. The numbers taught in the schools of Achill and Newport in Mayo was not specified. Where the 1821 census reported numbers, they seem to reflect total enrolments rather than average attendances or the numbers at school during a particular day or week. The more reliable 1824 returns refer to 'the number in the course of receiving education, and not merely the number who upon any particular day may be found collected in the school-room'. The 1834 returns also refer to the total number of children enrolled. The 1841 census data, on the other hand, include only those returned by the school authorities as 'making one appearance in school during a specified week'. The 1841 figures suggest very high attendance in the larger towns and cities—in Galway city, for instance, almost three-fifths of those aged 6 to 15 years were attending school—but substantial variation across counties. For all their weaknesses, the numbers are consistent with some rise in schooling during the pre-Famine decades. Applying the ratio of attendance to enrolment suggested by the data collected by the Commissioners on Public Instruction in 1834 to 1824 and 1841 suggests an improvement in literacy rates over the period, a conclusion corroborated by the rise in numbers of teachers from 11,823 in 1824 to 14,601 in 1841 and the information of literacy by age-cohort in the census of 1841.[29]

Comprehensive continuous data on the most obvious measure of living standards—wages—are lacking. However, Fergus D'Arcy has recently produced an index of the daily money-wage paid to unskilled Dublin building labourers. The index drops from 313 for the 1800s to 247 for the 1820s and 193 for the 1840s. Solar has compared Dublin Society and Poor Inquiry wage data for six counties; these refer to agricultural wages and imply a slight drop in nominal wage over a similar period. Other scattered data suggest constant or, at worst, slowly declining nominal wages. The cost of living over the same period has not been studied much, but John O'Brien has produced an index which uses the consumption basket of Cork workhouse inhabitants as weights. O'Brien's index averages 83.4 for 1825–9, 74.0 for 1830–4, 77.4 for 1835–9, and 74.6 for 1840–4. Solar's own subsistence indices show a substantial fall—of 25 to 30 per cent—in the cost of basic subsistence between the 1810–14 and 1825–9 and thereafter they move like O'Brien's.[30]

Comparing these estimates of the cost of living and the nominal wage data rules out, surprisingly, any sharp fall in real wages in this period. No allowance is made here for the trend in unemployment. What if the wage paid was increasingly an 'efficiency' wage? In other words, suppose that employers consciously paid workers more than the market clearing-wage, reckoning that the premium would be recouped through the effect of better diet on productivity? If such considerations bulked larger over time, recorded wage levels would be a distorted indicator of the trend in living standards. So far, however, this is only a plausible hypothesis.[31] Currently, the hard facts available on wage trends afford no *strong* support for immiseration.

The trends in recorded imports of certain consumer items not produced in Ireland—sugar, tea, tobacco—muddy the water further. When the likely effect of price changes on demand is allowed for, they are also consistent with some rise in average living standards between the Union and the Famine. This finding rests on three caveats, however. First, the exercise assumes that all changes in consumption may be accounted for by shifts in prices and incomes, thus ruling out changes in tastes. The applied economist has every reason to be sceptical of the non-economist who cavalierly invokes 'taste changes' to explain away consumption shifts. Mere assertion is not enough, though such changes may be notoriously difficult to identify. A second difficulty is that movements in the consumption of tobacco, tea, or sugar may be a poor reflection of the state of the very poor, who consumed them rarely: a rise in their consumption may thus simply indicate a rise in inequality. In the case at hand, the criticism applies more to tea and sugar than to tobacco, to which many of the poor were addicted even before the Famine. Third, the trend in smuggling—traditionally significant in the case of tea and tobacco—is almost by definition elusive.[32]

In Chapter 1, I invoked the results of recent research into the heights of Irishmen in the 1770s and during the Napoleonic Wars to argue that Irish males reaching adulthood in those years were taller than their English peers, and by implication reared on a healthier diet. Several analogous studies covering the pre-Famine decades have recently been published. They are summarized in Appendix 4.1. In general they show that the Irish advantage persisted. The Irish advantage was not due to higher living standards in the conventional sense of greater purchasing power; nevertheless these results indicated that Irish poverty was mitigated by a nutritious diet. That the Irish remained small by modern standards is a reminder of the stunting effect of childhood and adolescent diseases in an era of primitive medical technology. Had cures for childhood ailments such as diphtheria, measles, scarlet fever, toothache, and so on, been discovered by the mid-nineteenth century, it may be safely assumed that the British would have converted easier access to them into a height advantage over the Irish.

Recent research in another anthropometric area, the measurement of birth-weights, tends to support the evidence from heights. The link between the mother's health and the infant's weight is well attested, though unfortunately our information is on Irish-born women giving birth in America, not in Ireland itself. A study based on the records of the charity hospital records in Philadelphia (1848–73) shows that Irish-born mothers had heavier babies than other immigrant groups. This may tell us more about nutrition in the New World than in the Old, but it may well be partly because health and dietary habits were transferred from Ireland.[33]

William Hickey, prolific Wexford author on agricultural topics, wrote as follows of the connection between physique and a diet based predominantly on potatoes:[34]

That mealy potatoes constitute a nutritious and wholesome food, what hygeist can deny, who looks upon the fine specimens of the human frame which Ireland presents to his view, in tens of thousands, among the potato consuming peasantry?

Hickey's timing was unfortunate, since his plaudits were published in 1846, but the auxological studies reviewed above support his claim for the pre-Famine period, and imply that the Irish potato-dominated diet produced men and women who were tall relative to elsewhere. Within Ireland, it is true, greater potato consumption by the poor did not produce taller people; we have seen that the better-off were taller though they presumably consumed fewer potatoes, while the most potato-dependent regions did not produce the tallest men. Yet Irish people of all socio-economic backgrounds consumed considerable quantities of the root, and overall the outcome is another reminder that traditional apocalyptic accounts of pre-Famine Irish poverty may have been exaggerated.

The failure of the schooling and consumption measures outlined above to deliver a verdict in favour of impoverishment is somewhat surprising. My answer to this puzzle is that they refer to the entire population, *not* the rural and largely landless poor, the traditional focus of attention. For this rural proletariat, immiseration is likely. The mass of evidence gathered by the Poor Inquiry of 1835–6 supports it; and so does a great deal of other impressionistic evidence. But their poverty has often been misunderstood. We show next that though lacking most basic material comforts—decent clothes, housing, education—the Irish poor scored relatively well in another dimension, nutrition.[35]

4.4 An Energy-Accounting Exercise

Further insight into this important aspect of living standards on the eve of the Famine may be obtained from the 'energy cost accounting' framework applied by Robert Fogel to food consumption in England and France c.1800. This procedure involves two steps. First, an estimate of the aggregate calorific value of domestic food consumption is adjusted for the age-distribution of the population in order to calculate consumption per adult equivalent male. Then, second, an assumption about income distribution is invoked in order to infer likely consumption by income decile.

Solar has provided 'a rough account of where the Irish people got their calories' in the early 1840s. This estimate, which omits dairy and meat consumption and is based on an arguably over-cautious assessment of the aggregate grain acreage, nevertheless puts aggregate calorie (in kcals) consumption at 20.5 million daily, implying an average intake of just short of 2,500 kcals per day. But consumption varied by age and sex; applying the adjustment coefficient derived in Table 4.6 implies a mean intake of 3,168 (i.e. 2,477/0.7819) kcals per adult male consumption unit. Such a remarkably high level of calorific intake was due largely to the potato. It compares favourably with Fogel's estimates of 2,700 kcals for England in 1785–95 and 2,410 kcals for France in 1803–12, and is more than double that recently estimated for modern Bangladesh.[36] And there is further independent evidence for the massive calorific intake of the pre-Famine Irish: Crawford has invoked a 1839 survey of rural diets in thirteen poor law unions in Clare, Limerick, and Tipperary which put the daily intake of the average adult male labourer at almost 13 lb. of potatoes and about three pints of buttermilk daily, and pro rata for women. Such a diet would have provided adult males with 4,720 kcals! Even allowing for the likelihood that labourers fended on two meals a day during the winter months this would still return a total of well over 3,000 kcals.[37] True, there is more to a good diet than calories, but other evidence suggests that the pre-Famine Irish intake of protein and different vitamins was enough to guarantee an

Table 4.6. *Computing the calorific consumption per equivalent adult male*

Age interval (1)	Proportion in each interval (2)	Mean kcal cons. as proportion of that of males 20–39 (3)	(2) × (3) (4)
0–4	0.1346	0.4400	0.0600
5–9	0.1300	0.6883	0.0895
10–14	0.1231	0.8500	0.1046
15–19	0.1069	0.9000	0.0962
20–39	0.2840	0.8667	0.2641
40–49	0.0908	0.8233	0.0748
50–59	0.0639	0.7800	0.0498
60–69	0.0416	0.6933	0.0288
70+	0.0232	0.6067	0.0141
TOTAL			0.7819

Sources: Col.(1) uses the age-distribution given in the 1841 census, with a correction for those 'missing' in the 0–4 year age-group. Cols.(2) and (3) are taken from Fogel, 'Biomedical Approaches', 6.

adequate diet. Indeed, the quality of the protein stored in the potato is particularly high.[38]

The distributional implications of two levels of inequality imposed on the French and English data by Fogel are outlined in Table 4.7. Plainly, the distributional assumption chosen matters most for those at the top and bottom. Nevertheless, the outcome in even the 'high inequality' case suggests that only a very tiny fraction of Irish people starved in an average year and, indeed, that the poor could withstand a significant deficit in the harvest without undue excess mortality. This is consistent with the findings reported earlier that (a) the pre-Famine Irish were relatively tall, and (b) that their life expectancy was respectable by European standards.[39]

Several caveats are appropriate here. First, in estimating pre-Famine calorific intake, we cannot assume that the nutritional quality of pre-Famine foods matched that of modern varieties. Connell, a pioneer in the area, assumed that all potatoes have the same chemical composition. This may be legitimate for grain, but the evident preference of people for the premium Apple potato and even the Cup (hardy but coarser than the Apple) over the notorious Lumper in pre-Famine Ireland raises a question mark in the case of potatoes. In 1810 Townsend noted that the potatoes

Table 4.7. *An estimate of the distribution of Irish calorie intake before the Famine*

Decile	'Moderate egalitarian'		'Low egalitarian'	
	Daily kcal consumption	Cumulative (%)	Daily kcal consumption	Cumulative (%)
1. Highest	5 080	100	5 783	100
2. Ninth	4 124	84	4 399	82
3. Eighth	3 702	71	3 818	68
4. Seventh	3 399	59	3 413	57
5. Sixth	3 157	48	3 088	45
6. Fifth	2 925	38	2 802	35
7. Fourth	2 709	29	2 534	26
8. Third	2 487	21	2 266	18
9. Second	2 233	13	1 967	11
10. Lowest	1 812	6	1 496	5

Note: 'Moderate egalitarian' and 'Low egalitarian' reflect two hypothetical income distributions proposed by R. W. Fogel. The procedure followed is that outlined in Fogel's, 'Biomedical Approaches', 45, and 'Second Thoughts', 40.

eaten in Ireland were 'pleasant, mealy, and nourishing' compared to the 'watery and ill-flavoured' varieties prevalent in England.[40] Potato quality declined in Ireland thereafter, and on the eve of the Famine the very poor were often forced to rely on inferior varieties such as the Lumper. When radical English writer William Cobbett visited Waterford in 1834 he found that 'when men or women are employed, at six-pence a day and their board, to dig *minions* or *apple-potatoes*, they are not suffered to *taste* them, but are sent to another field to dig *lumpers* to eat.'[41]

Bourke, Ireland's foremost authority on the history of the potato, has collected a litany of criticisms of the Lumper, a few of which are worth reproducing here:[42]

The Irish are reduced to the necessity of entirely subsisting on the Lumper potato, a kind that grows somewhat better in the poor man's impoverished land than the potatoes of good quality. The Lumper is not indeed human food at all. Mix them with any other kind of potatoes and lay them before a pig, and she will not eat one of them until all the good kind are devoured, even if her hunger be not at all abated.

The watery Lumper, on which he [the labourer] knows from sad experience it is impossible for a man to work.

It is of a soft watery quality, and is both unwholesome and unpalatable food. [I]t approaches the nature of a turnip.

These comments date from the 1830s, after the Lumper had made heavy inroads in Ireland. How does the Lumper compare to today's varieties? The dry matter content (i.e. starch) in modern potatoes is quite variable: variety, climate, pests, soil, and agricultural practices all play a role. The food value of the potato was also a function of the weather and the kind of manure used.[43] Given its poor press, the 'watery' and ungainly Lumper probably contained somewhat less dry matter than other cultivated varieties. But did it contain less than modern varieties? And how widely was it consumed?

A critic of the Lumper noted in 1839 that cooking reduced its weight much more than better varieties, adding that its lower price reflected its inferior food quality. Now, elementary economic logic suggests that if the only difference between the Lumper and other varieties was carbohydrate content, the variety supplying carbohydrates at the lowest cost per unit would replace all the others in the market for potatoes. However, potatoes also differed in their seasonal availability, in their keeping quality, and, not least, in their taste. Since the Lumper scored poorly in terms of taste, the price premium commanded by a variety such as the Cup must exaggerate its relative nutritional advantage over the Lumper. Now between May 1843 and the end of 1845 the cheapest Lumpers fetched an average of 18.3*d.* per cwt. on the Dublin market, while the cheapest Cups cost 24.6*d.* The mark-down implied by these numbers—26 per cent—reflects a very conservative assessment of the Lumper's food content. The decision of the Killarney Board of Guardians in April 1845 to reduce the daily potato allowance by 1.5 lb. (from the previous norm of about 10 lb.) 'in consequence of minions being used instead of white potatoes' provides a better yardstick.[44]

The crucial question remains less how the Lumper compared with varieties such as the Cup than how it would rate against the underlying modern dry-matter estimates. It seems a fair bet that the Apple would beat today's popular varieties hands down. Yet inference is not enough. Crawford has done better, comparing the Lumper's weight-loss from cooking as reported by Hawley in 1840—2 ounces in every 16—with that of modern supermarket varieties. She found modern potatoes superior in this respect, and her estimates of calorific intake reflect this.[45] Austin Bourke has drawn attention to a more direct test in a Royal Dublin Society Prize Essay. This test involved measuring the specific gravity of samples of potatoes grown in 1833, and the outcome was as follows:

Variety	Specific gravity
Red Rose	1.099
Apple	1.116
Cup	1.096
Lumper	1.084

The conversion proposed by von Scheele *et al.*[46] produces dry-matter estimates of 27.8, 23.6, and 21.1 per cent for the Apple, Cup, and Lumper, respectively. On average, starch content works out at about 80 per cent of the dry-matter content. Since these estimates failed to control for soil type—the Lumpers had been grown on 'deep peaty soil', the Cup on 'deep friable loam', and so on—Bourke properly deemed them 'not above suspicion'. The Prize Essay also reported the specific gravities of small samples of a larger variety of potatoes:

Shaw's Seedling	1.060–1.081	Old Cruffle	1.092–1.097
Fox's Seedling	1.059–1.072	Cruffle	1.084–1.113
Cup	1.080–1.124	Long Black	
Lumper	1.067–1.104	Seedling	1.086–1.126
Apple	1.086–1.093	White Don	1.088–1.107
Lancs. Pink Eye	1.107	Red Don	1.070–1.081
Lenagly	1.108	Early French	
		Cruffle	1.110

The ranges quoted are quite wide, and the Lumper by no means comes out worst. The Lumper's reported specific gravity also stands up quite well against the range of 1.074–1.092 found in a test of nine varieties grown in the USA in 1958 and 1.067–1.091 in a test of eleven varieties harvested in 1959.[47]

A further check on the relative quality of potato varieties is possible. Though the Lumper has not been commercially cultivated for a long time, it was still grown in some districts in the 1920s, and specimens survive in a few 'museum' collections of potato varieties in Ireland and Scotland.[48] The Scottish Agriculture and Fishery Department's scientific services in Edinburgh has a rich collection of such varieties, and the Lumper has also been conserved in Ireland. During the 1991 season, officials at the Scottish Department kindly grew extra quantities of a range of modern and 'museum' varieties (including the Lumper), and measured their dry-matter content and specific gravities. In the experiment (the details are given in Appendix

4.2) the Lumper performed poorly compared to premium varieties, either modern or 'museum', but it measured quite well relative to modern supermarket varieties.

A second caveat concerns the diffusion of the Lumper, which had been introduced from Scotland in the 1800s. Before the Lumper, dozens of varieties were cultivated; Dubourdieu might claim in 1812 that each county had its own favourite.[49] The Lumper spread rapidly due to its higher yields, adaptability to poor soils, and reliability. It had made big inroads by the 1840s, but the common belief that the Irish relied on it almost exclusively on the eve of the Famine[50] must be qualified. Nearly all witnesses to the questionnaire on diet in the Poor Inquiry of 1835–6 mentioned potatoes as the main item in the diet. Twenty-one witnesses (from a total of over 1,500) were more specific about the *poor quality* of potato consumed in their area. One referred to 'that most unhealthy of vegetables, the lumper potato', another to 'a bad description of potato called lumper', a third to 'the worst description of potato', and so on. Such remarks were regionally concentrated; Galway produced four of them, Mayo five, Laois three, Cork three, and Carlow, Westmeath, Roscommon, Limerick, Kerry, Derry, and Tipperary one each. Moreover, the Tipperary reference was to 'some potatoes of the worst description called Connaught lumpers', and I have assumed that the Derry depiction of the 'Connaught cup, grown with very little manure, very hardy in its nature, and of a very solid description' also referred to the Lumper. Two of the Cork references were to coarse 'horse' potatoes, probably a synonym for the Lumper. While an *argumentum ex silentio* from the few references to poor-quality potatoes cannot be pressed too far, the implied non-universality of the Lumper reduces further the suspicion that Crawford's and Solar's conversions exaggerate calorific intake the regional spread. The sharp east–west gradient in the Lumper's distribution is also significant.[51]

The replies to a centenary inquiry into the Famine in folk memory contains several mentions of varieties found in the pre-Famine era. These accounts are not above suspicion, since they sometimes claim for the pre-Famine era later varieties no longer common or extinct by the 1940s. Moreover, some potato varieties—like some Irish dance tunes today—may well have been known by different names in different counties. The many names given included Green Tops, White Rocks, and American Sailors (Tousist, Kerry), White Tops (Carlow), Skerry Blues, Red Scotch Downs or Peelers, and White Scotch Downs (Westmeath), Thistlewhippers and Pink Eyes (Cavan), Prodestans (Erris, Mayo), Weavers (Kilkeel, Down), Leathers and Mingens (i.e. Minions) (Dún Chaoin, Kerry), Cups, Buns, Millers' Thumbs, and Derry Bucks (Drumholm, Donegal), and *Coipíní* (or Cups, Cill Chiaráin, Connemara). The Lumper was mentioned too, though rarely.[52]

Third, calories alone are an imperfect proxy for nutritional quality. However, the above comparison ignores the consumption of protein- or vitamin-rich items such as cabbage, fish (both fresh-water and marine, but notably herrings and mackerel), shellfish, as well as turnips, onions, rabbits, nettles, watercress, and wild fruit. Fish is mentioned in about one-quarter of the Poor Inquiry replies. Though rarely mentioned in the same source, and despite claims such as one from Kerry in 1800 that 'farmers scarce know what [it is]', I suspect that cabbage was more important than given credit for in the Poor Inquiry. References to cabbages being grown along ridge borders or plants being sold at fairs are frequent; a contributor to the *Irish Farmer's and Gardener's Magazine* in 1834 claimed that 'common cabbage' was 'long cultivated by every person having a perch of land'. Highly nutritious, cabbage was an ingredient in traditional potato-based dishes such as colcannon and stampy. Pre-Famine consumption levels are unknown, but if acreage and yield per acre matched those of 1854, cabbage production would have exceeded 350,000 tons. Arbitrarily— but generously—ceding 100,000 tons of this to animal fodder would still leave enough for an average annual intake 65 lb. of cabbage per head (or almost 1.5 lb. weekly per adult male equivalent). Like the potato, the cabbage crop was concentrated on smallholdings; in 1854 farms of less than thirty acres accounted for over half of it.[53]

Overall, Margaret Crawford's inquiries into pre-Famine diet suggest that not only did most people get the requisite calories through potatoes, flour, and oatmeal, but also that supplements warded off vitamin-deficiency scourges affecting the poor elsewhere such as scurvy, xerophthalmia, and pellagra. The 'exceptionally high values of protein' were due to the potato and to buttermilk—a drink 'not only nutritious and remarkably wholesome, but for some days after churning very palatable and agreeable'. But let us not get carried away; though Irish calorific and protein intakes may have been 'good' by contemporary standards, the Irish were still very unhealthy by today's standards, and lived brief lives by comparison.[54]

A fourth objection returns to the distinction between calorific intake and nutritional status. Perhaps the Irish 'needed' more calories because they worked harder? The study of rates paid for specific tasks such as harvesting and bricklaying in Ireland and Britain does not support the notion that the Irish worked more intensively in the pre-Famine period (see Chapter 13).

Though workers were paid much less on a daily or weekly basis in Ireland, piece-rates—denoting efficiency wages—were broadly similar on both islands. But perhaps the Irish may have worked for a longer part of the year on physically demanding tasks? There is a case to be made for agricultural labour at least. In pre-Famine Ireland labour-intensive spade cultivation often substituted for the plough, and the sickle or reaping-hook for the scythe. What difference did this make? A precise answer is impossible. The following account of a spade-digging contest held near Dublin in 1849 suggests an upper-bound on the area that might be dug in a day:

The digging match took place in a field adjoining the ploughings. The ground allotted to each man, a statute square perch, was dug in one hour and some minutes. There were fifteen competitors, who went to work more like madmen than anything else. I need not say they had their coats off; but they had their hats off, and every part of clothing they could possibly do without. Two or three of them fainted as they finished their work; six of them had to be blooded since the competition; and others are reported to be dangerously ill . . .

P.S.   Since the above was written I have learned that one of the diggers at the match, an able, well-conducted, good labourer named Grimes has died from its effects.

A statute acre contains 160 perches. Allowing for a ten-hour day, an acre at the rate of a perch per hour would have taken about two weeks' labour. This is not outrageous: Estyn Evans mentioned a rate of twenty days per acre, and the task rate of a penny per perch quoted in 1849 also matches this. In 1804 Coote claimed that planting an Irish acre in lazy-beds took twenty man-days, compared to three man-days and two horses for drills. These are averages: obviously, the work-rate depended in part on soil type. An English labourer, armed with a plough, could handle an acre or two in a day without difficulty. When it came to harvesting, the uneven surfaces left by the spade constituted a major obstacle for the scythe. The scythe represented a saving in labour-time of about one-half over the reaping-hook and the sickle.[55]

Unfortunately we can do little more than speculate as to the effect of these differences on aggregate labour requirements. The total acreage under grain, potatoes, and clover in Ireland in the early 1840s was probably about 7 million. The acreage under the same crops in England and Wales was almost double that. Ireland's male farm-labour force of about 1.6 million exceeded that of England and Wales (1.1 million). But even supposing that 4 million acres of Irish tillage land was ploughed, and one-third of the grain harvest reaped by scythe, the demands on the Irish labourer—

evaluating both at the same labour intensity per day—would have been considerably greater on this score. In Table 4.8, a rate of fifteen days per acre for spade-work, and two days per acre ploughed are allowed. The latter rate may seem high, but then most land was ploughed more than once. The labour involved in lifting fodder crops, proportionately greater in Ireland, is not included. The outcome suggests that in so far as these tasks are concerned, there is something to the point that the Irish required more calories. Moreover, agricultural work was more physically demanding than industrial, and a much larger proportion of Irish workers worked on the land. Such considerations temper somewhat the implication from piece-rates that the Irish 'needed' fewer calories. On the other hand, they must be set against the evidence on seasonal unemployment in Irish and English agriculture in the early nineteenth century, which shows that the problem was far more serious in Ireland.[56]

Another caveat refers to the problem of seasonal food shortages, already mentioned in Chapter 1. The Poor Inquiry painted a bleak picture of the 'hunger months' of June, July, and August:[57]

The distress of the peasantry is in proportion to the extent of time that thus intervenes, and the universal opinion that it is the most frightful evil in Ireland is but too strongly confirmed by the wretchedness that it annually renews or increase in the shape of regular periodic visitation which only varies from great privation to absolute famine, according the season, the price of food, employment and other local circumstances of the district.

Accounts of the poor resorting to nettles, wild mustard, and other weeds in bad seasons are plentiful. How endemic was such malnutrition? Data on the month-by-month variation in the number of births offer a limited,

Table 4.8. *Labour requirements in tillage*

	England and Wales	Ireland
Cropped acreage (m.)	13.8	7
Grain (m.)	7.2	3
Labour requirement		
(a) Spade/plough (m. days)	(13.8) (2)	(3) (15) + (4) (2)
(b) Harvesting (m. days)	(7.2) (1)	(2) (3) + (1) (1)
Total (m. days)	34.8	60
Male labour (m.)	1.1	1.6
Days per worker	31.6	37.5

indirect check on its extent in the following sense. Hunger is held to reduce libido and to diminish a population's ability to reproduce, though experts disagree on the power of these links. Nevertheless, if hunger was severe during the summer months in pre-Famine Ireland, it should have translated into a trough in births in the following spring. In Table 4.9 two measures of seasonality—the monthly coefficient of variation (CV) and the ratio of peak to trough months—are reported for Mokyr's national and western sample of Irish baptisms and for Wrigley and Schofield's sample of English data. Estimates for a sample of seventeen County Clare parishes where Catholic registers survive for the period 1837–40 and St Mary's parish in Limerick City are also given. Clare is an appropriate county, being heavily reliant on the potato and badly hit by the Famine, and population grew faster there during the 1820s and 1830s than in any other county.[58] Limerick offers an urban perspective, though only one-seventh of the population of pre-Famine Ireland lived in towns or cities. If a link between hunger and births is granted, there is no sign of it here in either rural or urban settings. Irish birth seasonality mirrored that of England rather closely, in terms of both timing and amplitude.[59] A variety of evidence thus supports the belief that the pre-Famine Irish were *relatively* well fed. The 'relatively' is important; by the standards of Ireland in 1920 or 1990 they lived short lives and had stunted physiques. Nevertheless, these findings should serve as correctives to a simplistic, apocalyptic view of Ireland before the Famine still current. Thus by two of the criteria (life expectancy and heights) set out by Livi-Bacci in his stimulating study of

Table 4.9. *Seasonality of births*

	Period	CV	Ratio
England	1750–99	8.4	1.32
	1800–37	6.3	1.26
Clare	1837–40	10.0	1.39
	1883–94	7.6	1.25
Limerick City	1746–99	5.0	1.14
	1820–39	5.0	1.22
	1861–96	7.8	1.20
Ireland	1837–45	8.1	1.27
Ireland (west)	1837–45	8.3	1.27

Note: Ratio refers to the ratio of the values in peak and trough months.

European population and nutrition, 'well-being' in pre-Famine Ireland exceeded that in several other economies. Yet Livi-Bacci's brief account of Ireland before 'the Great Famine of 1845' is unreconstructed, doom-and-gloom Malthus.[60] If this chapter has shown that Irish poverty was a more complex matter than this, it will have achieved one of its main aims.

The value of agricultural output on the eve of the Great Famine is discussed in Chapter 5. The figure suggested there—about £45 million—coupled with an estimate of landlord income and the size of the male labour force provides another perspective on living standards on the eve of the Famine. The £33 million non-landlord income was divided between 1.6 million male household heads and their families. One million or so of these were landless or near-landless labourers and cottiers. The variation in farm size suggests that the range of income earned by farmers was quite substantial. Perhaps something like the following distribution is not too farfetched:

$$200\,000 \; @ \; £60 = £12m.$$
$$400\,000 \; @ \; £25 = £10m.$$
$$1\,000\,000 \; @ \; £11 = £11m.$$

TOTAL   £33m.

The annual income allowed landless labourers here, £11, implies an average weekly income, net of any rent payments, of about 4s. (20p). Assuming an outlay of £1 on fuel and £6 on three tons of potatoes, this leaves a margin per household of £4 for sundries such as clothes and schooling. Again, this is an average, and would have been supplemented in some areas by income from spinning and weaving, fishing, or seasonal migration to Britain. The numbers betray considerable inequality in income distribution, and invite speculation about the scope for redistribution as a means of relieving poverty. Extensive research on today's Third World economies has found that small farms, by working the available land more intensively, typically produce more output per worker than large farms. Not only labour productivity, but total factor productivity too, tends to fall with farm size.[61] We cannot prove that pre-Famine Irish agriculture fitted the pattern just described; but let us assume that it did. Certainly, in both Ireland and in today's Third World the value of the fixed input (land) far exceeds that of capital inputs. This limits the potential damage from resource flight of any redistribution scheme. In economic terms, then, to assume that the aggregate output of Irish farming before the Famine would not have been reduced much in the long run by redistribution is not implausible. In that case, an egalitarian redistribution would have given each household about £25, while peasant proprietorship through the confiscation of landlord incomes only would have added £3–4 to the incomes of the bottom one million. Other combinations of rent and farm-size redistribution might be contemplated. However, while such counterfactuals are not implausible in economic terms, they are in political terms, since they featured on no political agenda before the 1840s. Utopian socialist William Thompson aside, the most radical demands of the era went no further than some controls on landlord excesses, and the provision of basic relief for the poor.[62]

The regional variation in average incomes was marked, and may well have been higher in the 1830s and 1840s than in the 1770s. Mokyr's estimates of male labour income by province in the mid-1830s give Leinster, the richest, a 60 per cent lead over the poorest, Connacht. Young's and Wakefield's wage data imply a far narrower spread.[63] Many travellers were struck by the lack of basic creature comforts in the west and south. The contrast with parts of the north-east was profound. Even at the height of the Great Famine the well-known surveyor Maurice Colles, while at work on the Londonderry estate in north County Down, found any tenant that he encountered 'ready without preparation to produce a bit of cheese, with bread, butter and beer for an unexpected guest'.[64]

Turning briefly from a regional to a comparative perspective, Mokyr has put Irish national income at about £80 million on the eve of the Famine.

Table 4.10. *Ireland c.1840 in the European mirror*

	Europe	Ireland
Crude birth-rate	38.8	39
Crude death-rate	28.8	24
Percent male LF in agriculture	72.9	70
Percent male LF in industry	10.1	15
School enrolment ratio	17	20
Urbanization	13.0	14

Note: Europe reproduces Crafts' data for economies at a per capita income of $250–300 (in 1970 US dollars). Irish school enrolment ratio defined as the fraction of those aged 5–15 enrolled at school; urbanization is measured by the 'civic' percentage of the total population.

Sources: Crafts, *British Economic Growth*, 55; Mokyr, *Why Ireland Starved*, 34–5; *1841 Census*, 438–40.

This means that income per head was roughly two-fifths that of the rest of the United Kingdom in 1840.[65] The comparison highlights Irish pre-Famine poverty, even if it probably exaggerates the real gap in incomes somewhat, since the prices of some goods, particularly food items and services, were lower in Ireland than in Britain.[66] Crafts suggests that average income in Britain in 1840 was worth $567, measured in 1970 US prices. If Ireland's 'real' income per capita (i.e. taking due account of the lower cost of living) was somewhere between $250 and $300, then it was roughly on a par with Finland's in 1840, Greece's in 1870, or Russia's in 1890—or Zaire's and Uganda's in 1970. Comparing Ireland on the eve of the Famine to the 'European pattern' outlined by Crafts suggests that pre-Famine Irish mortality was relatively 'low' and Irish literacy 'high', given the low average income level, but on the whole Ireland fits the pattern well.[67]

4.5 Helping the Poor

> Workhouse inmate: The lumpers are wet.
> Master: I'm sure they are far better than you'd get outside.
> Inmate: To be sure they are; if they weren't, do ye think I'd be giving
>   ye the pleasure of my company here?[68]

In Ireland, the late eighteenth and early nineteenth centuries saw increasing government involvement in the area of public health. The legislation that brought a 'new' uniform poor law to England and Wales in 1834 was replicated for Ireland four years later. However, there had been an 'old Irish poor law' of sorts before then, with its focus on provision through the civil parish and the Established Church. In addition, a combination of private charity and municipal initiative produced maternity, fever, and mental hospitals, houses of industry, and county infirmaries in the cities and bigger towns. The creation of a network of over 600 dispensaries after the Union meant that advice and rudimentary preventive care were within a few miles of most people. The conviction that refuse removal and sanitation reduced the spread of typhoid fever prompted Dublin city council to employ street-sweepers. The end result of all these developments was that, formally at least, public health provision in Ireland rivalled the best in Europe in the 1820s and 1830s. Eighteenth-century Protestant philanthropy and prosperity, which produced such famous institutions as the Rotunda Lying-in Hospital and St Patrick's (or Swift's) Hospital, partly explain this surprising outcome. Middle-class fears of unrest and of typhus and dysentery epidemics played their part too, being largely responsible for the fever hospitals and dispensaries. Such fears were well stoked by the crises of 1800–1 and 1816–19. Self-interest now dictated that hospitals, sanitation, and measures against itinerant beggars be funded out of taxes. The 'fear of 1817' prompted the Dublin House of Industry to employ scavengers to remove filth from the courts and backyards of the poor on a regular basis. The policy worked in the sense that harvest failures in 1822 and 1831 brought effective remedial action, and the incidence of fever and death was slight compared to 1816–19. When cholera struck in 1832, causing widespread panic, the better-off were told that their best safeguard was to help the poor. High though the cost in human lives turned out to be—the official death count was 46,175—the Board of Health claimed success for its preventive measures, arguing that the death-rate of 'other communities' had been much higher. Those 'other communities' did not include the rest of the United Kingdom, however, and the higher incidence of cholera deaths in Ireland relative to Britain was a straightforward reflection of Irish poverty.[69]

Though the focus of public health provision was on the symptoms rather than the causes of disease, on paper at least health care in Ireland before 1838 was generous.[70] The prospect of a comprehensive welfare system modelled on the English Poor Law of 1834 was another matter, and filled many taxpayers in Ireland with horror. The objectors included Daniel O'Connell, who believed Ireland was too poor for a poor law.[71] Fears that relief along English lines would bankrupt the country proved groundless, however, and the workhouse system installed in Ireland in the late 1830s and early 1840s was functioning broadly as intended by those who devised it when the Great Famine struck. Turnover in the workhouses was high, and few of them were stretched before the Famine. Thus at the beginning of 1844 the Cavan Union workhouse, which had opened for business on 17 June 1842 and had a capacity of 1,200, held only 541 inmates. Strabane (open 18 November 1841, capacity 800) held 231, Midleton (open 21 August 1841, capacity 800) 339. Workhouses in urban areas such as Dublin, Cork, and Belfast were busiest.[72] That the poor law's austere regime deterred all but the truly destitute is witnessed by the relatively small number of people seeking and being granted admission to the workhouses at any one time. The proportion of the population relying on in-house relief in Ireland on the eve of the Famine was much less than in England.[73]

Analysis of the admission registers of three workhouses—those of the Midleton, North Dublin, and Antrim Poor Law Unions—in the early and mid-1840s sheds some light on the incidence of poverty by age, sex, and marital status in pre-Famine Ireland. Midleton Union served a largely rural area in east County Cork, while the North Dublin Union was responsible for Dublin city north of the Liffey, and Antrim served a mixed rural and industrial area in east Ulster. The first pauper to enter the Midleton workhouse, on 21 August 1841, was one Maurice Doyle, a 47-year-old unmarried labourer who had lost the use of his limbs. By the end of June 1842 another 800 had followed Maurice. Table 4.11 describes them, as well as those admitted in the period between 21 August 1845 and 4 June 1846, and in the grim five months between 21 August 1846 and the end of January 1847. In all three periods old people were overrepresented, as might be expected. This was particularly so in the first period, but the middle period better represents the 'equilibrium' demand for places for the elderly. Males and females were present in almost equal numbers before the Famine, but women inmates were more numerous in the 15–49-year age-bracket, and men among those aged 50 years and above. The outcome implies that the gender gap in earnings and material comforts shifted over the life-cycle. Many of the younger female inmates were single mothers or mothers-to-be: indeed, virtually all the young mothers entering the Midleton workhouse were unmarried. Moreover, many of the married people entering the workhouse in these years, often with one or more children, did so without a partner. Another striking feature of the Midleton admissions register in the early years is the underrepresentation of married couples with young children and of older married people. None of the teenage inmates was married. Inferring the mean age at marriage of the population at large from the proportions of workhouse residents in the different age-groups who had married would produce a very misleading result! The numbers in Table 4.11 are consistent with the view that marriage, far from leading to impoverishment, provided security, and that 'irresponsible' marriages were the exception. Aggregate data on the age and sex of those relieved in Ireland as a whole mirror those reported here.[74] During the Famine, again as might be expected, the proportion of children rose; so too did the proportion of females in the total. The share of elderly admissions fell slightly, however.

The capacity of the North Dublin Union workhouse was more than twice that of Midleton's. When novelist William Thackeray visited it in the summer of 1842 most of the able-bodied male inmates had left for harvest

Table 4.11(a). *Paupers admitted to the Midleton workhouse, 1841–1846: age, sex, and marital status*

Age	Males				Females			
	S	M	W	Total	S	M	W	Total
1841–2								
0–19	161	—	—	161	143	—	—	143
20–9	21	5	—	26	46	9	5	62
30–9	5	4	1	10	12	18	15	45
40–9	16	14	5	35	13	17	27	58
50–9	13	8	8	29	11	8	9	28
60–9	21	26	30	77	6	5	25	36
70+	4	23	39	64	10	4	26	40
TOTALS	241	80	83	405	241	61	107	412
1845–6								
0–19	186	—	—	186	171	—	—	171
20–9	58	3	—	62	79	15	2	97
30–9	18	20	5	44	21	28	15	67
40–9	7	25	5	38	11	24	14	50
50–9	8	13	15	37	4	8	13	25
60–9	5	20	15	41	3	7	24	35
70+	4	5	26	37	3	1	12	17
TOTALS	286	86	66	445	292	83	80	462
1846–7								
0–19	431	—	—	431	378	—	—	378
20–9	68	6	—	75	126	27	5	160
30–9	22	18	4	47	80	61	37	181
40–9	18	41	7	70	18	39	44	103
50–9	11	20	22	54	7	18	26	54
60–9	22	18	35	81	8	9	25	45
70+	4	18	34	69	7	6	29	43
TOTALS	576	121	102	817	624	160	166	964

Notes: S = Single; M = Married; W = Widowed

work, but he was shown old men 'in considerable numbers', 'at least four hundred old ladies—neat and nice—in white clothes and caps, sitting demurely on benches' (some of whom stood up when the visiting party entered, to Thackeray's embarrassment), lots of younger able-bodied females with sly 'Hogarthian faces', and eighty babies in the nursery, attended by

Table 4.11(b). *Age distributions of inmates in Midleton* (percentages)

Age	1841–2		1845–6		1846–7		1841 population	
	M	F	M	F	M	F	M	F
0–9	22	20	24	19	31	21	27	26
10–19	17	14	18	18	22	18	23	23
20–39	9	26	24	35	15	35	30	30
40–59	16	21	17	16	15	16	15	15
60+	35	18	18	11	17	9	6	7

Sources: Cork Archives Council, BG 118/G/1; *1841 Census*, 192–3. The numbers in parentheses refer to those married at the time of admission. The numbers don't quite tally because the marital status of some inmates was not given. The 1841 data refer to Cork, excluding Cork City. Percentages have been slightly adjusted to allow for underreporting of infants.

their mothers.[75] Table 4.12 is based on admissions to the North Dublin Union during two periods soon after Thackeray's tour, 25 August 1845 to 2 February 1846, and 2 November 1846 to 2 February 1847. The outcome is broadly similar to Midleton. Again, old people were overrepresented, and older inmates were more likely to be men, younger adults more likely to be women. The preponderance of females among inmates aged 10 years or more was partly a reflection of the city's demographic structure: in 1841 56 per cent of Dubliners aged 10 or more were female. Deserted wives and young widows were more common in Dublin than in Midleton. The small proportion of women declaring a living spouse—37 per cent of those in their thirties, 25 per cent of those in their forties—is striking. Where were the 'fallen' women encountered by Thackeray? Perhaps they included some of the 'widows' and the 'married' women admitted without a spouse?[76]

Finally, Table 4.13 describes admissions to the Antrim workhouse, which first opened its doors in mid-September 1843. This workhouse was located in the confessionally and occupationally diverse area around Antrim town. Noteworthy aspects include the preponderance of children and old people (63 per cent of males, against 42 per cent in both Midleton and North Dublin) before the Famine. Again the great majority of women in their late teens and twenties were reported as single, though a significant proportion was listed as single mothers. I suspect that many of these

Table 4.12(a). *Paupers admitted to the North Dublin Union workhouse, 1845–7*

Age	Males				Females			
	S	M	W	Total	S	M	W	Total
1845–6								
0–19	304	—	—	304	188	5	—	193
20–9	62	2	—	64	80	29	20	130
30–9	42	8	9	59	30	47	52	129
40–9	34	12	18	65	17	20	41	78
50–9	17	13	49	79	4	4	36	44
60–9	9	5	52	67	9	2	46	58
70+	1	5	24	30	1	—	47	48
TOTALS	469	45	152	668	329	107	242	680
1846–7								
0–19	343	—	—	343	345	4	—	349
20–9	66	3	5	75	109	61	24	194
30–9	56	26	13	99	40	79	70	190
40–9	45	19	35	99	28	30	50	110
50–9	20	9	33	63	11	8	42	61
60–9	12	20	50	74	8	5	59	72
70+	2	5	35	42	5	3	34	43
TOTALS	544	72	171	795	546	190	279	1 019

Table 4.12(b). *Age distributions of inmates in North Dublin Union workhouse* (percentages)

Age	1845–6		1846–7		*1841 Census*	
	M	F	M	F	M	F
0–9	27	18	24	20	23	18
10–19	18	10	19	14	20	19
20–39	18	38	22	38	34	38
40–59	22	18	20	17	18	19
60+	15	16	15	11	5	6

Sources: NA, BG 78/2–5; *1841 Census*, 18–19.

Table 4.13(a). *Paupers admitted to the Antrim workhouse, 1843–7*

Age	Males				Females			
	S	M	W	Total	S	M	W	Total
1843–6								
0–19	245	—	—	245	227	—	—	227
20–9	13	1	—	14	39	6	5	51
30–9	11	1	11	24	25	15	35	75
40–9	11	7	6	24	41	21	10	72
50–9	13	8	11	32	11	2	13	26
60–9	13	18	20	55	8	5	19	33
70+	22	27	41	90	20	14	58	92
TOTALS	328	52	89	484	371	63	140	576
1847								
0–19	324	—	—	324	325	—	—	325
20–9	13	4	—	17	42	13	6	62
30–9	5	20	2	28	18	59	10	89
40–9	5	28	5	42	10	28	8	48
50–9	9	18	9	37	4	10	8	22
60–9	6	14	13	35	3	—	9	14
70+	7	2	21	30	3	3	26	35
TOTALS	369	86	47	513	405	113	67	595

Table 4.13(b). *Age distributions of inmates in Antrim workhouse* (percentages)

Age	1843–6		1847		*1841 Census*	
	M	F	M	F	M	F
0–9	33	21	35	31	27	25
10–19	18	18	29	23	25	23
20–39	8	22	9	25	26	28
40–59	12	17	15	12	15	16
60+	30	22	13	8	7	8

Sources: PRONI, BG 1/GA/1; *1841 Census*, 274–5 (County Antrim less Belfast and Carrickfergus). The admissions data refer to 19 Sept. 1843 to 18 June 1846 and 1 Jan. to 24 June 1847.

women, particularly those with more than one accompanying 'bastard' child, were really deserted wives. The Famine had a major impact on admissions: it produced a huge drop in the proportion of elderly people resorting to the workhouse and a big increase in the proportion of teenagers.

4.6 Conclusion

Over a decade ago, Mokyr's search for an answer to *Why Ireland Starved* led him to reject 'an overly pessimistic view of the Irish economy'. Against the ragged shoes, the bare feet, and all the squalor, must be set 'a diet, while monotonous and perhaps tasteless, probably richer than all but the most advanced regions of Europe', and the consequent good health and strength of the ordinary people.[77] Most of Mokyr's comments referred to levels of well-being rather than rates of change, though his ingenious index of impoverishment suggested a decline in living standards between 1815 and 1835. The findings of this chapter on the whole support Mokyr's. Yet while the outcomes of anthropometric and energy-accounting approaches guard against 'overly pessimistic' judgements, evidence on changes over time is more difficult to interpret. Schooling and consumption data may indicate some improvement, but the evidence on wages and the diffusion of the Lumper suggest stasis or immiseration in the decades leading up to the Famine. The conflict is probably more apparent than real, however, since the latter refer to the poor, while the former refer to either the population as a whole or the more comfortably off.

APPENDIX 4.1

Pre-Famine Heights, Health, and Welfare

Why not calculate mean heights on, say, a five-yearly basis between the Union and the Famine in order to track the trend in diet and health? There are several precedents for this procedure. New interpretations of eighteenth-century Austro-Hungarian economic history and of the trends in Swedish and British living standards are based on it. Floud, Wachter, and Gregory have also tracked the heights differential over time between Ireland, rural England, and Scotland. Their QBE estimates reveal a long-standing Irish advantage over the English; however, the gap narrowed between the 1790s and the 1820s, only to rise sharply thereafter. According to the authors, their estimates 'are sufficiently sensitive to track a strong negative impact of the Irish famine . . . [I]t is also interesting how strong a rebound is evident among Irish families who survived and stayed'. These are plausible findings, though Komlos's reworking of the Floud–Wachter–Gregory data offers a somewhat different synoptic view. Komlos, like Floud–Wachter–Gregory, finds that the Irish were taller than the English for most of the period between 1740 and 1850, but with the gap in his index being eroded in the early nineteenth century, and increasing again before the Famine: Table 4.A1.[78]

Table 4.A1. *Irish and English heights, c. 1780–1850 (Komlos's index)*

Cohort	Ireland	England	Gap
1780	99.2	99.1	+0.1
1790	99.1	98.9	+0.2
1800	99.2	98.8	+0.4
1810	99.5	99.1	+0.4
1820	99.4	99.0	+0.4
1830	99.0	99.1	−0.1
1840	99.0	98.9	+0.1
1850	99.2	98.6	+0.6

This closing of the gap after 1820 supports the finding of Irish immiseration at the lower end of the socio-economic scale before the Famine. The outcome is not conclusive, for the following reason: the comparison ignores the potentially serious selection biases associated with volunteer army data such as that of the EIC or the UK. These pose particularly awkward problems for time-series inferences, as the quality of recruits is sensitive to trends in unemployment and the degree of poverty, and to shifts in military requirements and in the relative status of soldiering. Thus a change in estimated mean height might reflect either a genuine improvement in health—or merely a loosening in labour-market conditions. Floud, Wachter, and Gregory recognize this problem, but dwell on the difficulty of measuring their soldiers' relative income.[79] The EIC data contain several warnings against the dangers of incautious time-series inferences. For instance, the rise in the quality of the EIC's intake in 1815–16 and the equally remarkable fall during the Sepoy Revolt of 1858 (when the minimum height requirement was reduced to 62 inches) were due to short-term shifts in labour supply and demand. Even at the best of times the Company accepted men with ailments such as defective teeth, stammers, or varicose veins. But among recruits deemed unfit for service in 1858 was one Archibald Smith, who had been 'at drill for eight weeks and although willing . . . from extreme awkwardness and apparent imbecility of mind totally incapable of learning his drill'. Cavalry recruit Martin Donohue proved no better; the Company's inspector at Warley barracks 'instantly remarked his imbecile expression of countenance, he has since evinced extreme silliness, and I am of opinion that this is his natural state of mind and that he will be worthless as a soldier'. Smith, Donohue, and some others like them were weeded out before embarkation for India, but their prior selection by recruiting sergeants desperate for men is symptomatic.[80] A cross-tabulation of mean height by age of the contrasting intakes in 1856–7, on the eve of the Sepoy Revolt, and in 1857–8 and 1858–60 makes the point more formally (Table 4.A2). On the eve of the Rebellion the Company was accepting only men considerably taller than population mean, but the news from India produced a dramatic drop in recruit quality. Comparing the mean heights of 20- and 21-year-olds in 1858–60 also suggests

Table 4.A2. *Heights of EIC recruits in the 1850s*

Age	1856–7		1857–8		1858–60	
	No.	Mean height (inches)	No.	Mean height (inches)	No.	Mean height (inches)
18	336	66.7	—	—	16	64.0
19	265	66.8	—	—	3	64.5
20	568	68.1	953	63.7	4596	64.3
21	302	68.2	372	63.5	1036	65.1
22	199	68.1	166	64.0	629	65.3
23	171	68.2	108	64.4	444	65.5
24	179	68.3	97	65.1	475	65.4
25	47	68.6	66	64.4	352	65.6
26	15	68.4	52	64.5	204	65.8
27	10	67.8	40	65.2	176	65.4
28	11	67.4	43	65.5	199	65.7
29	5	68.5	23	66.0	133	66.4
30	3	69.7	4	64.4	31	66.3
31+	6	—	2	—	16	68.5

that the frenzied recruitment campaign that ensued also produced teenagers who exaggerated their ages a little.

In October 1829, an EIC official wrote in reply to a query from Ireland: 'When you inform us about what time Michael Flanagan enlisted the enquiry shall be made about him, but without such information it would be impossible to know this individual among many Michael Flanagans in our Register.' The reply is a reminder of the strong Irish presence in the Company's forces. The EIC archive underlines Ireland's role as a fertile recruiting ground: between 1800 and the army's demise, Irishmen were nearly always more than twice as likely to enlist as Englishmen or Scotsmen. The Irish presence in the regular army was more in tune with population size. The ratio of Irish to English recruits in both armies also fluctuated in the short run, though movements in occupational distributions suggest that variations in recruit quality in both islands moved in tandem.[81] In Ireland, Dubliners were more likely to join the Company's army than men from any other region; London played a similar, though less important role, in England. Such overrepresentation of metropolitans is a common feature of volunteer armies.

The QBE algorithm was devised in part to correct for changes in the height requirements imposed by the authorities from time to time. To some extent the effect of the various biases may be reduced by controlling for the previous occupation and regional origin of recruits. One might focus, for instance, on Irish weavers or London labourers. Nevertheless, the sharp shifts in the occupational distribution of recruits over time is in itself worrying, since it implies that those calling themselves 'labourers' at a time of labour shortage may have differed from 'labourers' recruited when the labour-market is slack. Far-reaching inferences about trends in general health and welfare are therefore not warranted.[82]

Further analysis of the EIC data-base described in Chapter 1 illustrates the strengths and drawbacks of the anthropometric approach. Between 1802 and immediately after the Great Sepoy Revolt (1857–8) the Company enlisted over 80,000 men in the United Kingdom for service in India, the annual intake varying with military exigencies in India and labour-market conditions at home. The Company enlisted men from all corners of Great Britain and Ireland. Nearly all the men provided their previous occupation, and while labourers accounted for nearly one-half of the total, the list of declared occupations runs to some twelve hundred. These included some obscure or unusual ones (clicker,[83] gold and silver engine turner, buffer, leghorn presser, ostrich-feather maker) and some surprising ones (home missionary, gentleman, budget trimmer). The men's previous occupations are consistent with a relative decline in the quality of recruits in the 1850s. Irishmen declaring 'white collar' jobs—clerks, printers, teachers, etc.—accounted for one-eighth of the Irish intake in the 1830s and 1840s, but only half that during the 1850s. Second, there was a rise in the urban share of enlisted men. In 1802–15 fewer than one in seven of Irish recruits came from a big town or city background, and less than one-third of British; in the 1850s the proportions were nearly two-fifths and three-fifths, respectively. Poor conditions of pay and service in India were probably responsible: nominal wages in the ranks had hardly changed since the 1790s, and in the 1840s and 1850s soldiers were still earning less than 9 rupees (about £0.9) per month after stoppages for clothes and rations.[84]

Floud–Wachter–Gregory and Komlos focus mainly on whether the Irish were taller than the English. But what lay behind the differences in average height? Obviously, unconditional estimates of mean heights over the period as a whole are important, but the role of factors such as age, occupation, and urban–rural background may also be of interest in their own right. Besides, in so far as the skill and urban–rural composition of the recruits is partly due to the state of the labour-market, controlling for such factors should reduce the bias in estimates of the nationality gap. To this end Mokyr and I subjected the entire intake in different periods to regression analysis, the results of which may be summarized as follows.[85] The Irish height advantage was usually positive, but small: over the period as a whole it averages out at one-tenth of an inch. The results imply some whittling away of the Irish height advantage after 1815, followed by a mild recovery, and the outcome is consistent with the *relative* worsening in Irish diets in the pre-Famine decades. The height advantage of the Scots over both Irish and English, noted by Floud, Wachter, and Gregory, is confirmed. Rurality consistently produced taller men early on, though this premium had nearly vanished by the 1840s. A weaving background produced smaller men—a finding consistent with the historiography of the Industrial Revolution. The socio-economic background of men previously employed in jobs requiring literacy made them taller throughout; that advantage was accentuated in 1857–60 when the quality of unskilled recruits fell dramatically.

The data also invite a look at inter-regional comparisons. Dividing Ireland first into six regions—an industrial east Ulster (comprising counties Antrim, Armagh, and Down), a less-developed west Ulster, a 'peripheral' western region comprising Connacht and the Munster counties of Clare and Kerry, Dublin, the rest of Leinster, and a four-county east Munster—the Irish soldiers were subjected to separate regression analysis. The outcome indicated once more the robustness of the findings regarding the status of literate workers and weavers. The greater height of Leinstermen reflects the east–west gradient mentioned in Chapter 1. The small stature of Dubliners also stands out. East Munstermen were usually smaller than average also, and the men of east Ulster taller. No strong trends over time are discernible, however.

Surviving prison-register data provide an alternative snapshot of the heights of the Irish just before the Great Famine. Here I report the results of analysing two such registers. The first refers to the men and women recorded in the register for Clonmel gaol between 1845 and 1850.[86] These people lived in the garrison and market-town and its rural hinterland in south Tipperary and Waterford; they were accused of a panoply of crimes ranging from 'rolling a car on a footpath' through 'entering the house of John Dalton and killing three hens and cocks his property', being 'wandering strangers', 'trespass by pulling carrots', to grievous crimes such as rape and murder. The records reflect both the 'disturbed' state of the countryside and, through the large number of women charged with prostitution, Clonmel's status as garrison town. The socio-economic 'representativeness' of the sample is unclear, though probably it reflects a broader spread than the soldiers. That most of those listed in the register seemed to be first-time or once-off offenders—with

Table 4.A3. *The height by age-profile of Clonmel prisoners, 1841–1849*

Age-band	Men		Women	
	All	'W' only	All	'W' only
25–9	66.4 (521)	67.2 (171)	61.5 (176)	62.7 (16)
30–4	66.5 (386)	67.2 (93)	62.4 (160)	61.3 (22)
35–9	65.9 (168)	66.4 (43)	61.2 (39)	. . .
40–4	66.4 (188)	66.7 (43)	61.5 (105)	61.4 (5)
45–9	66.0 (84)	65.8 (25)	61.4 (28)	. . .
50–4	65.9 (89)	66.9 (21)	61.7 (27)	. . .
55–9	66.5 (44)	67.0 (11)	60.9 (8)	. . .
60+	65.4 (66)	65.7 (10)	61.0 (15)	. . .

Note: Height is reported in inches. . . . . indicates fewer than five observations. 'W' indicates an ability to read and write.

Table 4.A4. *Height, religion, and literacy of Kilmainham convicts, 1841–1849*

	Leinster	Munster	Ulster	Connacht
Height (inches)				
All convicts	65.1 (515)	66.2 (383)	64.6 (312)	65.3 (180)
All adults	66.5 (257)	66.7 (257)	65.9 (180)	65.9 (115)
Adult illiterates	66.1 (99)	66.3 (106)	65.7 (48)	65.4 (65)
Adults, read only	66.5 (53)	67.6 (44)	65.7 (48)	65.9 (8)
Adults, read and write	66.9 (98)	66.8 (107)	66.1 (72)	66.6 (34)
Adult Catholics	66.4 (194)	67.0 (199)	65.6 (70)	65.7 (81)
Adult Protestants	67.4 (28)	65.0 (8)	66.5 (59)	67.6 (5)
Literacy				
Adults	1.00 (250)	1.00 (257)	1.14 (168)	0.71 (107)
All Protestants	1.59 (44)	1.53 (15)	1.26 (93)	1.05 (6)
All Catholics	1.05 (394)	1.07 (304)	0.88 (124)	0.68 (127)

Note: The literacy index set illiterates at zero, those who could read at one, and those who could both read and write at two. The number of observation is given in parentheses.

the notable exception of the prostitutes—suggests that they should not be seen as belonging to some criminal lumpenproletariat.[87]

The mean height of adult men (those aged between 22 and 39 years) was 66.4 inches (Table 4.A3), impressive when compared to the estimates yielded by the QBE technique for other countries in the mid-nineteenth century.[88] Women were almost five inches shorter. The spread of ages in Table 4.A3 permits some tentative time-series inference. Allowing for the likelihood that the older men included there had 'shed' some height, men born $c.1820$ still seem to have been as tall as those born two or three decades earlier. In Clonmel literacy added an impressive one inch or so to mean male height, and half an inch to female.

Finally, Table 4.A4 summarizes the results of an analysis of a related source, the heights of transported convicts in the Kilmainham prison register. These are based on records of fourteen hundred men transported to van Diemen's Land between 1841 and 1849. The regional spread is good (40 per cent from Leinster, 29 per cent from Munster, 20 per cent from Ulster, and the rest from Connacht). The literacy information contained in the data also matches priors, though it indicates that Ulster convicts hailed from a relatively poorer background than those from other provinces. The outcome tallies well with the Clonmel data. The mean height of men aged 23 years and over was 66.3 inches. Literacy 'mattered', though less than in Clonmel. So did religion: the 552 Catholics aged 23 and over averaged 66.43 inches, the 111 Protestants 66.88 inches. Munstermen were tallest, Ulstermen and Connachtmen smallest.

The Results of the Hydrometric Analysis

The results of the Scottish Department of Agriculture's experiment were as follows:[89]

Table 4.A5. *The quality of potatoes according to the Edinburgh tests*

Variety	Content dry-matter	Content dry-matter (%)	Specific gravity
Control varieties			
Nadine	Very low	17.40	1.066
Arran Pilot	Low	22.00	1.090
D. Standard	Medium	19.90	1.079
Arran Consul	Medium high	25.00	1.106
Pentland Dell	Medium high	24.90	1.104
Kerrs Pink	High	26.30	1.114
Golden Wonder	Very high	>27.00	>1.115
'Museum' varieties			
Champion		>27.00	>1.115
Fortyfold		>27.00	>1.115
Gregor Cups		25.20	1.107
Lewis Black Potato		>27.00	>1.115
Lumper		24.20	1.101
Magnum Bonum		25.50	1.108
Myatt's Ashleaf		25.30	1.107
Raeburn's G. Cups		>27.00	>1.115
Skerry Blue		26.20	1.113
Yam		26.30	1.114

Because the summer of 1991 was dry and early, the dry matter content of many of the varieties ended up at the top end of the hydrometer scale—readings for premium varieties such as the Golden Wonder and the Champion (marked >) were off the scale completely. However, since the control varieties emerged more or less in the expected order, the figures reported for the selection of 'museum' varieties are reasonably reliable. By this criterion, the Lumper performs poorly compared to premium varieties, either modern or 'museum', but it measures quite well relative to modern supermarket varieties.

5

Farming on the Eve of the Great Famine: Output and Productivity

5.1 Agricultural Output

In thanking their architect, Thomas Larcom, for a set of Ireland's agricultural statistics for 1848, the noted English census-taker William Farr enthused, 'you have stolen a march on us in England—as you did in your comprehensive social survey of the census'.[1] Larcom's ambitious experiment was then one year old, the Great Famine having provided the initial spur. The detail provided in these first agricultural statistics is impressive: data on crop acreages and livestock by poor law union and barony, and on crop yields by county. From 1854 on, cross-tabulations by farm size were published for two decades. The precocity of this Irish experiment in data-gathering is striking. France, it is true, boasts a series going back to 1815, but it refers to cereals and potatoes only; Belgium and The Netherlands have spotty livestock statistics before 1845, but no published tillage data. In its comprehensiveness, the Irish experiment preceded a similar exercise in England and Wales by almost four decades.

The 1847 enumeration put the total acreage under grain at 3.3 million, that under potatoes at 0.3 million; it counted 2.5 million cattle, 0.6 million pigs, and 2.2 million sheep. The potato and pig numbers were dramatically reduced by the Famine. Still, the 1847 census, coupled with a variety of contemporary censal and price data and input–output estimates, forms the basis of several recent estimates of Irish agricultural output before and after the Famine.[2] All imply that output was worth about £40 million in the early 1840s. How good are these estimates? One obvious source of error and bias is that the technical coefficients used involve a good deal of informed guesswork. Second, there are good reasons for believing that, random errors aside, the early agricultural statistics err somewhat on the conservative side. An added reason why the aggregate figure of £40 million is too low is that it takes no account of turf, a significant item in pre-Famine Ireland. The early history of the statistics[3] and the importance of turf are interesting issues in their own right: let us take them in turn.

A consideration of the history of other Irish data-gathering exercises suggests that the early agricultural statistics gave less than complete coverage. Consider for a moment the lack of accuracy that marked other such pioneering data-collection exercises in Ireland. The shortcomings of the 1813–15, 1821, 1831, and 1841 population censuses are well known, and these shortcomings extend to various aspects of the 1841 agricultural data. Even post-Famine population censuses continued to suffer for decades from the underenumeration of infants and small children. Irish civil registration data were also notoriously unreliable in the early years, and nineteenth-century official emigration and seasonal migration series are also problematic.[4] The defects in these data can be put down variously to ignorance, understaffing, laziness, or fear of taxation.

The early reports of Registrar-General Donnelly, on whom responsibility for the agricultural census fell from 1851 on, reflect confidence in the agricultural statistics. Still, even though no reference is made to this in Donnelly's annual reports, coverage was probably not complete from the outset. That the police force was stretched is indicated by the break in the series in 1848: what Larcom later called the 'tumults of Ballingarry'—William Smith O'Brien's ineffective and short-lived 'rising'—was enough to bring data-collection in counties Tipperary, Dublin, and Waterford to a halt.

The House of Lords set up a select committee to examine the feasibility of collecting agricultural statistics in England in 1855. Donnelly's evidence to the committee was cautious, though consistent with less than complete statistical coverage in the early years. A few extracts are worth quoting:

I should state to your Lordships that information given is altogether voluntary; but though it is so, I have reason to believe, from various sources, that of late years much of the objection which originally existed, owing to prejudice and jealousy, has been gradually removed.

There was more jealousy, was not there, at the outset?—Yes; an impression prevailed on the part of the people that these enquiries were made for objects of taxation, and that if they made known their circumstances, it would lead to increased taxation. That prejudice I know existed to a considerable extent in some parts of the country. From several members of your Lordships' House, I beg to say, I received very great assistance in removing unfavourable prejudices.

There is no such jealousy now?—I believe the jealousy is very much diminished with regard to the agricultural statistics.

At present, do you find any indisposition on the part of the occupiers to give you the required information?—I have not been brought into much personal communication with the occupiers, except those in the immediate locality near

Dublin; but as far as I can learn from the landed proprietors of the country, their agents, and the constabulary themselves, I believe those prejudices are gradually dying away, and that each year they will diminish, unless some unforeseen difficulties arise.

A few years later Larcom, by then Under-Secretary at Dublin Castle, claimed that the opposition of 'a few jealous and crotchety people' had never been a great obstacle.[5] But others expressed their doubts about the accuracy of the returns in the early years. Even Larcom, their proud architect, confided in 1848 that 'the rates of produce must for a long time to come be a mere matter of opinion in Ireland, where so few take the trouble to record the produce of their farms.'[6] The *Irish Farmers' Gazette* ridiculed certain aspects of the 1850 crop returns, and as late as 1855 Richard Griffith wrote of complaints reaching him of 'the carelessness and inaccuracy of the police in giving their statements relating to the crops'. Some improvement in the numbers over time is thus plausible. Even if close attention to the ordnance survey maps meant that coverage of holdings was total or nearly so from the outset, that is not the same thing as accurate reporting of all acreage, yield, and livestock numbers. Nor is the evidence for improvement qualitative and indirect only; there are some tantalizing hints of better coverage of acreages and livestock in the early agricultural statistics themselves.

The increases in livestock numbers recorded between 1847 and 1853 were very substantial. In Connacht cattle numbers rose by 56 per cent and sheep numbers by 48 per cent between 1847 and 1853. Some increase in livestock numbers is to be expected, particularly if there was restocking to make up for animals disposed of at the onset of the Great Famine in 1846–7, but such increases seem very large, larger than any occurring over any subsequent seven-year period. In aggregate, the rise in the value of livestock in constant prices between 1847 and 1853 was about 30 per cent (here using 'official' 1841 prices), and would have required an investment in livestock alone of perhaps one-tenth of farm output annually. Overall, the reported acreage under crops also rose between 1847 and 1853, but this is accounted for by a big increase in the potato acreage from its trough in 1847. Individual county data suggest some anomalies. In Mayo, for instance, the acreage under crops rose by almost half in 1847–53 and by 30 per cent in 1849–53, and the cultivated acreage per farmer on farms exceeding an acre rose—this in a period when the agricultural labour force was drastically cut—from 2.4 acres in 1847 to 5.4 acres in 1853. Further circumstantial evidence for an improvement in coverage is that typically the number of animals aged less than one year in year t was considerably less than the number aged between one and two years in year $t + 1$. The problem is highlighted in the west, where the data in the early years are most likely to have been deficient. For example, in Connacht the ratio of one-year-old pigs counted in 1848 to pigs less than one year in 1847 was 1.25. The ratio dropped steadily thereafter to 0.78 in 1852-3, a pattern consistent with improving coverage over time.

A comparative perspective argues in the same direction. If the beginnings in England in the 1860s and in France in the 1810s brought teething pains, why not in Ireland? The shortcomings of the French official *Récoltes des céréales et des pommes de terre* are well known; first collected in 1816, they are generally conceded to have been defective for several years after that.[7] Turner and Coppock have pointed to serious shortcomings in English agricultural data-collection experiments in the 1790s and 1850s. Coppock has also shown that the continuous English series beginning in 1866 remained incomplete for several years. The key here is the implausible, continuous rise in the acreage in agricultural use in lowland counties, where the scope for reclamation was already very limited in the 1860s; the annual rise in Oxfordshire, for instance, averaged 0.7 per cent for over a decade.[8]

These English agricultural statistics were initially the responsibility of the Boards of Guardians. Holdings of less than five acres were excluded and filling the returns was voluntary. In Ireland, the constabulary were asked to collect data on all holdings; again, the supply of information was voluntary. The constabulary were given a few weeks in the summer to perform this task, and the average policeman (excluding those who worked in urban areas) had about one hundred farms to investigate under many headings. Alternatively, there was about one policeman for every 2,000 acres. These proportions varied across counties; for example, Mayo had a policeman for every 4,000 acres while Carlow had one for less than each 1,000 acres, Tyrone had 218 farms per policeman while Tipperary had fifty. There seems hardly any need here to invoke popular fear of the police or the farmer's perennial fear of taxation: the sheer size of the task facing an unexperienced police force in famine-time is enough.

There is little support either in Solar's trade data for the reported rises in livestock stocks. Juxtaposing Solar's estimates of aggregate beef exports (in thousand live-animal equivalents) and the annual enumerations shows that the rise in stocks was not matched by a rise in exports.[9]

There is a further reason for adjusting recent estimates of pre-Famine output upward. Throughout most of Ireland people relied on peat, or turf, for fuel. Nineteenth-century discussions about Irish bogs usually concentrated on their potential for reclamation or industrial fuel,[10] making it easy to forget their main function: providing fuel for the bulk of the rural population, or probably about a million families on the eve of the Famine. Turf production was an important part of the work-year: between cutting, drying, harvesting, and drawing home the turf, a labourer's annual supply required up to one month's work. Like the potato, the bulk of the turf harvest was not marketed. Turf varied considerably in quality and access,[11] but the information needed for a rough estimate of the value of output is available in the Poor Inquiry Report. An appendix to the report contains a great deal of comments such as the following from throughout the island:[12]

(Sligo): It would be a very poor cabin that would not burn 100 barrels in the year, and those, if bought, would cost 15*s*. or £1, and would take a man at least a fortnight to cut for himself, and together with the help of his wife and children in drying it.

(Clonlisk, Offaly): To an ordinary farmer the saving of his year's fuel would cost about £2. 10*s*., and the expense of drawing it home depends on the distance.

(Dundalk, Louth): The cost of fuel depends entirely on the distance from Dundalk for coal, and from the bogs for turf; if near to either, it may cost the ordinary farmer from £4 to £5 a year.

(Portnchinch, Laois): The expenses, in an average case, will be, perhaps, about £1. 10*s*.

(Talbotstown, Wicklow): To an ordinary farmer the cost of fuel may be about £5 annually, besides drawing, which at the average distance from the bogs, may be estimated at about as much more.

(Middlethird, Waterford): A farmer of twenty acres burns about fifty kishes of turf in the year, together with furze. The expense of drawing it home, labour etc. is about 1*s*. 6*d*. a kish, which makes the expense of fuel about £4. 5*s*.

(Aughrim, Galway): The bogs are plentiful enough, but I may say that they are closed against the poor, for turf is set at from 6*s*. to 8*s*. a perch, and three perches are little enough for any cabin.

The price and quantity consumed of turf varied widely across regions and by farm size. My reading of the evidence is that £2 per family would be a rather conservative estimate of the average cost per household.[13] Assuming a turf-using population of one million households yields an estimate of £2 million in aggregate, or about 5 per cent of total agricultural output. There is good reason for adding this sum to previous farm output estimates, since the main input into turf production was farm labour and the output constituted net value added in the conventional sense. As already noted in Chapter 1, abundant fuel was one of the factors which made life for the poor in Ireland bearable. Now, it might be argued that since turf is not a reproducible crop, except in the very long run, it should be excluded. But later estimates of Irish agricultural output have included turf, just as estimates of industrial output include coal or iron. In pre-Famine Ireland, where the constraint was not the supply of bogs but the summer labour needed to cut the turf, the argument hardly applies.

Recent estimates of output on the eve of the Famine have put it at between £39 million and £42 million; allowing for underenumeration and for turf production suggests a figure of about £45 million. A more dis-aggregated analysis of the output estimates shows that output *c.*1845 was largely made up of tillage items. The numbers rule out any big shift away from tillage between Waterloo and the Famine. Unfortunately, direct statistical evidence on the pasture–tillage split before the early 1840s is lacking, but both qualitative evidence and economic theory argue against consolidation on a substantial scale for most of the period under review. Thus several Irish experts giving evidence to the 1833 Select Committee on Agriculture referred to the rise in the tilled acreage since the peace. One of them claimed that wheat was spreading in Longford, not traditionally a corn county; others that the same held for parts of west Limerick, Clare, and Kerry. Two witnesses attested to the breaking up of old pastures in Mayo after 1815. Several of the county entries in Lewis's *Topographical Dictionary* (1837) also noted the spread of tillage. In Antrim, for example, 'a considerable portion formerly employed as grazing pastures is now under tillage', in Roscommon 'tillage has in later years been greatly extended', while in Wicklow 'cultivation has for many years been rapidly extending up the more improvable mountains'. Again, Mokyr's analysis of replies to a Poor Inquiry question about consolidation shows only sixty-seven of 1502 respondents declaring that consolidation was 'very widespread' or 'prevalent'. However, the evidence presented to the Devon Commission of the early 1840s suggests consolidation. The conflicting impressions gained from an analysis of the Poor Inquiry and Devon responses could reflect a genuine shift in the interim, but the greater objectivity of the Poor Inquiry witnesses, who were far more numerous and all of whom were responding to the same question, must also be stressed.[14]

The trend in the prices of pastoral products relative to those of tillage items also rules out any dramatic shift. Mokyr's statistical analysis of a tillage/pasture price ratio between the 1790s and the early 1840s reports a decline, but one too small to be distinguished from the annual fluctuations in the ratio. More recently, Solar has brought his rich array of newly constructed price series to bear on the issue. He found 'little support for the proposition that relative prices moved decisively in favour of pasture at the end of the Napoleonic Wars'. Instead he discoved a slight trend in favour of pasture that long pre-dated 1815, and a more marked movement from the early 1830s on. The trend in relative output prices alone would not have been decisive, however: a rise in wages relative to rent would also have dictated a shift towards pasture. However, such a rise is unlikely. As noted in Chapter 3 money wages declined between Waterloo and the Great Famine, while money rents more than held their own.[15]

This serves as a reminder of two points. First, swings into and out of tillage were nothing new in Ireland. Several eighteenth-century accounts lamented the displacement of *sculóga* or small-scale tillage farmers by cattle. Nicholas Taaffe in 1766 had regretted the dispersal of 'communities of industrious housekeepers who in my own time herded together in large villages and cultivated the lands everywhere, till as leases expired, some rich grazier, negotiating privately with a sum of ready money, took the lands over their heads'. Much later the Dublin Society surveyor of Mayo lamented the phenomenon there. The intensely commercial nature of Irish agriculture was responsible for such shifts.[16] Second, even when the shift towards tillage was at its zenith, some regions remained mainly pastoral. These included the rich grazing-lands of north Leinster and parts of east Connacht.

5.2 Agricultural Productivity: Comparisons and Trends

No careful itemized estimate of British agricultural output for this period exists. Some authors have rested content with economist J. R. McCulloch's guestimates of £80 million for crops and £61.6 million for livestock products, but McCulloch's crops estimate is much too high since it includes £9 million for clover (an input into livestock production) and makes no allowance for on-farm animal consumption of other crops. Deane and Cole have proposed a figure of £100 million *c.*1840, but an estimate of £120 million accords well with Allen's recent estimate for England in 1850 and Solar's for Scotland in the mid-1850s.[17] There is thus no doubting that land productivity, and especially labour productivity, were considerably higher in Britain in the early 1840s. The most generous comparison suggests that British output per worker was about double that of the Irish.

What of total factor productivity? A series of comparisons—with Scotland, Belgium, and Great Britain[18]—shows that, in a purely static sense, Irish agricultural resources were tolerably well allocated on the eve of the Famine. These studies compare factor inputs and output in each pair of countries. The British comparison suggests that while about one-half of Britain's edge in terms of productivity per worker may be accounted for by its higher land/labour ratio, and Britain's farmers were also better endowed with physical and human capital, a British lead in terms of total factor productivity is still likely. This British lead is confirmed by an alternative approach to total factor productivity, a comparison of input prices. Note that since Ireland had full access to British technology, Ireland and Britain could potentially have been on the same production possibility frontier. Farmers in both countries obtained similar prices for their produce; Irish prices were perhaps 5 to 10 per cent less, given transport costs. Given broadly similar prices, 'cheap' Irish labour should have produced a higher rent per acre in Ireland than in Britain for land of similar quality. This clearly was not the case: on the eve of the Great Famine, land in Ireland was worth about 16–18s. (80p to 90p), compared to 24–7s. (£1.20 to £1.35) in England.[19] Arthur Young had produced a similar gap. He estimated the Irish rent per acre at 10s. 3d. Irish currency or 9s. 6d. sterling (48p) in 1776–8, and his English tours produce an average of 13s. 4d. (67d.) for 1770.[20] If both land and labour were 'cheap' in Ireland, then total factor productivity in Ireland is likely to have been lower than in England. One possible reason for this, discussed further in Chapter 13, is that Irish labourers worked less hard or less long than British. However, that scenario refers to a two-input world, and British agriculture was presumably a good deal more capital-intensive than Irish in these decades.

The Belgian and Scottish comparisons return a striking verdict. They imply that the average worker in Irish agriculture may have produced less than his Belgian or Scottish counterpart, but this can be largely explained by the paucity of complementary resources. Given the doleful historiography, the point is important. It must not be stretched too far, however. Ultimately the issue becomes why Ireland's land/labour and capital/labour ratios were so low on the eve of the Famine. Nevertheless, the static productivity comparisons would seem to undermine traditional quick-fix panaceas for Irish backwardness. If Irish agriculture, factor input for factor input, was as productive as Belgian and Scottish, then explanations of that backwardness which dwell on the Irish peasants' notorious 'antipathy to labour' or incompetent farm management seem otiose. Recent research into pre-Famine farming practices is also more in tune with our productivity calculations. The verdicts of the Dublin Society surveys and the county reports in Lewis's *Topographical Dictionary* on Irish agricultural progress are broadly positive.[21] Only if Ireland is gauged by the demanding standard of English 'high farming' does MacCulloch's verdict against the Irish, that 'their extreme poverty is principally a consequence of their extreme sloth' carry much conviction.

Arthur Young's useful estimates of grain yields in the 1770s have already been discussed. Taken together with estimates of yields in the 1840s, they indicate an increase of about 20 per cent in the interim. This matches that occurring in contemporary England. Thus Irish yields continued to be high by contemporary standards in mid-century (e.g. compare France, where potato yields too were only half the Irish). Still, as noted in Chapter 2, the high yields were in part at least due to greater labour inputs, and overall output per acre of farmland was not so high.

The orientation of agriculture on the eve of the Great Famine was determined in part by protection. In the mid-1790s Ireland had supplied only 16.5 percent of Britain's corn imports. That percentage rose rapidly thereafter from 23 in the mid-1800s to 57 in the mid-1810s, 70 in the mid-1820s, and 80 in the mid-1830s.[22] This was partly the result of the Corn Laws. Not only did they impose hefty tariffs on foreign producers: since the tariff level depended on the price of corn in the British market, their unpredictability imposed an additional burden. The Corn Laws produced hothouse conditions for corn cultivation in Ireland, which produced far more grain than might be expected in competitive conditions from a country with such a damp climate. O'Rourke's simulation of the output and distributional consequences of the repeal of the Corn Laws in 1846 indicates that with continued protection at the level of the early 1840s' tillage output, instead of falling, would have been as high in the 1870s as it had been in the 1850s. As a consequence, there would have been work for another 100,000–200,000 men on the land. No wonder Irish landlords and tillage farmers were strident in their support for the Corn Laws in 1815, support that persisted until the Famine struck. In Roscommon one landlord accused those who favoured the repeal of the Corn Laws of 'seek[ing] to excite the passions of the lower orders of England against our last and only resource . . . after leaving Ireland nothing but Agriculture'.[23] Indirectly, the Corn Laws both encouraged and reduced the burden of Irish industrial decline after 1815. Their subsidization of wheat cultivation led to 'overcultivation' of the potato, given its role in the crop rotation. Thus though the Corn Laws benefited farmers before 1845, they also fuelled Ireland's eventual adjustment problems.

Inevitably the Famine has made the potato the villain of the piece. The irony is that though the drawbacks of non-storability and non-transportability were genuine, failures of the potato crop before 1845 were neither as murderous or as extensive as most historians have described. Even the notorious Lumper variety—reputedly prolific and suited to poor soils, but allegedly subject to wide variations in yield—did not deserve its bad reputation on its pre-1845 record. In a series of experiments carried out in Scotland less than a decade before the Famine the Lumper outperformed over one hundred other varieties for its yield, reliability, and leaching properties. The case for the potato must rest largely on inference, but Solar's statistical analysis of pre-blight French and other crop-yield data suggests that the potato's unreliability relative to other crops has been exaggerated and that repeated failures of Irish dimensions were unthinkable in the sense that they were beyond the realm of previous experience.[24]

Disaggregated data on farm output and productivity are very scarce. The survey of over one hundred farms carried out on the Courtown estate in north Wexford on the eve of the Famine is therefore of some interest. The survey reports landed area, rent due, and an estimate of the average output of tillage and livestock items. The numbers are interspersed with comments on the managerial skills of individual farmers. Farms in this area were fairly small, averaging 26 acres, and ranging in size from 4 to 110 acres. Crops grown included the standard hay, grain crops, beans, potatoes, turnips, and vetches. The data reveal no correlation between land quality and farm size. An analysis of the data shows that output per acre averaged £4.3, being highest on small farms, but the proportion of tillage items in total output was little influenced by farm size, and overall tillage accounted for nearly five-sixths of computed output.[25]

5.3 Landlords and Tenants

> My grandfather never saw [the estate] in his life. My father saw it but once, when he drove along the mail-coach road that skirts it in a carriage, stopped for half-an-hour to talk to the tenants who met him, and then drove back again. The agent was bad, and about 1838 turned out dishonest . . . [I]t was needful that some one should look after the estate.
>
> WILLIAM BENCE JONES, 1880

The Irish land-tenure system's part in holding back the agricultural sector was increasingly debated before the Famine. However, the solution eventually adopted half a century later—peasant proprietorship—was hardly a realistic option at this stage. The descendants of landlords dispossessed in the seventeenth century had come to terms with their reduced status, and tenant spokesmen articulated demands for 'fair' treatment rather than outright possession. Peasant proprietorship had hardly ever been considered by economists before Thornton and Mill in the 1840s. Nor was it a serious policy demand in Ireland. O'Connell's Repeal movement never envisaged it, and it took the trauma of the Famine to convert radical visionary James Fintan Lalor to wholesale land reform.[26] Reformers confined their critiques of landlordism to complaints about absenteeism and the widespread resort to eviction, often linking the latter to tenant underinvestment. Evictions were frequent before the Famine,[27] though probably as likely as not to be the work of farmers as of landlords. The landlord–tenant system could also cause tenant-induced disinvestment, however. Mokyr has juxtaposed the opportunistic tenant who ran down leasehold property with the predatory landlord who raised the rent when leases fell in. The latter was once a familiar figure in nationalist demonology, but the former has been usually overlooked. The following is Hely Dutton's account of the problem:[28]

In many parts of [Clare], chiefly the eastern and western extremities, where the soil in its present unimproved state is not adapted to wheat, oats is a very general crop, and frequently after manured potatoes, and the cultivation of this grain is continued until the ground is completely exhausted; in this state it remains for several years, producing little herbage, and of very bad quality, until it has produced a sufficient coverage to enable them to burn it again, and the same wretched course is pursued, whilst the agent (perhaps some young lawyer or attorney, totally ignorant of country affairs) permits his absentee landlord to suffer thus in his receipts; for, at the end of almost every lease, the ground comes in hands in this impoverished state, and it is by no means uncommon to burn ground four times during a lease of thirty-one years.

Townsend[29] similarly reported from Cork that 'towards the termination of a lease, it is a very common practice to pursue the system of exhaustion, which is most effectually accomplished by such as are not restrained from paring and burning'. In theory, the lack of security need not have been a drawback, if either (a) landlords over time earned a reputation for non-predation, and outgoing tenants were compensated for unexhausted improvements through some system such as tenant right, or (b) landlords carried out the fixed investment themselves. Nevertheless the general point remains that as long as ownership, management, and labour input are embodied in different people, there is scope for cheating, and resources are wasted in monitoring inputs and outputs.

In practice Irish landlords (with some notable exceptions) spent little on improvement before the Famine; the piecemeal land reclamation and the introduction of better farming equipment and new methods responsible for the output increases posited earlier were largely the work of the stronger tenants.[30] Though hard numbers are lacking, the percentage of the gross rental ploughed back into farming by landlords before the Famine was a good deal less than that reinvested in the post-Famine decades. Moreover, much of what landlords called improvement involved spending not on farms, but on 'churches, bridges, castles, hotels, courthouses, docks, wharfs', without, it is alleged, 'any ultimate benefit to the tenantry or improvement on the soil on which they live'. The sixth Duke of Devonshire, a 'good' landlord, lavished nearly £20,000 on Lismore Castle in 1811–14, and he and his father spent £71,277 on the town of Dungarvan between 1801 and 1820, with 'the single objective of ensuring that its political control remained in the Duke's hands'. This was by no means all waste, however: the building created substantial local employment, citizens of Dungarvan who voted for the Devonshires benefited from the extravagance, and local farmers gained from the new quays and markets. By definition, landlords were ultimately responsible for the location, shape, and upkeep of Ireland's towns and villages. This produced a link between the location of new and remodelled estate villages or towns and the wealth of associated landed estates. Hundreds of settlements were created and enlarged between the Restoration (1660) and the Famine. Inevitably some of the new towns failed (e.g. Rutland, Binghamstown), while the success of others (e.g. Fermoy, Ramelton) had less to do with heroic landlords than underlying economic trends or state involvement. Was the ensuing urban network 'optimal'? What role did traders and manufacturers play? Would more dispersed landownership have spurred on or retarded urban growth in appropriate sites? How far could spontaneous, higgledy-piggledy urbanization proceed without landlord interference? Appraisal of landlord performance in this area is a complex matter, awaiting analysis.[31]

Landlord investment in farms in pre-Famine Ireland was probably constrained by the small size of Irish farms relative to English. That does not absolve landlords as a group, however, since the size distribution of farms in 1815 or 1845 was partly the result of earlier landlord lethargy. Elizabeth Smith, wife of a west Wicklow landlord, provides a case in point.

Describing the plight of a tenant who married 'a sickly labouring lad who is often laid up, but to whom she has brought seven children . . . [living] in [her] mother's cowhouse where [the mother] had no right to put them and thus settle a whole family of beggars on us', Mrs Smith ruefully lamented, 'we did not look after things as we have learned to do now'.[32]

Absenteeism was another old chestnut. Estimates of the proportion of Irish land owned by residents of Great Britain on the eve of the Famine range from one-fifth to one-third (almost certainly an exaggeration). Mercantilist-inspired critics of the landlords pointed to the resultant drain of purchasing power as a brake on Irish development. Conspicuous consumption in Bath or London was at the expense of much-needed employment in Ireland. Hence Maguire's verdict on the spendthrift second Marquis of Donegall that 'a great landowner was important to a town such as Belfast because he employed more local people and spent more of his income locally than an absentee would have done'.[33] The classic contemporary riposte to this point is due to McCulloch, who repeatedly argued that it mattered little where the landlord spent the rent. Landlord consumption had to be paid for indirectly out of grain and livestock regardless. The argument is obvious in the case of imported goods, but what of the (non-tradable) bricks and mortar consumed by the likes of the Marquis of Donegall? There McCulloch invoked the classical economist's presumption of long-run full employment, whereby the Marquis's bricks and mortar were produced at the expense of some other goods and services (which would have been exported had he decided to have his mansion built abroad). McCulloch's model failed to address non-classical unemployment, due to structural or efficiency wage considerations.

Absenteeism was subject to considerable regional variation. Landlords tended to shun living on poor land and in remoter, thinly inhabited areas. This may have compounded the west's backwardness; on the other hand, on good land where scope for productivity gains were best, landlords were more likely to be resident. Comprehensive data are lacking for the pre-Famine period, though Mokyr has managed to extract an index of absenteeism from the replies to a Poor Inquiry questionnaire in 1835. The replies show absenteeism to have been most common in Ulster and Connacht; they also imply that nearly two-thirds of the absentees lived elsewhere in Ireland. Mokyr found absenteeism most prevalent in Longford, Leitrim, and Derry, and least common in Kildare and Westmeath. Since the proportion of absentees changed but slowly over time, Mokyr's index bears comparing with the detailed census of Irish landowners published in

1876. The 1876 census supports his findings. On a loose and somewhat arbitrary definition of absenteeism, it suggests that in the mid-1870s the share of all land owned by non-residents in a cross-section of counties was as follows: 10–15 per cent in Wexford, Tipperary, Antrim, and Down, less than a fifth in Westmeath and Kilkenny, over a quarter in Galway, slightly less than one-third in Kerry, Mayo, and Meath, well over one-third in Clare and Donegal, two-fifths in Derry, and half in Leitrim and Longford. The correlation between poor land and absenteeism is confirmed: for example, in 1876 one-fifth of all Donegal land was owned by five absentees, but that land was worth only one-tenth of the county valuation. In this respect, Derry is the exception that proves the rule, because the prevalence of absenteeism there was due largely to the London Companies, usually deemed caring landlords.[34]

The absentee–resident contrast was probably less important than that between spendthrift or insolvent landlords, numerous in pre-Famine Ireland, and those who invested some of their income on agricultural improvement. But residence was hardly the key to improvement: a good agent could be an effective substitute for a model resident landlord.[35] The 1841 census reveals considerable regional variation in the density of landlord proxies in the form of agents and stewards. While the Leinster counties of Kildare and Kilkenny had over thirty agents and stewards for every 1,000 farmers, Fermanagh, Donegal, and Leitrim had only two agents per 1,000 farms. Agents also effectively substituted for middlemen, and their greater prevalence in the east may thus reflect a tradition of direct letting. Strong inferences are hardly warranted, however; the ratio of agents and stewards to farmers in 'modern' east Ulster was less than in any Munster county.

Even if, as McCulloch insisted, *where* the landlord resided the rent mattered little for the Irish economy, the same hardly holds for the allocation of the rent between consumption and investment. Though aggregate data are lacking, Irish landlords were certainly conspicuous consumers, and their hospitality and eagerness to emulate their English peers provided a fair field for moneylenders and attorneys. One neglected aspect of landlord 'extravagance' is worth noting here, since its dimensions can be mapped at least approximately. Between the mid-eighteenth and mid-nineteenth centuries a craze for 'natural' or 'picturesque' landscapes prompted most Irish landlords to convert massive tracts of demesne land into leisure parks. As in England, the formal deerparks, fishponds, and carefully tended gardens of old gave way to a studiously unkempt landscape of grass and trees. Reeve-Smith's scrutiny of the early ordnance survey maps

suggests that by the mid-nineteenth century the total acreage converted
into more than 7,000 leisure parks approached 0.8–0.9 million acres, or
nearly 4 per cent of the total landed area. This omits land devoted to
demesne farming. The landscape parks tended to be located on prime
farmland. In some eastern counties the proportion of all land in leisure
parks reached 5 to 7 per cent; in counties Kerry, Leitrim, Mayo, and
Donegal, it was less than 4 per cent. The cost in labour of restoring land to
'nature' was considerable, and some of the conversion work had a relief
character. Yet, once created, the parks were lost to productive agriculture.
They should therefore be considered a cost of the land-tenure system. The
social cost measured in terms of aggregate agricultural output forgone—say
1 to 3 per cent—may seem trivial; viewed from another angle, the reallocation of 0.8–0.9 million acres of the best land would have kept 100,000
smallholders and their families in comfort.[36]

The surveyor of the Trinity College estate, Maurice Colles, informed the
Provost in 1839 that on college land 'in Iraghticonnor [County Kerry]
there is, I am confident, an interest five times greater than the rent paid'.
The reason was that most of the college's tenants were still middlemen.
About thirty tenants held the bulk of its lands, the most important of
whom were Lord Leitrim and Edward Conolly who shared over 40,000
acres in Donegal, and St John Blacker and Charles Launcelot Sandes, with
nearly 30,000 acres between them in Kerry. The rent paid by the middlemen was typically about one-third of the Poor Law Valuation.[37] Since
the Poor Law Valuation was considered an approximation to a 'fair' rent,
this left college middlemen—or middlewomen such as Mrs Anne Lyne
(2,730 acres in Armagh), Mrs Louisa Spread (1,707 acres in Kerry), and
Dame Sackvilla Johnson Walsh (1,265 acres in Tipperary)—plenty of scope
to make a comfortable living. In the late 1830s Daniel O'Connell (an
indulgent and slovenly landlord) was charging his Iveragh tenants over
£1,500 for Trinity College land on which he paid the College less than
£900.[38]

In its lackadaisical attitude towards middlemen Trinity College was
exceptional. The pre-Famine decades saw a marked shift towards direct
letting by head landlords. But this did not automatically constitute a step
forward for the agricultural sector, since the traditional view that middlemen
'presented an insurmountable barrier to the exertions of humble industry' is
no longer credited. For the most part the demise of the middleman meant
merely the reallocation of some of the economic rent to the head landlord.
Thus the London Companies, divorced from the direct management of their

estates in County Derry for two centuries, got rid of most of their middlemen in this period, but that mattered little for the tenants in terms of
rent paid or concessions granted. Nevertheless, leasehold tenures involving
middlemen continued to provide headaches for many landlords right up to
the Famine—and plenty of business for their lawyers. The following
account from the journal of John Benn-Walsh, absentee owner of about
10,000 acres straddling the Kerry–Cork border, is indicative:[39]

[Mr Gabbett's] connexion with Grange is a curious instance of the danger &
mischief of middleman interests. He is the son of a Cumberland gentleman of
independent fortune & is sheriff for the county this year. His father, who had been
to India, married a Miss Wiseman from the county of Cork & received as part of
her fortune a mortgage of the original lessee's interest of Grange. Mr Salkeld, the
father, subsequently published the equity of redemption in this mortgage & thus
became the representative of the original lessee, subject to several leases he had
previously made. The estate was, until these sad times, worth about £700 a year
and paid a head rent of £365 to me, a profit rent of £113 to Mr Salkeld, and the
remaining profits distributed among a number of sub lessees' mortgages, &c. My
head rent was always paid by Hawkes & Curtis who held together two thirds of the
lands. Latterly, Hawkes let the demesne to Mrs Clebburne, reserving the rents of
about £90 let to 3 tenants of the name of Mahony as his profit. My head rent of
£365 was thus paid in the proportions of about £225 by Mrs Clebburne & of £140
by Curtis. The real circumstances of this complicated tenure were never understood
either by me or by Mr Gabbett, Senior. It was always supposed by us that the
Hawkes's were the representatives of the original lessee Patrickson. But in these
bad times Mrs Clebburne got greatly in arrear & I brought an ejectment for £800.
Mr Matthew Gabbett, with great industry & sagacity, through the aid of the
registration courts, unravelled this tangled skein, & the liability for this arrear to
me is traced to Mr Salkeld, who is the only person in a position to redeem. He
wants to make various terms . . . I shall hold fast to the alternative: either let him
pay me my £800, or, by my holding where I am, the original lease to Patrickson &
all the complications resulting from them will be extinguished. There are several
other interests carved out of these. Mr Salkeld gave a lease of all the upper part of
the farm to a buttermerchant named Scanlan. This man failed & this part is in
Chancery & let to a tenant of the name of Magner, who has quite run it out. Mr
Lombard the clergyman has about 7 acres close to the parsonage house, & an old
man named Leary has 17 acres more of Curtis's part, but this is the general outline
of this complicated affair.

Many head landlords organized surveys and valuations of their estates in
the pre-Famine decades, but again more with a view to increasing their
share of the Ricardian rent than increasing output and productivity.[40]
Recent scholarship also returns a sceptical verdict on the long-standing
claim that Ulster custom or tenant right, by reducing landlord power,

facilitated capital accumulation in Ulster. The claim boils down to the double assertion that rents were lower in Ulster than in the rest of the country, and that tenants invested more of the proceeds than landlords would have done. Johnson and Kennedy's data on rent per acre in the 1830s, derived from the Poor Inquiry and reproduced below, seem to cast serious doubt on this version of the land-tenure hypothesis.[41]

Indeed it has been argued that tenant right, instead of reducing the landlord's share of the Ricardian rent, was a means of ensuring that stipulated rents were paid. While this fails to explain the determination of, or fluctuations in, the value of tenant-right, it probably contains an element of truth. As Coulter explained after the Famine:[42]

[Tenant right is] acquiesced in and encouraged by many agents and landlords because they look on it as the best security they can have for the payment of rent. If a tenant should fall into arrear, and be evicted from his farm, he is still allowed to sell his 'good will', and the arrear or rent and all his just debts are liquidated out of the purchase money, otherwise the landlord will not allow the transfer to be made.

In a frictionless world of zero transactions costs, economic theory holds that the choice of tenurial regime reflects agreement between the owner and user of land about the allocation of risk. Where labour is cheap, wage labour or sharecropping offer better insurance to the landless than fixed rent tenancy. Thus the choice of sharecropping is a symptom, not a cause, of poverty. Mokyr has raised the interesting question why sharecropping was not practised in pre-Famine Ireland. The variety of tenurial arrangements observed in Ireland—fixed money rent, conacre rent paid for in labour, the dairyman system of Munster—all seem to have forced the tenant to bear the brunt of variations in prices and yields. In practice, however, these systems offered some risk cover, because landlords granted abatements and allowed arrears to accumulate in bad years. And though in a bad year the

Table 5.1. *Rent per acre in Ireland, 1830s*

Province	Head rent (£ per acre)	n	Conacre rent (£ per acre)	n
Leinster	1.60	253	5.62	306
Munster	1.74	199	5.01	281
Ulster	1.60	152	6.52	171
Connacht	1.28	99	4.88	132

conacre tenant was forced to bear the full brunt of his poor potato crop, his labour was also presumably worth less in a bad year, and so he was insured to that extent.[43]

All in all, landlords achieved little for Irish agriculture in the pre-Famine era. If their penchant for 'political agronomy' has been exaggerated by populist historians, in the end they also failed to fulfil the role set out for them by one of their number, Lord Monteagle: 'Providence created landlords [to] keep down population.' Monteagle claimed that the good landlord's quest for 'as large as possible an amount of surplus produce' would mean that the land would hold 'only the number of persons necessary to enable it to produce the largest possible amount beyond their own subsistence'.[44] But were maximizing rentals and keeping down population compatible objectives before the Famine? The record suggests not, since rents continued to increase in real terms until the Famine. Irish landlords lacked the incentive, the power, or the imagination to fulfil their providential duty.

In the pre-Famine era one of the most constructive things that Irish landlords could have done was to help more of their poorest tenants to emigrate—as several of their Scottish counterparts did. Those who did so in Ireland were in a tiny minority. This explains why population continued to swell in the poorest parts of Ireland, while in the West Highlands of Scotland the annual rate of population growth fell from nearly 1.5 per cent in the 1810s to 0.5 per cent in the 1820s, and was negative in the 1830s. The Irish poor were eager to leave, granted the necessary seed-money, but employers (notably farmers) were unlikely to initiate assisted emigration schemes, and landlords were more interested in conspicuous consumption than in radical reform. That 'the safety-valve of emigration operated more effectively in the Highlands than in the poorer parts of Ireland' was largely due to the greater activism of Scottish landlords.[45]

Taken as a group, Irish proprietors were far removed from the cruel and destructive stereotype later painted by farmer and nationalist propagandists. Indeed, some modern historians prefer to depict them as victims or 'helpless giants'. Yet because they were powerless or unwilling to force radical change in the countryside, the landlords were exploiters in the sense of Karl Marx or Henry George that their removal in, say, the 1830s instead of the 1900s would have mattered little for agricultural progress. That point is usually missed in recent reassessments of the land–tenant system.

Land reform was constrained by a belief in the inviolability of property rights. The policy conclusions of the Devon Commission of 1843–5, a rich source of data for the economic historian, were extremely timid. Its evidence highlighted the cottier problem, but the Commission proposed no solution:

> We cannot disguise from ourselves the great difficulties of dealing by law with such matters, and the danger lest evils of this nature be aggravated rather than diminished, by too hasty attempts to remove them by legislation . . . we trust the exposure of such a state of things may lead to its remedy.

The landlord-dominated Commission proposed compensation for tenant improvements on eviction, but a cautious bill in this direction was quickly killed. The need for a smoother mechanism for transferring incumbered land was widely appreciated, but again nothing was done. However, in the end it is doubtful whether reforms along these lines would have boosted productivity much. More serious were the problems of distribution and overpopulation.

The traditional focus on land tenure tends to overlook the fact that a much more serious social problem in the pre-Famine era than insecurity of tenure for farmers was the plight of hundreds of thousands of landless and near-landless labourers employed on a system akin to bonded labour. The system required labourers to repay most or all of the rent on their potato patch or smallholding in labour dues. Most of these labourers rented from farmers rather than head landlords. Some landlords also paid their labourers mainly in land; Lord Inchiquin in Clare is a good example. Daniel Hanigan and his family supplied Inchiquin with 246.5 man-days of labour between November 1838 and October 1839 (over three-quarters of them during the busy months between April and August); at 10d. a day Hannigan earned barely enough to pay the £9. 10s. rent due on the family holding. Another labourer, Edward Dogherty, earned nearly £13 over the same period, working virtually full time; he had £4. 14s. stopped for rent.[46] The disincentive effects of such a system are surely clear, and the pitifully low and precarious shadow wages allowed labourers paid in potato conacre are a reflection of them. And yet conacre was a crucial cog in pre-Famine Irish agriculture: when it succumbed to *phytophthora infestans*, the emphasis on labour-intensive tillage also gave way.[47]

6

Communications, Banking, and Fishing,
c. 1815–1845

This chapter describes the contrasting evolutions of three unrelated sectors in pre-Famine Ireland. The first two saw considerable advances, assisting and being assisted by the integration of the Irish and British economies, but the third symbolized the backwardness of the rural economy. Though, as we shall see, the development of Ireland's mainline rail network barely preceded the Famine, communications both by road and boat improved, while developments in banking broadly mirrored those occurring in England. Legislation along English lines was crucial for the evolution of banking. I shall argue that neither of these sectors held back the development of the economy at large. However, our examination of the fishing industry will bring us face to face with the poverty that blighted the lives of most Irish people in these years.

6.1 Communications

Until well into the eighteenth century Ireland had virtually no public transport facilities. Roads were poor, trade limited, and travel in some areas considered dangerous. In mid-century, people travelling from Limerick to Dublin did so together on a chosen day:[1]

> It was posted on a sheet which was placed over a mantel-piece in the coffee room in Quay Lane, and those who intended travelling affixed their names to it. On the day appointed they all set out well armed and provided with the best means they could travel by. The journey {was} then performed in five days.

The following decades saw significant advances in communications both within Ireland and across the Irish Sea, and a reduction in the associated risks. The weekly Limerick–Dublin coach service which began about 1760 initially took four days to complete the journey. That was without a change of horses, but as the traffic developed stops for fresh horses became routine. Thus one traveller remembered being 'dragged by one miserable pair of garrans from Sligo, through Ballyshannon, Donegal, Raphoe, Derry, Newton Limavady, to Coleraine' c.1800; a decade later two pairs of horses were being kept at each of those towns. The streamlining of the government-run mail service and the provision of public funds and civil engineers for road-building played a role in improving passenger services. More and better roads were a precondition for a speedy and reliable postal service, and the total road mileage suitable for wheeled vehicles doubled between 1700 and 1850. Neglect and abuse in road-building and road-ownership by grand juries and turnpike trusts were highlighted, and gradually eliminated. The mail coaches became a byword for punctuality; contractors were fined a shilling for each minute's delay, and bad light, restive horses, and broken axles were no excuse. The far-flung coaching business of John Anderson of Fermoy, and the hotel, coach-building, and turnpike operations that it spawned, were built on a mail contract. Other coaching magnates such as Bourne, Purcell, and Bianconi also had mail contracts. Bianconi and Anderson were notable for basing their enterprises on inland towns; previously nearly all Irish stage-coaches had started from or ended in the capital. The first direct mail-coach services in Ireland, those between Belfast and Dublin and between Dublin and Cork, began in 1789. The cost of the services, in time and money, fell significantly thereafter in real terms: the average duration of the Belfast–Dublin journey fell from 20.5 hours in 1802 to 15.3 hours in 1815 and 13.5 hours in 1825, while the journey from Dublin to Cork, which took about two days in 1800 could be completed in 18.5 hours (by night) or 21 hours (by day) a few decades later. The times agreed by the post office and its contractors on all main-line routes were cut significantly in the 1820s. At the outset, the state of the roads limited speeds, but on the eve of the railway revolution the mail coaches could achieve an average speed of nine miles an hour on several routes.[2]

Most of the credit 'for the opening up of communications between Belfast and towns in the north of Ireland' has been claimed for private enterprise. The number of scheduled private coach services increased rapidly in this period. John McCoy started one between Armagh and Belfast in 1808; the trip of thirty-one Irish miles took seven hours, including the half-hour break in Lurgan, and cost 14s. 1d. (70p) inside and 7s. 7d. (38p) for those who risked braving the elements outside. McCoy also introduced a Belfast–Dublin service in the following year. In the south the Bianconi jaunting-car revolution of the 1810s, 1820s, and 1830s was more far-reaching than anything preceding it. Before Bianconi, the only form of public transport between Carrick-on-Suir and Waterford was 'Tom Morrissey's boat'. By 1836 the 'bians' were serving a busy network of 2,234 miles, and by 1843 3,800 miles, while imitators operated many other routes. Thus in 1844 residents of the town of Dungarvan (population 8,625 in 1841) had a choice of daily cars to Waterford, Clonmel, and Youghal, and there was also a daily service to Lismore.[3] These sociable cars were geared primarily towards a local middle- and lower middle-class clientele, but they also catered to the small but growing band of tourists heading west and south-west during the summer months. The cars were used and described with some affection by writers such as Thackeray, Inglis, and Kohl, who travelled around Ireland in the 1830s and early 1840s.[4]

Internal communications also improved in humbler though no less impressive ways. As Maria Edgeworth reported from Ballinahinch in Connemara in 1834:[5]

No mail coach road comes near here: no man on horseback could undertake to carry the letters regularly. They are carried three times a week from Outerard to Clifden, thirty-six miles, by three gossoons, or more properly bog-trotters, and very hard work it is for them. One runs a day and a night, and then sleeps a day and a night, and then another takes his turn; and each of these boys has £15 a year. I remember seeing one of these postboys leaving Ballinahinch Castle, with his leather bag on his back, across the heath and across the bog, leaping every now and then, and running so fast! his bare, white legs thrown up among the brown heath.

Before the revolution ushered in by Bianconi, the absence of mail coaches in the remote west, here noted by Edgeworth, could mean considerable expense and frustration for tourist and commercial traveller alike. Sir John Carr, who visited Ireland in 1805, recorded his irritation at being forced to pay £4 for a post-chaise from Limerick to Killarney. The Dublin lawyer who left a journal of a business trip to Cahirciveen in south-west Kerry in April 1824 expressed similar sentiments. An inside seat on the coach trip from Dublin to Limerick cost him £1. 15s., or about 3.5d. per mile. That presented no cause for complaint, but the journey became slow and costly from Limerick on. Securing 'an old gig and horse' as far as Tarbert (about 35 miles) cost £1. 5s. The lack of a regular conveyance to Tralee entailed a post-chaise costing £1. 10s. The final lap to Cahirciveen had to be completed on horseback. Considering that the horse's owner followed his client to secure the horse's return to Tralee, the cost (11s. 4d.) seemed reasonable, but the journey itself proved wearying to both man and beast. The horse's limbs were so swollen that the traveller feared for its life. The days of such exertions were numbered, however: from 1836 on, there would be a daily mail-car service, costing 6s., from Tralee to Cahirciveen. Even the remote west was affected by the coaching revolution, and there were regular services to Belmullet, Clifden, and Ballaghadereen before the Famine.[6]

The carriage of goods improved too. The cumbersome solid-wheeled Irish car, which had replaced the older slide car, in turn gradually gave way to iron-axled and iron-wheeled vehicles known as 'Scotch carts' that could carry loads twice as heavy. The carts or drays, which were common throughout the country by the 1810s, required tougher road surfaces. Such changes bespeak greater traffic density.[7] Yet on the eve of the Famine the number of horses and mules kept on holdings of an Irish acre or less—a rough proxy for those used in trade and industry—was only 49,144; in 1854 the number of horses used for 'traffic and manufactures' was 22,520, and the number of mules 18,601. While farm-horses might on occasion be diverted to non-agricultural use, these Irish numbers are small compared to British levels.[8] In assessing the reluctance of Irish entrepreneurs to build canals and railways, the implied thinness in the internal traffic of goods before the Famine should be borne in mind.

Pre-Famine commentators tended to praise the Irish road system, but sometimes with an eye to the conveyance of passengers rather than goods. The inefficiencies and inadequacies of eighteenth-century road-building have been documented by John Andrews in a classic contribution. The early roads, often ignoring gradients and contours, were not geared to heavy traffic, but as long as 'our whole inland carriage is . . . performed by small feeble cattle, either in high loads, which scarcely ever exceed two hundredweight, or on truckle cars . . . which . . . carry about four hundred-weight' this was not a problem. By the century's end the heavier Scottish cart was catching on, and by the 1830s loads of a ton per vehicle were commonplace.[9]

A great deal was achieved in this period not only in trunk-route con-struction, but also in 'secondary' road-building in the west. The Board of Works under Nimmo and Griffith added several hundred miles to the secondary network, opening up large tracts of north and east Kerry, north-west Cork, and west Connacht with stone-and-gravel roads.[10] On the eve of the Famine areas such as Glangevlin in county Cavan 'where there is no public road, and only one difficult pass [where] in some places a trackway is seen by which the cattle are driven out to the fairs'[11] were few. Increased production for the market was a likely consequence; Nimmo claimed that as a result of his efforts in Sligo 'houses [were] rising along the road, and tillage [was] finding its way to the summit of the hill', and Griffith pointed to the 'gaudy finery of Manchester and Glasgow' on display at Sunday mass within a few years of new roads in Munster as evidence of the change. The new roads also contributed to the campaign against rural insurgency and smuggling.

Nevertheless, Lee has painted a very unflattering picture of early nineteenth-century Irish transport, arguing that poor communications before the advent of the railway precluded most of the country from being a market economy. Lee produced several examples of high costs imposed by road freight, and tellingly quoted a report from an inspector on the proposed Dublin–Cork railway line to the effect that 'for the general exchange of commodities, the interior of this part of Ireland is virtually more remote than India or America'.[12] Hyperbole aside, how poor were inland communications?

Compared to Britain, Ireland might seem an unenthusiastic participant in the canal and railway revolutions of the eighteenth and early nineteenth centuries. Irish canal and navigation projects were few, and those few largely unprofitable. The Royal Canal, always a dubious proposition, went bankrupt in 1812, having linked Mullingar with Dublin; with government help, the cut was extended to the Shannon at Clondra. The new line was little availed of, though the Royal's traffic did expand modestly in the 1820s and 1830s. The Board of Control appointed to keep an eye on the Royal's directors in 1817 repeatedly criticized them for scrimping on repairs. The Boyne Navigation, which linked Slane and Navan to the Irish Sea, proved a flop. Traffic on the Shannon navigation north of Athlone was a trickle, and the income of even the Limerick navigation in its best years was insubstantial.[13]

Even in the north, the poor records of the Ulster (linking Lough Erne and Lough Neagh) and Coalisland canals justified the lack of enthusiasm for further projects. The Tyrone Navigation was 'indifferently attended to', and at one time choked up with weeds, and even the Newry, Ireland's first canal (1741–2), was unable to induce most farmers from using road carriage. By the late eighteenth century its inland section was in a very poor state. Virtually rebuilt by the Directors-General of Inland Navigation in the 1800s, it was slow to regain traffic diverted. In the mid-1830s the Lagan Navigation handled about only one-eighth of Belfast's estimated inland traffic, as the nearby roads competed with the waterway even for heavy bulky goods. The record of the Grand Canal Company was better. It carried about 5 million ton-miles in 1800 and about double that on the eve of the Famine. Even after the arrival of the railway it could compete in the traffic of grain, flour, and low-value bulky items such as building materials, dung, and turf.[14]

Ireland's waterways never experienced the traffic borne by British giants such as the Forth and Clyde or the Grand Junction, but the record of canals in the purely agricultural regions of Great Britain seems a more appropriate yardstick. In that league, the Grand Canal performed respectably. The canals' response to the coaching revolution brought on by Charles Bianconi and others in the 1820s was also spirited enough. From 1833–4 the Royal and the Grand ran scheduled passenger services which rivalled the coaches for speed. The era of this new technology was short-lived, alas. The last of the new boats was withdrawn in 1852, marking an end to less than two decades of 'galloping horses and surging fly boats'. Both the Grand and the Ulster canals faced intense competition from drays 'which ply with great regularity on all leading roads, and for fares extremely moderate'. For road carriage to compete successfully with water for freight was exceptional in both Britain and America in the nineteenth century. That it could some-times do so in Ireland was partly because it was the economy rather than the transport network *per se* that was underdeveloped. Geography mattered too; that people in Roscommon in the 1830s preferred to ship exports by 'bad roads' and 'inferior cars' from Galway and Sligo than by canal from Dublin was a reminder that nowhere in Ireland was very far from the sea.[15]

If Ireland's canal network was inadequate, this cannot be blamed on difficulties of eminent domain, since the law favoured prospective canal-builders over the owners of land. Nor can the lack of public funds be blamed. If the problem was one of constrained supply, might poor entre-preneurship be responsible? Lee suggested nearly three decades ago that 'there could be no more revealing indication of the inadequacy of Ireland's transport system in 1830 than her paltry 487 miles of navigable inland waterway, compared with England's 4534'. The comparison is a reminder that economic development cannot proceed far without adequate com-munications. Yet the poor record of those 'paltry 487 miles' in the pre-railway era suggests that the problem lay less with supply than with demand. Perhaps transport entrepreneurs were simply heeding Arthur Young's advice in the 1770s, to 'have something to carry before you seek the means of carriage'.[16] The Anglo-Irish comparison is misleading for two further reasons. First, Ireland lacked the coal deposits which were the *raison d'être* of the canals of the north-west of England and the Scottish central belt. Second, Ireland's shape and size meant that more of it was within reach of the sea than Britain.

Some railway projects had been mooted during the 1825 railway boom, including one involving Daniel O'Connell. In Tipperary Alexander Nimmo was engaged by resident landlords to investigate the viability of a line linking Cahir and Clonmel to the collieries at Killenaule. Nothing came of such schemes.[17] Many other projects were dreamed up in the following two decades, but few got far. The promoters of the Dundalk Western Railway (who included grandees such as the Earl of Roden, Lord Blaney, and Sir A. E. Bellingham) sought to connect the west and north-west with the port of Dundalk. They proposed a line from Dundalk to Ballybay first, 'as a matter of encouragement, not of speculation', to be worked by animal rather than locomotive power. Hardly surprisingly, they failed to raise the requisite capital. Other ventures to fall by the wayside included the Leinster & Ulster Railway Company, the Kilkenny Railway Company, and the Great Central Irish Railway Company. A rash of speculation on the eve of the Famine produced over one hundred new schemes in 1844–6, though only a quarter of these were authorized, and only seventeen had been embarked on by 1850. These included the Midland and Great Western Railway, which bought out the Royal Canal, using one of its banks for its permanent way from Broadstone in Dublin to beyond Mullingar, and the Great Southern Railway linking Dublin and Cork. When the Famine struck only the Dublin–Kingstown and the Ulster had been completed, a network of only sixty-five miles in all (compared to 2,235 miles in Britain).[18] Was this 'failure' of the railway to catch on in Ireland really due to the quality of the roads and the cheapness of coach and cart transport, or were there missed opportunities? Since the loss was made good between 1845 and 1852, the issue is hardly crucial for economic development in the long run. As for the waterways, surely the failure of many of those established by private enterprise to make ends meet is enough to explain the reluctance of others to follow suit?

Lee's account of an underdeveloped transport network hardly applies either to communications across the Irish Sea. When the *Rob Roy* began to ply the route from Belfast to Greenock on 13 June 1818, it was the first steamship in the world to service a scheduled seagoing steamship route. Before the spread of the steamship in the 1820s the only regular crossings of the Irish Sea were by mail-packet. Boats sailed 'when wind served', with the result that communication was rather erratic. The early routes, including the important Holyhead–Howth and Belfast–Glasgow routes, catered mainly for passengers. First to apply steam to the trade in goods was Charles Wye Williams' City of Dublin Steam Packet Company, which inaugurated the Dublin–Liverpool service in 1824. Henceforth Ireland's trade with the rest of the UK would be regular and year-round. Williams was the leading innovator in the business, in terms of both service and technique. There was undoubtedly some scope for monopoly profits at the outset, but the high fares charged only prompted new firms to enter the fray. In 1826 the British and Irish Steam Packet Company began a regular service on the London–Dublin route, and in 1836 a group of Dublin merchants created the City of Glasgow Sailing & Steam Packet Company to service the Dublin–Glasgow route. Two companies vied for custom on the Dublin–Cork route by 1827, Rogers Brothers claiming to provide the more 'reasonable' fare (15s. in a cabin, 7s. 6d. on deck) since they landed passengers on the quays at Cork, rather than at Passage. By the 1840s there were over one hundred crossings a week for man and beast, intense competition, and considerably lower fares. The proliferation of routes was a great boon to the trade in animals, fresh butter, eggs, and slaughtered meat. It made the large-scale export of fat cattle viable for the first time, and more and more of the butchers' meat of industrial Britain was Irish after 1820. Steam also encouraged more passenger movement; not least it provided quick passages, mainly from Drogheda and Dublin, for thousands of seasonal migrants to Britain. Steam did not replace sail; the sailing tonnage continued to rise for a time, but it was increasingly restricted to the carriage of bulky, low-value goods.[19]

In sum, communications is one area where Ireland made strides in the era under review. Perhaps there were external economies generated by transport that called for public initiative, particularly in rail. Perhaps too the failure of the rail network to get going in the 1830s was a sign of entrepreneurial failure. All the same, it would be far-fetched to blame Irish underdevelopment in the pre-Famine era on inadequate communications.

6.2 Joint-Stock Banking

As noted in Chapter 3, after a precocious start in the early eighteenth century, banking in Ireland remained in the doldrums until the 1790s. The suspension of gold payments in 1797 produced a revolution in the banking sector. Scores of banks and quasi-banks began to issue notes, mainly in small denominations, and usually convertible to Bank of Ireland notes on demand (at least in principle). The suspension of gold payments thus had the useful if unintended result of getting the Irish used to paper money and bank credit. This turned out to be no less true for Ulster, where landlords and businessmen had refused to accept paper for several years after the suspension. The Restriction had also usefully pointed to structural weaknesses in the banking system; the bank failures of 1814–15 and 1820 were widely attributed to an inadequate legal framework. Before 1824 no Irish bank other than the Bank of Ireland could have more than six shareholders, nor could any shareholder be involved in foreign trade. The result was small, undercapitalized banks. Increasing pressure ensued for a reduction of Bank of Ireland privileges and a system of joint-stock banking, and the Irish Bank Act of 1824 was the result. That Act paved the way for competition, though no Dublin-based joint-stock bank could issue notes or open branches in the Bank of Ireland's 'exclusion zone', which extended fifty Irish miles out of Dublin.

Between the end of 1825 and 1845 Irish banking was transformed. Almost immediately the Northern Bank, originally a private bank, was reorganized along joint-stock lines, and several other joint-stock banks were created. The most notable and pioneering of these was the Provincial Bank of Ireland, the brainchild of Englishman Thomas Joplin, founded in 1825 with a nominal capital of £2 million. The bank's aim was to employ English capital and Scottish expertise in opening up to banking those parts of Ireland poorly served by the Bank of Ireland. The Provincial was highly successful in this; by 1845 it had established thirty-seven branches throughout the country and was making healthy profits. Its staff was almost exclusively recruited from Scotland. In its early years, however, the Provincial had to face a series of runs on its branches in Munster. These runs, inspired by nationalist politicians, never constituted a serious threat but they increased costs. The Hibernian, also established in 1825, placed its headquarters in Dublin, within the Bank of Ireland's fifty-mile zone, and was therefore prevented from issuing notes: its ploy of issuing tokens which bore no promise to pay was successfully contested by the Bank of Ireland in 1827.[20]

Daniel O'Connell played a leading role in the creation of the National Bank of Ireland, which opened for business in 1834. The ethos of the new bank was less nationalist than 'liberal'; it chose to have its headquarters on London's Broad Street rather than in Dublin, and several of its directors were City gentlemen. The beginnings of the National, whose first managing director Lamie Murray (a disciple of Joplin) modelled it on the Provincial, were rocky enough. Early staffing policy left much to be desired, and reports of managerial fraud and incompetence at branch level are frequent in the early minutes. Thus John Taylor, who had been headhunted from the Provincial Bank at a salary of £800 plus a free house in 1835 to become manager of the Cork branch, had to be removed in 1839; 'irregularities' were reported from Ballinasloe, Ballina, Ennis, Tuam, Roscrea, Loughrea, Thurles, and Banagher. Nor did the bank's decentralized system of semi-autonomous branches acting as subsidiary companies work well. It was soon replaced. In 1836 the National's Court of Directors was reduced to the embarrassing step of seeking help from both the Bank of Ireland and the Bank of England. Less serious for the bank's overall viability, though another great embarrassment to his fellow-directors, were O'Connell's own gigantic borrowings from the bank— averaging nearly £30,000 in the late 1830s and early 1840s.[21] On the eve of the Famine, the National still lacked the solid reputation earned by the Bank of Ireland and the Provincial. Nevertheless, it braved these (and later) storms, and like its fellow joint-stock banks, grew in the pre-Famine decade.

The total number of bank branches or agencies rose from 14 in 1825 to 54 in 1834 and to 173 in 1845, and by the later date nearly all towns with a population of over 5,000, and several smaller towns too had their own bank.[22] The banks mopped up money that had previously been hoarded: in 1825–40 the Bank of Ireland received an average of £40,000 annually in gold guineas, though guineas had scarcely circulated in most of the island since the 1790s. The Bank of Ireland continued to dominate the banking scene, though its privileges were gradually being whittled away; in 1845 it still accounted for well over one-half the note circulation, and over three-quarters of the circulation of notes of £5 and above. There is circumstantial evidence that the Bank of Ireland was over-cautious in its branch policy in these years. The only Irish towns of 10,000 people or more without a bank branch in 1830—Dundalk, Drogheda, and Carlow—were within the Bank's fifty-mile zone, while a decade later the Bank had opened branches in only three towns in the 5,000–10,000 range—Youghal, Tullamore, and New Ross. The demand for banking services would therefore probably have been less fully met in the absence of competition from the other banks.[23]

Rivalry between the new banks and the Bank of Ireland could be quite intense. For some time before the Provincial Bank opened a branch in Youghal in August 1831, several of the town's most important merchants (who presumably had accounts in Cork) had been taking turns with supplying the group with cash. The Provincial's manager sought to untie the knot by prevailing upon Abraham Fisher, a prominent corn merchant, to open an account. The manager informed him that while overdrawing an account was contrary to the Provincial's rules, 'if he in the hurry of business should happen to overdraw his account I should not refuse him such occasional accommodation upon the understanding that when he did so overdraw the amount should be repaid by the end of the week'. The manager also undertook to discount three-month bills for Fisher to the value of a few hundred pounds during the corn season. Fisher duly opened an account in September.[24]

Banking in pre-Famine Ireland relied almost exclusively on an upper- and middle-class clientele; the number of accounts per branch tended to be small, and deposits typically substantial. The average opening balance at the Provincial Bank's Birr (then Parsonstown) branch during its first year was £250 (or £10,000 to £20,000 in today's money), while the humblest clients of the same bank's Youghal branch were small traders and merchants. Five accounts were opened on 8 August 1831, when the Provincial opened for business in Youghal; it took over a month for the number of accounts to reach twenty. The twenty included eight merchants, three engineers, two attorneys, two millers, two retired army men, a military paymaster, a chandler, and a medical practitioner. Again, among the early account-holders at the Bank of Ireland's Sligo branch, founded in 1828, farmers, professional people, agents, and Catholic priests dominated. The predominance of businessmen (mainly Catholic) among a sample of those signing the Dublin-based Hibernian Bank's account book in 1846 is striking. Almost 70 per cent of the total were merchants; professional men and manufacturers and builders with Catholic surnames made up the bulk of the remainder. Farmers accounted for over half of the account-holders of the Ulster Bank's Aughnacloy branch in 1852.[25]

The new banks performed the useful task of converting deposits, largely from rural areas, to loans in the towns and cities. Differences in the seasonality of demand for credit also allowed scope for intermediation. Thus, as Ollerenshaw[26] has neatly shown, in Ulster provision merchants were usually overdrawn early in the year but in credit in the summer months. Bill discounting had traditionally accounted for most of bank lending in Ireland. The new banks were more adventurous than their predecessors: banks were now sometimes prepared to risk lending on the security of individual promissory notes, and did so routinely against company stock and life assurance policies. The loans were short-term, typically for one year, but they could be rolled over. Munn[27] provides many examples of the more adventurous lending policies of the joint-stock banks. The selection set out in Table 6.1 makes the point.

Despite the occasional run, joint-stock banking brought a modicum of stability. In the pre-Famine decades the only major banking failure was Thomas Mooney's Agricultural & Commercial Bank, which was set up in 1834. The Agricultural & Commercial suspended payments in 1836, and was finally wound up in 1840. Among the new joint-stock banks, it was exceptional in that it attempted to extend banking to the lower-middle classes, both as investors and customers; perhaps its failure indicated, in part at least, that they were not ready for it. There was more to the Agricultural's demise, however. Mooney was considered a poor entrepreneur or, worse, a charlatan by the banking establishment. An anonymous but well-informed and devastating account of the Agricultural's history in the *Bankers' Magazine* cited an investigation by a Board of Auditors into the bank's finances in the wake of its collapse:[28]

We have found there was no efficient control over the branches, and that the system of inspection was most imperfect; a complete absence of plan for checking the accounts existed at the headquarters in Dublin; and the book-keeping has been

Table 6.1. *Some examples of pre-Famine bank loans*

Date	Bank	Customer	Amount	Period	Security
1829	B.o.I	Dublin Steam Pkt Co.	8 000	1 year	Joint promissory note
1840	—	Derry Steam Pkt Co.	7 000	15 months	Discounted bills
1841	B.o.I	Maynooth College	2 000	1 year	Minute and prom. note from three trustees
1841	—	Celbridge PLU	253	—	Poor rate
1845	—	Latouche & Co.	100 000	—	Govt. or B.o.I stock
1825	PBI	Pierce Mahony	4 400	—	370 shares in Bank
1826	—	Mr Shaw, Kilkenny	600	—	Government stock
1835	—	Mr Wright	20 000	—	Dutch stock
1840	RBI	St George Steam Co.	18 000	—	Discounted bill, later mortgage over ships

Note: B.o.I = Bank of Ireland; PBI = Provincial Bank of Ireland; RBI = Royal Bank of Ireland.

so faulty, that we are convinced no accurate balance sheet could at any time have been constructed.

According to the *Bankers' Magazine*, the manager of the Agricultural's first branch to open for business, that at Nenagh in north Tipperary, was a 'country farmer'. His modest investment in the bank had entitled him to the job. Other managers were equally incompetent, and still others were dishonest; those in Cork and Kilkenny helped themselves to salary increases and to loans on the basis of their IOUs. In the struggle for business with other joint-stock banks, particularly the National, 'the issues were unlimited and unchecked; the discounts were profuse'. Most historians echo the traditional scathing judgements of 'unmatched impudence and incompetency'. Only Barrow among banking historians has had a good word for Mooney and the Agricultural & Commercial. In a lively apologia for him, Barrow deemed Mooney a poor manager, but found little fault with his vision, and indeed surmised that had his bank succeeded the Great Famine would have been avoided. That is going much too far, since it forgets that, while a banking system may contribute to economic growth, in the end it is more a reflection than a determinant of the strength of an economy.[29] Daniel O'Connell's refusal to bail out Mooney is explained by the Liberator's leading role in the National Bank, and the Agricultural & Commercial's last-ditch plea to the Bank of England as 'proper guardian of the public credit' also fell on deaf ears.[30]

The banks typically provided only short-term credit, though, as noted, loans might be 'rolled over'. There was a complementary, informal market in longer-term loans. Alas, its size is unknown. Lawyers and scriveners were prominent players in this market, where term loans and mortgage leases were the typical instruments. Few moneylenders' account-books survive, but that of Hugh Waugh, a County Down practitioner, is an interesting exception. Between the 1810s and 1830s Waugh provided several loans, typically of several hundred pounds, to local gentlemen and businessmen. He charged a rate of interest of 5 or 6 per cent, reasonable in view of the repeated instances of procrastination and default in the accounts. In 1819 Waugh lent £20 Irish to Thomas and William Murphy on a promissory note. Several years later he noted the whereabouts of the Murphys, with a view to getting his money back, but had no luck: 'processed the Murphys to the January Hillsborough session in 1827. But not being able to procure a witness to prove the handwriting of the witness to the execution of their note and at present consider it as lost.' Something of the informal nature of Waugh's business is captured by his request in 1829 to a local clergyman for a loan of £700 at 5 per cent: 'The reason I am under the necessity of borrowing the above sum is in the course of the last year I lent a large sum, lately I purchased upwards of 200 Irish acres in this townland.'[31] Financial institutions other than banks might also occasionally delve into the market for loans. For example, in the early 1820s the European Life Insurance and Annuity Company undertook to provide Daniel O'Connell with a loan of £3,000 against an annuity of £365 per annum charged on O'Connell's lands.[32]

The modern vogue for banking deregulation has prompted some economic historians to seek reassurance in the 'free banking' experiments of eighteenth-century Scotland and nineteenth-century America. What of Ireland?[33] After all, before the Bank Act of 1845 any registered Irish banker had near-complete discretion over his own note-issue, with only the discipline of the Gold Standard to keep him in line. Moreover, as noted, several new banks entered the business between 1825 and 1845, and the Bank of Ireland found itself being seriously challenged for the first time. A director of the Hibernian claimed that his bank had forced the Bank of Ireland to handle country bills payable in Dublin, to open branches in the country, and to reduce its charge on discounts.[34] The banking sector in these decades certainly bore the hallmarks of dynamism and reliability. So far so good. Yet it is surely significant too that the new entrants failed to erode the high profits made by those longest in the business. Thus the dividends paid out by the Bank of Ireland (founded in 1783) continued to be very high, typically 8 to 10 per cent. Since not all profits were distributed, the return on capital was higher still. The Provincial Bank (founded in 1825, with headquarters in London), also fared well: after paying 4 per cent for the first four years, it increased its dividend to 8 per cent by 1835, a rate maintained till the 1850s. The Northern (1825) started off with 5 per cent, but by the early 1840s it was paying 10 per cent. Others had to be content with less, however; the Ulster (1836) paid 5–7 per cent in the late 1830s, while the Royal (1836) and the National (1834), both also late arrivals, typically paid only 5 per cent in the pre-Famine era.[35] Such data hardly betoken free entry and effective competition. Nor does the Bank of Ireland's success in preventing its Dublin rivals, the Hibernian and the Royal, from issuing banknotes, nor the concerted action of the Ulster banks in the 1830s to keep out further entrants. In Ulster even amalgamation was considered, but in 1839 the banks contented themselves with a formal cartel arrangement regarding customers and interest charges. The agreement survived into this century.[36] Again, as noted above, the Bank of Ireland retained a near-monopoly in the zone within fifty Irish miles (seventy statute miles) of Dublin: other note-issuing banks were excluded from doing business in that zone.

Finally, the Bank of Ireland's actions as a proto-central bank in this period also stretch the 'free banking' analogy. The Bank of Ireland seems to have acted as 'lender of the last resort' for the first time in December 1799, when the Dublin bank of Beresford & Company applied for help. One of Beresford's partners had signalled the desire to withdraw, and the Bank of Ireland agreed to accommodation to the tune of £80,000 on approved bills. It helped out on several occasions subsequently, particularly in 1814 and 1820. In 1814 the Bank resolved to do its utmost 'to prevent a public calamity'. In the wake of the numerous failures of 1820, it claimed that it had supplied 'every fair and legitimate demand for its notes from every quarter of the country, inasmuch that no Manufacturer, Banker or Otherwise, who could exhibit to the Bank of Ireland such property as the Bank could legally lend upon, has been disappointed'. The next major challenge came in 1836 when, amid general panic in banking circles in both England and Ireland, the Agricultural & Commercial Bank suspended payments, both it and most of the other joint-stock banks called on College Green for assistance. The Bank of Ireland obliged; the Belfast Bank was granted discounting facilities worth £103,000, while the Ulster received £60,000, the Hibernian £21,000, and the National £43,000 and the option of a further £70,000. Even the Agricultural & Commercial received help. The aggregate sum lent by the Bank of Ireland, over £0.25 million, was 6–7 per cent of its note-issue. Nor was that all: the Bank of England also intervened, transmitting gold coin from London, and lending against bills of exchange.[37] The Bank of Ireland did not continue to support Mooney's bank,[38] however, thereby indicating that help was not automatic. Whether any of the other banks would have been forced to close its doors for good without such assistance is a moot point, but the context is hardly one of 'free banking'. The contrast between 1836 in Ireland, when only one dubiously managed bank was forced to suspend payments, and the following year in the USA, when hundreds of banks failed, is an interesting one. Two important differences between American and Irish banking systems stand out. First, the Irish system was one of branch banking, the American largely one of unit banking. Their branch networks and greater capitalization gave the Irish joint-stock banks greater security. Second, the USA lacked a lender of last resort like the Bank of Ireland.

Peel's Bank Act of 1844 applied to Ireland to the extent that it ruled out the creation of new note-issuing banks in the UK. In other respects, for tactical reasons, Peel treated Irish and Scottish banking separately. The Bankers (Ireland) Act of 1845 (7 & 8 Vict., c.37) governed the course of commercial banking until the 1920s. The Act abolished the Bank of Ireland's fifty-mile exclusion zone. In its provisions on note-issue it was more lax than the 1844 legislation. Initially, it seems, Peel envisaged 20 per cent specie backing for existing note-issues, and full backing for any addition. In the event, the Irish legislation allowed all existing note-issuing banks a fiduciary quota based on existing circulation, with gold backing for additional notes. By thereby excluding the Royal and the Hibernian, the Act perpetuated an injustice born of the Bank of Ireland's previous monopoly. A proposal by William Smith O'Brien to allow any bank to issue notes on the security of government stock was defeated by 77 votes to 53. The allocation gave the Bank of Ireland almost 60 per cent of the fiduciary circulation, the Provincial 15 per cent, the National 13 per cent, and the Ulster banks another 13 per cent between them. Since the Irish banks (like the Scottish) were under no legal obligation to hold reserves, the new restriction would 'bite' only if their business expanded enormously.[39] Existing note-issuing banks were also allowed to continue their issues of small denomination notes. The legislation discriminated against potential entrants by denying them note-issuing privileges, and new entrants were few after 1845. The history of Irish banking in the post-1845 era is discussed in Chapter 14.

6.3 Fishing

> The fisheries of Ireland might prove a mine under water as rich as any under ground.
>
> SIR WILLIAM TEMPLE

In 1812 Wakefield, author of *Ireland Statistical and Political*, declared that discussion of how best to revive fishing in Ireland 'would require a volume'. His own rambling account found the native herring fishery in decline, and the white fishery dominated by foreign fishermen. Meanwhile, 'myriads of excellent fish' were left undisturbed off the coast of Galway and on the Nymph Bank south-east of Dungarvan.[40] Such neglect may have implied poor entrepreneurship, but Wakefield attributed the failure of the ambitious herring-fishing scheme of Donegal landlord-entrepreneur Burton

Conyngham to ecological factors, viz. 'the *cancer halecum*, with which the whole surface of the water seemed to be covered'. Conyngham's hare-brained plan, which had cost £38,000 of his own money and another £40,000 of the taxpayers', involved founding a fishing industry on the remote island of Rutland off the west coast of Donegal.[41]

Between 1819 and the late 1820s, the backward Irish fishing industry enjoyed a prosperity of sorts, underpinned by a system of bounties on boats and catches. During that period the Irish Fisheries Board spent about £0.25 million on bounties, boats and tackle, and piers. Both bounties and the Fisheries Board were disbanded in 1829, casualties of a growing commitment in Westminster to 'non-interference' in economic affairs. Though the system gave rise to some abuses, the Board defended it as vital to an infant industry.[42] Perhaps the Board was oversanguine as to what subsidies and infrastructural investment might have achieved in time; yet it was partly as a result of the policy shift in 1829 that the fishing industry was in such doldrums when the Great Famine struck. The 1841 census counted only 9,142 fishermen (and sixty-nine fisherwomen) in the whole of Ireland. Admittedly, these numbers exclude tens of thousands of part-time fishermen whose main vocation was farming, and who would have been returned as farmers or labourers in the census. A 'carefully revised enumeration' in 1836 counted 54,119 fishermen and 10,761 boats. Nevertheless, the failure of the seas around a land-hungry, poverty-stricken island to provide their main livelihood to fewer than 10,000 men has puzzled generations of commentators. To make matters worse, the poorest counties accounted for few of the fishermen. More than one in four of the total lived in the coastal counties of Leinster, while the extensive coastline of County Mayo provided employment for only 125 full-time fishermen in 1841. The Great Famine would soon inflict massive mortality and suffering on Mayo, as it would on other west-coast counties such as Clare (with 406 full-time fishermen in 1841) and Kerry (458). Besides, the whole of Ireland contained only two or three fish-curing establishments. Nor did the failure of the potato in 1845 and 1846 produce a headlong rush into fishing, though it was claimed that the fish were there for the catching. The Board of Works blamed a 'prejudice' against a diet based mainly on fish, and the fact that many fishermen had been forced by the potato failure to sell their capital in order to survive. The 'prejudice' may explain why the practice of storing salted and smoked fish for local use or export had never been widespread in Ireland. But what was most lacking was the 'solid basis of an existing trade'. With no ready outlets for freshly caught fish in most of the south and west in 1846 and no storage facilities, 'quantities of fish were allowed to rot on the shore, or were spread on the adjacent fields for manure'.[43]

Several reasons have been offered for the underdeveloped state of the Irish fishing industry. On the eve of the Famine, the Halls lamented:[44]

It is notorious that the teeming wealth conveyed by the ocean around their shores—easily rendered as productive as their soil—is neglected by the people, who cleave to old prejudices and customs with unaccountable bigotry; the consequence is that the Irish are the worst fishermen to be found anywhere; and that, not infrequently, even the markets of large towns are supplied by the activity and industry of their Scottish neighbours—the fish being caught a stone's throw away of the Irish strands.

Here the Halls lay the blame on Irish fecklessness and superstition, but elsewhere they allowed some room for an alternative explanation, the lack of proper equipment and infrastructure. Especially along the west coast, fishermen relied on small open boats, which forced them to stick close to land and produced fish unsuited for curing. In the late 1830s, it was claimed that no decked vessels fished along the coast between Killala and Newport, or between Westport and Galway. The Devon Commissioners in 1845 believed that the fishermen were in no position to raise the £300 required for an adequate boat and equipment. That is only part of the story. The lack of steady outlets for fish forced boat-owners to opt for dual-purpose open boats that could also be used to ferry cargoes of seaweed and turf. In addition, the lack of piers and quays ruled out decked vessels. In this version of the 'poverty-trap' argument, the fishermen themselves lacked the resources required to buy adequate boats and tackle and to build quays and curing stations. If landlords and entrepreneurs were unprepared to spend the money and 'create' the markets, surely then it was incumbent on the State to make good the absence? The Board of Works claimed that fishing piers built with public funds had brought 'very great benefit', but the industry could really not thrive in the west without the curing stations that would guarantee fishermen a steady market for their catches. But was the lack of curing stations and deep water facilities for large boats the main problem?[45]

Curiously, the history of the Irish fishing industry has been little studied.[46] The single most informative source on fishing before 1845 is the parliamentary inquiry of 1836, which provides details on landing and curing facilities and on the state of the catch at most points around the coast. That inquiry paints a rather bleak picture of the industry. It remarks of the long coastal stretch between the mouth of the Shannon and Malin Head:[47]

It is in this district that famines are of ordinary occurrence, and that the means of the fisherman are most completely inadequate to the profitable pursuit of his avocation. Here it is that the condition of the country offers the fewest auxiliaries to the philanthropist in his plans of improvement; and that the Commissioners have found the greatest difficulty in discovering any satisfactory or applicable measure of relief. Along the greater line of the cost the boats, both in size and in construction, are unfitted for encountering the uncertain and turbulent ocean; while the remoteness of the great towns leaves the fisherman (excepting those near Galway and Sligo) without a sufficient accessible supply of salt and of the means of curing the fish, should they arrive in great abundance on the shore.

However, geography gave the east and south-east coasts of Ireland, like the east coast of Scotland, a comparative advantage in fishing. Seas were rougher and the weather harsher along the 'tremendous coast' of the west.[48] True, natural harbours were few on or near the east coast, but those few—places such as Howth, Ardglass, Kilkeel, Arklow, or Dunmore East—not only offered both Irish and British fishermen safer seafaring conditions than did the western ports; they also provided better access to urban markets on both sides of the Irish Sea. This, after all, was the era before the railway, refrigeration, and steam-powered trawlers. Location is thus a more plausible explanation than culture as to why, after the Famine, eastern ports were to experience prosperity of sorts, while the western fisheries stagnated.

Fishing was the target of several unsuccessful private ventures. The Dublin Fishery Company was formed in 1818 'for supplying the Dublin market with fresh fish'. The company purchased eight forty-ton smacks, which it let out to captains in return for a share of the catch (first three-sevenths, then one-half). It earned a modest return for a short time, but its surviving minutes tell a tale of endemic personnel problems and erratic fish sales. By 1830, alas, its boats were sold off.[49] The 1836 inquiry described a short-lived company floated in England with a capital of £300,000 to operate on the south and west coasts of Ireland. This venture envisaged a series of curing stations, supplying fresh fish to London and Liverpool by well-boats 'on the model of those belonging to Barking on the coast of Essex', and, 'as a prospect of profitable speculation . . . curing fish for Portugal'. The National Coast and Deep Sea Fishing Company, which attempted to raise £0.5 million in 1825, hoped to combine offshore endeavour with whaling off Greenland.[50] Soon after the Famine, the London

& West of Ireland Fishing Company was launched 'having as a principal feature a steam-vessel as a 'carrier' which would collect fish . . . and ensure its delivery in good condition', but that effort foundered also.[51]

Yet another explanation given for the problems facing the pre-Famine Irish fishing industry is ecological. Fishermen frequently complained that the supply of certain varieties of fish, for whatever reason, was erratic or poor. During their investigations along the south coast the 1836 Fishery Commissioners were repeatedly told of a recent decline in herring catches. The basking shark (dubbed the sun-fish or *an liabhán mór* in Ireland) had been scarce for several seasons. Some witnesses blamed the mysterious movements of the fish themselves, while long-line fishermen blamed those using trammel-nets for over-fishing. However, the persistent annual invasions of Irish waters by Manx and Cornish fishermen is difficult to square with such claims, at least as far as varieties such as mackerel and herring are concerned.[52] The trend in fish prices, in so far as it can be ascertained, also argues against resource exhaustion. Elementary economic theory implies that if the price of fish rose faster than prices in general fish supplies may have been the problem. The trend in the ratio of one fish price series—that for dried ling presented to the 1835 inquiry by Messrs. O'Neill & Stokes, Dublin fish merchants—to an index of Irish cereal prices fails to support the hypothesis that fish supplies were drying up:[53]

1815–19	1820–4	1825–9	1830–6
100	115.3	82.3	104.2

A final point: the financial rewards from fishing, especially along the impoverished west coast, were meagre enough before the Famine. The 1836 inquiry conceded that 'wherever agriculture [was] pursued with ordinary industry and success', it provided a better living than fishing, and produced some scattered data on wages and gross income in an average year in support. A season's return for a seven-man boat ranged from £40 to £100 along the west coast, implying £5 to £12. 10*s*. per fisherman, and double that for the skipper. A north Mayo report put the average return per boat during the season at £2. 10*s*. to £3, or less than 10*s*. (50p) per man. Why blame the fishermen for fecklessness, if the returns were so modest and uncertain? Fishing on rough seas in open boats was dangerous and often unpleasant and unhealthy work.

Before leaving the fishing sector, the fate of the industry after the Famine deserves comment.[54] The numbers of men and boats declined. By the mid-

1870s the number of fishing-boats had dropped to about one-third of its 1846 level, and the number of men to less than one-quarter (Fig. 6.1). Against national decline, the east-coast summer herring fishery and the Kinsale-based spring mackerel fishery advanced for a time. The ports of County Down, accounting for one-third of the herrings landed in the last quarter of the century, were very active. The combined value of these drift-net fisheries reached £0.3 million in the 1870s, but only a fraction of this accrued to Irish boats, and the herring fishery went into sharp decline from then on. The mackerel fishery proved more resilient, and quantities of Irish cured mackerel were exported to the USA: nevertheless, the town of Kinsale, main port of the mackerel fishery, reached its peak population of 6,404 in 1871 and by 1911 was down to 4,020. The slump in herring fishing deterred owners from investing in new technology. As a result, in 1889 there were only three steam drifters fishing full time, and even twenty years later fishery inspectors were still advising trawlermen against investing in steamboats. Still, Ireland was a net exporter of fish in the 1900s and 1910s; its modest balance of trade in fish rose from £0.15 million in 1904–7 to £0.3 million in 1908–14, and £0.45 million in 1915–18.[55]

The west coast fishery remained small in the post-Famine decades, with most of the fishermen combining fishing and farming. Again, the lack of development was not for the lack of trying. Soon after the Famine a member of the Latouche family bought a steamer and brought some long-line fishermen over from England, but he soon 'gave up the business a considerable loser'. The London and West of Ireland Company was another casualty. The North West Fishery Company set up by Lord George Hill and others found the market for the fish they caught 'very poor'. A venture engineered by one Captain Symonds tried its hand on the west coast too, but failed 'with great loss to the originators'. After surveying this wreckage in 1866, Sir James Dombrain, ex-commander of the Coast Guard, was asked:[56]

Then if a private company, able and willing to put plenty of capital into the business, and to superintend it themselves, were not able to do anything for the fishermen of the west coast, is it not quite chimerical to think that the Government could do anything?

Dombrain's reply was that he could not think of any way of improving the west-coast fishery on a large scale. Having been personally stung in fishery speculations, he also felt that the west coast's fish resources had been exaggerated. Thus the matter rested for nearly thirty years. In 1890 the

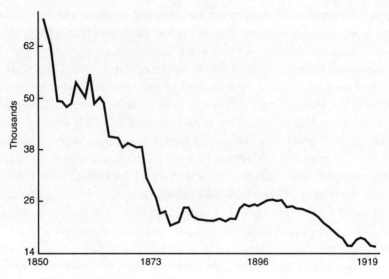

F I G. 6.1 Employment in the Irish fishing industry, 1850–1919

coastline between Lough Foyle and Castletownbere contained few boats capable of handling the quantity of nets then standard elsewhere. Open yawls and canvas-covered currachs were the common fishing vessels: the exception was Dingle, which had twenty decked sailing-boats. Along that part of the coastline administered by the Congested Districts Board (i.e. practically the entire coast from Malin to Kinsale), sales of fish in 1891 were worth only about £50,000. The Board vigorously encouraged the industry with capital grants, infrastructural investment, and marketing schemes, and by 1913 sales had more than trebled. They were to quadruple again during the First World War, but fell back dramatically after 1918.[57]

7

Trends and Fluctuations before the Famine

7.1 Economic Ups and Downs

Short-term fluctuations in the Irish economy before the Famine cannot be measured with precision, but the outlines may be gauged from a variety of contemporary data. For example, the half-yearly accounts of the Bank of Ireland help chronicle the ebbs and flows in economic activity after the mid-1780s. The Bank's income rose from less than £30,000 per half-year in the 1780s to over £100,000 in the 1800s, peaking at £229,357 (Irish) in the first six months of 1815. It fell off in nominal terms thereafter until the early 1820s, and the late 1830s saw a further fall (see Appendix Table 7.A1). The long-run evolution in the Bank's fortunes was a reflection both of macroeconomic trends and the evolving banking structure, but the numbers also reflect the severe downturns in the wake of 1815 and the Great Famine. The protracted decline in the bank's half-yearly income between the first half of 1846 and the second half of 1851 exceeded that for any similar period, and the early 1830s and the early 1840s also stand out as periods of recession.

Data on aggregate banknote circulation are available annually from 1833. Working on the presumption that the public's willingness to hold money is a function of the level of economic activity, then fluctuations from trend should identify periods of prosperity and recession. Fitting the data to a fourth-degree polynomial for the period 1833–1913 identifies 1840–3 and 1848–53 as depressed periods. That circulation should have dropped during the Great Famine comes as no surprise, but the drop from trend in the early 1840s (i.e. well before the Famine) echoes the period known to British historians as the 'hungry forties'.

The half-yearly profits accruing to agencies (or branches) of the Bank of Ireland between 1827 and 1852, reported in Table 7.1, also pinpoint good and bad periods. Unfortunately, the numbers in some half-years are approximations. Still, in so far as the profits reflect the level of activity in the previous year or so, they confirm downturns in the mid-1830s and

Table 7.1. *Bank of Ireland agents' profits*

Period	£	Period	£
		1827:2	28 350
1828:1	26 603	1828:2	27 600
1829:1	22 085	1829:2	20 000*
1830:1	20 000*	1830:2	20 000*
1831:1	22 373	1831:2	20 000*
1832:1	22 535	1832:2	20 000*
1833:1	21 882	1833:2	21 882
1834:1	20 052	1834:2	16 000*
1835:1	18 150	1835:2	16 000*
1836:1	20 152	1836:2	17 000*
1837:1	10 518	1837:2	8 000*
1838:1	11 512	1838:2	13 445
1839:1	17 839	1839:2	25 646
1840:1	21 460	1840:2	27 954
1841:1	31 021	1841:2	28 191
1842:1	24 001	1842:2	14 827
1843:1	13 234	1843:2	21 228
1844:1	17 320	1844:2	16 451
1845:1	21 282	1845:2	20 008
1846:1	30 266	1846:2	32 255
1847:1	34 958	1847:2	23 032
1848:1	18 237	1848:2	17 995
1849:1	11 713	1849:2	9 820
1850:1	−6 744	1850:2	4 861
1851:1	3 128	1851:2	1 497
1852:1	2 721		

Source: BofIA.   * entries are estimates.

early 1840s, when profits declined in four successive half-years (1836:1 to 1837:2 and 1841:2 to 1843:1). Again the Famine period comes out worst of all. The losses made in 1850:1—the only half-year to show a loss— reflect allowances made then for losses on bills due earlier, but perhaps it is the long-drawn-out nature of the downturn—virtually uninterrupted between 1847 and 1851—that is most striking.

These aggregate trends are bound to have left their mark on individual businesses. I give one example here. Morrissey's of Abbeyleix, a well-known 'stop' on the Dublin–Cork road, has been in business since the late eighteenth century, and details of its annual receipts in the 1830s and 1840s survive (shown in Table 7.2 to the nearest pound).[1] Note again the

Table 7.2. *Receipts at Morrissey's of Abbeyleix, 1835–1850*

Year	£	Year	£
1835	1 421	1843	2 903
1836	1 750	1844	3 337
1837	2 371	1845	4 021
1838	2 836	1846	4 536
1839	3 240	1847	3 507
1840	2 918	1848	2 448
1841	2 613	1849	1 826
1842	2 578	1850	2 086

slump after 1839 and the collapse in receipts during the Famine. The outline suggested by this data is broadly reflected in quite a different source, an index of property transactions derived by O'Rourke and Polak from memorials deposited in the Irish Registry of Deeds. While the memorials represent an amalgam of property transactions ranging from marriage settlements to leases on urban property and land sales, O'Rourke and Pollak are probably justified in arguing that the series reflects economic activity, albeit crudely. Their index rises impressively during the 1780s and mid-1790s, plummets during the troubled years of 1797–8, recovers to a new peak in 1813 and then falls off until the early 1820s. The index rises gently again until 1842, and remains low for the rest of the 1840s. New heights are scaled in the 1850s.[2]

Yet another window on short-term trends is provided by the bankruptcy data previously encountered in Chapter 3. Bankruptcy as a concept owes its origin to the fact that commercial life cannot proceed far in any society where creditors have no legal redress against cheating and debt evasion. However, genuine failures to discharge debts are bound to arise, and an efficient legal framework must seek to distinguish between the fraudulent and genuine business failure. The legal condition of bankruptcy extends back to the sixteenth century. The original bankruptcy laws treated the debtor very harshly indeed. A shift in the attitude to debtors is reflected in early eighteenth-century changes to the law.[3] The bankrupt's plight may still have been unenviable, yet it sought to protect the unlucky and incompetent businessman from the fate likely to befall other debtors. In this sense bankruptcy was deemed a privilege, since it ruled out the prospect of ending up in debtors' prison. Only businessmen who had kept accounts were entitled to avail of its provisions. The legislation covered only those involved in the trade of 'merchandise in gross or by retail, seeking their living by buying and selling [and] also scriveners, sales-masters, bankers, brokers and factors'[4] and only substantial creditors (those owed over £100) could plead for a commission of bankrupt. Thus only a fraction of business failures were covered. Creditors' meetings were held at the Royal Exchange in Dublin (or previously at the Tholsel). This presumably militated against creditors in remoter areas demanding a commission of bankrupt. Still, something may be learned from a time-series (Table 3.A1) and cross-section analysis of the data (Tables 7.3 and 7.4). Table 3.A1 above pinpointed 1788, 1793, 1801, 1806, 1810, 1814–16, and 1820 as crisis years; the number of bankruptcies declined thereafter, reducing the value of inferences from this source. The data show few striking long-run patterns. Dublin's dominant role in the bankruptcies is remarkable but, as mentioned, is probably accounted for in part by the way the law operated. Its share dropped slightly over time, that of Ulster hardly changed, while Munster's rose a little. The data also prompt an analysis by type of business. The categories adopted are rough-and-ready. Wood includes coopers but also timber-merchants, food and agriculture includes millers. The group 'other clothing' probably conceals substantial heterogeneity. It proved impossible to disentangle manufacturing pure and simple from trading, though such a distinction may be artificial in the context. The outcome, none the less, is interesting; it implies that growth was balanced across sectors in this period.

Table 7.3. *The regional breakdown of bankruptcies*

Period	Dublin	Munster	Ulster
1776–85	59.0	10.9	14.4
1786–92	58.0	16.4	12.6
1793–9	62.9	9.8	14.1
1800–4	52.7	17.0	16.4
1805–8	56.3	15.4	12.1
1809–12	50.4	19.8	15.8
1813–16	51.7	16.2	16.4
1817–23	49.5	18.1	18.4
1776–1804	58.2	13.0	14.4
1805–23	52.0	17.4	15.7

Table 7.4. *Bankruptcies by sector, 1776–1823* (percentages)

Sector	1	2	3	4	5	6	7	8
(a) Food, agriculture	2.2	1.8	3.3	4.1	5.5	2.8	5.3	5.5
(b) Drink	7.5	6.3	9.2	5.6	10.0	4.5	4.2	4.0
(c) Construction	1.3	1.4	1.8	0.5	0.7	0.7	2.2	1.5
(d) Textiles	2.9	4.3	5.5	4.7	6.9	5.2	5.3	4.2
(e) Other clothing	3.3	2.0	1.8	3.0	4.7	4.3	3.8	1.5
(f) Transport	1.5	1.1	1.8	1.2	2.4	2.5	1.8	2.7
(g) Metal	2.2	0.9	1.2	1.6	3.1	2.0	1.9	2.7
(h) Wood	2.4	1.8	2.0	1.4	3.1	2.0	1.9	2.5
(i) Textile trade	14.3	15.8	13.7	14.5	18.0	16.5	14.1	13.1
(j) Merchants	25.8	21.7	18.6	23.8	14.0	24.3	16.5	26.7
(k) FDT retail	12.8	18.7	10.2	13.0	12.4	12.8	11.6	8.8
(l) Other retail	14.6	12.6	17.3	16.6	11.8	14.0	15.8	14.7
(m) Wholesale	3.1	2.9	3.7	3.3	3.3	2.5	5.7	5.9
(n) Finance	3.3	4.5	6.3	3.5	2.4	2.0	3.3	2.9
(o) Printing, paper	1.1	1.4	1.4	0.9	0.4	1.3	2.2	2.1
(p) Misc.	1.2	2.8	0.8	2.3	1.3	2.2	2.7	2.5
(c) + (h)	3.7	3.2	3.8	1.9	3.8	2.7	4.1	4.0
(d) + (e)	6.2	6.3	7.3	7.7	11.6	9.5	9.1	5.7
(d) + (e) + (i)	20.5	22.1	21.0	22.2	29.6	26.0	23.2	18.8
(a) + (b)	9.7	8.1	12.5	9.7	15.5	7.3	9.5	9.5
(a) + (b) + (k)	22.5	26.8	22.7	22.7	27.9	20.1	21.1	18.3

Key: 1 = 1776–85;   2 = 1786–92;   3 = 1793–9;   4 = 1800–4;
    5 = 1805–8;   6 = 1809–12;   7 = 1813–16;   8 = 1817–23;

Note: FDT = Food, Drink, Tobacco.

As noted, the bankruptcy data highlight 1810 as a crisis year. In July of that year the Government set up a special commission to distribute £200,000 in grant aid on security to 'distressed manufacturers'.[5] Demand was brisk in the first few weeks; by year's end nine-tenths of the permitted sum had been lent out through the Bank of Ireland. The schedule appended to the commission's final report is of interest (see Table 7.5).

The absence of brewers, distillers, and millers among those aided is notable; help was geared overwhelmingly towards the textile sector. The small number of other concerns included paper manufacturers, a straw-hat maker, and a coach maker. The firms granted credits included some of the best known in the country; at the time of receiving them, their aggregate labour force numbered over 9,000, which they undertook to increase to

Table 7.5. *Public grants to industry during the crisis of 1810 (£s)*

Sector	Amount applied for by those granted relief	Granted on personal security	Granted on deposit of goods	Total granted
Cotton	94 600	80 700	1 000	81 700
Woollen	60 250	29 100	28 100	57 200
Flax spinning	14 500	14 000	—	14 000
Silk, worsted	4 000	4 000	—	4 000
Paper	12 700	9 100	2 600	11 700
Miscellaneous	6 500	5 500	—	5 500
TOTAL	192 550			174 100

nearly 12,000. This was no 'lame duck' scheme; unsold goods but not 'factories or other property of uncertain value' were accepted as collateral, and those granted loans paid everything back, indeed, the commission retired slightly in surplus. The data highlight the importance of cotton at this juncture, and of Dublin and its hinterland as textile centres (Celbridge, Prosperous, Leixlip, Balbriggan). The biggest and most persistent borrowers of all were the Celbridge woollen manufacturers, Atkinson and Haughton. The Irish Government had operated a similar scheme previously, in the disastrous year of 1793. A new orthodoxy would gradually take over, ruling out such crisis management. It was well articulated by the Chancellor of the Exchequer in 1820, when asked to ease the pressure in Munster: 'the principle of leaving commerce entirely free to its own operation should always be acted on, unless in cases of absolute necessity.' Nevertheless, help was forthcoming also in 1820. The Government bailed out Leslies' Bank, and Commissioners were appointed to administer loans totalling not more than £Ir0.5 million. Almost £0.3 million was advanced, and £0.1 million of the remainder was set aside in 1823 to promote public works and fisheries.[6]

7.2 The Climacteric of 1815?

Roy Foster, following the lead of Raymond Crotty, has asserted that 'if there is a watershed year in Irish social and economic history it is not 1846 but 1815'. Others have also stressed the severity and enduring character of the post-1815 crisis.[7] I do not seek to deny that crisis here. Yet there is a danger of magnifying a combination of the kind of temporary dislocation that often accompanies war's end (compare Britain after the First World War) and a series of poor harvests into a secular condition. The 1816–18 period, after all, was one of crisis for agriculture and of food shortage not only in Ireland, but in Britain and throughout Europe. The historiography of British agriculture in this period is instructive. The Board of Agriculture's *Agricultural State of the Kingdom, 1816* was almost apocalytic in its gloom. The slump in farm prices produced a chorus of complaints and pleas from farming lobbyists, and only dogmatic economists such as the young John Stuart Mill denied the reality of hardship in the short run. But historians believe that both the duration and the incidence of the post-war crisis in Britain have been exaggerated. Moreover, the crisis had a marked regional component, being worst in the heavy chalk-land soils of the east of England. In the reams of evidence presented to the series of parliamentary inquiries that followed, 'hardly a whimper was heard from dairy counties like Cheshire or Gloucester', and the rearing counties had little to complain of either.[8]

The Crotty–Foster assertion also attributes to 1815 changes which preceded that date and or were inevitable in any case. Thus though industrial decline in some parts of Ireland dates from the late 1810s and early 1820s, and therefore might plausibly be attributed to the slump that followed the peace, it seems much more likely that the war—by slackening the pace of the Industrial Revolution in Britain—merely postponed the day of reckoning. In much of Leinster and Munster industrial decline had set in earlier, in the 1790s and 1800s. The shift from 'frize' to coarse English cloths in rural Ireland was already underway by then, with its attendant consequences for employment, poverty, and income distribution.[9]

Trade data (Table 7.6) indicate that Ireland was holding its own relative to Great Britain up to the 1820s, with both imports and exports maintaining, or slightly increasing, their one-tenth share of the British totals. The increasing importance of agriculture in Irish exports (from 40 per cent of the total in the mid-1780s to 62 per cent in the mid-1820s) is as expected. The relative decline in re-exports from Britain to Ireland is also highlighted. Interestingly, too, though the share of manufactures in Irish exports to Britain fell over the period, Ireland's share in Britain's total imports of manufactured goods rose from 33.8 per cent in 1784–6 to 77.1 per cent in 1824–6. This is largely accounted for by the rise in Irish linen exports to Britain.[10]

On the agricultural front, agricultural output, valued in current prices, certainly fell in the wake of 1815. But the fall was basically due to a drop

Table 7.6. *British merchandise trade with Ireland, 1784/6–1824/6* (current values, £000s)

Date	Manuf.	Foodstuffs	Raw materials	Total	% of all British
A. Exports					
1784–6	531 (57)	119 (13)	274 (30)	924	6.8
1794–6	1 568 (69)	259 (11)	431 (20)	2 258	9.4
1804–6	2 551 (69)	204 (6)	951 (25)	3 706	8.9
1814–16	2 134 (60)	344 (10)	1 050 (30)	3 528	7.2
1824–6	3 145 (68)	576 (13)	887 (19)	4 608	11.5
B. Re-exports					
1784–6	6 (1)	730 (78)	197 (21)	933	25.9
1794–6	8 (1)	1 080 (77)	313 (22)	1 401	16.8
1804–6	5 (0)	1 085 (72)	427 (28)	1 517	15.4
1814–16	1 (0)	1 062 (64)	595 (36)	1 658	9.4
1824–6	1 (0)	810 (53)	708 (47)	1 519	15.8
C. Total exports					
1784–6	537 (29)	849 (46)	471 (25)	1 857	10.8
1794–6	1 576 (43)	1 339 (37)	744 (20)	3 659	11.3
1804–6	2 556 (49)	1 289 (25)	1 378 (26)	5 223	10.2
1814–16	2 135 (41)	1 406 (27)	1 645 (32)	5 186	7.8
1824–6	3 146 (51)	1 386 (23)	1 595 (26)	6 127	12.4
D. Imports					
1784–6	1 091 (46)	952 (40)	332 (14)	2 375	10.4
1794–6	1 600 (45)	1 692 (47)	299 (8)	3 591	9.5
1804–6	2 067 (42)	2 509 (51)	363 (7)	4 939	8.9
1814–16	2 031 (29)	4 416 (63)	608 (9)	7 055	9.8
1824–6	2 997 (32)	5 807 (62)	610 (6)	9 414	14.2

Note: Percentage shares in parenthesis.

Source: Derived from Davis, *Industrial Revolution and British Overseas Trade*, 88–106.

in food prices, not a fall in volume. The divergence in the trends in exports measured in current and constant prices (see Fig. 7.1) shows this. Moreover, while farmers as producers may have regretted the price slump, as consumers they will have welcomed the even greater fall in the price of manufactured goods. In the period under review, the terms of trade moved in Ireland's favour, benefiting those who complained loudest. Irish terms-of-trade data are not available for this period, but their direction may be inferred from (*a*) the movement in Solar's agricultural price index versus that in Imlah's UK import price index, or (*b*) the ratio of UK import to

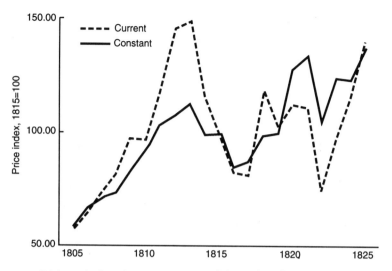

FIG. 7.1 Irish agricultural exports measured in real and current prices, 1810–1825

Source: Derived from P. M. Solar, 'Growth and Distribution', 239–40, 246. The current price series refers to net exports, the constant series to gross exports. Both are valued at Belfast prices, and set at 1815 = 100.

export prices. The first is the better gauge of the impact on Irish food producers, the second on the overall economy. The results (1800–4 = 100) are shown in Table 7.7.[11]

Nor can the decline of the fabled Irish provisions trade be pinned on 1815. The beef trade reached a maximum of 144,597 barrels in 1813 and tended to decline thereafter. The loss was soon made up by the more lucrative trade in live cattle. From the farmer's standpoint the British market, with its easy access and demand for fresh meat, was much preferable to those distant markets that placed little premium on quality produce—though the butchers and the coopers of Cork would not have agreed. Even if the demand for heavily salted beef in the colonies had remained constant after 1815, a ready sale on the lucrative British market for the fresh article, thanks to steam navigation, would have brought about a switch. Again, pork exports peaked in 1815, but the decline in pork was matched by the rise in bacon, ham, and live pig exports, while the gradual rise in butter exports was only briefly interrupted.[12]

Overall, the numbers suggest that the extended post-war crisis complained of by the landed interest was in large part a fiction born of special pleading. We must not be duped by the pleas of farmers and landlords,

Table 7.7. *Two measures of Ireland's terms of trade,*
1800–1835

Period	(a)	(b)
1800–4	100.0	100.0
1805–9	100.0	105.3
1810–14	123.5	120.1
1815–19	134.3	133.8
1820–4	139.7	126.3
1825–9	181.0	132.7
1830–4	205.4	148.3

Note: For derivation see text.

then as now effective propagandists. This is not to deny that severe short-term hardship may have been caused by temporary disequilibria such as the failure of nominal rents and other input costs to reflect the fall in output prices in the short run.

7.3 An Economy Grinding to a Halt before 1845?

The economy continued to grow in the post-war decades, though probably at a diminishing rate. A variety of other proxies for output such as bank deposits, linen exports, and canal traffic indicates an upward trend. Agricultural exports also rose markedly after 1815.[13] The extent of the increase in agricultural production is controversial, however. In an earlier study, I attempted to infer output growth from the trend in food exports and population between the Union and the Famine. My original guess—a rise of about 80 per cent—was derived as follows. The number of mouths to be fed in Ireland rose from 5 million to 8.5 million between 1800 and 1845. Over the same period, the value of Irish exports in real terms virtually quadrupled. Since Irish exports provided food for about two million people in Great Britain by 1845, ignoring changes in quality or quantity implies almost a doubling of output. We have seen in Chapter 4 that food intake, measured in kcals, in Ireland on the eve of the Famine was high, too high to make any substantial drop in the preceding decades plausible. However, switches from grain, beans, and meat to potatoes would not necessarily have entailed any drop in calorific intake. My estimate of an 80 per cent rise in output between the Union and the Famine allowed for this, leaving some margin for the quantity and/or quality of food consumed.

Solar's researches (still, alas, largely unpublished) suggest that this margin may have been too small. He infers sluggish output growth from the failure of agricultural rents to rise much between the 1800s and the 1830s. This squares with Ricardian economics: Ricardo claimed that in the absence of land-saving technological change, a rise in output leads to an even greater rise in rent levels. Alternatively, in a constant-factors-share Cobb–Douglas world, output and rent would have risen in line. Of course, it is necessary to distinguish here between nominal and real values. Agricultural prices dropped by about 27 per cent between 1810–14 and 1830–4 and by 19 per cent between 1810–14 and 1840–4.[14] What happened to nominal rents?

There are several ways of measuring the trend in income from the land. One is to use the evidence from estate accounts on new lettings. New lettings offer a better reflection of conditions at the time of contract than rents due. Solar suggests that the real value of new lettings rose by a quarter at most between the 1790s and the 1830s.[15] There is a catch, however: to the extent that such lettings were also leasehold, they would have attempted to capture expected returns in the future rather than actual returns to land at the time of letting.

A second measure is the rent received by head landlords. A shortcoming is that, given the prevalence of long leases in this period, many tenants paid rents contracted two or three decades previously, and thus possibly quite divorced from the economic value of their holdings. Thus this measure is hardly an ideal guide to the movement in the true value of the land, since it fails to distinguish between shifts in the economic rent and transfers from middlemen to head landlords. Solar finds that the change in rents due averaged 15–16 per cent between 1805–16 and 1823–38. This estimate is based on the records of forty-seven estates. While by far the most thorough estimate of rent trends so far, cross-estate variation was considerable, and a larger sample might yield a different result. Several excluded estates recorded substantial increases in these years. For example, the aggregate rent paid by tenants on the vast Trinity College estates rose from £10,500 c.1800 to £17,300 in 1829 and £24,000 by 1840. Rents paid on the Kenmare estate also rose in nominal terms between 1814 and 1845. In 1814 rents received on the Kerry and Limerick portions of the estate totalled £17,100. Admittedly, the £23,000–£24,000 paid in 1845 included sums paid by tenants on the Bantry section not included in 1814, but that section was made up mostly of bog and mountains. The Tipperary estates of the Earl of Dorchester, worth £8,000 gross around 1790, were yielding over £22,000 in the 1840s. On the other hand, rents due on the small north Donegal estate of Alexander Stewart fell from £2,850 in 1815 to £2,500 in 1844, though they had risen substantially between 1812 and 1815.[16]

The final measure discussed here is the movement in pre-Famine conacre rents. Potato conacre rents were typically much higher than other rents since they were exacted on small plots of prepared, well-manured ground. Prices quoted for potato-ground are plentiful, but very variable across and even within counties. Thus in 1800–1 the cheapest potato-ground in the barony of Iverk, Kilkenny, cost three guineas per acre, 'being a boggy waste, which was to be skinned and burnt by the tenants, the farmer ploughing it afterwards: the dearest potato ground ten guineas manured'. Wakefield (1812) provides a more comprehensive picture, and his data may be summarized as in Table 7.8. Since Wakefield's quotations refer to Irish currency and Irish acres, an average of somewhat over £5 (English) per statute acre is implied. Johnson and Kennedy's analysis of evidence in the 1836 Poor Inquiry on conacre produces a national average of £5.5 per statute acre in 1835. Taking averages of the scattered estimates presented to the Devon Commission (which again mostly refer to Irish acres) yields a figure of about £5.1 per statute acre for the early 1840s see Table 7.9.[17] A very modest rise in real terms between the 1800s and the 1840s is implied. Being subject to annual letting, conacre rents are free of the shortcomings described above. But conacre was in large part a payment for labour rather than land, so the numbers must in large part reflect labour-market conditions in these decades; besides some reduction in the quality of potato-land rented out is plausible.

Taken together, Solar's estimates imply a rise in the real value of rents received of about 20–30 per cent between the Union and the Famine.[18] From a Ricardian or Cobb–Douglas perspective, even such a rise is not easily squared with a big rise in agricultural output. Why did a 40 per cent rise in population—and presumably a bigger increase in agricultural employment—not force rents up more? Perhaps fears of cottier and labourer resistance deterred farmers from further increasing rents. On the other hand, the Ricardian inference of virtually zero output growth, or the Cobb–Douglas inference that output grew by no more than 30 per cent seem implausible too, since the implied drop in food consumption per head is scarcely credible. The movements in rent and output in post-Famine Ireland and early nineteenth-century England are a reminder that, in the end, inferences based strictly on Ricardo or Cobb–Douglas are not

Table 7.8. *The cost of potato conacre, c. 1810*

	Average (£)	SD	Observations
Leinster	8.8	1.2	19
Munster	11.0	3.9	8
Ulster	9.3	3.5	6
Connacht	8.0	1.6	7

Table 7.9. *Conacre rents in the mid-1830s and early 1840s*

	1835		Early 1840s		
	Av. (£)	n	Av. (£)	SD	n
Leinster	5.62	306	8.7	1.4	84
Munster	5.01	281	7.8	2.2	86
Ulster	6.52	171	8.3	1.3	29
Connacht	4.88	132	7.7	1.4	46
Average	5.49	890	8.1	—	245

Sources: Johnson and Kennedy, 'Nationalist Historiography', 29; Devon Commission. The 1835 estimates are per statute acre, those for the early 1840s per Irish acre.

warranted. In Ireland between the 1850s and the 1870s, rents rose less than agricultural prices but increased their share of output, while in England and Wales between 1800 and 1850 output volume increased by over 50 per cent (from £88 million to £135 million in 1815 prices), while nominal rents rose by about one-fifth.[19] On the eve of the Famine, aggregate head rents absorbed about £12 million of an Irish agricultural output worth about £45 million. If they accounted for £9 million out of £26–£27 million in 1800, a decline in rent's share from 34 per cent to 27 per cent is indicated. This would allow for a nominal increase in agricultural production of 70 per cent and a similar increase in real terms.[20]

A Liverpool corn merchant claimed in 1836, in the wake of a few years of low imports from Ireland, that 'the fact of the export of wheat not having increased is no proof whatever that the general growth has not increased very materially'.[21] Does this mean that exports (for which data are readily available) are a poor proxy for output (for which data are lacking) in the pre-Famine period as a whole? The answer is no. Data gathered by the constabulary on the quantities of wheat, barley, and oats sold on Irish markets between 1826 and 1835 are relevant here. The returns are by no means complete, and those that show a spurious stability have not been included in constructing the series that underlie Fig. 7.2. Despite the fluctuations, the graphs indicate a rise in grain production over these years. Sales and export data are highly correlated over the decade, though with the export series prone to fluctuate more.

Whether output growth decelerated in the late 1820s, 1830s, and early 1840s—or, more radically, was grinding to a halt—is an interesting and complex issue. A Malthusian perspective predicts deceleration through the law of diminishing returns. The slower population growth reported earlier suggests likewise, especially since population growth slackened most in areas of better land. The best evidence for deceleration is provided by the agricultural export series constructed by Solar. Solar's indices, which cover the 1780s to the 1860s, seem to suggest a levelling off from the mid- or late 1830s. Was Ireland approaching the dreaded zero-growth 'stationary state' envisaged by Ricardo?

The main difficulty with the stationary state hypothesis is that the period 1839–44 seems to have been particularly depressed, with the consequent danger that a run of poor figures could be mistaken for a trend. A Belfast newspaper, impatient for economic recovery in 1842, wondered whether 'this depression be the inevitable result of causes in constant, or constantly

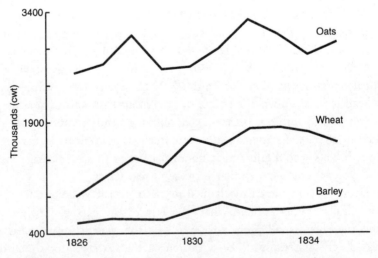

FIG. 7.2 Sales of oats, wheat, and barley on Irish markets, 1826–1835

recurring operation, or of the local temporary nature'. Around the same time at the other end of the island, in south Tipperary, Lord Donough-more's agent blamed low profits on two of his lordship's farms on cattle epidemics, a series of poor potato and grain harvests, and 'the failure of the orchards for the last three years'. Two years later a correspondent in the *Farmers' Gazette* blamed unfavourable seasons for the persistence of depressed conditions.[22] Crises were a feature right throughout this period. Most were linked to agricultural downturns (1800–1, 1812–20, 1837, 1839–43), but a few (1825–6) were 'imported' from Britain. In 1839–44 both domestic and external influences were at work: the series of bad harvests beginning in 1839 coincided with economic crisis in both Britain and America, reducing demand for Irish exports, notably linen. Other economic indicators, such as shipping tonnages cleared, bank deposits, Grand Canal Company traffic, and mining output, also tended to level off during the same period.[23]

Could a particularly depressed 1839–44 produce the 'mirage' of a stationary state? One simple test of this is to fit a regression equation with Solar's export series for 1805–38, and then forecast out of the sample for 1839–46. The result of doing so—estimating a polynomial with a trend term, trend squared, and trend cubed, and adjusting for serial correlation—is to banish the stationary state:

Year	1839	1840	1841	1842	1843	1844	1845	1846
Actual value	945	902	939	925	1070	996	1168	1038
Prediction	1127	1167	1204	1241	1279	1319	1359	1401

On the other hand, this exercise also suggests a secular deceleration in output growth. Moreover, focusing on the agricultural sector alone minimizes the likely deceleration in aggregate economic activity, given the reallocation of displaced labour from manufacturing to agriculture.

The discussion prompts a comment on productivity growth in agriculture during the period between the Union and the Famine, an issue discussed in some detail elsewhere.[24] Equating output growth with that in the number of stomachs filled implies a doubling over the period; the rise of 70 per cent adopted above is conservative, being compatible with a reduction in average Irish living standards, and a reduction in food consumption per capita of over one-fifth.

Let us suppose that labour input grew somewhat faster than population, reflecting the proportional shift out of cottage industries. Since population was 5 million in 1800 and 8.5 million in 1845 a rise in farm labour input of 80 to 90 per cent is suggested. Now let us assume as well that the capital stock rose in line with output, and that the output shares (α_i) of labour (L), land (T), and capital (K) were 0.6, 0.3, and 0.1. Then by definition total factor productivity growth (β) may be derived from:

$$q = \beta + \alpha_L.l + \alpha_T.t + \alpha_K.k$$

where lower-case refers to percentage growth rate. Now assuming $t = 0$ and $q = k = 0.7$, and substituting, yields:

$$\beta = 0.9.q - 0.6.l = 0.9(0.7) - 0.6(0.8) = 0.15.$$

This implies an average annual productivity increase of over 0.3 per cent, by no means astounding when compared to later European experience (discussed below in Chapter 11), but respectable by comparison with the most recent estimates of productivity growth in English agriculture during the Industrial Revolution (0.3 to 0.5 per cent per annum). An increase of four-fifths in both output and labour input would yield a productivity growth rate of 0.5 per cent. However, allowing the labour force to grow at 90 per cent and output at 70 per cent would prune down the increase to 0.2 per cent.[25]

APPENDIX 7.1

Half-Yearly Accounts of the Bank of Ireland

Table 7.A1. *Half-yearly accounts of the Bank of Ireland 1783:2 to 1866:2* (to the nearest £)

Date	£	Date	£	Date	£	Date	£
1783.2	21 874	1801.1	118 357	1818.2	174 774	1836.1	170 988
1784.1	19 251	1801.2	96 261	1819.1	192 970	1836.2	159 092
1784.2	22 183	1802.1	107 221	1819.2	181 600	1837.1	150 863
1785.1	25 537	1802.2	110 675	1820.1	181 445	1837.2	150 884
1785.2	26 046	1803.1	117 642	1820.2	165 647	1838.1	151 350
1786.1	26 768	1803.2	118 575	1821.1	194 310	1838.2	153 924
1786.2	27 871	1804.1	130 626	1821.2	192 169	1839.1	156 920
1787.1	26 788	1804.2	116 564	1822.1	194 049	1839.2	162 574
1787.2	28 117	1805.1	126 140	1822.2	186 091	1840.1	156 632
1788.1	29 672	1805.2	114 569	1823.1	194 643	1840.2	161 332
1788.2	26 787	1806.1	120 020	1823.2	202 435	1841.1	166 084
1789.1	28 009	1806.2	121 916	1824.1	203 419	1841.2	150 918
1789.2	27 431	1807.1	127 960	1824.2	205 178	1842.1	143 563
1790.1	28 513	1807.2	121 768	1825.1	209 657	1842.2	143 604
1790.2	30 563	1808.1	125 550	1825.2	208 270	1843.1	150 460
1791.1	34 478	1808.2	147 897	1826.1	183 324	1843.2	146 121
1791.2	36 365	1809.1	188 290	1826.2	178 309	1844.1	145 543
1792.1	37 471	1809.2	191 612	1827.1	210 222	1844.2	150 680
1792.2	38 908	1810.1	180 873	1827.2	203 017	1845.1	157 531
1793.1	39 254	1810.2	166 864	1828.1	186 175	1845.2	162 890
1793.2	39 952	1811.1	176 191	1828.2	185 415	1846.1	186 079
1794.1	57 125	1811.2	158 473	1829.1	185 268	1846.2	182 345
1794.2	44 270	1812.1	197 174	1829.2	176 302	1847.1	181 878
1795.1	51 444	1812.2	202 472	1830.1	198 020	1847.2	171 621
1795.2	48 604	1813.1	214 274	1830.2	165 672	1848.1	152 966
1796.1	63 007	1813.2	204 399	1831.1	177 357	1848.2	148 822
1796.2	54 429	1814.1	219 586	1831.2	168 225	1849.1	146 653
1797.1	50 003	1814.2	223 378	1832.1	166 866	1849.2	143 464
1797.2	73 679	1815.1	229 357	1832.2	169 929	1850.1	147 350
1798.1	60 285	1815.2	193 899	1833.1	166 772	1850.2	140 905
1798.2	60 894	1816.1	207 336	1833.2	169 475	1851.1	140 820
1799.1	72 189	1816.2	182 006	1834.1	164 806	1851.2	140 382
1799.2	95 129	1817.1	183 850	1834.2	167 058	1852.1	142 813
1800.1	105 313	1817.2	172 793	1835.1	169 549	1852.2	146 808
1800.2	115 790	1818.1	184 744	1835.2	166 759	1853.1	163 355

Table 7.A1. *Continued*

Date	£	Date	£	Date	£	Date	£
1853.2	174821	1857.1	219473	1860.2	181840	1864.1	216240
1854.1	187581	1857.2	226198	1861.1	221509	1864.2	216571
1854.2	178312	1858.1	180047	1861.2	169594	1865.1	188517
1855.1	186742	1858.2	165016	1862.1	150003	1865.2	193646
1855.2	183139	1859.1	165420	1862.2	148457	1866.1	259630
1856.1	208029	1859.2	167256	1863.1	157846	1866.2	252516
1856.2	184211	1860.1	173617	1863.2	169716		

Source: BofIA. British currency from 1826.1.

PART III

'An Gorta Mór': The Great Famine, 1845–50

> The population there so spreads, they say
> 'Tis grown high time to thin it in its turn
> With war, or plague, or famine, any way,
> So that civilisation they may learn.
>
> LORD BYRON, *Don Juan*

8.1 Introduction

Secondary references to Ireland's 'Great Hunger' or 'Great Starvation' are ubiquitous. The tragedy is still vividly etched in Irish and Irish-American folk memory, and a popular understanding of the Famine has become the stuff of history and even economics textbooks far and near. The long-term political consequences of that disaster in Ireland and among those of Irish descent further afield partly explain this interest, but it is also a reflection of the lateness of the Irish Famine by West European standards and, even more important, its context: the back garden of what would soon be dubbed the 'workshop of the world'. In the world history of famines the Great Irish Famine is perhaps best known of all.

Yet there is—or there was until a few years ago—a paradox. The Famine is the main event in modern Irish history, as important to Ireland as, say, the French Revolution to France or the first Industrial Revolution to England. Yet, at least until recently, secondary references to the Famine were out of all proportion to the amount of fresh research published. Irish historians tended to shy away from the topic, as a perusal of the main professional journals will show; no research monograph has appeared since that edited by Edwards and Williams over three decades ago, and little research in the professional journals either. Small wonder, then, that a recent best-selling survey of Ireland since 1600 should contain over three times as much on 'the ascendancy mind' or 'the politics of Parnellism' as on the Great Famine.[1] It was rather as if the profession had taken to heart

Sir Horace Plunkett's maxim that 'Irish history was for Englishmen to remember, for Irishmen to forget'. Ubiquitous amateur local histories, based on a combination of local sources and Cecil Woodham-Smith's *The Great Hunger*, can hardly be expected to fill the void. This silence, at a time when the research output of Irish historians has been considerable, is somewhat puzzling. It can hardly be blamed on the paucity of sources: they exist in abundance.

Meanwhile, popular understanding of the Famine in Ireland (as reflected, for example, in the film version of John B. Keane's *The Field*), still follows the populist-nationalist paradigm. In this oversimplified view, the excess mortality of the late 1840s was entirely, or almost entirely, due to a negligent government and cruel landlords. Exaggerated reports about 'coffin-ships' ferrying emigrants to their doom and about Queen Victoria's miserliness persist, and their mythic contribution should not be under-estimated.[2] It is the historian's function to debunk those myths, even when they are being put in the service of a 'good' cause. A case in point is the distorted account current today of an overnight trek in search of relief in County Mayo in 1849. The alleged march from Louisburgh to the bleak Doolough Valley is re-enacted annually as a focus for support for Third World famine relief, but the organizers' claim that several hundred people perished on the night of the original journey has little foundation.[3]

Folklore also evokes other sentiments. Several accounts relate how farmers and landlords who helped their starving neighbours during the Famine were rewarded by good luck later on. More explain the potato blight as a visitation on people who squandered the crop when it was plentiful, and the bountiful potato crop of the last pre-Famine year is recalled several times.[4] The belief that some particular area escaped lightly or suffered less than surrounding parishes and regions, a reminder of what more vigorous and effective relief might have achieved, also recurs frequently. But perhaps it recurs too frequently to be plausible, reflecting a subconscious communal scruple about famine deaths. After all, folklore also records that for a time the tragedy was somewhat of a taboo subject for some. But the taboo was hardly only about guilt: shared memories about the tragedy were very distressing for those who endured it. Survivors were reluctant to admit their dependence on the soup kitchen or *min déirce* (beggar's meal), or to confess that a member of their own household had died of starvation—though 'they were considered martyrs if they died of the fever'.[5] Still, the Famine was not hidden from memory: a centenary questionnaire organized by the Irish Folklore Commission in 1945−6 produced seven volumes of material, much of it specific and vivid, from all over the island. Most of this material awaits use and evaluation.[6]

In other key areas of Irish history, Irish historians have had considerable success in exorcizing the nationalist ghost.[7] By contrast, as a research topic the Famine remained, at least until very recently, virtually virgin soil. And yet, in their reluctance to look anew at the Great Hunger, Irish historians have not yielded to the nationalist interpretation of events. Until recently, the academic orthodoxy on the Irish Famine was not to be found in journals or research monographs, but in rather bland textbook accounts, book reviews, and university lectures. The impression gained from such sources is of a somewhat cautious and apologetic stance, very different in tone from the vivid accounts of Woodham-Smith or Robert Kee.[8] This is evident in several ways.

First, there has been a tendency in lectures and in the secondary literature to 'talk down' the Famine by reporting (though, it must be said, without supporting research) estimates of excess mortality much lower than the traditional figure of about one million.[9] The implication seems to be that the lower the death-toll, the less the blame. Elsewhere too—in Bengal in the 1940s and in the Soviet Ukraine in the 1930s, for example—one comes across instances of famine mortality being either hushed up or, conversely, 'talked up' for political reasons. Thus Sen[10] has argued for a toll of 3 million in Bengal, against the contemporary official estimate of half that. In the Ukrainian case, contemporary officialdom denied the very existence of a famine, but estimates today range from the 3 million or so indicated by economic-demographic research to the 7–10 million proposed in more ideologically charged accounts.

Second, and almost in contradiction, it is often asserted that massive mortality was inevitable in Ireland in any case, since by the 1840s a Malthusian subsistence crisis was overdue. The point being made here is that the backwardness of the Irish economy resulted in the inability of *any* bureaucracy, no matter how well-meaning, to cope. Sometimes the story has a nationalist twist to it, sometimes it amounts to no more than recounting Irish economic history as Malthusian inference. A related, relativist claim is that to expect any mid-nineteenth century government to have behaved like a decent twentieth-century social-democratic one is ahistorical or anachronistic. Even Roy Foster seems at pains to defend contemporary administrators, invoking sheer ignorance of the facts as an excuse for inaction.[11]

Third, several professional historians in Ireland have been unkind to, or dismissive of, writers such as Woodham-Smith and Kee whose accounts of the 1840s dwelt on graphical depictions of famine suffering and heartless policy-makers. Thus Daly has pronounced Woodham-Smith's depiction of the tragedy as 'highly dramatic and emotive', while for Foster she was no more than a 'zealous convert'.[12] Such criticism has failed to deter Irish readers, for whom Woodham-Smith's book has an enduring appeal that outweighs any analytical shortcomings. No doubt the historians' disapproval springs from a conviction that vivid accounts of suffering in the 1840s might prove divisive or, worse, promote terrorism in the 1980s and 1990s. Nearly 150 years after the event, the Famine is still a sensitive topic, with the result that home-grown academic accounts are rather bloodless, sanitized affairs.[13] But in their quest for 'objectivity' some Irish historians—subconsciously perhaps—have tended to trade nationalism for caution and conservatism.

Fourthly and finally, there has been the tendency to remove the Famine from the centre stage of nineteenth-century history. This has been done by arguing that trends traditionally attributed to it were inevitable in any case or already under way. And so it is held that a whole list of phenomena, ranging from the decline of the Irish language, demographic adjustment through emigration and lower nuptiality, and the shift from tillage to pasture, to the nuclear family household, impartible inheritance, and even the 'devotional revolution' in post-Famine Irish Catholicism, were already in evidence in 'backward Ireland' before 1845. Though certainly a useful historiographical corrective, this habit of treating the Famine as no more than a 'shock' or accelerator producing no fundamental long-run economic or social changes of direction seems an oversimplification.[14]

Against the somewhat reticent stance of home-grown historiography, there are the less inhibited assessments of outside historians, mainly American social and economic historians. Mokyr's vivid analysis of government outlays on Irish famine relief in terms of 'guns' versus 'butter' has attracted a good deal of notice. Echoing contemporary and later populist criticism, Mokyr has tellingly matched Treasury spending in Ireland during the Famine (£9.5 million) against the cost of the Crimean campaign (£69.3 million) less than a decade later. Much in the same vein, Donnelly spares a few kind words for nationalist John Mitchel, whose Swiftian outrage at official attitudes leaves home-grown historians cold.[15] But more important than the rhetoric is the freshness and analytical innovation of some of this work by outsiders. Best known is Mokyr's *Why Ireland Starved*, perhaps the most widely cited monograph in Irish economic or social history since

Woodham-Smith. Though familiar by now to historians and many third-level students in Britain and North America, it still has not attracted the careful scrutiny that it deserves in Ireland.[16]

The outlines of the tragedy have been well described elsewhere.[17] Nearly one-half of the potato crop of 1845 succumbed to a new mysterious fungus, *phytophthora infestans*.[18] The resulting privation produced few excess deaths, however; in counties such as Cork, Clare, Kerry, and Leitrim, where excess mortality would be severe later, people remained generally healthy until the summer or autumn of 1846. Near-total failure of the 1846 potato crop ushered in an extended period of disaster, made worse by harsh weather conditions. Nature played a cruel trick in 1847, when high yields per acre far from compensated for the greatly reduced acreage under potatoes. The high yields inspired the poor to give the potato another chance, but the 1848 crop was again almost non-existent. Excess mortality mounted from the summer of 1846 on and was at a peak in 1847–8, though it was to persist until 1850 or 1851 in some areas. Hunger-induced dysentery and typhus accounted for most of the deaths. Workhouse deaths, less than 6,000 in 1845, exceeded 14,000 in 1846, and 66,000 in 1847; they were still over 46,000 in 1850. The birth-rate also dropped during the Famine. The early phases of the crisis were well documented in the English press, and brought home by vivid, horrific illustrations in popular magazines, notably those by James Mahony in the *Illustrated London News*. Neither private charity, local transfers, nor the relief provided by central government in 1846–8—first through public works, then through soup kitchens—were sufficient to prevent mass mortality. Worse, from late 1847 ministers sought to renege on relief from central funds by placing primary responsibility on the local poor law. The ambitious administrative structure erected from early 1846 onwards probably could have achieved much more in terms of saving lives, given more resources to distribute in the early phase of the crisis. Mass emigration, another well-known feature of the Famine period, relied mainly on the resources of those travelling and their families. Though the Famine produced migrants from areas and groups that had been scarcely represented in the mass migration of 1815–45, nevertheless a poverty trap may well have prevented some of the very poorest from leaving. As a report from west Cork in 1847 explained, 'all the best of our people are flying to America, leaving behind them an inconceivable legion of idleness, filthiness and beggary to drag the whole nation into the gulph of Pauperism.' Emigration to the next world rather than the New World was the lot of many in that 'legion'.[19]

The wider economy soon felt the impact of the potato failure. Banknote circulation, a good barometer of the level of economic activity, had fallen to 62 per cent of its 1845 level by September 1848, and was to fall further in 1849; the decline in the circulation of Bank of England notes over the same period was only 13 per cent. All classes of society in Ireland were adversely affected by the Famine, though obviously not to the same extent. About one million perished as a result, mainly poor people. Though many landlords gave generously in time and money, and many more were bankrupted or in no position to help out, a third group of proprietors proved tough-minded and ruthless. Partly for this reason, partly because Irish proprietors, mainly Tory in politics, were vilified by Whig-radical propagandists, landlordism earned a poor reputation for its efforts during the crisis.[20] Excess mortality was exacerbated by an outbreak of cholera in 1849.

The rest of this chapter eschews a narrative account of the Famine tragedy, and instead focuses largely on demographic and economic aspects. Section 2 summarizes and reassesses recent literature on the demographic toll. Section 3 discusses the impact of political economy on relief policy. Section 4 assesses the relevance of Sen's entitlements approach to famine analysis, using the Irish Famine as a case-study, and contains a brief discussion of the Famine-induced increase in criminality. Section 5 summarizes recent contributions to the literature on post-Famine adjustment. Section 6 offers some concluding remarks.

8.2 The Demographic Toll

The demographic aspects of the Famine have received a good deal of scholarly attention, though here much remains to be done. Recent calculations of excess mortality follow the traditional method of calculating it as a residual, working from the 1841 and 1851 census totals (8.2 and 6.8 million) and estimates of 'normal' birth- and death-rates and of net emigration as starting-points.[21] Studies of famine-induced mortality elsewhere, notably in the Ukraine in 1933, must also link pre- and post-Famine censuses. It seems fair to admit that the most recent Irish estimates are on weaker ground than, say, those of excess mortality from the Great Finnish Famine of 1867–8, and on firmer ground than those from the Ukraine. Irish historians have betrayed an equivocal attitude to the measurement issue. Thus Kevin Nowlan, who 'ghosted' the introduction to Edwards and Williams's *The Great Famine*, claimed that 'all that matters is the certainty that many, very many died', but this did not prevent different contributors to the volume from providing their own (widely divergent) guesses. Similarly, Foster has cast doubt on Mokyr's recent estimates of excess deaths, and yet simultaneously invoked them to describe the famine's regional incidence.[22] As noted earlier, the question of excess mortality during the Great Famine tends to take on a political colour. Nationalists tended to highlight and exaggerate the toll in the past; more recently some revisionist accounts—without, it must be said, supporting evidence either—downplay it. In the case of the Ukraine the story is similar. There the regime denied even the existence of a famine at the outset. A recent collection of studies on the politically induced Ukrainian Famine by Serbyn and Krawchenko produces a much wider range than the Irish. Its specialist chapter on the topic (by Maksudov) suggests 4.4 million deaths from famine and terror combined between 1927 and 1938, but does not attempt to isolate famine deaths. However, Maksudov leaves open the possibility of under-estimation by as much as 1.5 million or overestimation by 2.1 million. In the same volume, the more strident James E. Mace asserts that a figure of 10 million from famine alone 'might well be closer to the truth'. Recent estimates by western scholars of excess mortality in China during the Great Leap Forward (1958–62) also straddle a wide range—from 16.5 million to 29.5 million.[23]

Providing some idea of excess mortality is desirable. While precision is beyond reach, estimates subject to a margin of error of scores rather than hundreds of thousands are possible. In order to get a handle on the demography of a counterfactual blight-free Ireland in the 1840s, Mokyr assumed that the average fertility and mortality levels which he calculated for 1821–41 would have obtained in 1841–51 in the absence of a famine. Boyle and Ó Gráda relaxed this 'stable' population assumption, but their estimate of excess mortality corroborates Mokyr's. Both confirm the traditional figure of one million excess deaths. If allowance is made for averted births, the toll is considerably higher. According to Mokyr, there were about 0.4 million missing births. Since he puts the famine-induced decline in the birth-rate at 8.7 per thousand annually over 1846–51, an average drop of over one-fifth in the normal birth-rate of 40 per thousand is implied. In Flanders, the birth-rate was about one-fifth below normal in 1846–8, in The Netherlands about one-tenth in 1846 and one-fifth in 1847.[24]

These numbers make the Irish Famine a considerably more serious affair than the Finnish famine of 1867–8. Excess mortality in Finland was less than 100,000 out of a population one-fifth the size of Ireland's in 1845. The difference is easily captured in another way: in Finland mortality trebled during one year, 1868, but the toll of the Irish Famine was equivalent to a doubling of normal mortality for a five-year period (1846–51). Relatively speaking, though, the Finnish famine was worse than two others in the late 1840s: that in Flanders which cost 50,000 lives out of a population of 1.4 million, and that in The Netherlands in which 60,000 out of 3 million perished. Of the same order as the Irish Famine in terms of excess mortality was the Ukrainian famine of 1933, which accounted for one-tenth to one-fifth of the population—depending on one's preferred estimate of excess mortality.[25]

Finally, by these standards, the 'Great Highland Famine' that hit north-western Scotland in the late 1840s hardly deserves to be considered a famine at all. According to its historian, Tom Devine,[26] whereas mortality was above trend in the rest of Scotland due to typhus and cholera, the Highlanders 'not only escaped starvation but also the worst effects of the epidemics . . . which raged elsewhere in Scotland'. Devine provides several good reasons for the greater impact of the potato failure in Ireland: a largely indifferent landed aristocracy, a far greater dependence on the potato, and an economy whose structure had failed to evolve like Scotland's. In addition, since only a small proportion of the Scottish population—mainly the 120,000-strong crofting community of An Ghaidhealtachd—was at risk, private charity could play a far more important role in Scotland than in Ireland. In these respects, the 'Great Highland Famine' had more in common with the localized Irish food crises of the 1890s than the Great Irish Famine.[27]

The age–sex incidence of the Irish famine has also been examined.[28] Excess mortality seems to have been more or less a multiple of non-crisis mortality. The old (i.e. those over 40) and the very young (i.e. those under 5) were more prone to perish, but that was the case in normal times too. As for the division by sex, the 'Tables of Death' in the 1851 census suggest that men were harder hit; for the period 1846–50, the census lists a total of 527,459 male deaths against 457,809 female.[29] Yet the scale of the difference is probably misleading; a comparison with data given in the same 1851 census for the early 1840s, and indeed also the data given in the 1841 census for the 1830s, suggests that female deaths were generally less well recorded than male. Calculating male and female deaths indirectly from censal and emigration data still implies that male deaths exceed female, but the difference was rather small (Table 8.1).

Table 8.1. *Excess deaths during the Famine, by age and sex*

Age groups	Males		Females	
	Excess deaths	Average population	Excess deaths	Average population
0–4	146 (29)	508 (14)	139 (29)	491 (13)
5–9	95 (18)	471 (12)	92 (20)	455 (12)
10–59	204 (40)	2 526 (68)	191 (40)	2 659 (69)
60+	66 (13)	211 (6)	52 (11)	234 (6)
TOTAL	511 (100)	3 716 (100)	474 (100)	3 839 (100)

Source: Boyle and Ó Gráda, 'Fertility Trends', 554–5.

The *timing* of famine mortality demands more attention than it has received. In terms of the duration of major demographic losses, the Finnish famine of 1868 and the Ukrainian famine of 1932–3 both seem to have been relatively brief affairs.[30] Like the Bengali famine of the early 1940s studied by Sen, the Irish Famine was much longer drawn out. In Bengal over half of the deaths due to the famine occurred after its official ending.[31] In Ireland, Treasury Under-Secretary Charles Trevelyan declared the famine over in the summer of 1847, but excess mortality lasted until 1850 at least, and was substantial in parts of the west. The absence of civil registration data has prompted Irish historians to deal with famine mortality *en bloc*, taking 1846–51 as a unit. Little has been written about the timing of deaths during this five-year period, other than noting the high incidence in 1849. Was the long-drawn-out character of the Irish Famine due to the inevitable aftershock of fever deaths, or would less stinting relief have reduced it? The issue requires further study but, in the west at least, several accounts imply that in 1849 literal starvation and the stinginess of the relieving authorities were still problems. In 1850 excess mortality was still high in Munster, the census tally exceeding 45 per thousand in Tipperary and Clare.[32]

The classification of famine deaths by cause in William Wilde's 1851 census cross-tabulations highlights the unimportance of literal starvation. This comes as no surprise: even in concentration camps, opportunistic disease and food poisoning killed many more people. The results are based largely on the assessments of survivors. This lends a downward bias to the results, since those who starved alone or entire families who starved left no

Table 8.2. *Reported starvation deaths in selected counties, 1844–1850*

County	1844	1845	1846	1847	1848	1849	1850
Kildare	0	2	3	2	4	8	14
Meath	1	4	11	23	31	27	21
Clare	13	20	44	133	238	286	241
Kerry	15	20	123	586	270	296	184
Donegal	5	6	44	99	49	32	17
Fermanagh	3	7	34	103	25	17	7
Mayo	51	79	293	927	885	784	373
Roscommon	8	20	123	480	306	188	65

Source: *1851 Census*, pt. 5: 'Tables of Death', ii (Dublin, 1856).

survivors to record them. Nevertheless Wilde's nosological data are sufficient to highlight trends by region and by year. The data reported in Table 8.2 confirm both the unimportance of literal famine in the Irish 'home counties' and its enduring impact in parts of the west. In Kildare and Meath starvation during the famine years hardly exceeded 'normal' levels; in Ulster, deaths tapered off after 1847, but in several Munster and Connacht counties the numbers of reported starvation deaths for 1849 and 1850 were substantial.[33]

The implication that famine-induced fever and diseases killed far more people than straightforward starvation is supported by medical opinion. The same held in Finland, where only 2.6 per cent of deaths in 1868 were put down to 'hunger' but over 60 per cent to typhoid fever. In Flanders hunger and starvation in 1845–7 gave way to typhus and cholera in 1847–9.[34] Yet massive disasters such as these are hardly promising material for pronouncing on the controversy between supporters of 'hunger' and 'epidemic' theories of pre-industrial mortality crises, for as the eminent Dublin physician, Dominic Corrigan, was fond of quipping, 'no famine, no fever'.[35] In Ireland, the proportion of deaths attributable to literal starvation was probably higher in the early stages, though the 1851 census 'Tables of Death' fail to corroborate this. They fail to confirm either MacArthur's claim that 'dysentery was rampant before fever had begun to spread', the ratio of deaths from dysentery to deaths from fever being much higher in 1849–50 than in 1846–8. However, the medical reports collected by William Wilde from scores of medical practitioners in 1849 are probably more reliable on this score, and they support MacArthur's sequence.[36]

Some details on the regional incidence of the Irish Famine have also been added. Mapping the proportion of the population on food rations at the height of the crisis by poor law union produces a striking pattern (Fig. 8.1). East of a line linking Wexford and Sligo the proportion rarely exceeded one-third. To the west of that line recourse to the soup kitchen was much greater, exceeding 80 per cent in much of Mayo and Galway. What of excess mortality? Mokyr has shown Cousens's pioneering estimates to have been flawed in a number of respects. Cousens's numbers are certainly too low in aggregate; but Mokyr also argues that, in relative terms, they overestimate deaths in the east and underestimate them in the west. There the verdict is less clear-cut, since Mokyr's own county estimates must also be regarded as tentative, based as they are on guesses about the county shares of emigration during the Famine. Mokyr's measures of county emigration rates rely largely on extrapolations from official data beginning in 1851. These data have been shown to underrepresent southern and western migrants in the wake of the Famine.[37] But such problems aside, it not clear why county migration during the Famine should have been so closely correlated with migration after 1850. Indeed a case could be made for an inverse correlation.

Mokyr's results are quite sensitive to the assumptions made about migration. For instance, assuming county rates 'derived from the shares in 1851 extrapolated back on the basis of trends 1851–5' produces an estimate of 66,000 excess deaths for the province of Leinster, while assuming rates 'derived from the shares of 1851–5 and the prefamine shares' yields 105,000.[38] Leinster mortality, admittedly, is most sensitive to the emigration assumptions: Mokyr's estimates of Leinster's share range from 6 to 10 per cent of the total. The estimates for Ulster are surprisingly high, typically 20 to 25 per cent of the total.[39] This seems implausibly high, since it implies that the famine's relative impact in Ulster was only a fraction less than in Munster. That runs against the impressions gained from workhouse deaths and from the 1851 census, and conflicts sharply with folk memory. Another feature of Mokyr's estimate is the truly massive Connacht mortality. *All* his estimates imply that 25 to 27 per cent of Connacht's 1846 population died of famine-related causes.

Mokyr had no trouble showing that the 1851 census commissioners' tally, based on retrospective reports by survivors, is biased downward. Deaths in workhouses and fever hospitals, though but a fraction of total deaths, are another potential guide to relative mortality. The 1851 census lists over 340,000 such deaths between 1841–51, the bulk of them

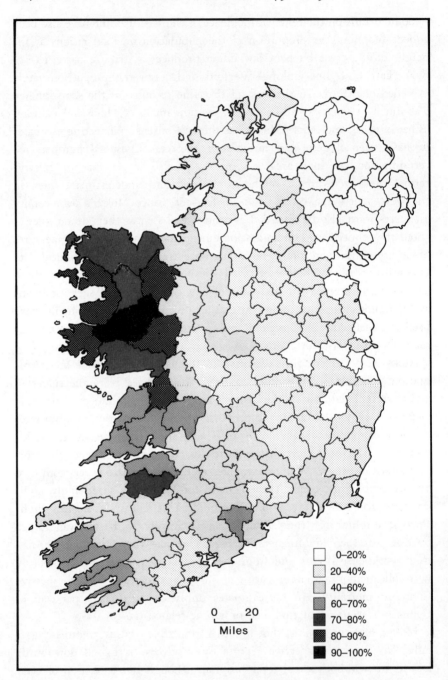

FIG. 8.1 Percentage of population on food rations in July 1847

occurring during the Famine. Cousens's estimate of county mortality[40] combines data provided by the census enumerators and institutions. This undoubtedly involves some double-counting. Cousens's adjustments for underrecording and normal mortality are also open to criticism. Still, taken separately, his census and institutional mortality data provide two further guides to county shares. As Table 8.3 shows, they tell a story remarkably different from Mokyr's. Not surprisingly, perhaps, the institution-based estimate underrepresents Connacht, but both alternative estimates revise Leinster and Munster upward.[41]

Even Mokyr's most conservative Leinster estimate makes it difficult to sustain the view that 'the Famine was less a national disaster than a social and regional one'.[42] *No* county in Ireland escaped excess mortality, though the Famine's impact was very uneven regionally. Still, both Cousens and Mokyr show that mortality was highest in the extreme west, high in Munster and south Ulster, and very low in Dublin and in east Ulster. Marked regional variation in mortality was also a feature of the Finnish famine. There mortality hardly rose at all in the north, but reached four times the norm in some provinces in 1868.

In his 'Deadly Fungus', Mokyr has proposed several explanatory variables in attempting to account statistically for the variation in excess mortality across Irish counties. The advantages of the county as a unit of analysis are twofold: first, there are thirty-two of them and, second, a considerable body of county-level data on relevant variables is available. However, one weakness of county-level analysis is appropriately discussed here, viz. county boundaries do a poor job of separating regions of clustered and dispersed rural settlement. They are therefore poorly geared towards taking account of a variable emphasized in the historical-geographic literature, the proliferation of tillage-oriented clustered rural settlements in certain parts of the country during the pre-Famine period. Such 'villages' were conducive

Table 8.3. *Estimates of famine mortality by province* (percentage of total)

	Leinster	Munster	Ulster	Connacht
Mokyr version 1 (iii)	6.0	28.9	26.6	38.4
Mokyr version 2 (ii)	10.4	31.4	17.8	40.4
Workhouses, etc.	21.3	44.0	16.8	17.9
1851 Census	18.3	35.4	19.3	27.1

Sources: Mokyr, 'The Deadly Fungus', 248–9; Cousens, 'Regional Death Rates'.

to the spread of fever and disease when the blight struck. As noted in Chapter 1, the origin and rationale of these dense huddles of households, often associated with common tenancies of dispersed open-field holdings (or *rundale*), is still debated, but the link between the concentration of rural settlement and excess mortality in the 1840s is surely plausible. To the extent that the prevalence of the system depended on farm size, dependence on the potato, or poverty, its effect on mortality variation may be proxied by such variables. Yet such a purely economic interpretation of settlement patterns goes too far: the role of history and culture in helping to determine settlement and inheritance customs in other parts of Europe has by now been well established by anthropologists. They can cite the Roman historian Tacitus on Germanic settlement patterns in the first century AD, describing differences that have endured in Alpine communities till this day: *colunt discreti, ut fons, ut campus, ut nemus placuit; vicos locant non in nostrum morem, conexis et cohaerintubus aedificiis, suam quisque domum spatio circumdat* (they settle apart where a well or a field or grove attracts them; instead of clustered buildings in our style, everyone surrounds his home with open space). Quantifying the impact of settlement patterns separately is not attempted here: McCourt's map of such settlements in the 1840s, based on a painstaking study of the early Ordnance Survey Maps, is not easily translated to a county-level variable such as 'percentage of rural households living in clustered settlements'—and indeed suggests the need for more disaggregated analysis.[43]

Karl Marx's quip that the Great Famine 'killed poor devils only' is not quite correct. As in 1816–18 and 1822, nobody was deemed safe from typhus in 1846–8, and indeed many reports suggested that attacks on the better-off were more likely to be fatal.[44] Froggatt has drawn attention to the 'staggering' mortality among the medical profession. In 1847 alone 191 medical doctors and students perished, three times the pre-Famine average. While such numbers may well reveal 'a committed and truly professional body of men', broken down by region they also suggest a massive mis-allocation of medical resources during the crisis. Almost one-third of the 1847 medical deaths took place in Ulster, but the death-rate among Ulster practitioners was only one in twenty. Connacht, where the fatality rate in 1847 was over one in ten and the need for medical aid far greater, accounted for only one-sixth of medical deaths. The number of physicians declined from 1,381 in 1841 to 1,223 in 1851. The decline was less than that in population, and in 1851 the east was still being far better served than the west (Table 8.4).[45]

Table 8.4. *Physicians per 10,000 population in 1841 and 1851*

	Leinster	Munster	Ulster	Connacht
1841	2.7	1.7	1.4	0.8
1851	2.9	1.8	2.1	1.0

These numbers again underline the relative unimportance of literal starvation during famines. Most of the excess mortality among the relatively well-to-do medical profession was due to 'fever' or typhus. Individual casualties among another middle-class group at serious risk from typhus, clergymen, have been documented, but overall excess mortality has not been studied. In a society riven by sectarianism and with a long history of petty discrimination against the majority religion, clergy of all persuasions were subjected to criticism and abuse by their rivals. Absentee landlord Denis Mahon of Strokestown, County Roscommon, soon to be assassinated at the behest of some of his tenants, attacked the local priests in 1846 for 'feasting and stuffing and praying'. However, the records provide ample evidence for the clergy's central role in administrating relief and pleading the cases of their communities. Indeed, the Quaker Central Relief Committee, at first reluctant to place local relief distribution in the hands of priests and ministers, soon realized that in many areas they were the only people able and willing to do the job. The death-rate of Catholic priests— twice the pre-Famine norm in 1847—gives the lie to the charge that they did not play their part during the crisis.[46]

8.3 The Famine and Political Economy

We are to have committees in each House on the Irish poor laws. They will contain illustrations valuable to a political economist. Experiments are made in that country on so large a scale, and pushed to their extreme consequences with such a disregard to the sufferings which they inflict, that they give us results as precious as those of Majendie.

NASSAU SENIOR (1848)

[Ireland] died of political economy.

JOHN MITCHEL (1861)

It is natural to begin with Malthus, for whom famine was 'the last, the most dreadful resource of nature'. Was the Irish Famine 'the ultimate Malthusian catastrophe', then, as pre-Famine Ireland was the 'the classic case-study in Malthusian economics'? Malthus concluded from his only visit there in 1817 that 'a population greatly in excess of the demand for labour . . . is the predominant evil of Ireland'. Ironically, he had nevertheless earlier explicitly ruled out a disaster such as the Great Famine in Ireland, predicting instead a greater recourse to moral restraint over time.[47]

Analytically, it makes sense to separate the 'malthean' (Maria Edgeworth's depiction) link between population and poverty from the issue of famine predictability. Considering poverty first, in time-series there can be little doubt but that as the population was growing, the living standards of the poor were falling (see Chapter 4). Yet—in so far as may be judged from scattered data and impressionistic evidence—crisis mortality was modest in pre-Famine Ireland, and the economy was showing some signs of coping with its many problems. The only rigorous test so far of the Malthusian model to Ireland has been Mokyr's *Why Ireland Starved*, which returns a sceptical verdict on Malthus. According to Mokyr, Ireland suffered in the 1840s because it was vulnerable to a disaster such as potato failure, but this vulnerability was not linked to overpopulation. Mokyr's test, which treats Ireland's thirty-two counties as hypothetical time-series observations, relates the land/labour ratio to income per capita. The focus on the land/labour ratio is correct: after his 1817 trip, Malthus stressed that 'the *land* in Ireland is infinitely more peopled than in England'. But against his own firm expectations, Mokyr failed to find evidence for the positive association between population pressure and poverty predicted by the Malthusian model. Surprisingly, this finding—the most revisionist finding in *Why Ireland Starved*—has been subjected to little close scrutiny so far. Patrick McGregor's recent 'Malthus After Mokyr' claims to turn Mokyr's results round simply by adjusting the land variable for quality. In arguing that Malthus was right after all, McGregor implicitly accepts Mokyr's ingenious ploy of inferring a time-series story from cross-section data. However, Liam Kennedy has proposed a methodological critique of this strategy. Kennedy points out that it assumes that Irish counties were both homogeneous and in effect insulated from one another economically. This can, at best, be only approximately true: even in the 1840s west Galway had less in common with east Galway than it had with Mayo, and the eastern and western parts of Cork and Donegal also presented remarkable contrasts. On the other hand, Kennedy argues from county rent data that the land market was well integrated. Moreover, if internal migration was low, then emigration and seasonal migration from the poor counties were a substitute.[48]

Turning to 'gigantic, inevitable famine', I have already argued in another place that it makes more sense to treat the Famine as unpredictable than as 'inevitable'. The sheer statistical improbability has also been stressed in recent work by Solar. Pre-Famine famines, treated since William Wilde's time as ever more menacing Malthusian warning shots, turn out to have been trivial compared to the Great Famine, and hardly intensifying over time. The famines of 1800–1 and 1816–18 killed about 50,000 people each, while public action effectively stalled the famine of 1822.[49] Here, Irish and Finnish histories have much in common.

The potato, of course, is the villain of the piece. Many subsequent accounts echo Malthus's and Cobbett's contempt for it as food unfit for humans and David Ricardo's worries about it being 'uncertain and liable to peculiar accidents'. Direct evidence on pre-1845 yield variability is lacking; the inferences in recent research from pre-blight crop yield data are indirect and must not be pushed too far. Still, Solar's analysis of pre-1845 French data indicate that while the potato was a slightly riskier crop than grain, (a) the trade-off was not huge and, (b) a serious crop failure two years in succession was far too unlikely to worry about.[50] The shortfall caused by *phytophthora infestans* in 1845—about 40 per cent—was at the limit of contemporary experience or memory, but it produced very little excess mortality.

This explains why previous potato failures in Ireland had not resulted in hundreds of thousands dead. The rural economy could cope with a poor potato crop, not without hardship but certainly without massive mortality. One reason for this is that potato-eating pigs, who consumed one-third or more of the normal crop, provided a buffer in bad years. The point is important, if only because it has been overlooked too often. In Finland, after all, a once-off 50 per cent loss of the rye crop in the wake of some less-than-average harvests earlier was enough to produce a famine: how much worse, one wonders, would the story have been had the harvest failed again there in 1868? In Ireland, the failure of 1846 was of a different order from anything ever before witnessed. Data collected by the police put it at a fraction of normal. Solar's canvas of contemporary yield data placed it 'far out of the range of actual or likely western European experience' in any food crop.[51]

Was Ireland merely 'unlucky', then? Focusing on yield variability and pre-Famine famines may suggest as much, but there is more to the story.

Although historians in the past have perhaps been unduly harsh on the potato, the verdict of recent research on the potato is hardly unqualifiedly favourable. Mokyr has suggested that potato failure could have more serious repercussions than a grain failure of the same dimensions since the potato was more expensive to store (in the form of pigs), and more difficult to transport. In the longer run, the potato inhibited the kind of commercial development that one associates with the grain trade.[52] And even if there is some evidence that markets were more integrated than this suggests, the notion that Ireland's 'potato people' were just unlucky can be also criticized by noting that Mother Nature saves her cruellest tricks for those least prepared for them. Thus the potato failure would have mattered less had Ireland been richer or more industrialized.

Recently Watkins and Menken[53] have questioned the role of famine as an effective positive check in the past. Not only, they argue, did famines typically fail to make a dramatic dent in population, they left a vacuum which was quickly filled. The Finnish famine may seem to fit this model: though the age pyramid continued to bear the scar of the famine for decades, aggregate population began to rise immediately again, and had made good its losses within four or five years. Indeed, Finland's natural increase was *higher* after its famine than before (nearly 1.5 per cent in 1869–74 against 0.84 per cent in 1857-66), and nuptiality also rose in the wake of the crisis.[54] Finland's population rose by somewhat over a quarter in the three decades before the famine, and by a half in the three decades after it.

Ireland does not lend much support to Watkins and Menken's claim. On the contrary, the Famine has often been defended for convincing the Irish of the need for 'moral restraint'. Several contemporary luminaries regarded it as an awful but necessary check,[55] and the living standards of the poor certainly rose in its wake. And yet, while the effect of the Great Famine on population was dramatic in the short run, and enduring in the sense that numbers continued to decline, much of the decline would have occurred in any case in the long run, through emigration and preventive check mechanisms. An added argument against regarding the Famine as a 'cure' is that for some decades after the crisis population decline was *lowest* in those parts of Ireland (i.e. the west) where, in Malthusian terms, the message from the Famine should have been driven home most firmly. Of course, this is a reminder of the extraordinary powers of a high rate of natural increase to restore, at least in part, 'lost' population growth.

Both birth and marriage rates plummeted during the Famine but, contrary to common belief, mean age at marriage in Ireland was not much affected. The proportion never marrying, probably already rising before the Famine (see Chapter 4), rose rapidly in the wake of the crisis. In a series of classic studies, Kenneth Connell linked this marriage-shyness of the post-Famine Irish to the Famine: it taught them the need for the Malthusian preventive check. Guinnane's alternative interpretation explains the decline in nuptiality in a non-Malthusian way: low nuptiality was the sign of higher living standards, not a preventive check reaction. The issue is discussed further in Chapter 9.

The role of relief policy has been studied more than any other aspect of the Famine. Much has been made of the policy shift that followed when Lord John Russell's Whig ministry succeeded Sir Robert Peel at the end of June 1846. The point holds, though it must be remembered too that the challenges facing the Whigs in 1846–8 were far greater than those dealt with by Peel in 1845–6. Some historians contend that to expect those in power in Whitehall in the 1840s to have spent more on famine relief is to impose anachronistic standards on them. That ignores how widespread was the belief in Ireland during the Great Famine that public spending was stinting and insufficient. Thus Mokyr's evocative Crimean War analogy has a respectable lineage: in their critiques of relief policy, the ailing Daniel O'Connell raised the £20 million compensation recently granted to West Indian, South African, and Mauritian ex-slave-owners, a Tory peer complained that 'England could find a hundred millions of money to fight the Grand Turk', and Edward Twistleton pointed to 'the expenses of the Coffre War'. On the other hand, even today, the welfare of the underclass and the famine-prone often plays second fiddle to military adventures. Finally, the suggestion that the threat of starvation in some part of England would have been handled differently merely echoes Dublin businessman Jonathan Pim's vain hope in 1848 that 'Cork is as Yorkshire; Mayo, Caithness, and Lancashire are equally objectives of imperial care'. Official reaction to the Lancashire 'cotton famine' of the early 1860s lends some support to Pim's claim. The ensuing crisis was slight and localized by comparison with that endured by Ireland fifteen years earlier, yet it prompted subsidized loans of £1.5 million for public works and a relaxation of the poor law.[56]

Establishment views on what could or should be done during famines have evolved since the mid-nineteenth century. Today, for instance, the notion that feeding the hungry during a famine can serve only to make matters worse would find few supporters,[57] but it was the firm belief of the youthful but already cocksure *Economist* in 1846–9. A good example of *The*

Economist's penchant for dogmatism was its reaction to the (surely reasonable) demand of a delegation from Cork to Whitehall in October 1846 for a living wage on the public works. For *The Economist*, paying people 'not what their labour is worth, not what their labour can be purchased for, but what is sufficient for a comfortable subsistence for themselves and their family . . . would stimulate every man to marry and populate as fast as he could, like a rabbit in a warren'. For Trevelyan, relief could lead only to 'general reliance on our depot, a general relaxation of private effort . . . and a general failure and disappointment in the end'. Such fears that relief might prove counter-productive on moral hazard grounds can be traced back to Malthus, but perhaps finds its most apocalyptic expression in a passage written by Nassau Senior during the Great Famine:[58]

For we may be sure that, if we allow the cancer of pauperism to complete the destruction of Ireland, and then to throw fresh venom into the already predisposed body of England, the ruin of all that makes England worth living in is a question only of time.

I know of no way of measuring the role of such statements in constraining relief, but their impact should nevertheless not be made light of. The notion that 'it is no man's business to provide for another' was made respectable by James Wilson of *The Economist*; Charles Wood, the Chancellor of the Exchequer, confided to Prime Minister Russell that he was 'perfectly ready to give [the Irish] as near nothing as may be';[59] Colonial Secretary Grey, another doctrinaire member of the Whig cabinet, held that 'Irish relief [could] not be granted in too rigid a manner';[60] and prominent members of parliament such as Roebuck and Brougham railed against Irish deceit.

Charles Trevelyan's *The Irish Crisis* was the most famous articulation of what the author of an excellent unpublished study of ministerial attitudes during the Famine has termed the 'moralist' attitude to the Irish problem.[61] Against the 'environmentalist' belief of a minority of the Whig cabinet (apparently including Russell himself) and officials that large-scale expenditure and governmental involvement was necessary to save Ireland, the moralists (notably Wood and Grey) held that forcing landlords to assume responsibility for the poor, either by employing them or by paying local rates for their support, was the only solution. Through Trevelyan, Senior, and others, the belief that things should be 'let take their natural course' gained 'a philosophical colour, and many individuals, even of superior minds, seem to have steeled their hearts to the sufferings of the people of Ireland, justifying it to themselves by thinking it would be going contrary to the provisions of nature'.

Another pointer to establishment opinion is the exchange between Tory-radical pamphleteer Poulett Scrope, a long-standing critic of *laissez-faire* dogmatism, and Richard Whately, Protestant Archbishop of Dublin, at the height of the crisis in 1848. In *A Few Words of Remonstrance and Advice Addressed to the Farming and Labouring Classes of Ireland*, Whately had vigorously accused the Irish poor of responsibility 'for the circumstances in which [they were] placed', pointing to their slovenliness, inattention to religious duty, and proneness to crime. The insensitivity of the timing was worse than the message, to which Scrope replied:

Do you mean that these poor people should be allowed to perish? I hope not. By knowing to what lengths the most amiable and humane men can be carried in a blind confidence in the stern dictates of an unbending theory . . . I do not feel quite certain on this point, Your Grace being . . . a disciple of that rigid school of anti-populationists . . . I cannot forget that the bigoted and prolonged opposition of these benevolent men—arguing in the pride of intellect, against the plain dictates of experience, humanity, and good sense—have by the influence of their high station and authority, protracted, for a quarter of a century at least, the denial to the poor of Ireland of, what all who are not obstinately committed to a false theory now recognize to be, their just birthright in the social institutions of the country.[62]

A key feature of official economic thinking during the Famine was that free markets could achieve more than any government agency. It is said that some of those who crossed the Irish Sea to plead the case for public charity were wont to return 'not with relief . . . but with excerpts from the fifth chapter of the fourth book of Adam Smith's *Wealth of Nations*'. Others were advised to read Edmund Burke's *Thoughts and Details on Scarcity*.[63] In Ireland, as in Belgium and The Netherlands, this belief in the power of markets led to the relaxation or complete removal of tariffs on grain imports.[64] In itself that was not a bad thing. But on balance, economic orthodoxy rationalized inaction and caution. Black's classic *Economic Thought and the Irish Question* has argued for a more benign verdict, but the interventionist and enlightened theories—or, following Montague, 'environmentalist' theories—which Black attributes to economists were far less influential on the ground than the doctrinaire version which emphasized the dangers of relief. That version was aired repeatedly in Parliament, and by influential journals such as *The Economist* and the *Edinburgh Review*. It was also applied with even greater rigour in The Netherlands in these years.[65]

Other aspects of Irish relief policy found echoes elsewhere too, notably the fear that overgenerosity might breach the principle of 'less eligibility'. Stories of individuals who were thriving on the works conditioned official attitudes:

At present (the task work system) is one entire system of abuse; thus in 'breaking of stones' the stones are frequently measured several times . . . The consequence of this is that men are sometimes receiving £1. 4*s*. per week; I say *receiving* for it is quite impossible that they could *earn* that amount by such kind of labour. Mr Stackpole . . . who is in the habit of employing fifty men at this time of year is tilling his land as best he can with girls; one family here obtained £4. 10*s*. in the week, and it is most difficult to prevent such.[66]

Of course, had the rates indicated here been typical, there would have been no famine, and Ireland would have been inundated with workers from Great Britain. In the same vein is Nassau Senior's use in the *Edinburgh Review* of 'somewhat detailed statistics' from the electoral divisions of Belmullet and Binghamstown, and the union of Kilrush. According to Senior, so corrupted by relief had the people in these areas become that in 1847 there were only '2,375 acres producing food consumable by man [in] a district containing a larger area than the county of Middlesex, and a larger population than the county of Rutland'. No hint here that the bulk of the land consisted of bogs and exposed, barren hills! This is a good example of Senior's penchant for drawing apocalyptic (and mischievous) inferences from irrelevant case-studies.[67] That relief was preferable to starvation, of course, is not to deny the likelihood that relief had negative side-effects, or that fears about the effect of the works on farm-work were genuine. The truth about the connection between relief, wages, and work effort during the Famine must have been complex, but has not been studied. The typical farm-worker in pre-Famine Ireland had been paid a potato wage not much above subsistence. Either he spent most of the work-year covering the cost of renting a plot of manured potato-ground (or conacre), or else he was paid a money wage so low that the only subsistence he could afford was potatoes. The conacre system so central to the farmer–labourer nexus before 1845 was very severely dented by the potato blight, as labourers sought to renegotiate, or simply reneged on, their contracts for labour in return for diseased potatoes. Farmers tended to let workers go. This is reflected in the precipitous drop in the potato acreage after 1846.

But the deals that farmers made with those they retained have not been studied in the Irish context.[68] During the Famine, there is some presumption that farmers would pay their workers—the minority they retained— more money or more land for a substitute crop in order to keep them efficient.

At the height of the Famine, the public sector through the Board of Works replaced the farmers as the main employer of labour: at the peak in March 1847 the Board employed over 700,000 people.[69] The Board has been criticized for failing to target the areas and the people most in need. Daly has pointed to anomalies such as proportionately more of the Board's money being spent in parts of Kildare and Kilkenny than in west Cork or Leitrim. In paying its masses of mainly adult male workers, the Board attempted to apply a piece-rate system, but this produced further delays and injustices. The sheer inability to perform physically demanding work had a drastic implication for the system of task-work: it meant that those in greatest need were least likely to benefit. One report tells of how in February 1847 a gentleman-farmer who was prepared to offer workers 16d. (7p) a day failed to lure any from the public works which were paying only 10d. (4p), though 'they were wretchedly off for provisions for themselves and their families'. What could explain this 'most incomprehensible extent of vicious propensity'? A senior official explained to Trevelyan:

It is now beyond a spirit of idleness and unwillingness to work; there is a *physical incapability*. An engineer in Kerry reports, that with the wretched objects who come to the works, he is ashamed as an engineer of the *smallness* of the task he gives them, and as a man, viewing the condition of the labourers, of the *largeness* of the task . . . I have *not a doubt* that the poor wretches are incapable of doing the work for the 1s. 4d., although by *appearing* and remaining through the day, they can gain their 10d.

Officials realized the problem, but were clearly unhappy with the implication that it might make more sense to pay the weak for doing nothing than have them wielding shovels and axes on the roadside:

We are not now paying for labour, but paying money to enable people to feed themselves. The prostration of strength in many incapacitates them from *earning* a fair day's pay, and the consequence is that they are only entitled to a small sum, or else they are paid subsistence without a return for it. The task-work system, or the one nominally so styled, must soon be exploded.[70]

Yet in London, the Treasury and its supporters were obsessed by the abuse occasioned by the task-work system and the potentially high wages obtain-

able from it. Corruption and favouritism were undoubtedly rife. Landlords, priests, overseers, and magistrates vied with one another in placing
dependants on the works; money earned was sometimes spent on whiskey
instead of on food. But that was surely not the main point. The Board of
Works' accounts reveal that in late 1846 and early 1847 it paid its workers
on average 12*d.* to 13*d.* per day. Though this exceeded the pre-Famine norm
for unskilled rural wage labour, the rise in food prices made it a starvation
wage. Mere subsistence for a family of four or five during the winter of
1846–7 cost at least 2*s.* or 3*s.* a day, before making any allowance for
clothes or lodging:

8*d.* per diem is unquestionably the usual rate of wages of this part of the country
in *ordinary* seasons, though many persons, and perhaps all of the better classes, are
now paying at higher rates.[71]

A County Roscommon inspecting officer wondered 'what was a man to do
on eight pence with a large family, and he the only one to work out of
it . . . a question I would earnestly call the attention of the Government
to'. The east Galway songster Peatsaí Ó Callanáin posed precisely the same
question from the perspective of those at risk:

Gan ór gan airgead, gan chreidiúint shaolta,
Gan tnúth le tréan againn ach amháin le Dia,
Ach muintir Shasana ag tabhairt pái lae dhúinn,
Dhá bhonn ar éigin gan deoch gan bia.

Is iomaí teach a bhfuil ochtar daoine ann,
Is gan fear le saothrú ach aon duine amháin,
Siúd pingin don duine acu, gan caint ar an tSaoire,
Agus lá na díleann níl faic le fáil.[72]

It is only fair to say that 'the Government' never tackled this fundamental problem. The average wage paid on the public works during
1846–7 was simply not enough to keep a destitute family alive, and
hundreds of thousands of households had few resources with which to
supplement that wage. The lack of purchasing power at this stage was
crucial, since the ensuing hunger spread dysentery and disease.

On top of such shortcomings, an added fear, particularly once the very
harsh winter was over, was that the public works were attracting labour
away from agriculture. The works were officially deemed a failure by early
1847, and historians have by and large concurred with this verdict. However, this should not be taken to mean that public works are inherently
unable to cope with famine crises. Evidence from recent Indian experience

suggests the contrary. There the success of famine prevention in recent decades has been put down largely to an effective system of entitlements protection, in which public works have always had pride of place. A comparison suggests several defects in the Irish schema. Besides the early linkage between the wage paid and effort, and the stinginess of the reward, the Irish system, unlike the Indian, failed to guarantee 'work for all who want[ed] it'. In Ireland most of those employed were men, though the Board eventually felt obliged to employ destitute women and children, while many people holding even small amounts of land were excluded. 'A man was often forced to quit out of physical weakness, but there were others watching for that to happen so that they would get their turn.'[73] Thus it was never the case even in the worst-hit parts of Ireland that 'virtually the whole population of entire villages was employed on relief works'. Nor was there the same obsessive concern in India with 'reproductive' projects: for example, the relief works organized during the Maharashtra drought of 1972–3, which employed nearly 5 million workers at their peak, produced a metal scrap mountain of nearly 30 million cubic metres.[74] In the end, one suspects that had the Irish poor—like those of Maharashtra and other more successful famine prevention efforts—been given more generous allowances on the public works (or through some other means), and always been paid on time, markets would have worked well enough to induce a greater inflow of the necessary food.

The decision taken in March 1847 to replace public works by direct, but in effect non-transferable, food grants, anticipates modern theoretical discussion on the choice between rationing by price or by quantity. Cash transfers might seem preferable since they increase consumer choice. In this instance consumer choice was not trusted: the soup (really a maize-based gruel or slop) was thought to minimize cheating since it was not easy to transport and resell. The effective price was increased by making many people suffer the indignity and nuisance of having to travel and queue for hours for food. At its peak in the summer of 1847 the scheme was doling out over 3 million meals daily, yet another reminder of the capacity of the bureaucracy to reach the needy. The bureaucratic apparatus erected during the Famine was indeed a marvel. Soup-kitchens and public works reached the remotest areas. The point deserves emphasizing, because it means that neither poor communications (compare the situation in parts of Finland in 1867–8) nor a weak bureaucracy can be blamed for the famine: given the political will to spend more money, the relief framework erected *could* have been marshalled to distribute more aid.

Historians have rated the soup-kitchen scheme highly, but (like Treasury under-secretary Trevelyan at the time) they may have been too quick to do so, because the drop in deaths during the soup-kitchen period—the late spring and summer of 1847—had a strong seasonal component to it. And, though the food content of the diet still awaits definitive analysis, it has been plausibly claimed that liquid food was little help to people already weakened by malnutrition.[75]

Public policy attempted to ensure that private charity would not be crowded out. However, private charity was never equal to the task of preventing famine. Initial enthusiasm soon gave way to 'donor fatigue' or 'compassion fatigue'. Thus the Society of Friends (or Quakers), whose Central Relief Committee played a key part in famine relief efforts in Ireland in 1846–7, conceded after a year that 'government alone could raise the funds, [and] carry out the measures necessary in many districts to save the lives of the people'. The message failed to strike home, for in 1849 the Prime Minister urged the Quakers, unsuccessfully, to undertake another Irish relief campaign. Experience with private charity in today's Third World mirrors the Irish example: despite continued hardship in Africa, most European relief agencies saw a fall-off in their incomes in 1986 after the bumper years of 1984–5.[76] Private charity, it seems, may cope with a short crisis, but not a prolonged one. In Ireland, alas, official anxiety to declare victory over the Famine in mid-1847 probably added to the problem, by giving the wrong signals to some remaining potential donors.

While interesting in terms of abstract theory, and indeed worth bearing in mind in the formulation of an efficient relief scheme, these moral hazard and 'crowding out' considerations obsessed contemporary administrators, who nevertheless did not attempt to quantify them. They may have been correct about the *direction* of the responses to relief and cheap food, but they seemed unconcerned about their *sizes*.

This prompts a final point. The most obvious questions about Irish famine relief—how many lives were saved by actual outlays and how much more would it have cost to save some or most of the lives lost—are probably unanswerable. Does the spatial coincidence between relief and mortality mean that relief was ineffective, or that mortality in the blackest spots would have been even greater otherwise? Perhaps detailed local study and comparative insights will answer such questions. Only the rough outlines of the cost function may be guessed at: a huge initial commitment required to keep famine fever at bay, and a rising marginal cost to saving further lives. Timing would have been a crucial aspect: a given sum spent on food in late 1846, before fever became universal, would have saved more lives than the same sum six months later.

8.4 Food Entitlements and Crime

> I shall be very much obliged to you to call at Bassetts Gunmaker Parliament St and make him send to you a small mahogany case he has of mine containing a six barrel pistol.
>
> ROSCOMMON LANDLORD, 1847[77]

Sen has drawn attention to several twentieth-century famines where 'people starved to death without there being a substantial rise in food prices'.[78] Price rises, of course, are the norm. In Bengal in the 1940s foodgrain prices reached four to five times the pre-Famine norm for some months; in Bangladesh in 1974 they doubled. In Ireland the prices of all potato varieties rose fourfold between 1845 and 1847, though the price of grain only doubled. In Finland in 1867–8 the story is somewhat more complicated: the official prices used to convert tax-grain to money rose by less than one-third, but market prices doubled.[79] Such rises bespeak a supply-side shock. Yet several scholars have suggested the relevance of Sen's 'exchange entitlements' hypothesis to the Great Irish Famine. Sen argues that the most plausible reason for famines—the sheer lack of food—overlooks the evidence from many case-studies elsewhere of mass starvation in the midst of plenty. Sen's own Bengal in the 1940s contained enough food in the strict arithmetical sense for everyone, yet 3 million died. His less detailed studies of recent famines in Ethiopia and the Sahel argue in the same direction, and others have pointed to more examples. Elsewhere Sen has invoked no less an authority than economist David Ricardo against the claim that famines cannot occur in conditions of 'superabundance': Ricardo's reference was to the Irish famine of 1822.[80]

Sen's criticism of what he has termed the Food Availability Doctrine is not that food shortages do not cause famines, but that they are far from being the only cause. Yet given the crude facts of the Irish case—most of the normal potato crop of fifteen million tons destroyed or not planted for several years in succession—the prima-facie case for the Food Availability Doctrine is strong. The potato had accounted for a quarter of Irish agricultural output, and the shortfall was certainly not made good by a rise in corn or livestock output. Perhaps Sen's entitlements view might be defended in the following sense. Ireland had long produced a food surplus (largely of grain and livestock products), which was exported. Though the potato crop after 1845 was only a fraction of normal, in theory there was still enough of the 'surplus' products—corn, butter, and meat—to feed everybody. True, much of the 'surplus' was exported, but the fraction exported declined during the Famine and, what is more, some of the proceeds from exporting beef and wheat were used to pay for the massive imports of cheaper food after 1846. On the other hand, *any* appreciable outflow of grain can only reflect a lack of entitlements in Ireland.[81]

Solar's calculations of food availability before and during the Famine at first sight seem to support Sen's characterization of famines as crises of entitlements rather than strict lack of food. Solar's estimate of food supply during the Famine (reproduced below as Table 8.5), which allows for maintenance of the capital stock in tillage, might be interpreted as implying that the food shortfall was not dramatic. Indeed had all horses remained unfed during the Famine period, there would have been even more food to hand in 1846–51. However, as emphasized by Solar himself, his data treat the period 1846–51 as a block, and thereby muffle the food supply problems of 1846–7 in particular.

A second problem with such political arithmetic is that it must ignore the dynamic consequences of redistribution: redistribution in one year might have induced (or forced) farmers to reduce output in the next. In the end, the strongest argument in favour of Sen's approach is that the unit of analysis matters: treating Ireland as a full-fledged part of the UK supports the thesis that entitlements should be considered in conjunction with food availability. This recalls once more the old nationalist chestnut that the threat of famine in Devon or Yorkshire in the 1840s would have been handled differently from one in Mayo or Clare.

Table 8.5. *Irish food supplies, 1840–1845 and 1846–1850* (in 1,000 m. kcal/day)

	1840–5	1846–50
Irish production (*less* seed and horses)	32.1	15.7
Less exports and non-food uses	−11.8	−3.1
Net domestic supplies	20.3	12.6
Plus Imports	+0.2	+5.5
TOTAL CONSUMPTION	20.5	18.1

Source: Solar, 'The Great Famine', 123.

In another sense, the Irish Famine differed from the famines described by Sen. Implicit in Sen's scenario is a zero-sum game. Since aggregate output is not much affected, what those affected adversely lose, others must gain. But few can have *gained* from the Great Irish Famine. The most obvious losers were the poor who perished and their kin. But at the other end of the spectrum few landlords escaped unscathed either. The 49 per cent drop in the note-circulation of the Provincial Bank, the landlord bank *par excellence*, between mid-1846 and mid-1849 tells its own story. A few landlords, such as Dennis Mahon of Strokestown, murdered at the behest of some of his tenants, paid the ultimate price.[82] For the rest, there was a great deal of variation both within and across regions. Mokyr's sample of estates passing through the Encumbered Estates Court in the wake of the Famine offers some insight into the regional impact of crisis-induced bankruptcy. This suggests—plausibly—that the worst-affected landlords lived in the south and the west. Rather less plausible is the implication that landlords in the region comprising Donegal, Fermanagh, Tyrone, Leitrim, Roscommon, and Sligo escaped lightly (Table 8.6).

Presumably the degree of local destitution was crucial, since it influenced both receipts and outgoings. Moreover, the fewer tenants holding directly, the better from the head landlord's point of view. In such cases—the Kenmare and Trinity College estates are good examples—middlemen eager to hold on to their leases were more apt to cushion the head landlord from ruin. Yet surprisingly few studies exist of the trend in rent receipts during

Table 8.6. *Landlord insolvency by region: evidence from the O'Brien rentals*

Region	O'Brien sample (%)	Total acreage (%)	Total arable (%)
North-east	16.2	15.5	18.2
North-west	2.1	18.9	15.7
Centre	15.2	10.7	13.3
East	10.5	11.8	14.8
South	32.7	25.1	25.4
West	23.2	18.1	12.6
	100.0	100.0	100.0

Sources: Mokyr, *Why Ireland Starved*, 92; *1841 Census*, xiii.
Regions as defined by Mokyr.

the Famine. Solar's analysis of landlord incomes ends with the Famine, as does Maguire's of the Downshire estates, and Robinson's of the London Companies' estates in County Derry. Donnelly's study of seven Cork estates (including the massive Devonshire estate) shows 84 per cent of the rent due being collected between 1846 and 1853, but the estates in Donnelly's survey probably weathered the storm better than most.[83]

More complex is the farmers' case. Most farmers had relied on some hired labour before the Famine, and what they gained in terms of cheaper land was almost certainly outweighed by what they lost in cheap labour and cheap potatoes. Probably only heavily land-intensive farmers— sometimes dubbed graziers in Ireland—gained. Most ancillary trades suffered too.

A salutary feature of Sen's approach is its focus on class and distributional considerations, too long taboo in Irish historiography. It invites Irish historians to look more deeply into the part played by farmers, shopkeepers, and townspeople—or, more generally, the middle classes—in preventing or exacerbating mortality. The rate-in-aid controversy of 1849– 50 betokens a low degree of interregional solidarity at a late stage in the crisis.[84] Moneylenders, probably inevitably, earned a poor reputation: yet if borrowers who survived on credit were forced to pay high premia, that was partly in order to compensate for the defaulters who perished. On a more local level, *comhar na gcomharsan* (helping one's neighbour) often did not extend to farmers lending a hand to landless labourers during the Famine. Folklore instances the generosity of many individuals, but there is ample evidence too of the better-off ruthlessly protecting their property. Donnelly notes that 'the records of the great famine are replete with anti-social behaviour and gross inhumanity—committed by wealthy farmers and shopkeepers against the poor, by the poor against others of their own class, by parents against their children, and by sons and daughters against their parents.'[85]

This brings us to another traditional explanation for mass mortality: the people did not resist enough during the Famine. Radical nationalist Michael Davitt later accused them of 'wholesale cowardice' as if, like in Belgian Flanders, 'the people, pious and sober, resigned themselves to their fate'.[86] The crime statistics suggest that though they may not have resisted enough, resist they certainly did. The resistance was for the most part spontaneous and unorganized, by individuals or small groups against other individuals. Shops and stores were also plundered in classic 'moral economy' fashion, and petty larceny was widespread. The propertied took counter-

Table 8.7. *Crimes reported during the Great Famine* (1844 = 100)

Year	1845	1846	1847	1848	1849	1850	1851
All crime	128	196	332	223	236	168	145
Burglary	97	269	561	279	134	73	141
Robbery	124	257	559	588	460	409	319
Rape	89	92	31	52	34	65	43
Homicide	95	116	145	117	139	95	108
Cattle- and sheep-stealing	79	368	1 223	821	993	585	448

Source: NA/SPO, *Return of Outrages*. The data exclude the Dublin Metropolitan Area.[87]

Table 8.8. *Reported crimes, 1844–1847*

	1845	1846	1847
Jan.–Feb.	1 236 (1 108)	1 555 (1 412)	5 082 (2 246)
Mar.–Apr.	1 352 (1 219)	1 500 (1 351)	4 469 (1 980)
May–June	1 617 (1 531)	1 226 (1 096)	4 208 (1 904)
July–Aug.	1 201 (1 097)	956 (830)	1 551 (1 029)
Sept.–Oct.	972 (892)	2 246 (1 838)	1 640 (1 283)
Nov.–Dec.	1 184 (1 054)	4 327 (2 258)	

Source: PRO, T64/367A/3. The numbers in brackets exclude cattle-stealing.

measures. The number of crimes outside Dublin rose from 8,000 in 1845 to over 20,000 in 1847. Data on committals show a similar rise. The disruptions brought by the Famine may have presented ordinary criminals with new opportunities, but the details show that the upsurge was due more to desperation than to pathological criminality. A Treasury minute chronicles reported offences month by month; the aggregate number rose sharply only in the autumn of 1847, with offences such as cattle-stealing and burglary to the fore (Table 8.7). Indeed some seem to have engaged in petty crime in the hope of being sentenced to transportation: reports back from Australia noted that many of those sent out were 'wholly unfit for ordinary convict association and treatment, owing partly to their youth and partly to their general good conduct'. Opponents of the abortive 1849 Cattle and Sheep Stealing (Ireland) Bill claimed that 'harsher' penalties would only increase the incidence of the crimes in question.[88] Contemporary police and prison records convey the nature of the typical crime during 1847–9 more evocatively than the printed statistics can. Petty theft of items such as sheep, pigs, potatoes, turnips, flour, bread, and cloaks predominate. The same sources show that many of those arrested had died before being brought to trial or while serving their sentences. Among the hundreds charged and committed for theft before the Cork assizes of 1847 were five members of the Keeffe family. Two of them had perished before they could complete their six-week terms. Others who perished in prison included 48-year-old John Sexton, convicted for turf-stealing, and John Guinee (aged 15), convicted for stealing and killing a sheep. Denis Lane was found dead in his cell after being brought in for 'forcibly taking meal from carmen'.[89]

Thieving and robbery without violence surged after 1845, but the numbers of those charged with serious violent crimes (e.g. murder and rape) changed by much less (see Table 8.7). The higher share of illiterates and married people among Famine criminals and the higher average age of those committed also imply desperation. An analysis of County Clare transportees in 1839–40 and 1846–8 supports the view that Famine criminals were 'different': the numbers convicted of larceny and stock-stealing, in particular, were much higher in 1846–8. The law dealt harshly with the guilty. Hangings rose from an average of six in 1843–6 to seventeen in 1848–9, and the number of people sentenced to seven years' transportation from 485 to 1,853.[90] In Flanders and The Netherlands too, crime increased during the 1840s, if to a lesser extent. There too resistance was largely poorly planned, and severely punished.[91]

Though often accused of fomenting sedition, the Catholic Church clergy, largely manned by the sons of strong farmers, frowned on violence and, with a few exceptions, eschewed radical demands on behalf of the poor. They opposed the operation of the quarter-acre clause, however, and surviving correspondence in support of relief suggests Trojan work by them (and indeed by clergy of all denominations). Irish politicians also counselled moderation; perhaps they were too moderate. Sometimes at local level they were the unwitting agents of Whitehall stringency. Many of the guardians presiding over the stingiest poor law unions were middle-class Repealers, not Protestant landlords. Again, few Irish members opposed the passage of the Gregory clause in Westminster. There is ample scope for further research here by cultural, social, and local historians.[92]

8.5 Economic Aftermath

One of the best-known chapters in the first volume of Karl Marx's *Das Kapital* contains an interesting discussion of economic trends in post-Famine Ireland. Unfortunately Marx's attempt to use Ireland as a case-study in the 'general law of capitalist accumulation' founders on extra-polations from a series of particularly bad years between 1859 and 1864. By comparing the agricultural statistics in these years with those of the early 1850s, Marx could argue that depopulation and decline had persisted in Ireland, and blame labour-saving technological change in farming. The statistical basis for his story, however, rests on an atypically depressed period. In particular, the potato crop was less than two-thirds of its post-Famine average in 1860–2, and by mid-1863 farmers had £26 million wiped off the value of their output by a combination of crop failures, a fall in livestock numbers, and poor prices.[93]

Yet if these depressed years are interesting for having misled Marx, they are also notable for another reason. Curiously, neither famine nor disease resulted from such a persistent slump in prices and output, and numbers entering the workhouses hardly rose. Donnelly has pointed to the role of increasing commercialization and the availability of credit.[94] Censal data do indeed hint at a minor commercial revolution after the Famine: in Connacht, the number of grocers, victuallers, and kindred tradesmen per thousand population rose from about 1.0 in 1841 to 1.4 in 1861. But far more important was the population thinning done by the Great Famine; according to Fitzpatrick's calculations, the number of male agricultural labourers had dropped from 1.2 million or so in 1845 to 0.9 million in 1851 and 0.7 million in 1861.[95]

Another of Marx's assertions, that landlord income was absorbing an increasing share of a declining output, is closer to the mark. Yet the basis for this was not his 'law of primary capitalist accumulation', whereby labour-saving technical change relentlessly impoverishes the working class; rather, it was the rise in the relative price of land-intensive produce in the 1850s and 1860s.

In his dissertation and in a number of related articles Kevin O'Rourke has recently posed the question, 'Did the Great Famine Matter?' in the precise sense suggested by Crotty in *Irish Agricultural Production* in 1966, i.e. would the population decline popularly associated with the Famine have occurred in the long run in any case?[96] For Crotty, as noted in

Chapter 7, 1815 rather than 1845 marked the chief turning-point in nineteenth-century economic history: the Famine only accelerated changes already in train. Data lacunae and the exigencies of model-building prompted O'Rourke to confine his analysis to the agricultural sector. Perhaps the best-known feature of Irish agriculture after the Famine is the radical shift away from labour-intensive tillage (largely grain and potatoes) to livestock. Was the associated decline in labour requirements induced by the Famine, or was it—as Crotty maintained—the product of changing world-market conditions? The rise in livestock products far outstripped that in tillage products after 1840. O'Rourke refers to the hypothesis that the observed, exogenous relative shift in livestock prices between the early 1840s and the mid-1870s caused the observed decline in employment as the 'Crotty hypothesis'.

O'Rourke's work marks the first application of a computable general equilibrium (CGE) model to Irish economic history. The great advantage of CGE is that it offers the closest thing to a controlled *ceteris paribus* experiment that an economist can perform.[97] The technique involves subjecting a model of the agricultural sector on the eve of the Famine to the long-run price shocks actually observed in the wake of the Famine. The model's twenty-seven equations attempt to capture the agricultural technology implied in contemporary accounts and recent estimates of agricultural output, taking care to capture the technical aspects of pre-Famine agriculture. The convenient assumption that agricultural workers earned a constant-utility real wage and consumed a fixed amount of potatoes per head implies a straightforward link between the money wage and the price of potatoes.[98] Experimentation with the choice of input–output coefficients and elasticities of substitution in production and consumption yielded a consistent benchmark model of the agricultural sector. Having set up a working model of the sector c.1845, O'Rourke was then able to examine the effects of shifts in output prices and factor inputs on aggregate output and product mix, and on factor allocation and factor rewards. Manipulation of the model opens up that might-have-been world, a post-1845 Irish farm sector free from potato blight.

The Crotty hypothesis implies that the 45 per cent decline in employment between the 1840s and 1870s was due to exogenous price shifts. However, O'Rourke's simulations produce a surprise here; they suggest that agricultural employment would have risen as a result of such a relative price change alone. The range of the rise, from 6 to 29 per cent, is a function of the assumptions made about the various elasticities in the model. The reason for this surprising result is that a rise in labour-intensive potato consumption as animal feed would have been induced. Besides, the price change would have caused a relative decline in the price of labour relative to other factor inputs. Presumably grafting an industrial sector to the model would moderate the rise in employment: still, O'Rourke's finding is an arresting antidote to interpretations that view the Famine as 'unimportant'.

Since the Famine simultaneously rid agriculture of over 200,000 small-holdings and drastically reduced the tilled acreage, it might seem a good example of the workings of the Rybczynski theorem of international trade theory, which 'predicts that a reduction in the endowment of a factor (in the case at hand, labour) will reduce by a greater than proportionate amount the output of the good intensive in that factor (tillage) and will increase the output of the other good (pastoral produce)'. O'Rourke's model returns a mixed verdict on the appropriateness of the Rybczynski theorem. He simulates the 'shock' of the Famine by imposing a 29 per cent reduction in labour input on the model, but holding output prices constant. While the output mix moves as predicted, aggregate pastoral output declines, contrary to Rybczynski. However, as O'Rourke is quick to concede, there are more factors in his model than traded goods, 'which leads the Rybczynski theorem to break down'.[99]

Unlike that other famous ecological 'shock', the Black Death, *phytoph-thora infestans* inflicted enduring and substantial damage on the Irish economy's capital stock. It did so in the sense that it reduced the average yield of tillage land until an antidote was discovered in the 1880s—and indeed it still causes problems and imposes costs.[100] O'Rourke therefore also subjected his pre-Famine model to a potato yield 'shock'—a 50 per cent cut in the potato yield per acre. His simulation suggests that such a shock, considered in isolation, would have reduced agricultural employment by 9 to 14 per cent, depending on the supply and substitution elasticities used. By allowing a 50 per cent drop in yields, O'Rourke attributed the decline in yields after 1845 exclusively to the blight. This assumes too much. That the drop in labour input after the Famine, by forcing a shift from the spade to the plough and less manuring, was partly to blame, may be gauged by noting the size of the yield increase that followed the diffusion of the spraying-machine in the 1890s. Yield per acre rose from 3.0 tons in the 1870s to 3.6 tons in the 1880s and 1890s and only 4.5 tons in the 1900s—less than the 100 per cent implied by O'Rourke. Nevertheless, even a decline of one-quarter—from, say, 6 to

4.5 tons, would have had a non-negligible effect on agricultural employment. O'Rourke also imposed the yield and labour input shocks, along with other quantifiable shocks, simultaneously. The results were more impressive than those for either the yield or the Rybczynski shock in isolation. Overall, the view that the Famine merely accelerated shifts which would have occurred in any case is not vindicated.

8.6 Conclusion

The 'convergence' of national productivity and average income levels remains an important element in the credo of most economists. Since the technology of rich economies is available to the poor, and the labour of the poor is there to be tapped by the rich, self-interest and competition should make the incomes of the poor eventually match those of the rich. Whether trends in the real world today bear out such hopes is a much-debated question.[101] For an earlier era, the Great Irish Famine is a grim reminder of how narrowly the benefits of the first Industrial Revolution had been spread by the 1840s. Nearly a half-century of political and economic union had made little or no impression on the huge gap between Irish and British incomes, nor was it enough to shield Ireland from cataclysm.

I have already referred several times to the Finnish famine of 1867–8 for comparative perspective. This was truly the 'last great subsistence crisis of the western world'. The Irish famine surpassed the Finnish in its intensity, in its duration, and in its long-term impact. In Finland, about 0.1 million out of a population of 1.6 million died, in Ireland one million out of 8.5 million. In Finland, the crisis was limited to one bad year, in Ireland excess mortality was substantial for four years. In Finland, the cereal crops failed badly once; in Ireland, the potato failed disastrously several times, and took half a century to regain its pre-Famine vigour. The roles of politics and relief seem to loom much larger in the historiography of the Irish than of the Finnish famine, perhaps because London was much closer to events, both geographically and administratively, than Moscow. In other ways, there are obvious parallels and contrasts worth pursuing: differential impact by region, the causes of death and of variation in deaths by age and sex, the functioning of markets and communications networks. In both countries, politicians and bureaucrats have been blamed, and rightly so, for acting in a doctrinaire and ungenerous fashion. In the wake of the First World War, both Ireland and Finland were prised away from the empires that long coveted them. Irish anti-imperial resentment long outlasted Finnish, though perhaps for reasons that had little to do with the Famine. The difference is captured symbolically in the contrasting fates of the statue of Queen Victoria that once graced Leinster Lawn in Dublin and that of Tsar Alexander II, whose reign straddled the Finnish famine. Victoria is now half a world away in Australia, but Alexander still dominates one of Helsinki's most elegant squares.

PART IV

PART IV

9

Population and Emigration, 1850–1939

9.1 Demographic Trends

The Great Famine set off a population decline unmatched in any other European country in the nineteenth century, a decline that lasted in Ireland as a whole until the 1900s, and that has continued in some rural areas until this day. It is often seen as the Great Famine's most enduring legacy. The Famine certainly provided the spur, but the persistence of the decline is perhaps better explained as a consequence of Irish poverty relative to both Great Britain and America in 1800, 1850, and 1900. Here neighbouring Scotland provides a useful analogy. Though the population of Scotland as a whole grew, that of its Highland counties peaked in the mid-1840s or even before, and continued to fall for a century, while numbers in its far northern counties fell by over one-third between 1861 and the 1940s.[1]

Ireland's population decline was largely a rural phenomenon. Between the Famine and the First World War, the country's rural and small-town population dwindled from 7 million to less than 3 million, and the share of towns and cities of 2,000 people or more—a very generous definition of urbanization—rose from one-seventh to one-third. By 1914 nearly one Leinsterwoman and one Leinsterman in every two lived in such towns, but the pace of urbanization was most dramatic in Ulster, where the urban percentage soared from 9 in 1841 to 38 in 1911. One city—Belfast—was largely responsible for the rise, and Belfast also accounted for over half the increase in Ireland's urban population in these decades. By 1911 the population of Belfast (386,947) had outstripped Dublin's (304,802),[2] and Derry (rising from 15,196 in 1841 to 40,780 in 1911) had been promoted to the second division of Irish cities. Only one province, Connacht, remained overwhelmingly rural. Most Connacht towns saw their population dwindle between 1841 and 1911, but the proportional decline in the towns—28 per cent—was small when compared to the 59 per cent outside them. If urbanization is defined by the number of people living in towns and cities of 20,000 people and above, the story is not very different: in Ireland as a whole the total living in the small number of places in this category more than doubled over these years, reaching nearly a million by 1914.[3] Taken together, these are important changes, but it is the fate of the rural population that has attracted most attention from economic and social historians.

The creation of Northern Ireland and the Irish Free State in 1921–2 produced two distinct yet overlapping demographic regimes. The population of the Free State fell by 5 per cent between 1911 and 1926, but by only 0.1 per cent between 1926 and 1936. In the latter period Leinster's population rose by 6.2 per cent. In Northern Ireland population rose by 0.5 per cent in 1911–26 and 1.8 per cent in 1926–37, though with marked variation across counties. Armagh (−9.6 per cent), Fermanagh (−12.1 per cent) and Tyrone (−10.8 per cent), substantial losers over the period as a whole, had more in common with Donegal (−9.5 per cent) or Longford (−9.1 per cent) than they had with Antrim (+4.5 per cent), Dublin (+6.0 per cent), or Down (+2.4 per cent). As before, the urban share of the population rose, both north and south. By the mid-1930s well over half the people of Leinster and of Northern Ireland lived in towns of 2,000 people or more. Munster occupied an intermediate position, with the town and urban share rising from 25.6 per cent in 1911 to 29.3 per cent in 1936. Connacht and the three Free State counties of Ulster remained overwhelmingly rural (Table 9.1).

For Kenneth Connell, the Famine effectively fulfilled its Malthusian educative mission by putting an end to the 'haphazard, happy-go-lucky marriages of the eighteenth and early nineteenth centuries'. The land legislation of the 1870s and later served only to make the peasant still more 'ambitious and calculating', and substituted a 'disciplined marriage geared to his ambition'. Connell's has become the standard classroom story.

Table 9.1. *Population North and South, 1901–1936* (000s)

Year	26 Counties	6 Counties	Total
1851	5 112	1 441	6 552
1881	3 870	1 305	5 175
1901	3 222	1 237	4 459
1911	3 140	1 251	4 390
1926	2 972	1 257	4 229
1936–7	2 968	1 280	4 248

Curiously, a rise in mean marriage age does not account for much of Ireland's post-Famine population decline. Fitzpatrick's measure of the trend in the age at marriage—the movement in the 'singulate mean age at marriage' (Table 9.2)—rules out much change in the mean marriage age in the wake of the Famine, though the mean did rise towards the end of the century. By contrast, the post-Famine rise in celibacy was dramatic. Eastern counties such as Meath and Kildare were most affected at first; generally the rise in the proportions never marrying was greater in 1881–1911 than in 1851–81. In Connacht in 1851 only 8.2 per cent of women and 7.4 per cent of men aged 45–54 years remained single, and in 1881 only 9.5 and 10.9 per cent, but by 1911 the proportions had risen to 17.9 and 25.4 per cent and by 1926 to 18.5 and 29.7 per cent.[4]

Why the decline in nuptiality? Connell's classic interpretation links the Malthusian lessons taught by the Great Famine with the growing desire of Irish country people for higher living standards. The price they paid was impartible inheritance and an end to the subdivision of farms. The change increased intrafamilial tension, as brothers curried for fathers' favours and daughters vied for dowries; it also made for delayed marriages. Such sibling rivalry provided a ready-made theme for writers such as novelist Seán O Faoláin and dramatist T. C. Murray.[5]

Table 9.2. *Nuptiality in Ireland in the nineteenth century*

SMAM for generations born between 1821 and 1861			% never married, aged 45–54 years		
Year	Males	Females	Year	Males	Females
1821	30.1	26.2	1841	10.2	12.5
1831	30.3	27.3	1851	12.1	12.6
1841	29.9	26.5	1861	14.7	14.3
1851	30.4	26.7	1871	17.0	16.5
1861	31.0	27.5	1881	17.1	17.1
			1891	20.0	18.5
			1901	23.8	21.9
			1911	27.3	24.9

Sources: D. Fitzpatrick, 'Marriage in Post-Famine Ireland', in A. Cosgrove (ed.), *Marriage in Ireland* (Dublin, 1985), 129–30; Fitzpatrick and Vaughan, *Irish Historical Statistics*. SMAM (singulate mean age at marriage) is the average age at which those marrying between the ages of 15 and 50 years ceased to be single.

The timing and regional incidence of the rise in celibacy, just described, do not square well with a 'shock therapy' interpretation. Connacht was worst affected of all provinces by the Famine, yet the propensity to marry there was slowest to change. Guinnane has recently proposed a different interpretation of marriage trends in Ireland in the later nineteenth century. Jettisoning Connell's doleful explanation of Ireland's high and rising mean marriage age as a sacrifice or preventive check along Hajnal–Malthus lines (see Chapter 1), Guinnane treats peasant marriage as just one of a range of possible strategies geared towards achieving security in old age. Thus those growing old in the post-Famine decades might rely on the help of their children, but alternatively they might have saved up instead of marrying, and then be in a position to retire or hire help in old age. The farmer who could afford to do so might forgo the trauma of an arranged marriage, knowing that later he would be able to realize the value of his holding, or else afford to hire a farmhand in his declining years. In this view, celibacy, far from being a stigma, was to be valued, and farmers with large holdings were more likely to exercise that option. Marriage being an inferior good, labourers and small farmers chose marriage and children instead. Thus, the gradual decline in Irish nuptiality after the Famine indicates a *rise* in rural living standards. For Connell, late marriage was a precondition for material betterment, for Guinnane it was a consequence. These different interpretations are easily captured by a diagram familiar to students of economic demography.[6] In Fig. 9.1 the mortality and fertility rates are plotted against the real wage. In the left-hand panel a shift in the upward-sloping fertility schedule from f_1 to f_0 reflects the lesson taught by the Famine: the

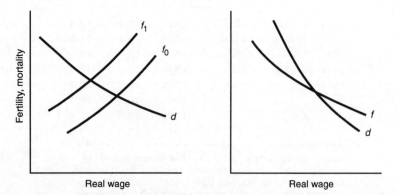

FIG. 9.1 Modelling the post-Famine decline in nuptiality

result is a decline in the equilibrium fertility rate and a rise in the standard of living. In the right-hand panel, the downward slope of the fertility schedule reflects marriage's status as an inferior good; a rise in the standard of living could either increase or decrease the rate of population growth, depending on the real wage. The direction of population change depends, however, on the slopes of the fertility and mortality schedules.

In cross-section, Guinnane's sample of farm households from the 1911 census suggests that the more prosperous parts of Meath and Wicklow:[7]

developed higher levels of permanent celibacy as a perverse result of their economic development. The larger farms of these areas augmented the ability of their occupiers to find substitutes for families, reducing the incentive for farmers themselves to marry; and the larger farm created places for more unmarried dependants, including siblings, servants and other relatives.

Many of those who never married, Guinnane points out, were well-off household heads: their decision to remain single would not seem to have been forced on them. His own data sample, derived from four scattered rural areas (two in Leinster, one each in Munster and Connacht), is consistent with this interpretation in cross-section; most notably, the proportion of bachelor farmers rose with farm size. However, this ingenious (but 'frankly speculative') model squares poorly with nation-wide data from 1926 and 1936. Table 9.3 shows that celibacy tended to *fall* with farm size, though hardly markedly, in the Irish Free State in both 1926 and

Table 9.3. *Proportions of 45–54-year-old farmers never married across farm size, 1926 and 1936*

Farm size (acres)	1926					1936
	Leinster	Munster	Connacht	Ulster	Total	Total
1–	43.0	32.7	20.9	22.6	27.0	28.5
5–	39.9	23.2	17.2	29.6	24.6	30.3
10–	31.8	20.1	16.3	27.6	21.7	28.0
15–	29.2	17.8	15.2	25.0	19.9	26.0
30–	26.1	14.2	15.1	26.6	18.5	24.1
50–	25.5	12.8	17.5	25.6	17.8	22.4
100–	25.5	12.9	21.5	27.1	18.8	22.6
Over 200	21.9	15.2	27.6	23.4	19.7	21.3

Source: *1926 Census*; *1936 Census*.

1936. The rise in celibacy between the 1920s and the 1930s does not support the model either, since this was a period of downward pressure on rural living standards (see Chapter 17). The traditional interpretation is also supported by Arensberg's statistical analysis of the family histories of 200 County Clare families 'since famine times'. That analysis showed 'families without farms or with very small and "backward" ones were forced to extinction through celibacy': late marriage and permanent celibacy—the preventive check—worked as outlined by Connell. Finally, modern evidence also suggests that poor economic conditions reduce Irish marriage rates.[8] A further drawback of both Guinnane's and Connell's interpretations of post-Famine marriage patterns is their undue focus on male strategies, as if there existed a limitless supply of women willing to marry the men if required.

The emphasis placed by some historians on rising expectations of what constituted a decent standard of living in the post-Famine era[9] supports a more Connellite interpretation of the decline in nuptiality. If increasing emigration and literacy—proxies for 'modernization'—stiffened the tenantry's resolve to better their lot, presumably by the same token it strengthened the preventive check. In consequence, some marriages that would have been previously viable were ruled out. Smaller farms, instead of being subdivided as before, after the Famine were increasingly passed on to neighbouring nieces and nephews, or were merely sold off.[10] Incomplete rural households containing two or three unmarried brothers or sisters were common in rural Ireland until recently. According to this view, they were a transitional phenomenon, sacrifices to the community's rising aspirations rather than—as envisaged by Guinnane—wishes fulfilled for those immediately concerned.

9.2 Fertility Change

> I am just twenty eight years old married nine years today and the mother of six children so I feel have done my bit and only wish I could be in London to go to your clinic.
>
> LIMERICK MOTHER, 1923[11]

> The poor have childher and to spare,
> But with the quality they're rare,
> Where money's scarce the childer's many,
> Where money's thick you'll scarce find any.
> W. M. LETTS, Songs from Leinster (1913)

Among the scores of letters from Irish correspondents to English family planning campaigner Marie Stopes in the 1920s and 1930s, one of the most striking came from a young man who confided that he 'had always thought that if you talked too much with girls or made chums with them too much God would send a child'. If such ignorance was commonplace in Ireland, one may well wonder why Irish fertility was so high! Against this, a common theme is that once the Irish learned how it was done they did not know how to stop. Access to the new contraceptive technology (and quack abortifacients) being diffused in Britain after 1900 was very restricted in Ireland. An Englishwoman married to a Corkman declared to Stopes in 1923 that 'Cork is such an old-fashioned goody-goody place that they would not sell you what you wanted if they thought it was for a wrong purpose'. At the same time, an analysis of the Stopes correspondence[12] also indicates that the demand for family limitation in inter-war Ireland was still low, being greatest in the north and among the Protestant middle class.

The transition from a demographic regime marked by high birth- and death-rates to one of low fertility and high life expectancy is a symptom of 'modernization'. In most of western Europe this transition began in the second half of the nineteenth century. The subject has been the focus of much recent debate among social and demographic historians. One model of the demographic transition emphasizes the role of 'the earlier termination of childbearing', another 'the deliberate spacing of children within marriage'. These alternatives are known as 'stopping' and 'spacing' in the professional literature. Strong support for the 'stopping' hypothesis is provided by John Knodel's study of fourteen German villages in the nineteenth century. While marital fertility declined, the mean interval between births changed but little in most villages, suggesting that couples 'stopped' only when they reached their desired family size. Equally striking in their support for the rival 'spacing' approach are the findings of Marcel Lachiver for a sample of parishes in the Parisian basin. These show mean birth-intervals of about two years dominating in the mid-eighteenth century, before the onset of the transition, reflecting the 'biannual rhythm of births'. However, from the 1760s on, the percentage of birth-intervals in the 31–48-month range increased in all areas, and by the 1820s and 1830s intervals of four years or more accounted for one-half of the total.[13]

Where is the Irish role in these controversies? To the extent that Ireland was a slow and reluctant participant in the European fertility decline of the late nineteenth century, its place is on the sideline.[14] Analysis of the 1911 population census by Coale and others convinced them that effective birth-control hardly existed in Ireland then. Teitelbaum's study of the Irish equally indicates little shift in Irish marital fertility before the First World War (for the definition of I_g see Chapter 4). Such results have prompted generalizations such as 'the declines that occurred after 1920 were in Ireland and the southern and eastern periphery of Europe', or '[Ireland was] an extreme case where marital fertility did not decline before the 1920s',[15] reinforcing Ireland's status as demographic odd-man-out.

The story does not end there, however, because the fertility estimates underlying it are marred by their reliance on uncorrected birth-registration data. Though collected since 1864, the registration of births, marriages, and deaths in Ireland was defective well into this century. My own alternative fertility estimates[16] indicate that though the Irish fertility transition was slow—indeed it is still in progress—it had commenced well before the First World War. By 1911 marital fertility was about one-tenth less than thirty years earlier. Invoking early twentieth-century Irish fertility patterns as a benchmark for 'natural fertility' or the absence of birth-control is therefore not warranted. As early as 1881 there was significant variation across counties in marital fertility, with lowest levels in the north-east, and highest in Connacht and north Munster.

Recently Paul David and his collaborators have used the fertility returns of the Irish population census of 1911 as a benchmark for an alternative approach to fertility measurement. This approach, which they have dubbed Cohort Parity Analysis (or CPA), highlights the importance of distingui-shing between 'stopping' and 'spacing' as alternative family limitation strategies.[17] Traditionally, accounts of the fertility transition emphasize 'stopping', i.e. the decision to control fertility only after some target family size has been met. However, David and his team argue for the role of 'spacing', which entails more control over the timing of births within marriage. Couples might decide, for example, to have no children until they could afford adequate housing, or to interrupt family formation while the wife engages in temporary employment, or recovers from a difficult pregnancy. When the contraceptive technology available to couples (as throughout most of Ireland before the First World War) is unreliable, greater recourse to spacing as a precautionary measure might be expected. CPA infers the extent and timing of birth-control within marriage from distributions of married women by number of children born. The technique and the detailed results are spelt out in detail elsewhere.[18] Using the 'rural' element reported in the Irish census of 1911 as a 'model', David et al. were able to identify a substantial minority of married couples in Irish urban areas practising birth-control in 1911. However, the level of aggregation forced on the CPA estimates by the published censal data conceals the fall in Irish marital fertility that was taking place even in rural areas before the turn of the century, and the marked contrasts to be found within the 'rural' population.[19]

Studies of nineteenth- and twentieth-century fertility decline in other European countries have highlighted differences across class, region, and religion. In Ireland today, alas, the discussion of such differences is almost bound to take on a political dimension.[20] There are some recent findings worth reporting. First, an examination of the fertility gap between Catholics and Protestants in rural Ulster based on the 1901–11 manuscript census returns reveals only very weak signs of the gap that would prompt a Northern Ireland government half a century later to seek exclusion from the provisions of a generous British family allowance scheme, since the scheme would disproportionately benefit Catholics. Second, a cross-county analysis of the variation in marital fertility suggests explanatory roles for religion, farm size, and emigration. The implied effect of religiosity across counties, evaluated at the mean, was not large: religious affiliation alone 'explains' less than a third of the variation in cross-county fertility at this juncture. The association between fertility and emigration is interesting; an economic interpretation of this might be that the returns in emigrant remittances induced parents to 'save' for old age through large families. A more cultural explanation would argue that the outlet of emigration reassured pious parents who worried about their ability to provide for a large family.[21]

Third, the public use status of the 1911 manuscript census schedules also invites the measurement of family limitation in local populations at the turn of the century. A study based on three areas, composed of clusters of District Electoral Divisions (DEDs) in three very different parts of Ireland, yields some interesting contrasts. The first area was a traditional rural area in Clare, the great majority of women were married either to farmers or farm labourers, but a smattering had married teachers, policemen, and so on. The second area included mainly rural parts of Tyrone, a northern, confessionally mixed county. Again the husbands' occupations were mainly agricultural, but a minority of the men were engaged in the textile industry. The choice for an urban middle-class area was the comfortable Dublin suburb of Rathgar. In 1911 Rathgar had a large non-Catholic population. Clusters of DEDs large enough to yield a population of about 600 women who had married since 1901 were collected in each case. The women were then subjected to CPA, using Clare as the model population. The contrasting outcomes in Clare and Tyrone, both largely rural areas, confirmed that rural Ireland was far less homogeneous than David and his co-authors imply. Both Tyrone and Rathgar contained a considerable proportion of couples controlling family size relative to Clare.[22]

Regression analysis using the same data suggested further regional differences. Again, signs of family limitation early in marriage proved weakest in Clare. The data also suggested connections between the prevalence of 'spacing', on the one hand, and occupation and religion, on the other. While labourers' wives in Rathgar were more likely to control fertility early in marriage, the wives of Tyrone labourers were less likely to 'space' than the wives of farmers. Religion seems to have influenced fertility in Rathgar, though not in Tyrone; but religion in Rathgar was probably a proxy for education and class. Finally, since by implication more Rathgar and Tyrone couples were planning family size, it came as no surprise to find that they were more likely to 'replace' lost children than Clare couples.[23]

By the 1930s 25 per cent of women in their late forties, as well as 30 per cent of the men, had never married. On the Princeton I_m scale, the Irish Free State was at 0.369 in 1936, compared to 0.503 for England and Wales in 1931, 0.613 for France in 1931, and 0.519 for Italy in 1936.[24] Marital fertility was relatively high in Ireland, however, with the result that the birth-rate of about 20 per thousand was unexceptional by contemporary European standards. Marital fertility continued to decline in the inter-war period. By 1936 I_g had dropped to 0.570 (compared to 0.440 in Scotland and 0.292 in England in 1931) in the thirty-two-county area. Marital fertility in the Free State (0.607) was considerably higher than in Northern Ireland (0.483), and higher than in any other western European country in the 1930s.[25] An unusually detailed survey of births in Dublin in the early 1940s highlights the contrasting pace of the fertility decline among rich and poor. Only 5.9 per cent of births to upper-middle-class women were seventh parity or higher; for the wives of unskilled workers, the percentage was 22.6.[26]

In Northern Ireland the fertility transition had an interesting consequence: by the end of the period surveyed here, it had helped to halt the long-standing decline in the Catholic share of the population (Table 9.5). The decline had been largely the product of greater emigration from the poorer Catholic areas, but the subsequent rise was due to the Catholic distaste for contraception. The county reports of the 1937 Northern Ireland census betray some signs of worry in official quarters on this score, drawing

Table 9.4. *Irish nuptiality and the birth-rate*

Province	aged 45–9 never-married (%)		Birth-rate
	Males	Females	
Leinster, 1926	33.1	26.8	22.3
Munster, 1926	32.6	22.7	20.4
Connacht, 1926	32.8	19.2	19.4
Ulster (3 Cos.), 1926	38.7	27.1	19.7
26 Cos., 1926	33.4	24.2	20.6
26 Cos., 1936	34.7	25.7	19.6
26 Cos., 1946	33.4	26.3	22.9
26 Cos., 1951	32.0	26.3	21.2
Northern Ireland, 1926	24.7	25.4	21.9
Northern Ireland, 1937	22.9	25.7	19.8
Northern Ireland, 1951	20.5	23.8	20.7

Source: Derived from Census Reports, 1926–51.

Table 9.5. *The Catholic share of Northern Ireland's population, 1834–1981*

County	1834	1861	1881	1901	1926	1961	1981
Antrim	28.2	27.4	25.3	23.0	22.1	26.3	—
Armagh	47.7	48.8	46.4	45.2	45.4	47.3	—
Down	34.4	32.5	30.9	31.3	30.6	28.6	—
Fermanagh	53.5	56.5	55.8	55.3	56.0	53.2	57
L'derry	43.4	45.3	44.4	45.2	47.5	50.6	55
Tyrone	54.7	56.5	55.5	54.7	55.5	54.8	58
TOTAL	42.0	40.9	38.0	34.8	33.5	37.2	39.1

Sources: For 1834, Mokyr, *Why Ireland Starved* datafile; for 1861–1926, Vaughan and Fitzpatrick, *Irish Historical Statistics: Population 1821–1971* (Dublin, 1978); for 1981, D. E. C. Eversley and V. Heer, *Estimate of Catholic Population of Northern Ireland* (Belfast, 1985). The districts used in 1981 do not in general follow county boundaries; the estimates given for the three western counties are approximate.

attention to the possibility even where (as in County Tyrone) they could find no evidence for it. In rural Ulster generally (including the three southern border counties of Cavan, Donegal, and Monaghan),[27] the gap between Catholic and non-Catholic marital fertility in the 1930s was small, but it was already quite marked in Belfast. The census report for Belfast

County Borough noted the 'significance' of how the six wards with the highest Catholic populations were also those with the highest ratio of young children to married women of child-bearing age. This ratio was almost twice as high in Smithfield and Falls wards, where Catholics accounted for over nine-tenths of the population, as in largely Protestant Ormeau and Windsor; the Falls' edge over the Shankill was over 50 per cent. The report provides the data for a more formal test. Regressing *Fert* (the ratio of children under 3 years to the number of married women under 45 years) on *Cath* (the Catholic share of the population) in the city's fifteen wards produced:[28]

$$Fert = 402.7 + 305.46Cath$$
$$(21.33) \quad (6.30)$$

$$R^2 = 0.75, \; t\text{-statistics in parentheses}$$

An attempt at controlling for socio-economic factors by including a variable describing housing congestion failed to improve on this result.

9.3 Emigration

> On the right lives Henry Sheeran, a deserving and prosperous man, with a strong wife and five children. But one son was in the police, one was in Canada, and a girl was serving in a draper's shop in Lismahee.
>
> SHAN BULLOCK (1931)

The historiography of European emigration in the nineteenth century is massive, but it can claim few models or 'laws' that capture the inter-temporal and interregional contrasts. Irish emigration was distinct in several respects.

(1) *Dimensions*

The outflow—about 4 million between 1850 and 1914—was enormous by international standards, and large enough to give rise to predictions such as Engels's in the late 1860s, that 'if this goes on for another thirty years, there will be Irishmen only in America'. The sentiment became a cliché; forty years and 2 million emigrants later, French writer Paul-Dubois might still warn that 'emigration will soon cause it to be said that Ireland is no longer where flows the Shannon, but rather beside the banks of the Hudson River, and in that "Greater Ireland" whose home is the American Republic'.

These statements highlight both the size of the Irish exodus and the large share of the USA in it. But they must be qualified in two respects. First, both ignore the substantial fraction of Irish emigration destined for the UK. The ratio of Irish-born in Britain to Irish-born in North America—0.42 in 1861, 0.38 in 1881, 0.37 in 1901, 0.46 in 1921— reflects the abiding importance of Britain as an asylum for the Irish emigrant. Second, the rate of emigration was in long-run decline when both statements were made. On the other hand, the human outflow was even greater than the official statistics reveal. This is largely because emigration from Ireland to Britain was poorly recorded. Between the Famine and the 1890s the Irish overseas emigration rate exceeded that recorded for any other country.[29]

The importance of migration in Ireland is illustrated by the fact that much of the decade-to-decade variation in the rate of population growth is accounted for by the behaviour of the net external migration rate (Table 9.6). Both emigration and population change were much more variable than the rate of natural increase (birth-rate *minus* death-rate).[30]

(2) A 'female' emigration

Irish emigration was more female than any other major outflow from nineteenth-century Europe. It is sometimes claimed that this was a re-flection of the particularly miserable life facing young women in post-Famine Ireland. More specifically, the case has been made that changes in Irish farming patterns, induced by a combination of market conditions,

Table 9.6. *Population change, natural increase, and net emigration* (annual rate per 1,000 population)

Period	Population change	Natural increase	Net emigration rate
1861–71	−6.9	+8.3	−15.2
1871–81	−4.5	+8.0	−12.5
1881–91	−10.9	+5.3	−16.3
1891–1901	−7.4	+4.5	−11.9
1901–11	−2.6	+5.6	−8.2
1911–26	−3.7	+5.2	−8.8
1926–36	−0.1	+5.5	−5.6
1936–46	−0.4	+5.9	−6.3
1946–51	+0.4	+8.6	−8.2

embourgeoisement, and technological change, reduced women's entitlements relative to men's. Now, to the extent that the new technology saved on sheer strength and muscle—as in the case of reaping and threshing—it boosted women's comparative advantage over men. Thus the case for deterioration rests on a division of labour that was partly determined by culture. Joanna Bourke has shown how this worked in the case of poultry management, traditionally the woman's responsibility on the farm. Prosperity meant chasing the chicken and hen from the kitchen, to fields far from 'territory convenient for female workers and into distinctly male territory'. The transfer of butter-making from the dairy to the creamery worked in the same direction.[31] It must be said that the apparent rise in the ratio of female to male agricultural wages after the Famine does not support the notion of the relative impoverishment of Irishwomen (see Chapter 10). Nor were the prospects for women utterly bleak outside agriculture. In textiles, the shift from handloom to powerloom weaving tended to involve the replacement of some male by female labour, and the demand for women as nurses, teachers, and nuns grew.

Remember that migration is a function of wage differences or relative incomes; the higher Irish ratio could equally have been the function of relatively better prospects for Irishwomen in receiving countries. Earnings data are scarce, but those collected by the Dillingham Commission in the USA in the 1900s return an average of $8.24 per week for Irishwomen, and $2.09 per day for Irishmen. The implied gap is probably less than that obtaining in Ireland at the time (see Table 10.1 below). If so, women had relatively more to gain from emigration. The Dillingham Commission data also imply that Irishwomen fared no better in America relative to their menfolk than women from elsewhere, since the average for all males was $2.19 a day, and for all females $7.90 a week. Those data refer to manufacturing only. In the service sector the fluency and literacy of Irishwomen in the English language opened up job prospects as nannies and secretaries not open to many other immigrants. These are factors noted by Hasia Diner, who suggests (anticipating Guinnane in this respect) that the high mean marriage age of Irish immigrant women—high by American, though not by Irish, standards—in the USA was a reflection of their independence and improved status.[32] The narrowing of the gender gap in earnings in the USA across the nineteenth century thus surely explains *some* of the rise in the ratio of female to male emigrants. The reduction in the cost of a passage is also likely to have prompted more women to leave.[33] Another plausible reason is that high rates of both female and male permanent migration reinforced each other (see below). With so many men (women) leaving, it made sense for more Irishwomen (Irishmen) to try their luck on the Irish-American marriage market. The high proportion of departing young adults in turn reduced the attraction of return migration.

Most emigrants were in their late teens or early twenties. On average, women left slightly earlier than men. Guinnane holds that the earlier departure of women around the turn of the century was due to an 'asymmetry of opportunities reflect[ing] the preference for male heirs and a lack of employment opportunities for women in rural areas'. If so, a glance at data from periods either before or after Guinnane's period implies that the asymmetry was of long standing. In a large sample of pre-Famine transatlantic emigrants, the ratio of unaccompanied men aged 15–19 years to those aged 20–4 years was about 30 per cent, while for women it was nearly 70 per cent. Over a century later the Commission on Emigration (1956) again revealed the relative youthfulness of female emigrants. The latest available data, for the year ending April 1988, show that 76.2 per cent of female emigrants were aged less than 25 years, but only 64.8 per cent of the males.[34]

This earlier departure of Irishwomen is akin to—and plausibly linked to—their lower marriage age. Perhaps, borrowing a leaf from Becker's model of marriage and the family,[35] Irishmen in the past reached independence and maturity later than Irishwomen. An alternative explanation for both the lower mean age at marriage and the earlier departure of Irishwomen runs as follows. Suppose that, for whatever reason, men had a greater preference for marrying younger women than women had for marrying younger men. Then in a context where half or more of the menfolk emigrated, the earlier the women left, the better their chance of finding a suitable partner among the male emigrants.[36]

Another exceptional feature of Irish emigration—or at least its transatlantic component—was the small proportion of return migrants. Data on returning 'Yanks' and repeat emigrants are lacking, and they may have been more numerous than we suspect. Nevertheless, they were still a small minority of those who left: the emigrant 'wake' was not for nothing. The contrast with most other places in Europe is marked: in the 1860–1930 period, one-fifth of Scandinavians and two-fifths of English and Welsh emigrants returned, while in the early twentieth century, almost one-half of Italian emigrants returned home eventually. Dudley Baines has linked high rates of return migration with urbanization in the sending country.

On this reckoning Ireland's failure to industrialize deterred more Irish emigrants from returning.[37]

(3) Costs and benefits, push and pull

The costs and benefits of emigration have long been bones of contention. That emigration benefited the emigrants is strongly implied by their revealed preference for their new homes. As noted, the rate of return migration was low, and emigrant remittances were an important matter. Victorian civil servants produced estimates of them annually from 1848 on. Their numbers—after a little correction, an average of £0.8 million to £1 million a year, or £50 million over 1850–1900—impressed historian Arnold Schrier, who noted that in the 1850s and 1860s remittances far outstripped spending on poor relief. In fact, Schrier's numbers are probably conservative. An American calculation referring to 1907 put the annual flow to the UK at $25 million or about £5 million, and since the Irish accounted for almost three-fifths of UK-born American immigrants in the 1900s, it seems fair to assume that at least half of this was destined for Ireland. Assuming a figure of £3 million from all sources implies an inflow equivalent to 2 to 3 per cent of national income before the First World War.[38]

The earnings gap between receiving and sending countries exaggerates the gains from emigration to the extent that most of the Irish who emigrated, by exchanging rural for urban living, were moving to less healthy environments. Preston and Haines have shown that child mortality was considerably higher among the Irish in America than in Ireland in the late nineteenth century. Their estimates of $q(5)$—the probability of dying between birth and age 5—in Ireland and among Irish-Americans c. 1900 are as follows:[39]

Ireland	0.14
Dublin	0.21
Belfast	0.19
'Rural Ireland'	0.12
First generation Irish in USA	0.25
Urban	0.25
Rural	0.20
Second generation Irish in USA	0.20
Urban	0.22
Rural	0.09

The Irish in Britain were also more prone to die young. Though these differentials affected the migrants only vicariously through their offspring, the diseases and poor living conditions that gave rise to them must also have adversely affected adult health. The Irish in the New World were well fed; the high mortality was less a reflection of poverty than of inadequate medical know-how and problems in urban public health.

The literature on the gains and losses from emigration remains inconclusive. Against the clear gains to those who left, for those who remained the gains from remittances and reduced land hunger had to be weighed against the putative losses stemming from input complementarities. One frequently mentioned source of loss is the life-cycle effect. Its starting-point is the individual who on average balances consumption and production over his or her lifetime. The young person incurs upbringing debts till adolescence or later, which he will repay the State in taxes and his parents and his own children in kind. However, emigration means that the 'debt' may never be repaid in full, since typically it is the very young and the elderly, those who are in a strict sense a burden to the community, who are least likely to leave. This was always the case in Ireland, a point not lost on critics:[40]

The producing part of our population is being driven out by emigration. What would naturally be the producing part of the population—the young and the able-bodied people—are being driven out by emigration, and we have to carry on the service of education to deal with the young people and the service of old-age pension for the older population. We are spending on education, say, four and a half million per year and we must remember that we are doing that largely for the benefit of foreign countries. We are saving the American people, who get a larger share of our younger people than other countries, the cost of education that would fall upon them if they had to educate their own citizens.

A recent guestimate puts the cost to Ireland of the life-cycle effect at about £0.5 million annually on the eve of the Famine, after allowance for the return flow of emigrant remittances.[41] So far, similar calculations have not been made for the post-Famine period. I suspect the life-cycle loss would have been proportionately greater for a time, since both the size and age-structure of the outflow was 'worse' after the Famine. On the other hand, emigrant remittances also rose substantially.

Putative losses from the 'brain-drain' or 'skill-drain' effect have also long been stressed by those opposed to emigration. Their worries are reflected in the remark of Charles Oldham, professor of economics at University College, Dublin, in 1914: 'There is in Ireland a perpetual survival of the unfittest, a steady debasement of the currency.'[42] Even though most of those young men and women who emigrated after the Famine were described as 'labourers' or 'servants' in both emigration returns and passenger lists, common-sense intuition suggests some selection bias towards the more talented. Is it not fair to assume that the emigrants were less risk-averse than those who stayed, less shy or inhibited, and more determined and ambitious?[43] Such qualities have eluded direct statistical testing. Though the presumption for a human-capital drain remains, a few caveats are necessary. First, the loss of redundant skills such as, say, handloom weaving or coopering is not at issue. Second, if opportunities for the ambitious and the talented were lacking at home, then no loss was incurred either. Third, if parents trained their children specifically for skilled employment abroad, then the human-capital loss was part of the inter-generational transfer discussed above, and the losses to complementary factors would have been small. Why still others among the talented and the skilled chose emigration instead of the rewards available (by implication) to them at home is a complex issue. Perhaps they simply had a comparative advantage in emigrating over their brothers and sisters. But if skilled workers were relatively well paid in nineteenth-century Ireland (as often claimed: see Chapter 10), then comparative advantage also suggests that those with skills should have been less likely to leave.[44]

With so many different effects at work and data scarce, constructing and computing a full-fledged model to account for the causes and consequences of post-Famine migration flows seems almost pointless. Hence the appeal of the 'atheoretical' Granger–Sims approach to the question whether emigration 'caused' domestic incomes to rise or fall. The test involves running a current wage variable on past values of itself and on lagged values of the emigration rate. If the standard chi-square test for exclusion of the emigration rate variables is positive, then there is a statistical presumption that they 'caused' variations in the wage rate. The sum of the lagged emigration rate coefficients denotes the direction and size of the effect. One exercise along these lines assumed that Irish and British labour-markets must have been reasonably integrated in the post-Famine period. Since emigration from both islands to the USA was important, it used Irish plus British emigration as the dependent variable, and an estimate of UK wages for the lagged exogenous variables. The effect of emigration on the wage rate turned out to be very small but positive. Another recent econometric study of nineteenth-century emigration focuses on the determinants of the intercounty variation in emigration rates. The outcome suggests, as might be expected, that the poorer the county and the faster the rate of natural increase, the higher the outflow.[45]

A further enduring topic of controversy concerns the relative importance of 'push' and 'pull' factors in influencing people's decisions to leave. Against the claim that domestic misery was mainly responsible for emigration, there have always been those prepared to maintain that 'emigration has been due more to attraction from abroad than repulsion from within'. Even as far as the period 1815–50 is concerned, there is room for debate: as we have seen in Chapter 2, the living standards of the majority in Ireland probably fell, while working-class living standards in Britain after 1815 improved.[46]

During the Famine, the issue is clear-cut; trends in living standards abroad were hardly uppermost in the minds of emigrants. However, by definition thereafter 'pull' must have dominated, since emigration persisted despite slowly improving conditions at home.[47] In other words, had living standards in Ireland remained static after 1850, emigration would almost certainly have been greater than was actually the case: 'push' factors served over time to reduce rather than increase the emigration rate. The point becomes clearer when 'push' is associated with shifts in the emigration supply schedule, and 'pull' with shifts in the demand schedule. In Fig. 9.2 let *DD* and *SS* be the demand and supply schedules in terms of the North

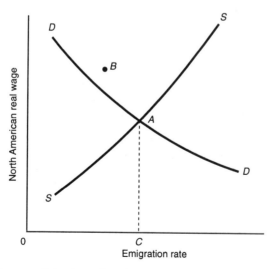

FIG. 9.2 Push vs. pull in the wake of the Great Famine

American real wage. Suppose A (which alone may be observed) represents the situation in the 1850s, indicating an emigration rate of OC. Since the real wage available to potential emigrants rose between the 1850s and 1870s, while the emigration rate declined, a point such as B is indicated for the later date. Only an inward shift in the supply schedule (negative 'push')—or an inward supply shift combined with some outward movement in the demand schedule—can produce a consistent new equilibrium. A few numbers help flesh out the argument: between the mid-1850s and 1910 the American real wage rose by two-thirds or more, while the emigration rate from Ireland fell from about 12 to 6 per thousand.

O'Rourke's finding[48] that after mid-century the trends in real wages in the USA and London do a good job of accounting for the variation in nominal wages in Ireland, while domestic factors seem powerless to explain it, supports this emphasis on 'pull' factors in accounting for the trend in the migration rate. O'Rourke has also provided a computable general equilibrium analysis of the push–pull issue. Using a twenty-three equation model of Irish agriculture in the 1850s, and manipulating it to yield the actual outcome in the 1870s reinforces the case for 'pull' factors.

(4) Emigration and regional incomes

In the literature of development economics, emigration is sometimes seen as a means of widening income differentials within the sending country. This may occur if those living in the richer areas and the more talented are more prone to leave. As noted in Chapter 4, Irish emigration arguably operated in this manner in the pre-Famine period. The evidence from other European countries is mixed. Nineteenth-century Denmark seems to fit the standard model, but neither Baines for England and Wales nor Carlsson for Sweden could find a connection between emigration rates and county incomes. It was once thought that a poverty-trap hindered migration from the west of Ireland in the immediate post-Famine decades, but more recent research depicts Irish emigration as a means of narrowing regional differentials, and raising relative living standards from the Famine on. The gradual decline in the emigration rate from the 1850s on (though with a big blip in the 1880s) is a reflection of this.

Post-Famine data support this interpretation. Defining *Emigr* as the proportionate cohort-depletion of those aged 0–15 in 1881 by 1911, *Hsg* as the proportion of 3rd- and 4th-class housing in 1881, *Dub* as a dummy for Dublin, and *Wage93* as the agricultural wage rate in 1893, produces the following result:

$$Emigr = 0.543 - 0.0019.Wage\,93 + .00496.Hsg - 0.2166.Dub$$
$$(4.27) \quad (-2.13) \qquad\qquad (4.53) \qquad\qquad (-3.01)$$
$$R^2 = .714, F(3, 28) = 23.31$$

The lower the wage, and the higher the proportion of poor housing, the higher the proportion of the cohort lost. Defining *Dwage* as the wage change between 1893 and 1911 implies 'convergence', albeit weakly:

$$Dwage = -0.197 + 0.6169.Emigr + 0.2869.Dub$$
$$(-1.40) \quad (2.49) \qquad\qquad (1.87)$$
$$R^2 = .180, F(2, 29) = 3.18$$

The variation in emigration rates across counties has been quite persistent until this day, a reminder that emigration has failed to entirely erode the gap in regional incomes.[49]

(5) Seasonal migration[50]

The temporary migration of Irish harvest workers to agricultural regions of Great Britain had been substantial since the early nineteenth century. It continued to be important after the Famine; indeed it probably increased for a time. Its regional breakdown did not change much; men and women from Mayo and west Donegal always accounted for the bulk of the movement. Seasonal migration between different regions in Ireland declined with the Famine, however. The character of the migration also changed in several respects between the 1840s and the turn of the century. The virtual elimination of migration from west Munster and south Ulster is one obvious difference. Seasonal migration from the extreme west grew; in the 1890s, a majority of the young men of the Rosses, Gort a' Choirce, Fanad and Ros Goill—'congested' areas of poor land—were travelling to Scotland annually. Another change was more variation in the length of stay. Before the Famine the bulk of the migration was for three or four months at most, but in the post-famine period for some the absences might last almost the whole year. In west Donegal in the 1890s, 'a large number of men go to obtain general work in Scotland as soon as their own crops have been put in and others go for the Scotch harvest only. The time of return also varies; some return in October, others at the end of the year, and others not until it is time for the spring work on their holdings in Donegal.' That statement implies the next point, namely, that the migration was gradually becoming less seasonal, and less closely tied to agricultural conditions in Britain. Around the turn of the century many from the Rosses were working 'in oil refineries and other miscellaneous occupations', while a sizeable minority of Clonmany men boarded smacks in Dundee rather than opting for the more traditional sort of seasonal work. Finally, women seem to have contributed more to the temporary flow in the post-Famine decades. They did not necessarily work with or accompany the men; indeed female migrants from Achill in Mayo tended to go to Scotland on the 'gaffer' system, while many of their menfolk headed for Lancashire, Cheshire, and Yorkshire. With the diffusion of the mechanical reaper, working the scythe gave way to potato picking, fishing, and longer terms away.

There is a sense in which seasonal migration continued to reinforce the socio-economic status quo.[51] The migrants were predominantly from small farm families, and their income and part-time labour kept those farms viable. The local economies of Mayo, west Donegal and a few other places associated with seasonal migration were characterized during the 1850s and 1860s by increases in the numbers of agricultural holdings; in Newport Poor Law Union in Mayo, for example, the number of holdings over an acre rose from 1,852 in 1851 to 2,614 in 1870, and in Swinford, also in Mayo, from 6,960 to 7,564 over the same period. The acreage under potatoes rose, and, in pockets here and there, even population. To take an admittedly extreme example, in eight electoral districts in north-west Donegal situated between Dungloe and Gort a' Choirce, population rose from 14,923 in 1841 and 16,107 in 1891. People continued to marry young, and the proportion of never-marrieds remained low. All this was in rather marked contrast to immediate post-Famine developments in the rest of Ireland. However, the apparent reversion towards pre-Famine conditions was insufficient to keep emigration in such areas down below the national average during the 1850s and 1860s. It seems more likely that the emigration statistics do not capture the whole outflow from the western counties.

Seasonal migration rose temporarily in the 1890s but declined steadily after the turn of the century. By then refinements in reaper technology had made human harvesters uneconomic even at subsistence wages in most of Britain's arable areas. With the resultant relative decline in summer and autumn wages, more and more migrants found the seasonal trek no longer worth while. By 1937, when the tragic deaths of ten seasonal workers from Achill in a miserable bothy in Kirkintilloch evoked a national outcry, the once-massive outflow had dwindled to less than 10,000. About one-fifth of these were hired as potato-lifters, the remainder for general agricultural labour; the average take-home pay was about £20.[52]

Should the long drawn-out decline in seasonal migration to Britain be regarded as a symptom or cause of 'modernization' in the west? The question cannot be properly answered without comprehensive data on the trend in incomes, which are still unavailable. A tentative answer is 'both'. On the one hand, the very persistence of the migration after the Famine suggests that resistance to emigration remained strong. Migration provided 'a way of keeping a grip' on one's home-place.[53] According to the Irish Registrar-General in 1887, 'in old times they used to earn a good deal of money—they used to get about £15 a head but they now don't get anything like it. I believe it is now about £10'. Despite the decline, tens of thousands continued their annual journey for a time. It was a harsh and rough routine; the hours were long, and though 'gaffers' reduced search costs for the workers, they also sometimes exploited the weaker and the vulnerable among them. On the other hand, detailed data on 29 western rural districts in the mid-1930s shows a positive correlation (+0.517) between the rate of migration for agricultural work and the rate of migration for domestic and industrial work. That is because the latter outflow represented 'persons who would normally have gone to America if emigration to that country were possible'.[54] The decline in seasonal migration thus reflected both betterment at home for some and increasing recourse to permanent migration for others.

9.4 Conclusion

The contrasts between the demographic patterns described above and those described in Chapters 1 and 4 explain why Ireland has for so long been an 'outlier' in the population history of Europe. From a regime where population growth was for a time among the very fastest in Europe, after 1850 Ireland switched to one marked by negative population growth, accompanied by levels of celibacy and maritial fertility which were to become, again, unusual by European standards.[55] No wonder Ireland has been a magnet for many historical demographers! It seems natural to link the radical nature of these swings, though not their direction, to the Great Famine; no other nineteenth-century European society endured such an ecological jolt. But if the Famine set off the process, the ensuing decline in numbers played an important part in the rise and 'convergence' in living standards discussed in Chapter 10.

IO

Living Standards after the Famine

From the Famine onwards, on the basis of practical evidence, Irish *per capita* incomes rose more rapidly than English.

L. M. CULLEN[1]

Tráthnóna Dé Sathairn ag dul faoi don ngréin
Sea do chonaic mé lánún i ngarraí leo féin
Bhí an bhean tí go casaoideach ag cur síos ar an tae
Is níor mhaith leis an bhfear í bheith ag trácht air.

COLM DE BHAILÍS[2]

10.1 Trends

English economist Nassau Senior had expected the Famine to kill 'not more than a million people, [but] that would scarcely be enough to do much good'. He had guessed the toll correctly, yet saw 'neither poverty, nor overpopulation' on a visit to Cork in 1852. The Famine had done its work: Harriet Martineau's jaunty *Letters from Ireland*, an account of impressions gained (and some prejudices confirmed) on a fleeting tour in 1854, makes the same point. The complacent, unsympathetic tone may grate, but the Famine's part in improving the lot of most people who survived is indisputable. Wages rose significantly in the wake of the crisis, and neither exogenous price changes nor agricultural improvement can fully account for this. However, the Famine alone would have provided only temporary relief from growing population pressure; had it not been for continued emigration and a falling birth rate, Senior might have been closer to the truth! The rise in wages persisted: Bowley's indices of nominal farm labourers' wages more than doubled between 1850 and 1894. In the three southern provinces the rise was particularly striking in 1850–70, and the data point to a fairly steady decline in regional wage dispersion in the Irish agricultural labour market (see Table 10.1). True, these estimates take no account

Table 10.1. *Estimates of nominal wages* (pence per week)

Year	Mean	Coefficient of variation
(a) *Bowley/Fitzpatrick*		
1777	42	0.22
1829	61	0.15
1845	56	0.17
1850	58	0.16
1860	84	0.15
1870	94	0.11
1886	112	0.12
1893	113	0.11
1894	128	0.13
1911	129	0.07
(b) *Ten farm sample*		
1850–9	72.6	
1860–9	82.3	
1870–9	95.7	
1880–9	107.6	
1890–9	117.5	
1900–3	127.1	

Sources: (*a*) derived from Bowley, 'The Statistics of Wages', 400–1, and Fitzpatrick, 'The Disappearance of the Irish Agricultural Labourer', 81, 90; (*b*) *Report on Agricultural Labourers in the United Kingdom*, 135.

of changes in the cost of living, and the labourer's cost of basic subsistence was certainly higher after the Famine than before it. Fitzpatrick goes further: 'it seems probable that the fully employed labourer of 1911 obtained less satisfaction from his more varied meals, despite modestly increased money wages, than had his counterpart of 1860.' Fitzpatrick did not construct a cost-of-living index, though he noted that the blight-induced rise in potato prices and the increasing scarcity of potato ground had forced labourers to shift from potatoes to more expensive oatmeal stirabout. No doubt there was something to this, but the shift was not all price-induced; the cross-section evidence from the pre-Famine period (discussed in Chapter 4) implies that the shift from potatoes to oatmeal was also linked to an increase in income.

Agricultural wages were still much higher in Britain than in Ireland in the 1890s and 1900s.[3] The same did not hold for industrial wages in the cities. A wide-ranging wage survey conducted by the Fiscal Inquiry Committee in 1923 indicates that by 1914 skilled workers in Ireland were paid almost as much as their British peers (Table 10.2). The gap in wages for unskilled work in the towns was still substantial, though, about one-quarter. Adjustment for the higher cost of living in towns and cities is

Table 10.2. *Money wages in Ireland and Britain, 1914* (shillings per week)

Industry	Ireland	Gt. Britain
Skilled and semi-skilled work		
Railways (5)	35.0	36.6
Cycle manufacture (5)	36.2	43.0
Constr. engineering (3)	34.7	38.1
Agr. machinery (6)	23.8	33.3
Printing and binding (5)	33.3	35.3
Furniture (6)	38.1	38.9
Coach-building (7)	35.8	38.7
Average	34.9	37.7
Labourers (male)		
Constr. engineering	19.0	20.0
Agr. machinery	15.0	22.0
Jute	15.0	22.3
Coach-building	16.0	20.0
Tanning	16.0	29.0
Flour milling	18.0	22.0
Furniture	16.0	22.5
Biscuit man.	18.0	20.0
Confectionery	16.0	26.0
Average	16.6	22.6
Labourers (female)		
Biscuit man.	9.0	11.5
Margarine	7.0	11.7
Jute	11.6	15.3
Binding	10.0	13.0
Tobacco	12.0	17.0
Confectionery	7.0	13.0
Average	9.4	13.6

Source: *Reports of the Fiscal Inquiry Committee*, App. A. The numbers in parentheses refer to the number of trades; simple averages are reported.

unlikely to eradicate the gap between Irish agricultural and unskilled urban wage levels. The gap, further discussed in Chapter 17, suggests less than competitive labour-markets. Qualitative evidence from the Irish service sector corroborates this: the rural gentry still wielded considerable power in nominating men for the armed forces and the police, while in the towns businessmen were in a good position to land railway and banking jobs for trusted clients and friends.[4]

The meliorist view is also strongly supported for part of this period by the real wage index constructed by O'Rourke, which rises from 105.1 in 1855–7 to 164.6 twenty years later. Turning to another labour-market, D'Arcy has reported a rise of 60 to 80 per cent in the money wages of Dublin building craftsmen's labourers between the 1850s and 1890s, when the cost of living in the city was probably declining. The evidence from the skilled trades in Cork City is more equivocal: hefty increases of one-half or more for plumbers, printers, and bakers between 1850 and 1890, but modest rises of less than one-fifth for founders and cabinet-makers.[5]

The impressive rises in tobacco, tea, and sugar consumption were largely due to higher incomes, and the rise in travel by train also contained a consumption element. Even the occasional shopping journey to town or city brought its pleasures, and not only in lower prices and greater variety. The number of train journeys per inhabitant rose from 1.7 in 1860 to 3.9 in 1885 and 7.1 in 1913 (in Britain the numbers were 6.6 in 1861, 21.6 in 1885, and 34.9 in 1913). The growth of holiday resorts such as Bray and Portrush (whose populations more than doubled between 1851 and 1911) owed much to the railway, and also bespoke rising living standards among the urban lower-middle and middle classes. McCorry's history of Lurgan suggests another, unusual index of amelioration: the decline in the percentage of Catholic funerals unsupported by offerings from 59 in the late 1860s to 30 in the 1880s and 18 in the 1890s.[6]

Official returns describing the trend in small savings between the 1880s and the 1910s offer some further support for melioration (see Table 10.3). Intended as an inducement to working-class saving, the generous deposit rate offered by the post office also attracted many savers from further up the socio-economic ladder. The number of people holding accounts in post office and trustee savings banks in Ireland more than quadrupled between 1881 and 1912, and the rise in the amounts deposited was almost commensurate (from £3.8 million to £15.5 million). The numbers do not mean an equivalent rise in net savings, because this mode of saving was still new in much of Ireland in the 1880s. Post offices had been doubling up as

Table 10.3. *Irish post office savings, 1881–1912*

	1881	1896	1907	1912
Savings accounts per 10,000 population				
Leinster	86	229	378	449
Munster	47	124	219	271
Ulster	69	168	277	322
Connacht	17	51	110	143
Average deposit (in £s)				
Leinster	18.3	16.7	15.0	14.6
Munster	30.9	27.6	24.5	24.3
Ulster	28.6	27.9	27.6	26.9
Connacht	27.7	31.0	32.6	33.1

Source: 'Tables Showing . . . the Number of Depositors'
Accounts', BPP 1913 (272) [LVII], 915.

savings banks only since 1861, and many towns and villages were still without their post office twenty years later. For example, the small village of Carna in south Connemara had no post office in 1881, but the number of depositors there grew from 11 in 1896 to 38 in 1907 and 57 in 1912. Lisdoonvarna's single post-office saver in 1881 had over £30 in his (or her) account; by 1912 the town had 102 accounts averaging £26. As the habit and the facility spread, undoubtedly many savings were shifted from under the mattress to the nearest post office.[7] Nevertheless, focusing only on those towns and villages with a post office in 1881 reveals a healthy growth in the number of accounts between then and 1912. In Clare, for example, the number of accounts in such places nearly trebled between 1896 and 1912. Even if the average value of those Clare deposits rose only marginally, from £33.1 in 1896 to £33.2 in 1912, the aggregate rise is telling. The numbers also imply relative improvement in the west: though Connacht's population fell by almost twice the national average between 1881 and 1912, the share of Connacht savers in the value of monies put aside in post office and trustee savings banks rose from 4.9 to 9.3 per cent.[8]

The trends in literacy and housing quality also imply betterment after the Famine. The proportion of people aged over 5 who claimed that they could read increased from 47 per cent in 1841 to 53 per cent in 1851; the proportion reached nearly nine-tenths in 1911. Letters written and newspapers and magazines read increased in tandem, and the number of newspaper editors and writers quadrupled between 1861 and 1911. The growing prosperity of Eason & Son, Ireland's version of W. H. Smith, stemmed from the improvements in literacy and transport facilities.[9] Housing also improved. The single-room cabins in which over one-third of rural families had lived in 1841 were unusual by 1911. In 1861 one rural family in ten still lived in what the census commissioners deemed 'fourth-class' accommodation—meaning, roughly, one room per family. Half a century later only 1 per cent did. The percentage of families living in third- and fourth-class housing fell from 63 to 29.[10] This is far from denying the persistence of poor housing conditions, particularly in the cities. In the early 1860s a City Hall official described the housing of Dublin's poor in terms that echoed Whitelaw in the 1800s and Willis in the 1840s:[11]

We may safely venture upon the average of eight persons to each house, which gives us 64,000 people out of a population of 249,733, 50,000 at least of whom reside in a fetid and poisonous atmosphere. The dwellings of the poor are chiefly confined to about 450 lanes, courts, and alleys, and about sixty streets. The worst districts are the Liberties on the south, and the parish of St Michan on the north side of the city . . . The entrance to the courts is very narrow—a sort of great stench valve, or over-ground sewer. As a general rule, there is a green slimy steam oozing from a surcharged and choked-up cess-pool, through which the visitor is compelled to wade.

Four decades later, the French writer Paul-Dubois chose the percentage of families living in one-room tenements in 1901 as an index of housing decadence. In Dublin the percentage was 36, in London 15, in Cork 11, in Belfast 1. The contrast between Dublin and Belfast is striking. In booming Belfast speculators had produced the purpose-built 'two-up, two-down' housing schemes so characteristic of that Victorian city; in Dublin the demand for working-class housing was met by 'house-jobbers' who bought up dilapidated buildings formerly used by artisans or located in areas no longer fashionable, and relet them by the room. Still, on the eve of the First World War working-class housing in Dublin had become a scandal, not so much because conditions were worse than those described above, but because they had failed to keep step with what was considered 'decent' housing standards elsewhere.[12] Though the average number of families per house had fallen from 2.5 in 1861 to 1.8 in 1911, 'dear, dirty Dublin' had the worst urban slums in the UK (and in north-western Europe) in the 1900s and 1910s. Bad housing was complemented by poor food, irregular employment, and a high incidence of typhoid fever and tuberculosis. Dublin's lack of a strong industrial base made it harder for women to find work. Ironically this kept down infant mortality, because it meant that most mothers could breast-feed their children.

Lee's estimate of the growth rate of Irish national income between 1848 and 1914 (0.5 per cent per annum) places Ireland at the bottom of the European growth league. Combining Mokyr's revised estimate of national income $c.1845$ (about £80 million) and the estimate for 1914 proposed in Chapter 15 (£135 million) implies a higher growth rate—0.7 per cent in current price terms between 1845 and 1914. Since this was, broadly speaking, a period of falling prices, and Irish income declined between 1845 and 1848, growth in real terms probably exceeded 1 per cent over 1848–1914. Even 1 per cent was unimpressive by British or broader European standards. Yet at the same time, the numbers also suggest both betterment and convergence—a rise in Irish income per capita from about two-fifths to somewhat short of three-fifths of the British over the period. Emigration on a scale leading to population decline reconciles the sluggish growth in aggregate output and the substantial growth in income per capita. Put in another way, the numbers mean that average incomes in Ireland almost trebled between 1845 and 1914.[13]

Though conditions certainly improved for those who stayed at home, an analysis of farm inheritance patterns suggests that those selected for emigration by their parents were considered the fortunate ones. Their exclusion from wills, coupled with the largely one-way flow of remittances, bear testimony to this. The low rate of return emigration reinforces the point. The emigrants were the luckier ones, not only because they were materially better off, but because much of the fun or 'crack' seemed to travel with them. None the less, the distinction between levels and rate of change is significant here. Since the rate of emigration tended to fall over time, a narrowing in the gap between incomes at home and abroad is indicated. Indeed O'Rourke's comparison of real wage changes in Ireland after the Famine and in the USA confirms this.[14]

There was an impressive increase in another proxy for living standards, the average duration of life, in Ireland after the Famine. Life expectancy, under 40 years on the eve of the Famine, had reached 50 years by the early 1870s and 58 years by the 1920s. Connachtmen (62.3 years) and Connachtwomen (62.6) were now likely to outlive Dubliners (51.5 and 55.8) by several years.[15] Usher and Williamson have proposed a framework for assessing the consequent increase in 'true' living standards.[16] In Fig. 10.1 let A on IC_0 represent the situation facing the average individual in 1840. This individual would have been equally happy with any point along

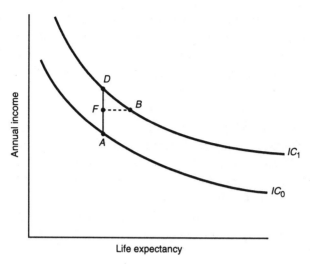

FIG. 10.1 Longevity and living standards

IC_0. Let B represent the outcome in 1914. Then DF is the share of the rise in 'true' living standards attributable to increasing life expectancy.

Empirical implementation of this framework requires some special simplifying assumptions. Thus Williamson's estimates embody assumptions about the elasticity of annual utility with respect to annual consumption and the share of longevity gains attributable to exogenous influences. Williamson's 'best guess' is that the rise in English life expectancy between the 1780s and the 1850s—from about 35 to 40 years—accounted for only a tiny fraction—1-2 per cent—of the 'true' rise in living standards over that period. However, he finds that the greater rise in life expectancy in 1851–1911 accounted for 10–15 per cent of the 'true' rise. Since the rise in Irish real incomes, conventionally defined, exceeded the English in these years, and the rise in the expectation of life was similar, Williamson's English estimates provide an upper-bound estimate of added longevity's contribution to the 'true' rise in Irish living standards between the Famine and the First World War. Still, the added premium on living standards of, say, 10 per cent or so should not be ignored.

Post-Famine data on heights are plentiful. Here I summarize the results of an analysis of four datasets, two taken from the records of Castlebar and Kilmainham prisons in the early 1880s, a third from Kilmainham in the late 1900s, and a fourth from Castlebar in the 1910s.[17] The Castlebar prisoners were mainly Mayo-born and nearly all Catholics. A majority were charged for crimes such as drunkenness, assault, and begging. But 82-year-old John Hopkins, an illiterate weaver, was charged with 'causing the death of Pat Jordan by bleeding him not being a qualified surgeon', and the charges ranged from debt to sedition. Several of the younger female prisoners, especially those charged more than once, were probably prostitutes. The mean height of adult men was about 66.5 inches. Cross-tabulations show mean height falling off after age 30 or so, but this probably springs from adverse selection in the kind of men included: alcoholics and vagrants were particularly numerous among the older prisoners. My analysis of 859 Mayo prisoners in the 1880s showed men being about five inches taller than women. Being able to read and write added about 0.8 inches to height, and not being a Catholic 0.4 inches. The last result means little, however, since it derives largely from the heights of wayward English-born soldiers and sailors.

The Kilmainham prisoners of the 1880s, all male, hailing from a much wider range of birthplaces, and including a far higher proportion of non-Catholics, are the basis for the regression results in Table 10.4. They show

Table 10.4. *Explaining the variation in male heights and BMI: The Kilmainham sample, 1882–1885*

Variable	Height total sample	Height age 20+ only	BMI total sample	BMI age 22+ only
Constant	59.77	65.22	19.54	23.58
	(137.32)	(107.62)	(33.44)	(25.28)
Age	0.339	0.064	0.183	0.019
	(14.26)	(2.09)	(5.79)	(−0.47)
AgeSq	−0.004	−0.001	−0.002	0.000
	(−13.46)	(−2.74)	(−5.08)	(0.33)
Dub	−0.558	−0.647	−0.239	−0.209
	(−3.88)	(−4.47)	(−1.25)	(−0.94)
Foreign	0.414	0.392	−0.660	−0.599
	(1.13)	(1.09)	(−1.36)	(−1.06)
Liter	0.162	0.200	−0.057	0.102
	(2.21)	(2.67)	(−0.58)	(0.87)
Religion	−0.503	−0.554	−0.485	−0.897
	(−1.88)	(−2.17)	(−1.40)	(−2.41)
R^2	0.110	0.032	0.068	0.019
n	2 002	1 514	686	491

that literacy was a much weaker predictor of height in Dublin in the 1880s than in the west, but perhaps the most striking result is how much smaller, after controlling for age, literacy, and religion, were Dubliners. Cross-tabulations reveal that the adult westerners in the sample were as tall as the Mayomen measured in Castlebar around the same time. Little had changed in Kilmainham by the late 1900s: the mean heights of adult non-Dubliners was 66.5 inches, that of Dubliners almost an inch less. The mean height of first-time prime-age male Castlebar prisoners charged between 1910 and 1918[18] was just short of 67 inches, that of women charged over the same period 62 inches.

A backward glance at the results presented in Chapter 4 reveals little change in the mean height of Dubliners between the 1840s and the 1900s, but a modest improvement in that of rural men. The difference is probably an indication that conditions improved more in post-Famine rural Ireland than in the city.[19]

The Kilmainham records also report the weights of prisoners from 1884 on. These are the basis for the estimates given below of the Body Mass Index (BMI)—defined as Weight/Height^2. This alternative anthropometric index reflects 'the balance between intakes and the claims on those intakes'. While the mean height of a population is the product of dietary intake during childhood and adolescence, BMI reflects the balance between food and energy requirements at the time of measurement. In Fogel's parlance, people who are short relative to modern North American or West European standards are deemed 'stunted', while people with low BMI are 'wasted'. The 'ideal' BMI level varies with height; Fogel puts it at about 26 (measuring height in metres and weight in kilograms) for men under 66 inches. The results of modern clinical research invoked by Fogel suggest that Kilmainham BMI—about 23—on the low side. The outcome by age is as shown in Table 10.5.

Table 10.5. *Kilmainham BMI levels, 1884–1885*

Age-group	Dublin	Rest-of-Ireland	All Ireland
20–4	22.9 (107)	22.6 (44)	22.8 (151)
25–9	23.2 (86)	23.3 (37)	23.2 (123)
30–4	23.0 (41)	23.4 (25)	23.1 (66)
35–9	22.8 (31)	23.3 (19)	23.0 (50)
40–4	23.6 (20)	23.8 (26)	23.7 (46)

Analysis of a group of Kilmainham prisoners charged in 1908 reveals little change: for men over 20, BMI was 22.9 for non-Dubliners and 23.1 for Dubliners. In Mayo in the 1910s BMI was also 23. The most plausible explanation for low BMI is that the data include men who, though they may have been reasonably fed while growing up, tended to neglect their own health in adulthood; that many of the prisoners in the sample were charged with crimes such as drunkenness, vagrancy, petty thieving, and assault may be a pointer here. By the BMI measuring rod, men born in Dublin were no more disadvantaged than the rest.[20]

Another strand of anthropomorphic research has focused on the trend in birth weights as a gauge of social change and living standards. As a report by the World Health Organization claims, weight at birth[21]

in the first place . . . is strongly conditioned by the health and nutritional status of the mother, in the sense that maternal malnutrition, ill-health and other deprivation are the most common causes of retarded fetal growth and/or prematurity, as manifested in low birth weight (LBW). In the second place, low birth weight is, universally and in all population groups, the single most important determinant of the chances of the newborn to survive and to experience healthy growth and development.

Though the claim stands, the range of historical evidence on birth weights unearthed so far has been slightly disappointing.[22] Nevertheless, an analysis of birth weights at Dublin's Rotunda maternity hospital seems to provide some solid indication of an increase in living standards in the city between 1874–99 and 1900–30. Though biological variables pack much more explanatory punch than 'economic' variables in accounting for the variation in birth weight, still, after controlling for everything else Rotunda babies born in the later period were about 100 grams heavier (3,350 grams) in 1900–30 than in 1874–99 (3,250 grams). Moreover, the proportion of low-weight children, i.e. of less than 2,500 grams, dropped from 9.8 per cent in the first period to 6.8 per cent in the second. This is interpreted as 'compelling evidence' of betterment in the diet of Dublin's poor. The main results of the study's regression analysis of the variation in birth weight during the 1869–1930 period are worth reporting. The dependent variable is birth weight in grams:[23]

Exogenous variable	Coefficient
Constant	2968.4(*)
Male child dummy	119.6(*)
Year of birth 1900–13	110.9(*)

Year of birth 1914–20	73.5(*)
Year of birth 1921–30	106.9(*)
Birth order	14.7(*)
Mother's age	5.7(*)
Father domestic servant	62.6(*)
Winter	−30.8(*)
Resided in north Dublin	−37.1(*)
Resided in 'Dublin poor core'	−56.3(*)
Mother ill at delivery	−411.6(*)
Father's occupation skilled	25.6
Year of birth 1869–73	27.6
Mother married	46.1
Resided in south Dublin	−30.4

I have reported those variables producing statistically significant (which are asterisked) or sizeable coefficients. The outcome shows that male birth contributed 120 grams to birth weight, each year of a mother's age 6 grams, and each increment in birth order 15 grams. Year-of-birth dummies suggest improvement over time, and there are plausible geographical and socio-economic effects too. These results bear comparison with a companion analysis of birth weights in Vienna's Krankenhaus between 1865 and 1930:[24]

Exogenous variable	Coefficient
Constant	2,716.5(*)
Male child dummy	129.7(*)
Year of birth 1916–22	−68.1(*)
Year of birth 1923–30	156.3(*)
Birth order	37.5(*)
Mother's age	6.2(*)
Domestic servants	80.9(*)
Autumn	47.3(*)
Lower Austrian address	−55.2(*)
Lower Austrian origin	32.0
Working-class Vienna address	−24.9(*)
Bureaucratic, clerical occupations	43.9
Professional, managerial occupations	133.8(*)

Comparing the constant terms—2,968 against 2,717 grams—might seem to mean that Rotunda mothers and their children fared better than

Viennese in these years. That is not quite correct; the absence of a dummy variable for ill mothers in Vienna must pull down the Viennese constant term, and standardizing on Lower Austrian origin (+32) and the poorer parts of Dublin (−37.1) would also lower the gap. Unconditional estimates for a broader sample of cities show that Dublin birth weights were bracketed by those for other European cities in the nineteenth century.[25] In some other respects the Dublin and Vienna results are similar. Mother's age and the sex dummy return reassuringly similar coefficients. The substantial difference in the birth-order coefficients—15 grams versus 38 grams—is interesting, however. It is a reminder that available birth-weight data should be interpreted with some caution, being subject to varying selection biases that are difficult to explain. This is because nineteenth-century birth-weight data are almost invariably the product of maternity hospitals. Regression analysis helps to control for shifts over time in the catchment areas and socio-economic composition of such hospitals. But a problem with the Rotunda data is that the spread of its out-patient 'districts' system after mid-century—whereby healthy mothers gave birth at home with the help of specially trained Rotunda nurses—led to a disproportionate number of difficult births being handled in the hospital itself. Against this, as the danger of puerperal fever receded and maternal mortality declined, the hospital became less exclusively a haven for poor mothers. Such factors must have influenced average birth weight, reducing somewhat the value of comparisons across place and time. Thus the lower value of the Rotunda's birth-order coefficient may well reflect the relatively poorer health of higher parity mothers who used the hospital.

Curiously, information on a single year over a century earlier indicates little change in Dublin birth weights since the 1780s: a 1786 study by Rotunda Master Joseph Clarke produced figures of 7.4 lb. for males and 6.8 lb. for females (an average of 3,200 grams). Finally, one finding in a study of American birth weights is worth mentioning here. An analysis of the weights of children born in Philadelphia's almshouse between 1848 and 1873 found that the babies of Irish-born women, though smaller than those of American-born women, were substantially bigger than those of other immigrant women.[26]

In Ireland as elsewhere, discussion of past living standards is too often conducted in terms of men's wages alone. Yet it is often urged that the status of women worsened after the Famine; their weakening marriage prospects after 1850 and the female character of Irish emigration, noted in Chapter 9, are seen as consequences. Hitherto, the discussion has been largely impressionistic and anecdotal: hard data on wages and consumption patterns are few. Table 10.6 offers no more than a tentative, introductory outline. All the data refer to agricultural wages; Wakefield's are a blend of daily and annual rates, those for 1860 are weekly, those for 1926–30 half-yearly. The comparison therefore assumes that the relative cost of the in-kind component in earnings was the same as the ratio of cash payments. That probably balances the comparison in the 1920s against women, since items such as a bed or a room should have cost the same for both. Further refinement is not attempted here. Women's marriage prospects, arguably another proxy for well-being, undoubtedly dropped in the post-Famine decades. However, *relative* well-being is the issue, and by that criterion men's prospects worsened relative to women's. Thus the proportion of 45–54-year-old men who had never married rose from 12.1 per cent in 1851 to 27.3 per cent in 1911; among women in the same age-group the rise was from 12.6 to 24.9 per cent. In Connacht, the poorest province, the contrast in fortunes was greater—from 7.4 to 25.2 per cent for men, from 8.2 per cent to 17.9 per cent for women. Presumably higher female emigration improved the marriage chances of those remaining at home. Literacy trends also indicate relative improvement in women's status: the substantial gap between the proportions of males and females able to read and write in all four provinces in 1861 had been virtually eradicated by 1911.[27] Women's expectation of life also rose after the Famine, though in this regard Irishwomen still fared worse in the 1920s than women else-

Table 10.6. *The trend in the male/female farm wage ratio, c.1810–1930*

Province	c.1810	1860	1926–30
Leinster	.59	.55	.59
Munster	.57	.58	.72
Ulster	.47	.55	.70
Connacht	.48	.55	.68
Ireland	.55	.56	.67

Sources: c.1810: Wakefield, *Ireland*, ii; *Return of the Average Rate of Weekly Earnings of Agricultural Labourers* [2] (1862), ix; *Statistical Abstract 1934*, 41. The 1810 data are my own averages of the observations collected by Wakefield. They exclude one Meath outlier. The 1926–30 data refer to the average rates per half-year, including full board and lodging, and are based on a three-county Ulster.

where. In the long list of country data reported in the 1926 Saorstát census only in Ireland was the expectation of life from one to 22 years of age worse for females than males.[28]

In sum, a whole series of proxies for living standards—wages, consumption, literacy, life-span, height, birth weight—argue for betterment between the Famine and the First World War. The period also seems to have witnessed a narrowing in the regional variation in welfare, and in the gap between men and women.

10.2 Good Times, Bad Times

Though the post-Famine decades were a period of growing prosperity for the average Irishman and Irishwoman, progress was by no means uninterrupted. In a small, largely agricultural, open economy, the poor harvests of 1859–64, 1879–81, and 1890–1, 1894–5, and 1897–8 were bound to provoke hardship, and this hardship is reflected in the emigration statistics for those years. Other data also reflected peaks and troughs in economic activity. For example, economists regard the public's demand for money as a good barometer of the level of economic activity. Year-to-year changes in banknote circulation for 1845–1914 are shown in Fig. 10.2. Troughs during the Famine, in 1860–3, 1877–80, 1883–7, 1891–2,

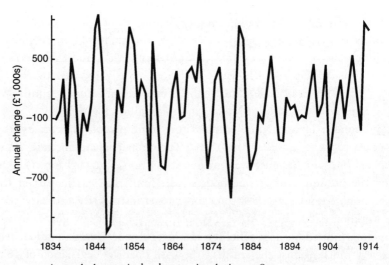

FIG. 10.2 Annual change in banknote circulation, 1834–1914

1896–8, and 1904–5 are discernible. Short-term dips in the Irish Exchequer balance held at the Bank of Ireland in Dublin also point towards bad
years. Drops in 1858–62, 1876–9, 1886, 1889–91, and in 1900–1 are
indicated. Remittances to the Treasury from Ireland tell a similar story. A
new index of property transactions reveals broadly synchronous downturns
in 1859–61, 1881–2, 1891–2, and 1902–3.[29]

    Though no post-Famine recession matched that of the late 1840s, those
of the early 1860s and 1879–81 were serious enough. An Ulster Bank
circular of 1863 reflects the gravity of the first of these. The state of the
country, it declared[30]

has not been in so critical a condition since the year 1847. Three successive bad
harvests have reduced farmers—particularly the smaller class—to a very low ebb.
The country shopkeepers, who are dependent upon the farming and labouring
population, cannot collect the money due to them, while the traders carrying on
business with small provision dealers in Lancashire and the North of England must
have been doing a very unprofitable trade.

Yet the crisis of 1859–64 produced nothing like the hardship or unrest of
the late 1840s. This 'non-famine', so soon after the cataclysm of the Great
Famine, is of special interest. The detailed agricultural statistics invite
gloomy inferences. The potato crop was less than two-thirds its post-
Famine average in 1860–2, and by mid-1863 farmers had £26 million
wiped off the value of their output by a combination of crop failures, a fall
in livestock numbers, and low prices. Dairy farmers were in a particularly
bad way. Yet neither famine nor disease resulted. Donnelly has attributed
this to the role of increasing commercialization and the availability of
credit. The link is plausible, but far more important was the population
thinning done by the Great Famine. The ranks of those most at risk in the
1840s, the cottiers and labourers, had been greatly reduced by the late
1850s: the number of male farm labourers had dropped from 1.2 million or
so in 1845 to 0.9 million in 1851, and 0.7 million in 1861.[31]

    The number of workhouse entrants rose from 46,000 in February 1859
to nearly 67,000 in February 1863. The proportionate increase in the
numbers on outdoor relief was greater still (from 1,463 to 8,751). After
1863 the pressure on the workhouses eased, but this was in part at least
because more unions resorted to outdoor relief instead. By February 1867,
the workhouses contained 59,000 people, and the poor law guardians were
providing limited outdoor relief for another 19,000. Though outdoor relief
was very much against the spirit of the Irish poor law legislation of 1838,
by 1867 only thirty-three poor law unions out of 163 provided no outdoor

relief at all. Nevertheless, poor relief in Ireland was hardly liberal at this time. Though year-to-year fluctuations in admissions and in the average number on relief provide sensitive barometers of economic trends in Ireland, the relatively low numbers relieved in Ireland in this period (1 per cent or less of the population from the mid-1850s on, compared to 4 per cent in Britain in the 1860s and 2 per cent in the 1900s) reflect Irish poverty, not Irish well-being. The numbers do not reflect well on the generosity of Irish poor law guardians and property-owners.[32]

The crisis of 1879–81, induced by a combination of bad harvests and low prices, sparked off the Land War and a bout of mass emigration. Once again, the associated rise in the number of workhouse inmates is a sure sign of increasing privation. Local relief distribution committees bombarded the main charitable relief agency, the Mansion House Committee, with 'duly authenticated' stories of privation. In Cushendall in the Glens of Antrim 'people were impoverished to an extent unknown since '47'; in Glangevlin in Cavan 'very many [were] actually starving'; in Carna in west Galway 'many hundreds must have died but for the aid of the Mansion House Committee'; in Knock in Mayo there was 'terrible destitution; people half-starved'. Privation was undoubtedly greatest in the west, where living standards were lowest, and where the harvest failure in Britain reduced earnings from seasonal migration. That it was not confined to the west is indicated by the following account from Fivemiletown in south Tyrone:[33]

Mr Graham informed me that a friend of his dropped into a cabin on the Aughentaine estate last week. There were four little children round a fire on which a small saucepan was simmering. The saucepan contained a handful of Indian meal stirabout, barely a meal for any one of them. The eldest child, a bright little girl of ten years, was nursing a baby which was crying piteously. The visitor spied a heap of bare straw in a corner, and, on closer investigation, found stretched upon it, without a sack or blanket covering of any kind, the dead body of their mother.

Other individual cases of deaths attributable to the crisis might be cited, yet once again there was no excess mortality on a significant scale. The civil register, though incomplete, supports the hypothesis that no community was hit by literal starvation in 1879 and after. During the 1880s the combined death-toll from relapsing fever and starvation was only a few dozen. More generous relief, properly targeted, was partly responsible for this. The self-congratulatory account of the Mansion House Committee claimed that for the first time a famine had been 'grappled with and got under by the almost unaided arm of private benevolence'. The Committee had raised an impressive £0.2 million, including substantial sums from as far away as Hong Kong and Hyderabad, and it estimated that in total over £0.8 million in charitable donations had been allocated by late 1880. Yet the role of the State was more than commensurate. Gladstone's Whig–Liberal administration, which assumed power in summer 1880, quickly made up for the undue caution of Disraeli's Conservatives. Between 1879 and 1884 ministers spent £2.6 million on a crisis that was minor compared to the Great Famine. Though the sharp rise in the numbers relieved in workhouses—1.1 million in 1874–8, 1.7 million in 1879–83—reflects acute distress, workhouse deaths rose less (from 55,554 to 62,277). Mass emigration relieved the pressure on those who stayed. Also important, the Gregory Clause of 1847, which at the height of the Famine had excluded from relief entitlement those holding over 0.25 acres of land, was set aside, and never again applied in time of crisis. Again in 1886, Indian meal and seed potatoes were being distributed in remote pockets such as Achill, Clare Island, and Inishboffin. In mid-February 1880 the government agreed to authorize relief for *all* destitute people, landless or not, thereby putting an end to that callous exercise in imposing the principle of 'less eligibility'. Again in 1890–1 £0.2 million was spent on public works to relieve a local crisis: at their peak the works employed 16,000 people in an area whose total population hardly exceeded 100,000. Another £0.3 million was spent on seed loans, in an effort to wean cultivators away from traditional blight-prone varieties in favour of the Champion. Public works became the norm: 'not a year passes', complained Chief Secretary Balfour, 'without frantic appeals to start relief works'. Further grants and loans were given in 1897–8 and 1904–5, though on slightly less generous grounds. Relief gradually came to permeate the rural culture. As one Donegalwoman put it later, *Ba mhinic an focal* relief *i mbéal an phobail le linn m'óige: bealtaí* relief, *brioscaí* relief, *éadach* relief, *agus mar sin de.*[34] Moreover, emigration, much of it subsidized, soared in 1879–1881; the outflow and the ensuing remittances relieved the pressure on those who remained.

The west suffered further distress in 1890–1, 1894–5, and 1897–8, eliciting loud protest from Maud Gonne, criticism of rural moneylenders or gombeenmen from some Irish members of parliament, and vivid fictional cameos later from Pádraig Ó Conaire (in *Páidín Mháire*) and Liam O'Flaherty (in *The House of Gold*).[35] Not only did timely relief help prevent people from dying of famine-related causes in the 1880s and 1890s: the crises provided an impetus for preventive action such as the creation of the Congested Districts Board, the construction of light railway lines in the west, improvements in public health, and—though of less tangible benefit—the Recess Committee of 1895. That the resources required for such improvements were more plentiful in the 1880s and the 1890s than in the 1840s must not be forgotten. But public attitudes had shifted too. Finally, it should be stressed that even the worst of these 'famines' was insignificant compared to the Great Famine. 'Hold the harvest' was the popular slogan in 1879–80; the great tragedy of the Famine was that the labourers and cottiers had no harvest to hold.[36]

Farming, Commercialization, and Convergence, 1850–1914

11.1 Agriculture and Land Tenure

> Himself and the lady used try and keep the tenants in with them as much as they could. They did not like to fall out with them. Lady Gough used have men employed making roads or 'drives' through the property, so that she could be showing off her property to the friends that used to come see her. She used spend the day driving around in her coach like that.
>
> FORMER TENANT ON THE GOUGH ESTATE, SOUTH GALWAY[1]

> May heaven forgive those who represent the Irish tenant as an innocent, simple being, unable to take care of his own interests or make a bargain for himself. A more barefaced fiction was never put forward.
>
> WILLIAM BENCE JONES, CORK LANDLORD[2]

This period has been the main target of the 'new history' of Irish tenurial relations. If the gist of Solow's influential study of the Land War was that the protracted struggle that began in 1879 was unnecessary, Vaughan's assessment went further, considering its outbreak a fluke, and its outcome at best a draw from the tenants' standpoint. Further, it is claimed, landlord exploitation cannot explain the origins of the Land War, nor can it be proved that the tenants won the battles of 1880–2 or 1887–90. The struggles of the 1880s and 1890s, far from putting an end to evictions, only provoked many more of them, and failed to reduce rents significantly. In the short run at least, a coalition of tough landlords fought tenants to a draw in the Plan of Campaign (1886–91). Worse still, according to Solow, the Land War put an end to landlord investment and distracted farmers from the business of farming.[3] While the Irish plotted and fought, the Danes and the Dutch increased their hold on the British market for dairy and pork products.

Indeed, the 'new history' of the Irish Land War has virtually transposed the heroes and villains of traditional populist accounts. On the one hand, the stereotype of the predatory, cruel landlord now applies only to a handful of bullies such as the third Earl of Leitrim, Donegal's George Adair, south Galway's Earl of Clanricarde, Tipperary's Scully of Ballycohy, or Cork's Arthur Smith-Barry. The old stereotype has been replaced by that of the benign proprietor, who, though hardly in the vanguard of change himself, gave progressive tenants a fair field.[4] On the other hand, the 'hillside men' have been effectively deromanticized, one account linking their nocturnal activities to '*machismo* and sexual frustration', another relegating them to 'a form of rural gangsterism', and a third accusing them of mafia-fashion 'arbitrary and cruel punishment without due process'. In the new orthodoxy, the 'redressers' have replaced the landlords as the villains of the piece.[5] Far from being inevitable or prompted by landlord wrongs, the Land War followed almost three decades of tenurial peace and growing prosperity. Recent research in this anti-populist, anti-deterministic vein credits the genius of Parnell and Davitt with converting a downturn no worse than an earlier one in 1859−64 (described in Chapter 10) into a revolutionary situation: without them there would have been no Land War.

The 'revisionist' literature on Irish land tenure briefly summarized above was an overdue reaction to the populist anti-landlord bias of traditional historiography. In reality, post-Famine landlords rarely resorted to eviction, and when they did so it was nearly always for non-payment of rent. The numbers evicted closely mirrored agricultural conditions, and over one-quarter of those evicted between 1855 and 1880 lost their holdings in the four hard years of 1861−4. Nor did proprietors pursue a policy of predatory rent increases. Rents rose less than agricultural prices, and rent levels were such that 'if the farm has not been run out, and no big leak like drink exists', the average tenant could ride out even the worst years.[6] Landowners now gave more value for their money, paying more attention to the day-to-day running of their estates and to agricultural improvement than did their fathers and grandfathers. On these important matters, it took 'revisionism' to set the record straight. But in its defence of landlords' reputations and its implicit assertion that the Land War was unnecessary, the focus of the new historiography remained firmly traditional. For the economic historian, surely the main point about the Land War is not whether landlords were 'fair' or 'hard'—even the 'fairest' of them absorbed a hefty proportion of output—but the economic cost of the shift in tenurial regimes and the ensuing political changes. Other nineteenth- and twentieth-century rural social revolutions exacted a high cost in lives, in physical destruction, and in efficiency losses. In that respect, Ireland did not fare so badly. 'Inflated images of [landlord] self-importance notwithstanding',[7]

Irish farmers coped with the challenges of the late Victorian and Edwardian eras, and incurred no drop in their real incomes in the process. What is striking nearly a century later is how easily the system imposed by the sword in the seventeenth century was eliminated in the late nineteenth and early twentieth centuries, and how few traces it left.[8]

Though the post-Famine period contained stretches of bad years (see Chapter 10), Irish agriculture suffered no long-term depression like that endured by the heavy clay regions of England after the mid-1870s. In Ireland, the period was one of innovation (particularly in dairying), increasing regional specialization, rising potato yields (the product of new varieties and spraying), and buoyant livestock and butter exports. The post-Famine rise in the ratio of livestock to beef prices implies an improvement in cattle quality and size, an improvement confirmed by direct evidence.[9] Tory conciliation policies also helped by putting an end to the uncertainty surrounding the land question, and by producing a separate Irish Department of Agriculture and Technical Instruction in 1899. Under Horace Plunkett and his successors, the Department defined its brief broadly, gathering data, and fostering agricultural instruction and product quality improvement.[10]

In Chapter 5 we noted some pitfalls in the early agricultural statistics. However, the data collected from the mid-1850s on are probably no less reliable than those assembled by the Central Statistics Office today. They form the basis of Turner's recent output and productivity estimates.[11] Converting historical data on acreages and livestock numbers to output estimates is always a tricky matter, and future scholarship will no doubt produce more refined estimates, based on new evidence about input coefficients, seed ratios, carcass weights, milk yields, and so on. Still, Turner's continuous output series is the most comprehensive to date, and is the starting-point for our look at agricultural performance. Turner's numbers are summarized in Table 11.1, where columns (1) and (2) report two alternative measures of the growth in output per worker. The implied annual increase in agricultural output per worker over the half-century, about 0.7 per cent, is hardly sensational, but belies stories of stagnation from both land reformers and landlord apologists. Column (3), which divides nominal output per worker by the Statist–Sauerbeck wholesale price index, is an attempt at capturing the ensuing rise in the purchasing power of the rural community. The picture there is of considerable improvement, brought about by a sharp rise in the price of Irish agricultural produce relative to the cost of living. Column (4) highlights the re-

Table 11.1. *Output and productivity in Irish agriculture between the 1850s and the 1910s*

Period	(1)	(2)	(3)	(4)	(5)
1850–4	89.0	92.0	74.3	65	—
1855–66	94.0	91.8	82.3	45	—
1867–76	100.0	100.0	100.0	38	100.0
1877–85	99.0	101.4	117.1	28	99.9
1886–93	102.0	114.0	133.0	26	96.6
1894–03	110.5	129.1	154.8	23	99.7
1904–13	124.7	135.3	177.3	21	90.3

Notes: (1) Real output per head of agricultural labour force
(2) Real output per head of 'farm' population
(3) Nominal output deflated by SSPI
(4) Tillage share in total output
(5) Real GB output per head of agricultural labour force

Source: Turner, 'Agricultural Output and Productivity', 427.

markable change in output mix between the 1850s and the 1910s, a change prompted by shifts in the ratio of livestock to tillage prices and rising labour costs. That change is also captured by the raw agricultural statistics that form the basis for Turner's estimates. Thus the acreage under hay rose by three-quarters between the 1850s and the early 1910s and cattle numbers by a third, while the acreage under grain and potatoes was halved. Column (5), based on Ojala's assessment of British agricultural output trends, lends a comparative perspective. Turner's numbers imply that productivity growth, though far from headlong, was faster in the 1880s and 1890s than in the pre-Land War decades. They also imply little change in output per worker before the 1880s. Again, Turner's estimate of total factor productivity change puts it at −0.3 or −0.4 per cent per annum between the early 1850s and the early 1870s, at 0.2 per cent c.1875–95, and at 0.6 per cent between the early 1890s and the First World War. The trends in labour and total factor productivity in these decades fail to support Solow's 'revisionist' assessment of the period between the Famine and the Land War as one of improvement in Irish agriculture and of the Land War as a costly distraction. However, Vaughan has criticized the output numbers underlying the findings for the 1850s and 1860s, claiming that Turner biased the outcome downwards by placing too high a value on potatoes. Since potatoes were a contracting crop in these decades, using inflated prices understated growth. My own estimates indicate a rise of about one-fifth in labour productivity over roughly the same period, or about 1 per cent per annum, and a similar rate of increase between the 1870s and the 1920s.[12] Either way no dramatic deterioration in the wake of land reform is indicated.

Farm productivity was boosted by a drop in the number of holdings exceeding one acre from 570,338 in 1851 to 485,455 in 1911 (the number of farmers fell by even more), and in the percentage of holdings containing 15 acres and less from 49 to 40. Nor did peasant proprietorship stem the outflow from farming: the number of farm-holdings in Ireland, north and south, fell from 461,164 in 1901 to 395,676 in 1930. The fall in the number of farmers, male and female, was again greater, from 399,387 to 337,939. The chief mechanical innovations included the reaping, mowing, threshing, and potato-spraying machines, and the centrifugal separator. The spread of the creamery system and, in remote areas, smaller separators, boosted productivity in the dairying regions. Dairy farmers were often berated in these years, it is true, for not maintaining milk supplies during the winter months. In Ireland cows typically calved in spring. The alternative of winter calving would not only have guaranteed a winter supply of milk: it would also have boosted overall yields as the fresh spring grasses prompted the cows to produce a 'second spring' of milk. The result was underutilized facilities and the loss of British markets to the Danes when prices were highest. That issue still awaits resolution, but the comparative advantage that the Irish climate gave Irish dairy farmers in opting for spring calving is obviously an important part of the answer. Winter dairying produced higher milk yields, but it also required higher inputs of labour and capital.[13]

Detailed analyses of regions and individual farms have been few. Two studies of farms in the east of the country merit mention here. Vaughan's analysis of the records of grazier Edward Delany implies stasis—at least in so far as output per acre is concerned—on one substantial Meath holding. On Delany's original holding at Woodtown, beef output fluctuated around 230 cwt. annually between 1851 and 1899. However, output per worker probably expanded, since Delany increased his income, not by cultivating more intensively, but by buying up neighbouring farms. Admittedly data on labour outlays are lacking. Delany's accounts, stretching over nearly half a century (1852–99), show that the gross return on animals purchased was highest in the 1850s and 1860s, though movements in his net income cannot be estimated in the absence of rent data.[14] Some further hints of a rise in output per worker over roughly the same period are offered by the

Another Danish Invasion.

ERIN (to Irish Farmer taking his winter nap)—"Wake up, man, and drive these invaders from your door!
If it was the British Government you would be holding meetings of protest all over the country. I suppose
you are waiting for Home Rule to come. If you wait for that day you won't be troubled to make much butter."

["During certain months of the year Irish butter merchants lose the British market altogether—they have no supplies to send.   During the entire
twelve months the Dane, on the other hand, holds the market ; when the Irishman comes forward in the season he is very much in the position of the
man who is trying to capture a new market.   This is a decided disadvantage alike to Irish merchants and producers.   To cope with the Dane on level
terms it is, we submit, absolutely necessary to adopt the method so successfully employed by our most formidable rival, and that is winter dairying."
—*Extract from Leading Article, "The Irish Independent," May 25th, 1910, on the meeting of the Council of Agriculture, which was held at the National
University of Ireland, Earlsfort Terrace, May 25th.   Mr. T. W. Russell, Vice-President of the Department of Agriculture, presided.*]

PLATE I. In the 1890s and 1900s indolent Irish farmers were commonly
accused of ignoring the profits obtainable through winter dairying. In truth, the
small premium offered by creameries for winter milk probably would not have
justified the costly switch from summer dairying (*The Lepracaun*, June 1910)

Barrington farm at Fassaroe, near Bray. The Barringtons, who specialized
in tillage, kept exceptionally detailed accounts, and Richard Barrington
presented a paper largely based on them to the Statistical Society in late
1886. His focus was low output prices and rising labour costs, but his data
also imply that the cost in man-days of cultivating an Irish acre of grain
and green crops moved as shown in Table 11.2.[15] The introduction of
reaping and threshing machinery explains the decline in labour requirements in grain. The implied rise in output per man-day between the 1830s
and the mid-1860s (presumably when the new machinery was being introduced) was 57 per cent for wheat, 25 per cent for oats, and 51 per cent for
barley. The output per man-day of potatoes and turnips, heavily reliant

Table 11.2. *Cost per acre of Irish crops (in man-days), 1837–1885*

Period	Wheat	Oats	Barley	Potatoes	Turnips
1837–46	37.6	33.2	40.1	66.7	43.6
1847–56	33.4	31.0	34.4	54.5	34.9
1857–66	24.0	26.9	26.5	67.4	40.3
1867–76	24.9	23.9	24.4	64.8	43.1
1877–85	22.5	26.8	25.8	63.2	42.3

on manual labour throughout the period, hardly changed, however. The published data are silent on trends in yields per acre, but these may be inferred from the farm accounts. Barrington's presentation to the Statistical Society was prompted by a series of disastrous years at Fassaroe. Profits in 1883–5 had averaged £29 a year, against an average of £555 in 1868–82. Part of the problem was that wheat and barley yields were less than half the norm in 1882; the wheat crop was also poor in 1884 and 1885. Low prices compounded the difficulties.[16] Over the longer run, however, wheat and oats yields rose slightly. Potato yields in the 1870s barely matched pre-Famine levels, but they rose impressively in the 1880s and 1890s.[17]

While Irish agriculture may have done well relative to British, its record was less impressive by broader European standards. In European agriculture, the period under review was one of strong land-saving bias, with innovations such as the mechanical cream-separator and co-operative marketing raising the small farmer's productivity most. The huge drop in cereal prices and the continuing rise in agricultural wages presented obvious challenges, but opportunities too in terms of cheaper inputs and increased demand. Danish farmers are renowned for having capitalized on these changes, but comparative assessments of the record by Geary and by Staehle showed Irish agriculture in a surprisingly favourable light. Both found that between the 1850s and the 1900s the Irish increased labour productivity as fast as the Danes 'whose success in raising their productivity is generally considered as unique'. The finding prompted Geary's surmise that the Irish experience reflected a west European 'norm'. O'Rourke's recent Danish–Irish comparison is less reassuring, but if Britain provides a 'soft' yardstick, perhaps Denmark was at the other extreme? Van Zanden's study of agricultural output and productivity change between 1865–74 and 1905–13 in fifteen European economies provides an answer. It confirms Ireland's performance relative to Britain's, but also shows that Irish aggregate output per hectare

was low and output per head modest by European standards both in the
1860s and the 1910s, and that the growth rate in output per head was less
than average. However, a more realistic estimate of the decline in the
agricultural labour force tempers this (implicitly) harsh assessment of Irish
agriculture. Assuming a decline of 25 to 30 per cent for 1870–1911
instead of van Zanden's 19.5 per cent would push Ireland up to the middle
of the league table (Table 11.3).[18]

A final point about land tenure concerns farmers as borrowers. On
balance, Irish farmers were creditors rather than debtors to the banks. Yet
individual farmers required loans from time to time to tide them over a
period of low prices, buy machinery and land, engage in building and
drainage schemes, and so on. Bank lending to farmers in these decades
consisted largely of short-maturity bills. As the Munster Bank's chairman
explained to shareholders in the 1870s:

He could take him (i.e. any shareholder) any day he pleased to a country Branch and
show him a sheaf of bills it would take him some time to count and those bills would
be for sums ranging from £10 to £50 or £60 and up to £100 and a great many of these
bills had the drawers' marks on them for in many instances they could not sign their
names. But they were all farmers. It was a usual thing, to have lots of these bills
unpaid when due.

Such loans helped farmers cope with the seasonality of farm income/
expenditure and gave them greater discretion over the timing of their sales.
However, an alleged drawback of the Irish landlord–tenant system was
that as long as landlords held title to the land, banks were reluctant to
extend larger sums to farmers using land as collateral. Given the obvious
appeal of land as security, and since in Ireland tenants rather than landlords

Table 11.3. *Productivity growth rates in European
agriculture*, c.1870–1914 (% p.a.)

Country	Production per head	Production per hectare	Total productivity
Denmark	1.37	1.62	1.31
Britain	0.46	0.01	0.19
Germany	1.58	1.72	1.53
Ireland	0.69	0.14	0.36
Europe	0.57	0.90	0.65

Source: Van Zanden, 'The First Green Revolution', 229.

carried out the lion's share of farm investment, the point seems well taken. Before peasant proprietorship it is asserted that banks did not refuse farmers money; they provided loans such as those described above on the personal security of a few neighbours, and the sums involved were typically small. Should the switch to owner-occupancy not have provided a remedy? Not in the short run, perhaps, since the effect of land purchase was that most farmers were already heavily in debt to the Irish Land Commission, though on concessional terms. But even in the case of farmers with unencumbered title, it has often been argued[19] that the shift to peasant proprietorship failed to produce an improvement on the credit front. Why? In part because participation in forced land sales could make trouble for creditors. As a Longford witness put it to an inquiry into agricultural credit in 1914:[20]

I consider the difficulty which banks, or other persons taking mortgages, have on a forced realisation of their security, make it practically impossible to borrow a sixpence on land security . . . the timidity of the people, in the existing condition of things, about interfering in a forced sale, naturally prevents banks or others from advancing money, and thereby supplying capital for the reasonable and proper development of agricultural business.

As a consequence, it is said, the banks continued to insist on the cumbersome system of personal securities. The irony was that before farmers 'could fully enjoy the implications of landownership, they had to learn to view land as something that could be bought, sold, or seized, like any other commodity'. As long as they refused to recognize the rights of creditors, they remained more dependent than was good for them on butter-merchants and small-town gombeenmen (see below), paying unnecessarily high rates for advances. The official banking inquiries of 1926 and 1938 both returned to this point.[21]

Surviving bank records suggest that the point has been somewhat over-argued. They show that even before the land legislation banks often lent substantial sums to farmers on the security of leases, assignments, life policies, copies of wills, or even deeds of marriage settlement. After the Wyndham Act of 1903, which cemented the move towards owner-occupancy, land certificates issued by the Land Commission were often used as security. Some of the titles held as security were distinctly shaky from a legal standpoint. Nevertheless, while it is true that banks rarely proceeded to dispossess farmer-debtors, holding on to leases and certificates at least made it cumbersome for such clients to sell or otherwise legally dispose of their property without paying some or all of their bills out of the proceeds.[22] The argument is analogous to that made about tenant right in Chapter 5.

Aggregate data on bank lending to farmers are lacking before the 1930s. At the end of 1935 advances to people whose main income derived from farming totalled £13.8 million. That sum was spread over 125,000 borrowers, or nearly half the total number of farmers. Less than 6,000 loans were considered irrecoverable, though the average bad loan greatly exceeded the average size of all loans (£110). The farm population as a whole, with combined deposits (excluding current accounts) worth £36 million, continued to be a substantial creditor to the banking system.[23] In the end, if some contemporaries criticized the banks for being over-cautious, others believed that indebtedness was a baneful byproduct of owner-occupancy.

The winners in the social revolution of 1879–1903 were the farmers, not the farm labourers. The wealthier farmers, best informed and with most to gain from peasant proprietorship, played a prominent part in the struggle. This explains why, when several of his best-off tenants refused to pay their rents in full in 1880, Cork landlord William Bence Jones noted that 'it was easy to guess who were readers of newspapers'. Unlike their Continental counterparts, Irish agricultural labourers won no concessions in terms of land in the wake of the Land War, though this is hardly the full explanation for their virtual demise. The very titles of two recent studies, 'The Agricultural Labourer: A Marginal Figure' and 'The Disappearance of the Irish Agricultural Labourer'[24] tell their own story. As predicted by Michael Davitt, the outcome of the Land War traded one form of inequality for another, and gave rise to new social tensions. These tensions found parallels elsewhere in Europe at this stage. In Ireland they lay behind the creation of the Congested Districts Board and the Land Commission, but their ultimate resolution brought the landless and the western smallholder little joy. A less restrictive franchise before 1917 would have favoured the smallholder and farm labourer: in Denmark it gave the *husman* considerable political clout. The socio-economic composition of the votes that produced the Irish parliamentary party was hardly pro-labour, however; it closely anticipated that which would later produce Cumann na nGaedheal and Fine Gael. The Irish Labour Party, on the other hand, originally owed much to support from farm labourers.[25]

11.2 Commercialization

In the 'forties and 'fifties men and women wore homespun that defied time and weather, wove their own linen from home-grown flax, grew

wheat, barley, rye, and ate it or fed it to the beasts, did more
spadework in one season that they did now in ten. No slops of tea for
them, no sour bread from Belfast sent down in hampers, no yellow
meal and prairie-fed bacon from the States.

SHAN BULLOCK, *After Sixty Years* (1931)

The increasing commercialization of the economy, here lamented by
Fermanagh-born Shan Bullock, deserves separate treatment. As explained
in Chapter 2 pre-Famine Ireland did not lack markets and traders, though
most of them were strictly small-scale. Traders camped on the fair-green
and on the streets outnumbered those with capital invested in shops and
warehouses. In 1841 the thirty-two counties contained almost 27,000
'huxters' and 'dealers', besides the 18,000 shopkeepers and shop assistants
who operated from fixed establishments. Dublin's Moore Street and Thomas
Street and Cork's Coal Quay are remnants of an era when, even in Dublin
and Belfast, the informal traders dominated; butchers too tended to operate
outdoors for public health reasons. The city of Cork contained, besides 188
merchants (all men), 97 grocers (including 18 women), 346 shopkeepers
(212 women) and their 177 shop assistants (92 women). Women dominated
the street-trading 'huxters and provision dealers' (417 women out of a total
494), and 'dealers' (453 out of 578), who constituted the majority of Cork
traders. Most towns also contained their artisan-traders: tailors, bootmakers, bakers, dressmakers, and so on. Thackeray's account of the lower
end of the retail market in pre-Famine Limerick bears quite a resemblance
to that of Third World countries today:[26]

To return to the apple-woman: legions of ladies were employed through the town upon
that traffic; there were really thousands of them, clustering upon the bridges, squatting
down in doorways and vacant sheds for temporary markets, marching and crying their
sour goods in all the crowded lanes of the city. After you get out of the Main Street the
handsome part of the town is at an end, and you suddenly find yourself in such a
labyrinth of busy swarming poverty and squalid commerce as never was seen—no, not
in St Giles's, where Jew and Irishman side by side exhibit their genius for dirt. Here
every house almost was a half ruin, and swarming with people: in the cellars you
looked down and saw a barrel of herrings, which a merchant was dispensing; or a sack
of meal, which a poor dirty woman sold to people poorer and dirtier than herself: above
was a tinsman, or a shoemaker, or other craftsman, his battered ensign at the door, and
his small wares peering though the cracked panes of his shop.

Seventy years later, the picture had altered considerably. The proportion
of the population living in towns of 1,500 or more rose from about one-
sixth in 1845 to one-third in 1914 and, almost by definition, increasing
urbanization brought greater commercialization. Kennedy has noted that

the number of innkeepers, publicans, and grocers per thousand population rose from 4.5 in 1881 to 5.7 in 1911. Alternatively, the number of shopkeepers and dealers per thousand population rose from 5.3 in 1871 to 7.5 in 1911. Indeed, some have gone so far as to criticize the increase in commerce as excessive.[27] The massive increase in bank deposits—from about £8 million in 1850 to £43 million in 1900—also bespoke increasing commercialization. So did the rise in rail traffic; between 1849 and 1912 revenue from freight rose from £175,000 to £2.1 million, while passenger numbers quintupled. Freight tonnage doubled between the early 1870s and the early 1910s.[28]

Modern retailing ranges from the department store that sells virtually everything to the small, highly specialized establishment. Little shops in Brussels and Paris sell nothing but mushrooms of various sizes and shapes. In Venice others specialize in making and selling carnival masks. Dublin has its specialist coin-shop and its Celtic bookseller. Such specialization requires a modicum of prosperity; the artisan-traders and meal-mongers of pre-Famine Ireland catered for more frugal tastes. Gradually they gave way before a flood of factory-produced clothes, shoes, and bread. In the bigger towns most of the peripatetic dealers gave way to the pub-grocery, and stores carrying a narrow range of products ceded business to 'monster shops' or department stores such as Clerys and Arnotts. In smaller towns and villages, the process followed a familiar pattern. In mid-century, poverty and self-sufficiency kept the range of items regularly bought and sold in small-town shops narrow. As living standards improved, the range might increase for a time, though it would tend to contract eventually as the general stores gave way to more specialist traders. Thus in nineteenth-century rural Ireland the archetypal retailer was the grocer-publican, who combined general shopkeeping with the tasks of dispensing drink, moneylending, and the purchase and sale of farm produce such as eggs. But such traders too were victims of the process described here. One consequence was the splitting up of the trades of publican and shopkeeper.

Analysis of the surviving ledgers and daybooks (itemizing all charge transactions in chronological order) of traders helps illustrate the pattern outlined. Here, I report on a few case-studies. The first refers to sales in a general store in the east Mayo village of Kilkelly between January and May 1880. Six items—sugar, tea, tobacco, flour, Indian meal, and whiskey—dominated the store's daybook in that difficult period. The listed items accounted for nearly three-quarters of all transactions, with fertilizer and seed, oatmeal, bread, and bran accounting for most of the rest. Other items to feature from time to time included lamp oil, biscuits, candles, cakes, and fortified wine. Tea was usually sold by the ounce, costing 3*d*. or 3.5*d*. In this five-month period coffee is mentioned 17 times, soap 13 times, beer 38 times, and so on. Items represented once included a quilt, a pair of trousers, a scarf, a dose of Epsom salts, a piece of rope, vinegar, flannel, and a crucifix. Eggs, turf, and labour (at the low rate of 9*d*. a day) were accepted in lieu of cash for purchases, and amounts of cash (typically small) often lent. Flour sales greatly outnumbered those of bread, and no sales of potatoes or milk were recorded. The sales of meal and flour, as well as those of seed and fertilizer, were proportionately much more important in April–May 1880 than in the previous three months, presumably a reflection of the very poor 1879 potato harvest (see Chapter 10). Butter featured only once and bacon only twice over the five months. Thirty-seven years later, in early 1917, the five items dominating in 1880 accounted for less than one-fifth of all transactions, and the shop was supplying a variety of hardware goods, animal feed, clothing and fabrics (worsted, sateen, velveteen, plaid, linenette), as well as quantities of bacon and jam, and brand name goods such as Jeyes Fluid and Clarendo.

The second shop is in Urlingford, a Kilkenny village on the main Dublin–Cork road. Its surviving records go back to 1870. In early 1870 spirits, tea, sugar, tobacco, candles, and soap accounted for well over half of this shop's transactions. Other items to feature included ale and porter, sherry, biscuits, coffee, thread, leather, lamp oil, starch, penknives, note-paper, and even lemons and arsenic. Sales of items such as nails, latches, locks, timber, iron, and steel provided a clue to the shop's future as a hardware specialist. Yet four decades later drink still accounted for one-fifth of transactions (with stout and Bass ale now complementing whiskey), and specifically hardware items for only about one-third.[29] The daybooks of a pub-grocery in Coagh, County Tyrone, reveal the same broad pattern. The range of items bought in 1870 reflected a spartan lifestyle, but by 1914 Irish bacon, polish, tins of salmon, margarine, and currants were common purchases.[30] Our final example is Morrissey's famous establishment in Abbeyleix, not far from Urlingford. Early in this century Morrissey's was the leading supplier to the local landed gentry, and this is reflected in a price-list issued in 1908. The listed items included several varieties of curry paste and powder, figs, caviar, saffron, pistachio kernels, chow-chow preserve, and housemaids' gloves and gauntlets. But the earliest surviving daybook, that for 1918–19, again indicates the dominance of staples such as bread, tea, sugar, butter, and soap: they together accounted for over half the items charged. Also featuring prominently were oil, matches, candles, and flour.

Another consequence—or corollary—of greater commercialization was greater regional specialization in economic activity. The dealers, shops, and mail traders who displayed and encouraged the purchase of imported wares played their part in the decline of native Irish industries. The effects are also to be seen in the agricultural statistics. Cheaper transport and better market outlets meant that agricultural output was bound to vary more from region to region. Specialization should lead to an increase in the inter-county variation in output mix. And, indeed, the coefficients of variation across counties for the acreage under cereals rose from 0.53 in 1850–5 to 0.71 in 1905–10; that for cattle numbers rose from 0.47 to 0.77 over the same period. Within the cattle industry, the specialization patterns outlined in Chapter 2 intensified. For example, the ratio of cows to other cattle aged over one year in 1927 in Meath, Ireland's premier grazing county, fell from 0.20 in 1854 to 0.08 in 1911 and 0.11 in 1926.[31]

In common with other classical economists, Adam Smith believed that the forces being described here would produce a reduction in the rate of return on capital. Smith's prognosis, unlike those of Ricardo and Marx, was not predicated on technological change: the falling rate of profit followed from the greater competition that accompanied the widening of markets. The ensuing commercialization, he argued, would also lower interest rates.[32] Post-Famine Ireland would seem to fit Smith's model. Describing conditions in the west of Ireland soon after the Famine, journalist Henry Coulter repeatedly lamented the exploitation of 'usurers' and 'harpies' who charged the poor interest rates equivalent to 50–100 per cent per annum. The money, Coulter argued, was advanced virtually risk-free, since the canny moneylender 'always takes care to have two or three names on the IOU'.[33]

Perhaps Coulter exaggerated the rates charged by such moneylenders, but his account of the early 1860s bears comparison with Kennedy's analysis of inquiries made thirty years later. Kennedy's estimate of the interest charged by the typical small-town shopkeeper is based on the Congested Districts Board's *Baseline Reports*. These reports were confidential local surveys of conditions in the west of Ireland in the 1890s; they contain a good deal of information on budgets, employment conditions, and living standards. Kennedy's analysis of the gap between the cash and credit price charged by the shopkeepers in the congested districts implies a modal interest charge of 10–15 per cent per annum. Even given that the cost of administering the loans was low, the charge seems modest. One catch is that it fails to take account of the likelihood that in discharging their debts in farm produce such as eggs or butter, borrowers were under the added disadvantage of having to sell to the same trader. Besides, since the evidence also suggests that the premia charged by the local trader (or gombeenman) were not justified by greater risk, some degree of extortion seems likely in the remoter areas. The effective rate was certainly a good deal higher than the nominal rate charged by the commercial banks. On the other hand, the local trader had the double advantage of being accessible and being in a better position to recognize the prospective borrower's credit rating.[34]

One of the aims of the founders of the Irish Agricultural Organisation Society (IAOS), Ireland's rural co-operative movement, was to reduce the power of the small-town trader. Shopkeeper-publicans and butter-merchants detested the IAOS, though co-operative activists probably had an exaggerated notion of the gombeenman's power to exploit. This is indicated by the fate of their co-operative banks, which had been set up in the 1890s and 1900s in the west as antidotes to the gombeenman. The 5 per cent rate that they charged was not viable: most of the banks failed after the IAOS lost its government subsidy following a political wrangle in 1907.[35]

The *Baseline Reports* also indicate that the influence of the local trader-usurer was on the wane in the 1890s. The following report from the Rosses area in west Donegal is instructive:[36]

Credit dealing was almost universal some few years ago, but now, as far as I can judge, half of the purchases of the district are cash transactions, and both buyers and sellers are glad of the change. May, June, and July are the months in which credit is most largely given in ordinary years, but in a year in which the potato crop is bad, or in seasons when the rate of wages for migratory labourers is low, credit is sought for much earlier, often as early as January. There are different prices for cash and credit dealings, but interest for delay of payments in credit transactions is not charged—for instance, supposing that twelve shillings per bag is the cash price per meal, the credit price would be 13s. 6d., payable in the following November, when most of the migratory labourers return home. . . . Eggs are nearly always exchanged at market prices for tea, sugar, or tobacco, and, as shopkeepers make a much larger profit on tea than on other commodities, they naturally prefer to give tea rather than any other commodity in exchange for eggs.

In the Glenties area, where 2s. (10p) per six months on a bag worth 15s. (75p) was general in the 1890s, the CDB's inspector was told that 5s. (25p) and 7s. 6d. (38p) a bag had been charged formerly, 'but competition has reduced that exorbitant rate'. Shopkeepers who had been in the habit of imposing hefty interest charges on anything sold on credit, were gradually forced to give free, or almost free, credit with no questions asked, to counter the threat of competition from increasingly accessible shops in the bigger towns and cities, and from mail-order firms further afield. By the 1920s most such shopkeepers would have preferred cash dealings, but credit facilities (and long hours) kept them some of their customers.[37] In the cities and larger towns, in Ireland as elsewhere, there was a protracted struggle between specialized retail outlets and all-purpose department stores. Innovations introduced by the latter included half-made or ready-made clothes and piece goods, marked prices instead of haggling, money-back guarantees for dissatisfied customers, opportunities for potential customers to browse, and periodical 'sales'. The 'monster' shops which drew the fire of Dublin's traditional traders in the early 1850s were in effect half-way houses between the specialist and the department store. Though hardly a match for pioneers such as Boucicaut's *Le Bon Marché* (1852) or Bainbridge's of Newcastle (1841), they offered lower prices and greater variety to cash customers. Dublin's first of these 'leviathan houses of trade' opened for business in the 1820s; by mid-century it had several. McSwiney and Delany's New Palatial Mart, precursor of Clery's, opened its doors in 1853.[38]

11.3 Integration and Convergence?

Allied to the commercialization and specialization described above was the increasingly open character of the Irish economy in the nineteenth century. Massive overseas emigration (1 to 2 per cent of total population annually) and capital movements (annual transfers between Ireland and England worth about 2 per cent of Irish national income) are two well-known aspects of this. Irish interest rate movements followed British, and (as we shall see in Chapter 13) British entrepreneurs chased after Irish profits. The share of commodity trade in Irish national income also grew. Merchandise exports in the mid-1830s were worth perhaps £12–13 million annually, or less than one-fifth of national output.[39] By 1913 the ratio of exports to national income was half or more, very high by international standards.

Traditional neoclassical trade theory predicts that international commodity flows will bring commodity prices closer, and that commodity price equalization will cause factor prices to converge. The implied presumption that economic integration would cause income differentials to narrow and poorer economies to 'catch up' has been the focus of a good deal of research in the last decade, not least by economic historians. Theory offers other scenarios too, however. The presence of scale economies and imperfect competition may delay or even prevent economic integration between strong and weak economies from yielding convergence or catch-up.[40] Did the closer links between the Irish and British economies narrow the gap in Irish and British living standards in the nineteenth century? The record is mixed. Retardation rather than convergence would seem a more accurate characterization of pre-Famine Ireland—along, indeed, with other parts of Europe's periphery. Trade liberalization and transport improvements after 1800 gave the expected fillip to the volume and range of goods exchanged, but signs of a convergence in wages and living standards are hard to find. In Britain, economic historians still debate the dimensions of the real wage increase after 1800 or 1815, but in Ireland real wages seem to have barely held their own. Similarly, as noted in Chapter 5, the Anglo-Irish gap in land rents failed to narrow in the pre-Famine era. Again, the rate of emigration was impressive by European standards in the pre-Famine decades, but the outflow was greatest where the 'need' for it was least. Both before and during the Great Famine, the landless poor were less likely to emigrate than those with even limited capital, and better-off counties supplied a disproportionate share of those leaving. The result was probably increasing inequality in regional incomes. This botched adjustment prompts the wistful speculation that had factor markets behaved in textbook fashion in these years, i.e. had they been more competitive and more quickly and fully integrated, the Irish would have been spared the worst of the Great Famine. The necessary equilibrating process was just taking too long—as Keynes, in a grimly appropriate quip, predicted that it sometimes would. All this presupposes competitive markets. If manufacturing was subject to scale economies and concentration, then the presumption in favour of convergence is weaker. Growing economic integration might merely mean the shift of manufacturing industry from 'small' to 'large' economies, leaving the 'small' economies to specialize in farming and non-tradables:

Where good agrarian alternatives existed which would become relatively more profitable on the basis of comparative advantages arising from stronger industrialization elsewhere, a reversal to agriculture, or de-industrialization of a positive kind, was likely. The tendency was reinforced if the initial rural industry had been relatively weak and dispersed and without a strong export market. The de-industrialization of parts of Bavaria and Central Germany, Eastern Westphalia, Lower Normandy, Brittany, and Languedoc might be explained in this way. Behind it was ultimately the effective competition from more advanced regions, which in c.1815–30 meant generally Great Britain.[41]

Much of Ireland might have also been included in the list. If external economies are absent in farming, the gap between 'small' and 'large' economies might even widen. In such cases migration from the 'small' economy may be necessary to promote convergence—if workers can afford, or are allowed, to leave. This kind of model would seem to help explain why pre-Famine Ireland failed to converge.

The history of the post-Famine era provides stronger support for the convergence hypothesis. Across most of the globe, this was a period of unprecedented trade liberalization, factor movements, and transport innovation, and economic historians have detected strong signs of commodity and factor-price convergence. Ireland was very much part of the process. Prices on Mark Lane and in Smithfield, relayed by telegraph, dominated agricultural markets all over Ireland, and farm output reflected market signals with the necessary lags. As noted in Chapter 9, county emigration rates now worked in the required direction, producing an exodus from the poorer counties. Short-term fluctuations in the migration rate and the destinations of migrants were extremely sensitive to labour-market conditions abroad. Within Ireland, the regional variation in living standards narrowed, and living conditions improved relative to Britain after the Famine, though slowly. Irish income per capita rose from about two-fifths to somewhat less than three-fifths of British between 1845 and 1914. (It still had reached only two-thirds by the 1980s.) As shown in Chapter 10, Irish wages also rose relative to British. On the eve of the First World War, British industrial workers still had an edge (Table 10.2), but the British lead was much smaller for skilled work (8 per cent) than for unskilled work, male or female (about 36 and 45 per cent, respectively.)

There are signs that the wage-gap for most kinds of factory work had disappeared altogether by the 1920s, though farm labourers—admittedly a diminishing band—were still paid far less in Ireland (see Chapter 17). However, it is important to remember that it took more than commodity and factor movements between the two islands to achieve even this partial convergence. Had the safety-valve of emigration to America and other distant destinations not been available, the gap between Irish and British living standards would have been even greater in the 1910s or 1920s.

12

Industry, c.1780–1914:
An Overview

Before this generation dies, it must have made Ireland's rivers navigable
and its hundred harbours secure with beacon and pier, and thronged
with seamen educated in naval schools, and familiar with every rig and
every ocean. Arigna must be pierced with shafts, and Bonmahon
flaming with smelting-houses. Our bogs must have become turf
factories ... Our coal must move a thousand engines, our rivers a
thousand wheels.

THOMAS DAVIS, *c.*1845

Out of 177 Irish weeklies there are only 6, it is said, which use Irish
paper. If one buys picture-postcards in Dublin one finds printed on
them, 'Designed in England and printed in Prussia'.

L. PAUL-DUBOIS, 1911

12.1 Introduction

The common perception of nineteenth-century Ireland is of an economy
overwhelmingly dominated by agriculture. This squares poorly with the
census of 1821, where over two-fifths of Irishmen and Irishwomen declaring an occupation were 'chiefly employed in trades, manufactures, or
handicraft'. Nor was non-agricultural employment confined to the north-
east. The provincial percentages ranged from 55 in Ulster and 43 in
Connacht to 33 in Leinster and 24 in Munster. The predominance of
industrial occupations in east Ulster, which was experiencing its own
industrial revolution at the time, comes as no surprise. The percentages
'chiefly employed in trades, manufactures, or handicraft' in the baronies of
O'Neilland East (76) and West (72) in County Armagh, Iveagh Lower (63)
and Mourne (62) in County Down, and Dungannon (63) in County Tyrone
speak for themselves. However, 'trades, manufactures, or handicraft' also
accounted for over half of all recorded employment in several baronies in
the south and west of the province, particularly in Donegal. The same held

for several rural baronies in north Connacht. In the 'Yeats Country' half-barony of Carbery Lower the percentage was 51; in the barony of Leitrim (in the county of the same name) it was 54. In the remote Mayo barony of Burrishoole, the percentage reached 57, yet Burrishoole contained only one town of any note, Newport-Pratt, with a thousand people. The implied importance of non-agricultural occupations in such largely rural areas was due mainly to the textile sector.

In Burrishoole, Carbery Lower, and places like them, industrial employment was a sign of both land hunger and commercialization. In Tyrone such pressures had forced small farmers to sit down at night to weave a couple of yards of cloth in order to make ends meet. Describing an earlier era, Charles O'Hara's survey of Sligo explained how farmers' wives and daughters had taken up spinning when graziers began to bid up land-rents. Such responses in turn encouraged landlords to grant leases to weavers and factors to 'scavenge' the countryside for linen.[1] Across the whole island, the spatial spread of cottage industry is not so easily explained, though (as in other parts of Europe in this period) it seems to have been inversely associated with land quality. Cottage industry was more likely to be found where the soil was poor. The specialization thus reflected the law of comparative advantage.

Besides such rural proto-industry, in the late eighteenth century Irish cities and towns contained hundreds of factories and workshops, embodying traditional and modern technologies. As explained below, the new inventions of the Industrial Revolution caught on quickly in Ireland. In addition, more traditional industries such as glass- and paper-making, the production of woollens and silks, printing, coopering, sugar-refining, milling, tanning, brewing, and distilling were important, though they catered largely for local markets. Many of them faced decline in the following century or so. This chapter outlines the history of some of these industries; the following chapter considers the advantages and disadvantages of Ireland as an industrial location.

12.2 Cotton

Cotton had been produced in a small way in Ireland since the 1750s, encouraged by a government bounty on mixed fabrics. The new Arkwright spinning technology caught on quickly. The famous experiment with spinning-jennies in the Belfast workhouse in 1778–9 was followed by a rash of other concerns in the early 1780s, both north and south. Ireland's precocity here is worth stressing: France had its first modern spinning-mill by 1778, but the USA, Russia, Switzerland, and the Low Countries had to wait until the 1790s.[2] And although Belfast's cotton mills are well known for having temporarily almost wiped out that city's linen industry, the impact of the new technology was apparently even greater in the south at first.

Robert Brooke's venture into mechanized cotton-spinning at Prosperous in County Kildare in 1780 'suddenly raised an obscure and scanty trade into a great national manufacture'. Others quickly followed Brooke's lead, and substantial spinning-mills were set up in Dublin's Liberties, and at Balbriggan and Malahide. Weaving-factories sprang up too, particularly in the Liberties. However, the early growth of the industry in the Dublin area was of the hothouse variety, marked by inexperience, incompetence, and failure. That Brooke was no businessman is indicated by his choice for a factory on a virgin site in the middle of a bog twenty miles from Dublin. Nevertheless, in an era of lax public accountability, he obtained vast subsidies from the public purse for a time. When his request for further support was refused in 1786, his project collapsed. Cotton production in Balbriggan and Malahide did not survive long either. The Balbriggan works switched to flour-milling, and Lord Talbot's planned cotton village at Malahide became a bathing-resort. In Cork—where the new technology had made great strides in the 1780s and 1790s—the two great cotton concerns, Sadleirs' and Deaves', failed in 1801; the first of these, founded in Glasheen in 1781, had been the biggest in the country at its peak. These failures did not mark the end of the cotton industry in the South, however. Several other landed proprietors tried their luck, and by 1802 there was enough yarn to occupy 7,500 looms in Leinster and another 3,000 in Munster. A year or so after the collapse of cotton-spinning in Cork city, George Allman opened a massive mill in nearby Bandon. This provided the yarn for a corduroy industry that employed about 2,000 weavers for almost three decades. Allman was forced out of business in the mid-1820s, and when no buyer could be had for his massive building, it was gutted and its spinning-machinery sold for scrap. During the Great Famine, the former mill was used as an auxiliary workhouse.[3]

Sadleirs' belief that 'cotton seems the best adapted system to this part of the kingdom of any ever attempted in it' was predicated on a home market protected by tariffs and high transport costs. By contrast, the success of the Allman enterprise in Bandon, albeit temporary, stemmed from its specialization in coarse cloth directed at both home and foreign markets. The

productivity growth of the English cotton industry and the gradual elimination of protective tariffs proved too much, however, and by 1830 there
was little left of the southern industry.[4]

In the Belfast region, despite less auspicious beginnings in the Belfast
workhouse, the cotton industry progressed much more rapidly. By 1811,
according to Dubourdieu, 15 steam-powered, 12 water-powered, and 6
horse- or hand-powered mills had been constructed in Belfast. The 150,000
spindles working in the city and its hinterland produced enough yarn to
employ 2,000 spinners and 11,000 weavers. The progress of cotton was
partly at the expense of linen, which was slower to mechanize. The growth
of the Irish cotton industry may be gauged from the trend in raw cotton
and yarn imports (Table 12.1). Comparison with British raw cotton consumption suggests that Irish cotton output was about 5 to 7 per cent of
British c.1790 in volume terms and 4 per cent three decades later; since the
average quality of British output was higher, a value comparison would
increase the British advantage. Comparison with Belgium provides another

Table 12.1. *Imports of raw cotton wool and cotton
yarn, 1780s–1820s* (3-year average, in cwt.)

| Period | Belfast, Cork, Dublin | | National |
	Wool	Yarn	Total (Yarn + Wool)
1781–3	3 981	41	4 384
1784–6	6 920	144	7 329
1787–9	11 680	454	12 599
1790–2	14 823	1 923	17 591
1793–6	11 267	2 663	14 833
1796–8	9 226	3 680	13 653
1799–1801	13 226	5 275	19 333
1802–4	14 372	8 240	25 514
1805–7	21 862	8 011	31 680
1808–10	39 038	8 304	48 283
1811–13	33 114	9 296	46 675
1814–16	20 395	5 592	27 777
1817–19	25 778	10 564	37 820
1820–2	33 318	14 874	49 934

Source: Dickson, 'Aspects', 105, 108.

bench-mark: as late as 1810 the Irish cotton industry was producing twice as much as its vaunted Flemish counterpart.[5]

Thus a series of huge Irish cotton works—those of Brooke in Prosperous, John Orr at Stratford-on-Slaney (county Wicklow), and the Sadleir brothers in Cork, being most spectacular—were successful for a time. The Stratford mill had cost £40,000 to build: in 1809 it had an imported labour force of 500, engaged in weaving imported yarn, printing, and finishing.[6] Irish precocity is also evident in the statistics of failure: bankruptcies in cotton were an annual event from the mid-1780s on, as they were in Britain. The failures are also pointers to the southern interest in cotton, with southern firms accounting for the bulk of failures well into the 1800s.[7]

Despite the failures, Irish cotton production continued to rise in volume (though not in value) until the 1820s. Its southern branch was largely founded on coarse cottons and printing, the northern on finer cloth and bleaching. In the south of Ireland decline set in around 1810, and produced severe hardship for workers not easily absorbed elsewhere. An 1834 petition on behalf of Dublin's remaining 500 handloom weavers claimed that there had been 9,000 cotton weavers working in 'factories' in the city and immediate hinterland in 1800. Their long list of failed entrepreneurs included Samuel Jackson of Bride Street (with 400 looms), bankrupted in 1826 and 'now very poor'; Quaker Thomas Barrington of Cork Street (100), who had failed in 1814 and was 'lately seen drawing an ass with cows' milk on it in New York'; James Greenham, also of Cork Street (700), who had failed in 1814 for £42,000 and twelve years later for another £15,000; Edward Clarke (1200), who had built a factory village outside the city at Palmerstown, had gone bankrupt around 1810, and died 'in despondency'; William Cotton of Francis Street (450), who had sunk his profits in land and retired in the early 1820s. Bridget Maguire of Ardee Street (350), also evidently knew when to bail out, dying a wealthy woman in 1821. The weavers placed all the blame on tariff reduction.[8] In the north the industry was hard hit by the commercial crisis of 1826. Yet the notion that cotton production in Belfast was about to collapse just when, luckily, the wet spinning process arrived on the scene has been vigorously contested by Frank Geary. Geary's scrutiny of surviving archival material from the late 1820s (notably the letter-books of James Boomer & Company) convinced him that Belfast's cotton mills were still quite competitive in the 1820s, and indeed continuing to increase their output and develop new markets outside the UK. Wet spinning gave Belfast a comparative advantage in flax, however. Accordingly, though existing cotton-mills comfortably covered their variable costs and took their time to decide about shifting to flax, new investment concentrated on linen. In the 1830s, while Boomer continued to produce both linen and cotton, over twenty other mills in the Belfast region converted from cotton to flax.[9] By the 1840s the Irish cotton industry still employed a few thousand mill and factory hands and a few thousand indigent handloom weavers. The former included the employees of Malcolmsons of Portlaw (see below).[10] By century's end, Belfast had only one cotton-mill left, the Springfield Spinning Company. That mill had survived by producing 'the finest thread that could be procured from any place'.[11]

The demise of the Irish cotton industry need not be blamed on under-capitalization or technological conservatism. Irish mills, it is true, clung to water as their main energy source, but that was not necessarily a sign of backwardness (any more than using water as a source of electricity in Norway is today).[12] The most plausible explanation for decline is also simple. Though the survival of small mills in Lancashire into the 1840s and later suggests that cotton yarn and cloth were not subject to marked economies of large-scale production, there is no doubting the presence of agglomeration economies at industry level (see Chapter 13). These gave producers for the 'large' British market a competitive advantage over producers for the 'small' Irish market. In addition, the increased economic integration that followed trade liberalization and improvements in transport was bound to take its toll of those Irish producers who relied largely on domestic consumers. Tariffs and the risk and uncertainty attending sailing vessels had effectively insulated the Irish market for cotton for a few decades, but with steam navigation delivery time could be calculated 'onto an hour'.[13] For Belfast producers, the story is less straightforward; they exported a considerable proportion of their output, and Geary has argued that they benefitted from the external economies normally associated with Lancashire. If so, the industry would have survived longer but for the prospect of greater success in linen.

12.3 The Malcolmson Enterprise

The survival and prosperity of the famous cotton mill founded by David Malcolmson at Portlaw, County Waterford, in 1826 for half a century or so is awkward for generalizations about the decline of the cotton industry and Irish deindustrialization generally. The Malcolmsons were a Quaker family who, in the course of the nineteenth century, built up a multinational, multifaceted business. David Malcolmson was born in Lurgan in 1765, and migrated south to Clonmel around 1785 to manage a Quaker-owned flour mill. He soon became a prosperous miller in his own right, and by the 1820s the Malcolmson mill, reputedly the finest in Ireland, processed half the corn harvest of Tipperary and adjacent counties.[14] David Malcolmson was also the guiding genius behind the family-financed vertically-integrated venture at Portlaw. The Portlaw firm was born in 1825 out of a fear that a relaxation of the Corn Laws would damage the family grain business in Tipperary and Waterford. The advice of fellow-Quaker James Cropper transformed that fear into a concrete plan to convert a derelict site on the river Clodiagh into a modern spinning-mill.[15] By the early 1830s the mill's only surviving accounts show it selling over £18,000 worth of cotton annually.[16] For several decades the firm prospered. The Malcolmsons imported bales of raw cotton and exported the finished product in their own steamships; in the mid-1840s the business at Portlaw involved sixty trips a year by seagoing vessels of 100–150 tons and one hundred and fifty by open boats of 30–40 tons. The plant was an impressive one by the standards of the day:[17]

Some idea may be formed of the extent of this factory, from a reservoir on the roof, 260 feet in length by 40 feet in width, from which water in the event of fire can be discharged to extinguish it. The machinery is driven by three large water-wheels, aided by three powerful steam-engines, whose united force is equal to 300 horses.

By the mid-1850s the workforce at Portlaw was spinning over two million pounds of raw cotton and producing six million yards of calico annually. Portlaw then contained one-sixth of the spindles, nearly two-fifths of the horsepower, one-half of the labour, and over one-half of the looms employed in the entire Irish cotton industry. David Malcolmson built a foundry on the site, and kept a benevolent but despotic eye over the workforce, most of whom lived in the purpose-built village of Portlaw. Portlaw had 3,647 inhabitants in 1841; the population of Clonegam parish (which included Portlaw) rose from 1,186 in 1821 to 4,759 in 1841. The trends were as shown in Table 12.2 between 1841 and 1881. At its peak in the 1850s Malcolmsons' mill employed over 1,600 workers, more than half of them female, and their single firm was apparently importing more raw cotton than the entire Irish industry had done in the 1800s.

The closure of the mill at Portlaw was bound up with the failure of a much larger family enterprise. When the Malcolmson dynasty's business collapsed in 1876, it comprised spinning-mills in Belfast and Manchester,

Table 12.2. *The population of Portlaw, 1841–1881*

	1841	1851	1861	1871	1881
Clonegam	4 759	5 031	4 373	4 276	2 436
Portlaw	3 647	4 351	3 852	3 774	1 891

an ironworks in Waterford, a salmon fishery near Limerick, steamship interests in London and Glasgow, and a variety of other smaller concerns. Malcolmsons' Neptune Iron Works produced the first steamship (the *European*) to carry live cattle from North America to Liverpool, and the *Una* was one of the first ships to pass through the Suez Canal. Plant and machinery at Portlaw accounted for only one-tenth or so of all assets.[18] Was the Waterford mill dragged down by losses in other parts of that enterprise, or, conversely, had it been cross-subsidized from profits in other ventures? The issue has so far not been determined. Certainly, other parts of the business were losing money. Thus in the early 1870s those running the Malcolmson-owned Milford Spinning Co. in Belfast were having trouble disposing 'of their consignments abroad under their old name', and another family firm undertook to sell their goods for them at the lowest prices obtaining in Belfast. Malcolmsons' Belfast creditors insisted in 1876 that 'the Milford Mill should be closed fortwith, as the continuance of the trading has undoubtedly caused, and is causing, a serious loss to the estate'.[19] The withdrawal of capital shares by the widow of one partner in 1858 and by the trustee of another's son in 1867, and the collapse of the banking firm of Overend Gurney, had a broader impact. William Malcolmson's unwise partnership with one Robert Fennell, a lunatic who had made purchases resulting in big losses, added to the woes. A family memoir notes that the family's fortunes took a turn for the worse with the death of Joseph Malcolmson, the senior partner, in April 1858, while leaving open whether earlier success 'was through shrewd foresight or the general prosperity of trade or merely through good fortune while under his control'. The salmon-fishery at Limerick absorbed thousands of pounds in litigation, and Malcolmsons' costly involvement in the Galway Line—the project to link Galway and North America by steamship—was a 'dead loss' from the start. In the end, Malcolmsons' liabilities exceeded £0.5 million against assets of £0.2 million.

The available factory returns (Table 12.3) would seem to rule out any

Table 12.3. *Malcolmson's, Portlaw: capacity and employment, 1856–1878*

Year	Spindles	Looms	Power		Employment			
			Steam	Water	Youths	Females	Adult M	Total
1849	26 055	626	150	350	167	764	431	1 362
1856	27 000	900	150	150	199	922	527	1 648
1861	30 292	940	200	200	252	853	307	1 412
1867	43 253	844	320	200	153	816	536	1 505
1870	41 792	837	320	240	121	727	482	1 330
1874	41 908	812	n/a		196	709	430	1 335
1878	41 234	782	n/a		33	213	90	336

Source: *Return of the Number of Factories and Workshops Authorised to be Inspected under the Factory and Workshops Act . . .* , various years.

drastic falling off in activity at Portlaw before the mid-1870s. Yet the American Civil War (1861–5) undoubtedly disrupted the firm's export markets and raw material sources in the USA—the Malcolmsons had backed the Confederacy, where most of their commercial links were, and had even attempted to beat the blockade imposed by Union forces—and the post-war increase in the US tariff on cotton forced the firm to rely more on British purchasers.[20] Soon Malcolmson Brothers' main Manchester connection, Messrs. John Stewart & Co., 'being aware of the great depression of cotton manufacture in the south of Ireland', was seeking better guarantees for its credit.[21]

Much of the story is still shrouded in mystery. Few company records survive, and the massive Malcolmson enterprise still awaits its historian. Thus it is too soon to reject outright the hypothesis that the isolated factory-village of Portlaw, like the Owenite commune at Ralahine, provides a hint of broader possibilities unfulfilled. Alas, that is unlikely. The reminder that one or two swallows do not make a summer prompts the following query: if the Portlaw cotton enterprise was basically sound, why did it fail to thrive under new management? After Malcolmsons' collapse its Portlaw plant was reorganized as the English-owned Portlaw Spinning Company, but neither output nor employment ever recovered their earlier levels. The new owners at Portlaw failed to find alternative export markets. As a result, the population of the parish of Portlaw dropped from 4,276 in 1871 to 2,436 in 1881. The last bobbin stopped turning in 1904, and the mill was converted into a tannery.[22]

12.4 Linen

Linen and woollen goods had been Irish staples for centuries. From the sixteenth century on, the linen tunics (*léinte*) and the loose woollen cloaks (*bratacha*) and gowns of the native Irish had gradually given way to flannel waistcoats, frieze breeches, and woollen petticoats and greatcoats, and to linen shirts and shifts and sheets. Domestic producers responded to changing fashions.[23] Irish textile production consisted mainly of coarse cloth for the home market, though since late medieval times fine-spun Irish linen yarn had won an excellent reputation abroad. The immigration of handloom weavers specializing in fine yarn from northern England into east Ulster in the wake of the 1641 Rebellion had nicely complemented local flax-spinning skills, paving the way for Huguenot Louis Crommelin's enterprises in the 1690s. The Irish Linen Board was created in 1711, and became the vehicle of regulations and bounties encouraging the cultivation of flax and the production and export of high-quality linens. Boosted by the removal of the British tariff on Irish plain linens in 1696 and by buoyant British demand, Irish exports of linen cloth rose sixtyfold from 0.3 million yards in 1700 to 18.7 million yards in 1780. While the bulk of fine-linen broadcloth output was exported, mainly from Ulster, poorly bleached narrow 'bandle' linens continued to be produced for the domestic market in the rest of the island.[24]

Spinning flax by hand, a task reserved for women, was probably the single most important source of non-agricultural employment. Male weavers supplied coarse cloths (including shirts made from tow yarns) for local consumption, and sold their better pieces to Ulster drapers for sale further afield. Yarn was sent north-east too for weaving in Ulster, often for export. Brown (that is, unbleached) linen markets in north Connacht and west and south Ulster expanded rapidly in this period: in 1817 the market at Westport was attended by '4,000 to 5,000 persons [who] appear dressed in their best clothes, each occupied in the disposal of flax yarn, linen, etc.'. Mayo at the time boasted five linen markets and six bleach-greens, and Sligo had another two. Leitrim's one linen market, that at Ballinamore, hardly deserved the name, but the county contained eighteen yarn-fairs and four bleach-greens. Cavan and Monaghan still accounted for one-eighth of Ulster brown linen sales in 1821, and Louth's sales rivalled Down's. Counties Longford and Cork between them sold more than Mayo.[25]

Despite such evidence of regional dispersion, linen obviously counted for more in Ulster than anywhere else. Even before the opening of Belfast's own White Linen Hall in 1785—a ploy by the city's merchants to divert the trade away from Dublin and Newry—Ulster was famous for its range of handwoven linens. The Linen Hall was a monument to the handicraft stage of linen production, however; the water-powered cotton-mill being built nearby by Wilson and Grimshaw embodied a technology that was not adapted to fine linen yarn until the 1820s, and between the 1780s and the 1820s cotton rather than linen was the 'glamour' industry in Belfast. Though linen production continued to advance in outlying areas, mill cotton displaced hand-spun linen yarn in the town's handlooms. Linen exports, which had more than doubled between the late 1750s and the mid-1780s, continued to increase until the early 1790s, but stagnated thereafter until the 1820s.[26] With spinning and weaving techniques in linen remaining traditional, the main sources of productivity growth in the linen industry before the 1820s lay in bleaching and finishing. The cost of bleaching fell from about 2d. per yard in mid-century to 1.25d. in 1809. The change entailed heavier fixed investment and more working capital, and marked the end of the independent bleacher-weaver.[27]

In 1821 three east Ulster counties (Tyrone, Armagh, and Antrim) accounted for over half of all Irish linen market sales. Yarn sales were more widely dispersed. In retrospect, it is easier to see how such dispersion as there was could not survive the centralizing tendencies of the Industrial Revolution. Within Ulster the fine-linen weavers of the Dungannon– Newry–Belfast 'linen triangle' were best located to take advantage of the fine yarns produced by the wet-spinning process introduced in the 1820s. As Robert Williamson, merchant and bleacher, explained to an inquiry into the linen trade in 1825:[28]

Nor is it possible to direct capital generally over Ireland for mill-spinning; I should think that the new manufacture would rather fix itself in those portions of Ireland that are richest, and extend the other [i.e. hand-spinning] back to those unfortunate districts that have not the linen manufacture or any other.

Alas for the peripheral proto-industrial districts, Williamson's hopes were not realized. Areas such as Mayo and south and west Ulster were doubly disadvantaged—far from mechanized raw material, and far from mass markets. The minority of fine-yarn spinners in the periphery could not compete with the mills, and coarse-yarn spinners could not compete with cotton. Instead of exporting cloth, they switched to exporting seasonal migrants and grain. In the late eighteenth century the manufacture of coarse linen cloth for local use had been an important industry in north

Connacht and south Ulster. Linen was also exported to Leinster and Ulster in the form of hand-spun yarn, merchants from those provinces obtaining their supplies in the markets of Galway, Sligo, and Mayo. But in County Leitrim in 1837, only four bleach-greens remained in operation, producing about 32,000 pieces 'chiefly for the English market'. According to Lewis's *Topographical Dictionary* (1837) linen was still the staple of County Sligo, but in decline; four bleach-greens between them produced nearly 40,000 pieces a year, 'principally shipped for England and destined for the American market'. Three years later Caesar Otway found Sligo's linen hall sold to a hotel-owner, who had rented it out as a warehouse; on market-days a few spinners hawked hand-spun yarn through the streets, and the weavers had turned to what other work they could find. The value of linen cloth sold in Mayo fell from £81,640 in 1816[29] to a few thousand pounds by the 1840s, and the triumph of wet-spinning in the Belfast area put an end to yarn exports to Ulster. Again, Meath had supplied the Drogheda market with coarse linens 'to clothe the Negroes' in the 1800s, and Drogheda itself had been a hive of weaving activity. In 1816 Louth was the fourth county in Ireland for linen, after Antrim, Armagh, and Tyrone. Its trade centred on Drogheda, but three decades later, Drogheda's once-thriving linen sector, founded on coarse handloom weaving, was on its last legs, unable to compete with machine-woven textiles from across the water.[30] Within the province of Ulster the market sales of brown linens showed no sign of market localization before the 1820s; the shares of aggregate linen sales of the top four Ulster markets rose from 33.1 per cent in 1783 to 36.6 per cent in 1820, those of the top ten from 57.8 to 59.9 per cent.[31] Weaving in the outlying areas went into serious decline thereafter. The number of webs sold on Derry's market fell from 29,432 in 1810 to 22,184 in 1820 and 10,460 in 1837. In 1840 it was claimed that all markets except those at Ballymena, Ballymoney, and Coleraine had greatly declined.[32]

Shifts in the regional origins of former weavers recruited by the East India Company in Ireland reflect the increasing localization of the textile sector. Before 1815 only slightly more than one ex-weaver in four hailed from counties Antrim, Down, or Armagh, but by the late 1840s the share of those counties had reached three in four. Before 1830, the other six counties of Ulster had supplied more weaver-recruits than those three counties that would henceforth dominate the textile sector. In western Ulster, as in Leinster and Munster in the 1820s and 1830s, the decline of linen weaving led to substantial enlistment among weavers; by the 1850s, when the spread of the power-loom prompted the enlistment of many

Table 12.4. *The recruitment of Irish weavers by the EIC Army, 1802–1860*

Period	EU	WU	WEST	DUBLIN	EM	ROL
1802–19	214 (27)	258 (32)	63 (8)	62 (8)	68 (8)	136 (17)
1819–31	68 (15)	84 (19)	38 (9)	52 (12)	106 (24)	99 (22)
1831–47	44 (31)	20 (14)	15 (10)	17 (12)	25 (17)	23 (16)
1847–60	320 (78)	34 (8)	18 (4)	8 (2)	21 (5)	10 (2)

Note: EU = East Ulster (Antrim, Armagh, Down); WU = rest of Ulster; WEST = Connacht + Clare + Kerry; EM = rest of Munster; ROL = rest of Leinster. Row percentages in parentheses.

Ulster weavers, weaving in the rest of the island had already virtually given up the ghost. The 1841 census confirms the key role of linen in east Ulster. If we assume that most of those described as 'weavers' and 'spinners' in the list of occupations worked with flax, then easily half of those employed outside agriculture and related occupations were in the linen industry. The rise in Irish flax-mill and factory employment—a tenfold increase from 9,000 in 1839 to 90,000 in 1917—was almost entirely confined to Ulster.

This was also a crucial period for the expansion of the linen industry. Exports of linen cloth had failed to rise much during the Revolutionary Wars, but reached a new peak of 55.8 million yards in 1818. Between 1825–9 and 1850–2 cloth exports rose from 44.7 million yards to 64.6 million yards. The rise was modest when compared to that of UK cotton exports, which quadrupled over the same period.[33] On the eve of the Industrial Revolution the linen industry was widely dispersed, producing varieties of yarn and cloth from home-grown flax, mainly on a domestic basis. The 1790s and 1800s were a period of stasis for linen, as capital and labour were diverted into cotton. Subsidies from the Irish Linen Board prompted several manufacturers to install spinning-frames *à la* Arkwright, but the machinery was ill-geared to flax fibres, and could produce only coarse yarn. The mechanization of higher yarn counts, in which Ulster specialized, became viable with the introduction of wet-spinning in Leeds in 1824 (the technique had been invented in France in 1810). The industry's centralization in mills followed, beginning with the erection of water-powered flax-mills at Chapelizod outside Dublin and at Mount Caulfield near Newry in 1826. The more famous mills at Darkley in south Armagh, Castlewellan in County Down, and at Ballyclare and Glynn in County Antrim were built soon after, and Mulhollands' shift from cotton- to flax-spinning followed in 1828–9. By the mid-1830s Belfast had ten substantial steam-powered spinning-mills, four of them located on the Falls Road; a decade later the capital sunk in the fifty or so mills in operation was worth nearly £2 million.[34] Even the spinning of the very highest quality yarn soon succumbed: while the price of 14^{00} yarn dropped from 17.5d. (7p) in 1830 to 13.5d. (5.5p) in 1852, the drop in fine 24^{00} yarn plummeted from 8s. 6d. (42.5p) to 2s. 10d. (14p) (or almost 70 per cent). Domestic spinning, which had been widely dispersed across Ulster and north Connacht early in the century, had declined dramatically as a source of income by the early 1840s. Linen weaving was not mechanized till the post-Famine era, but the regional spread of weaving was affected by the revolution in spinning: the cost of shipping mill-spun yarn to peripheral areas such as Donegal, Cavan, Sligo, and Mayo, which had no spinning-mills of their own, inhibited merchants from supplying yarn to weavers. Adapting the technology of power-loom weaving to medium and fine linen yarn—in which Ulster specialized—was a challenge not overcome till the 1850s. The rise in hand-loom weavers' wages in the wake of the Famine accelerated the diffusion of power-loom weaving: the number of the new looms, most of them powered by steam, rose from 58 in 1850 to over 17,000 by 1875. The industry continued to expand thereafter, largely on the basis of the technology already in place by the 1860s.

Scotland was often seen as Ireland's rival in linen, but in practice the two linen industries were complementary, with each country adopting 'its own peculiar branch'. This had long resulted in an interesting example of two-way trade:[35]

Notwithstanding Scotland is so great a linen country, it appears that the value of the linens she takes from Ireland is above half of all her imports from that country. On the other hand, Ireland takes not much less linens of other sorts from Scotland; kenting, alone, amounting to £40,235, and lawns to £11,175 in the year 1783. This should remove jealousy: it shows that different fabrics of the same manufacture may flourish in neighbouring countries to the advantage of both.

Trade statistics for the early 1850s show further signs of two-way trade, Ireland being a considerable exporter and importer of both flax and linen yarn. The linen industry had also long ago given rise to a trade in flax-seed, since the trade-off between flax and seed quality led most Irish flax-growers to sow for fibre only and allow others to specialize in seed.[36]

Solar suggests that Belfast's increasing control of marketing predated its pre-eminence as a production centre, and indeed encouraged the localization of linen production in the Belfast area.[37] By 1841 only Belfast,

Drogheda, and Carrickfergus of the nine borough towns rated as textile towns. In all three towns textiles accounted for over one-fifth of occupied workers; everywhere else the proportion was less than 5 per cent. An analysis of sub-occupations in the textile sector shows far greater 'complexity' in Belfast and nearby Carrickfergus than elsewhere by 1841. Spinning and weaving accounted for a much higher proportion of textile work in towns such as Galway (94 per cent), Cork (68 per cent), and Kilkenny (72 per cent) than in Belfast (44 per cent) or Carrickfergus (49 per cent). In the two last-mentioned, the importance of ancillary occupations such as bleaching, dressing, and dyeing accounted for the difference. One plausible implication of this is that the east Ulster industry was large enough to generate external economies of scale (see Chapter 13).

In the end, though the development of the linen industry was an Irish success story, linen failed to generate the employment in Ireland that cotton did in England. The number of workers employed by the Irish linen industry at its peak—about 90,000 during the First World War—was dwarfed by the half a million and more employed by the British cotton industry. Yet the relative impact of linen on the smaller and poorer Irish economy was significant. In the mid-1820s linen accounted for just over a quarter of Irish exports to Britain, and in the mid-1830s for about the same fraction of all Irish exports.[38] By comparison, cotton accounted for over two-fifths of total UK exports in the 1820s and nearly one-half in the mid-1830s.[39] However, Bielenberg's estimate of the net value of linen output in the early 1840s (£5 million) means that it was worth 6 or 7 per cent of national income on the eve of the Famine, exceeding cotton's 4 per cent of British national income between the early 1820s and the mid-1840s.[40] The Irish estimate is based on placing an assumed average price on exports and on an assumed domestic consumption of four yards per person. Gill had estimated average consumption at six yards per person about 1821: a switch to cotton accounts for the decline in domestic consumption.[41]

During the nineteenth century, the output of Irish linen yarn and finished cloth rose only modestly by the standards of the British cotton industry. Was this because the fall in the price of linen failed to match that of cotton goods? Table 12.5, which compares Sandberg's quality-adjusted cotton price index and the price per yard of exported linen, shows cotton gaining on linen before mid-century, but the decline in linen prices thereafter matched that of cotton. The range in linen prices reflects the difference between the rates for plain and fancy linen. Throughout, linen was the costlier fabric. That it was not wiped out reflects the fact that linen

Table 12.5. *The trend in linen and cotton prices, 1815–1913*

Year	Cotton			Linen
	Grey cloth price index (1)	Cloth quality (2)	(1)/(2) [1845 = 100] (3)	(in old pence) (4)
1815	403.2	124.1	325.9	16 to 18
1835	163.3	107.4	152.0	12.7
1845	100.0	100.0	100.0	—
1853	99.5	91.4	108.9	7.6 to 9.0
1875	106.5	85.9	124.0	7.6 to 8.2
1898	61.3	91.0	67.4	5.0 to 5.9
1913	94.2	92.3	102.1	7.2 to 8.0

Sources: Cotton computed from Sandberg, *Lancashire in Decline* (Columbus, Ohio, 1974), 239–43, using a base of 1845 = 100. The quality index follows Sandberg's Assumption (1) for 1845–98 and assumption (2) for 1815–45 and 1898–1913. Linen prices were taken from Gill, *Linen Industry*, 225 n.; 1836 Irish Railways Commission, *Report*, App. B(10), 91; the trade statistics for 1853–1913.

and cotton were not perfect substitutes. For many purposes, though, they were close substitutes, and difficult to tell apart, and bogus linen goods made of cotton or blends were a common complaint. Only in the exceptional circumstances of the early 1860s were linen goods produced to look like cotton.[42] By the 1870s and 1880s cotton had largely displaced linen in shirts, bed-sheets, and even various other uses. The spread of the sewing-machine in these years gave cotton an added comparative advantage, as durability became less important. Linen, a common household fabric early in the nineteenth century, had become a costly item by its end.[43]

Employment in the Irish linen industry was at the expense of employment in the same industry in the rest of the UK. Yet unfortunately for Ireland linen was less subject to the centralization pressures that gave England almost the entire UK cotton industry by the end of the nineteenth century. As a result in 1890 Ireland's share of total UK employment in linen was still only three-fifths. Nor was the demand for linen as buoyant as the factory employment data indicate, since the 1850 figures exclude the still substantial number of outworkers in the linen industry. The failure of output to advance much beyond the levels achieved by the 1870s also tempers linen's contribution.

In both spinning and weaving, it took a few decades before the new technologies of Arkwright, Crompton, and Cartwright could be adapted to linen. Irish experimentation with 'dry'-spinning in the 1800s and 1810s was a failure, and the technique of softening flax fibres in water before submitting them to the jenny—'wet'-spinning—was introduced to Ireland only in 1826–7. Handlooms still dominated linen weaving in mid-century. Scattered experiments with power-loom weaving had all proved commercially unsuccessful, and the 1850 factory returns reported only one weaving-factory using power-looms. Fine quality products such as serviettes and tablecloths were still being woven by hand half a century later, both in the weavers' homes and in factories. In the 1900s the handloom factory of John S. Brown & Sons at Ardoyne was using the same wide looms that had been installed eighty years earlier! The Ardoyne weavers' practice of coming and going as they liked during working hours evoked another echo of earlier days. The Ardoyne factory employed no more than a few score men; the weaving of fine cambrics and damasks by hand still employed a few thousand men and women in Counties Down, Armagh, and Antrim in the 1900s. Linen handloom weaving was fast becoming marginal by then, however: aggregate wages paid to Irish handloom weavers fell from £220,000 in 1893 to £55,000 in 1910.[44] Further evidence of the recalcitrance of flax in the face of technical change would soon be seen in Ulster's rejection of ring-spinning and the automatic loom. Even in the 1950s rings accounted for only 5 per cent of total capacity, and the extra costs of preparing the yarn for the automatic loom were deemed to outweigh any savings. The fineness of the yarn required in Ulster ruled out the ring, except 'in the coarser end of the trade'.[45]

Another important feature of the Irish linen industry was its marked localization within the island. By 1918 Irish spindles were distributed among 50 owners, of whom 17 were in Belfast, 4 in Drogheda, 1 in Cork, 1 in Dublin, and the rest in Ulster. In weaving, it was the same story: by 1912 Belfast held 22,000 of Ireland's 37,000 power-looms, and the rest of Ulster another 13,000.[46]

Linen's growth was largely founded on markets abroad. Before the First World War about three-quarters of Irish linen output was sold outside the UK and 70 per cent of that in the USA. Linen yarn and linen goods accounted for over one-fifth of Irish exports.[47] Stories of huge profits being made in linen were commonplace. Boyle cites a contemporary who spoke of 'profitable returns of well nigh fabulous percentage', and who claimed that one firm's profits 'equalled the value of the entire premises and plant' for two years running. Though data are sparse, early entrants into mill spinning presumably earned high returns on their capital. Huge profits were also made during the cotton famine induced by the American Civil War in the early 1860s: the profits of flax-spinners Gunning & Campbell, for example, rose from under £7,000 in 1861 to over £21,000 in 1864. However, the number of entries and exits is consistent with a good deal of competition—there were 35 mills by 1839, about 80 by 1853, and 82 by 1868—and, typically, margins were tight and failures plentiful after the boom of the Civil War, when both exports and production declined. Though the Irish linen industry held its own against foreign competition, a combination of changing fashions and the rise of protectionism in Europe prevented it from growing as fast as before. In 1875–6 the spectacular collapses of William Spotten & Co. and Lowry, Valentine & Kirk were followed by several others. Further bankruptcies followed in the 1880s. A spokesman for the Belfast industry in 1884 confessed that four of the city's twelve joint-stock spinning-mills had been unable to declare a dividend for some time, and that the share values of several had fallen drastically.[48]

Like the English cotton industry, Ireland's linen industry included both vertically integrated plants and plants specializing in either spinning or weaving. William Barbour & Sons of Hilden (just south of Belfast) and Dunbar, McMaster & Co., whose huge plant straddled the River Bann north of Banbridge, produced thread and were therefore engaged in both spinning and doubling. In the late 1880s Barbour & Son employed nearly 40,000 spindles and 2,000 horsepower in Ulster, and acquired a subsidiary in Paterson, New Jersey. The firm of Dunbar, McMaster, founded in 1836, was renowned for the extremely high quality of its yarn and thread. In the 1880s, besides providing high-count yarn for looms in southern Europe, they were producing 'gilling twines for the Adriatic', 'twine for salmon-

Table 12.6. *No. of spindles in the linen industry* (000s)

	Ireland	Scotland	England
1850	396	303	266
1871	896	317	270
1918	956	150	33

fishing in British Columbia', and so on. Both Barbour & Son and Dunbar, McMaster were massive concerns. In general integrated mills were larger than specialized mills, more likely to be steam-powered, and to spin lower-count yarns. The twenty integrated (spinning and weaving) plants in operation in 1868 contained over half again as many spindles as the sixty concerns confined to spinning only.[49] Though vertical integration might be expected to minimize co-ordination problems, the very persistence of specialized firms in Ulster into the present century bespeaks a technological rationale for them.

As Brenda Collins has noted, undue emphasis on spinning and weaving has led historians to overlook the contribution of the making-up trades in the textile sector. In parts of Ulster, notably in Down, Derry, and Donegal, embroidering or 'flowering', sewing, and dressmaking offered thousands of women an alternative to spinning. The location of flowering in Down owed much to its being originally an offspring of the textile industry. The flowerers worked on a task-rate basis for Scottish firms, and their output was sold in London and further afield as 'Scotch work'. The 1841 census returned over 20,000 seamstresses and dressmakers in Down (and another 4,000 in Antrim). Their number reached a peak of 31,000 in

Table 12.7. *Factories and employment in cotton and linen, 1850–1890*

	1850		1874		1890	
	Plants	Workers	Plants	Workers	Plants	Workers
Cotton						
E & W	1753	291 662 (88)	2542	440 336 (92)	2406	492 547 (93)
Scotland	168	36 325 (11)	105	36 104 (8)	124	34 873 (7)
Ireland	11	2 937 (1)	8	3 075 (1)	8	1 375 (0)
TOTAL	1932	330 924	2655	479 515	2538	528 795
Linen						
E & W	135	19 001 (28)	141	22 327 (17)	59	8 886 (8)
Scotland	189	28 312 (41)	159	45 816 (36)	136	34 222 (32)
Ireland	69	21 121 (31)	149	60 316 (47)	162	64 475 (60)
TOTAL	393	68 434	449	128 459	357	107 583

Sources: BPP 1850 (745) [XLII], 455; 1875 (393) [LXXI], 57; 1890 (328) [LXVII], 169. Percentages given in brackets.

1851, but fell back rapidly thereafter, particularly in the wake of the financial crisis of 1857, which ruined the most important of the Scottish merchants, D. & J. McDonald. Sewing maintained its importance as an employer further west, though under another guise, shirtmaking.[50]

In west Ulster after 1850, the shirtmaking industry assumed an increasingly important role. The area had no strong tradition in shirts (though it did engage in sewing) when William Scott and the Scots duo, Tillie and Henderson, set up factories in Derry. The industry quickly adopted the sewing-machine, and was transformed from five 'unpretentious' factories in the 1850s to a massive industry with thirty-eight factories in the 1900s, along with a network of over 100 rural branches. The number of shirtmakers and seamstresses in Derry City in 1911 was 2,772. In the manufacture of white shirts, the industry produced an interesting marriage of urban and rural labour. Factories in Derry and Strabane produced the component pieces, which were then dispatched with the requisite buttons and thread to shirt stations throughout Donegal and north-west Derry and made up by outworkers. In 1881 there were 6,406 shirtmakers and seamstresses widely spread throughout County Donegal, and another 7,263 in Derry. The two counties provided work for over 15,000 in 1891, but only 7,883 in 1911. (The number of women employed in other outworking trades in Donegal and Derry—fancy goods, embroidery, millinery, and dressmaking—followed a similar pattern, rising marginally in the 1880s to 6,536 in 1891, and then dropping to 3,943 in 1911.) The Congested Districts Board Baseline Reports, reflecting conditions in the mid-1890s, attributed the decline to the McKinley tariff, while several Donegal witnesses appearing before the Royal Commission on Congestion in 1906–8 lamented the industry's decline, blaming foreign competition and changing fashions. Part of the outworkers' problem was that they relied on the contracting market for plain white shirts. The result was a sharp fall in piece-rates. In 1907 the value of output still exceeded £1 million, with exports worth about half that sum.[51]

12.5 Wool

The eighteenth century has usually been seen as a difficult period for the Irish woollen industry, hampered by the English mercantilist legislation of the 1690s and by rising wool prices. In reality, the legislation hurt only the urban producers of 'old and new draperies', and the perennial complaints about the industry's problems reflect their concerns. Others still found markets at home for coarse friezes and flannels, and abroad for worsted yarn. As late as 1798 it was claimed that 'the inhabitants of the South and West are to a man clad in woollen'. If that was nearly true, then the post-1740s population explosion guaranteed a rising demand for woollens. In times of war such as 1776-83 and after 1793, there was an added military demand for woollen clothing.[52]

Wool-spinning was typically a part-time rural female activity. Weaving was a male occupation, whether carried on in rural homes for purely local needs, or in the towns of the south and south-east. Different towns developed their own specialisms—Carrick-on-Suir was famous for fine quality 'rateens', Kilkenny for blankets, Cork for a wide range of cloths. Organization differed too. In Carrick the industry was dominated by independent artisans, but in Cork the industry was organized on more capitalist lines: manufacturers such as Mahonys of Blackpool imported wool from Connacht, employing rural labour to card and spin it, and city weavers to produce the cloth. The woollen industry employed several thousand people in Cork City and its hinterland during the Napoleonic Wars. Cork manufacturers responded to the challenge of the Industrial Revolution by importing the new technology: both Martin Mahony and Lane's, the two biggest concerns, and several others applied the spinning-machinery that had transformed the industry in Yorkshire. However, the Cork industry contracted after the peace of 1815, and was in deep crisis in the late 1820s. In towns such as Kilkenny and Carrick it was a similar story. Kilkenny's output of blankets more than doubled in value between 1800 and 1821, and by the latter date eleven woollen factories employed nearly 800 people between them (in a city of 23,000 people). The drop of one-fifth in population in the 1830s is a measure of the crisis that followed. In Carrick decline had set in earlier, and the challenge of competition was met by reducing quality ('stretching the woollens to augment the measurement') and by cutting wages, ploys which failed to save the industry. Wakefield (1812) maintained that, despite the decline of wool-producing centres such as Kilkenny and Carrick, the production of woollens was 'evidently' on the increase, and he put the rise down to rising population and 'a greater degree of luxury among the inhabitants'.[53] However, imports of Yorkshire woollens and worsteds increased a great deal between 1810 and the mid-1820s, when slack trading on the domestic market led to a flood of exports to Ireland. The measure of the outside challenge is captured

Table 12.8. *British textile and cotton exports to Ireland, 1784/6–1824/6* (£000)

Period	Wool		Cotton		Linen
	Cloth	Yarn	Cloth	Yarn	
1784–6	182	—	31	—	96
1794–6	570	—	74	335	28
1804–6	628	—	136	332	7
1814–16	761	95	151	101	33
1824–6	1 056	89	286	210	25

Source: Davis, *The Industrial Revolution and British Overseas Trade*, 94–8.

by the rise in value of British woollen exports to Ireland, which in the mid-1820s accounted for one-fifth of all British woollen exports and was worth three times that of cotton and linen imports combined.[54]

The woollen industry recovered after the battering it received in the 1820s, albeit slowly. The number of mills rose from 11 in 1850 to 61 two decades later and 82 in 1899. Most of these were small, water-powered affairs: Comerford claims that they were 'the factories of an earlier age reopened in response to moderately encouraging market conditions'. That cap hardly fits a firm such as Martin Mahony & Co. which had moved from Cork itself to Blarney in 1824, and whose famous 'Blarney Tweed' was being woven some decades later with looms powered by three 145-hp turbines and two auxiliary steam-engines. By the 1890s the Blarney mills were employing over 700 people, possibly more than any other industrial employer in the south of Ireland. The modest blanket factory erected in Dripsey (near Coachford) presents a more mixed picture. Its modern face was represented by its reliance on the latest turbines and looms, but as the manager explained in 1907, its small size precluded much specialization of tasks:[55]

I design; I go out and sell almost every yard we make; I come back and see the goods are made *right*, and up to time, etc. Our book-keeper is an expert dyer! and our principal foreman is 'everything else'! If we had to pay a separate manager, designer, dyer, book-keeper, traveller, etc., we would be swamped.

By 1902 the number of mills had risen to 114, employing over 3,000 persons. The Census of Industrial Production of 1907 put gross output at

£0.6 million and net output at £0.2 million. In 1920 Riordan counted eighty-five mills spread over fifty-three towns. The industry was widely scattered around the country. The numbers and the spread bespeak a dualistic structure of a few large concerns and many small ones, but in County Cork at least, Bielenberg has correctly noted that a successful transition to factory-based production had been accomplished.[56] Curiously, this staple industry relied largely on imported Australian wool; the bulk of home-grown wool, being too coarse for machine use, was exported.

The production of woollen goods was slower to succumb to the factory than either cotton or linen. In south Kerry in the 1900s local home-spinners and weavers of wool combined to produce 'Kenmare homespuns', 'well spun and woven, but poor in colouring and pattern'.[57] Knitting heavy woollen socks and weaving coarse tweeds were important ancillary occupations in the north-west. Such work never paid well: the old women of the Rosses in west Donegal referred to their knitting-needles as *ceithre chró-iarann na boichtineachta* (the four crowbars of poverty).[58] The number of Donegalwomen described as 'hosiery manufacturers' rose from 78 in 1881 to 303 in 1901, and fell back to 97 in 1911. Female woollen-cloth manufacturers declined from 573 to 422 and 220 over the same period. In the long run homespun, handwoven tweed, despite the best efforts of the Congested Districts Board, could not compete with the output of the factories. Even in Donegal on the eve of the First World War it provided poorly paid part-time employment for no more than a few thousand people. Not even a Royal Warrant from Edward VII could save the Kenmare homespuns.[59]

12.6 Shipbuilding

In the 1840s and 1850s the output of the entire Irish shipbuilding industry, whose main centre was Cork, averaged 2,000 tons annually. By the early 1910s two Belfast firms, Harland & Wolff and Workman Clark, were producing over 150,000 tons between them each year, and accounting for 8 per cent of world output. The achievement is all the more astounding given Belfast's awkward topography. If the city's earlier success with textiles owed little to its location—the site where the Farset joined the Lagan had been selected in the early seventeenth century for its strategic, not its economic, value—then, as Pollard and Robertson have noted, Belfast also seemed an unlikely centre for shipbuilding in the nineteenth century: 'the shipyards were located 12 miles from the sea, on a river narrower than the

Thames. Coal had to be imported from Ardrossan, steel from Great Britain or the USA, and timber from Canada and Norway.' This may be misleading in that it conveys the impression that Belfast was twelve miles up a narrow river. Nevertheless, shipbuilding would never have been viable in Belfast had not the city's Ballast Board and their successors, the Harbour Commissioners, engaged engineering contractor William Dargan to make the necessary cuts between the city and the sea. This recalls the decision in 1783 to build a linen hall by public subscription, so that Belfast might capture the trade in linens from Dublin and Newry. In both cases private enterprise obtained an initial fillip by a dose of municipal 'socialism'.[60]

Belfast had no strong tradition in shipbuilding, even though Scotsman William Ritchie had established a yard for building wooden ships there in 1791, and in 1841 the city provided employment for almost as many shipwrights (177) as Cork (91) and Dublin (91) combined. Fortunately for Belfast, Cork's concentration on wooden ships and its industrial and commercial stagnation virtually ruled out a future for it in the construction of iron ships.[61] The Queen's Island site acquired by Harland & Wolff in 1859 was the by-product of Dargan's excavations. Initially known as Dargan's Island, it had been developed as a shipyard only six years earlier. The credit for this goes to the Harbour Commissioners, who prepared the site for Messrs. Robert Hickson & Co. Soon Queen's Island was about to witness one of the most spectacular engineering successes that Ireland has known. Edward Harland, Hickson's manager, acquired the site, and the partnership created by Harland and Gustav Wolff in 1861, who were joined by William Pirrie (later to head the firm) and Walter Wilson in 1874, was a crucial part of the story. The firm was technologically very innovative, and by 1890 was producing the fastest liners in the world. The ill-fated *Titanic*, built at Queen's Island in 1908–11 for the White Star Line, and weighing over 46,000 gross tons, was the largest ship in the world in its day. Harland & Wolff were also responsible for the *Iroquois*, the largest oil-tanker ever built when launched in 1907. The firm spun a complex web of interlinking partnerships with shipping-lines and with ropemaking and engineering concerns, and its growth was also aided by a secret commission business. Workman Clark, founded across the Lagan in 1879 by two former Harland & Wolff managers, was also an important concern in this period. Though always smaller than its more famous rival, and producing smaller ships, Workman Clark grew faster in the 1890s and 1900s than Harland & Wolff. In 1893 Workman Clark bought out a third Belfast shipbuilding and engineering concern, McIlwaine & McColl, whose yards lay next to Harland & Wolff. McIlwaine & McColl, founded by two Dubliners, had started out as engineers and ship-repairers, but since the 1870s had been constructing iron barges, tugboats, and even a paddle-steamer. They had been the only Belfast shipbuilders to construct and fit their own engines, a tradition continued by Workman Clark after the take-over. Between the late 1870s and 1913 the average annual growth rate of output of Workman Clark and Harland & Wolff combined was nearly 8 per cent.[62] That most of the growth was financed out of capital supplied by the partners and their families is an indication of the huge profits made. Belfast's developing industrial infrastructure, based on shipbuilding and textiles, meant that intermediate products such as ropes and rigging, woodwork, and metallurgical products could be supplied locally. Low wages and high-quality workmanship, too, have been cited as factors underlying Belfast's success.[63]

There was never any prospect of Dublin rivalling Belfast's massive shipbuilding industry, and in the late nineteenth century Dublin lacked even the repair facilities to service its own merchant fleet. In 1900 the Port Authority and city fathers took action, and a property at the Alexandra Basin was leased to a company headed by two Scotsmen. For over two decades, the Dublin Dockyard Company combined repair work and ship-building. The shipbuilding was intended at the outset to help fill in slack periods between repair contracts. Output included the *Dun Aengus*, built in 1912, and other small craft for local clients, but orders also came from as far away as British Columbia and Chile. In the end the company was a victim of inter-union rivalry and post-war deflation.[64]

12.7 Distilling[65]

There were, admittedly, some successes besides shipbuilding and linen. For a time, distilling seemed one such success story. But the increase in whiskey output was erratic: by the 1900s output was only double that of the 1840s, and stagnated thereafter. Nor could distilling ever provide the kind of employment of which industrial revolutions are made. At no time was distilling a significant job-provider. In 1870 thirteen distilleries employed 1,416 workers; in 1907 the census of industrial production returned a work-force of 2,423 in the industry. Distilling required a good deal of capital, and the bigger distilleries were impressive edifices.

On the domestic front, demand conditions were not congenial in the post-Famine period. Population was declining, the temperance campaign of the early 1840s had an enduring impact on consumption, and an increase in the excise duty from 6s. 2d. (31p) to 8s. (40p) per gallon in 1858 (leading to the harmonization of Irish and British duties) hardly helped either. The progress of the industry in the second half of the century was against a background of a steadily falling consumption per capita in Ireland, from 1.1 gallons in 1857 (extremely high by modern world standards) to 0.63 gallons in 1910. By 1907 Irish whiskey accounted for one-quarter of UK output, and the industry's growth was perforce very much export-based. In 1887 there were 28 distilleries in operation (see Appendix). In 1919 there were 23 in existence, 11 of them in the six counties that would soon constitute Northern Ireland, though the number operating was probably smaller.

Even against this background of rising output historians have found cause for complaint. Whiskey production methods had remained virtually unchanged for centuries until the diffusion of the new technology patented by Irishman Aeneas Coffey in 1830. Coffey's method revolutionized distilling in the long run, but, ironically perhaps, Irish distillers were slow to adopt it. The new method was ideally suited to making industrial alcohol and gin, but when first applied to whiskey-making, it combined oats and other cereals (including maize from the 1860s on) to produce a spirit that was cheap but barely drinkable. By the 1860s experimentation produced potable whiskey blends consisting largely of patent spirit. Traditionalists argued that the cheaper patent-based product was 'chiefly drunk by the Dram Drinkers, who wish to get drunk at the cheapest rate, and whose corrupted stomachs prefer the harsher spirits'.[66] It is important to emphasize that the outputs of the two processes were different. The traditional pot still produced what was known as malt whiskey, though the mash rarely consisted of malted barley alone: Irish pot-stillers always worked from a mixed mash, a practice which may have forced them to run the spirit through three stills to make the product drinkable. It is claimed, correctly, that most Irish distillers rejected the patent still on the grounds that it produced an inferior product. Irish distillers, moreover, possibly held a comparative advantage in the original malt product: thrice-distilled Irish malt was smoother than Scotch, and thus less in need of blending with tasteless patent spirit. There was thus still a role for the old technology, with which Irish whiskey became almost synonymous in export markets. But the alleged trade-off between taste and quantity was costly: in the 1880s the proprietors of Bushmills, clinging to the 'tedious, troublesome, and expensive' pot still, conceded that it required ten times as much fuel as the patent method. Besides costing more fuel to produce, pot-still alcohol required more time in cask, because it contained more of the secondary constituents. The Irish practice of running the spirit three times through the stills, rather than twice as in Scotland, further increased the cost of the Irish product. Most Irish distillers, even when they blended, prided themselves on their pot-still malt;[67] the bigger Scottish distilleries, meanwhile, acquired an increasing share of the export market, particularly the English and American, with their blended whiskies. By 1887 Scotland's two largest distilleries—the Port Dundas in Glasgow and the Caledonian in Edinburgh—were grain whisky concerns, and many of the smaller malt whisky producers were playing the subsidiary role of providing a blending base for such giants. Nor were the Scots content to compete with the Irish on export markets: in 1878 the Distillers Company took over the failed Dublin & Chapelizod Distilling Company (earlier a cotton-mill owned by William Dargan), renaming it the Phoenix Park Distillery Limited, and began to produce pot-still whiskey for the Dublin market.[68]

Rivalry between patent and pot-still distillers led to a controversy about the very definition of 'whiskey'. Irish and Scottish malt distillers, forced by

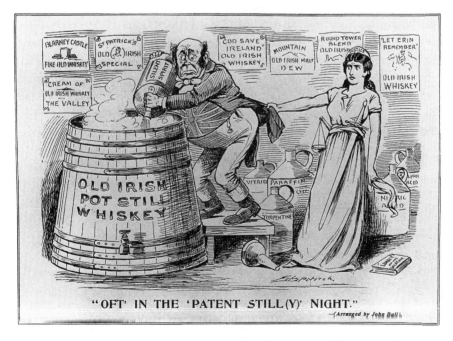

PLATE 2. Rivalry between patent and pot-still distillers was intense in the 1900s (*The Lepracaun*, March 1906)

technology to mature their own product for several years, tried to make bonding for a minimum period compulsory for all. This was no more than a piece of straightforward trade protectionism. An inconclusive parliamentary report followed in 1909, but in 1915 Lloyd George finally introduced compulsory bonding in the Immature Spirits (Restriction) Act. By then the Scots had largely won the battle for the English market for whiskey (see Table 12.9).

The apparent correlation between the spread of blended whisky in Scotland and that country's increasing domination of the world market for whiskey is sometimes noted. However, though accounting for a declining share of Scottish output, Scottish malt producers also held their own against the Irish. More importantly, the juxtaposition obscures the reality that by 1890 the output of Irish (mainly northern) patent whiskey had outstripped that of pot still, and in 1900 accounted for over two-thirds of all whiskey Irish production (see Fig. 12.1). True, pot-still producers accounted for the great majority of distillers—23 out of 30 in 1900—but their output had been declining both in relative and absolute terms for a few decades. Three of the northern Irish patent distillers formed the United Distillers Ltd. in 1902, and discussions with the remaining producers led to the creation of the Irish Distillers' Association cartel in 1905. Neither this nor the agreement with the giant Edinburgh-based Distillers Company in the same year (and the consequent price rise) could quite counteract the major problem facing Irish distillers, the dramatic decline in spirit consumption in Ireland after 1900. Perhaps some future analysis of the industry will exonerate the Irish pot-still producer, as recent case-studies have sought to do for the Victorian mule-spinner, ironmaster, and ammonia

Table 12.9. *English imports of spirits from Ireland and Scotland* (million gallons)

Year	(1) Scotland	(2) Ireland	(1)/[(1) + (2)]
1880	1.8	1.6	0.53
1888	2.2	1.5	0.59
1900	7.1	4.2	0.63
1910	4.4	1.8	0.71

Sources: G. B. Wilson, *Alcohol and the Nation* (London, 1940), App. F, 418 (cited in I. A. Glen's introduction to a 1969 repr. of Barnard's *The Whisky Distilleries of the United Kingdom*).

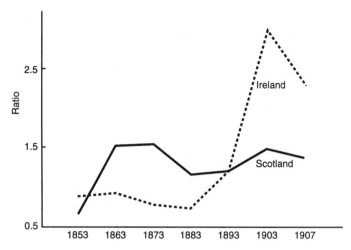

FIG. 12.1 Ratio of patent to pot-still spirit, 1853–1907

producer. At least the Irish pot-still distilleries outlasted their northern patent-still rivals. But that part of the story is less important than the poor performance of the Irish patent distillers relative to their Scottish rivals. In sum, the decline of the Irish distilling industry can hardly be blamed on the wrong choice of technique only; the Irish, North and South, lost out to the Scots on both patent- and pot-still fronts. A more plausible explanation for the lacklustre Irish performance is the lack of marketing: it is difficult to think of a single Irish distiller that built up the kind of overseas distribution network that characterized the leading Scottish blenders. The Scots also invested more heavily in the blending side.[69]

An inquiry into the quality of whiskey served in public houses in working-class areas throughout the UK and at fairs and markets in the west of Ireland in 1908 seems to imply that the Irish pot-still distillers' concern for quality was not shared by consumers. Only six of the thirty establishments sampled in Ireland (and none of those sampled in Britain) served pure malt as whiskey, though it is true that some others tried to dupe customers on that score. Samples taken in Cappawhite labelled 'First Quality Irish Whiskey' and in Offaly labelled 'Pure Old Irish Whisky— Distilled in Ireland from Home-Grown Barley and Malt' turned out to be raw patent spirit, with at most a touch of malt for flavouring. Nearly all the samples were artificially coloured with caramel or coal tar. Nor did malt, though more expensive to produce, command a higher price in the establishments visited in Ireland. Both the cheapest and the most expensive establishments in the sample—in Crossmolina (20*d*. a pint) and Feakle (42*d*. a pint), respectively—served a half-and-half blend. The study provided information on the alcoholic strength (percentage proof), intensity of colouring (on a scale from 1 to 6), and malt content of the spirit served in all thirty locations. In the regression reported below price was measured in pence, proof in percentage points, and a value of one was put on patent spirit and of six on pure pot-still, with the intervening range representing blends of varying proportions.

$$Price = 33.84 - 0.091 Proof + 0.701 Colour - 0.101 Quality$$
$$(2.47) \quad (-0.55) \quad (0.98) \quad (-0.23)$$
$$N = 30; \quad R^2 = 0.05; \quad t\text{-statistics in parentheses}$$

The outcome—small, weakly determined and wrongly signed coefficients, and virtually zero explanatory power—is not inconsistent with the claim of the 1909 inquiry that 'working men prefer patent-still spirit, or at least . . . they will not pay anything more for the superior article'.[70]

   Bielenberg's recent study of Locke's Distillery at Kilbeggan blames a combination of exogenous forces (falling alcohol consumption, rising excise duties) and lackadaisical management for that concern's poor record and ultimate demise. However, as he notes, this midland distillery also went through a golden age of a kind. John Locke, a Kilkennyman, had taken over the distillery on the River Brusna as a barely going concern in 1843. The earliest surviving daybook, which covers the 1860s and early 1870s, chronicles the transformation from a distillery catering almost exclusively to local needs to one with important clients in Dublin, Limerick, Armagh,

Table 12.10. *Orders for Cork Distillery Company whiskey, 1859–1937*

Period	Total	Munster	Rest of Ireland	GB	Other
Mar.–May 1859	1 225	1 206 (98)	5 (0)	14 (1)	0 (0)
Mar.–May 1871	2 427	2 251 (93)	7 (0)	168 (7)	1 (0)
Mar.–May 1890	2 548	2 348 (92)	34 (1)	158 (6)	8 (0)
Mar.–May 1902	2 111	1 972 (93)	29 (1)	108 (5)	2 (0)
Mar.–May 1937	3 144	2 779 (88)	365 (12)	— (—)	— (—)

Source: Cork Archives Council, CDC papers (packets 5, 125, 144, 165). Since the 1859 and 1937 data refer to spirit sent out of stock, and the 1871–1902 data to orders won either on Monday–Wednesday–Friday or Tuesday–Thursday–Saturday, and the totals are not strictly comparable. The 1937 data also exclude foreign orders, if any. The data refer to the number of orders. Percentages in parentheses.

Table 12.11. *The output of Irish distilleries, c.1887*

Distillery	Year founded	Output (1000 gals.)	Method
1. Bow St Distillery (Jameson)	1780	1 000	P
2. John's Lane Distillery (Power)	1791	900	P
3. Thomas St (George Roe), Dublin	1757	2 000	P
4. Marrowbone Lane (Wm. Jameson), Dublin	1797	900	P
5. Jones' Road Distillery (DWD)	1873	560 (600)	P
6. Phoenix Park, Dublin	1878	350 (350)	P
7. Cassidy's, Monasterevan	1784	203	P
8. Tullamore	1829	270	P
9. Lockes, Brusna	1757	157	P
10. Nun's Island, Galway	c.1815	400	P
11. Limerick Distillery	early 19C	300	P
12. North Mall, Cork	1779	510	P
13. Midleton	1825	1 000	P
14. Glen, Cork	c.1880	60	P
15. Allman's, Bandon	1826	500	both
16. Birr	1805	200	P
17. Bishop's Water, Wexford	1827	110	P
18. Dundalk	early 19C	700 (800)	both
19. Dunvilles, Belfast	1869	1 500	both
20. Irish Distillery, Belfast	incomplete in 1887		patent
21. Avoniel, Belfast	1882	850	patent
22. Upper Distillery, Comber	1825	150	P
23. Lower Distillery, Comber	1825	150	P
24. Coleraine	1820	100	P
25. Limavady	early 19C	250	P
26. Abbey St (Watt's), Derry	1826	1 260	patent
27. Waterside, Derry	?	200	P
28. Bushmills	1784	100 (100)	P
TOTAL		14 680	

Notes: Some details have been slightly corrected. Output in 1891–2 is in parentheses. P = indicates pot still. Evidently some distilleries exaggerated their output to Barnard, since official returns of the total number of gallons of proof spirits distilled in Ireland in the late 1880s are lower. In 1889 three of Dublin's distilleries—George Roe, Jones' Road, and W. Jameson—amalgamated. Barnard's inquiry suggests that the Irish distilleries were not wanting in size: even the smallest of them, the Glen distillery, was bigger than several highland malt distilleries.

Sources: Alfred Barnard, *The Whisky Distilleries of the United Kingdom* (London, 1887); *Industries of Ireland, 1: Belfast and the Towns of the North* (London, 1891); *Stratten's Dublin, Cork and South of Ireland* (London, 1892).

Bradford, Liverpool, and elsewhere. The distillery somehow failed to capitalize on this breakthrough, for on the eve of the First World War it was still a minor producer, selling about 50,000 gallons per annum, less than one-third the output claimed in Alfred Barnard's *The Whisky Distilleries of the United Kingdom* for the late 1880s. By the new century its clients were spread more widely (but thinly) throughout Ireland, and small markets had been developed in the USA and even among the Irish in Buenos Aires.[71] Presumably the other distilleries who succumbed to competition in the early twentieth century had failed to achieve even that much, though their histories and that of the surviving Irish distilleries remain to be written. The sales analysis books of one of these—the Cork Distillery Company's concern at Morrison's Island, producer of Paddy Flaherty whiskey—reveal a distillery firmly set in its ways during the period surveyed here. Only later did CDC seriously attempt to conquer Irish markets outside Munster.[72]

12.8 Other Industries

The output of the brewing industry trebled between the 1850s and 1914. About 40 per cent of output was exported at the end of the period, when beer and ale accounted for 3.2 per cent of all exports. That success was largely associated with one brewery, Arthur Guinness, by 1914 the largest in the world; it then accounted for about two-thirds of all Irish output and the bulk of exports. For a time after the Famine Guinness's rivals seemed to cope: their share of total Irish beer exports rose from 68 per cent in 1855 to 70 per cent in 1868. But this is to take no account of the Dublin brewery's increasing domination of the domestic market after the Famine. The other brewers, over a score of them still well scattered throughout the island in 1914, catered largely for local markets. Cork's brewers fared best; between 1844 and 1898 the quantity of malt used by them—a fair proxy for output—more than quadrupled. Through amalgamation and reliance on the rail network, they were able to win and hold on to much of the Cork city and county markets. Still, at the beginning of the new century the combined output of Cork city's surviving brewers, Murphy and Beamish & Crawford, was only one-eighth that of Arthur Guinness, with virtually all sales confined to Munster.[73]

Whiskey and beer relied largely on domestically produced raw materials. This was also true at the outset of another industry, flour-milling, a growing industry in the pre-Famine period. The bounty on flour sales to Dublin introduced in 1758 had provided an incentive to mill flour, and the following decades saw the output rise considerably. More important were the spurs given to flour production after 1800 by Napoleon's continental blockade, the Corn Laws, and steam navigation. Exports of flour grew from 25,000 cwt. annually in the 1800s to over 750,000 cwt. in the early 1840s. Scores of mills were built; the biggest, such as those at Slane, Milford (near Carlow), and Clonmel were technologically very sophisticated, and impressed travellers. When built in the 1760s, the Slane mill had been one of the largest anywhere, and probably remained the largest industrial structure in Ireland for some decades; bigger still were some early nineteenth-century mills, which could handle 30,000–40,000 barrels of flour annually.[74] Even in the 1830s new mills were being erected or old ones enlarged in places as far apart as Cahirciveen, Cavan, and Gorey.[75]

The industry was bound to suffer from the declining grain acreage after 1846. Exports were down to 160,000 cwt. in 1860–7, and American competition and roller-milling technology posed new challenges from then on. American wheat, being harder, required less drying, and the metal rollers produced a finely ground product much faster than the old mill-stones. Most of the Irish milling industry succumbed. Some newly built mills in port towns such as Belfast, Limerick, and Cork coped by applying the new technology to American and native wheat and grinding maize into animal feed. The Limerick firm of J. N. Russell & Sons, which had been milling wheat since 1810, adapted by building a roller-mill at Newtown Pery that was nine storeys high and driven by a 350-hp steam-engine.[76]

Other industries were of lesser significance. Paper-making was still expanding in mid-century, though even then it employed less than 1,000 people. In 1907 a labour force of 570 produced less than £0.2 million worth of paper. In the late eighteenth century the production of local editions, many pirated, of English works was a mainstay of the Dublin book trade. The Copyright Act of 1801 put an end to this, and Irish imports of British books quadrupled within a decade. In the longer term rising literacy created a growing demand for home-produced printed matter, but the number and circulation of Irish newspapers remained small until mid-century. Circulation rose impressively thereafter, as the telegraph and political mobilization gave home-produced papers an advantage over the English competition. As a result the number of newspaper editors and journalists rose from 259 in 1861 to 1,108 in 1911. That the boom in newsprinting easily compensated for any falling off in bookprinting is suggested by the rise in the number of printers from 1,755 in 1841 to

3,420 in 1871 and 4,722 in 1911. With some justice, then, Riordan might claim in 1920 that printing had weathered the storm.[77] Another industry to weather the storm was tobacco. Traditionally the production of 'roll' and 'twist' tobacco had been small-scale and widely dispersed: the 1841 census counted 548 'tobaccotwisters' spread over twenty-seven counties. Mechanization led to centralization, and by the 1900s Belfast, Dublin, and Dundalk accounted for the lion's share of output. Ireland became a net exporter of manufactured tobacco, and for a time the Belfast multinational of Gallaher Ltd. was the largest tobacco-producer in the world. Less successful in the long run were industries such as glass, salt, and sugar-refining. Glass had been manufactured in both Cork and Waterford since about 1780, but the industry was at a low ebb in both cities by 1840, and had ceased altogether a decade later. Dublin still had 146 glass-workers in 1841, and Belfast 74, but their industry was feeling the lash of Belgian and British competition. In 1852 only three glass-houses survived, two in Dublin and one in Belfast. The output of these three producers may have matched that of a much larger number of firms operating in the early 1830s in terms of weight, but this takes no account of illicit glass-houses, and the undoubted deterioration in the quality and value of output. Glass-bottling (in which home producers had a comparative advantage) was virtually all that remained of the industry by 1920.[78] The Royal Irish Sugar Beet Company began operations at Mountmellick in 1851 with a capital of £120,000, commanding the approval of Kane and others, but lasted barely a decade. The growth of brewing and distilling was unable to prevent the number of coopers from falling from 9,375 in 1841 to 6,186 in 1871 and 2,219 in 1911.

12.9 Industrial Decline?

> There is not, in all the history of our country, a more melancholy reflection than that suggested by the manufactured objects in [the Cork] Exhibition.
>
> *Irish Quarterly Review*, 1853[79]

The balance between British and Irish industry was already shifting in Britain's favour in the late eighteenth century. This is reflected in the contrasting reactions of British producers to the prospect of free trade in the early 1780s and in 1799–1800. In 1780–2 the Irish Parliament had imposed a 12.7 per cent tariff on imported calicoes and yarns and a 5 per cent bounty on home sales and exports. The severe economic depression and high food prices that hit Dublin manufacturers and workers in 1783–4 prompted demands for higher, matching tariffs against British imports. The joint response of the Dublin administration and prime minister Pitt was a series of 'commercial propositions' to liberalize Anglo-Irish trade. For Pitt and his supporters the propositions had a dual logic. First, like the Anglo-French commercial treaty to follow, they were an exercise in the new economics of Adam Smith.[80] Second, they would foster closer political union between the two kingdoms. The propositions provoked noisy and effective opposition from British manufacturers, however. The protesters included Mathew Boulton and Josiah Wedgwood, and England's cotton and linen manufacturers: a Lancashire petition against the move gathered 80,000 signatories. At issue were the advantages accruing to Irish manufacturers from lower taxes and cheap labour. In retrospect such English fears may be difficult to take seriously, yet they are a reminder that England's future role as 'workshop of the world' was not foreseen, even if it was predestined, in 1785. Pitt's proposals were duly defeated. In 1799–1800 it was the turn of Dublin industrialists to protest loudest against outside competition, and Article 6 of the Act of Union of 1800 (see Chapter 3) reflected their concerns—though it did not satisfy them.[81] The shift in Ireland's trade balance with Britain in manufactured goods is symptomatic. In 1784–6 Ireland exported nearly twice as much industrial produce in value terms to Britain as vice versa, but exports were level in the mid-1790s, and British manufactured exports to Ireland always greater thereafter. The range of British exports was greater too; while linen accounted for the bulk of Irish exports, in the mid-1820s textiles accounted for 54 per cent of British, ready-made clothing items for 12 per cent, iron and metal goods for 17 per cent, and other manufactures for the remaining 18 per cent.[82]

Though certain Irish industries declined after the Union, economic historians deny cause and effect, for several reasons. First, though Irish industry expanded in the 1780s and 1790s, the decades of 'Grattan's Parliament', protection of the domestic market by tariffs had little to do with it, and (as we have seen) decline in most sectors long post-dated the union. Second, the pre-Union duties would have been too small to counter the massive technology induced price decreases in textiles in the early nineteenth century. Third, Irish industrial expansion could not have proceeded on the domestic market alone; access to the British and American markets was crucial to success stories such as linen, shipbuilding, and beer.

Fourth, the protection of selected industries would almost certainly have increased costs for others.[83]

The adjustment problems besetting the Irish economy after Waterloo were thus exacerbated by industrial decline throughout much of the island. As noted above, the 1821 census still revealed substantial non-agricultural employment in counties that would eventually become predominantly agricultural. That almost half those credited with occupations in over-whelmingly rural counties such as Mayo and Leitrim in 1821 were 'chiefly employed in trades, manufactures, or handicraft' is striking evidence of this. In Monaghan the proportion was even higher—56 per cent. Decline was uneven both in timing and extent, and cannot be charted with precision because output and trade data are limited, and the occupational categories used in 1821 and 1841 differ. Besides, the 1821 census provides no breakdown of sectoral employment by sex. The 1821 census returned 1.17 million people (or 41 per cent of those given occupations) as 'chiefly employed in trades, manufactures, or handicraft', while the 1841 census returned nearly three-quarters of all families as 'chiefly employed in agricul-ture'. Comparing the 1821 and 1841 censuses shows that counties with a high proportion of females in manufacturing employment in 1841 ex-perienced proportionately the greatest job-losses in manufacturing. Were these also the counties with the highest proportions of female spinners in 1821, or was male employment more at risk in them in 1821–41? We don't know, but both explanations probably hold, since the spread of flax-spinning by machine in Belfast and its hinterland in the 1820s and 1830s is held to have reduced the viability of weaving, mainly a male occupation, in outlying rural western and north-western counties.[84]

Meanwhile, the slow pace of town growth would seem to have ruled out much industrialization in the towns; between 1821 and 1841 the propor-tion of people living in towns of 2,000 people or more barely rose, and fell in the provinces of Connacht and Munster. Yet comparing the 1.17 million in manufacturing employment in 1821 with the 0.9 million listed as 'ministering to clothing' in 1841, plus the 0.16 million 'ministering to lodging, furniture, machinery, etc.' suggests that industrial decline, very broadly defined, before the Famine may have been relative rather than absolute. If, as seems likely, a combination of new techniques and longer hours made labour productivity rise in these decades, the argument for some output growth is strengthened.[85] Relative decline at national level is not in dispute, however, and the absolute decline in poor counties such as Mayo—from 78,000 in 1821 to 46,000 in 1841—was real enough.

By mid-century, when Great Britain was celebrating its claim to be the workshop of the world at the Crystal Palace Exhibition, Irish industry had certainly fallen far behind. The contrast between the London Exhibition of 1851 and the Irish Industrial Exhibition of 1853 (brainchild of William Dargan, railway engineer and entrepreneur) is more than symbolic. Dargan's scheme cashed in on the vogue for exhibitions, following the London model closely. However, the huge crowds who visited the show-grounds by Merrion Square, in effect, were presented with a display of Irish industrial decline. By and large, the catalogue of exhibits offered a gloomy assessment of Irish manufacturing. In the engineering and textile areas, most of the manufacturing exhibitors were British. The same held for agricultural machinery; cheek by jowl with implements from the great English engineering firms of Ransome and Crosskill, one found 'sheep netting, made by the Irish peasants', 'a net for confining sheep on pasture, &c., made of shreds of bog deal', or a 'model of a horseshoe for a contracted foot' from a County Dublin inventor. That section of the exhibition prompted *The Times* to note that there were 'not half a dozen good implement makers in all Ireland'. The numerous exhibits of lace and crochet-making reflected aristocratic patronage or workhouse labour, 'the kind of manufacture that in England has been displaced by machinery'. Most Irish exhibitors were strictly small-time producers, or else importers of English wares.[86]

A comparison fifty years earlier would have produced a more equal outcome. But if the Dublin industrial exhibition suggests Irish industrial decline, did the trend continue thereafter? Before turning to a litany of hypotheses seeking to account for the lack of industrial progress in the following chapter, let us note at this point the danger of explaining away too much. Bielenberg's recent comparison of Irish industrial output in the 1840s and the 1910s implies some *increase* in aggregate output over the period, with the progress of textiles (notably linen), shipbuilding, brewing, and distilling more than matching the decline in other sectors. *Relative* decline is not in dispute, however. While Irish output held its own over these decades, UK industrial output quadrupled.

In general the period is not well served by industrial output data. Nevertheless, the trend in staples such as whiskey and beer can be captured by excise statistics, and estimates also exist for some other industries (e.g. linen, shipbuilding). Factory inspectors' returns (1870), trade data (from 1899 on), and the census of industrial production of 1907 throw some light on aggregate industrial trends. The official factory returns collected in 1870 for the whole of the UK demand careful handling, but also provide some useful detail. These statistics are incomplete: while intended to provide a full enumeration of factories and workshops, the workshop details were only 'partially received'. In Ireland workshop owners seem to have been particularly remiss, for in eleven counties no returns at all were furnished to the authorities. Perhaps this explains why Table 12.12 implies that Irish plants were on average larger than British plants, and better provided with energy. Still, the data are probably tolerably accurate for those industries coming under the provisions of the Factory Acts.[87] In 1870 these included textiles, foundries, letterpresses, breweries, distilleries, glass-making plants, potteries, and several others. The data confirm that though the factory system had effectively substituted for traditional industry in the north-east, throughout most of the south, west, and east hardly anything of significance remained. Thus only twenty-six plants were recorded for County Cavan, employing in all 213 persons, and two of these were tobacco factories, employing eighty-three persons between them. In counties

Table 12.12(a). *Irish and British industry, c.1870: Factory returns, aggregate data*

	Gt. Britain	Ireland
Number of plants	128 150	3 129
Horsepower (hp)		
Steam	945 927	31 013
Water	45 741	9 879
Employees	2 416 905	123 890

Table 12.12(b). *Irish industry, c. 1870: Factory returns*

Sector	No. of plants	Power (hp) steam	Water (hp)	Employment
Textiles	1 749	25 032	8 293	86 564
Metal	193	1 722	192	12 086
Leather	111	49	—	1 055
Chemicals	69	412	—	2 335
Food	85	2 066	412	5 257
Building	27	407	—	2 708
Paper	27	245	652	1 450
Misc.	678	1 080	330	12 475
TOTAL	3 129	31 013	9 879	123 890

such as Kerry and Clare the figures tell an even gloomier tale. Kerry could claim only a tiny flax-mill, three letterpresses, and two tobacco factories, employing forty-eight workers in all. In Clare three woollen factories and a letterpress accounted for a recorded labour force of thirty-one. The persistence of water-power in Ireland, particularly in the textile industry, is highlighted: in 1870 it provided nearly one-fourth of Ireland's recorded horsepower, but only one-twentieth of Britain's. The 1870 statistics suggest that Irish industrial horsepower was about 4.2 per cent of the UK total. In 1907, the first census of industrial production put the Irish share at 2.5 per cent. Since the coverage of the 1870 statistics was probably less complete for Ireland than for the rest of the UK, the drop from 4.2 to 2.5 per cent underestimates the true extent of Irish decline.

The impression of post-Famine industrial stagnation is confirmed by another source, the official lists of joint-stock companies established in Ireland during the 1850s and 1860s. True, over the next half century nearly 3,000 companies were registered in Ireland under this legislation, with a total nominal share capital of £109.6 million, and the survival rate of Irish companies was somewhat higher than that of English. However, this was mainly due to the smaller share in Ireland of risky propositions specializing in finance, land, or mining. Though many of the earliest of these Irish joint-stock ventures were small, established private companies seeking a public 'shell', they probably contain a fair cross-section of the new investment projects being started at the time. In 1868–9, for instance, of the fifteen limited companies registered in Dublin, five were municipal gaslight concerns, while the rest included the Limerick Masonic Hall Company, the Tyrone Loan Company, and the Newry Steam Packet Company. Three years later, thirty new companies had registered, but only two of these were substantial, the City of Cork Steam Packet Company and the Dublin Whiskey Distillery Company, with nominal capitals of £300,000 and £100,000. The others included the Valentia and Cahirciveen Steam Ferry Company, the Clew Bay Steam Navigation Company, the Londonderry Omnibus Company, Portrush Townhall and Assembly Company, the Larne Fishing Company, and two more gaslighting concerns. Practically all the joint-stock investment was in communications, lighting, building, and mineral prospecting.

Such quantitative impressions are supported by Sir Robert Kane's admission in 1884 that he 'could scarcely name a branch of industry that has not either become extinct or much more limited in its sphere, since the publication of [his] book' [in 1845]. The list of Irish manufacturing

Table 12.13. *Gross industrial output in Ireland (1907) and the 26 counties (1912) (in £000)*

	1907 Ireland (1)	1912 26 Counties (2)	(2)/(1) (3)
Grain milling	7 186	5 321	0.74
Bacon curing	3 755	3 955	1.05
Butter, cheese, margarine	4 066	3 085	0.76
Brewing & malting	5 197	7 036	1.35
Spirit distilling	1 416	438	0.31
Bread & biscuits	3 646	1 637	0.45
Woollen & worsted	769	684	0.89
Mines, quarries	258	156	0.60
Engineering implements	890	193	0.22
Iron, steel, ships, vehicles	4 942	377	0.08
Textiles (except woollen)	15 836	347	0.02
Clothing, millinery	4 622	841	0.18
Boots & shoes	264	132	0.50
Dyeing, cleaning	303	28	0.09
Paper, stationery, &c.	355	143	0.40
Printing, publishing, &c.	1 337	830	0.62
Soap, candles	357	167	0.47
Chemicals, drugs, paints	834	871	1.05
Public utility services	2 904	1 242	0.43
All others	7 839	2 257	0.29
TOTAL	66 839	29 257	0.44

Sources: Census of Industrial Production, 1907; Census of Industrial Production 1926 and 1929 (Dublin, 1933), xxi.

exporters prepared by the Department of Agriculture and Technical In-struction in 1911 continues the story. The list, the result of notices and advertisements circulated by the Department, contains details of about 270 firms, presumably the bulk of going concerns at the time, and is a good guide to the industrial state of the country and of geographical concen-tration. Two-thirds of the firms listed were located near Belfast or Dublin, and half in what would soon become Northern Ireland. Most of Leinster, Munster excluding Cork, and Connacht contained few manufacturers in-terested in exporting. Table 12.13 provides a useful impression of the relative position North and South on the eve of the First World War. The 1907 and 1912 returns are not strictly comparable—note that in a few cases gross output in the South in 1912 exceeded all-Ireland output in 1907! Nevertheless, the comparison clearly shows that, excluding food and drink, the south was virtually without industries at this time. It confirms that Ulster's success was built on linen, engineering, and shipbuilding, linen being by far the most important of these in terms of job creation. The contrasting fortunes of the north-east and the rest is also a reminder that though decline relative to Britain is hardly in doubt, the growth of industrial output in the north-east after mid-century may well have compensated for decline in the rest of Ireland.[88]

Industry, c.1780–1914:
Problems and Prospects

Historians and others have suggested many reasons why most of Ireland failed to industrialize in the nineteenth century. One, long popular with nationalist writers, blames the mercantilism that preceded the Act of Union of 1800 and the imperialism of free trade that followed it. In the eighteenth century England is supposed to have stifled Irish industry by preventing the Irish from exporting their wares, in the nineteenth to have done the same by preventing the Irish from imposing tariffs. Such arguments no longer carry much conviction. They are held to exaggerate the damage caused by prohibitions against Irish wool and cattle exports, and to forget that both the prosperity of the late eighteenth century and the crises of the early nineteenth were largely independent of commercial policy. The nationalist version was also poor economics: it ignored the deadweight losses that would have stemmed from protection and the undoubted benefits that free trade conferred on agriculture and linen.[1]

Other hypotheses include Ireland's paucity of natural resources, the 'lack of private enterprise', and the risks to life and property there. Some historians deny that the lack of coal and iron was a disadvantage; others might counter, with Bielenberg, that 'the European industrialists of the nineteenth century took the view that it was easier for labourers to go where coal and iron are abundant and cheap (even if economists and economic historians have not).'[2] The hypothesis that Ireland's lack of industry was due to entrepreneurial failure (or Ulster's success to entrepreneurial flair) is another argument with a wider European resonance. Both Britain's early start and her later inability to match German and American competition have been put down to the quality of her entrepreneurs. The claim that Irish industry languished for the want of venture capital is really also one about poor entrepreneurship. Another line of reasoning worth exploring is the role of luck: recent economic models of 'path dependence' have given greater respectability to sheer serendipity and 'small historic events'. Yet another reason given is that Ireland's peripheral location, far from centres of large population, placed it at a disadvantage from the start.

The success of the north-east has prompted cultural explanations and a role for Ulster tenant right in encouraging accumulation in the north-east.[3] If recent research suggests that the spatial correlation between tenant right and industrialization was weak, then at least the industrial revolution in the north, a region with a strong Presbyterian ethos, would seem to provide ammunition for Weber–Tawney 'Protestant ethic' arguments. Within the north, Presbyterians tended to dominate the linen industry: in 1795, 'almost every shilling [was] in the hands of Protestants'. The hypothesis is worth considering even if, as Lee has noted, Protestantism did not save Ulster from relative decline in the twentieth century.[4] Clearly, there is no shortage of explanations. In this chapter we dwell on some of Ireland's alleged advantages and disadvantages in Europe's race to industrialize.

13.1 Resource Constraints

> Dr Kane shows that the precious baltic iron, for which from £15 to £35 per ton is given, could be equalled by Irish iron smelted by Irish turf for six guineas per ton.
>
> THOMAS DAVIS[5]

Just before the Famine, Dublin scientist Robert Kane denied that a lack of natural resources could explain Ireland's failure to industrialize along British lines. He based his claim in part on an oversanguine assessment of the country's coal and peat resources. Even so, coal might also be imported, and Kane tried to show that the cost of shipping it from Britain would have added only marginally to aggregate costs. The point was rejected in the 1860s by economist William Neilson Hancock, who asserted that 'Irishmen ha[d] no ground to complain of a relatively greater progress, so far as it is founded on natural advantages of coal and iron, and the numerous manufactures dependent on them, which Great Britain is fortunate enough to possess to a much greater extent than Ireland'. Who was right? In the early decades of the nineteenth century coal could be had close to the pithead in regions such as the central lowlands of Scotland and South Wales for about £0.25 per ton.[6] The price on the Dublin quays was three or four times that, and carriage to most parts of the city cost another £0.10–0.20 per ton. Nevertheless, recent assessments by Mokyr, Geary, and Ollerenshaw side with Kane. They argue that energy constituted only an insignificant fraction of total cost, and that any disadvantages on that front were outweighed by the cheapness of Irish labour. Businessmen might economize on the scarcer resource; in Belfast in the 1880s it was said that 'perhaps from the shrewdness of the millowners, more care was exercised in the economical production of steam power than in any other town in the three kingdoms'.[7] Unfortunately, direct comparisons based on business records are scarce. One such, an 1843 letter from a Glasgow mill-owner to the owner of the York Lane cotton-mill in Belfast argues, rather loosely, for a Scottish cost advantage of £200 (£312 versus £112) out of a total outlay of £10,000 from cheaper coal; more important was the Scottish cost advantage in spinning labour. Estimates of production costs in the Belfast linen industry in the early 1870s put the cost of coal at 5 to 10 per cent of the total.[8] While such numbers seem to support Kane's point, 2 or 3 per cent of total costs nevertheless might mean 20 to 30 per cent of the average return on capital. Besides, the comparisons refer to Belfast, and the cost of coal some miles inland would have been substantially higher (see below). For other industries, the cost of coal bulked larger. It was claimed in 1830 that the cost of coal had forced the virtual abandonment of glass-making, sugar-refining, and salt production, and 'of some other articles in which coal is largely consumed'.[9] Moreover, the record of industrialization within Great Britain suggests that there is something odd about Kane's argument; industry there settled largely near the coalfields. When coke-smelting replaced charcoal, the iron industry came to be concentrated on coalfields near iron ore deposits. The distribution of steam power also mirrored that of coalfields. In the Low Countries too, the differing rates of industrialization of Belgium and Holland in the early nineteenth century seem to have had a lot to do with the location of resources of coal and iron.[10]

In pre-rail Britain overland carriage ten miles from the pit could double the price of coal; a rate of 6d. per ton-mile was common. In 1844 Kane felt 'obliged to estimate its minimum amount at 3d. per ton per mile' in Ireland, but again that was before the railway. In 1866 the cost of carrying a ton of coal for a mile by horse and dray was estimated at 6d., but at only a penny per ton-mile by rail and even less by canal. However, even at such improved rates coal produced in Munster or Connacht could not be sold in Dublin for less than 25s. per ton. Dubliners relied instead on imported coal costing 14–15s., twice the price paid in Glasgow and Leeds. In the end one can only agree with Johnson and Kennedy, that 'it cannot be seriously maintained that if Ireland had possessed the mineral resources of the Ruhr it would not have been a more industrialized country.'[11]

Coal is not merely an input, it is an output in its own right.[12] The point is a reminder that Ireland's rather meagre coal deposits—to be found mainly in Counties Kilkenny, Tyrone, Leitrim, and Laois—were also actively worked in the nineteenth century. During its period of peak prosperity in the second quarter of the nineteenth century, the Tyrone coalfield at Coalisland was producing 20,000 to 30,000 tons annually and providing work for about 250 men. Costly cartage and competition from turf limited the size of the market, however, and the awkward structure of the coal-seams added to the difficulties. The Tyrone Coal Mining Company (which yielded 0.2 million tons between 1873 and 1875) hoped to turn a resource base of 33 million tons into making Ulster self-sufficient in coal, but was soon prey to flooding problems and exaggerated expectations. Mining activity in Tyrone staggered on, coming to a halt in 1910. Two further efforts were made at reviving the Tyrone coalfield, in the 1920s and the 1950s, though without lasting success.[13] The Kilkenny (or Leinster) coalfield was centred on the bleak plateau around Castlecomer. Its anthracite provided the lion's share of Irish coal output, but it was better suited to industrial than domestic use, 'the fire it made [being] cheerless to the eye, and exceedingly unpleasant to the smell'. Castlecomer also catered for a local market, and its remote location meant that it could not compete with imported coal on the east coast. The Halls put the output of Kilkenny coal at 115,000 tons (including 75,000 tons of culm) annually in the early 1840s, but sounded a bleak note on the colliery's prospects. According to Kane the Munster coalfield was 'the most extensive development of the coal strata in the British Empire', but efforts at working it proved costly and fruitless. For a time, the Arigna field was held to contain vast mineral wealth, but the sad fate of the Arigna Iron and Coal Company put paid to that dream. Isaac Weld's withering account of the dashed hopes for north Connacht 'where thirty millions of tons of fine coal, suitable to every possible use, were supposed to lie disregarded within the bowels of the earth, together with beds of iron stone, capable, with the aid of capital, of converting this district into another Carron' is much more to the point.[14] Even Kane, the great optimist, conceded that future Irish industrialization could not be based on Irish coal alone. Aggregate Irish output data are available from 1854. They reveal a story of absolute and relative decline (see Table 13.1).[15]

Table 13.1. *Irish coal output, 1854–1914*

Year	Tons	% of UK output
1854	148 750	0.9
1864	125 000	0.5
1874	139 213	0.3
1884	122 431	0.3
1894	112 604	0.2
1904	105 637	0.1
1914	92 400	0.1

In *The Industrial Resources of Ireland* (1845) Kane also enthused about the value of copper, lead, and precious metal deposits.[16] He was not alone, yet in truth Ireland's mineral resources were meagre by British standards in the nineteenth century. (The wealth of modern mines such as Tynagh, Navan, and Galmoy would remain hidden until developments in remote sensing techniques and conceptual geology and geochemistry would make prospecting covered deposits viable). None the less, known deposits generated considerable interest and activity throughout the century, and all the fields mentioned by Kane were targets of speculation. As in the twentieth century, most of the money and expertise involved in Irish mining came from outside the country. Companies with grandiose names such as the Mining Company of Ireland, the Associated Irish Mine Company, the Royal Irish Mining Company, the Imperial Mining Company, and the Hibernian Mining Company, and local enterprises such as the Berehaven Mining Company, the West Cork Mining Company, the Kenmare Mining Association, the Mountcashel Iron Ore Company, and the Arigna Iron Company, came and went. The Mining Company of Ireland, formed in 1825, fared better than most. Its directors included scientists Whitley Stokes and Francis Barker, and businessmen Joseph Pim and Jeremiah Haughton. Spending nearly £48,000 in its first half-year, it took out leases on forty-three widely scattered mining properties (including ones at Dalkey, Ballycorus, and Knockmahon).[17] The story of the Associated Irish Mine Company, which raised a capital of £50,000 in 1798 to operate the copper mines at Cronebane and Tigroney in County Wicklow, captures the precarious nature of most Irish mining ventures. Started up by investors from the Liverpool–Macclesfield area, the Company prospered at first and paid an 8 per cent dividend in 1806. The English directors, delighted with the results, voted gifts of silver plate and salary increases for the management at Cronebane. It was a different story when the price of copper plummeted in 1807 and profit turned to loss. Production soon stopped. Efforts at selling the mine and associated leases for £1,700 in 1818–20, when 'everything [was] going hourly to decay and ruin', failed. The Company struggled on under new ownership, and every improvement in the price of copper brought renewed activity. It was finally dissolved in 1882.[18] Another Wicklow mine, that of the Hibernian Mining Company at nearby Ballymurtagh, yielded about 6,000 tons a year in the early 1840s. Copper was also mined around Allihies on the bleak and remote Beara peninsula. Between 1812, when ore was first discovered, and 1842, 88,000 tons were produced there. The location dictated that plant and supplies be brought in and the ore sent out by sea, while the awkward situation of the ore veins themselves soon required the use of steam-engines. The owners claimed an output of 6,000–7,000 tons in the mid-1830s, but the take fell back considerably before the Famine. The Allihies mine went through repeated ups and downs thereafter. Production dropped from 8,358 tons in 1863 to 1,807 tons in 1870, when a rise in the price of copper prompted a brief recovery. When the mine closed in 1883, a victim of foreign competition and resource depletion, it seemed like the end of the road for Allihies, and plant was auctioned off. Yet a succession of investors took turns in seeking to make a go of what was left of the deposit, until another price decline put an end to mining in 1930.[19] Perhaps the single greatest commercial disaster in Irish mining history was the London-based West Cork Mining Company, which undertook to pay the huge sum of £165,000 for the rights to Lord Audley's mines near Ballydehob in west Cork in 1836, but managed to produce only 173 tons of ore before being swamped in litigation. That company was the brainchild of one Joseph Pike, an ex-bankrupt swindler.[20] The mines around Bonmahon (County Waterford) proved more successful, lasting from 1824 until the dismantlement of the works in 1884; total production reached over 9,000 tons in 1843. At their peaks both the Waterford and Beara concerns claimed to give employment to about a thousand men. But copper extraction in Ireland was costly, and aggregate output (perhaps 25,000 tons on the eve of the Famine) was always modest compared to that of Cornwall (145,688 tons in 1838). Irish output in the 1880s and 1890s averaged less than 100 tons annually; in 1900–13 it averaged 1,000 tons.[21]

Lead-mining was also tried, though on a smaller scale. Quantities were taken sporadically in Wicklow and Wexford by the Mining Company of Ireland, and smelted at Ballycorus (County Dublin) from the early nineteenth century on. The deposits at Silvermines near Nenagh were not exploited, but small quantities of lead were taken in Down, Clare, and Kerry. An official source named a mine in County Armagh, which yielded a single ton of dressed ore, as Ireland's only working lead-mine in 1916: in 1918 that distinction passed to the mine at Abbeytown in County Sligo.[22] Iron ore was tried too. In the 1870s the Antrim iron-ore field attracted both local and English entrepreneurs. But the output was too small— somewhat over 200,000 tons at the peak around 1880—to justify the construction of smelters, and the ore mined in the Glens was all sent unprocessed to England. Antrim also contained the UK's only deposits of bauxite, but output remained very small.[23] The 1841 census counted 3,096 miners (including 52 women). Wicklow accounted for 721 of these, Tipperary for 439, Waterford for 385, and Cork for 321. Kilkenny, the main coal-mining county, employed 416, and Tyrone 169 more.[24] Some increase in employment in the post-Famine decades is indicated, since the Inspector of Mines put the total employed in metalliferous mining in 1873 at 3,212. Numbers declined rapidly thereafter, however, to 1,245 in 1883 and 617 in 1898.

To summarize: the nineteenth century saw a good deal of mining activity in Ireland. Richard Griffith wrote in 1828 of 'wandering English miners of the lowest order, and worst character'[25] who had attempted to reopen ancient mining sites in the previous half-century. More respectable prospectors, Irish and British, followed in their wake, and by the end of the century most of the accessible deposits were exhausted. Grenville Cole's geological memoir of 1922 mentions about 500 sites, scattered over virtually all counties, which had been worked at one stage or another since about 1800.[26] Yet all in all, Irish mines were at best marginal propositions, worked only when the market for the relevant metal was very buoyant, as with copper in mid-century and iron ore a few decades later. A great deal of money was invested—and lost—in mining activity.[27]

What are the broader implications of this story? First, we have seen that substantial capital and expertise, both native and foreign, were devoted to the Irish mining sector during the nineteenth century, despite the risks involved. Production techniques were adapted and developed to suit local conditions. In several cases, the inglorious demise of one set of investors early in the century failed to deter others from trying their hand later. If that much is true of mining, is it not reasonable to infer that capital would also have flown into other ventures, had the prospects been as promising? Perhaps there was 'something special' about mining as a magnet for speculation? That question cannot be addressed here, though the onus is surely on those who believe this to prove their case.[28] Second, despite considerable expenditure of capital, not much mineral wealth was found or generated. In so far as deposits of coal and metal helped industrialization, Ireland was at a disadvantage relative to most west European economies. Perhaps this is why Kane tried to have it both ways in *The Industrial Resources of Ireland*: arguing (implausibly) on the one hand that Ireland was well endowed with natural resources, and (more plausibly, though hardly convincingly) on the other, that natural resources were not crucial for industrialization.

13.2 The 'Turf Question'

'Dá mbeadh prátaí is móin againn, bheadh an saol ar a thóin againn.'[29]

AN IRISH PROVERB

A 1920 estimate put the endowment of turf (as peat is usually termed in Ireland) in Irish bogs three to four billion tons, or 250 times the then annual total fuel requirement. The best bogland—'red bog'—was to be found in the central limestone plain, north of a line between Wicklow and Galway and south of one between Dublin and Sligo, but practically every county had some peat deposits. The role of turf as a domestic fuel and as an important ingredient in agricultural output and in pre-Famine living standards has already been discussed (in Chapters 1 and 4). But if coal was lacking, surely those vast expanses of turf, extending to some three million acres in all, also represented a viable alternative as a source of industrial energy? Curiously enough, the government-appointed Bogs Commission of 1809–14, whose pioneering researches into peat deposits still impress today, was more concerned with the agricultural potential of reclaimed bogland than the fuel potential of the turf itself. But to authorities such as Kane, for whom 'our bogs may become, under the influence of an enlightened energy, sources of industry and eminently productive', the prospects were good. Much later in 1921 an inquiry on behalf of the First Dáil's Department of Scientific and Industrial Research reached an equally optimistic conclusion. But there have always been the doubters too. Of these perhaps Edward Wakefield is the most celebrated; the most extreme must be R. Dennis, who held in 1887 that 'the bog-covered surface of Ireland would be far more valuable in almost any other character', and who could think of 'nothing worse, save the glaciers of Switzerland or the lava-beds of Sicily'.[30]

Throughout the nineteenth century the bulk of this 'resource' remained untapped by industrialists, and what was cut—about 5–6 million tons annually—was being harvested by hand along age-old lines, almost exclusively for household use. On 97 per cent of Connacht farm households as late as 1917 turf was the sole fuel used; in Leinster a majority then used coal. The only regional traffics worth a mention were along the Grand Canal to Dublin and between south Connemara and fuel-starved north Clare and Aran. The former reached 30,000–40,000 tons annually around mid-century, about 0.5 per cent of contemporary consumption nation-wide. In the 1910s the only railway companies to carry turf were the West Clare Railway (about 5,000 tons per annum) and, in a local way in north Kerry, the Great Southern and Western.

Did neglect of the peat bogs, then, represent a lost opportunity? For Wakefield the issue was simple. That factories did not develop next to the bogs was 'a decisive proof that the expense of this kind of fuel has been too great to admit of any such improvement'. And the basic issue is one of the respective costs of turf and coal as household and industrial fuels; the mere *presence* of turf is not enough. The calorific content per ton of coal is well over twice that of turf, so in order to compete turf would have had to cost at most less than half as much as coal at consumption point. But that is not all: a cubic metre of coal produced five or six times as much heat as the same quantity of turf, implying far lower storage, carriage, and operating costs. Turf, ton for ton, was more expensive to transport, and suffered more in transit.[31] Besides, turf yield tended to be quite variable from season to season, descending to one-half or even one-third the norm in a very wet year, and turf was cheapest in remote and desolate areas where the substantial external economies of urban location were unavailable. That turf cost less per standardized unit than coal on the Bog of Allen was no consolation to the entrepreneur considering setting up in Cork City. A more realistic price ratio, then, might be 1:4 or 1:5—and the scattered data in Wakefield and elsewhere suggests that turf was generally not that cheap in Ireland. In 1844 Kane reported that furnace coal along the east coast cost 12s. per ton, while turf, excluding transport, cost 4s. per ton. But in 1855 manufacturers in Galway and Limerick preferred to pay £1 per ton, 'and often much more', for coal than use local supplies of turf.[32] In

1915, loading and transport charges added 5s. 6d. to the cost of Ticknevin turf (6s.) in Dublin.

An important point: the lack of success in developing peatbogs for industrial use during the nineteenth century was not for the want of trying. The list of failures is an impressive one, spanning many decades and many different processes. Turf not just as fuel, but turf as fertilizer, turf as animal litter, turf as brown paper, turf as hardboard, all were attempted by hopeful businessmen. Firelighters were made by soaking hardened turf in inflammable liquid. Kane was heavily involved in the turf-distillation factory set up at Kilberry near Athy in 1849, which proved a costly failure just a few years later. The efforts at smelting iron ore with peat coke at Newtowncrommelin in County Antrim in 1843 and at Creevelea in County Leitrim in 1854–8 also proved unsuccessful, though here perhaps the poor supply of iron ore was part of the problem. The redoubtable J. P. O'Gorman Mahon MP created quite a stir once in the House of Commons, when he exhibited some candles made from turf to fellow members in the chamber, but it turned out that they cost a guinea each to make!

Among the exhibits at the Dublin Exhibition was a working model by a Castlecomer inventor of 'an apparatus for converting dried peat into charcoal'.[33] The paper produced at Callenders' mill at Celbridge contained 66 per cent turf fibre, and was reputedly of excellent quality. For a short time this plant turned out more wrapping paper than all other Irish paper-mills combined, and provided employment for forty to sixty people, but the high costs of shipping and purifying the turf, of which only one-tenth was usable in any case, led to bankruptcy in 1905. The irony is that here Ireland was at the forefront of innovative activity both at process and product level. The Irish Amelioration Society, incorporated by Royal Charter amid much publicity, using the patent of one Jasper Rogers for converting turf into peat fuel and charcoal, hoped 'to employ constantly and most beneficially thousands of the half-starved and half-naked peasantry'. At Derrylea near Portarlington a new method of pressing peat was introduced in 1866; a 'first' has also been claimed for the method introduced by Williams at Cappogue in 1844 for converting peat into fuel by pressure, and for that of making sieve turf by Buckland in Sligo in 1863. Dennis could claim with some justice in 1887 that 'there is hardly any natural substance the use of which has been made the subject of so much experiment as peat'. All the experiments failed, and, as the Department of Scientific and Industrial Research conceded in 1921, the bogs were being used then as a fuel source only when coal was unavailable. That

Department, sick of 'magical schemes', focused on whether the best-located turf could compete with coal. The record was such that 'the public has lost confidence in any scheme for the utilization of the bogs, and it would be difficult to attract private capital for such work'.[34]

Turf had been employed fitfully for industrial purposes during the nineteenth century, for example by the steamers who plied the Shannon for a time in the 1840s and 1850s, and—most famously—by Messrs. Hamilton Robb at their factory at Portadown. The early nineteenth-century owners of the distillery at Kilbeggan relied on turf before the town was linked to the Grand Canal. Turf was used on a limited scale for kelp and lime-burning, for drying corn, and for driving threshing-machines, stone-crushers, and sawmills. But the overall record is such that a search for hidden reasons for why turf was not used more widely, such as difficulties surrounding turbary rights and compulsory purchase,[35] seems superfluous. When the Irish Amelioration Society began to operate the bogs at Derrymullen, they were besieged with offers by landed proprietors like the Marquis of Sligo, Lord Freyne, and General Caulfield, hoping to see their wastes similarly used. Turf was given every opportunity to prove itself as an industrial fuel during the nineteenth century, and it failed.

13.3 Entrepreneurship

Another reason advanced for Ireland's failed industrialization is the poor quality of its entrepreneurs. Dublin Quaker Jonathan Pim, no mean entrepreneur himself, exempted Ulster businessmen, 'more willing to embark in manufactures, and to devote the requisite care and attention to the management of their business'.[36] For students of the British economy in the late Victorian era the accusation against the Irish entrepreneur has a hint of *déjà vu* about it. In Britain's case, the new textbook conventional wisdom established in the late 1960s and 1970s holds that the lack of good entrepreneurs did not constrain Britain's growth after mid-century. The broad implication of both macroeconomic growth accounting exercises and a series of industry and firm case-studies is that suitable entrepreneurs were not lacking when there was a profit to be made. However, the case is not closed: more recent reassessments of the British cotton and iron industries undermine somewhat the panglossian inferences drawn from earlier investigations.[37]

The detailed research required to weigh such conflicting claims has only begun in the Irish case. Caskey's revisionist study of Ulster businessmen after 1850 finds their performance 'erratic'. Even in linen failures were frequent, the return on capital low, and prosperity dependent more on exogenous factors than on entrepreneurial acumen.[38] Outside Ulster, the tanning industry is an oft-cited case of opportunities missed. In the south of Ireland tanning had long been a very important industry, boosted by the ready supply of hides from the provisions trade. Bandon once had boasted seventeen tanneries and Cork had forty-six in the 1830s. Yet at the Irish Industrial Exhibition of 1853 the representation was 'altogether left to a few of the tanners of Dublin'. In 1892 there was a solitary tannery left in Bandon, and in 1907 the whole of Ireland accounted for only £87,000 out of a UK leather production total of £18 million. Cullen has blamed the decline on a failure to adopt new technology, echoing Sullivan's lament that '[the tanners were] in many cases tanners by accident, and usually gentlemen by profession, and knowing just that the skin of animals and the infusion of bark makes leather, but considering the process by which it is made to be the peculiar domain of the workman.' The Irish allegedly clung to a traditional technique that produced a superior article, 'but the price of the rapid-tanned leather appealed to the attenuated purses of the populace'. Alas for Irish tanners, shoe and boot manufacturers were happy with the cheaper leather. But before blaming the tanners entirely for their own demise, it should be noted that the decline of the Cork victualling trade and the switch to exporting Irish cattle on the hoof reduced their ready supply of hides. They may also have suffered from a decline in the Irish boot and shoe industry. Employment in the footwear industry fell from 55,000 in 1841 to 32,000 in 1871 and only 13,000 in 1911. The 1841 data refer to boot- and shoe-makers, but many of those recorded in 1911 were probably cobblers.[39]

The early history of the Irish railway system, wherein the bulk of the initial risk capital was provided by British investors, provides another instance of Irish reluctance to take risks. The return on early ventures was high, and latecomer Irish investors were forced to buy in at a substantial premium.[40] The early history of gaslighting in Dublin tells a similar tale of missed opportunities on the part of Irish capital. Irish people showed little interest in the shares of the Hibernian Gas Light Company in 1823, and accordingly lost out when the company was taken over by the London-based United General Gas Company a few years later at a premium of £22 a share.[41] Our survey of the brewing and distilling industries revealed instances of 'satisficing' behaviour on the part of Irish businessmen, seemingly content with servicing a purely local clientele while their rivals in Dublin and Scotland sought out markets abroad. But the argument must not rest on a few such case-studies.

If first-rate native capitalists were wanting, why did outsiders not avail themselves of the lost opportunities? The answer is that many did, for the history of Irish manufacturing in the nineteenth century shows that entrepreneurial mobility across the Irish Sea was considerable.[42] Indeed early Irish industrialization was almost synonomous with the importation of techniques, finance capital, entrepreneurs, capital goods, and even skilled workmen. An early example is the Scotsman Nicholas Grimshaw, who introduced twist-milling to Ireland in 1784. Grimshaw had also been involved in setting up the spinning-works at the Belfast Charitable Institution in 1777. Examples multiply thereafter. The first cotton-mill in Lisburn was set up in 1790 by a Yorkshireman, James Wallace, who was also responsible for importing the first Boulton and Watt steam-engine, while most of the workers at the Stratford-on-Slaney textile works came from Ulster and Scotland, and their employer John Orr had previously been a muslin-producer in Paisley and a mill-owner near Hillsborough (which he left when he could not obtain a lease).[43] The cotton manufacturers attracted to Balbriggan by its landlord in the 1780s were Lancashiremen; Robert Gemmill of Lambeg was a Scotsman; according to Dubourdieu, a Yorkshireman was making machinery parts (mainly rollers, spindles, bobbins, and chains) for local cotton manufacturers in Lisburn early in the nineteenth century. Charles Walker, who set up a lace-factory in Limerick in 1829, was from Oxford. Fine linen thread-making, 'as stated on the best authority', was introduced to the Lisburn area in the late eighteenth century by the Scot, John Barbour. The owners of Drogheda's Westgate linen-mill hailed from Preston. Coxon, who built a cotton-mill next to the Boyne near Navan, was English. The huge mills built in Bangor, County Down, in 1803–6—the second of them was deemed 'more extensive than any hitherto erected in Ireland'—were the work of a Scot, McWilliams, in partnership with an Irish textile manufacturer and the local landlord. The Ulster muslin and embroidery sectors were largely controlled by Scottish firms. James Fisher, a Lancashire businessman, was responsible for exploiting the iron-ore mine at Glenravel in the Glens of Antrim in the 1860s and 1870s. Much earlier, in 1798, the people and the capital behind a much larger mining venture, the Associated Irish Mining Company, came from the north-west of England.[44] John Arnott, co-founder of the retailing firm bearing his name and later owner of the *Irish Times*, was a native of Scotland.[45] Robert Gordon, who is supposed to have spent £60,000 on a

We wish the new Company every success, but we don't like the look of the graveyard.

PLATE 3. If insurance companies failed in Ireland, it was not from the want of trying. The same could have been said of mining ventures (*The Lepracaun*, May 1908)

series of fruitless farming and manufacturing ventures outside Cork in the 1780s and 1790s, was also a Scot, as were William Tillie and John Henderson, the driving forces behind the Derry shirtmaking industry, which boomed after mid-century. In other sectors, it seems to have been the same story. John Anderson—the Cork entrepreneur whose coaching and other ventures earned him a fortune during the Napoleonic Wars, though he was to lose it in their wake—was also a Scotsman.[46] Charles Bianconi, another coaching magnate, hailed from northern Italy, while the driving force behind joint-stock banking in Ireland in the 1820s was Englishman Thomas Joplin. Later on, Yorkshireman Edward James Harland relied on the help of a Liverpool-German financier and the German Gustav Wolff to set up Harland & Wolff. The principals of the Belfast Ropework Company, founded in 1872 and soon to be the largest concern of its kind in the world, included Wolff and a son of Samuel Smiles.[47] Many more examples might be given. Unfortunately, the census reports fail to capture in sufficient detail trends in the occupational make-up of the foreign-born, but they indicate an increasing inflow of foreigners. People born outside of Ireland accounted for 0.42 per cent of Ireland's population in 1841, 0.79 per cent in 1851, and 1.35 per cent in 1861. In 1926 foreigners accounted for over 10 per cent of employers, managers, and foremen in several industries in the Irish Free State, including textiles, drink, 'other apparel', electrical apparatus, printing, and watch- and glass-making.[48]

Perhaps the inflow implies that native enterprise was lacking. But enterprise was a mobile input, so the grosser failures of indigenous and local entrepreneurs probably would have been capitalized on by competitors from across the Irish Sea or elsewhere in Ireland. That entrepreneurs and capital moved into some sectors and areas—though not in others—may be evidence that those factors were not lacking, but that profitable opportunities for them were.[49]

Historians have long debated the role of religious minorities and ideology in economic development.[50] At first sight Ireland offers sad proof of the Weber–Tawney link between Catholicism and laggard economic performance. Though Ireland as a whole was not short of non-Catholics— Presbyterians, Methodists, and other Nonconformists accounted for one-tenth of total population in the mid-nineteenth century—that 95 per cent of Nonconformists lived in Ulster would seem to clinch the link between the old religion and economic backwardness. That link did not escape nineteenth-century observers, several of whom pointed to the greater industry of non-Catholics. And still, in so far as religion influenced the supply of entrepreneurs, the rest of Ireland was not left short. County Dublin had 15,000 Nonconformists, and over a quarter of the people living in the city and suburbs were non-Catholics. The Irish Quakers, according to Arthur Young 'the most sensible class in the kingdom', never numbered more than a few thousand, but they played a disproportionate role in business in both northern and southern Ireland, as their co-religionists did in Britain, moving from place to place as profit dictated. The Pims, the Malcolmsons, the Richardsons, and the Greers are but the best-known examples: Friends' finance was central to Ireland's first railway and to the Royal Bank of Ireland, and Friends also founded the great textile concerns at Portlaw and Bessbrook. Over the years, many Quakers left Ireland for Britain and America but, again, there is a presumption that fewer would have emigrated had the opportunities been present in Ireland. The same kind of argument might be applied to Ireland's late nineteenth- and early twentieth-century Jewish community. In the wake of the Tsar's anti-Semitic 'May Laws', the number of Jews in Ireland jumped from 472 (394 of them in what would become the Irish Free State) in 1881 to 3,769 (3,006) in 1901, and rose further to 5,038 (3,686) in 1926. Many of the immigrants depended on peddling and moneylending for a living; their descendants progressed to more sedentary forms of trading, manufacturing, and the professions. The Irish immigration was but a minuscule part of a movement that saw hundreds of thousands of Jews trading eastern Europe for places as far apart as Buenos Aires, Johannesburg, Montreal, London, and New York, and establishing enterprising and prosperous communities in all of them. Ireland's Jewish community remained small by comparison, and was to shrink from the 1920s on. The most plausible reason why more Jews did not settle or remain in Ireland is that profitable business opportunities were fewer there.[51] Overall, in so far as 'trade is not fixed to any species of religion as such, but rather to the heterodox part of the whole'—William Petty's claim—Ireland was better positioned than many nineteenth-century European economies.[52]

The role of religious minorities such as the Quakers is but one aspect of the Weber–Tawney hypothesis. The broader point is one about societal ethos. Could the signs, noted below, that the nineteenth-century Irish did not work as intensively as the British, be put down to the lack of a Protestant work-ethic? Perhaps, but there are several arguments against. The first concerns timing. Most historians now consider the evangelical Protestantism that sought to make England sober and hard-working to have been a product of the Industrial Revolution, not a precondition. The worshippers of St Monday were no papists. The work-ethic in the north-east of Ireland was also just as plausibly the product as the agent of economic development. Arthur Young's well-known depiction of Armagh weavers, that 'a pack of hounds is never heard but [they] all leave their looms and away they go after them by hundreds' matches Wakefield's belief that Ulster Presbyterians were as leisure-prone as Catholic southerners. Again, the saying that 'a dear peck of meal makes a cheap pack of yarn', with its message of backward-bending labour supply, referred to Protestant Ulster weavers. In the same vein, a co-owner of the massive York Street Mill conceded as late as 1833 that 'the people here are more irregular in their habits of punctuality and they are as yet scarcely accustomed to this factory system'. Second, nineteenth-century Irish Catholicism produced its own brand of reformer aplenty (Father Mathew being best known). Priests were prominent and effective in the campaigns against faction-fighting, excessive drinking, and other boisterous pastimes.[53] Finally, our analysis of work-intensity, reported below, hardly indicates that the province of Ulster was 'better' than the rest of Ireland in that respect. Protestant Ulster was different, of course, but perhaps this had less to do with religious ideology than with the circumstances of its colonization and settlement? After all, Ulster's industrial trump-card, fine-linen weaving, reflected the origins of its immigrants, not their religious beliefs, and Catholic poverty must have limited Catholic accumulation, partly explaining why Catholics were underrepresented in trade and industry. The temptation to return a verdict of 'not proven' on this particular cultural explanation is strong.[54]

Yet east Ulster people had long differed in another way which may have helped in the long run: more of them could claim some rudimentary literacy. In 1841 only 23.7 per cent of Antrim people aged 5 years and over could neither read nor write, while in Down and Derry the percentages were 27.8 and 29.9. The next-placed counties were Dublin and Carlow, far behind at 37 and 38.7 per cent. The spatial correlation between literacy and Presbyterianism is evident in the census of 1861, the first to provide the necessary detail. The correlation reflects how seriously Protestants, and Presbyterians in particular, took the ability to read the 'holy word'.[55] Half a century later, the spread of elementary schooling had nearly obliterated the literacy gap among younger people, but for the whole of the nineteenth century east Ulster had the edge in literacy. The immediate relevance of literacy to the conduct of farm- and mill-work may be debatable, but literacy clearly reduces transactions costs both between consumers and producers and between employers and employees in many ways, and both economists and economic historians stress the importance of human capital formation (of which literacy is an important part) in economic growth.[56]

Religion may also have mattered in other ways. Kennedy has raised serious questions about the role of another alleged link between Catholicism and underdevelopment—the diversion of risk capital into unproductive church investments[57]—but more plausible, if also more elusive, are the potential links between sectarianism or discrimination and economic performance. These might have taken several forms: rent-dissipation in the quest for privilege, reduced work-effort from disadvantaged workers and entrepreneurs (to be balanced against more effort from the gainers), selective emigration, or higher transactions costs born of mutual mistrust. Testing for such effects is notoriously difficult, and must be left to some future research agenda.

13.4 Crime and Economic Activity before the Famine

It is unfortunate for Ireland, that the cruelties and excess which occasionally occur, by finding their way into the newspapers, give a character to the country which is by no means correct.

JAMES CROPPER, 1825[58]

On announcing a new coaching service linking Dublin and Cork in 1808, the owners deemed it worth noting 'as an inducement to passengers' that their vehicle was 'lined with copper'. The famous highwayman, Ned Brennan of the Moor, was active along part of the route at that time; he was caught shortly thereafter, and hanged. Yet a few decades later, the American evangelist Asenath Nicholson spent much of 1844 and 1845 travelling around Ireland alone, by coach and on foot. 'The Irish', she wrote in her travel journal, 'their enemies would have it, are murderers; they will kill a person for a few shillings.' Her own experiences convinced her that this was nonsense.[59] The Italian-born coaching magnate Charles Bianconi would have agreed. Surveying over forty years of doing business in the south of Ireland, Bianconi claimed in 1857 that though his cars had travelled round the clock 'often in lonely and unfrequented places', never had the 'slightest injury been done by the people to [his] property, or that entrusted in [his] care'. Such accounts may indicate improvement with time, yet the dominant impression left by influential commentators and historians is that pre-Famine Ireland was a violent place where law and order were virtually non-existent. According to historian Galen Broeker, on the eve of the Famine 'violence and crime remained at what was undoubtedly a higher level than in any other area of western Europe.' In economic terms the outcome was predictable: 'the insecurity of property in Ireland, whether real or supposed, assist[ed] in increasing the number of the Irish emigrants to Great Britain, inasmuch as it prevent[ed] the English and Scotch capitalist from transmitting materials to be manufactured in Ireland.' During the Great Famine, asserted Archbishop Whately of Dublin, the Irish poor paid the price. They had deterred potential investors, when it had been 'in [their own] power to attract money into Ireland by making it safe to employ it here'. Armagh land-agent William Blacker claimed that agricultural improvement had been 'completely put an end to' after an 'agriculturalist had twice narrowly escaped assassination'.[60]

This widespread belief that endemic violent criminality stymied Irish economic progress finds support in many individual reports of murder and intimidation.[61] Yet, though it is difficult to test formally, that belief was almost certainly exaggerated. The notion of endemic lawlessness receives little support from the several hundred replies from all over the island in 1835–6 to the following query from the Poor Inquiry assistant commissioners: 'Has your parish been disturbed or peaceable since the Peace in the year 1815?' An analysis of the replies suggests (see Table 13.2) that only a tiny fraction of respondents deemed their area very disturbed. Another 15 per cent or so noted periodic unrest related to tithes, factions, or secret societies. These included references to the Rockite movement in 1822–3, the Terry Alts in Clare in 1830–1, and the Tithe War of the early 1830s. Well over half of the respondents declared their areas free of unrest, while the remainder noted exceptional or occasional trouble.

Differences in legal regimes, in the reporting of crimes, and in the efficacy of law and order make either cross-section or time-series comparisons of historical criminal statistics risky. Still, on the eve of the Famine, reasonably reliable data were being assembled in both Ireland and England. These indicate that pre-Famine Ireland was a violent place by the standards of the 1990s. Curiously, though, they also indicate that the crime rate then was not much higher than in the 1850s, supposedly a quiet decade. Moreover, by the standards of mid-century England the record was not bad either. Violent crimes against property and the person were somewhat more common in Ireland than in England and Wales on the eve of the Famine, but the differences were not striking (see Table 13.3). The Irish propensity to murder barely outstripped the English. The higher incidence of crimes against the person reflects the far greater frequency of ritual faction-fighting and interfamilial brawling in Ireland. McCabe has put it well: 'the likelihood is that Irish society was merely rowdier than elsewhere in the British Isles.'[62] Such crimes, 'mindless' in the sense that

Table 13.2. *Rural unrest: Evidence from the Poor Inquiry*

Category	Leinster	Munster	Ulster	Connacht	Ireland
1. No unrest	204 (47)	206 (52)	424 (81)	79 (48)	913 (60)
2. Occasional	135 (31)	108 (27)	91 (17)	49 (30)	383 (25)
3. Faction, tithe	83 (19)	75 (19)	12 (2)	28 (17)	198 (13)
4. Disturbed	15 (3)	10 (3)	0 (0)	7 (4)	32 (2)

Source: *Poor Inquiry*, App. E, 1–393. Percentages in parentheses.

Table 13.3. *Annual average committals in Ireland, 1844–1846 and England and Wales, 1841–1845*

Category of crime	Committals		Committals per 100,000 population	
	Ireland	E & W	Ireland	E & W
Murders (I), homicides (E & W)	107	281	1	2
Other crimes against person	5 140	2 194	61	13
Against property with violence	1 156	1 962	14	12
Against property without violence	6 289	23 849	74	146
Malicious offences against property	206	214	2	1
Forgery, offences against currency	103	545	1	3
Miscellaneous	5 397	1 338	64	8

Source: Ó Gráda, 'Poverty', 131.

they had no clear economic focus or target, hardly interfered directly with investment in manufacturing.

Over the nineteenth century as a whole, the link between capital inflow and the crime rate is very loose. On the one hand, the hundreds of British capitalists who tried their luck in Ireland before the Famine were not deterred by stories of crime and outrage. Some of them may have believed that crime was on the wane in the pre-Famine decades. On the other hand, the well-attested decline in the crime rate after the Great Famine produced no spurt in foreign investment. Yet the impact of crime on capital inflow is largely a matter of outsiders' perceptions, and it is reasonable to suppose that influential commentators such as Nassau Senior and Campbell Foster, *The Times* correspondent of 1847, induced exaggerated fears of Irish criminality in some nervous investors.[63] Further research may reveal how damaging such accounts really were. Meanwhile, one guide to investors' perceptions is the property insurance premia paid by Irish houseowners, traders, and industrialists in the pre-Famine period. If the business records of the massive London-based Sun Insurance Company are any guide, the Irish premia were no higher than those paid by their British counterparts. The Sun Insurance Company operated throughout Ireland in the 1830s and 1840s. Its records show that it was very sensitive in its pricing policy to fire-inducing risks such as thatched roofs and steam-engines. However, the different categories of risk paid the same premia in Ireland as elsewhere in the UK. Thus private houses of brick, stone, and slate were insured at a rate of 18*d*. per £100 throughout, thatched houses at a rate about three times that, and spinning-mills at about £1 per £100 insured.[64] This suggests that, at least in the eyes of one highly successful insurance business, the perceived risk of incendiarists was no higher in Ireland than in the rest of the UK.

Trends in crime are difficult to extract from the confusing and incomplete police and court statistics of the period. McCabe infers little change in the rates of indictment for homicide, rape, and serious assault between the 1800s and 1840s, and a slight drop in 'agrarian' crime from these data. Mokyr's statistical analysis of committal data for rural areas between 1826 and 1838 suggests that 'law and order were deteriorating at a rate of almost 3.7 per cent per year', but he also notes a fall in the conviction rate from 123 per 100,000 population in 1831 to 89 per 100,000 in 1831–45. Unreported crime is the great imponderable, though an increasingly professional police force should have reduced its incidence over time. If some decline in crime did occur, it was largely the product of better policing, as the maintenance of law and order passed from often ramshackle and arbitrary baronial forces to provincial (1822) and national (1836) control. Though peasant attitudes to the new armed constabulary were ambivalent or even hostile on occasion, particularly during the Tithe War, recourse to the police for redress and protection increased over time. Even in the far west, McCabe has argued, the people had begun to 'assimilate statutory legal norms' before the Famine.[65]

Agrarian crime earned separate attention in the official statistics, and was a constant focus of comment. It was subject to marked regional variation. The extreme east and some of the extreme west were almost immune, as was much of the north; worst affected in the pre-Famine decades was a belt of counties stretching from Waterford to south Ulster. If unrest is interpreted as a reaction to modernization, then a chronological pattern whereby the locus of unrest gradually moved from mature east to less developed west is suggested. Not until the 1870s and 1880s would Connacht be similarly affected. If this spatial interpretation lacks precision, it must be said that efforts at 'explaining' the variation in crime across counties statistically have so far come to nought. Qualitative accounts of the unrest have not been short of explanations either. The traditional emphasis on 'moral economy' and communalist ideology has given way to accounts that stress the individualistic motivation of agrarian crime. Regional research has yielded a plethora of case-studies defying class considerations, best interpreted as family or local feuding. At the same time, recent eclectic interpretations allow roles for both the labourer–farmer struggle, and that between tenant and landlord.[66]

Nearly always local and reactive, in some years agrarian unrest reached epic proportions and assumed a 'moral economy' character. In County Clare in 1831 the authorities recorded a total of 3,280 offences (including 658 illegal meetings, 420 attacks on houses, 323 administrations of illegal oaths, 156 robberies, 224 'assaults connected with ribbonism', and 28 homicides). Most of these offences were linked to the Terry Alt rebellion which peaked in that year. The number of offences dropped to 371 in 1832, and Clare remained quiet between then and the Famine. Though fanned by the excitement of county politics, the Terry Alt uprising, like the contemporary Captain Swing revolt in England, was basically a labourer's protest, which sought to block moves by farmers and landlords that would reduce the demand for labour. In Clare, the 'festive' side of the agitation involved the turning up of land recently put down to grass. Murder and intimidation also played their part. However, military force and the judicious use of repression quelled the rebellion before the end of 1831. Though Clare was far from being crime-free after 1831, it witnessed nothing like the Terry Alts ever again.

In the history of utopian socialism, the Terry Alt unrest is notable for having prompted one Clare landlord, John Scott Vandeleur, to expedite his plans for an Owenite commune at Ralahine in the south of the county. Vandeleur was driven by desperation: his land steward had been a victim of the Terry Alts, murdered allegedly for attempting to introduce a mechanical reaper from Scotland. Just a few months before embarking on the new scheme, Vandeleur himself was one of thirty Clare magistrates to petition for the re-enactment of the Insurrection Act in the county to relieve 'the awful insecurity of life and property' there.[67]

What of crime in the towns, where industrialization was most likely to occur? In the late eighteenth and early nineteenth centuries Irish urban artisans had a reputation for being troublesome, and industrial sabotage and militant trade unionism were also invoked as factors in industrial decline. The brutal methods with which 'combinations' enforced their views often captured the headlines.[68] The awkward locations chosen by some of Ireland's pioneering industrialists in the late eighteenth century— Prosperous, Stratford-on-Slaney, Balbriggan, for example—might be interpreted, in part at least, as a defensive anti-union strategy. Most crafts in the towns and cities seem to have been highly unionized, and entry and demarcation were strictly enforced; perhaps this gave 'new' towns such as

Belfast an advantage over 'old' ones with a history of labour organization (e.g. Dublin, Cork). Moreover, skill differentials in wages were higher in Ireland than in Britain, and several commentators put this down to greater Irish union power. It was not that simple, however. In the first place, union power did not prevent employers of either persuasion from discriminating against workers on religious grounds, and the influence of the craft unions in places like Dublin must have been constrained by their own sectarianism. Secondly, labour-market conditions alone would account for the relatively higher wages of Irish craft workers, since unskilled workers were more plentiful in Ireland.[69] Thirdly, the argument should be considered in a comparative context. The power of local craft 'combinations' in Britain was also considerable, a point not lost on Kane.[70] For much of the period reviewed here Irish craft unions were engaged in a desperate defensive struggle, and union power was lessening over time.

How effective was such unrest—or the threat of such unrest—from the perspective of the 'redresser'? Donnelly has argued that 'it was a fairly low risk strategy, and that those who pursued it were content with temporary gains'. Eiricksson shows that social protest during subsistence crises produced results, influencing the behaviour of both large farmers and government. The motives were complex and varied. Some of those who fought, such as the original Terry Alts, sought to impose a code that was widely understood locally, by preventing the free operation of a land market that might yield evictions, consolidation, and higher rents. The Rockite uprising in Munster in the early 1820s was sparked off by unrest on the Courtenay estate in west Limerick. The Caravats of east Munster sought to protect the status of rural labourers in the area; part of their brief was to intimidate large farmers and harvest labourers from the west. After the Famine 'the first thing' a Longford seasonal harvester seeking work in parts of Meath had to do was to join 'one of the Societies, like the Molly Maguires or the Fenians . . . it was the same . . . as joining a Trade Union'. Such movements and conflicts were often marked by a loose, resentful nationalism but, just as important, they contained strong elements of class conflict, and sought to influence landlord and farmer decision-making. Historians believe that they reduced the shift to pasture in parts of Ireland after 1815.[71] In hindsight this raises a difficult counterfactual question: did the threat of violent reaction prevent Irish landlords from engaging in clearances and emigration schemes in the manner of their Scottish Highland counterparts, and thereby worsen the ravages of the Famine?[72] Perhaps so, though the question begs two points. First, it assumes that Irish tenants would have resisted any emigration schemes along Scottish lines on offer. The massive success of the Peter Robinson emigration scheme, which settled over 2,000 people, mainly from the north Cork region, in Upper Canada in 1825, negates this. Robinson had to choose from 50,000 applicants, and 'never had a more unpleasant duty to perform than of making the selection'. Far from deterring people, the tense and violent atmosphere in the area seemed to increase the number of would-be emigrants. Not only did these poor people leave peaceably: as news of the scheme and others like it spread, 'countless petitions' on behalf of others eager to emigrate reached London.[73] So if landlord-assisted emigrants were few between 1826 and 1845, the problem was less one of low tenant demand than landlord supply. Second, the question ignores pre-Famine Ireland's high eviction rate (already noted in Chapter 5 above). The number of families ejected in Ireland greatly outnumbered that settled in the New World by Highland landlords. In 1839–43 (admittedly a period of economic hardship) clerks of the peace recorded over 20,000 land-connected civil bill ejectments; if the households affected were of average size, this would have meant more than 100,000 people.

13.5 Low Wages, Cheap Labour?

Several historians of European industrialization have stressed the role of cheap labour in fostering modern industry. It is a key element in Mokyr's comparative analysis of nineteenth-century industrialization in the Low Countries. In Mokyr's account, high wages in The Netherlands were a legacy of Dutch economic pre-eminence in the mercantilist era. In the late eighteenth century neighbouring Belgium was poor by comparison. But when the new textile technology became available in the Low Countries in the 1790s, low Belgian wages enabled Belgian industrialists to reap supernormal profits during the transition from domestic industry, reinvest the proceeds, and thereby make a much faster transition to economic maturity than The Netherlands. Within England too, before industrialization wages were lowest in the north, the cradle of the Industrial Revolution.[74]

But where does this leave pre-Famine Ireland, surely also well endowed with cheap labour? Mokyr has recently addressed the issue. Noting that real wages in Ireland were far lower than in Britain, his proposed solution to the puzzle recalls Young's point (later echoed by Kane) that Irish 'labour is low priced but by no means cheap'. Mokyr attempts to account for the observed variation in wages across Irish counties by focusing on proxies for human capital. Controlling for urbanization (which might be expected to increase the nominal wage), and the prevalence of cottage industry (generally associated with low wages), Mokyr finds that any of three proxies for literacy—(i) the proportion of adult males declaring an ability to read and write in 1841, (ii) an age-heaping index (defined as the proportion of men aged 30–4 years reporting their age as 30 in 1841), and (iii) the proportion of teachers per adult male employed—carries considerable explanatory punch. This indicates that wage variation across Ireland was largely influenced by productivity or efficiency differences.[75]

Might the wage gaps between Irish and English or Scottish workers be similarly explained? Direct productivity comparisons between Irish and English workers engaged in similar tasks would clinch the issue, on certain conditions. First, the quality of output must be the same. Second, the complementary factors used must be the same: for instance English ploughmen workers might be paid less per acre ploughed, because they were using more horses and better equipment. The requisite data are scarce, but Clark[76] has produced a comparison for wheat reapers *after* the Famine, c. 1860 (Table 13.4).

An alternative way of tabulating the same data produces Table 13.5. The implication is striking enough: the lower daily wages of Irish (and Southern English) agricultural labourers in this period were largely accounted for by their lower productivity in the fields.[77] Within Ireland, the evidence from Connacht is too skimpy—a single observation—to overturn the impression that the effective cost of labour did not vary much within Ireland. Admittedly, the evidence on labour costs is not all one way. Lee's analysis of the construction costs of railways in Ireland and England in the 1840s and 1850s suggests that it cost twice as much to build a mile of permanent way in England as it did in Ireland in the 1840s. While cheaper land and

Table 13.4. *Work intensity in Irish and English farming,* c. 1860

Place	No. of observations	Winter wage (bu./day)	Reaping (acres/day)	Yield (bu.)	Reaping (bu./day)
Ireland	20	.18	.24	23	5.6
S. England	54	.27	.31	26	8.2
N. England	17	.34	.45	27	12.6

Source: Clark, 'Productivity Growth without Technical Change in European Agriculture'.

Table 13.5. *Harvest wages and piece-rates in Ireland and Britain, 1860*

Area	Weekly wage		Harvest wage		Cost of mowing an acre of hay		Cost of cutting and reaping an acre of wheat	
Ulster	6.69	(9)	11.31	(9)	3.75	(7)	9.13	(6)
Leinster	6.56	(8)	14.44	(8)	3.90	(6)	11.72	(6)
Munster	6.56	(9)	12.56	(9)	3.23	(8)	9.91	(8)
Connacht	5.00	(1)	9.50	(2)	3.70	(1)	7.41	(1)
Ireland	6.49	(28)	12.48	(28)	3.60	(20)	10.09	(21)
England	10.83	(71)	17.91	(61)	3.58	(70)	11.48	(67)
Scotland	12.40	(15)	17.73	(12)	3.08	(3)	9.44	(8)

Source: *Gardeners' Chronicle*, 28 Apr. 1860, 392–3. No adjustment has been made here for either yield differences (somewhat higher in Britain) or dietary supplements (worth more in Britain). Irish acreage measures have been converted to British where appropriate. Number of observations in parentheses.

single-track lines explain part of the difference, for Lee a key element is that Irish labour effectively cost only half the English price.[78]

But what of the pre-Famine period? Construction and farming offer some further comparative task-rate data. In building, the system of 'value-and-measure' whereby a professional measurer assessed the quantity of work performed by different tradesmen, had probably been introduced into Ireland during the Restoration. It lasted until the mid-nineteenth century and, as a result, eighteenth and early nineteenth-century manuals and business archives provide a good deal of data on recommended or actual task-rates paid to tradesmen such as painters, plasterers, masons, and bricklayers. Bryan Bolger, a noted Dublin 'measurer', valued tradesmen's work for the wealthy who employed them to build, repair, and decorate private houses and workplaces. In the process, Bolger surveyed the work of many of the tradesmen who built Georgian Dublin, providing us with evidence on rates by the square, perch, or yard, for workmanship only or (increasingly) for work and materials between the late 1780s and 1815. The rates quoted by Bolger correspond quite well with those in published measuring books such as Hodgson's *Complete Measurer* (1779) or Stitt's *Practical Architect's Ready Assistant* (1819). Such sources suggest that in the building trades at least Irish labour was not so 'cheap'. It is interesting that this should be so in construction, a non-tradable activity.

The Practical Builder and Workman's Companion gave the labour cost of a perch of stonework c.1821–2 'in northern and southern Ireland' as 46*d*. (28*d*. for the mason and 18*d*. for his attendant). It listed brickwork at 36*d*.

outside Dublin and at 40*d*. in the metropolis. A perch required 240 bricks. It put the cost of working a rood in England—4500 bricks—at five days or £2 (£1. 5*s*. for the bricklayer and 15*s*. for his attendant), but allowed 6.5 days for the 'best manner work'. The lowest Irish rate quoted exceeds the first of the two English rates by 40.6 per cent and the second by 8.3 per cent.

The best single source on pre-Famine piece-rates is Wakefield, who collected a considerable amount of piece-rate data on his Irish tour of 1809–11. His *Ireland Statistical and Political* contains rates for masons and fencers (by the perch), slaters (by the square), mowers (per acre of grass), and blacksmiths (horseshoeing). Some of his findings, collated by province, are given in Table 13.6. While the rankings by trade are not consistent across provinces, rates in Connacht were generally lowest. Is it a coincidence that Wakefield's endearing depiction of farm labourers who wasted 'half the time in *gossiping* either with the overseer or among themselves' refers to Connacht? A few decades later, Weld would note how in Roscommon 'congregations of workmen' planting or digging potatoes were 'ordinarily scenes of much cheerfulness'. Nor were Connachtwomen any different: Wakefield was greatly amused by 'gangs of young women employed in hay-making or in gathering potatoes, indulg[ing] in the same propensity, joking and laughing with the overseer the whole day'. He also noted that 'Irish labourers never work singly. [T]he people there have a sympathy of feeling, which makes company necessary for those at work.' Much in the same vein, the nostalgic depiction of work rhythms in the early 1800s given in the Ordnance Survey Memoir for Dungiven in County Derry has labourers 'leaping, jumping, wrestling [and] dancing' for 'two or more hours' after their midday meal, with many of them spending 'the early part of the night in singing Irish songs and telling old stories in turn'.[79] Such accounts cannot be ignored. Nevertheless, the statistical results provide little ground for arguing that real wages in any of the provinces were low enough to give it a substantial cost advantage over the others.

Was Irish farm labour cheap by British standards? The following comparisons offer some clues. First, Wakefield's average for mowing grass— about 40*d*. per statute acre—bears comparison with those reported in the Board of Agriculture surveys for several British counties around the same time. These range from 30*d*. to 60*d*. in Wiltshire (1811) and 30–3*d*. in Rutland (1808) to 42*d*. in Durham (1810) and 48*d*. in Ross and Cromarty (1810). The 22–3*d*. per acre quoted by Tighe for mowing grass in

Table 13.6. *Some Irish task-rate data, c.1810–1811*

	Leinster	Munster	Ulster	Connacht
Masons (pence per day)	36.7 (4.9) *n* = 23	37.9 (6.5) *n* = 12	34.2 (4.5) *n* = 13	32.3 (3.6) *n* = 7
Carpenter (pence per day)	37.8 (6.4) *n* = 22	38.1 (6.7) *n* = 13	32.6 (3.4) *n* = 7	34.3 (4.5) *n* = 7
Masons (pence per perch)	20.4 (5.0) *n* = 20	25.1 (8.4) *n* = 10	25.0 (4.8) *n* = 11	19.8 (4.7) *n* = 6
Slaters (pence per day)	41.0 (7.1) *n* = 23	40.0 (6.6) *n* = 12	37.0 (4.6) *n* = 10	34.3 (7.2) *n* = 7
Slaters (pence per square)	101.1 (18.5) *n* = 19	86.4 (18.2) *n* = 10	97.2 (22.6) *n* = 13	104.4 (19.0) *n* = 6
Fencing (pence per perch)	28.6 (12.9) *n* = 14	22.9 (10.7) *n* = 8	23.8 (10.6) *n* = 10	16.3 (2.4) *n* = 4
Mowing grass (pence per Irish acre)	72.8 (15.5) *n* = 22	70.0 (11.5) *n* = 11	66.7 (17.2) *n* = 12	64.1 (13.5) *n* = 7
Mowing grass (pence per ton)	21.4	19.3	21.5	20.3
Horseshoeing (pence per horse)	39.8 (4.2) *n* = 21	40.4 (5.8) *n* = 12	39.1 (4.2) *n* = 11	43.2 (5.5) *n* = 6
Harvest labour (pence per day)	22.6 (5.8) *n* = 23	20.0 (4.8) *n* = 11	19.2 (5.5) *n* = 13	16.3 (3.7) *n* = 6
Threshing (pence per day)	16.1 (4.7) *n* = 20	20.4 (4.5) *n* = 11	14.2 (2.5) *n* = 12	13.7 (4.5) *n* = 6
Labour, *c.*1776–8 (pence per day)	7.4 (1.4) *n* = 9	6.0 (0.4) *n* = 12	7.3 (1.1) *n* = 12	5.5 (0.4) *n* = 6

Sources: Wakefield, *Ireland*, ii. 208–30; Young, *Tour in Ireland*, ii. 38–9 (App.). Standard deviations in parentheses. In calculating the piece-rate for Leinster slaters, three extreme outliers have been omitted. The slater's 'square' was 100 square feet. The quotations for fencing by Stratton (Dundalk), and Phelps (Limerick) were excluded. In estimating the cost of mowing grass Phelps's quotation was again excluded, and the two lowest Cork estimates were assumed to refer to statute acres. The cost of mowing a ton of grass is based on the average reported yield 1847–54. *n* = number of observations. The rates for shoeing a horse include the cost of the iron.

Kilkenny in 1790[80] compares with 16–24*d*. in North Wales (1790s), 22–30*d*. in Renfrewshire (1792–5), 30*d*. in Northumberland (1793), and 24–30*d*. in Leicester (1794). Second, turning to the cost of reaping an acre of wheat, in Thompson's 1802 survey of Meath the cost of reaping and stooking an Irish acre is given at 90–108*d*. (Irish). This is equivalent to

76–92*d*. (English) per statute acre, and compares with 78–90*d*. in Rutland (1808), 96–108*d*. in Cheshire (1808), 103*d*. in Norfolk (1804), and 90*d*. in north Wales (1800s). Third, Thompson's estimate for the cost of threshing wheat in Meath is 12–14*d*. (Irish) or 10–12*d*. (English) per 20-stone barrel in 1802. This compares with estimates of 57*d*. per quarter for north Wales (1800s), 30*d*. per quarter for Rutland (1808), 9*d*. per bushel for Durham (1810), 40.5*d*. per quarter for Norfolk (1804), and 18–24*d*. per quarter for Cambridge (1804).[81] In general, these sources suggest that (unskilled) day labour was much cheaper in Ireland than in Britain, often 50 per cent less. The margin on task-rates was a good deal smaller, however, though very variable.

Why was 'cheap' Irish labour unproductive? One possibility, noted above, is that their complementary inputs of capital—their flails, scythes, horses, and ploughs—were of poorer quality, so that more Irish labour was expended per task performed. This could hardly be the whole story, given the relative importance of labour and other inputs. Neither health nor strength presumably had much to do with it, if (as argued in Chapters 1 and 4) the Irish seem to have been as well endowed with calories as the British at this juncture. Nor has a causal link between productivity and schooling—which would tell against the Irish—been established in this context. How, then, is the apparently lower intensity of Irish labour explained? What of the cultural explanation implied by Wakefield, linking lower work-intensity with the greater Irish proclivity for amusement and chat? Nobody would accuse the pre-Famine Irish of emulating the ancient Athenians, of whom it was said that they 'knew no holiday except to do their work and deemed the quiet of inaction to be as tedious as the most tiresome business'. Though economists tend to be sceptical of such claims, they cannot be ruled out, even though they are difficult to test.

13.6 Economies of Scale, External Economies, and 'Path-Dependence'

Over a century ago Alfred Marshall devised the concept of external economies of scale in order the square the presence of competition between firms with increasing returns to scale at the industry level. In Marshall's view, the cost savings that accrued from the growth of an industry stemmed from the development of ancillary industries and services. An increase in the demand for the output of some industry (e.g. cotton) not only increased the number of firms, but also produced backward linkages in terms of information, capital goods production, a skilled work-force, and so on (e.g. specialized warehousing and transport services, machinery workshops). The following account of the engineering workshops of Belfast provides a vivid example:[82]

[They] surrounded by mills and manufactories [and] were daily visited by those employing them, who thus saw the progress made in the execution of their orders, and by pointing out their requirements, and the defects of the previous machines, enabled the machinists to introduce every known improvement and, as far as possible, remedy previous defects.

Even in the absence of such external economies, unavoidable excess capacity or input lumpiness may yield decreasing costs over a certain output range. Inventions and the introduction of new technologies also produce scale economies at low levels of output. Now consider the following possibility: the first firms in an industry start up by 'historical accident', even randomly perhaps, in one or two locations. Others firms emerge in their wake. Eventually, this produces Marshallian external economies of scale: as a location gains more firms, it also gains useful infrastructure, its labour-markets deepen, specialized legal and financial services appear. Spare parts and out-of-stock items become available locally, reducing inventory costs. Information becomes cheaper. And so the process is cumulative. Industrial specialization in the early-chosen town or region, at the expense of late starters, is the result. In a series of publications, economists Brian Arthur and Paul David have formalized versions of such a story, stressing the importance of 'path-dependence' and historical 'small events' in explaining the spatial pattern of industrialization. Agglomeration economies are a key ingredient. The outcome is non-predictable, however: a different set of early events could have steered the locational pattern into quite a different outcome, so that settlement history is crucial. Here the locational system generates structure as it grows. It can follow divergent paths, and possess a multiplicity of outcomes. Industrialization might occur in an area not necessarily best suited to it, and indeed at a cost in terms of aggregate resource allocation. To paraphrase Arthur, traditional explanations of Irish backwardness would focus on factors such as wage levels, the lack of natural resources, restrictive government policy, or the quality of entrepreneurship. The 'historical path-dependence' view would emphasize instead the localization of the textile revolution within Ulster and parts of Great Britain as largely, though not wholly, the result of chance. Chance events and key personages—earlier plantation settlement patterns or the random location decision of a talented entrepreneur, for example—gave these areas an initial lead, which made choosing them very advantageous to those who followed.[83]

The presence of scale economies suggests other historically plausible scenarios also. Thus the gradual elimination of trade barriers, either artificial or real, between a small 'peripheral' economy such as Ireland and a major economy such as Britain could 'tip' the sector subject to scale economies (manufacturing) towards the centre, and force the periphery to specialize in a sector not subject to such economies (farming). Alternatively, the combination of high shipping costs and scale economies may insulate (or even promote) industry in a high-cost location (e.g. Ireland), but falling shipping costs will eventually prompt a shift to a low-cost location (e.g. England). A distinct but related model of localization has recently been proposed by Krugman. Krugman's model differs from the Arthur–David model, first, in that its focus is on savings in the industrial sector as a whole rather than in a particular industry within it. Second, it is concerned with pecuniary rather than technological externalities. In this model, industry will tend to locate in areas of high population, and the consequent savings from agglomeration stem from reduced transport costs. As in the Arthur–David approach, cumulative circular causation plays a part, and industry gradually concentrates on regions lucky enough to have got 'a head start'.[84]

Such models help explain the 'relentless tendency towards geographical specialization and concentration' which marked the UK textile industry during the Industrial Revolution. Their intuitive appeal in the Irish case must also be obvious. In accounting for the decline of the Irish cotton industry, Dickson mentioned traditional factors such as the absence of coal and the decline of the colonial trade, but gave pride of place to considerations such as those just discussed. The success of the Irish linen industry may be traced back ultimately to 'small historical events'—the immigration of skilled weavers from northern England to east Ulster in the mid- and late-seventeenth century and the abolition of import duties on Irish linens in 1696. O'Malley has urged the disadvantages of a late start more generally: in nineteenth-century Ireland smaller industries were gradually edged out by their British rivals, and newcomers found it increasingly difficult to compete. Conversely, Ollerenshaw and McCutcheon have linked the success of the Ulster linen industry to the economies gained from the development of ancillary industries such as engineering, and Durie and Solar have emphasized the importance of marketing economies to

Ulster.[85] Krugman's framework is a reminder that the cost of getting output to consumers may bulk just as large as that of getting raw materials such as coal and cotton to the producer. In 1800 the Irish accounted for almost one-third of the population of the UK, though their share of the market for most industrial products would have been considerably less. Ireland's population share dropped thereafter, from 31 per cent in 1841 to 17 per cent in 1871 and less than 10 per cent in 1911. The contrast between an impoverished and failing Irish home market and the expanding and increasingly affluent domestic market across the Irish Sea, draws attention to the role of demand-side factors. In terms of Krugman's core-periphery model, the causation between that decline and industrialization ran both ways. The moral of Krugman's model is that the Famine, by reducing the domestic market, may have spurred on deindustrialization, and it also helps explain why what little Irish industry remained was concentrated on the east coast.

Firm evidence of scale economies and learning-by-doing effects in nineteenth-century Ireland is hard to come by, and so far the relevance of such models is in the realm of plausible speculation. The fate of scientific instrument-making in Dublin provides one concrete example:[86]

In olden times, opticians made a much greater proportion of the articles they sold. Today [i.e. 1944] many of them make nothing. Some who, like ourselves and Yeates, manufactured a number of various instruments have found it impracticable to do so today. Yeates made the last big attempt about 1890, but they were forced to market most of their products through English firms and they lost money. The home market is too small, and because of the advance of science the variety is too great. A world market is needed, and this requires not merely highly-educated scientific brains, but also large organising ability and great capital resources. One of my sons went through the works of the largest English makers of engineering instruments about 4 years ago. He saw rows of theodolites, each valued at about £100, and was informed that they were manufactured in batches of not less than 50 instruments; a smaller number was not economic. Fifty of these instruments would be sufficient for 25 years' demand in Eire.

Here remoteness from markets put paid to an industry. The case of the Pneumatic Tyre and Booth's Cycle Agency, established in Dublin in 1889, and soon renamed the Dunlop Rubber Company, provides another example of locational disadvantage. A series of complaints from Dublin corporation about fumes and smells was the ostensible reason for the company's move to Coventry in 1895, but the real reason was the desire to be near big markets for bicycles and capital.[87] On the other hand, the successful industrialization that occurred in the north-east arguably owed something to the process described by Arthur and David. Belfast's proto-industrial textile sector had given it the advantage of being the principal textile port since the 1780s. The temporary success of the cotton textile revolution was important, since it prepared the way for linen mills. It was during the cotton era that Belfast became 'the warehouse of the North'. Cotton's success virtually wiped out Belfast's linen industry for a time; it is estimated that between 1791 and 1806, the number of looms employed in linen in the city and its immediate hinterland dropped from 129 to four while those in cotton rose from 522 to 629.[88] When linen re-established itself with the introduction of the wet-spinning process in the 1820s, its focus was very much on Ulster. Meanwhile, Ulster's engineering industry developed in tandem. Besides the usual bleaching, printing, and dyeing works to be met in any textile centre, Belfast contained by the late 1830s 'various manufactories for machinery, iron-forges, and other chymical products . . . together employing about a thousand persons'. The local foundries soon began to invent and construct machinery specifically geared to local conditions. In 1834 the Belfast Foundry claimed to be the first firm in Ireland to have produced wet-spinning machinery. The Ordnance Survey Memoir for the Antrim parish of Carnmoney (1838–9) noted that Bell and Calvert's mill near Belfast was the only one completely reliant on Irish machinery; its steam-engine and spinning-machinery had been made at the Belfast Foundry. Soon Belfast machinery makers such as George Horner, James Scrimgeour, James Mackie, and James Combe of the Falls Foundry were supplying local engineering needs, and exporting substantial quantities in addition. Foremost in this respect were the last-mentioned, who had started off in business in 1845 as suppliers to the railway industry. Their owners included members of the Barbour linen dynasty and they were employing 1,200 workers by the early 1880s:[89]

Invention after invention, improvement after improvement, have emanated in a long and continuous succession from this great establishment: and the results achieved and the perfection attained by the firm in the production of every description of machinery and apparatus for the preparing and spinning of flax and its kindred fibres, hemp, jute, &c . . . have made for Messrs. Combe, Barbour, & Combe, Limited, a renown and position in which it is hardly too much to say they stand unrivalled.

Finally, it is important to bear in mind that the victory of the Belfast region was not merely at the expense of Dublin and 'outside Ulster', but of the linen centres of Yorkshire and Scotland too. Linen was very much a gainer from Ulster's location. But on balance, location was probably more a disadvantage than advantage to Irish industry. Being on the periphery of such a powerful industrial nation could have been a disadvantage in the Krugman sense, but also in the sense that most of the external economies were being reaped in Britain.

13.7 Conclusion

Marx's famous preface to *Das Kapital* reminded his German readers: *de te fabula narratur* (this story is about you)! Marx was by no means alone in his belief that late economic developers would tread the path previously trodden by others. The stage-theory approach to economic history has been around since the Physiocrats, and the efforts of many less developed economies at replicating the industrialization of mature economies have been partly based, implicitly, on such an approach. Ireland is no exception. An alternative interpretation proposed by Gerschenkron emphasizes instead the systematic variety of routes to economic maturity. Backward economies in a hurry to industrialize or 'catch up' find themselves short of capital and entrepreneurs, and tend to substitute government involvement, foreign capital, and deferred consumption.[90] Gerschenkron's framework presumes a degree of political autonomy lacking in Ireland under the Union, but it fails to explain the policies pursued by successive governments after 1922 either. Cumann na nGaedheal (1922–32) fostered agriculture, while Fianna Fáil's commitment to industrialization was tempered by De Valera's idyll of the 'Ireland that we dreamed of' (see Chapters 15–17). Crafts' model of 'industrialization in an international context' also highlights variety in economic development. Its context is Great Britain in the early nineteenth century, where (he claims) agricultural productivity grew at an unprecedented rate of almost one per cent.[91] Why, then, did Britain not specialize in farming? Because industrial productivity grew faster still, so that Britain's comparative advantage lay in manufacturing. Note, however, that this is neither a sufficient nor a necessary condition for Britain's choice. If industrial productivity rose even faster relative to agriculture elsewhere, the logic of comparative advantage would *eventually* have dictated specialization in farming for Britain! Empirical support for Crafts' interpretation thus requires information about industrial *and* agricultural total factor productivity growth rates *both* in Britain and in other countries.[92] A tall order! Nor does Crafts account for the origins of comparative advantage: interpretations along Arthur–David lines are not excluded. The general point holds, however. If Britain was destined for an industrial revolution

based on cotton and steel, other countries must choose a different development path. Might such a model, which requires some economies to
modernize without industrializing, apply to nineteenth-century Ireland?
After all, for some comparative advantage must have lain in agriculture: for
Ireland and Denmark, perhaps? Only future comparative research will tell.

The 'deindustrialization' of southern Ireland in the nineteenth century
had a significant influence on the economic agenda of the Irish Free State in
the 1920s and 1930s. Implicit in that agenda was an interpretation that
rested on commercial policy and entrepreneurial failure. That free trade had
ruined Irish industry had been argued repeatedly by nationalists since
1800, and thus one of the first measures of the Cumann na nGaedheal
regime was to set up a tariff inquiry. Cumann na nGaedheal subsequently
became wary of tariffs, but after 1932 Fianna Fáil pursued a vigorously
protectionist policy. The high cost of the ensuing tariff-induced industrialization, discussed in detail in Chapters 15 and 16, has a direct bearing on
the economic case against the Act of Union. It suggests that protection in
the early nineteenth century could have succeeded in saving some manufacturing jobs, but only at a high cost to consumers and other producers.
By pursuing an active role in industry and capital formation, the Free State
also implicitly accepted the notion of native entrepreneurial failure. Our
own survey returns a verdict of 'not proven' on this hypothesis. Though it
is easy to cite examples of entrepreneurial incompetence, they beg two
questions. First, how representative are they? In Chapter 12 we produced
several counter-examples indicating considerable entrepreneurial effort even
in cases where the prospects of reward were not good. Second, did other
entrepreneurs capitalize on the mistakes? The answer, as we have seen, is
that they often did.

Other explanations found wanting included the lack of law and order and
the anti-business Catholic ethos of the country. Another in this category,
discussed in Chapter 14, is the lack of venture capital. Hypotheses which
seem to count for something, though they still need to be convincingly
proved, are those stressing Ireland's lack of resources, particularly of coal
and iron, and the geographical propinquity of the 'workshop of the world'.

14

Banking and Industrial Finance, 1850–1939

14.1 A Capital-Starved Economy?

> That the prosperity of Ireland could best be advanced by the introduction of capital, in some sense not exactly defined, was a safe generalisation, sure to command popular assent, in England or Ireland.
>
> R. D. C. BLACK, 1960[1]

Shortage of capital, particularly venture capital, was another common explanation for Irish industrial retardation. The argument stemmed in part from the allegedly high set-up costs of new industries during the Industrial Revolution: the lack of a proper capital market allegedly put the new technology out of reach of late-starting Irish entrepreneurs or forced them into small-scale ventures. The trouble with this claim is that the capital invested in 'traditional' businesses by Irish merchants, warehouse-owners, brewers, and flour-millers in the nineteenth century often exceeded that required to set up cotton or linen enterprises. Table 14.1, which reports the insured values of plant and equipment belonging to a range of Irish manufacturing and wholesaling firms in operation in the early 1840s, provides some examples. It includes some considerable concerns, notably in brewing, distilling, and milling. This suggests that, given entrepreneurial acumen, had textile-mills been more remunerative than flour-mills, more of them would have been built instead. In support, Geary's case-study of early nineteenth-century Belfast suggests that the city's cotton mills were no less capitalized than their more successful British counterparts.[2]

Nor can shortage of capital mean that savings were lacking, since Ireland already possessed a highly developed banking system in mid-century, and on the eve of the First World War had more bank branches per head than either France or England. The savings marshalled by the banks—about £60 million in the 1900s—were impressive, and their growth since the 1870s had kept pace with the rest of the UK. Most of these savings were channelled into short-term loans in Ireland or invested by the banks on the London discount market. But this did not necessarily represent a misallocation of capital away from Irish business: it may simply indicate that returns were higher abroad. The geographical spread of Irish holdings of British government securities in 1922 is relevant here: residents of Ulster held only 9 per cent of the total, presumably because they had better things to be doing with their money.[3]

During the nineteenth century the transmission of capital from Dublin to London and vice versa was easy and inexpensive. Stock bought in London could be transferred to Dublin and then sold on the Dublin stock exchange. As a result the capital markets of Ireland and Britain were closely integrated. Between 1818 and 1863 £62 million of worth of gilt-edged stock moved from London to Dublin, while £39 million flowed out. Irish holdings of British gilts declined thereafter, investors transferring their capital to foreign bonds and the home share market. In 1862 the paid up value of the joint-stock securities listed on the Dublin stock exchange was only £4 million; the figure reached £5.3 million in 1881 and £17.2 million in 1897. The range of companies represented on the exchange by the 1890s was quite wide; that few textile and engineering concerns were included was due less to capital supply constraints than to a lack of demand.[4]

Foreign capital was also available to Irish enterprise. Over two-thirds of the capital invested in the Provincial Bank in the 1830s was British. Nearly one-third of the Hibernian's original shareholders were English. The National was founded largely on English money, and many of the Royal Bank's important shareholders were English Quakers. While the Dublin & Kingstown and Ulster railways raised nearly all their capital in Ireland, the promoters of the Dublin & Drogheda relied on British investors for half of theirs. Foreign capital was crucial thereafter, playing a major role in the railway investment boom of 1845.[5]

The 1870 factory returns (Table 14.2) indicate that horsepower per man employed, our imperfect but best available proxy for capital-intensity, was lower in Ireland in most sectors than either England or Scotland, but the differences were generally small. The profile suggested by these data is of an Irish industrial sector which mirrored the rest of the UK rather closely in terms of plant size and power usage.

14.2 The Joint-Stock Banks

Bank managers in the 1990s provide a much wider range of financial services than their nineteenth-century predecessors. Nowhere has the change been greater than in lending activity. Like the English commercial banks,

Table 14.1. *The insured value of selected firms, c.1840–1845*

Concern	Activity	Insured for (£)
Nicholson *et al.*, Lisburn	Spinning and bleaching	4 000
Catherine Walsh, Youghal	Pawnbroker	2 150
Michael Walsh, Dublin	Haberdasher and trimming manufacturer	7 200
Stevenson, Falls	Cotton-spinners	15 620
Greer, Clonmel	Flour-millers	5 000
Gilmore, Belfast	Provisions merchant	5 000
Workhouse, Enniskillen	Poor Law Guardians	9 000
Murphy, Limerick	Wine and spirit merchant	3 650
Peat, Dublin	Warehouseman	4 200
Smith & Smyth, Drogheda	Merchant	6 500
Devereux, Wexford	Brewers and distillers	7 617
Samuel Robinson, Clara	Miller and farmer	2 400
McDonnell, Dublin	Paper marchant	6 050
Sweetman, Dublin	Brewers	21 000
Gartlan, Carrickmacross	Distillers	12 500
O'Neill, Limerick	Corn merchant and brewer	3 000
Purser & Briggs	Brewers	5 800
Lawlor, Dublin	Provisions dealer	3 760
Bourke, Dublin	Woollen manufacturer	3 200
Cole, Bowen Court	Brewer	3 750
Leppers, Belfast	Cotton-spinners	2 000
Forsythe, Derry	Merchants	7 650
William Andrews, Dublin	Woollen merchant	20 300
O'Connor, Dublin	Wine merchant	6 550
John Lynch, Dublin	Miller	6 000
Delany, Boyne Mill	Miller	11 600
Galavan, Dublin	Woollen merchant	8 900
Beamish & Crawford, Cork	Brewers	28 837
Lewis Reford, Belfast	Merchant	10 200
D'Arcy, Dublin	Brewer	6 000

Source: Records of the Sun Fire Insurance Company (Guildhall Library, London). All the data refer to the early 1840s.

until half a century or so ago the Irish joint-stock banks liked to create the impression that providing investment loans to industry, even term loans of a year or two, was not their function. The stereotype was of institutions specializing in short-term, often seasonal, loans, particularly to traders, industrialists, and farmers. The banks created an aura of caution around

Table 14.2. *Plant size in Irish and British industry, 1871*

Sector	Plants	hp per plant	hp per employee	Employee per plant
Cotton				
Ireland	14	11.2	.37	297
England	2 371	121.1	.69	175
Scotland	98	205.3	.65	316
Wool				
I.	61	19.1	.78	24
E.	1 550	33.4	.51	65
S.	218	42.7	.40	106
Flax				
I.	154	149.7	.42	357
E.	155	62.7	.49	128
S.	191	126.8	.49	261
Foundries				
I.	64	14.2	.20	72
E.	1 310	16.1	.33	48
S.	144	17.7	.14	123
Shoes				
I.	251	0	0	6
E.	8 865	0	.01	6
S.	3 266	0	.01	3
Glass				
I.	8	0.5	.02	33
E.	213	18.5	.20	92
S.	19	6.4	.07	84
Brewing				
I.	19	3 .8	.30	103
E.	860	5.2	.31	17
S.	123	3.9	.18	21
Distilling				
I.	13	53.4	.49	109
E.	16	29.5	1.34	22
S.	44	11.5	1.43	20
Artif. manure				
I.	—	13.1	0.33	40
G.B.	—	7.7	0.42	19

Source: 1870 Factory Returns (BPP 1871 (LXII)).

themselves, and the real bills doctrine—restricting credit to short-term lending on trade bills to solvent customers—was part of the image. In principle, loans were for three months, loans for longer periods being deemed unsafe. In the words of one apologist, lending for even six months 'would not be banking, but money-lending'.[6] The banks were often criticized for such a narrow definition of the banking function. They were also criticized for putting governments before business clients when it came to lending money. Of course, investments in bonds and consols made perfect sense to banks eager for liquidity, and the Irish banks were only mimicking English behaviour by lending on the London money market. But did they overdo it?

Comprehensive data on lending policy are lacking, but the banks' published balance-sheets are indicative. Table 14.3 presents the ratio of advances (including bill discounts) to deposits and notes (where applicable) in 1903–4, 1913–14, and 1923–4 for the nine joint-stock banks. This involves comparing part of the bank's assets to the lion's share of their liabilities. One point stands out. Though subject to short-term and seasonal fluctuation, over time the ratio dropped in all cases, as banks switched their asset portfolios from advances and discounted bills to government paper. In opting increasingly for such safe outlets, the banks lay themselves open to the charge of becoming mere rentiers.[7] The banks and their defenders justified such portfolios in terms of the need for liquidity. But that is hardly a convincing reason for the fall in the typical ratio from about 0.7 in the 1890s to 0.4 in the 1930s.[8] Did the reduction in the ratio reflect an increasing conservatism on the part of the banks, or was it a necessary reaction to a shift in the composition of loans from bill discounts to advances? Did the increasing attraction of alternative investments such as bonds and Treasury Bills play a part? Or was it simply a case of a reduction in the demand for advances relative to supply?

Complaints against the banks endured. In the 1920s they prompted De Valera's Fianna Fáil party to promise an official investigation on attaining power, and the Commission of Inquiry on Banking, Currency and Credit (1934–8) was the result. Fianna Fáil also created the Industrial Credit Company in 1933 in order to plug an alleged gap in the market (see Chapter 15). Data supplied by the banks to the Banking Commission in January 1935 revealed that only 8.5 per cent of all bank advances in the Irish Free State went to manufacturers, builders, and railway and other transport concerns, as against 27 per cent to farmers, and another 22 per cent to wholesalers and retailers. Moreover, the 8.5 per cent is likely to

Table 14.3. *Ratio of advances plus discounts to deposits plus notes, Irish joint-stock banks, 1873–4 to 1933–4*

Bank	1852–3	1863–4	1873–4	1883–4	1893–4	1903–4	1913–14	1923–4	1933–4
Bank of I.	—	—	—	·53	·55	·54	·52	·34	·34
National	·76	·79	·74	—	·71	·72	·62	·45	·42
Provincial	—	—	—	·70	·60	·63	·66	·45	·42
M & L	—	—	—	—	·80	·67	·55	·52	·47
Royal	—	—	—	—	·55	·66	·74	·64	·57
Hibernian	—	—	—	—	·84	·91	·75	·49	·49
Belfast	—	—	—	—	·80	—	·66	·59	·49
Northern	—	—	—	—	·74	·72	·57	·65	—
Ulster	—	—	—	·86	·70	·73	·64	·48	·40

Sources: Calculated from reports in *Bankers' Magazine*; Hall, *Bank of Ireland*, 400–1. The Bank of Ireland's earliest balance-sheet refers to 1885. The banks did not synchronize their financial years until the late 1920s, while only some presented half-yearly balance-sheets. The Munster & Leinster data refer to 30 June.

have consisted of short-term loans, and to have been lent to established firms.[9]

Yet some of the wilder criticisms of the banks were quite off the mark. The critic who argued in 1884 that 'many an Irish capitalist would be glad to invest in Irish manufacture instead of trade, if he would receive at the commencement of his venture that aid by cash credit which the trade receives by goods credit'[10] failed to note how much riskier it was to provide venture capital than to discount trade bills for an established firm. Spokesmen for the banks might note that it was precisely those banks who combined borrowing liquid funds from depositors with lending to risky industrial concerns—the Tipperary Bank, the National Discount Company—that had failed. Moreover, undue focus on the fixed capital aspect ignores the importance of working capital requirements. As Sidney Pollard has noted in a well-known contribution, 'the problem of finding capital was largely a problem of finding circulating capital for stocks of raw materials, work in progress, and finished commodities, and for rents, interest and wage payments, and the like'. Others have chronicled the difficulties faced by firms short of working capital in the early stages of the Industrial Revolution, before the emergence of joint-stock banking.[11] A related point here is that the Irish (and English) banks' reluctance to mix short- and long-term lending should not have prevented other institutions from engaging in more speculative ventures.

In a spirited defence of the Irish banks Ollerenshaw has contrasted the negative impression left by parliamentary inquiries and by populist criticism with findings based on bank archives. On the whole, he suggests, joint-stock banks performed their task of providing short-term credit well in this period. They had to be sensible and cautious, but they were also flexible and resourceful in their dealings. Ollerenshaw's defence of the Irish banks tallies with that of historians of British and American nineteenth-century banking.[12]

The evidence from the banks' archives shows that advances to business also grew during the period. Banks were quite willing to lend on a short-term basis to established manufacturers. For instance, the Cork Distilleries Company's credit limit at the Provincial Bank in the mid-1880s was £40,000—or well over a million pounds in today's (1993) money. Around the same time the troubled Tullamore distillery of B. Daly & Co. owed the Bank of Ireland £32,054. A Limerick provisions merchant had been granted a discount line of £40,000 in 1854. The Provincial allowed Belfast's York Street Spinning Mill an even greater sum in the 1860s—£60,000—and

was to be badly hit in 1875 by failures in the textile industry. When the
Northern Spinning and Weaving Company collapsed in 1887, it owed the
Northern Bank £29,500. The Royal, long banker to Dublin-based railway
and canal companies, was owed over £107,000 by the Dublin, Wicklow
and Wexford Railway in 1868. During the Overend Gurney crisis, the
Bank of Ireland extended Malcolmson Brothers' line of credit to £100,000.
The Bank of Ireland lent Harland & Wolff £30,000 towards its new engine
works in 1879. In 1904 the same bank lent Workman Clark & Co.
£100,000 for seven years, and a few years later sanctioned a massive loan of
£230,000 to the same firm on the guarantee of its three directors to finance
the construction of a ship for the Oriental Steam Navigation Company. In
the event Workman Clark were 'so flush of funds' that a year later they had
not availed of the accommodation. On a more modest scale, accounts kept
by the manager of the Maghera branch of the Ulster Bank in the early
1860s show a willingness to tide textile firms over difficulties caused by the
American Civil War. Again, Boyle has shown how bank loans accounted
for over half of the total liabilities of several failed Ulster linen firms in
the 1870s. Examples of substantial loans to manufacturers might be
multiplied.[13] In general, the bank archives do not confirm the stereotype of
the over-cautious institution bent on short-term loans. In the north-east in
particular, where the demand for more flexible lending was greatest,
accommodation was not lacking. Specific complaints from businessmen
were rare. Ollerenshaw instances the case of textile machinery, where
banking facilities for exporters fell short: since export sales in that sector
were normally once-off affairs and involved large sums of money, the banks
were naturally wary of the bills offered by distant and unknown purchasers.
German banks, 'in close touch with outside markets', had no such fears.
The result was that at least one Belfast engineering firm lost important
contracts in Serbia in 1913. Yet it would be rash to blame the banks for
the loss: their lack of information in a particularly thin market might
explain their reluctance to be involved in it.[14]

The six Irish banks accorded continued note-issuing rights in 1845—the
Bank of Ireland, the Provincial, the National, and the three northern
banks—were still around in 1914, as were the Royal and the Hibernian.
Only the Munster & Leinster (founded in 1885) was relatively new. The
banks continued to differentiate their products in modest ways in the post-
Famine decades. The Dublin-based Royal had begun by catering primarily
for the capital's Protestant business and professional people, a service the
Hibernian had performed for Catholics. Both were handicapped by the

lack of note-issuing privileges. The Royal acquiesced, but the Hibernian repeatedly complained and sought to break out of its Dublin fastness in the 1870s through expanding its branch network and offering attractive terms to lenders and borrowers. The London-managed Provincial continued to serve a largely landed and professional clientele, its dull annual reports consisting largely of surveys of the latest agricultural statistics and harvest forecasts.[15] That the Munster & Leinster was a byword for caution in the 1880s and 1890s was predictable, given the failure of its previous incarnation (see below): branch managers were allowed full discretion on advances under £100 only. The Munster & Leinster was very much the farmer's bank, and the fluctuations in the ratio of its advances to deposits reflected the ebb and flow of business in rural and small-town Ireland. In the 1890s and 1900s it was the leading bank of the new agricultural co-operatives. At the outset its lending was in the form of discounting small bills, though the shift to fluctuating overdrafts was well under way before 1914. By then the Munster & Leinster was as much part of the establishment as the rest, its impressive new head office on Cork's South Mall reflecting its standing. Banks tended to either nationalist or unionist in ethos. The Bank of Ireland, the Provincial, and the Royal rarely employed Catholics in senior positions, and during the wave of branch expansion in the late 1910s some Ulster Catholics hoped the Munster & Leinster would take on the 'Orange Belfast banks' in the north. It was said of the luckless London & Irish Bank, which claimed to be 'entirely free from any sect or party', that 'it failed to enlist the influence or sympathy of either'.[16]

There remains a question about the degree of interbank competition. Stories of the repeated jockeying for business accounts and the publicity surrounding shareholders' meetings bespeak healthy rivalry in the banking sector. So do the fortunes of the Bank of Ireland in the wake of the 1845 Bank Act, when the Bank lost custom at the expense of its rivals, particularly the National Bank. An internal inquiry in 1864 forced two changes in Bank of Ireland policy: the payment of interest on deposits and a commitment to opening up new branches. Judging from note-issue data (Fig. 14.1), these stemmed the decline in the Bank's share of banking business. The Hibernian Bank's determination to expand its branch network in the mid-1870s and press its case for a note-issue also bespoke a competitive environment. The Munster Bank too, founded in Cork in 1864, instilled a dose of competition by paying a higher rate on deposits and by opening up new branches in the south. The rivalry over new branches was real enough.[17]

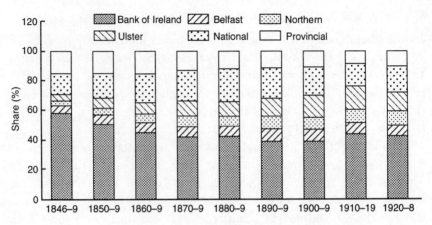

FIG. 14.1 Note-issuing banks' share of total circulation, 1846–1928

Yet this was hardly textbook competition. Once the Bank of Ireland began paying interest on deposits, the Irish banks (with the exception of the Munster and the Hibernian in its aggressive phase) tended to follow the lead of the Bank of Ireland in determining charges. The Irish rate was typically 1 per cent lower than the English. On occasion this arrangement broke down, as in 1903–4 when a fierce struggle led to favoured customers winning terms considerably better than the published rates. After a series of heated meetings between bank representatives, the established practice of rate-fixing was reimposed. The relative stability of the note-issuing banks' shares of the aggregate note-issue from the 1870s is more consistent with informal collusion than cutthroat competition. Shares were perturbed during the First World War, with the Bank of Ireland gaining at the expense of the rest, and the circulation of the Ulster banks rose relative to the rest over the longer haul (a reflection of the greater economic dynamism of that province). Yet, all in all, the relative positions of the banks changed remarkably little. Throughout, the Bank of Ireland and the National remained first and second in terms of note circulation, and the Belfast and Northern shared the bottom. The rank ordering of all nine joint-stock banks' shares of deposits and advances changed seldom either.[18]

A second limitation on competition was that the Bank Act of 1845 restricted the right of note-issue to those banks already issuing notes. This put prospective entrants at a disadvantage, and the Hibernian and Munster Banks complained accordingly.[19] The Munster had been founded in 1864, too late for note-issuing privileges, while the Hibernian, though founded in 1825, was a victim of the Bank of Ireland's pre-1845 monopoly of the

Dublin note-issue. The point about note-issue, given the requirement of 100 per cent backing at the margin, should not be exaggerated; nevertheless, it is surely significant that none of the note-issuing joint-stock banks relinquished the privilege in the decades under review here.

Third, Ollerenshaw's excellent study of the three Ulster joint-stock banks implies that their high profits stemmed in part from an effective cartel that managed to keep southern intruders at bay. As early as 1825 the Belfast-based banks and the Provincial were party to an agreement on deposit rates, and an arrangement between the three northern banks 'for mutual non-interference' in the matter of competition for deposits and branch expansion was agreed on in 1870. This entailed no bank opening a branch within five miles of one already established by another, though exceptions were stipulated. The market for new branches was divided up by agreement; for example, in 1877 the Belfast Bank opened a branch in Donegal in return for conceding the Ulster a branch in Larne. The cartel withstood the pressure of increasing demand for banking services in Belfast; in 1882, the banks decided that the Belfast Bank open a branch in the city's Markets area, the Northern in the Shankill, and the Ulster by the Falls Road. Earlier agreements were consolidated in a formal document in 1886. That document prohibited managers from canvassing for the transfer of accounts, and confirmed the policy on new branches. Despite occasional breaches and complaints, the agreement stuck, and was reflected in the banks' dividends. In sum, the notion that banking stability in Ulster at least was purchased at the expense of free competition has much to recommend it. In the south there was more competition, though its extent was lessening over time. It must not be forgotten, however, that this was the era of rationalization and amalgamation in banking in England too. In Scotland the joint-stock banks had operated a cartel since the 1840s through the General Managers' Committee, which determined lending and borrowing rates; non-price competition was constrained by bans on soliciting and advertising.[20]

Moreover, while the joint-stock banking system, with the Bank of Ireland at the helm, prided itself on its stability, it was not entirely scandal-free or panic-proof either. Three incidents stand out. The first concerns the Tipperary Joint Stock Bank (founded in 1838), which in early 1856 fell victim to the long litany of forgeries and swindles engineered by its leading light, John Sadleir. Sadleir's frauds had included selling bogus company shares and fictitious deeds to landed property; he had also managed to build up a huge overdraft without proper collateral. The mystery is why it took so long to find him out. The collapse drove Sadleir to suicide, and cost the Tipperary Bank's shareholders £0.5 million. It placed the entire Irish banking system under severe pressure for a time.[21]

The second major scandal centred on Sir Joseph Neale McKenna, chairman and managing director of the National Bank in the 1850s and 1860s, and several of his co-directors. For the most part, this period had been one of expansion for the National Bank. However, the directors engaged in a series of dubious investments in the 1860s, while seeking to diversify some of the bank's business out of Ireland. To this end they greatly increased its capital and took on several highly speculative accounts. The National Bank was seriously compromised by the failure of the Bank of Hindustan, China, and Japan, which closed its doors in 1866, and rumours persisted of investments in risky projects in France and far-away Peru. From mid-1865 on confidence in the bank fell, and deposits and current accounts declined. Its share of total note circulation fell too, and the value of its stock dropped drastically relative to that of the other banks (see Fig. 14.2). McKenna survived for a few years through bullying and bravado, but he and his associates (including a son of economist David Ricardo) lost the confidence of the proprietors in 1869 and were removed from the board. They left the National with bad debts of between £300,000 and £400,000 and a grossly excessive paid-up capital. An influential deputation of Irish shareholders criticized its lavishly rewarded directors for extravagance, and blamed them for overpaying a top-heavy staff. The shareholders deemed the bank's officials 'more men of pleasure than of business [with] ideas and . . . habits entirely above their position', and demanded more devolution from London to Ireland. McKenna was accused of lending money to companies whose security was 'in a great measure the speculation upon which [they had] borrowed'. His less flamboyant successor, William Massey, signalled a more cautious policy in future with the declaration that the 'the proper place for speculation was certainly not in connection with a banking establishment'. Still, though confidence in the National in the City of London took some time to re-establish, its future was never seriously in jeopardy.[22] The value of its stock and dividends were gradually restored after McKenna's dismissal. Even McKenna's fortunes recovered; he represented Youghal in Westminster between 1874 and 1885 and Monaghan South until 1892![23]

Thirdly, the suspension of payments by the Munster Bank in July 1885 marked the last failure of a major Irish bank. The brainchild of a group of Cork City industrialists and merchants, the farmers and traders of the south

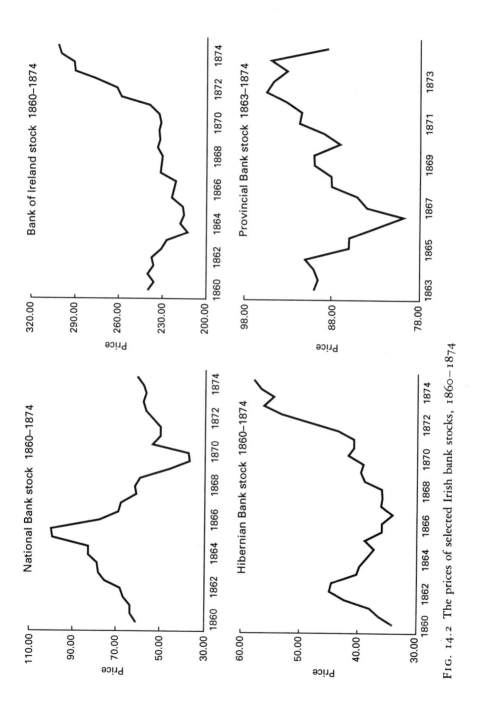

FIG. 14.2 The prices of selected Irish bank stocks, 1860–1874

were the bank's mainstay. The Munster vigorously competed for deposits, and its high ratio of advances and discounts to deposits (generally over unity) indicates that it was also readier to discount bills than its competitors. By the end it had forty-three offices, 19,000 creditors, and 22,000 debtors. Recurrent complaints about the bank's inadequate liquidity by the *Irish Banker* from 1876[24] did not bring the bank down: what destroyed it were rumours emanating from alienated Dublin shareholders about directors helping themselves to huge unsecured loans. The resignation in July 1884 of long-serving chairman, William Shaw MP, one of the prime targets, and the sudden acknowledgement of substantial long-standing bad debts were not propitious. Not even the accession to the board of the influential and upright James J. Murphy of Lady's Well Brewery in July 1884 could save the Munster, though Murphy was chiefly responsible for the bank's rapid reincarnation in the form of the Munster & Leinster. The Munster's problems in 1884–5 were exacerbated by the reluctance of debtors to repay on time loans due to an apparently doomed institution, and after weeks of pressure, it was forced to close its doors on 14 July 1885. On that day the amount due by debtors (£2.7 million) was considerably in excess of deposit and current accounts (£2.2 million). To make matters worse, a fortnight later one of the Munster's managers in Dublin, Robert Farquaharson, fled the country on the discovery of fraud to the tune of £70,000. In the ensuing proceedings William Shaw and two co-directors were forced to declare bankruptcy, and Shaw spent his last years 'in seclusion and under shadows of commercial and domestic misfortune'.

Ironically, despite the resulting losses to shareholders, events were to prove that the Munster Bank was basically solvent. The failure sent shivers down the rest of the banking system. Irate supporters of the Munster accused the Bank of Ireland of 'strangling' their bank, and forced a run on several branches of the Bank of Ireland in Tipperary, withdrawing over £300,000 in a few days. It took the shipment of £1 million in coin from the Bank of England to halt the run. But worse was to come. At its half-yearly meeting of December 1885, a day after Gladstone's statement in support for Home Rule, the Bank of Ireland declared a 10 per cent dividend, 2 per cent less than shareholders had expected. Bank stock, worth 336 in early 1885, had fallen to 306 by the beginning of December; it now plummeted to 249 by the year's end. Another Irish bank in some trouble around this time was the Hibernian Bank. Once again, an ex-director had compromised the bank's liquidity. Dividends were low or non-existent for a few years, and the value of the bank's shares plummeted. As a result shareholders were extremely nervous: when one of the bank's 'runners' absconded with £2,000, its shares immediately dropped by 5 per cent—even though the loss was fully insured. The Hibernian was to pull through after a few tough years. Not even the Ulster banks were immune from the prevailing uncertainty; the crisis prompted the banks to agree to 'diminish . . . the existing rivalry and [come] to a more complete and friendly understanding as to allowances, rates and charges'. The agreement lasted until October 1917.[25]

The failure of the Munster Bank raises again an issue previously addressed in Chapter 3, the evolution of the Bank of Ireland's role as lender of last resort. Evidently the Tipperary Bank was beyond saving, though its collapse placed several other reputable banks under pressure. La Touche's requested a loan of £30,000 from the Bank of Ireland, and the National Bank and the Belfast Bank sought reassurance that help would be forthcoming if necessary. The Bank of Ireland duly obliged, and the storm passed without recourse to special accommodation. The Bank of Ireland was forced to act again in 1865–6 when the Irish banking system was rocked by the failure of the London bank of Overend, Gurney & Company. Early in 1866, La Touche's, the Hibernian, the Royal, and the Munster were granted accommodation. The Bank of Ireland went further, overstepping the classic lender of last resort function by granting special overdraft privileges to several large business including Malcolmson Brothers and the City of Dublin Steam Packet Company. The Bank's claims to have done its best to save the Munster Bank in 1885 are less convincing. True, the Bank had helped to the tune of £0.4 million before finally pulling the plug on the Munster, but questions in Westminster from Cork City MP, one Charles Stuart Parnell, about the Bank of Ireland's alleged negligence elicited the following important communication to the Bank of Ireland from Chancellor of the Exchequer Hicks-Beach:[26]

Her Majesty's Government cannot but consider that the Bank of Ireland occupies not only the leading but also an exceptional position among [Irish banking] institutions.

It is not merely, in common with a few other banks, entrusted with the issue of notes, but to it is also confided the management of the public debt, and the custody of the Exchequer balance. These are privileges which give it the first place in the monetary world of Ireland, but there are privileges which entail also special responsibilities. The public will expect that, in the hour of difficulty, an institution so exceptionally placed will also take the lead in the adoption of measures to avert diaster and maintain public confidence, and should such expectation not be fulfilled, they may not improbably demand a reconsideration of exclusive rights.

Her Majesty's Government desire to acknowledge the value of the assistance rendered by the Bank of Ireland in the present crisis . . . It must however be a subject of regret that the remaining banks of issue have not so far as my Lords are informed, co-operated actively with the Bank of Ireland in its efforts to restore confidence. They also are privileged institutions, and it lies upon them to justify the retention of a privilege, which goes far to create a monopoly in their favour, by proving that they may be trusted in times of difficulty to take their share of risk and responsibility.

Hicks-Beach evidently believed that the Bank of Ireland had been over-cautious in its dealings with the Munster Bank. Events were to prove him right, to the extent that in the end the Munster & Leinster Bank, which emerged from the ashes of the Munster Bank, repaid all outstanding liabilities.

In emergencies such as those of 1856, 1866, and 1885, the Bank of Ireland was certainly in a dilemma. Potentially at least, its duties as outlined by Hicks-Beach conflicted with its quest for profits and markets as a commercial bank. Supporters of the Munster Bank could accuse the Bank of Ireland, however unjustly, of 'a treacherous desire to grasp at the business of a rival concern'.[27] The issue arose again in 1904 in connection with the collection of annuities due from farmers under the Wyndham Act. The Act stipulated that the Bank of Ireland receive the annuities, but this presented opponents with the cue to articulate anew their objections to the Bank of Ireland's privileges. Why not devise a more equitable collection scheme? Why not rotate the government account among the joint-stock banks as was done in Scotland? The official reply was simply 'because [the Bank of Ireland] keep[s] all the government accounts and because of the relations that exist between the government and the Bank'. The Bankers' Magazine, supporting the demand for fairer play, noted that the Bank of England had distanced itself from 'the everyday business of the country, and contents itself with the more important operations that fittingly fall to the duty of a State bank'. However, since the Bank of Ireland continued to compete with the other Irish banks for private business, its claims on a monopoly of the government account were far less compelling. In the decades before the First World War the Irish banking system groped towards one solution to the dilemma—a banking system led by the Bank of Ireland, but founded on agreed rates and informal market-sharing. As discussed below, the Irish Free State was confronted with the issue again after 1923.[28]

Table 14.4. *Bank deposits in the UK, 1871–1914* (£m.)

	Ireland	Scotland	England and Wales	Total
1871	25.9 (5.8)	65.1 (14.6)	355.6 (79.6)	446.5
1881	29.8 (5.9)	78.6 (15.7)	392.8 (78.4)	501.1
1891	39.3 (6.3)	92.1 (14.7)	495.2 (79.0)	626.6
1901	48.8 (5.9)	107.4 (12.9)	676.8 (81.2)	833.0
1914	71.1 (6.4)	129.6 (11.7)	899.9 (81.0)	1 110.6

Source: Ollerenshaw, 'Aspects of Bank Lending', 223 (percentages in parentheses).

The role of merchant banks in providing Irish business with more long-term finance after the Famine has not been properly studied, though it probably did not count for much. Massive loans such as those made by the Merchant Banking Company of London to the Belfast textile firm of William Spotten & Co. in the 1870s were exceptional.[29] The stock market, ploughed back profits, and private borrowing were the usual means relied on in both Ireland and Great Britain for industrial finance.

14.3 Banking in the New Ireland

The creation of the two Irish States in 1921–2 had little immediate effect on the banking sector. Commercial banking in the twenty-six counties in the inter-war period continued to be dominated by eight joint-stock concerns, viz. the Bank of Ireland, the Munster & Leinster, the Provincial, the National, the Royal, the Hibernian, the Northern, and the Ulster. The Belfast Banking Company ceded its southern branches to the Dublin-based Royal in 1923, and the three Belfast-based banks had the lion's share of northern business. Bank deposits in Ireland were very high relative to national income. In 1932 they were worth almost £42 per head of population, compared to £48 in Britain, £40 in New Zealand, £22 in Denmark, and £72 in the USA. The bulk of deposits in Irish banks consisted of accumulated savings rather than funds for financing current spending, bearing out Andrew Jameson's quip that 'the Irishman is temperamentally a depositor, not an investor'. Other savings outlets, such as savings certificates and trustee savings banks were less developed. In Ireland such outlets absorbed £5 per head of population, compared to £22 in Britain, £33 in Denmark, and £40 in New Zealand. The banks converted the deposits into liquid resources, held for the most part on the London money market. Thus the deposits indirectly put Ireland in a very strong financial position.

In November 1913 the Bank of Ireland had proposed a system of rates 'to be embodied in a formal agreement to be signed or sealed by all the Banks'. However, the Munster and Leinster Bank did not attend the meeting that ensued, and the support of the Royal and the Hibernian was not forthcoming. The remaining banks considered a limited agreement, not binding in places where one of the banks not party to the agreement had a branch. But nothing seems to have come of this. At the outbreak of the First World War the banks agreed privately 'that each would retain its existing business but would not canvass for or encourage business away from any of its competitors'.[30] The rivalry about branches was renewed at the war's end, and dozens of new banking outlets were created in the 1918–25 period. An amusing sidelight on this is obtained from a minute from the general manager of the Royal Bank to his board in August 1921:[31]

I received information a few days ago that the Hibernian Bank was opening a branch in the above town, and, in accordance with the policy of my directors of extending operations by opening branches in certain towns, I thought that this was a good opportunity for the Bank to open an office in Blessington. We have a considerable number of clients in the neighbourhood of Blessington, and I felt that it would not do for us to overlook this fact.

As my informant told me that the Hibernian Bank were opening on Friday I felt that if we were to move at all, it was imperative that the branch should be opened at once, if possible before our competitors. Under the circumstances I was unable to lay the proposition before the Board. The only course open to me was to ring up Mr Jellett (the Chairman) at his private residence, which I did on Monday, and he took me to Blessington that evening, and we secured premises, which enabled us to open on Thursday, one day before the Hibernian Bank. I attended at Blessington on the opening day, and am convinced that the prospects are most promising.

Yet a series of developments in 1918–19—a request from the Chancellor of the Exchequer that all the Irish banks hold interest rate on deposits to 3 per cent, the prospect of serious industrial unrest, and the uncertain future status of Irish banknotes—made for increased co-operation between the banks on other fronts. This co-operation was institutionalized in 1920, when the southern banks joined together with representatives of the three northern banks to form the Irish Banks' Standing Committee. The Committee would meet quarterly (and more often when necessary) to agree on rates for overdrafts, loans, and discounts, and to discuss other matters of common concern. As seen from Table 14.5, the shares of the different

Table 14.5. *Deposits and advances of the nine joint-stock banks, 1893–1938* (in percentages of the total)

Period	BofI	Prov	Natl	Hib	M&L	Royal	Belfst	North	Ulster
Deposits									
1898–1903	19.3	9.9	23.4	6.0	7.9	4.1	8.7	7.7	13.0
1903–8	19.4	9.6	22.5	6.1	8.7	3.6	8.4	7.8	13.8
1908–13	19.7	9.3	21.7	6.1	9.2	3.0	8.8	8.0	14.2
1913–18	17.4	9.3	21.6	6.5	10.8	2.9	8.1	8.1	14.0
1919–24	16.6	8.6	21.2	7.4	14.5	2.9	9.1	7.8	12.0
1924–9	17.4	8.4	21.2	7.0	14.1	3.9	8.3	7.8	11.9
1929–34	17.7	8.2	21.1	6.6	14.3	3.7	7.8	8.1	12.4
1934–8	18.2	8.6	21.2	6.1	13.9	3.7	8.1	8.0	12.2
Advances									
1898–1903	17.7	10.2	27.0	7.0	6.0	3.1	8.7	7.5	12.9
1903–8	19.6	9.7	25.0	7.1	6.9	3.0	8.5	7.3	13.1
1908–13	20.7	9.6	21.5	6.5	7.2	2.9	9.7	7.6	14.3
1913–18	19.3	10.9	21.4	6.2	8.5	2.9	10.4	7.6	12.8
1919–24	15.8	8.5	19.9	5.7	13.3	3.6	11.7	9.8	11.7
1924–9	15.2	7.3	18.7	7.4	14.2	4.5	10.2	11.1	11.4
1929–34	16.7	7.4	19.5	6.8	13.7	4.5	8.9	10.8	11.7
1934–8	16.9	8.3	20.6	7.1	13.5	4.7	8.0	9.7	11.1

BofI = Bank of Ireland   Hib = Hibernian Bank
Prov = Provincial Bank   Natl = National Bank
M&L = Munster & Leinster Bank   Royal = Royal Bank
Belfst = Belfast Banking Company   North = Northern Bank
Ulster = Ulster Bank

Note: The calculations exclude deposits in the National Land Bank (1919–27) and its successor, the National City Bank, a tiny fraction of the total. See Hall, *Bank of Ireland*, 352. The Belfast Banking Company passed its southern business to the Royal in 1923, and this is reflected in the numbers. The data refer to all the banks' business, within and outside the Irish Free State.

banks of deposits and advances did not budge much during the 1920s and 1930s.

In the 1920s and 1930s, banking developments were largely conditioned by the operation of the Standing Committee. That gentlemen's agreement quickly acquired teeth. Not only did it set rates; members agreed in March 1920 to a scale of charges on cheques lodged in overdrawn accounts, and in May to an annual charge of one guinea (21*s.*) on current accounts. These measures led to considerable customer dissatisfaction, but they stuck. Scales such as those shown in Table 14.6 from February 1922 give an impression

Table 14.6. *Banks' pricing policy, 1922* (rate %)

Bank of England rate	2	2.5	3	3.5	4	4.5	5	5.5	6	6.5	7	
Irish Banks' rate			4	4.5	5	5.5	6	6	6.5	7	7.5	
Standard overdrawn accounts			5.5	5.5	6	6	6.5	7	7	7.5	8	
Deposits (*a*) Ordinary			1.5	1.5	2	2	2.5	3	3	3.5	3.5	
(*b*) £500–£1,999			1.5	2	2	2.5	3	3.5	3.5	4	4	

of the banks' pricing policies during the inter-war period. The 4 per cent margin between standard overdraft and deposit rates seems wide. Indeed, Irish rates were usually less attractive than those on offer in England, and there were repeated complaints in the press and from customers about the spread between borrowing and lending rates. Delegations of businessmen[32] and farmers were met with a stock answer; the effective spread was narrower than people believed, and Irish customers gained in other ways. Yet the Standing Committee's enduring concern with the loss of large deposits to English banks tells its own tale. Geoffrey Crowther's report to the Standing Committee (see below) found claims against the banks exaggerated, but conceded that the typical borrower was paying 'slightly more' in Ireland than in England, though it was in their treatment of the small depositor that the banks were 'weakest in face of criticism'. Individual banks grumbled at aspects of the Standing Committee's rate structure, but none seems to have systematically reneged on it.[33]

Setting standard bank charges was by no means the Standing Committee's only function. It also set out the terms for bank underwriting of government loans, and represented the banks in attempts to fend off regulation and competition. Early contacts between the Committee and the Department of Finance were none too cordial. At one stormy meeting in 1923, several members of the Committee wondered if the 'two young gentlemen [meaning civil servants Joseph Brennan and J. J. McElligott] who waited on them spoke with authority'. The banks were at first reluctant to underwrite government loans without a British Treasury guarantee, a politically insensitive demand that they did not continue to insist on. In the event, the Government managed to raise the required £10 million without much support from the banks. After Brennan's departure to the Currency Commission in 1927, the whole burden of negotiating the Government's case fell on McElligott. Feeling isolated, McElligott obtained the assent of his minister, Ernest Blythe, for a second-in-command from the British Treasury.[34] Nothing came of that, but McElligott was to prove himself an able bargainer in later bouts. The terms of the second national loan of 1930 were also the outcome of tough negotiation between the joint-stock banks and the Department of Finance, the banks again taking a gloomier view of the Government's creditworthiness than the outcome warranted. In November 1933 the banks wanted to know how the money sought in the next national loan was to be spent. Typically the banks sought a commission of 1.5 per cent to manage and underwrite the loans. The banks' attitude to the Financial Agreement of 1938 and the ensuing loan was relief. The National Bank's representative on the Standing Committee urged the banks' support for the Government, declaring the National's willingness to take up its quota of a 3.5 per cent loan at 99 or even par if the other banks went along. The other banks proved tougher, forcing 3.75 per cent at par, but were content with a 1 per cent commission. The loan was considerably oversubscribed.

Did the banks' cartel result in poor service at high prices? One might have expected a hard look at this question from the official inquiries of the 1920s and 1930s. However, if Irish public opinion was unfairly prejudiced against the banks, both official inquiries into money and banking, the Parker–Willis Commission of 1926 and the second Banking Commission of 1934–8 (on which more below and in Chapter 17) were arguably too 'soft' on them. In the case of the former, 'packed' with bank representatives, and established in a hurry in order to provide a blueprint for exchange-rate policy and seignorage, this is no surprise. The banks feared much worse from the second inquiry, a Fianna Fáil creation, and tried hard at first to quash it. Failing in that aim, they proceeded to 'capture' the inquiry through the selection of indulgent commissioners. The Majority Report defended the banks by arguing that cartels like the Standing Committee were commonplace elsewhere, citing examples from Scotland, Britain, and the USA. Amazingly for a commission appointed to 'examine and report on the system in Saorstát Éireann of currency, banking, credit, public borrow-ing and lending', the 1934–8 inquiry failed even to cross-question repre-sentatives of the Irish banks in public,[35] while witnesses critical of the banks were subjected to vigorous questioning by bank supporters of the Commission. The Commission's only references to the Standing Committee[36] were defensive and apologetic, holding that 'it is not to the ultimate interest of the public that competition should take the form of a competitive reduction of charges and an increase of the rate of interest paid upon deposits'. Perhaps so, but there were points worth at least discussing. For example, the higher rates charged by Irish banks for loans and the slow growth of the system might seem prima-facie evidence for a misallocation of resources. Second, the inflated socio-economic status of bank officials and bank managers might be interpreted as the fruits of rent-seeking behaviour. Thirdly, the power of the Standing Committee to prevent individual banks on occasion from expanding branch networks because of objections from other members also suggests some degree of monopoly power. For instance, in September 1937 three banks—the Provincial, the Northern, and the Belfast—sought permission to create several new branches in and around Belfast. A meeting of the Standing Committee deferred consideration indefinitely, on the basis that this would open the door to 'unrestricted competition of a harmful nature to the offices already established in or near these areas, and of doubtful advantage in the long run to newcomers'.[37] Fourthly, the Commission, content to report overdraft rates issued to it by the Standing Committee, failed to see through—or to note—the banks' strategy of not increasing rates while the Commission deliberated.

The Irish banks' consolidated balance-sheets for the 1930s (supplied by the Standing Committee to the second Banking Commission with some reluctance) bear comparison with those of the London clearing banks. In 1931 in evidence to the Macmillan Committee spokesmen for the English banks stated that their aim was to lend out 50–60 per cent of deposits in the form of advances, a target which they failed to meet in subsequent years. English bank advances fell from £988 million in 1929 to £961 million in 1936–8, and the share devoted to manufacturing, building, and transport fell from 33.6 per cent to 25.6 per cent, prompting one banking historian to conclude that the economic recovery of those years 'was not being financed by clearing bank advances'.[38] Table 14.7 compares aggregate Irish and British balances. In value terms, advances in the Irish Free State hardly budged between 1931 (£44.7 million) and 1936 (£44.1 million), and the share of 'manufacturing, building, railways, transport, etc.' was less than one-tenth, or about £4 million.[39] The Irish banks repeatedly argued that their low ratio of advances to deposits was a necessary precaution, given the size and origin of most of their deposits. Their very risk-aversion brought stability, even in the absence of a recognizable lender of last resort. But the numbers leave room too for an alternative hypothesis, viz. the cartel allowed the banks to leave money with the discount banks which might, with more effort, have realized higher returns from business customers.

Three considerations possibly mitigate such criticisms of the bank cartel. First, the banks' monopoly was countered by a powerful trade union, the

Table 14.7. *Assets of the Irish and London Clearing Banks, c.1930–1938* (as a percentage of deposits)

	Irish banks		London clearing banks	
	1931–3	1934–6	1928–30	1936–8
Cash	9.5	10.8	11.2	10.6
Money at call at short notice	6.3	5.5	8.2	7.4
Bills discounted	6.7	4.2	14.7	12.9
Investments	49.9	52.4	14.4	27.7
Advances	40.8	41.3	52.0	41.2
(in IFS)	(25.5)	(26.9)		

Sources: 1934–8 Banking Commission, *Report*, 99; Michael Collins, *Banks and Industrial Finance in Britain*, 73.

Irish Bank Officials' Association. Virtually all managers and clerks were members of the IBOA, which would have been quick to capitalize on bank disunity. In the absence of the cartel, any single bank in a labour dispute would have been an easy target for the combination of a strong union and greedy business rivals. It might therefore have been slower to innovate. The problem with this argument is that the IBOA seems to have been quite adept at eating into the monopoly rents created by the cartel; in the inter-war years, Irish bank clerks were better paid than their British peers.

Second, the banking sector was in the doldrums in the 1930s, and the need for some rationalization was widely conceded. A confidential report to the Standing Committee in 1932 by a youthful Geoffrey Crowther, future editor of *The Economist*, highlighted the issue. Crowther found that the Irish Free State had 33 per cent more banking premises per head of population than Britain. Concerted action aimed at streamlining the branch network would result in higher profits, and enable the banks to pay a higher rate on deposits. In the following year, the Ulster Bank offered to produce at any time a list of branches that it was willing to close, and the 'redundancy of banks' was repeatedly discussed by the Standing Committee in the next few years. The results were rather disappointing, and a concerted effort to effect branch closures was not made until 1938. Individual banks played bargaining games. The Bank of Ireland's articulate Lord Glenavy was the most vocal supporter of a system of branch closures, but the Belfast Bank declared satisfaction with the *status quo*, while the Munster & Leinster thought this was a matter for bank-to-bank horse-trading. The authority of Per Jacobsson, a fellow member of the Banking Commission, was invoked by Glenavy and Sweetman. Jacobsson had indeed told them that on a journey through the south and west with McElligott and Brennan in 1935 he had been impressed with the large number of bank branches, and counselled 'friendly agreement' between the banks as the best solution. Eventually the Munster & Leinster conceded.[40] The result was an agreement engineered by the Standing Committee in 1939 to close twenty-five branches in twenty-three counties.

Third, the small share of bank lending destined for manufacturing in the 1920s, if not in the 1930s, probably reflected a lack of demand more than an unwillingness on the part of the banks to do business. In support, the spokesman for the Irish Chambers of Commerce told the Parker–Willis Commission that the banks were meeting business needs, and denied that there was an unrequited demand from their members for long-term credits from their members. The Commission accepted this, adding the proviso:[41]

It is not yet certain how far the country may desire to attempt industrialisation . . . [W]e recognize that for a brief period to come it may be deemed necessary that some special provision in the way of credit facilities should be continued for the assistance of new or struggling industries which otherwise could not succeed in attaining a firm basis in operation.

Though it played a leading part in the Standing Committee—indeed such an agreement was largely its idea, and meetings were held at Bank headquarters, usually with the Bank's governor in the chair—the position of the Bank of Ireland remained rather special in the new Ireland.[42] Banker to the Dublin Castle administration for well over a century, the Bank of Ireland's ethos had been strongly Unionist and Protestant; in the 1920s, its Court of Directors was still dominated by earls, baronets, and captains. The Bank had not prepared for the creation of the Irish Free State, and indeed in January 1922 was obliged to seek urgent advice from the Bank of England. In London, Montagu Norman could offer little consolation, urging the creation of an independent Irish central bank on the model of the Reserve Bank of the Union of South Africa. The Bank of Ireland's Governor could only reflect that Norman was 'obsessed with the pre-eminent position and conservative position of the Bank of England'.

None the less, the Bank of Ireland adapted well to political change. It accepted the invitation from General Michael Collins, as Minister of Finance of the provisional government, to become financial agent for the new administration. A few months later, in the course of a dispute with the British Treasury, 'the Court . . . animated by the feeling that in the new conditions arising out of the establishment of the Irish Free State individual interests should not be pressed to the possible advantage of the body politic, deem it a wiser and more patriotic course to merge their interests in the nation at large'. This is more than could be said at this stage of some of the other banks, deemed by Andrew Jameson to be 'quite out of touch and sympathy with Free State affairs'. The new Government broached terms for short-term advances first with the Bank of Ireland; early in 1923 Liam T. MacCosgair (*alias* W. T. Cosgrave), Collins's successor, was seeking accommodation to the tune of £0.5 million, and in June the Bank of Ireland joined the other southern banks for the first time, not without some trepidation, in tiding over the Government. The Bank of Ireland was unhappy with its allocation of consolidated banknotes in 1926, but its anachronistic claim for a share based on the terms of Peel's Act of 1844 rather than on a business share in the mid-1920s was a non-starter. (The Bank's share of total Irish banknote circulation had fallen from 60 per cent in 1845 to about 45 per cent in 1880; it was still about 45 per cent in 1920–2.) Meanwhile the Bank of Ireland's monopoly of government business rankled with the other banks. If the Bank's top men were Unionist by sentiment, they worked hard at relations with Free State ministers.[43]

The Bank of England on occasion treated its Irish sister as a kind of satellite central bank. Cordial, informal relations were maintained between the likes of Jameson and Glenavy in Dublin and Sir Ernest Harvey, Norman, and Niemeyer in London. Threadneedle Street always notified College Green by telegram of changes in bank rate, and the Bank of Ireland and the other Irish banks adjusted their rates without fail to maintain a margin between their minimum rate and the announced London rate. In April 1924 the Bank of England provided further evidence of the Dublin bank's special status. Governor Norman was then engaged in one of his major feats of banking diplomacy, the creation of a new German bank to finance foreign trade in the wake of the hyperinflation of 1922–3. The Bank of England undertook to find half the required capital, and asked the Bank of Ireland 'as a central bank to accept participation in the loan'. The Bank of Ireland duly complied, placing £0.25 million at the disposal of Threadneedle Street. Senior officials of the Irish bank corresponded freely with their London counterpart on issues such as the chairmanship of the Currency Commission,[44] the Currency Commission's London agency (which the National Bank was seeking), Irish debt finance, and banking legislation.

The Bank of Ireland sought reassurance on the findings of the Crowther report, a report described by Brennan as an *ex parte* statement against the proposal to set up a central bank. Henry Clay reassured Glenavy that Ireland did not need a central bank, adding that 'machinery for its own sake [is] one of the most futile causes of waste and dislocation to which this age is addicted', while Norman declared himself to be a 'champion' of the Bank of Ireland.[45]

Yet politics in the end ruined the special relationship between College Green and Threadneedle Street. Just a few days before the outbreak of the Second World War, a nervous Bank of Ireland Court sent Deputy Governor Sir John Keane to London for assurances. Keane's visit began cordially enough with an interview with his London counterpart, B. G. Catterns, Catterns playing down Irish fears regarding the unavailability of foreign exchange and a moratorium on assets. The rest of the minute is worth quoting in full:[46]

At this point Mr Catterns retired temporarily, and on his return was accompanied by the Governor, Mr Norman, who said that notwithstanding the long and intimate relations between the two institutions he was not prepared to commit the Bank of England by promising to come to the assistance of the Bank of Ireland in an emergency of the nature under discussion. As an ordinary banking transaction there would be no question whatever about making an advance to the Bank, but in an emergency situation there was an important principal [sic] involved. The Bank of England looked upon Eire as a Dominion, and if it accommodated the Bank of Ireland in a crisis, there would be no reason why they should withhold similar assistance from the other Dominions—the Bank was not prepared to concede this principal [sic]. Mr Norman stressed the view that the Bank 'whose centre of gravity was in Eire' should look to their own Treasury or the Currency Commission to help them over difficult periods. Sir John pointed out that the position in Eire did not admit of a solution in that way, as the Treasury came to the Bank of Ireland when it was short of funds, and the Currency Commission was not a lender of the last resort. Mr Norman then urged that as Eire was a separate political entity it should have a Central Bank of its own. He went on to say that 'two of your friends' (emphasising the word 'friends') had already approached the Bank of England for a similar assurance which the Bank of Ireland was seeking, but the Bank could not admit the principal [sic] in their case either.

After some further general remarks on the provisions of the Currency Act in regard to Consolidated Bank Notes and Legal Tender Notes, the interview terminated.

Later Mr Catterns urged the confidential nature of the information afforded as to the foreign exchange arrangements which had been discussed by His Majesty's Treasury and the Eire Government, and suggested that in any conversations which the Bank of Ireland might have with the latter, no reference be made to the fact that such information was in our possession.

For the Bank of Ireland, this was the signal that the Irish banks could no longer expect the Old Lady of Threadneedle Street to act as their lender of last resort. Legislation creating an Irish central bank followed in 1942.

14.4 Company Legislation

Curiously, Ireland had an apparent advantage over the rest of the UK in the field of company legislation: whereas limited liability came to Great Britain only in the mid-1850s, the Anonymous Partnership Act of 1782 provided for general limited liability in Ireland. The preamble to the Act reflected the bullishness of the 'patriot' Parliament:

Whereas the increasing of the stock of money employed in trade and manufacture must greatly promote the commerce and prosperity of this Kingdom, and many persons might be induced to subscribe sums of money to men well qualified for trade, but not of competent fortune to carry it on largely if they were allowed by the profit or loss of trade for the same, and were not deemed traders on that account, or subject thereby to any further or other demands than the sums so subscribed.

The Act envisaged companies formed by acting and 'anonymous' partners for the 'purpose of buying and selling in the gross, or by wholesalers, or for establishing or carrying on any business for any term not exceeding fourteen years'. Losses incurred by the anonymous partners could not exceed the sums they invested. The total capital subscribed might range from £1,000 to £50,000. The Act produced 125 partnerships during the pre-Union period, accounting for a total capital of over £340,000, of which one-third was supplied by the active partners. The 1801–15 period saw the greatest concentration of activity under the Act, with 234 companies worth a total of £1.2 million being set up. The pace of registration fell off after then, with no new companies being registered in some years. Charles Wye Williams's pioneering City of Dublin Steam Packet Company availed of the Act in 1823 on an initial capital of £24,000.[47] Between 1834 and 1854 only eighty-three concerns were registered, with a total capital of less than £150,000. The failure of the legislation to generate greater capital accumulation was invoked in evidence in 1854 as an argument against limited liability in Britain, but restrictive clauses in the Irish legislation have also been blamed for that failure. A Belfast witness claimed that 'its provisions are so loose and have been interpreted so illiberally by our Courts of Law that no lawyer would advise his client to take advantage of the Act'. The limited duration of partnerships formed under the Act and the exclusion of mining and retailing have also been mentioned. Besides, the Act was restricted to companies with a capital of £50,000 or less: the agreement which increased the capital of the City of Dublin Steam Packet Company to £230,000 in 1833 required special legislation. These are supply-side arguments; the subsequent history of joint-stock companies in Ireland suggests that there was a demand-side aspect to the story as well.[48] Whatever it was about the Act's shortcomings that so little Irish and British capital availed of it before the Famine suggests the lack of profitable opportunities.

The company legislation of 1856 and 1862 greatly facilitated the formation of limited liability companies in the UK. It seems to have had an impact in Ireland too, to which it also applied; in the next half-century or so 2,850 companies were registered under the Company Acts, with a nominal share capital of £110 million (compared to slightly over £2 million under the Anonymous Partnerships Act). Most were small and confined to servicing and processing, with gas and mining, hotels, and transport companies bulking large. Still, some substantial concerns were floated. In the 1890s in particular, the Irish investor seems to have shed the caution pinpointed by Lee for the 1840s:

No sooner does a company come with its £1 shares offered at par . . . than benevolent speculators push up the quotation to a big premium, in some cases as much as 200 or 300% in a very few hours and this inflation in patent rights must in a great many directions result in loss and disappointment . . . We are given to understand that promoters whose antecedents are not altogether pleasant in regard to bringing out undertakings in London and the provinces in this country have devoted their attention to the unsophisticated Irish. This attitude to the Irish is really a *boulversement* of the old fashion cry of 'no Irish need apply'.[49]

Manufacturing was 'but sparsely represented' in these issues, but this was probably due to factors other than a want of capital. The problem with capital was less one of supply than of demand.[50]

PART V

15

The Economic Performance of the Two Irelands, 1921–1939: Issues and Evidence

The late Government was able to solve, partially, its unemployment problem by the annual emigration of 25,000 or 30,000 young people. That is ended. Those 25,000 or 30,000 people who, in other years, found an outlet through the emigrant ship are remaining at home or have to be provided for at home.

SEÁN LEMASS, 1932[1]

I am not sure that we did not attack the problem from the wrong angle . . . I have already expressed the view that the law of comparative costs should continue to govern agricultural policy . . . But in regard to manufactures, some concession might perhaps have been prudently made to sentiment.

GEORGE O'BRIEN[2]

15.1 Income

Questions about the relative incomes of the citizens of European economies today may be answered quickly by reference to official Eurostat or OECD data. Sometimes comparisons along these lines (as with Italy's *sorpasso* of the UK in the 1980s, or Norway's threatened overtaking of Sweden in the 1990s) give rise to bouts of national self-congratulation or self-doubt. Assessments of the relative performances of economies in the past must rely on more approximate, retrospectively constructed data. In the case of Ireland, the construction of historical national accounts remains at an embryonic stage. Mokyr's revised estimate of Irish national income in the early 1840s (about £80 million) and Cullen's of gross national product on the eve of the First World War (£150 million) imply that Irish income per head rose from about two-fifths to over three-fifths that of Great Britain between those dates. The implied trebling in Irish purchasing power seems impressive enough, even if much of it was achieved at the expense of a decline in population.[3]

Cullen's estimate implies an average income from GNP of £34, at a time when British GNP per head was about £55. If the Irish were still poor by British standards in 1914, how were they faring by European standards? The question is an important one, since it influences any broader assessment of the record since then. Denmark, a frequent focus of comparison, provides a useful bench-mark. Danish GNP in 1914 has been put at 2,276 million kroner. At an exchange rate of 18 kroner to the pound, this means a per capita income of about £44.5, or 30 per cent more than the Irish level. A more refined comparison, adjusting for deviations from purchasing power parity, is not possible at this stage. Another perspective is gained by linking the Irish estimate to Crafts' estimates in 1970 dollars of GNP per capita in several European economies in 1910. Ireland (at $776) was much poorer than Denmark ($1,050), Switzerland ($992), Germany ($958), or The Netherlands ($952), but ahead of Sweden ($763) and Norway ($706), and well clear of Italy ($548) and Spain ($547). Maddison's alternative estimates of Danish, Swedish, and British 1914 GDP per head in 1985 dollars, adjusted for purchasing power—$3,037, $2,450, and $4,024— produce a similar ranking, since assessing Irish income to scale with British gives a figure of $2,490. Ireland's lead over Sweden and Norway (if not Denmark) in 1914 might be taken to reflect poorly on subsequent Irish performance.[4]

At first sight, Cullen's figure of £150 million is not easily squared with official estimates of £23 million for net Irish industrial output in 1907 and £59 million for net agricultural value added in 1912, particularly since the agricultural estimate is gross of feed and fertilizer inputs (worth perhaps £8–9 million in 1912).[5] However, much of the apparent inconsistency is explained away by the following factors:

(1.) The 1907 Census of Industrial Production counted plants in Ireland employing a total of 291,304 workers, but the 1911 census of population reported more than double that number (613,397) in industrial occupations. While both sources reported similar totals for certain sectors (textiles, paper and printing, chemicals), the later source included far more workers in the construction and the food and drink sectors. The 1911 census also included a large miscellaneous sector, with nearly 12,000 dealers and shopkeepers, 4,000 factory workers, and 150,000 general labourers. Presumably the census included retired and unemployed workers as well; Bielenberg has suggested a deduction of 35,000 to allow for these and the 'misallocated' dealers and shopkeepers.[6] Comparing export data with those in the 1907 industrial production data also suggests some anomalies. For example, Irish exports of whiskey and other spirits were worth £2.3 million in 1907, but the 1907 census returned a gross output of only £1.4 million and a net output of only £0.5 million. Paper exports (mostly from Larne) were worth £0.16 million, but gross output was recorded at £0.19 million and net output at only £0.06 million. A further complication is that the productivity of industrial workers included in 1907 probably exceeded that of those omitted, who were more likely to be employed in small plants and factories, or to be part-time workers. An estimate of £40 million for aggregate industrial output would allow those included in 1907 a productivity margin of 29 per cent, an estimate of £36 million a margin of over two-thirds.

(2.) The 1911 census (corrected as above) reported 578,397 employed in industry, and 780,867 in agriculture. The tertiary sector (i.e. the professional, domestic, and commercial categories) employed 423,026—or 31 per cent—more. Given an agricultural output of £50 million, and assuming that productivity in the service sector matched that of the primary and secondary sectors, would mean adding 31 percent—i.e. £(36 + 50)(0.31) to £(40 + 50)(0.31)—or £26.7 million to £28 million—to the total. That would increase the aggregate estimate to something between £113 million and £118 million. However, both UK and later Irish Free State data suggest that the assumption of equal productivity is a cautious one: in the UK in 1920 output per worker in the tertiary sector was over one-third greater than in the rest of the economy, while in 1926 output per worker in the non-traded sector (i.e. services plus construction and utilities) of the Irish Free State was over one-half greater than that of the agricultural and industrial sectors combined. Increasing the estimate range to one of £118 million to £123 million would seem appropriate.[7]

(3.) The industrial output estimate reflects the situation in 1907. However, the economy grew between 1907 and 1914. Banknote circulation rose from £6.4 million in 1905–8 to £7.7 million in 1911–13; bank deposits rose by over a fifth; the value of exports rose by 23 per cent and of imports by 21 percent, and general merchandise carried by rail rose from 6.0 million tons in 1907 8 to 6.7 million tons in 1912 13. It seems fair to assume a rise in industrial and service sector output in the interim.[8]

(4.) The above estimates make no allowance for forestry and fishing for which another £1 million or so might be added.

These considerations suggest that Cullen's estimate of £150 million is somewhat on the high side. A lower figure in the £130–140 million range for pre-war Irish GNP would also be easier to square with the presumption that the Irish economy grew faster than the British between 1914 and the mid-1920s. Opting for a tentative figure of £135 million would increase the pre-war Danish lead over the Irish to almost half (£44.5 vs. £31) and allow Sweden, if not Norway, to edge ahead of Ireland. It would place Irish per capita income at 57 per cent, rather than 62 per cent, of British in 1914. While still implying convergence, the revised figure would mean that average Irish incomes had grown less rapidly since the Famine—though they would have still quadrupled since 1845.[9] A per capita income 57 per cent of Britain's would place Ireland as follows in Maddison's league table for 1913:

Great Britain	100	Italy	52
Ireland	57	Netherlands	79
Denmark	75	France	68
Sweden	61	Germany	65
Norway	52	Belgium	81

So much for size; what of structure? The structure of the Irish economy in 1914 differed rather markedly from the stylized 'European pattern' derived by Crafts a decade ago. Table 15.1 sets Crafts' norm for an economy with a per capita GDP of $800 (US) against the Irish record on the eve of the First World War. Ireland's birth- and death-rates turn out to have been low by this criterion, its schooling rate high, and its rate of urbanization low. A comparison between the Irish Free State, created in 1921–2, and the European pattern would emphasize Ireland's relative rurality and literacy.[10]

The partition of the island in 1922 dictates that the two economies henceforth be discussed separately or comparatively. T. J. Kiernan, a pioneer in the field, estimated the expenditure on national output of the Irish Free State at £167.5 million in 1926, while Duncan put it at £161.7 million in 1929.[11] Kiernan's estimate seems too high, since it implies that by the mid-1920s average Irish income had jumped to over two-thirds the British level, or 94 per cent if agriculture is excluded. O'Rourke's corrections reduce Kiernan's estimate to £143.1 million or £48 per capita, about 57 per cent of British. This accords well with Kennedy et al., who have suggested 55.7 per cent for the Irish Free State and 61.8 per cent for Northern Ireland in the late 1920s.[12]

Table 15.1. *Ireland c.1914 and 26 cos. c.1926 in the European mirror*

	Ireland 1914	Irish Free State, 1926	'European norm'
Birth-rate (per 1,000)	22	21	31.0
Death-rate (per 1,000)	15	14	20.6
Urbanization (%)	34	32	41.1
LF in agriculture (%)	43	51	44.2
Schooling (%)	53	53	47.4
Male LF in industry (%)	31	11	33.4
Agriculture's income share (%)	38	34	28

Note: 'European norm' as defined in Crafts, *British Economic Growth*, 55. All-Ireland income per head *c*.1914 and Irish Free State income per head *c*.1926 are assumed to have been worth about $800 (1970 values).

Sources: Most of the 1926 data are taken from *Statistical Abstract*, 1931. The IFS agricultural income share is that given by Duncan for 1929. Urbanization in Ireland is defined as the percentage living in towns of 2,000 (1,500) in 1911 (1926).

Official national accounts for the 1920s and most of the 1930s are lacking. The only series that extends over this period is that by Duncan. This indicates a growth in real GNP of 13 to 17 per cent between 1926 and 1938, but allocates the lion's share of the growth to the 1926–31 period. Duncan's estimates have been criticized by Kennedy *et al.*, who have no quibble with the growth rate for the full period, but find the distribution of the growth between the 1920s and the 1930s implausible. Their tentative correction of Duncan's industrial price deflator suggests real growth of 10 per cent in 1931–8, and correspondingly lower growth in 1926–31. The correction, which is more easily reconciled with the sectoral trends revealed in the *Statistical Abstract*, marks quite a revision of the traditional understanding of the inter-war economy.[13] In particular, it goes some way towards undermining the over-doleful assessments of the 1930s by Duncan and others.

Irish banking statistics for the period are less reassuring. The pre-1932 data are approximate, but they show that between 1926 and 1931 the aggregate deposits of Irish banks in the twenty-six-county area rose by only 0.1 per cent, while between 1931 and 1939, the rise was virtually zero. These are unimpressive numbers compared to those of the London clearing banks, whose deposits rose by 5.8 per cent in 1926–31 and by almost 20 per cent in 1931–9. Since the rate of inflation was about the same in both economies during the period, a *relative* decline at least in Irish fortunes seems to be indicated. The failure of Irish deposits to rise in the 1930s was put down to the depressed state of Irish agriculture by the Majority Report of the 1934–8 Banking Commission.

Reference to the picture in Northern Ireland removes some of the gloom cast by the Southern data. In Northern Ireland deposits and cash balances fell marginally between 1926 and 1931, and dropped from £44.9 million in 1931 to £44.4 million in 1937. Other Free State bank data tell a more cheerful story: the total sum of notes, bills, and cheques cleared rose from £274 million in 1932 to £324 million in 1938, while the circulation of legal-tender notes rose from £6.9 million to £10.2 million over the same period.[14]

While the depressed state of southern agriculture in the 1930s is not in doubt, three further reasons for the failure of deposits to rise must be considered. The first two have less to do with the level of aggregate demand than with the structural transformation of the economy in the 1930s. First, the 1934–8 Banking Commission and others claimed a role for 'a higher degree of home investment'.[15] Certainly, there was much more activity on the Dublin stock exchange in the late 1930s than ten years earlier. Between 1933 and 1938 the Industrial Credit Company, founded by Fianna Fáil to plug a gap in the provision of industrial finance, organized public issues worth £4.4 million, and another £0.25 million was raised without its help.[16] A further £6 million or so was raised privately in these years. The result was a substantial increase in the paid-up capital of Irish joint-stock companies. Between 1926 and 1932 paid-up capital had risen modestly, from £35.7 million to £37.7 million; by 1938 it had reached £49.0 million. Emboldened by tax concessions and the buoyant market in Irish shares, Irish investors provided most of the capital. The process helped to spread the investment habit. But did it result in a net withdrawal of deposits from the banks? In theory, in a closed economy no such withdrawal is likely, since the expenditure of the proceeds of stock issues and other forms of company borrowing should have led to the creation of roughly equivalent flow of deposits, as the vendors of capital equipment banked their receipts. True, if the new joint-stock companies had spent the proceeds on imported capital goods, a net reduction in the deposits in the banking system would have resulted. The trade statistics show no sign of the necessary increase in the value of capital good imports, however: by one definition, such imports averaged £5.6 million in 1928–31, £5.0 million in 1932–5, and £6.4 million in 1936–8.[17] Overall, the sums involved are small compared to aggregate bank deposits in the Irish Free State (£114 million in 1938).

The second reason given for the sluggishness of bank deposits, that investors in Irish Government debt, culminating in the Financial Agreement Loan of 1938, financed their investments by withdrawals from the banks, is theoretically more plausible, and the sums involved more significant. The liabilities of the Free State Government rose from £13.9 million in 1923 to £31.8 million in 1932 to £61.4 million in 1939, and most of this debt was internally financed.[18] Finally, the 1930s saw a big increase in deposits in the post office savings bank—£4.2 million in 1932, £10.7 million in 1939. An interest rate substantially higher than the ordinary rate paid by the commercial banks in the 1930s produced the rise.

Nevertheless, the sluggishness of the Irish banking sector, north and south, reflects, above all, the failure of the two economies to grow as fast as other European economies in those decades. On the eve of the First World War, per capita incomes were about the same in what were to become Northern Ireland and the Irish Free State. Between 1926 and 1938 Irish Free State incomes dropped from 58 to 51 per cent of the UK level, and Northern Ireland's from 60 to 51 per cent.[19] These declines occurred in two Irish economies that became more different in these years, and the underlying causes were quite different. The North's main problem was its staple industries (linen and shipbuilding); as noted below, its agricultural sector performed better than the Southern.

15.2 New Leaders, New Policies?

One of the ironies of Irish history in the 1920s is how a group of tough but talented gunmen became the staid and rather conservative rulers of a newly independent Irish Free State. Setting aside the rhetoric of their fighting days, these men opted instead for continuity and caution in economic affairs. The Cumann na nGaedheal Party that assumed power in 1922 followed the path of low taxation and an outward-looking commercial policy based on pursuing Ireland's comparative advantage in pastoral agriculture. The new Irish pound continued to exchange at par with sterling, and the temptations to run down foreign assets in the interest of industrialization or to form a separate Central Bank were avoided. The 'triumph of pragmatism over dogma' also embraced fiscal policy. A majority of ministers were relieved to see pleas for tariffs to foster Irish industry being rebuffed first by the Fiscal Inquiry Report of 1923,[20] and later stymied by a slow-moving Tariff Commission, which limited itself to protection for a curious amalgam of items such as candles, glass bottles, and rosary beads. The ethos of the new Dublin civil service, in large part a carry-over from the previous administration, was very much conditioned by the 'Treasury view'. Opposition demands for policies that would shift—or distort— farming away from livestock towards tillage and greater self-sufficiency (and thereby tilt the balance in favour of smaller farmers and farm labourers) were rejected. Most of this went against the traditional nationalist grain.[21] Prudence and caution were bywords in the 1920s: the decision to engage the German engineering company Siemens to build a hydroelectric station on the Shannon, regarded as very daring at the time,[22] was far from typical. As a result, at the start of the Great Depression southern Ireland stood out as an exceptional place for two reasons: it was ruled by Europe's longest-serving democratic government, and it could claim (with some exaggeration) to be one of the world's last free-trading nations.

The combination bespoke a steep learning curve in the art of economic management. Yet what followed in 1932–8 under the new Fianna Fáil government has been seen alternatively either as an exercise in economic fanaticism or doughty resistance to economic and political bullying by a powerful neighbour. If mistakes were made by both regimes, might they be excused by noting that past history and external conditions constrained policy both in the 1920s and 1930s? The issue in part is why it took so long to learn from those past mistakes. But there is an added twist to the argument: perhaps the clumsy policies of the 1920s and 1930s had their own rationale in terms of political economy?[23] After all, while Cumann na nGaedheal policies bore all the signs of being grounded in orthodox economic theory, they also happened to suit most of the party's voters. During the 1920s, as later, Cumann na nGaedheal drew much of its core electoral support from the urban middle class and the more substantial farmers. Its early appeal to a broader constituency—most of those weary of six years of armed rebellion and civil war—was being whittled away from the mid-1920s on.[24] Fianna Fáil policies too, as we shall see, were grounded in sound politics as much as in unsound economics.

Yet in retrospect, some economic historians tend to see the decade or so of Cumann na nGaedheal caution as a kind of 'golden age' relative to what followed. Economists would find much to commend in the rejection of protection, cheap money, foreign borrowing, and budget deficits. By con- trast, the era of the more populist and nationalist post-1932 Fianna Fáil

Governments tends to be viewed as a 'lost generation'. Fianna Fáil under the ascetic, Gandhi-like De Valera were associated with high tariffs, the World Depression, and an agricultural sector in crisis. When Fianna Fáil brought new value-judgements to bear on industrial policy and agricultural specialization, prices were made to reflect 'political ideals, [not] economic realities'.[25]

The dichotomy oversimplifies, for three reasons. First, it overlooks Cumann na nGaedheal's noisy abandonment of its commitment to free trade from 1929–30 on. Indeed, Cumann na nGaedheal had been giving way to protectionist pressure ever since Fianna Fáil's first electoral successes, and was encouraged in this by some of its own back-benchers. On economic matters, at least two members of the cabinet (Richard Mulcahy and J. J. Walsh)[26] held views close to Fianna Fáil's, and in November 1927 President Cosgrave was boasting that 55 per cent of non-agricultural imports were dutiable, and that the result was over 10,000 new jobs without any rise in prices! Had Cumann na nGaedheal clung to power after 1932, it would have undoubtedly become even more protectionist, and in this it would have been following a world-wide pattern. Events were forcing it into interventionist experiments frowned upon earlier. Within the administration, the Ministry for Industry and Commerce prepared the way, producing tables that listed employment gains due to tariffs already imposed and the value of imported items that might be protected in future. Cumann na nGaedheal's spokesmen, notably the voluble Patrick Hogan, liked to claim in 1930 and 1931 that their attitude to protection was pragmatic rather than dogmatic:[27]

We have tariffed, on the admission of anybody who has examined the matter, almost fifty per cent of our tariffable imports. And that is called Free Trade? I accept that definition of Free Trade.

Thus the worsening economic situation in 1930–1 put the Government in the unfortunate position of seeming to mimic Fianna Fáil policy whenever it tried remedial measures.

Secondly, the general election of August 1931 produced a UK 'National Government' of Conservatives and renegade Liberals and Labourites committed to protecting British agriculture, and particularly those products in which Irish farmers specialized (livestock and dairy products). This greatly reduced the appeal of the Cumann na nGaedheal policies of the 1920s. In the context of depression-induced unemployment and a virtual halt to emigration, those policies—which had failed in any case to produce the 'abundant rural employment' promised by Ireland's Stolypin, Patrick Hogan[28]—could not have endured.

Thirdly, when Fianna Fáil were finally defeated in 1948, their successors —a coalition including many former Cumann na nGaedheal ministers—did not jettison protection, but persisted with the established policies. Indeed, a sort of consensus had emerged much earlier. *The Economist* noted that the election of July 1937 was a 'singularly tame one, principally because there does not seem to be very much difference between the policies of the two main parties'. Cumann na nGaedheal (now born again as Fine Gael) had become reconciled to the political wisdom of tariffs, and promised even more costly social welfare programmes than Fianna Fáil. So the issues discussed here are not straightforward party-political ones.

Nevertheless, it makes sense to treat the post-1931 period separately. The break is symbolized by the increasing bulk of the official publication describing the Irish tariff regime. In the late 1920s Irish tariff regulations could be described in ten pages, and Ireland still rivalled The Netherlands and the UK as a low-tariff economy. A decade later, the protectionist schedules took over 100 pages to list, though, in mitigation, quotas were relied on much less in Ireland than elsewhere.

Viewed narrowly, the contrast between the 1920s and 1930s is remarkable. Yet a comparative perspective shows that though Ireland was atypical of new post-1918 nation-states for its economic liberalism during the 1920s, Irish policies were hardly extreme by international standards after 1929. For example, the League of Nations estimated that 17 per cent of Irish imports were subject to licence or quota restrictions in 1937. In France the percentage was 58, in Switzerland 52, in Belgium 24, in Norway 12, and in the UK 8.[29]

In one superficial sense that would appeal to old-time nationalists; Fianna Fáil for a time represented an 'improvement' over Cumann na nGaedheal. Ever since 1846 the population of the area that constituted the Irish Free State—east Ulster was exceptional—had been declining. Self-government in the 1920s made no difference, but the early years of Fianna Fáil rule saw the trend reversed. It almost seemed as though an assertive nationalist administration could turn things around. However, the rise in population was seen at the time rather as a challenge than an achievement, and it was not sustained. The rise was the result of net emigration to North America turning negative in the early 1930s,[30] and partly explains the greater preoccupation with unemployment and job-creation under Fianna Fáil.

Nevertheless, economists' assessments of twenty-six-county performance after 1932 have been almost uniformly negative, and Fianna Fáil found few economists ready to defend it at the time. The qualified support given by Keynes to Fianna Fáil—much to the embarrassment of the Dublin economics establishment—was exceptional.[31] But the dearth of quantitative research into the post-independence period—and especially of reliable national income data—rules out definitive assessments and comparisons. Given the paucity of official data before the mid-1920s, studies of trends in sectoral output, employment, and living standards during the first decade of independence are few. Nevertheless, I shall argue below that while the pre-1932 administration had much to be proud of in the political sphere, its economic achievements were modest.

15.3 Agriculture

> There is the Ireland of the North, where the land is, comparatively speaking, poor land and the climate cold, where the farmers are shrewd, intelligent men, who have made the most of their circumstances. The farms are trim and well kept. The land is well tilled. There is an air of prosperity about the country. There is the Ireland of the South, where the land is better and the climate milder, and the people, possibly to some extent because nature has done so much for them, less energetic; where the steadings are ill-kept and the land badly tilled, and waste and neglect are much in evidence.
>
> A SCOTTISH FARMER, 1906[32]

The above statement, made on behalf of a group of touring Scottish farmers in 1906, reflects a common and enduring perception. In the past, the presumed Northern edge was linked to the alleged advantages of its tenurial system. This traditional interpretation of Ulster superiority is no longer widely accepted (see Chapter 4). I shall show below that, first, the northern advantage over the south on the eve of peasant proprietorship was a mirage and, second, that the switch in tenurial regimes coincided with a relative improvement in the efficiency of northern agriculture.

Irish farmers seem to have responded lackadaisically to the opportunities presented by the First World War. Though the value of farm produce, food, and drink exported rose from £41.6 million in 1914 to £78.3 million in 1918, exports declined in real terms, and failed to make good the vacuum left by the collapse of Danish and Dutch exports. Ireland also lost out relative to the USA and Canada. These were prosperous years in rural

Ireland, none the less; a well-known poet was moved to claim that during the First World War 'money grew on the tops of bushes'.[33] The prosperity is reflected in the accounts of two substantial estate farms, Lord Clonbrock's at Ahascragh in east Galway, and the Dunmore farm on the Ormonde estate in Kilkenny. On the former the balance on account rose from an annual average of £660 in 1910–13 to £2,310 in 1914–19; on the latter, the standard pattern of small or negative profits was transformed into an average profit of £4,000 between 1914–15 and 1920–1.[34] By contrast, farmers faced hard times in the early 1920s. In order to convince cabinet colleagues of this, Hogan used a study carried out in his own department, based on 1920 data derived from eighteen farms. That study estimated aggregate revenue from output, labour outlays (valuing farmers' own labour at the going rate for agricultural workers), and other expenses. Deducting the last two items from the first produced an estimate of farmers' residual income in 1920. This then was compared to what residual income would have been in 1914 and 1922, using the same input and output data. The outcome suggests a negative residual in 1922. The minority of farmers employing wage-labour were presumably worse hit than others. Admittedly, the simulation may exaggerate farmers' discomfort, since it excludes adjustments in response to input and output price changes, but the impression given of depression is accurate. The same picture is evident in the fortunes of the demesne farm at Clonbrock. In an account-book that covers the period between the late 1870s and the 1940s, 1921 was the first year to return a negative balance (see Fig. 15.1).[35]

Agriculture recovered thereafter. Exports in 1924 were inflated by the effects of the civil war, but cattle exports (the best barometer of rural prosperity) rose by 27 per cent in volume and 12 per cent in value between 1925 and 1930. Butter, fresh pork, and sheep exports rose too. 1931 was a bad year, however, and the 1932–8 period was dominated by the effects of a shift in government policy and the 'Economic War'.

The earliest official estimates of Irish agricultural output date from 1908 and 1912. The second of these may be used as a basis for calculating Southern output and for evaluating output and labour productivity growth North and South between 1912 and the mid-1920s. The result is reported in Table 15.3, along with figures for 1938. The comparison required certain adjustments to the raw data, in particular allowing for turf in 1912.

The comparison produces a rather unexpected result: evaluating output in both areas at domestic prices, agricultural output per worker was slightly higher in the South in both 1912 and 1926. Indeed, the gap

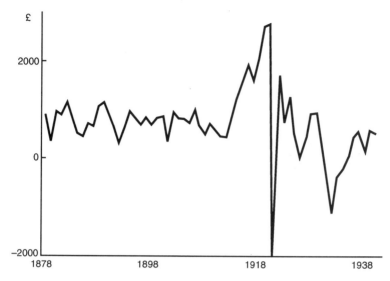

FIG. 15.1 Annual balance on the Clonbrock Estate farm, 1878–1938

Table 15.2. *Hypothetical farm revenues, 1914, 1920, 1922*

Year	Imputed to labour	(%)	Residual farmer income	(%)	Total revenue from 18 farms
1914	4 303	(49)	4 471	(51)	8 774
1920	11 789	(44)	15 099	(56)	26 099
1922	10 614	(120)	1 762	(20)	26 888

Source: UCDA, P35b/2, 4.

widened between those dates, but during the subsequent decade or so the South lost most of its advantage. Excluding turf revises the story somewhat: the South maintained its edge up to the 1920s, but had lost it by the 1930s.

Governmental policy in the South in the 1920s favoured agriculture: for Patrick Hogan 'national development [wa]s practically synonomous with agricultural development'. Hogan, articulate and energetic, enunciated a strategy based on increasing the quality of output through brand-names for eggs and butter, improving the breeding stock of milch cows and pigs, and promoting agricultural education at all levels. Believing that 'the beef trade is merely a second best', his wager was on the progressive milk- and bacon-

Table 15.3. *Agricultural output North and South, 1912 and 1925–6*

	All-Ireland	26 Counnes	6 Counnes
1912			
Livestock (£m.)	45.2	37.2	8.0
Crops (£m.)	14.9	10.1	4.8
TOTAL (£m.)	59.1	47.3	12.8
Labour force (m.)	0.977	0.765	0.212
Output per worker (£)	60	62	60
1925–6			
Livestock (£m.)	60.2	48.4	11.8
Crops (£m.)	14.3	11.1	3.2
TOTAL (£m.)	74.5	59.6	15.0
Labour force (m.)	0.847	0.648	0.199
Output per worker (£)	88	92	75
1938–9			
Livestock (£m.)	52.0	38.9	13.0
Crops (£m.)	15.1	13.0	2.2
TOTAL	67.1	51.9	15.2
Labour (m.)	0.761	0.586	0.175
Output per worker (£)	88	89	87

Sources: Derived from O'Connor and Guiomard, 'Irish Agricultural Output'; *Statistical Abstract* (Dublin); *Ulster Yearbook* (Belfast).

producer. Yet the response of farmers to Hogan's slogan of 'one more cow, one more sow and one more acre under the plough' was disappointing. Between 1922 and 1932 the number of cattle enumerated fell by 8 per cent and the acreage under the plough by 17 per cent, and crop yields failed to improve much. It would seem that the aim of raising agricultural efficiency was not achieved.[36] Another measure of evaluating performance, the trend in Ireland's share of the British market of the main agricultural products, confirms this impression. Butter's share rose from 8.7 per cent in 1924 to 9.1 per cent in 1928; that of eggs fell from 23.1 to 19.6 per cent. That of cattle fluctuated from year to year, but registered no sustained increase.[37]

It takes no elaborate calculation to show that the South's advantage over the North hardly stemmed from greater endowment of physical capital. The difference in buildings and outhouses was apparently small—rateable value per worker was about £10 both North and South—but the agricultural census of 1908 implies that Northern farmers had considerably more machinery at their disposal. The North's share of the all-Ireland labour force then was about 22 per cent, but the North had 30.2 per cent of all steam- or gas-engines, 71.6 per cent of horse-drawn sprayers, 70.7 per cent of threshing-mills, 38.5 per cent of cultivators and grubbers, 26.2 per cent of ploughs, 40.8 per cent of drill-ploughs, and 25.1 per cent of reapers and mowers.[38] Adjusted for land quality, the land-labour ratio was only marginally higher in the South.

The South's productivity advantage was not to last, however. Table 15.4 summarizes agricultural output growth (using domestic prices as deflators) in the North and South between the 1920s and 1960s.

Why did Southern agriculture do so poorly in the 1930s? One stern critic of Fianna Fáil economic policy claimed that policy errors had reduced agricultural output by a quarter. They did so partly by distorting output through the wrong price incentives,[39] but mainly through losing the British market in the silly political wrangle known as the 'Economic War' (on which more in Chapter 16). A recent comparative exercise by Gillmor, which focuses on the increasing divergence in the pattern of output in the two Irelands after 1932 and proposes an 'index of dissimilarity', provides a useful way of highlighting the output 'distortion'. The index is computed as follows. Output is divided into the six sectors given in Table 15.5. The percentage differences in each sector's output share are then added, and their sum divided by two. The resulting number can range from zero (when there is complete correspondence) to 100 (complete divergence). Gillmor's index rose from 13.3 to 24.3 between 1926 and 1938.[40] Now, from a strictly theoretical standpoint, there is no presumption that the price shifts

Table 15.4. *Agriculture in Ireland, North and South, 1920s–1960s*

	North		South	
	dQ/Q	dL/L	dQ/Q	dL/L
1926–38	+29	−7.2	+5	−10.5
1938–48	+12	−7.0	−1	−7.0
1948–62	+71	−32.3	+22	−14.5
1926–62	+150	−42.0	+30	−29.0

Source: Ó Gráda, 'Irish Agriculture North and South'.

Table 15.5. *Agricultural output in the two Irelands, sectoral shares*

Year	North				South			
	1926	1938	1960	1985	1926	1937	1960	1985
Tillage	21.6	12.0	9.1	6.6	14.6	19.0	20.4	11.3
Milk	19.4	17.3	17.0	27.8	24.1	24.0	23.1	36.5
Cattle	23.2	14.9	21.1	40.8'	24.3	22.4	30.3	38.8
Sheep	4.3	3.5	5.8	4.1	5.0	6.6	7.0	4.0
Pigs	9.3	29.9	28.3	10.5	16.0	13.5	11.4	5.7
Poultry	22.3	22.4	18.7	10.2	15.9	14.6	7.7	3.7

Sources: Gillmor, 'The Political Factor'; *Statistical Abstract 1939*, 70.

generated by one set of policies under one regime (the Southern) should do more harm than the shifts generated by different policies under another (the British). However, part of the critique resurrected a long-forgotten argument from Adam Smith's *The Wealth of Nations*. In a discussion of the ratio of cattle to grain prices, Smith argues that a certain relation must be kept between them if any improvement in agriculture is to take place:

The price of butcher's meat . . . and consequently cattle must gradually rise till it gets so high, that it becomes profitable to employ the most fertile and best cultivated lands in raising food for them as for raising corn . . . Till the price of cattle has got to this height, it seems scarce possible that the greater part, even of those lands which are capable of the highest cultivation, can be completely cultivated. In all farms too distant from any town to carry manure from it, that is, in the far greater part of those of every extensive country, the quantity of well-cultivated land must be in proportion to the quantity of manure which the farm itself produces; and this again must be in proportion to the quantity of cattle raised on it . . . The increase of stock and the improvement of land are two events which must go hand in hand . . . Of all the commercial advantages . . . which Scotland has derived from the union with England, this rise in the price of cattle is, perhaps, the greatest.

In support of his claim that 'Adam Smith's contention [was] abundantly illustrated' by Irish agriculture, Johnston produced data showing the ratio of oats to beef prices in Ireland almost twice as high in 1934–7 as at any time in the previous half-century. The argument seems to be that up to 1932–3 a free market generated the near-constant ratio of oats to beef prices required by technology. However, politics thereafter drove the ratio out of kilter, making Johnston conclude with the rather apocalyptic predic-

Table 15.6. *26-County output in own and 6-County prices (£m.)*

Year	(1) 26-County prices	(2) 6-County prices	Price ratio i.e. (2)/(1)
1926–7 (A)			
Tillage	11.2	9.8	.875
Livestock	46.7	50.4	1.079
TOTAL	57.9	60.2	1.039
1926–7 (B)			
Tillage	11.2	11.4	1.018
TOTAL	57.9	61.8	1.067
1935–6			
Crops	11.6	11.2	.966
Livestock	30.9	37.2	1.204
TOTAL	42.6	48.4	1.137
1948–9			
Crops	33.7	31.6	.938
Livestock	85.9	83.1	.967
TOTAL	119.6	114.7	.959

Source: Calculated from official output data, using the implicit prices where possible. Otherwise (e.g. turf, 'other vegetables') (2) was evaluated at Southern prices.

tion of 'a gradual but increasingly rapid decline of our national agriculture'.[41] One informal way of making sense of this argument is to remember that tillage and livestock were each an input for the other: the supply of manure and draught animals limited tillage acreage and yields, while livestock output was constrained by crop supplies. In the short run the trade-off between tillage and livestock along the transformation schedule might be generous, as with *DD* in Fig. 15.2. However, the long-run trade-off might be a different story, perhaps like *EE*. In that case the shift from *G* caused by a shift in relative prices might be to *H* in the short run, but to *J* (inside the original factor price frontier) in the long run. While perhaps a plausible representation of what Smith and Johnston seem to mean, the move implies a degree of myopia on the part of policy-makers. This kind of contrast between short- and long-run trade-off is probably much less today than it was in the 1930s, when it was intensified by tariffs on tractors and fertilizers. In the short run at least, the distortions probably hurt least the mixed, mid-sized farm. The promotion of wheat favoured

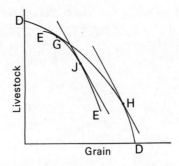

FIG. 15.2 The long- and short-term trade-off between tillage and pasture sectors

Source: Ó Gráda, 'Irish agriculture north and south', in Campbell and Overton (1991), 450

large, eastern farmers, but the benefits of another subsidized crop, sugar beet, were more widely spread, beet being grown in quantity in Galway and even Mayo. The western smallholder continued to produce meagre quantities of oats, potatoes, and young cattle, so the farmer's dole introduced by Fianna Fáil counted for much more to him than protection. The movement in the size distribution of holdings in the 1930s indicates big drops at the top and bottom of the distribution, and an increase in the number and share of farms in the 30–100-acre category.

15.4 Industry

The conviction that the Act of Union had deprived Ireland of an industrial base was part of the nationalist creed. George O'Brien branded its Articles 6 and 7 simply 'the economic provisions which English statesmen devised for the extinction of Irish independence'.[42] Ironically, the claim that the political settlement of 1920–1, by partitioning the island, did so for the new Saorstát Éireann carries greater conviction. Cumann na nGaedheal set little store by industrial development, and employment and output in manufacturing may well have fallen during their years in power. The exasperation of President Cosgrave, who was moved in July 1926 to refer to Irish businessmen as 'antique furniture', is symptomatic, but Cumann na nGaedheal's timid experimentation with tariffs brought disappointing results in so far as new business and employment was concerned.[43] During the Cosgrave years emigration remained substantial, as the towns failed to mop up excess labour in the countryside. How did industrial employment fare in the 1930s compared with the 1920s? This is a controversial issue.

The Census of Industrial Production implies virtual stasis in industrial employment in the 1920s and a substantial rise in the 1930s. It reports the net value of output in transportable goods industries rising from £16.4 million in 1926 to £18.2 million in 1931 and £24.8 million in 1937, while employment rose from 57,758 in 1926 to 62,608 in 1931 and 99,656 in 1937. However, critics have interpreted the population censuses of 1926 and 1936 as implying no net improvement in employment. In FitzGerald's view, the extra employment reported in the annual industrial censuses was a mirage, a reflection of better statistical coverage over time. Daly, on the other hand, has argued that the population census reports of 1926 and 1936 are consistent with an increase. As Table 15.7 shows, once the construction sector is excluded the verdict hinges largely on a rise in jobs for women. Yet whatever the change over the 1926–36 decade as a whole, the contrast between the pre- and post-1932 periods remains. After all, if better coverage accounted for some of the alleged increase in employment after 1931, it must have equally concealed a decline in industrial employment before then.[44]

Table 15.7. *Employment change in industry. Censal data 1926–1936*

Sector	1926				1936			
	At work		Out of work		At work		Out of work	
	Male	Female	Male	Female	Male	Female	Male	Female
Food	16 189	5 448	2 576	545	18 981	6 294	3 416	617
Drink	8 107	561	1 321	40	6 351	543	807	14
Tobacco	856	1 208	87	144	924	1 316	60	82
Textiles	2 913	4 854	633	884	3 139	4 202	318	299
Clothing	13 257	14 764	859	672	15 567	22 781	1 075	1 102
Skins, etc.	1 758	90	202	10	1 749	312	142	28
Wood	13 557	502	1 505	70	13 685	755	1 463	66
Metals, etc.	11 806	436	1 299	43	12 320	865	1 206	78
Vehicles	10 006	232	2 139	18	9 074	200	1 268	10
Chemicals	1 920	512	327	48	2 596	1 191	322	83
Paper	4 791	2 426	731	357	6 090	3 345	556	183
Building	36 131	325	13 519	52	55 430	334	22 027	31
Bricks	667	39	230	8	1 642	305	401	15
Gas and electricity	2 396	66	400	2	4 550	278	708	4
Other mfg.	915	405	166	55	2 776	1 106	398	90
TOTAL	125 269	31 868	25 994	2 948	154 874	43 827	34 167	2 702
TOTAL (excl. building)	89 138	31 543	12 475	2 896	99 444	43 493	12 140	2 671

There are other indications of a contrast between the 1920s and 1930s. A good example is the trend in industrial issues on the Irish stock exchange. Between 1922 and 1930 there had been only one public issue of shares, and that for only £15,000. By 1933 there were twenty-four quoted Irish industrial companies with an aggregate capital of £5 million. By 1939 there were seventy-eight companies, with a combined capital of almost £10 million. The *Times Issuing House Year Book* recorded three new Irish companies in 1933, nine in 1934, twelve in both 1935 and 1936, and ten in 1937.[45]

Industrial policy in the 1930s was better geared towards generating employment throughout the country in the short run than towards building up a self-supporting Irish industrial sector. The preoccupation with regional dispersion reflects this. Practically every town was promised its own factory or factories, ruling out scale economies and external economies, and virtually guaranteeing that the new plants would be parochial in their ambitions. The example of the Bristol-based shoemakers, Woodingtons, who had established a tariff-hopping factory in Drogheda in 1932, is instructive. In order to guarantee their supply of leather uppers, Woodingtons also requested permission to build a tannery in Drogheda. The Department of Industry and Commerce replied that Drogheda was already well looked after, and recommended a series of other distant towns to the Drogheda concern. In the end Woodingtons' tannery was built in Gorey.[46]

Dublin was the first choice of most businessmen. Besides accounting for a substantial chunk of the home market, it also had good communications, the biggest pool of skilled labour and services, and convenient access to government departments. Policy discriminated against Dublin for sociopolitical reasons, though firms displayed a marked preference for the metropolis, nevertheless. But, granted the commitment to decentralize, should the Department of Industry and Commerce not have tried harder to encourage centres of specialization elsewhere? In the footwear industry, for example, why not build on the concentration in Louth, instead of establishing plants in Ballinasloe, Killarney, Tralee, and Clonmel and Edenderry? This example is a reminder of the role of local businessmen in dictating location. The 'fiercely independent' footwear producers were all for dispersion in the 1930s, failing to unite on issues such as access to raw materials. Hilliards of Killarney, who had been importing footwear for decades, established a boot factory in 1934; however, like others, they were effectively forced to buy their leather from the tannery at Portlaw, and closed their plant temporarily in protest.[47]

Table 15.8 is derived from data assembled in the Department of Industry and Commerce in 1948. The interim between 1932 and 1947 should have provided most of the firms included here enough time to 'grow up', but the picture is of an economy still dominated by minuscule plants. Almost three-quarters of those listed employed fewer than twenty workers. Excluding such tiny concerns, the average firm still had a labour force of only eighty-two. In 1948, the 'giants' among these minnows were Córas Iompair

Table 15.8. *Firms and employment by county in protected industries*

County	All firms			Plants employing 20 or more	
	(1) Firms	(2) Jobs	(2)/(1)	Firms	Employees per firm
Carlow	13	314	24	4	63
Dublin	516	17 815	35	111	54
Kilkenny	6	295	49	3	94
Kildare	25	1 474	59	10	136
Laois	9	324	36	3	88
Louth	52	2 579	50	13	177
Longford	4	59	15	1	44
Meath	23	422	18	8	35
Offaly	15	1 125	75	8	137
Westmeath	11	360	33	2	137
Wexford	12	532	44	7	71
Wicklow	21	1 226	58	8	89
Clare	14	720	59	5	122
Cork	100	3 376	34	32	90
Kerry	17	204	12	1	110
Limerick	28	1 033	37	6	146
Tipperary	27	2 077	77	12	123
Waterford	33	1 667	51	13	114
Galway	28	892	32	7	102
Leitrim	13	247	19	4	43
Mayo	22	627	29	9	61
Roscommon	10	272	27	3	82
Sligo	12	269	22	4	56
Cavan	16	662	41	7	88
Donegal	32	551	17	7	54
Monaghan	13	415	32	6	63
TOTAL	1 072	39 537	37	294	82

Éireann's assembly and repair works, Dunlop (with a labour force of 1,200), Comhlucht Siúicre Éireann's sugar-processing plants (336 in Mallow, 320 in Tuam, 312 in Thurles), Rawsons' of Dundalk (625), Clondalkin Paper Mills (513), Cement Limited in Drogheda (510), Salt's of Tullamore (408), Roscrea Meat Products (348), Peter Kennedy's main Dublin bakery, Mianraí Teoranta at Doolin in west Clare (338), Irish Tanners at the old Malcolmson site in Portlaw (328), and Munster Shoes of Clonmel (327). Of these, three were semi-State concerns, and another two tariff-hopping foreign subsidiaries.[48]

In this respect, the experience of the Free State is a far cry from Gerschenkron's famous model of the 'big spurt', whereby the backward economy bent on rapid industrialization relies on foreign capital and expertise, and economizes on scarce entrepreneurship through 'giantism', or large plants.[49] The Irish experience differs from textbook models in another way. As explained in Chapter 13, in the past early industrialization has been typically associated with regional specialization or 'localization'. External economies of scale are the usual reason given. Ulster linen and Lancashire cotton are obvious examples. In theory, such a pattern should cause a minority of towns and cities to grow much faster than the rest, yielding an increase over time in the variation of town and city populations. Deindustrialization might be expected to have the opposite effect, as towns revert to serving local markets. What was the effect of Free State industrial policy? While Table 15.8 fails to bear out the contention of a job-creation bias against Dublin in the 1930s (since nearly half the new jobs were created there), none the less the new factories were evidently very widely dispersed throughout the country. This held even for individual industries; though Louth accounted for over half the labour force in the shoe industry, seven other counties also had shoe factories in 1948. Small hosiery and clothing manufacturers were also widely dispersed. As a result, the size distribution of Irish towns became, if anything, less dispersed in the 1930s and 1940s.[50]

The industrial censuses imply a levelling off in output and employment by the late 1930s. Saturation of the home market by tariff factories had been achieved by then, and the 'exuberant' phase of development was over. This is confirmed by Table 15.9, based on another table prepared by the Department of Industry and Commerce in early 1948.[51] But not only was output growth not sustained: productivity growth in manufacturing was very poor in the 1930s. According to Kennedy, output per worker in the Southern industrial sector grew at only 1.2 per cent per year in 1926–38,

Table 15.9. *Employment in 1932, 1939, and 1947 in those protected industries 'which expanded considerably' since 1932*

	1932	1939			1947		
	Total	Male	Female	Total	Male	Female	Total
F, D, and Tobacco	14 177	10 181	6 592	16 773	11 092	7 568	18 660
Textiles	4 092	3 030	4 263	7 293	3 676	4 573	8 249
Apparel	8 830	5 749	15 125	20 874	6 795	17 638	24 433
Leather	263	817	203	1 020	1 379	296	1 675
Wood	4 661	6 061	931	6 992	5 937	931	6 868
Metal and machinery	1 152	1 466	583	2 049	1 514	474	1 988
Iron and steel	2 398	4 435	366	4 801	2 767	411	4 178
Vehicles and parts	685	3 305	358	3 663	3 687	354	4 041
Chemicals, etc.	2 189	2 480	889	3 369	2 360	1 137	3 497
Paper and printing	4 471	3 618	3 406	7 024	4 233	4 207	8 440
Bldg. materials	1 202	2 267	343	2 970	2 806	260	3 066
Misc.	1 228	1 596	1 668	3 264	1 924	2 177	4 101
TOTAL	45 348	45 365	34 727	80 092	49 170	40 026	89 196

Source: NA/SPO, 'Establishment of Industries', S. 11987B.

compared with 3.8 per cent in 1946–66. The contrast between the two periods might plausibly be put down to isolationist economic policy alone, though in Britain over the same period the record is more or less the same: industrial output per worker grew by 1.8 per cent in 1924–37, by 1.5 per cent in 1937–51, and by 4.6 per cent in 1964–73.[52]

Returning to manufacturing output growth in aggregate, in the South labour productivity failed to grow at all in the 1930s, and was much lower in the mid-1940s than in 1932. The effect of the Second World War on supplies of materials and equipment, and government policies aimed at maintaining employment in face of declining output were responsible for this. An industry-by-industry comparison with Northern Ireland only rubs salt in the wound: in about two-thirds of the twenty sectors with comparable data, output per worker grew faster in the North in the 1930s and 1940s. Kennedy has argued that the poor performance of Southern industry was partly due to the low skills of new workers, partly to the huge rush of small new firms induced by sudden, dramatic tariff increases. An added factor after 1939 was the Government's urging that firms hold on to workers, in effect a form of 'work-sharing'. By that criterion, static productivity was something to be welcomed. An added consideration is that since the new protected firms could afford to be less competitive than those already there before 1932, a reduction in aggregate productivity might be expected.[53]

The story in Northern Ireland was very different. Employment in manufacturing industry there stagnated in the inter-war period: if building and contracting are excluded, there was a drop of 4.6 per cent in 1923–39. The difficulties faced by the North's long-established staples, shipbuilding and linen, forced the unemployment rate up to 18.2 per cent in 1923 of the insured non-agricultural labour force in 1923, and over one-quarter in the 1930s.[54] 1914–19 were boom years for Belfast shipbuilders, with employment in the yards rising from 20,000 to 29,000. Excess capacity in world shipping became serious from 1920 on, and UK shipbuilders were particularly hard hit by Scandinavian and Japanese competition. The UK share of world output fell from 60 per cent before the First World War to 38 per cent in 1930–8. Belfast held its share of UK production, but its output fell from 1.4 million gross tons in 1906–14 to 0.9 million in 1921–9 and 0.7 million in 1930–8. Employment plummeted from 24,000 in 1923 to 8,000 in 1934, recovering to only 10,500 by 1939. No ships were launched from Queen's Island between December 1931 and May 1934. Workman Clark was forced out of business in 1935. Harland & Wolff's fared better, its involvement in the development of the marine diesel engine standing it in good stead in the 1920s, and it remained one of the world's leading producers. The 1930s were more difficult, though the company tried hard to combat adverse world market conditions through diversification. It did not benefit much from Admiralty business until 1939.[55]

For Northern Ireland's other staple, linen, the inter-war years brought crisis and contraction. Part of the problem was changing tastes: 'the modern demand for novelty' was at the expense of 'articles of distinction and durability' made of linen. The consequences were particularly bleak for producers of bedlinen, beadspreads, shirts, and the like. Relative price movements in the 1920s did not help.[56] There is a controversy as to whether the organization of the industry compounded the difficulties. On the one hand, the linen industry remained one of small, specialized plants. As late as 1954 Northern Ireland's 'linen complex' still contained 298 establishments employing twenty-five persons or more. The industry was accused of refusing to 'think vertically', and of clinging to 'old-fashioned' techniques. On the other hand, scale economies were not important, and in any case there was a good deal of informal integration through interlocking directorships. Ulster linen maintained its share on both export and domestic markets in the inter-war period. But the glory days of Belfast and its hinterland as a first-rank industrial region were over.[57]

The histories of industry in the two Irelands in the 1930s were thus very different. In the South the dominant pattern was the 'hothouse' growth of small plants reliant on a protected home market; in the North, crisis by the 1930s for an industrial structure 'most insecurely founded' on linen and shipbuilding. Protection was never an option for Northern Ireland, but there were other choices. From 1932 on, a policy aimed at industrial diversification led to the subsidization of sites and rates, interest-free loans, and improvements in industrial infrastructure.[58]

Northern Ireland Agricultural Output, 1925–1926 to 1948–1949

The following tables are based for the most part on information summarized in the *Ulster Yearbook*. They provide estimates of volume change for two pairs of years, using both base- and end-year prices. The results reported in the text are based on an average of the two.

Table 15.A1. *NI agricultural output, 1925–1926 and 1938–1939*

Item	In 1925–6 prices		In 1938–9 prices	
	1925–6	1938–9	1925–6	1938–9
Cattle	3 496	2 208	3 488	2 203
Sheep	595	1 152	243	471
Pigs	1 399	6 709	925	4 435
Poultry	575	1 314	404	924
Milk	2 919	2 817	2 658	2 565
Eggs	2 755	3 318	1 988	2 394
Wool	59	95	32	52
Wheat	41	35	16	14
Oats	165	205	105	130
Barley	15	13	10	9
Potatoes	1 280	880	1 358	942
Flax	638	425	470	313
Hay and Straw	130	93	89	64
Grass Seeds	540	278	598	308
TOTAL	14 607	19 550	12 384	14 824
Change (%)	+38.8		+19.7	

Table 15.A2. *NI agricultural output, 1938–1939 and 1948–1949*

Item	In 1938–9 prices		In 1948–9 prices	
	1938–9	1948–9	1938–9	1948–9
Cattle	2 203	3 079	4 718	6 593
Sheep	471	279	1 980	1 172
Pigs	4 435	1 130	14 811	3 373
Poultry	924	1 910	2 727	5 637
Milk	2 565	3 545	9 139	12 629
Eggs	2 594	3 999	8 372	13 984
Wool	52	35	220	147
Wheat	14	4	61	18
Oats	130	101	480	374
Barley	9	18	42	83
Potatoes	942	1 867	3 091	6 127
Flax	313	626	580	1 160
Hay and straw	64	43	134	89
Grass Seeds	308	330	672	721
TOTAL	14 824	16 966	47 027	52 307
Change (%)	+14.4		+11.2	

16

Commercial Policy and the Economic War

> We believe that Ireland can be made a self-contained unit, providing all the necessities of living in adequate quantities for the people residing in the island at the moment and probably for a much larger number.
>
> SEÁN LEMASS, 1932[1]

16.1 Trade

The Irish Free State contributed more than its share to the world-wide 'trade destruction' of the 1930s. While the combined merchandise trade (imports plus exports, measured in gold US dollars) of fourteen other small European economies dropped by 54 per cent between 1929 and 1938, that of the Free State fell by 64 per cent.[2] Few other countries fared worse than Ireland by this measure. Irish economists, then and since, have argued that the damage suffered by Ireland during the Great Depression was also more than commensurate; worse still, that it was largely self-inflicted, the product of mistaken economic policies. In this largely policy-oriented chapter we recount some of their arguments.

We have already seen how Cumann na nGaedheal started out in the 1920s as virtual free-traders. This was partly because, in the words of the Fiscal Inquiry Commission of 1923, 'the volume of industry which is anxious to obtain a protective tariff is small compared with that which desires no change in the existing system'. The infant industry argument had been part of the nationalist economic canon, but the Commission rejected it with the damning rejoinder that 'the experimental period is with most [Irish industries] a thing of the past'. The problem, the Commission reasoned, was debility rather than extreme youth.[3] The rather timid experimentation with tariffs that followed in the mid- and late 1920s might, none the less, be interpreted as support for infant industries seeking their comparative advantage in the long run. The same could hardly be said for

Fianna Fáil trade policy after early 1932. Infant industry protection would have been geared towards a limited number of potential export-oriented industries, but the ambitions of the diverse, numerous, and small concerns supported by tariffs after 1932 rarely went beyond the home market.

Policy was directed less at protecting existing industry, senile or otherwise, than at fostering new industry. Tariff protection and capital support for new enterprises (through the Industrial Credit Company, founded in 1933) were combined with the Control of Manufactures Acts of 1932 and 1934, legislation which aimed at preventing foreign businessmen from setting up 'tariff factories' in Ireland in order to circumvent the tariffs. Official data suggest that the policy 'worked': the growth in manufacturing employment and output was about one-third between 1932 and 1938. Indeed, they suggest rises in private sector output and employment never equalled since in such a short period. Critics[4] have urged that the data reflect at least in part better statistical coverage over time. There is something to this: but by the same logic, there must have been a decline in manufacturing jobs before 1932, and thus the contrast between the pre- and post-1932 periods holds.

Fianna Fáil sought to reserve the domestic market for Irish capital, and indeed the new firms were geared very much toward the home market. What was insufficiently realized at the time is that the policies of creating employment through protection and of protecting Irish capitalists through the Control of Manufactures Acts were in conflict. From an employment standpoint, the more the foreign capital and enterprise flowed in, the better. Seán Lemass, their chief architect, gradually realized this, but in the meantime it seems that many businessmen found ways of circumventing his legislation.[5]

The charge of excessive tariff protection in the 1930s, frequently urged, is supported by Ryan's finding[6] that the average import tariff in the Irish Free State quintupled, from 9 to 45 per cent, between 1926 and 1936. There is no doubting the tilt towards protection, but Ryan's numbers must not pass without quibble. Part of the difficulty is technical: the measurement of protection, like that of the cost of living or the standard of living, typically faces an index number problem. Ryan dismissed the easiest measure of protection—aggregate tariff revenue as a percentage of the value of merchandise imports—on the ground that it effectively gives prohibitive tariffs zero weight. Yet his own alternative measure—based on 1924 import weights—is hardly free of bias either. Trade patterns were radically different in the mid-1930s, and to the extent that the shift in composition was in response to tariff-induced relative price changes, Ryan's weights produce an upper-bound estimate of protection.

A simple example will illustrate the difficulty. Suppose there are two economies with identical trade patterns before protection. Both import £10 million of Good A and £5 million of Good B. Now let both impose tariffs of 60 per cent on A and 20 per cent on B; as a result imports change as in Table 16.1. Plainly, using pre-tariff weights produces an average tariff rate of [(6 + 1)/15] or 46.7 per cent in both countries. However, an index based on post-tariff weights would mean 60 per cent for Country I and 40 per cent for Country II. This is because of Country I's failure to switch out of the heavily tariffed Good A. Generally, the less elastic the demand for the most heavily tariffed imports, the more protectionist the impact of the tariffs will seem, using post-tariff weights.

Ryan conceded some other shortcomings of his estimates. First, the inclusion of *only* items tariffed in either 1936 or 1938 lent his estimates an upward bias. Second, the results measured a notional protection level, i.e. 'the height that *would* obtain if no mollification of the tariff burden were legally possible' (my emphasis); the rate obtaining in practice would have been lower. Third, changes in data categorization forced Ryan sometimes to apply the duties 'to a wider class of goods than seemed proper'. These are significant reservations.

The distinction between tariffs imposed largely for revenue purposes and those with protective intent is also relevant. An informal manipulation of the 1926 and 1936 import data (see Table 16.2) that excludes beer, spirits, wine, and tobacco from both the duties and import totals, and calculates an average tariff rate (T/M) from the remaining items suggests a rise from less than 3 per cent in 1926 to 16.7 per cent in 1936! Though such numbers are no substitutes for Ryan's, they suggest that his are too high.[7]

Ryan linked the Irish economy's poor performance relative to the British

Table 16.1. *Tariffs and imports: hypothetical outcomes*

	Good A	Good B
Imports before (in £)	10	5
Tariff rate (%)	60	20
Imports after		
Country I	10	0
Country II	5	5

Table 16.2. *Tariff revenue and imports, 1926 and 1936* (£000s)

	1926			1936		
	Imports	Duties	T/M (%)	Imports	Duties	T/M (%)
Beer	181.9	217.3	119.5	410.0	309.5	75.7
Spirits	205.1	688.8	335.8	178.7	581.0	325.1
Wine	331.5	240.1	72.4	218.2	187.0	85.7
Tobacco	513.0	3 225.2	628.7	1 069.0	4 234.9	396.2
(1) Totals	1 232.0	5 071.5	411.6	1 875.9	3 734.1	199.1
(2) All	61 286.1	6 852.2	11.2	39 912.6	10 083.2	27.1
(1) − (2)	60 054.1	1 780.7	3.0	38 036.7	6 349.1	16.7

Sources: *Statistical Abstract*, 1931 and 1939.

economy, as indicated by contemporary unofficial estimates of Irish national income, to Irish tariff policy. The British economy recovered very impressively after the suspension of gold payments in September 1931, but Irish growth seems to have been sluggish. Without seeking to deny Ireland's poor economic performance, this comparison also begs several questions. First, across Europe the connection between freer trade and faster growth in the 1930s was no means clear-cut. Tariffs produce inefficiencies and increase costs, but they also boost domestic demand. Second, as noted in Chapter 15, there is some doubt about the national income data underlying Ryan's comparison. Third, 'two-horse race' comparisons can be misleading: other economies also performed poorly during this period (e.g. Netherlands, Belgium, France, Northern Ireland), while several (e.g. Finland, Australia, Denmark, USSR, Norway) recovered more impressively than the UK.[8]

The tariff regime hurriedly constructed in the 1930s was far from scientific; it was the product of horse-trading between prospective industrialists and government officials eager to increase employment. The following minute from an official in the Department of Industry and Commerce, referring to requests from Dundalk shoe manufacturers John Rawson & Sons (Ireland) Ltd. to import certain raw materials duty-free, reveals how concessions were made, and the costs of processing and winning them:[9]

Division 'D' has no objections to the grant of exemption for 9 months for *wood spool heels* and for six months for *glace kid and patent leathers*. It was suggested that the Co. should be referred to O'Callaghan & Son Ltd and Irish Tanners Ltd for *dressed welting shoulders*, and for *suedes* to Plunder & Pollock and for fancy leathers to the Dickens Co. Licence Section has since been satisfied by production of documentary evidence that these required materials are not available from home sources and Licences have been recommended. Licences have also been recommended for *light bends* and for *wood heels* and *fibres covered with celluloid* and *extended fibre stiffeners* and *elongated heels* on production of inability to secure here. Evidence has also been furnished that the 3 *cements* are not procurable here. Exemption may therefore I think be given for all the leathers to 30th June next and for the remaining items to 30th September next.

The best defence of the cumbersome tariff regime remains political pragmatism—the means, however crude and awkward, of creating jobs that were required for social stability. In the 1930s critics of protection were very slow to produce alternative quick-fix schemes. The deflation urged by Department of Finance mandarins was liable to create serious social tension, and was largely ignored both by Cumann na nGaedheal in 1930–1 and Fianna Fáil later. On the other hand, Keynes's support for deficit spending on public works was also considered heresy by the Dublin intellectual establishment. Even within Fianna Fáil tariffs seemed more respectable than budget deficits. As a result, nationalist policies that might have never reached the statute book were now deemed pragmatic as stopgap measures.

Keynes's cautious support for job-inducing tariffs in Ireland echoed that made by an Irish economist, Isaac Butt, in the 1840s:[10]

If, in any case, the effect of obtaining commodities from abroad be to leave labour or resources unemployed at home, it is perfectly clear that in every such a case it does not follow that you add to the entire revenue of the country, by resorting to other countries for what you require, even though you may obtain it cheaper and better than at home. There must be a calculation of profit and loss; the profit is the measure of the superiority of what you import over what you could raise at home, but the loss is the entire value of what you must export to pay for it. This argument is unanswerable *in every instance in which, by resorting to foreign countries, either labour or resources are made unprofitable at home*. If the labour or the resources that are so discouraged, are turned to other purposes the loss must obviously be diminished by the value of the product which in their new employment they will yield.

Butt favoured temporary tariffs when the labour-market was slow to adjust. Yet (like Keynes) he warned against tariffs 'injudiciously and rashly enforced'.

Several caveats about Fianna Fáil job-creation should be noted. First, many of the new jobs were not in protected industry but in the construction of subsidized housing and social infrastructure, financed through taxation and the repatriation, though on a modest scale, of external assets. Second, Census of Industrial Production data suggest that job-creation in manufacturing had run out of steam by 1936–7, by which time home-based firms had saturated the domestic market. These infant firms showed no inclination to seek markets abroad. Thus as a policy of fostering sustained, cumulative growth, protection was hopeless. Third, the jobs created in the 1930s exacted a cost in jobs lost as Ireland moved towards freer trade again from the early 1960s. To that extent the policies of the 1930s involved a sort of intergenerational trade-off. Fourth, as the British economy gathered steam from 1932 on, emigration from Ireland grew apace, as if factor movements substituted for movements of goods. This reduced the job-creation rationale for tariffs, though it raised another familiar problem. The cost of Irish emigration, in terms of loss of skilled personnel and life-cycle effects, has already been discussed in Chapter 10.

16.2 The 'Economic War', 1932–8

> The economic war will exhaust neither side; it is more injurious to Ireland in times of peace and may be more injurious to England in times of war and rumours of war.
>
> *Spectator*, 5 April 1935

> The Council regards with increasing anxiety the effect of the present unequal struggle with Great Britain, which, if continued, must lead, by a rapid process of financial exhaustion, to the annihilation of our external trade and the permanent and substantial diminution of our internal trade.
>
> DUBLIN CHAMBER OF COMMERCE, 21 November 1932[11]

> It was to a great extent a bluff... We had these catch cries of the Minister that we could get markets elsewhere; that we could cut off Britain's supplies and would have Great Britain on her knees in no time... The Fianna Fáil Government has made a demonstration to the world of exactly what our strength is.
>
> PATRICK McGILLIGAN, TD (1935)[12]

The 'Economic War' was a phoney war: no blood spilt, no diplomatic relations severed. In an era when trade warfare was commonplace throughout the world, this particular Anglo-Irish row received scant attention outside Ireland and the UK. Yet the term 'Economic War' was a boon to the new Fianna Fáil administration. The 'war' began with the refusal of

Fianna Fáil to continue paying certain 'land annuities' arising out of the Treaty settlement of 1921. These annuities, a tax levied on Irish peasant proprietors to pay for the cost to the (British) exchequer of compensating Irish landlords, had been paid in full by Cumann na nGaedheal. Fianna Fáil questioned the fairness of the annual payment of £5 million on both legal and moral grounds. The British rebutted the legal claim with the counterclaim that the annuities were really payments between tenants and their former landlords, with both Governments merely acting as inter-mediaries, but expert legal opinion was split.[13] On rhetorical grounds, Fianna Fáil's case that Britain should have been more understanding at a time when Britain was seeking favours in own debt repayments from the USA, was a stronger one. For Ireland the annuities represented a consider-able drain, about 3 per cent of national income. Moreover, thousands of militant farmers had been forcing the Irish Government's hand, by refusing or being unable to make their payments to the Irish exchequer. Still, when the Irish Government failed to honour the July 'gale' in 1932 the UK immediately imposed special duties of 20 per cent on livestock in order to raise the money. When the rates originally set proved too low, they were raised to 40 per cent on livestock and 30 per cent on other agricultural products,[14] enough to bring in the £5 disputed million per annum. Fianna Fáil retaliated by imposing special duties on British imports and export bounties on certain Irish agricultural products.

Another complicating factor was the quotas imposed from January 1934 on the import of Irish live cattle into the UK. Whether Ireland, ruled by a friendlier regime, i.e. Cumann na nGaedheal, would have been exempt from these quotas is a moot point. The Department of Finance did not believe so, and *The Economist*, whose sympathy for Fianna Fáil's predicament sprung from its own deeper hostility to protection for the British farmer, conceded that 'whether [Irish farmers] choose Dominion or republic, their trade with great Britain will be safe only so long as it suits the greed of the British farmer'. Canadian, Australian, and New Zealand farmers would have concurred.[15] In Ireland it was argued that the impact of the quota on farmers was more serious than that of the special duties, especially since the Irish Government softened the blow of the latter with export bounties. In any case, the combined effect of the 'Economic War' and cattle quotas was to make the 1930s a much rougher period for the Irish farmer than it would have been. In partial equilibrium terms, the losses depend on the elasticities of demand and supply for imports and exports. More specifically, the lower the Irish elasticity of supply and the higher the Irish elasticity of demand for British imports, the smaller will have been the loss incurred by Ireland. At the outset, Irish spokesmen stressed the danger of alternative import markets to British coal-producers, and the reliance of British cattle-fatteners on Irish supplies. In Britain, the liberal *New Statesman and Nation* echoed the same sentiments:[16]

An examination of Anglo-Irish trade during the last fortnight suggests that the British Government will be lucky if it receives 15 per cent of the revenue it anticipated when it imposed the duties. Such meagre receipts as there are will in any case be mainly paid for, not by Ireland, but by the British consumer. Meanwhile, the Free State is transferring its coal orders to the Continent and seems likely to make quite a useful little revenue out of the tariffs imposed on British exports to Ireland. Whether in these circumstances the British Government's policy will lead to the overthrow of De Valera we do not venture to prophecy. But it must result in increased unemployment in England, and in distress in Ireland . . . And the joke, if anyone can be found to laugh at it, will be that the Land Annuities, in so far as they are paid at all, will be paid by the British consumer.

True, individual British businessmen (notably south Wales mine-owners) complained of the loss of the Irish market. The Coal–Cattle pacts of 1935–7, the first break in the 'War', were geared in part towards them. Yet it is highly unlikely that this scenario described by the *New Statesman and Nation* materialized. The trends in the price of store cattle in the UK and in Ireland[17] show that Irish producers suffered more than British consumers.

The mid-1930s marked the nadir of farmer welfare in the South in the present century. The plunge in conacre or eleven-month rents, a sensitive indicator of farmer expectations, tells the tale. Conacre rents in the Limerick area fell from nearly £2 per acre in 1930–2 to just over £1 in 1934–5. The decline was by no means entirely due to the 'Economic War', however. A confidential minute prepared by the Department of Finance in June 1934 concluded that Irish farmers' living standards had dropped by 15 per cent between 1929 and 1933, but that the decline would have been 13 per cent in the absence of any dispute. It estimated the decline in farmers' income to have been £4 million gross, and £2.2 million net in 1993–4, adding that non-payment of legal liabilities for rates and annuities reduced the net fall by half.[18] Though it may have been little consolation to Irish farmers who absorbed the full effect of the price differentials, at least the £5 million collected by the UK customs did not represent a net loss, since the Irish authorities held back the annuity payments.

A simple cost-benefit analysis is in order. Let us focus on Irish exports for purposes of illustration. If the demand for Irish produce was very inelastic, then British consumers would have absorbed most of the increased duty. Some claimed this for live cattle. But the evidence fails to support it: prices in Ireland dropped by the full extent of the special duties. In that case the loss is the producer surplus resulting from the fall in Irish prices. The relevant parameter estimates are unavailable, but at a guess, it was £1 million to £2 million. In Fig. 16.1 let KJD be the demand for Irish exports before the special duties, and LH the demand after they are imposed. Let HJS be Irish supply. The British Treasury recoups the annuities through KGHL, and the loss in producers' surplus is GJH. Now suppose the value of Irish exports (LHNM) was £12 million, and KGHL was £5 million. Then if the export supply elasticity is unity, it is easy to show that GJH is worth £1.25 million. (A relatively low elasticity, at least in the short run, is indicated by the failure of cattle numbers to fall in face of such price shocks.) Doubling the elasticity would double the loss.[19] If the loss in consumer surplus was roughly the same, then what is at stake is the loss of £2 million to £5 million a year in return for the settlement of spring 1938, which cancelled the annuities in return for a lump-sum payment of £10 million. This is evidently a crude exercise, but a more sophisticated computable general equilibrium estimate of the loss by O'Rourke yields a similar outcome.[20]

Estimates of the present value of the outstanding Irish debt in 1938 ranged from £40 million to £100 million. These numbers posed a dilemma

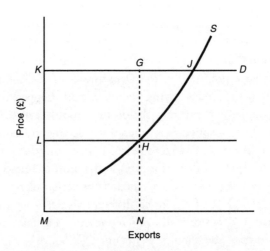

FIG. 16.1 Partial equilibrium analysis of the 'Economic War'

Table 16.3. *UK trade with four agricultural economies, 1924–1938*

	Ireland	New Zealand	Denmark	Netherlands
Imports as a percentage of all UK imports				
1924	4.4	3.5	4.3	3.7
1930	4.4	4.2	5.6	4.0
1931	4.5	4.2	5.8	4.4
1932	4.0	5.1	6.2	3.3
1933	2.8	5.1	5.6	2.9
1934	2.4	5.2	4.8	3.0
1935	2.6	4.9	4.5	3.2
1936	2.5	4.9	4.2	3.1
1937	2.1	4.6	3.8	3.2
1938	2.6	4.9	4.4	3.4
Exports as a percentage of all UK exports				
1924	5.9	2.5	2.9	3.2
1930	6.0	3.1	3.0	3.3
1931	7.8	2.9	2.8	3.5
1932	7.1	2.8	2.7	3.3
1933	5.2	2.6	3.3	3.4
1934	4.9	2.9	3.4	3.1
1935	4.8	3.1	3.2	2.7
1936	4.8	3.9	3.4	2.8
1937	4.1	3.9	3.3	2.9
1938	4.3	4.1	3.4	2.8

Table 16.4. *British agricultural imports (1927–9 = 100)*

	Empire imports				Other			
	1931	1934	1935	1936	1931	1934	1935	1936
Meat	117	123	130	138	117	81	73	70
Dairy	135	170	171	163	112	114	107	116
Eggs	106	100	83	81	104	72	85	107
Wheat	106	116	111	165	114	76	7X	29
Veg	102	123	131	127	172	70	77	92
Fruit	133	196	205	186	115	43	71	47
TOTAL	117	137	137	152	116	84	82	75

Source: Ruth L. Cohen, 'The Increase in Food Imports in 1936', *Farm Economist*, 2/6 (1937),
110–12.

for the negotiators, for the desire for a once-and-for-all settlement was matched by the fear on the British side that the Irish Government would be unable to raise such sums. The fear had some basis, since the recent Fourth National Loan—for £6 million at 3.6 per cent—had been somewhat of a flop, and about half of it had to be taken up by the underwriters. In 1938, however, the sum agreed on was raised with ease for 3.75 per cent as the Financial Agreement Loan. From this perspective, the agreement was a useful outcome from the Irish standpoint.

Ireland suffered much more in economic terms than Britain during the 'Economic War'. Though those worst affected were a minority of strong farmers (never noted for their support of Fianna Fáil), *all* farmers were affected. Small farmers in the west and south provided the young cattle fattened on the pasture lands. Civil servants on both sides increasingly pressed ministers to come to terms, but the timing of the settlement is best explained by British eagerness to end the conflict. If the Irish 'won' the war, it was for political reasons. There were other more important things to worry about in 1938. The Anglo-American commercial dispute of 1807–8 provides a useful analogy. Frankel has shown, using some rough-and-ready terms-of-trade data, that Britain suffered more than the USA from the embargo. But the USA had political reasons for wanting to settle. Similarly, Britain could have continued to hurt the Irish economy, but had sound political reasons for appeasement in late 1937 and early 1938. 'Critic' in the *New Statesman and Nation* put it like this: 'What made us sane at last? Hitler. That's the answer. The bully remains a bully until he is frightened by a bigger bully.'[21] Comparing Irish trade patterns in the 1930s with those of other mainly agricultural countries traditionally reliant on British markets suggests that (*a*) British policy 'hurt' Ireland more than them, and (*b*) Ireland fared much worse than other Empire economies (Tables 16.3 and 16.4).

Despite early hopes, the trade statistics show little sign of a loosening during the 1930s of the ties that bound the Irish economy to the British. The substantial drop in recorded imports from Northern Ireland (over 10 per cent of the total in 1930–1, 4.4 per cent in 1935–6) was probably in part a reflection of increased smuggling. The UK absorbed over 90 per cent of Irish exports throughout the 1930s, and continued to be Ireland's dominant trading partner. Ireland's terms of trade deteriorated significantly (by about 20 per cent) between 1932 and 1937, recovering quickly again at the end of the 'Economic War', while Britain's improved slightly during the same period.

Cattle Smuggling: A Mitigating Factor?

During the 1930s as before, most Irish trade was with Great Britain. But given the extensive land border between Northern and Southern Ireland, the emergence of a substantial smuggling trade after July 1932 might be anticipated. The distortions caused by the European Community's Common Agricultural Policy have had such an effect in the two Irelands in recent years. And indeed at the height of the 'Economic War' *The Economist* (26 October 1935) quipped (though without supporting evidence) that about nearly one hundred thousand cattle were taking part 'in conducted tours across the border under the guidance of experts in the smuggling profession'. Hilarious anecdotal accounts survive.[22] David Johnson has matched contemporary trade, consumption, output data to produce estimates of cattle smuggling (Table 16.A1). On the face of it, these numbers support *The Economist*, but they seem difficult to square with contemporary price data, which indicate that the price differential between North and South matched the size of the British tax closely. How does one square the claim of a British minister that 'the price of fat cattle of over 18 months in Naas (in the Irish Free State) was £7. 10*s*. per head, while in Camlough (in Northern Ireland) it was £13. 10*s*. per head',[23] with a Northern Ireland magistrate's quip that 'everyone knew that this smuggling was going on wholesale and a very good example was provided by the last Camlough fair, of which one man had said that one might as well be in Ballina as not 5 per cent of the animals were home produced'.[24] Northern and Southern Irish and British official data support the minister. In face of the massive smuggling, how could such price differentials persist? Indeed Johnson shows that the price differential was *greater* from mid-1934, at the peak of the smuggling trade, than later.

The standard Bhagwati–Hansen model of smuggling shows that smuggling may improve welfare if it narrows the gap between tariff-distorted and world prices, though this is by no means inevitable. But their model lacks a spatial dimension, and handles the coexistence of illegal and legal trades (a central feature of the Irish case) awkwardly.[25] A simple model which seems to capture the most important features of the present case presumes that the demand for Irish exports abroad (i.e. in the UK) was perfectly elastic at price P. Thus the domestic price was $P-t$. The supply schedule of smugglers reflects the increasing costs faced by the industry; some smugglers may have been able to smuggle at little or no cost (e.g. because they lived along the border or had local contacts) thus pocketing t as a rent. The smuggling industry's supply was like SS in Fig. 16.2. Smugglers as a group thus captured JGH in producers' surplus, and provided GJ of total exports JK. In this scenario, there is no presumption that smuggling reduces Irish economic welfare. The producers' surplus was a gain at the expense of the UK

Table 16.A1. *Cattle smuggling in Ireland in the 1930s*

Year	Estimate of cattle smuggled into NI (000s)	Recorded imports from Irish Free State to NI (000s)
1932–3	33	133
1933–4	58	118
1934–5	93	146
1935–6	54	153
1936–7	17	142
1937–8	31	135

Source: Johnson, 'Cattle Smuggling', 56, 62.

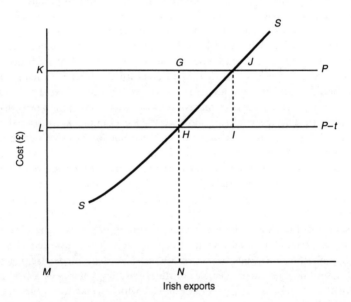

FIG. 16.2 A simple model of smuggling

Treasury (which lost GJIH). How much of it accrued to Ireland during the 1930s depends on the smugglers' nationality.

In the context of Ireland in the 1930s it is plausible to suppose that any smuggling will have attracted primarily cattle raised near the border. Could the smuggling trade have been so monopolized that its benefits were confined to the smugglers? Pre-1932 price data belie the common belief that the regular cattle trade was heavily controlled by buyers' 'rings': the margins between Irish and British prices are too narrow for that. But perhaps working the border illegally was different, at least at the outset. The issue is worth further research, for if Johnson's smuggling estimates are near the mark, they suggest that the cost of the 'Economic War' is exaggerated by the calculations above—even if the benefits of smuggling were very thinly spread within Ireland.

The simple approach outlined here explains what might appear at first glance a curious feature of the agricultural statistics of the 1930s. Smuggling seems to have left no impact on the county agricultural statistics of the period. The year-to-year trends in livestock numbers in border counties were like those elsewhere. Had smuggling benefited farmers, we would have expected those near the border to have done best relatively, and to have built up bigger herds. But since as we have posited, the benefits were limited exclusively to the smugglers themselves, the failure of the data to reflect this does not rule out smuggling. Finally, though smuggling helped reduce the burden of the 'Economic War', it was only a small part of the story since most cattle continued to be shipped direct to Britain.

The Economic Performance of the Two Irelands, 1921–1939: Macroeconomic Policy and Living Standards

17.1 Fiscal Policy

> In an effort to cope with unemployment we have increased tariffs, we have fostered tillage, we have subsidised dairying and pigs and live-stock production, we have developed the sugar-making industry; we have raised the prices of agricultural commodities, we have shortened the working hours of the employed and given them holidays with pay, we have introduced quota restrictions and established virtual monopolies. We have more regimentation, more regulation, more control everywhere. And more unemployment.
>
> SEÁN MACENTEE, c.1938[1]

There was something paradoxical about economic policy under Fianna Fáil in the 1930s. The responsible minister, Seán MacEntee, was a strong fiscal and monetary conservative, who fought hard against cheap money, public works, and government intervention generally. With few allies in the cabinet, he found himself being repeatedly overruled, and threatened to resign on several occasions. In 1937 he complained that 'so far as the Minister for Finance was concerned his part was to be that of a cypher, except when the bill was to be paid at which time he might be permitted to figure in the more active role of a scapegoat'. MacEntee clearly felt that he was losing the battle for fiscal rectitude.[2]

Nevertheless, the statistical record hardly suggests that Fianna Fáil fiscal policy in the 1930s was reckless. True, under Cumann na nGaedheal both taxes and spending fell in nominal terms until 1929–30, while they rose slightly under Fianna Fáil (see Fig. 17.1). The most important boosts to Fianna Fáil spending included unemployment insurance and assistance (up from £0.2 million in 1933–4 to £0.9 million in 1934–5), public works (from £0.6 million in 1931–2 to £0.9 million in 1938–9), and old-age pensions (from £2.7 million in 1931–2 to £3.5 million in 1938–9). Neither regime quite balanced its books. Cumann na nGaedheal had failed

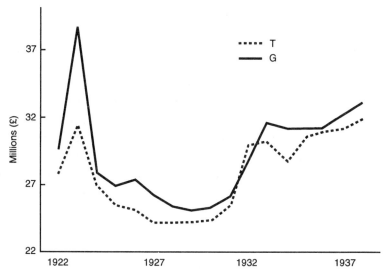

FIG. 17.1 Exchequer revenues and issues, 1922/3–1938/9

to balance the current budget in all years except 1931–2. Exchequer issues
on central fund and supply services also exceeded receipts under Fianna
Fáil. Yet even setting aside the recurrent claim that some of the outgoings
listed under current spending were 'of a capital and productive character',
the average deficits in 1932–9 represented only about 3 per cent of
spending. The real difference between Fianna Fáil and Cumann na nGaedheal fiscal policies was not fiscal recklessness versus fiscal rectitude, but that
Fianna Fáil had fewer reservations about raising revenues to financing
higher current spending. Thus the 1920s were a period of retrenchment,
the 1930s of mild budgetary expansion.

Both administrations borrowed for capital spending purposes. The
national debt (capital assets less liabilities) rose from less than £10 million
in March 1924 to £16.1 million when Fianna Fáil took over. Fianna Fáil
had increased it to £30.9 million by March 1939. The lion's share of the
latter rise (£10 million) was accounted for by the Financial Agreement Loan
of 1938. On the eve of the war, the debt still represented less than £10 per
head or about one-fifth of national income. Nevertheless, its 'singular rate
of increase' and its size relative to a selection of countries were harshly
criticized in the Majority Report of the Second Banking Commission of
1934–8 (on which more below). 'The contrast is still more unfavourable to
the Free State if the inquiry be extended to the important point of the

weight of taxation.' Accordingly, 'no increase whatever beyond the existing volume of net dead-weight debt should be permitted, and that volume should be reduced from year to year at such rate as general financial circumstances permit'.[3] The Banking Commission's fears reflected its gloomy assessment of Irish economic prospects, and it selected a few small Baltic and Scandinavian economies with lower debt ratios to drive the point home. Yet a more broadly based comparison than the Report's shows that Ireland's debt situation in the late 1930s was no cause for worry. Table 17.1 shows that Ireland's ratio of receipts to debt in the late 1930s— almost two-thirds—placed it sixth out of twenty-two of Europe's smaller economies. Besides, Ireland was one of only four countries listed with no foreign debt, and its credit rating on the US bond market was very high.[4]

Were private savings crowded out? The trend in interest rates suggests not: the Irish banks' minimum lending rate remained at 3 per cent between July 1932 and the outbreak of war, and the gap between it and English bank rate held steady.[5] The trend in the yields on bonds suggests problems on a related front, however. Nevin has detected a 'distinct widening' in the gap between the flat yields (i.e. the coupon divided by current market value) on Irish and British government securities in 1932. Whereas the initial gap before 1932 might be put down to the lower liquidity of Irish bonds, the widening might plausibly be interpreted as an indication of investor nervousness about inflation, debt repudiation, or currency depreciation in Ireland. Nevin put the gap down to the British policy shift to cheap money rather than to Fianna Fáil policy, arguing in particular that the conversion of the huge 5 per cent War Loan to a 3.5 per cent basis dragged down the British average after 1932: 'the narrowness of the gap before 1932 was partly a reflection of this fact that a single, enormous stock was dragging the British list down; the width of the gap thereafter, on the other hand, is a reflection that this enormous issue was tending to push the British list up.'[6] The trouble with this interpretation is that it conflicts with the law of one price: after all, Irish and British securities remained close substitutes for the Irish investor throughout these years.

An examination of the movements in bond prices during 1932 allows us to decide between the rival interpretations. Note that the election which brought Fianna Fáil to power took place on 16 February 1932. Fianna Fáil's commitment to repudiating the land annuity payments and to increasing employment through a combination of protection, price supports, and public spending had been widely publicized during the preceding campaign. Thus if the investor's fear of Fianna Fáil explains the widening, it

Table 17.1. *Ireland's public debt in comparative perspective*

Country	Foreign debt as a percentage of total	Receipts as a percentage of debt
Austria, 1937	56.7	56.0
Belgium, 1939	32.0	19.7
Bulgaria, 1939	44.0	29.8
Denmark, 1939	54.2	46.3
Spain, 1935	4.2	20.5
Estonia, 1939	90.3	83.0
Finland, 1938	30.3	136.8
Greece, 1938	73.6	26.9
Hungary, 1938	69.2	82.9
IRELAND, 1938	0.0	64.6
Latvia, 1938	78.8	117.6
Lithuania, 1938	60.4	233.2
Norway, 1938	43.7	42.0
Netherlands, 1938	0.0	21.4
Poland, 1938	51.8	47.6
Portugal, 1938	44.3	28.2
Romania, 1938	66.5	26.9
Sweden, 1938	0.0	59.3
Switzerland, 1938	0.0	19.6
Czechoslovakia, 1938	17.8	19.1
Turkey, 1938	35.1	63.8
Yugoslavia, 1938	60.4	52.7

Source: *Statistical Year-Book of the League of Nations 1939/40* (Geneva, 1940), 239–61 (Tables 113–14).

should show in the data for February (or even a little earlier, as the likelihood of a Fianna Fáil victory grew) rather than in late June or early July, when the British bond conversion took place. Here we look at the week-to-week movements during 1930–2 in the official price of Irish Second and Third National Loan and UK 4 per cent Victory Bonds.[7] Graphing the outcome (Fig. 17.2) clearly shows that the gap widened early in 1932, implying that investor apprehension of Fianna Fáil was to blame.[8] Overall, however, Fianna Fáil may be absolved of fiscal irresponsibility in the 1930s. On the contrary, more might have been done along classic Keynesian lines. Early in 1933 Keynes himself had recommended spending 'to make Dublin, within its appropriate limits of scale, a splendid city fully

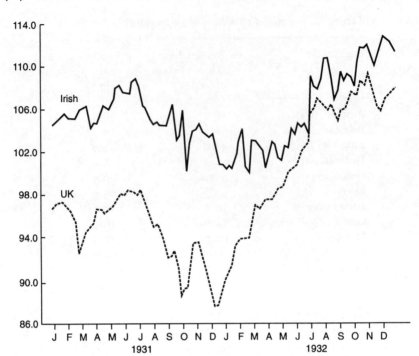

FIG. 17.2 Irish and UK security price trends, 1931–1932

endowed with the appurtenances of art and civilisation of the highest standards'. Anticipating one of the key messages of the *General Theory*, he attempted to reassure an audience in University College, Dublin, which included both De Valera and the leading lights of Cumann na nGaedheal, that 'money thus spent would not only be better than any dole, but would make unnecessary any dole'.[9] However, Fianna Fáil strategy relied more on job-creation through tariffs rather than on deficit spending.

17.2 Monetary Developments

> Having proved to the satisfaction of any normal person that in our circumstances a central bank was not by any means necessary, it goes on to argue that, nevertheless, we must have a central bank, and the principal reason which appears to have been given is that central banks are the fashion.
>
> JOSEPH JOHNSTON[10]

The hallmark here was caution. As John Pratschke has remarked of the 1920s, 'such changes as occurred in this decade were of an institutional character, and did not immediately affect monetary policy weapons to any extent'. In the commercial banking sphere it was the same story, and the Irish banks 'continued to regard their balances in London . . . as the ultimate basis of their credit'.[11] The same might be said of the 1930s. Despite the enduring popular appeal of currency schemes, both Cumann na nGaedheal and Fianna Fáil administrations were reluctant to meddle with monetary practice. The paradox is that as a result, the Irish joint-stock banks were left without any proper lender of last resort, and the Irish Free State was left little discretion in monetary policy. And yet no major Irish bank failed or even experienced any serious pressure in this crisis-ridden period. This is a remarkable achievement.[12]

The posture of the two major official inquiries into monetary policy options, the Parker-Willis Commission of 1926–7 and the Commission of Inquiry into Banking Currency and Credit of 1934–8, was orthodox and conservative. Policy was no different; it sought simply to maintain the sterling link while gaining revenue from an Irish note-issue. Yet on the question of central banking there was some ambivalence. On the one hand, though central banks were very much the flavour of the day after 1918 (recommended to emergent nations by the League of Nations and the Genoa Financial Conference of 1922 and enthusiastically supported by the Governor of the Bank of England, Montagu Norman), the Irish Free State seemed not to succumb to the temptation of creating its own until 1942. On the other hand, the Currency Commission, the statutory non-political institution created in 1927 to manage the new Saorstát pound, was granted the most important responsibilities of the textbook central bank—those of defending the value of the domestic currency and generating seignorage revenue for the Government. To that extent, the Currency Commission was a central bank by another name. The ambivalence stemmed in part from a conviction that outside the Irish Free State—and to some extent within it—central banks were being promoted as antidotes to backward or unduly risk-averse commercial banking systems. Accordingly, creating an Irish central bank might be seen as both a slight and a threat to the long-established commercial banks.[13]

The Government quickly enacted most of the advice of the Parker-Willis Commission of 1926–7, of which the American economist Henry Parker-Willis was chairman. That Commission was dominated by bankers and their allies. Besides Parker-Willis himself, it included two sympathetic civil servants, four representatives of the Irish banks, and an ex-chairman of the Commonwealth Bank of Australia. Andrew Jameson of the Bank of Ireland, a wily old campaigner, was the original choice for chairman. Though he could understand the choice, given his 'reputation of being an old-fashioned conservative', he turned down the offer. Jameson's refusal to serve as chairman reflected his fear that he would be heading a Commission whose recommendations would weaken the Bank of Ireland. Instead, he served as that bank's representative on the Commission, and ended up by being the sole dissenting voice to the majority report.[14]

The Parker-Willis Commission deemed that, first, the soundness of Irish financial institutions vitiated the need for an Irish central bank.[15] Second, it held that the virtual absence of a domestic money or capital market ruled out an independent Irish monetary policy. Such a market might develop, but could not be forced. In making this last point, the Commission was doing no more than paying its dues to the orthodoxy that 'the success of central banking depends largely upon the condition of the capital market in which it is practised'.[16] Now, Britain's peculiar institutional framework made it natural for the Bank of England as *de facto* central bank to control credit through open-market operations. But London's situation was quite exceptional; central bank control of the commercial banking system through reserve requirements or moral suasion, without the intermediary of a money market, was much more important elsewhere. Indeed orthodoxy did not prevent Norman's roving ambassador, Sir Otto Niemeyer, from recommending a central bank for New Zealand in 1930. That there was 'no bill market, no short-loan market, and, generally speaking, no money market in the full sense of the term . . . [did] not constitute insuperable objections'. But the Parker-Willis Commission held to the belief that something along British lines would have been the Free State's only central banking option.[17]

More important than the quality of the commercial banking system or the lack of a money market, the Irish banks' links with London and the commitment to maintain parity with sterling arguably ruled out an independent monetary policy in any case.[18] Instead of a full-fledged central bank, the Parker-Willis inquiry therefore proposed the creation a quasi-central bank, an institution responsible for a domestic currency backed one hundred per cent by sterling notes, short-maturity British government securities or gold as the only fundamental change required.[19] In addition Irish banks were to be allowed a consolidated issue in lieu of the fiduciary issue allowed under the Bank Act of 1845. The Commission made no provision for either bill discounting or advances. The Government's account remained with the Bank of Ireland. Even such modest changes were too much for Andrew Jameson, who kept up an anguished correspondence with Niemeyer and Norman in Threadneedle Street while the Commission deliberated. Neither shared his misgivings about its findings, however. Norman waxed enthusiastic about the proposal the Saorstát pound be backed by Treasury bills, and Jameson was left to produce his own minority report.

The resulting Currency Commission (1927–42) guaranteed that the seignorage from note-issue belonged to the Irish authorities. Was the sum at stake worth the trouble? The seignorage accruing to Britain between 1922 and 1928 was put at about £0.5 million a year in a claim set out by the Irish Government during the 'Economic War'. This figure was reached by allowing a return of 5 per cent on the £3.9 million of British currency in circulation and another 5 per cent on the £5.5 million of British Treasury bills held by Irish banks as backing for note-issue above the fiduciary allowance.[20] The estimate is probably too high; the net annual receipts of the Currency Commission in the 1930s from dividends, interest payments, and payments on consolidated banknotes, were about £0.2 million, or 0.1 to 0.2 per cent of national income.[21] Brennan and his colleagues were unhappy with the low return on British Treasury bills. In March 1929 he wrote for information from the Bank of England about the 5.5 per cent being offered by two London merchant banks, but was told that the Governor disapproved of any proposal to place with discount houses money intended as backing for a sterling-based currency. Some months later Brennan mentioned 'in confidence' that there had been a good deal of talk in Dublin about lengthening the maturity date of permissible backing for the Legal-Tender Note Fund, and the Currency Commission was given the right to include longer-term paper in its portfolio. The share of Irish legal-tender notes and coins in the total supply of outstanding money rose steadily, reaching about two-thirds by 1939.[22]

The seeds of an Irish bond market were sown by the small clandestine loan raised by the First Dáil in 1919. By 1937 the national debt had risen to £73 million, of which £24 million was in marketable National Loan bonds and £27 million in Land Bonds. Despite some government encouragement, this was still far from enough to create an active two-way market. Very small transactions were not a problem, but the sale of even £30,000 of National Loan might take a month to complete in the mid-

Table 17.2. *Fiduciary issues in 1845 and 1928* (£m.)

	1845		1928	
Bank of Ireland	3.738	(58.8)	1.705	(28.4)
National	0.852	(13.4)	1.365	(22.8)
Northern	0.243	(3.7)	0.243	(4.1)
Provincial	0.928	(14.6)	0.649	(10.8)
Ulster	0.311	(4.9)	0.419	(7.0)
Belfast	0.282	(4.4)	—	
Hibernian	—		0.439	(7.3)
M & L	—		0.852	(14.2)
Natl. Land Bank	—		0.055	(0.9)
Royal	—		0.273	(4.6)
TOTAL	6.354	(100.0)	6.000	(100.0)

Note: Figures in parentheses are percentages.

1930s. Such a market was little use to the Irish banks, who dealt in the London market to the tune of several hundred thousand most weeks. For example, the Bank of Ireland's short-term loans of £0.3–0.5 million to the London discount houses of Alexander, National Discount, and Union Discount stood in sharp contrast to its sales through Dublin stockbroking firms of a few thousand pounds' worth of National Loan or Land Bonds. As for markets in local industrial shares, they were typically slow. An order to sell shares at about the last quoted price might take three or four days 'as luck would have it, but it is possible you may have to wait'.[23] Nevertheless, there was much more activity on the Dublin stock exchange in the late 1930s than ten years earlier. Between 1933 and 1938 the Industrial Credit Company organized public issues worth a total of £4.4 million (including £1.5 million for Comhlucht Siúicre Éireann in three instalments, £0.7 million for Cement Ltd., and £0.5 million for Ranks (Ireland)), and another £0.25 million was raised without its help. Such sums, along with the £6 or so million raised privately in these years helped to spread the investment habit.[24]

The overvaluation of sterling relative to foreign currencies after 1925, by deflating the British economy, also had a deflationary effect on the Irish economy.[25] However, it seems unlikely that higher costs in Ireland than in the UK dictated a devalued Irish pound in the late 1920s. Overall, the logic of maintaining the link with sterling in the inter-war era was compelling, since Irish foreign trade was almost exclusively with the UK, and Irish and British labour and capital markets were closely integrated. Nevertheless, the British decision in September 1931 to suspend gold payments was a serious blow to Ireland. Such a decision had been on the cards, and the Currency Commission had considered converting some of its sterling balances and securities (which totalled £7.5 million at the time) into gold or gold-backed currencies. Brennan visited the Bank of England just over a week before the suspension, and noted that the Currency Commission intended not to renew £0.5 million of Treasury bills falling due that week, and another sum due the following week. This was done in order to leave open the option of asking the Bank to set aside the equivalent in gold. The Bank of England's representative, Leveaux, counselled a gradual build-up of any gold reserve, arguing that it would be 'most unfortunate' if foreigners were given the impression that 'a distrust of sterling were entertained by those so nearly allied to us'. Brennan and the Currency Commission failed to act out of loyalty to the Bank of England on that occasion. A few days later a chastened Brennan met Niemeyer in Threadneedle Street, wondering whether he should not then buy gold, and noting the Irish banks' apprehension about withdrawals. But that was after the horse had bolted.[26]

Seven years later, with war in prospect, the Currency Commission acted more boldly. On 12 September 1938 Brennan phoned to place an order for £2 million of gold bars in return for Treasury bills. Some months later the Currency Commission placed an order for $2.5 million, to be transferred to its credit at the National City Bank of New York. A Bank of England official noted that the commercial banks were likely to want dollars too, in which case 'we stand to lose . . . not £8 millions of Irish reserves but something like £80 millions now held by the Irish banking system in sterling'.[27] British fears of wholesale conversions of Irish assets into dollars were not realized.

In 1931, for Irish holders of sterling assets (estimated to have been worth £200 million at the time), the 25 per cent depreciation of sterling that followed suspension constituted, in theory at least, an equivalent capital loss. Their disappointment at what was seen as a breach of trust on the part of Britain was widely shared:[28]

September 20, 1931, was the end of an age. It was the last day of the age of economic liberalism in which Great Britain had been the leader of the world . . . Now the whole edifice had crashed. The slogan 'safe as the Bank of England' no longer had any meaning. The Bank of England had gone into default. For the first time in history a great creditor country had devaluated [*sic*] its currency, and by so doing had inflicted heavy losses on all those who had trusted it . . . Hitherto devaluation had been the prerogative of improvident debtor countries. Great Britain was a powerful creditor country, yet she had sacrificed, with apparently little regret, the fundamental principle of an international capitalist system, the sanctity of contracts.

However, most of Ireland's external sterling assets could not have been easily converted into some safer currency, so the implied loss of £50 million or so constituted a mere paper loss. More important, part of the loss must have been short-term only, since the sterling value of the assets probably rose to compensate for the depreciation. The dollar, which may have looked a good prospect in late 1931, was soon to depreciate even more than sterling. Still, the collapse of the gold standard provided the new Fianna Fáil administration with the opportunity to set up a public inquiry into monetary and banking policy. Finance Minister MacEntee, his permanent secretary McElligott, Brennan (Chairman of the Currency Commission), and representatives of the commercial banks protested at both the timing and the need for an inquiry. Brennan's objection typically contained an element of catch-22: while insisting that no change should be contemplated before exhaustive investigation, he urged that even rumours of an investigation would cause panic. Efforts to quash the inquiry were of no avail, but mention in its draft terms of reference to the 'effective control of internal and external credit' and the 'operations and methods of the joint-stock banks in regard to credit facilities' (which had alarmed MacEntee and the banks) were dropped.[29]

The Commission of Inquiry into Banking, Currency and Credit was established in late 1934 after a good deal of spadework. The Government certainly could not be accused of packing the membership with radicals. The arch-conservative Brennan sought to spike its guns by keeping its membership small and biased towards commercial banking interests. Though he did not altogether succeed in this, his role was nevertheless paramount. Brennan was the new body's chairman and the main architect of its majority Report. Other influential members included George O'Brien of University College, Dublin, Per Jacobsson (then with the Bank for International Settlements, later president of the IMF), and Theodore Gregory of the London School of Economics. The two last-mentioned were chosen as foreign experts, Jacobsson at the suggestion of the Bank of England:[30] Charles Rist and Gustav Cassell had been invited first, but both declined. Keynes had been briefly considered; his Finlay lecture supporting protection and deficit spending cannot have helped his chances.[31] Gregory and Jacobsson were both conservative in banking matters. The bishop selected, Most Revd. Dr William McNeely, was 'unaware of any reasons why he should have been appointed, except to add an atmosphere of respectability to the conference'.[32] Brennan, who feared a commission dominated by academics rather than 'practical men', had fought very hard to get Jacobsson.

The members of the Commission had worked well together. As Jacobsson noted at the end, 'some curious bonds of friendship have been established, irrespective of religion or political tendencies'.[33] Overall, the Commission proved very indulgent to banking interests, and there was a good deal of behind-the-scenes contact between the banks and individual Commission members during the Commission's deliberations. Thus Glenavy (repeatedly) and even Gregory urged the banks to hold their rates until the Commission had reported. With Brennan at the helm, a conservative report was guaranteed.[34] The Commission's Majority Report looked back with nostalgia on the gold standard era, and the associated 'great advance in world production, international trade and international investment'.[35] It saw little to support in the policies in fashion in the 1930s. It showed little enthusiasm either for an Irish central bank, though in the end it proposed that the Currency Commission be granted limited powers to engage in open-market operations, and recommended an unspecified name change to reflect this central banking feature. The question of other standard central banking responsibilities—lender of last resort and custodian of the Government's accounts—was not broached. The Majority Report saw the main function of any central body as a restraining force on the Government of the day on monetary matters. Any experimentation with the exchange rate was once more ruled out as leading to uncertainty and futile, and the Commission saw no real role for a money market in Dublin. No wonder, then, that Glenavy's addendum to the Majority Report interpreted its findings as meaning that 'nothing whatever is wrong with the system in Saorstát Éireann of currency, banking and credit'.[36] Or as The Economist's correspondent in Dublin put it:

The conclusions of the Commission bear all the earmarks of a compromise. The present Currency Commission (whose functions are virtually limited to the issue of currency and the holding of sterling assets against the notes issued) is to be renamed and its functions are to be enlarged. But the enlarged functions are not to include those usually attaching to a Central Bank. For example, there is to be no attempt to create a money market in Dublin, the commercial banks are not to be under the obligation of keeping reserve deposits with the new institution, and it is not even to take over the Government from the Bank of Ireland. In short, the Currency Commission is to have a new title and a research department, and that is all. It seems to be an admirable solution of the problem, which should please politicians and bankers alike.[37]

The 1934–8 Banking Commission's Majority Report was widely—and correctly—seen as a thinly veiled attack on the policies of Fianna Fáil. The Report sounded a warning about the balance of payments threat posed by industrialization, and was chary of the rise in public debt resulting from Fianna Fáil's social programme and the running down of foreign assets. The rhetoric of the Report anticipated that of the annual reports of that body only furtively anticipated by its authors, Ireland's Central Bank. The Government chose to ignore the Report, and it took the threat of war to produce central banking legislation. In the end, the Central Bank Act of 1942 was a compromise between, on the one hand, Brennan and the Department of Finance, and the majority of ministers on the other. Ironically, Clause 50 of that Act left open a possibility ruled out by the Banking Commission: the Central Bank's right to special deposits from the commercial banks. The aim of this clause was to induce the bank to repatriate some of their external assets for the purpose of investment at home.[38]

The Majority Report of the Banking Commission coyly noted that the legislation of 1927 did not envisage the Currency Commission providing advice to the Government, 'and it does not seem to have been the habit of the Government to consult the Commission on financial questions generally'. The Commission also noted the lack of co-ordinated research into economic and monetary trends, and proposed the creation of a research department in the monetary authority.

17.3 Relative Performance

If the Majority Report of the 1934–8 Banking Commission was an irritant to de Valera and Fianna Fáil, the settlement of the 'Economic War' proved a boon. The chief architect of tariff protection in the 1930s, Industry and Commerce Minister Seán Lemass, quipped that it didn't matter who started the 'Economic War', 'the main thing is that we won it'. Another minister (Seán T. O'Kelly, later to become President) bragged that 'we had whipped John Bull' and would 'do it again'. In the tense and heady atmosphere of the 1930s, such rhetoric counted for much. But if nationalist fervour favoured Fianna Fáil, so did the economic effects of their policies, at least in the short run. Industrial workers and businessmen gained from protection, as did those who were entitled to Fianna Fáil's more generous social welfare. The notion that Fianna Fáil backwoodsmen 'neglected' the cities, especially Dublin, is a myth. Lemass and O'Kelly both represented largely working-class Dublin constituencies, and Fianna Fáil's share of the Dublin vote increased considerably during the 1930s. Small farmers, who were prepared to make temporary economic sacrifices, were shielded from the worst effects of the 'Economic War' by tillage subsidies, dole payments, and land transfers. Together this coalition of small farmers, the new bourgeoisie, and urban workers was numerous enough to give de Valera the greatest victory of his long political career in the general election of 1938. While Fianna Fáil had successfully targeted 'the urban poor and the twenty-five acre farmer', a prominent Cumann na nGaedheal spokesman was left to lament at the height of the 'Economic War':[39]

One of the misfortunes of the present situation is that the economic war is hitting most severely the very section of the people most favourable to the English connection, they are suffering relatively far more than the bulk of those on whose votes the fates of governments depends.

The policies of the 1930s were thus not quite as irrational, politically or economically, as most commentators insisted at the time. The problem lay less with the pursuit of such policies in a context of world-wide trade destruction and unemployment than the determination of both Fianna Fáil in 1945 and the Coalition Government in 1948 to continue with them in the altered post-war circumstances. Their limitations should have been obvious by then.

But let us end on a comparative note. Recent studies by Eichengreen and Sachs and by Bernanke and James have emphasized the importance of exchange-rate policy during the Great Depression. The studies show that economies which depreciated soonest and most staged the best recoveries in the 1930s. By this reckoning British policy was a notable success, and France's loyalty to gold in the 1930s costly. In their study Eichengreen and Sachs regressed a series of measures of recovery against depreciation over the 1929–35 period. They found that depreciation boosted the volume of manufacturing output and exports, restored business confidence (as reflected by the movement in Tobin's q, the ratio of an index of security to industrial output prices), dampened real wage increases, and increased the money supply. The model suggests that the sterling depreciation of 1931–3 should have given a fillip to the Irish economy.[40]

Adding Ireland as an eleventh observation to Eichengreen and Sachs's sample of ten European economies produces the result shown in Table 17.3. Plainly, in comparative terms Irish economic performance in the 1930s was unimpressive. The outcome shows Ireland confirming the pattern indicated by Eichengreen and Sachs for employment and industrial output (if one is to credit the Irish Census of Industrial Production), and real wages. However, Irish exports fell off dramatically in real terms, despite sterling's depreciation relative to most other currencies in the sample. Moreover, viewed against the experience in the economies examined by Bernanke and James, Irish bank deposits and advances grew very modestly relative to the depreciation against gold. Taking together the 1920s and the 1930s, the performance of the Irish economies, North and South, was very poor by international standards.

17.4 Living Standards and Unemployment

Economic well-being in the Irish Free State in the 1920s was largely determined by conditions in the UK. In the 1930s the slump in world agricultural prices, rising trade barriers, and the 'Economic War' were added considerations. Official wage series present a confusing and con-

Table 17.3. *Reduced form regression results*

	Adjusted R^2		Elasticity	
	Without Ireland	With Ireland	Eichengreen and Sachs	Ireland
(1) Export volume	.558	.405	−0.68	+0.88
(2) Industrial production	.561	.514	−0.50	−0.71
(3) Real wages	.268	.305	0.40	0.04
(4) Tobin's q	.467	.291	−1.03	−1.78
Bank deposits	.282	.308	−0.54	−0.10

Sources: (1)–(4): variables as defined in Eichengreen and Sachs, 'Depreciation and Economic Recovery'; data kindly supplied by Barry Eichengreen. Irish data taken from *Statistical Abstract*. Irish elasticities use averages of 1929 and 1935 values. (5): data on commercial bank deposits taken from Mitchell, *European Historical Statistics*, 692–5. All data refer to 1929–35.

flicting picture of levels and trends over these 'years of the great test'. Agricultural wage data (see Table 17.4) imply no sustained growth in real wages between the early 1920s and the late 1930s. Farm labourers continued to be very poorly paid; their average half-yearly wage of £16 in 1938 bears comparing with the cost of a cheap suit (£1.50), blouse, shirt, or jumper (50p), silk tie (10p), lunch (10p), or bed and breakfast (38p) in a modest hotel. The end of the 'Economic War' gave a boost to farm wages as well as to farm incomes generally. Trends in certain other wage categories seem to imply modest improvement at best. Data supplied to the International Labour Organisation provide the rates for a 48-hour week in Dublin in 1926, 1931, and 1938 (Table 17.5).[41]

We have already seen in Chapter 10 that the gap between Irish and British industrial wages in 1914 was small. A noteworthy aspect of the ILO data is their implication that Irish real wages for both skilled and unskilled labour *exceeded* British in the 1920s and 1930s by a slight margin (and Swedish, Norwegian, and German, by a considerable margin). The Anglo-Irish gap is captured in Table 17.6, which also points to a big gap between

Table 17.4. *Agricultural wage trends, 1923–1939*

Year	(1) Cash wage s. d.	(2) Half-yearly wage £. s.	(3) COL	(1)/(3)	(2)/(4)
1923	28 6	16 10	180	103.1	100.8
1924	26 3	14 13	183	93.4	89.1
1925	25 3	14 2	188	87.4	83.5
1926	25 0	14 18	182	89.5	88.0
1927	23 6	13 17	171	89.5	90.1
1928	23 6	13 14	173	88.4	88.1
1929	23 6	13 14	174	88.0	87.6
1930	24 6	14 7	168	94.9	95.0
1931	24 3	14 1	157	100.6	99.6
1932	23 6	13 15	153	100.0	100.0
1933	22 3	12 13	149	97.2	94.5
1934	21 0	12 6	152	90.0	90.0
1935	21 3	12 3	156	88.7	86.7
1936	21 9	12 11	159	89.1	87.8
1937	22 0	13 1	170	84.2	85.4
1938	27 3	16 0	173	102.5	102.9
1939	27 6		173	103.8	

Source: *Statistical Abstract*; *Irisleabhar Trádáil na hÉireann*, May 1930, 116–17.

Table 17.5. *Wages per week in Dublin 1926, 1931, and 1938 (in shillings)*

Category	1926	1931	1938
Bricklayers, masons	90	86	94
Painters	86	82	90
Carpenters	91	84	92
Compositors	55.6	55	62.7
Cabinet-makers	91	88	90
Fitters	75	75	81.2
Labourers (engineering)	55.2	56	61.4
Labourers (building)	64	60	68
Labourers (printing)	84	84	94.9

Table 17.6. *Wages for unskilled work in Irish and English cities, 1931–1938* (pence per hour)

	Local authority labourers		Building labourers		Labourers (electrical)	
	1931	1938	1931	1938	1931	1938
Cork	13.75	15.96	13.50	16.00	—	15.50
Dublin	16.00	17.45	15.00	17.00	12.00	17.18
Dundalk	12.75	12.58	10.50	13.50	—	12.50
London	16.00	15.72	15.00	15.75	15.75	17.00
Manchester	13.00	13.96	14.00	14.75	13.25	14.89

Source: See text.

urban and rural unskilled workers' pay in Ireland. The gap is already present in the wage data gathered in 1923 by the Fiscal Inquiry Committee, which indicate that it emerged during the First World War. Those data reveal that, as in Britain, the wages of unskilled workers, men and women, rose more than those of skilled workers after 1914. They also imply, remarkably, that unskilled labourers in Dundalk, a small town, earned nearly twice as much as farm labourers in the 1930s.[42]

Was the Irish advantage merely a reflection of poorer employment prospects in Ireland? Would adjustment for differences in social welfare regimes, taxation, and purchasing power redress the balance? Only further detailed research can tell. Meanwhile the data imply that those workers who continued to migrate in numbers to Britain in the 1920s and 1930s were likely to have been 'outsiders' from the countryside, unable to break into market for blue-collar jobs in the cities and towns.[43] The data also explain why industrialists seeking tariff protection complained about high labour costs, and help to account for the failure of Irish wages to rise like British in the 1930s: British wages had some catching up to do! So did wages in Northern Ireland, which also fell behind after 1914.

The widening gap between Irish and British unemployment rates in the 1980s and early 1990s is frequently commented on. Consistent, comparable data are unavailable for the 1920s and 1930s. Irish Free State unemployment statistics are notoriously difficult to interpret, since legislative changes affected the numbers far more than did real factors. According to the author of a minority report to the Banking Commission Report of 1938, 'it is a matter of regret that the figures relating to unemployment before the later months of 1932 are worthless, while, owing to the operation of a series of Unemployment Period Orders, under which certain classes are not registered during the summer months, the figures since 1935 are by no means complete.' When the visiting Swedish expert, Per Jacobsson, tried to make sense of the trend in Irish unemployment in December 1934, he was soon disabused by R. C. Geary: 'Long talk in the afternoon with Geary of the Statistics Office . . . I asked him about unemployment. He said the so-called Unemployment Assistance Act (1933) ought to have been called Distress Relief Act. The real employment is up by 24,000 as compared with last year.' The following account from Dundalk in July 1934 is symptomatic:[44]

An increase of 150 in the live register was due, in addition to the operation of the Unemployment Assistant Act, to the fact that the bus repair depot of the Great Northern Railway Company closed down temporarily and also to the fact that a number of women and juveniles registered in anticipation of work at the local boot factories.

The erratic movements in the numbers of registered unemployed at the end of each year were thus the joint product of cyclical trends, unemployment insurance, and a perverse 'encouraged worker' phenomenon. Comparing the returns of people out of work in the 1926 and 1936 census reports suggests that unemployment rose from 6.0 per cent of the labour force in 1926 to 7.1 per cent in 1936. The census also suggests a significant rise in long-term unemployment (Table 17.7). Given the more generous unemploy-

Table 17.7. *Unemployment > 1 year as a percentage of total unemployment*

Area	1926		1936	
	Male	Female	Male	Female
Dublin City	38.2	32.9	52.9	34.2
Dublin suburbs	34.0	25.4	46.3	39.1
Cork City	46.7	36.3	57.8	45.7
Limerick City	44.9	39.6	46.4	43.2
Waterford City	35.3	22.6	46.4	34.1
Other towns > 1,500				
Leinster	34.6	27.6	34.3	33.9
Munster	33.7	23.2	37.0	35.2
Connacht	26.7	17.0	26.6	26.0
Ulster	25.5	24.1	27.7	38.5
Rural				
Leinster	18.8	16.7	22.5	21.5
Munster	16.7	15.5	21.8	25.1
Connacht	13.0	15.8	15.8	17.9
Ulster	13.4	14.2	17.8	25.5
TOTAL	27.8	25.4	33.9	31.1

ment assistance regime introduced by Fianna Fáil, the rise probably reflects a shift in supply rather than demand in the interim. The answers given by employees to a special query in the 1936 census (Table 17.8) provide yet another perspective on the incidence and duration of unemployment in the previous years, though it must be said that the mean duration given seems too short to be credible. In sum, our information on unemployment is currently too confused and contradictory to warrant inferences about living standards.

Other proxies for living standards, ranging from life expectancy and nutrition to cinema admissions or attendance at big sporting events, imply slow but steady improvement both North and South. The average lifespan in the South rose from 57.7 years in 1926 to 58.9 years a decade later, and in the North from 55.7 to 58.5 years.[45] Though there was no overall improvement in infant mortality, the rate in urban areas declined during the 1920s and 1930s. So did the death-rate from tuberculosis. Numbers receiving second- and third-level schooling, another barometer of living

Table 17.8. *Extent and duration of unemployment in 1936*

	No. of employees out of work	Percent replying	Percent never out of work	Estimated av. duration of unemployment
Irish Free State	210 383	65.6	87.0	3.2 weeks
Dublin area	74 029	76.7	90.0	2.5 weeks
Rest of Leinster	46 388	57.6	86.2	3.1 weeks
All Leinster	120 417	69.2	88.8	2.7 weeks
Munster	59 714	62.0	83.8	4.0 weeks
Connacht	17 662	53.9	86.3	3.3 weeks
Ulster	12 590	64.3	84.0	2.8 weeks

Source: *1936 Census*, vi. 126–7.

standards, rose. A further popular proxy for the trend in living standards is motor vehicle ownership, where again comparing Northern and Free State data provides some perspective. Between 1923 and 1932 car ownership rocketed in both the South (286 per cent) and the North (245 per cent); but between 1932 and 1939 the rise in the South was only 47 per cent, that in the North 99 per cent. The implication of greater progress in the North is probably valid, if tempered by one important consideration: the imposition of a heavy tariff on cars in 1932 increased the price of cars in the South relative to the North.

Such improvements failed to obliterate poverty. Deeny's pioneering studies of the nutritional status of Lurgan linen-workers in 1938–9 painted a very bleak picture of conditions in the industrial North. His analysis (with Harold Booker) of 202 male weavers 'typical of many linen workers in Northern Ireland' found 54 per cent of them clinically malnourished; his female sample of 205 fared even worse at 58 per cent. In confirmation, the average BMI of the entire male sample was 20.3, and that of the under-nourished sub-sample 19.5, against a recommended level of 26 (see Chapter 10). The low average height of the men in Deeny's sample (66.5 inches with their boots or shoes on) is also worth noting.[46]

Housing conditions also improved in this period. In the early twentieth century Ireland still contained some of the worst slums in Europe. The situation in Dublin was particularly bad, though something had been achieved before 1921 by philanthropy and the municipal corporation. Table 17.9 shows Cumann na nGaedheal in the 1920s marking time, but one of

Table 17.9. *Houses built under State-aided schemes, 1922–1939*

	(a) Private persons and public utility societies, no. of rooms			(b) Local authorities, no. of rooms				Total
	3	4	5	2	3	4	5	
1923–4	*	*	*	30	—	30	404	*
1924–5	26	112	374	—	8	199	748	1 467
1925–6	103	529	1 672	—	82	95	900	3 381
1926–7	126	632	1 710	67	185	64	927	3 711
1927–8	97	359	1 283	—	28	330	27	2 124
1928–9	117	431	1 489	—	156	359	181	2 733
1929–30	150	466	1 743	24	75	831	135	3 424
1930–1	250	598	1 408	—	35	716	8	3 015
1931–2	437	922	2 130	75	52	1 518	87	5 221
1932–3	86	189	729	56	71	1 047	3	2 181
1933–4	340	789	2 309	33	1 331	2 134	22	6 958
1934–5	1 031	1 740	3 748	84	1 490	5 106	54	13 253
1935–6	1 597	2 139	4 303	36	1 481	4 552	176	14 284
1936–7	1 786	2 216	4 268	164	1 125	4 742	63	14 364
1937–8	2 388	2 975	4 044	43	432	4 371	44	14 297
1938–9	2 135	3 082	4 868	340	806	5 601	185	17 017

Source: Compiled from *Statistical Abstract*, various years.

the most impressive of Fianna Fáil's achievements in the 1930s was in housing.[47] The new housing estates such as Crumlin and Cabra in Dublin and Gurranabrahar in Cork marked a big improvement on the inner-city slums such as Dorset Street and The Marsh. The following description of one family unwilling to move captures the worst of what the others left behind:[48]

Mrs X, aged 34, on her 13th confinement was found to be living with her husband and ten children in one small room which was nearly completely filled by a double bed. Mr X got casual work as a Dock Labourer earning about 30/— per week. The eldest son earned 10/— per week as a messenger, and the Society of St Vincent de Paul was giving a small weekly allowance. Two of the children had recently returned from a sanatorium, and the patient had chronic nephritis. It was hopeless for the mother to regain her health in such surroundings; consequently she was supplied with suitable nourishment from the Samaritan Fund until she was strong enough to be transferred to a Convalescent Home, and given clothes for herself and the baby, who was cared for by relatives. On investigation it proved impossible to get this family better housing accommodation as they had repeatedly refused to move to one of the new housing estates on the outskirts of the City because of the distance from the Docks; and so, like many others, they are waiting for one of the new flats in the centre of the City.

The Free State also acquired some of the trappings of a proto-welfare State. Cumann na nGaedheal affected a flintier attitude to social welfare— its Finance Minister Blythe cut the old-age pension in 1924, and Industry and Commerce Minister McGilligan told the Dáil in the same year that 'it is no function of Government to provide work for anyone . . . people may have to die in this country and die through starvation'.[49] Fianna Fáil's more progressive stance, which included improved old-age pensions and a small farmers' dole, may not have saved lives, but it provided modest welfare cushions for the poor and won popular support. Though Fianna Fáil had been the target of a frantic 'red scare' campaign from Cumann na nGaed- heal in 1932, the true effect of its policies was to 'blunt the appeal of political extremism'. In Dublin Fianna Fáil became the party of the working class.[50]

APPENDIX 17.1

Irish and British Bond Prices in 1930–1932

The series selected for analysis were UK Victory Bonds (4 per cent), and Irish Second National Loan (5 per cent), and Irish Third National Loan (4.5 per cent). The British series is the average weekly price quoted in the *Stock Exchange Weekly Intelligencer*; for the Irish data, each Wednesday's official price (or next day's price if there was no quotation on Wednesday) as reported in the *Irish Times* was chosen. The first two series cover the full three years (157 observations), the Irish Third Loan the period from mid-June 1930. The unit root hypothesis could not be rejected in the case of any of the series. However, the standard Sargan–Bhargava and Augmented Dickey–Fuller tests for co-integration reject the hypothesis that Irish (*Irish2* and *Irish3*) and British (*UK*) series are co-integrated. The results of the Sargan–Bhargava DW tests were as follows:

Regression	DW	Regression	DW
Irish2 on *UK*	0.228	*UK* on *Irish2*	0.146
Irish3 on *UK*	0.137	*UK* on *Irish3*	0.803
Irish3 on *Irish2*	0.912	*Irish2* on *Irish3*	0.982

(*Note*: Critical values for DW ($n = 100$) are 0.511 (1%), 0.386 (5%), and 0.322 (10%))

The 'break' in the gap between *Irish2* and *UKAV* was identified by choosing the specification of a (0, 1) dummy variable that added most explanatory power to a regression of *Irish2* on *UK*, a constant and a time-trend. Changing the value of the dummy variable from 0 to 1 at the very beginning of 1932 produced the best result. This suggests that investors (like many commentators) had anticipated a Fianna Fáil victory by then, and discounted bond prices accordingly.

BIBLIOGRAPHY

The items included here bear directly on Irish economic history. The reason for the bibliography is twofold. First, it may help those interested in further reading and study. Second, many of the listed items are frequently cited throughout the book. In the interest of saving space, such items are allowed only an abbreviated reference in the text. Full references are given in the text to primary source material and to cited works not listed in this bibliography.

Published works

Key to journals cited below and in the text:

AgHR	*Agricultural History Review*
DHR	*Dublin Historical Record*
EHR	*Economic History Review* (2nd series)
DHR	*Dublin Historical Record*
ESR	*Economic & Social Review*
EEH	*Explorations in Economic History*
EJ	*Economic Journal*
IESH	*Irish Economic & Social History*
IG	*Irish Geography*
IHS	*Irish Historical Studies*
IT	*Irish Times*
JCHAS	*Journal of the Cork Historical & Archaeological Society*
JDSS	*Journal of the Dublin Statistical Society*
JEH	*Journal of Economic History*
JEEH	*Journal of European Economic History*
JIH	*Journal of Interdisciplinary History*
JIBI	*Journal of the Institute of Bankers of Ireland*
JKAHS	*Journal of the Kerry Archaeological & Historical Society*
JPE	*Journal of Political Economy*
LTD	*Samuel Lewis, Topographical Dictionary of Ireland*
NHI	*New History of Ireland*
OSMI	*Ordnance Survey Memoirs of Ireland*
OEP	*Oxford Economic Papers*
PDDE	*Parliamentary Debates Dáil Éireann*
PS	*Population Studies*
PRIA	*Proceedings of the Royal Irish Academy*
RSAIJ	*Royal Society of Antiquaries of Ireland Journal*
SH	*Studia Hibernica*

Aalen, F. H. A. (1992). 'Health and Housing in Dublin *c*.1850–1921', in Aalen and Whelan (1992), 279–304.

Aalen, F. H. A., and Kevin Whelan (eds.) (1992). *Dublin City and County: From Prehistory to Present*, Dublin: Geography Publications.

Adams, William F. (1932). *Ireland and Irish Emigration to the New World from 1815 to the Famine*, New Haven, Conn.: Yale UP.

Akenson, Donald H. (1981). *A Protestant in Purgatory: Richard Whately Archbishop of Dublin*, Hamden, Conn.: Archon Books.

——— (1988). *Small Differences: Irish Catholics and Irish Protestants, 1815–1922, An International Perspective*, Kingston and Montreal: McGill-Queen's UP.

Alison, William Pulteney (1847). *Observations on the Famine of 1847 in the Highlands of Scotland and in Ireland, as Illustrating the Connection of the Principle of Population with the Management of the Poor*, London: Blackwood.

Allen R. C., and C. Ó Gráda (1988). 'On the Road Again with Arthur Young: English, Irish and Scottish Agriculture During the Industrial Revolution', *JEH*, 48/1: 93–166.

Anderson, Ernest (1951). *Sailing Ships of Ireland: A Book for Lovers of Sail, being a Record of Irish Sailing Ships of the Nineteenth Century*, Dublin: Morris.

Anderson, Michael (1988). *Population Change in Northwestern Europe 1700–1850*, London: Macmillan.

Andrews, J. H. (1964). 'Road Planning in Ireland Before the Railway Age', *IG*, 5/1: 17–41.

Anon. (1805). *Considerations on the Silver Currency, relative to Both the General Evil Affecting the Empire, and the Present Enormous Evil in Ireland*, Dublin: Miliken.

Arensberg, C., and S. Kimball (1965). *Family and Community in Ireland*, Cambridge, Mass.: Harvard UP.

Armstrong, David L. (1989). *An Economic History of Agriculture in Northern Ireland 1850–1900*, Oxford: Plunkett Foundation.

Barrington, R. (1887). 'The Prices of Some Agricultural Produce and the Cost of Farm Labour for the Past Fifty Years', *JSSISI*, 9: 137–53.

Barrow, G. L. S. (1970). 'Justice for Thomas Mooney', *DHR*, 24/1: 173–88.

——— (1972). 'Some Dublin Private Banks', *DHR*, 25/2: 38–53.

——— (1975). *The Emergence of the Irish Banking System 1820–1845*, Dublin, Gill & Macmillan.

Barry, Colm (1941–2). 'Irish Regional Life Tables', *JSSISI*, 16: 1–13.

Bell, Jonathan, and Mervyn Watson (1986). *Irish Farming 1750–1900*, Edinburgh: Donald.

Bielenberg, Andy (1991*a*). *Cork's Industrial Revolution 1780–1880*, Cork: Cork University Press.

——— (1991*b*). 'The History of Lockes Distillery Kilbeggan 1757–1958', mimeo.

——— (1992). 'The Growth and Decline of a Textile Town: Bandon 1770–1840', *JCHAS*, 97: 111–19.

Black, R. D. C. (1949–50). 'Theory and Policy in Anglo-Irish Trade Relations, 1775–1800', *JSSISI*, 18: 312–24.

——— (1957*a*). 'William James Pirrie', *Threshold*, 1/1: 58–67.

——— (1957*b*). 'Irish History and the Great Famine', *Threshold*, 1/2: 51–9.

——— (1960). *Economic Thought and the Irish Question 1817–1870*, Cambridge: Cambridge University Press.

—— (1969). *A Catalogue of Pamphlets on Irish Economic Subjects 1750–1900 in Irish Libraries*, Belfast: Queen's University Press.

Bourke, Austin (1993). *The Visitation of God?*, Dublin: Lilliput.

Bourke, Joanna (1987). 'Women and Poultry in Ireland, 1891–1914', *IHS* 25/99: 293–310.

Bourke, P. M. A. (1964). 'The Emergence of Potato Blight, 1843–6', *Nature*, 203: 805–8.

—— (1965). 'The Agricultural Statistics of the 1841 Census of Ireland: A Critical Review', *EHR*, 18/2: 376–91.

—— (1968). 'The Use of the Potato in the Pre-famine Ireland', *JSSISI*, 12/6: 72–96.

—— (1969). 'The Average Yields of Food Crops in Ireland on the Eve of the Famine', *Journal of the Department of Agriculture*, 66: 3–16.

Boylan, T. A., and T. P. Foley (1992). *Political Economy and Colonial Ireland: The Propagation and Ideological Function of Economic Discourse in the Nineteenth Century*, London: Routledge.

Boyle, Emily (1976). 'The Linen Strike of 1872', *Saothar*, 2: 12–21.

Boyle, Phelim P., and C. Ó Gráda (1986). 'Fertility Trends, Excess Mortality, and the Great Irish Famine', *Demography*, 23: 543–62.

Brunicardi, Niall (1987). *John Anderson Entrepreneur*, Fermoy: Éigse Books.

Budd, John W., and Timothy Guinnane (1991). 'Intentional Age-Misreporting, Age-Heaping and the 1908 Old Age Pensions Act in Ireland', *PS*, 45: 497–518.

Burke, Helen (1987). *The People and the Poor Law in Nineteenth-Century Ireland*, Littlehampton, Sussex: Women's Education Bureau.

Burton, W. G. (1989). *The Potato*, 3rd edn. London: Longman.

Cameron, Charles (1908). *How the Poor Live*, Dublin: Figgis.

Cameron, Wendy (1976). 'Selecting Peter Robinson's Emigrants', *Social History/ Histoire Sociale*, 9: 29–46.

Campbell, B. M. S., and M. Overton (eds.) (1991). *Land, Labour and Livestock: Historical Studies in European Agricultural Productivity*, Manchester: Manchester University Press.

Canning, Paul (1985). *British Foreign Policy towards Ireland*, Oxford: Oxford University Press.

Clark, Gregory, and C. Ó Gráda (1991). 'Cheap Labour and Irish Industrialization', mimeo.

Clarkson, Leslie A. (1981). 'Irish Population Revisited, 1687–1821', in Goldstrom and Clarkson (1981), 13–36.

—— (1987). 'The Demography of Carrick-on-Suir 1799', *PRIA*, 87C: 13–36.

—— (1989). 'The Carrick-on-Suir Woollen Industry in the Eighteenth Century', *IESH*, 16: 23–41.

—— and E. Margaret Crawford (1988). 'Dietary Directions: A Topographical Survey of Irish Diet, 1836', in Mitchism and Roebuck (1988), 171–92.

Coe, W. E. (1969). *The Engineering Industry of Northern Ireland*, Newton Abbot: David & Charles.

Cohen, Marilyn (1990). 'Peasant Differentiation and Proto-Industrialisation in the

Ulster Countryside: Tullylish 1690–1825', *Journal of Peasant Studies*, 17/3: 413–32.

Colby, William (1837). *Ordnance Survey of the County Londonderry*, 1, Dublin: Hodges and Smith.

Collins, B. (1988). 'Sewing and Social Structure: The Flowerers of Scotland and Ireland', in Mitchison and Roebuck (1988), 242–54.

—— (1991). 'The Organisation of Sewing Outwork in Late Nineteenth Century Ulster', in Maxine Berg (ed.), *Markets and Manufactures in Early Industrial Europe*, London: Routledge, 139–56.

Commission of Inquiry into Banking, Currency and Credit (1938). *Reports*, Dublin: Foillseacháin Rialtais.

Connell, K. H. (1950). *The Population of Ireland 1750–1845*, Oxford: Oxford University Press.

—— (1967). *Irish Peasant Society*, Oxford: Oxford University Press.

Connolly, Sean (1982). 'Religion, Work-discipline and Economic Attitudes: The Case of Ireland', in Devine and Dickson (1983), 235–45.

—— R. A. Houston, and R. J. Morris (1994). *Conflict, Identity and Economic Development: Ireland and Scotland 1600–1939*, Edinburgh: Donald.

Coulter, Henry (1862). *The West of Ireland: Its Existing Condition and Prospects*, Dublin: Hodges & Smith.

Cousens, S. H. (1963). 'The Regional Variation in Mortality During the Great Irish Famine', *PRIA*, 63C: 127–49.

Crawford, E. M. (1984). 'Dearth, Diet and Disease in Ireland: A Case Study of Nutritional Deficiency', *Medical History*, 28: 151–61.

—— (ed.) (1989). *Famine, the Irish Experience 900–1900: Subsistence Crises and Famine in Ireland*, Edinburgh: Donald.

—— (1991). 'Epidemic Diseases in the Great Famine of Ireland 1845–50', mimeo.

Crawford, W. H. (1972). *Domestic Industry in Ireland: The Experience of the Linen Industry*, Dublin: Gill & Macmillan.

—— (1975). 'Landlord-Tenant Relations in Ulster, 1609–1820', *IESH*, 2: 5–21.

—— (1988). 'The Evolution of the Linen Trade in Ulster before Industrialisation', *IESH*, 15: 32–53.

Crotty, Raymond D. (1966). *Irish Agricultural Production*, Cork: Cork University Press.

Cullen, L. M. (1967). 'Problems of the Interpretation and Revision of Eighteenth Century Irish History', *Transactions of the Royal Historical Society*, 5th ser., 17.

—— (1968a). *Anglo-Irish Trade 1660–1800*, Manchester: Manchester University Press.

—— (1968b). 'Irish History Without the Potato', *Past and Present*, 40: 72–83.

—— (ed.) (1969). *The Formation of the Irish Economy*, Cork: Mercier.

—— (1972). *An Economic History of Ireland from 1660*, London: Batsford.

—— (1977). 'Eighteenth-Century Flour Milling in Ireland', *IESH*, 4: 5–25.

—— (1979). 'Germination and Growth' in Share (1979), 23–60.

—— (1981). *The Emergence of Modern Ireland*, London: Batsford.

—— (ed.) (1984). 'Landlords, Bankers and Merchants: The Early Irish Banking World, 1700–1820', in Murphy (1984), 25–44.

—— (1988). *Easons: A History*, Dublin: Eason.

—— (1992). 'The Growth of Dublin 1600–1900: Character and Heritage', in Aalen and Whelan (1992), 257–77.

—— and F. Furet (eds.) (1982). *France et Irlande*, Paris: Éditions de l'EHESS.

—— and T. C. Smout (eds.) (1978). *Comparative Aspects of Scottish and Irish Social and Economic History 1660–1900*, Edinburgh: Donald.

Daly, Mary E. (1982). 'Social Structure of the Dublin Working Class', *IHS*, 23/90: 121–34.

—— (1984a). 'An Irish-Ireland for Business: The Control of Manufactures Acts 1932–4', *IHS*, 24/94: 246–72.

—— (1984b). 'Government Finance for Industry in the Irish Free State: The Trade Loans (Guarantee) Acts', *IESH*, 11: 73–93.

—— (1984c). *Deposed Capital: An Economic History of Dublin 1860–1913*, Cork: Cork University Press.

—— (1986). *The Great Famine in Ireland*, Dundalk: Dublin Historical Association.

—— and D. Dickson (eds.), (1990). *The Origins of Popular Literacy in Ireland: Language Change and Educational Development 1700–1920*, Dublin: Dept. of Modern History, TCD.

Daniel, T. K. (1976). 'Griffith on his Noble Head: The Determinants of Cumann na nGaedheal Economic Policy, 1922–32', *IESH*, 3: 55–65.

D'Arcy, Fergus (1989). 'Wages of Labourers in the Dublin Building Industry, 1667–1918', *Saothar*, 14: 17–34.

Daultrey, S.-G., David Dickson, and C. Ó Gráda (1981). 'Eighteenth-Century Irish Population: New Speculations from Old Sources', *JEH*, 52/3: 601–28.

Davis, Ralph (1979). *The Industrial Revolution and British Overseas Trade*, Leicester: Leicester University Press.

Day, Angelique, and Patrick McWilliams (1990–). *Ordnance Survey Memoirs of Ireland*, Belfast: Institute of Irish Studies.

De Courcy Ireland, John (1981). *Ireland's Sea Fisheries: A History*, Dublin: Glendale.

Deeny, J. (1939–40). 'Poverty as a Cause of Ill-health', *JSSISI*, 16, 75–84.

—— (1989). *To Cure and to Care: Memoirs of a Chief Medical Officer*, Dublin: Glendale Press.

—— and H. S. Booker (1939). 'Clinical and Social Survey of Male Linen Weavers', *British Medical Journal*, 1: 267–78.

Delany, Ruth (1973). *The Grand Canal of Ireland*, Newton Abbot: David & Charles.

—— (1986). *A Celebration of 250 Years of Ireland's Inland Waterways*, Belfast: Appletree Press.

Delany, V. T. H., and R. Delany (1966). *The Canals of the South of Ireland*, Newton Abbot: David & Charles.

Devine, Tom (1993). 'Why the Highlands Did Not Starve', in Connolly, Houston, and Morris (1993).

Devine, Tom, and David Dickson (eds.) (1983). *Ireland and Scotland: Parallels and Contrasts in Economic and Social Development*, Edinburgh: Donald.

Dickson, D. (1977). 'Aspects of the Rise and Decline of the Irish Cotton Industry', in Cullen and Smout (1978), 100–15.

—— (1979). 'Middlemen', in T. Bartlett and D. Hayton (eds.), *Penal Era and Golden Age*, Belfast: Ulster Historical Foundation, 162–85.

—— (1986). *New Foundations Ireland 1660–1800*, Dublin: Helicon.

—— (ed.) (1987). *The Gorgeous Mask: Dublin 1700–1850*, Dublin: TCD History Workshop.

—— 'Catholics and Trade in Eighteenth-Century Ireland: An Old Debate re-visited', in T. Power and K. Whelan (eds.), *Endurance and Emergence: Catholics in Ireland in the Eighteenth Century*, Dublin: Irish Academic Press, 85–100.

—— (1991). 'No Scythians Here: Women and Marriage in Seventeenth-Century Ireland', in M. McCurtain and M. O'Dowd (eds.), *Women in Early Modern Ireland*, Edinburgh: Edinburgh University Press.

—— C. Ó Gráda, and S. Daultrey (1982), 'Hearth Tax, Household Size and Irish Population Change 1672–1821', *PRIA*, 82C: 125–81.

Donnelly, J. S. (1975). *The Land and the People of Nineteenth-Century Cork*, London: Routledge & Kegan Paul.

—— (1988*a*). 'The Great Famine 1845–52', in Vaughan (1988), v. 272–371.

—— (1988*b*). 'The Kenmare Estates During the Nineteenth Century', *JKHAS*, 21 (1988), 5–41.

'Doyle, Martin' (1831). *An Address to the Landlords of Ireland*, Dublin: William Curry.

—— (1846). *The Labouring Classes in Ireland: An Inquiry as to What Beneficial Changes May be Effected in Their Condition*, Dublin: McGlashan.

Dublin Mansion House Relief Committee (1881). *The Irish Crisis of 1879–80*, Dublin: Browne & Nolan.

Dubourdieu, John (1812). *Statistical Survey of the County of Antrim*, Dublin: Graisberry & Campbell.

Duncan, G. A. (1939–40). 'The Social Income of the Irish Free State 1926–38', *JSSISI*, 16.

—— (1940–1). 'The Social Income of Éire 1938–40', *JSSISI*, 16.

Dwyer, Gerard, and C. Lindsay (1984). 'Robert Giffen and the Irish Potato', *American Economic Review*, 74: 188–92.

Edwards R. D., and T. D. Williams (eds.) (1956). *The Great Famine: Studies in Irish History*, Dublin: Browne & Nolan.

Elliott, Bruce (1988). *Irish Migrants in the Canadas: A New Approach*, Kingston and Montreal: McGill-Queen's University Press.

Eversley, David (1981), 'The Demography of the Irish Quakers, 1650–1850', in Goldstrom and Clarkson (1981), 57–88.

Fanning, Ronan (1978). *The Department of Finance*, Dublin: Institute of Public Administration.

—— (1983*a*). 'Economists and Governments: Ireland 1922–52', in Murphy (1984), 138–156.

—— (1983*b*). *Independent Ireland*, Dublin: Helicon.

Feingold, William L. (1984). *The Revolt of the Tenantry: The Transformation of Local Government in Ireland, 1872–1886*, Boston: Northeastern University Press.

Fetter, F. W. (1955). *The Irish Pound*, London: Allen & Unwin.

—— (1959). 'The Politics of the Bullion Report', *Economica*, 26: 99–120.

—— (1965). *The Development of British Monetary Orthodoxy 1797–1875*, Cambridge, Mass.: Harvard University Press.

Fitzgerald, Garret (1959). 'Mr Whitaker and Industry', *Studies*, 48: 138–50.

Fitzpatrick, David (1980). 'The Disappearance of the Irish Agricultural Labourer', *IESH*, 7: 66–92.

—— (1984*a*). *Irish Emigration 1820–1914*, Dublin: Irish Economic and Social History Society.

—— (1984*b*). 'Irish Farming Families Before the First World War', *Comparative Studies in History and Society*, 25: 339–74.

—— (1986). 'Marriage since the Famine', in Art Cosgrove (ed.), *Marriage in Ireland*, Dublin: College Press.

—— (1992). 'Famine, Entitlements and Seduction in Ireland, 1846–1851', mimeo.

Floud, R., K. W. Wachter, and A. Gregory (1990). *Height, Health and History: Nutritional Status in the United Kingdom, 1750–1980*, Cambridge: Cambridge University Press.

Freeman, T. W. (1956). *Pre-Famine Ireland: A Study in Human Geography*, Manchestor: Manchestor University Press.

French, E. A. (1990). 'The Origin of General Limited Liability in the United Kingdom', *Accounting and Business Research*, 21/18: 15–34.

Geary, Frank (1981). 'The Rise and Fall of the Belfast Cotton Industry: Some Problems', *IESH*, 8: 30–49.

—— (1989). 'The Belfast Cotton Industry Revisited', *IHS*, 26: 250–67.

—— (1992). 'The Act of Union, British-Irish Trade, and Pre-Famine Industrialisation in Ireland', TS, University of Ulster.

Geary, Laurence M. (1986). *The Plan of Campaign 1886–91*, Cork: Cork University Press.

Geary, R. C. (1951). 'Irish Economic Development since the Treaty', *Studies*, 50.

Gillmor, Desmond (1989). 'The Political Factor in Agricultural History: Trends in Irish Agriculture 1922–85', *AgHR*, 37/2: 166–79.

Goldstrom, Max, and L. A. Clarkson (eds.) (1981). *Irish Population, Economy and Society: Essays in Memory of K. H. Connell*, Oxford: Oxford University Press.

Grant, James (1990). 'The Great Famine and the Poor Law in the Province of Ulster: The Rate-in-Aid Issue of 1849', *IHS*, 27: 30–47.

Gray, Peter (1992). 'Potatoes and Providence: British Government Responses to the Great Famine', TS.

Green, E. R. R. (1949). *The Lagan Valley 1800–50: A Local History of the Industrial Revolution*, London: Faber & Faber.

—— (1957). 'James Murland and the Linen Industry', *Threshold*, 1/3: 48–53.

—— (1963). *The Industrial Archaeology of County Down*, Belfast: HMSO.

Green, E. R. R. (1971). 'History of the Belfast Grain Trade', *Proceedings of the Belfast Natural History and Philosophical Society*, 2nd ser., 8: 38–47.

Gribbon, H. D. (1969). *The History of Water Power in Ulster*, Newton Abbot: David & Charles.

Guinnane, Timothy (1990). 'Coming of Age in Rural Ireland at the Turn of the Twentieth Century', *Continuity and Change*, 5/3: 443–72.

—— (1991*a*). 'Rethinking the Western European Marriage Pattern: The Decision to Marry in Ireland at the Turn of the Twentieth Century', *Journal of Family History*, 16/1: 47–64.

—— (1991*b*). 'Economics, History, and the Path of Demographic Adjustment', *Research in Economic History*, 13: 147–198.

—— (1992*a*). 'Age at Leaving Home in Rural Ireland, 1901–1011', *JEH*, 52: 651–74.

—— (1992*b*). 'Inter-generational Transfers, Emigration and the Rural Irish Household System', *EEH*, 29/4: 456–76.

—— and R. I. Miller (1992). 'Bonds without Bondsmen: Tenant-Right in Nineteenth Century Ireland', mimeo, Princeton University.

Hall, F. (1949). *The Bank of Ireland 1783–1946*, Hodges Figgis: Dublin.

Hall, S. C., and Mrs A. M. Hall (1845). *Ireland, Its Scenery, Character*, London: How & Parsons.

Hannigan, Ken (1992). 'Wicklow in the Famine Years', *Wicklow Historical Journal*, 1/5, 37–56.

Harrison, Henry (1934). *The Anglo-Irish Economics War of 1932–1934. The Game of Beggar-My-Neighbour: Who Wins?*, London: Irish News and Information Bureau.

Hayes, Samuel (1797). *Essays in Answer to All the Queries on the Culture of Potatoes*, Dublin: Sleator.

Hill, Jacqueline R. (1981). 'Artisans, Sectarianism and Politics in Dublin, 1829–48', *Saothar*, 7: 12–27.

Hochberg, Leonard, and David W. Miller (1990). 'Peelers and Peddlers: Spatial Hierarchies in Pre-Famine Ireland', paper delivered at ACIS annual meetings, Madison, 13 Apr. 1991.

Hoffman, Elizabeth, and Joel Mokyr (1983). 'Peasants, Poverty, and Potatoes: Transactions Costs in Prefamine Ireland', in G. Saxonhouse and G. Wright (eds.), *Technique, Spirit and Form in the Making of the Modern Economy: Essays in Honour of William N. Parker*, Greenwich, Conn.: Greenwood Press.

Hoppen, K. T. (1984). *Elections, Politics, and Society*, Oxford: Oxford University Press.

—— (1989). *Ireland since 1800: Conflict and Conformity*, London: Longman.

Horner, Arnold (1992). 'From City to City-region – Dublin from the 1930s to the 1990s', in Aalen and Whelan (1992), 327–58.

Horner, John (1920). *The Linen Trade of Europe during the Spinning-Wheel Period*, Belfast: M'Caw, Stevenson & Orr.

Hynes, Eugene (1978). 'The Great Hunger and Irish Catholicism', *Societas*, 8: 137–56.

Irish University Press, British Parliamentary Papers, 'Famine' Series (8 vols.), Shannon, Ireland: Irish University Press.

Jameson, J., *et al.* (1878). *Truths about Whisky*, London: Sutton Sharpe.

Johnson, David (1979). 'Cattle Smuggling on the Irish Border 1932–8', *IESH*, 6: 41–63.

—— and Liam Kennedy (1991). 'Nationalist Historiography and the Decline of the Irish Economy: George O'Brien Revisited', in Sean Hutton and Paul Stewart (eds.), *Ireland's Histories: Aspects of State, Society and Ideology*, London: Routledge.

Johnson, James H. (1988). 'The Distribution of Irish Emigration in the Decades Before the Great Famine', *IG*, 21: 78–87.

Johnston, Joseph (1934). *The Nemesis of Economic Nationalism*, Dublin: P. S. King.

—— (1937). 'Price Ratios in Recent Irish Agricultural Experience', *Economic Journal*, 47: 680–5.

—— (1951). *Irish Agriculture in Transition*, Dublin: Hodges Figgis.

Kee, Robert (1981). *Ireland: A History*, London: Weidenfeld & Nicholson.

Kennedy, K. A. (1971). *Productivity and Industrial Growth: The Irish Experience*, Oxford: Oxford University Press.

—— T. Giblin, and D. McHugh (1988). *The Economic Development of Ireland in the Twentieth Century*, London: Routledge.

Kennedy, Liam (1978). 'Retail Markets in Rural Ireland at the End of the Nineteenth Century', *IESH*, 5: 46–63.

—— (1981). 'Regional Specialization, Railway Development, and Irish Agriculture in the Late Nineteenth Century', in Goldstrom & Clarkson (1981), 173–94.

—— (1983). 'Studies in Irish Econometric History', *IHS*, 23/91: 193–213.

—— (1991). 'Farm Succession in Modern Ireland: Elements of a Theory of Inheritance', *EHR*, 44/3: 477–99.

—— and P. Ollerenshaw (eds.) (1985). *An Economic History of Ulster 1820–1939*, Manchester: Manchester University Press.

Kennedy, R. E. (1973). *The Irish: Emigration, Marriage, and Fertility*, Berkeley, Calif.: University of California Press.

Keynes, J. M. (1933). 'National Self-sufficiency', *Studies*, 22: 177–93.

Kiernan, T. J. (1927). 'The Irish Free State Tariff on Footwear', *EJ*, 37: 312–17.

—— (1930). *History of the Financial Administration of Ireland to 1817*, London: King.

King, Lord (1803). *Thoughts on the Restriction of Payments in Specie at the Banks of England and Ireland*, London: Cadell & Davies.

Kohl, J. G. (1844). *Travels in Ireland*, London: Bruce & Wyld.

Komlos, John (1992). 'The Secular Trend in Nutritional Status of the Population of the United Kingdom, 1730–1860', TS.

Lee, Joseph J. (1971). 'The Dual Economy in Ireland 1800–50', *Historical Studies*, 8: 191–201.

Lee, J. (1982). 'Patterns of Rural Unrest in Nineteenth-century Ireland: A Preliminary Survey', in Cullen and Furet (1982), 223–37.

—— (1973). *The Modernisation of Irish Society 1848–1918*, Dublin: Gill & Macmillan.

—— (1981). 'On the Accuracy of Pre-Famine Censuses', in Goldstrom and Clarkson (1981), 37–56.

Lees, Lynn (1979). *Exiles of Erin: Irish Migrants in Victorian London*, Manchester: Manchester UP.

Linehan, Thomas (1991). 'History and Development of Irish Population Censuses'. *JSSISI*, forthcoming.

Lynch, Patrick, and John Vaizey (1960). *Guinness's Brewery in the Irish Economy 1759–1876*, Cambridge: Cambridge University Press.

Lyon, Stanley (1947–8). 'Natality in Dublin in the Years 1943, 1944, and 1945', *JSSISI*, 18: 57–77.

Lyons, F. S. L. (ed.) (1983). *The Bank of Ireland*, Dublin: Gill & Macmillan.

McAfee, W. S. (1987). 'The Population of Pre-Famine Ulster: Evidence for the Parish Register of Killyman', in P. O'Flanagan, P. Ferguson, and K. Whelan (eds.). *Rural Ireland: Modernization and Change, 1600–1900*, Cork: Cork University Press, 146–61.

—— and V. Morgan (1981). 'Population in Ulster, 1660–1760', in Peter Roebuck (ed.). *Plantation to Partition: Essays in Honour of J. L. McCracken*, Belfast: Blackstaff.

McAleese, D. (1971). *Effective Tariffs and the Structure of Protection in Ireland*, Dublin: Economic and Social Research Institute.

—— (1977). 'Do Tariffs Matter? Trade and Specialization in a Small Open Economy', *OEP*, 29: 117–27.

McArthur, W. A. (1944). 'Famines in Britain and Ireland', *Journal of the British Archaeological Association*, 3rd ser., 9: 66–71.

McCarthy, R. (1992). *The Trinity College Estates 1800–1923*, Dundalk: Dundalgan Press.

McCaughan, Michael, and John Appleby (eds.) (1989). *The Irish Sea: Aspects of Maritime History*, Belfast: Appletree.

McCracken, Donal (1984). 'The Management of a Mid-Victorian Irish Iron-Ore Mine: Glenravel, County Antrim, 1866–1887', *IESH*, 11: 60–72.

McCutcheon, W. A. (1965). *The Canals of the North of Ireland*, Newton Abbot: David & Charles.

—— (1980). *The Industrial Archaeology of Northern Ireland*, Belfast: HMSO.

McGregor, Patrick (1984). 'The Impact of the Blight on the Pre-Famine Rural Economy of Ireland', *ESR*, 15/4: 289–303.

—— (1989). 'Demographic Pressure and the Irish Famine: Malthus After Mokyr', *Land Economics*, 65: 228–38.

McMahon, Deirdre (1983). *Republicans and Imperialists: Anglo-Irish Relations in the 1930s*, New Haven, Conn.: Yale University Press.

MacNeill, Eoin (1932). 'Developments since Independence', *Foreign Affairs*, 10: 235–49.

McParland, Edward (1972). 'The Papers of Bryan Bolger, Measurer', *DHR*, 25: 120–131.

Maguire, W. A. (1983). 'A Resident Landlord in His Local Setting: The Second Marquis of Donegall at Ormeau, 1807–1844', *PRIA*, 83C: 377–99.

Marmion, Anthony (1858). *The Ancient and Modern History of the Maritime Ports of Ireland*, 3rd edn., London: Cox.

Martineau, Harriet (1854). *Letters from Ireland*, London: Chapman.

Meenan, James S. (1970). *The Irish Economy since 1922*, Liverpool: Liverpool University Press.

—— (1980). *George O'Brien: A Biographical Memoir*, Dublin: Gill & Macmillan.

Meldrum, A. H. (1979). 'The Development of the Irish Exploration and Mining Industry', in Irish Mining and Exploration Group, *Irish Mining and Exploration Conference*, Dublin: Confederation of Irish Industry, 29–49.

Milne, Kenneth (1964). *A History of the Royal Bank of Ireland*, Dublin: Figgis.

Mitchison R., and P. Roebuck (eds.) (1988). *Economy and Society in Scotland and Ireland 1500–1939*, Edinburgh: Donald.

Mokyr, J. (1980*a*). 'The Deadly Fungus: An Econometric Examination of the Short-term Demographic Impact of the Irish Famine', *Research in Population Economics*, 2: 237–77.

—— (1980*b*). 'Industrialization and Poverty in Ireland and The Netherlands: Some Notes Toward a Comparative Case Study', *JIH*, 10/3: 429–59.

—— (1983*a*). 'Uncertainty and the Pre-Famine Economy', in Devine and Dickson (1983), 89–101.

—— (1983*b*, rev. edn. 1985). *Why Ireland Starved: A Quantitative and Analytical History of the Irish Economy, 1800–1850*, London: Allen & Unwin.

—— (ed.) (1985). *Economics and the Industrial Revolution*, Totowa, NJ: Rowan & Allenheld.

—— (1991). 'Dear Labor, Cheap Labor, and the Industrial Revolution', in P. Higonnet, D. S. Landes, and H. Rosovsky (eds.), *Favorites of Fortune: Technology, Growth, and Economic Development since the Industrial Revolution*, Cambridge, Mass.: Harvard University Press, 177–200.

—— and C. Ó Gráda (1982). 'Emigration and Poverty in Prefamine Ireland', *EEH*, 19: 360–84.

—— —— (1988). 'Poor and Getting Poorer? Irish Living Standards Before the Famine', *EHR*, 41: 209–35.

—— —— (1989). 'The Heights of Irishmen and Engishmen in the 1770s', *Eighteenth Century Ireland*, 4: 89–98.

—— —— (1993). 'The Heights of the British and the Irish *c.*1800–1815: Evidence from Recruits to the East India Company's Army', in J. Komlos (ed.), *Anthropometric History*, forthcoming.

Mollan, Charles, William Davis, and Brendan Finucane (eds.) (1985). *Some People and Places in Irish Science and Technology*, Dublin: RIA.

—— —— —— (eds.) (1986). *More People and Places in Irish Science and Technology*, Dublin: RIA.

Morgan, V. (1973). 'The Church of Ireland Registers of St Patrick's Coleraine as a Source for the Study of a Local Pre-Famine Population', *Ulster Folklife*, 19: 56–67.

—— and W. McAfee (1984). 'Irish Population in the Pre-Famine Period: Evidence from County Antrim', *EHR*, 27: 182–96.

Moynihan, Maurice (1974). *Currency and Central Banking in Ireland 1922–60*, Dublin: Gill & Macmillan.

Munn, Charles (1983). 'The Coming of Joint-stock Banking in Scotland and Ireland *c.*1820–45', in Devine and Dickson (1983), 204–18.

—— (1983). 'The Emergence of Central Banking in Ireland: Bank of Ireland 1814–50', *IESH*, 10: 19–32.

—— (1981). 'Bank Credit for Industry in Scotland and Ireland', unpublished.

Murphy, A. E. (ed.) (1984). *Economists and the Irish Economy from the Eighteenth Century to the Present Day*, Dublin: Irish Academic Press.

Murray, Alice (1903, 1970). *Commercial Relations between England and Ireland*, New York: Burt Franklin.

Neary, J. P., and C. Ó Gráda (1991). 'Protection, Economic War and Structural Change: Ireland in the 1930s', *IHS*, 27/108: 250–66.

Nicholas, S., and Deborah Oxley (1991). 'The Living Standards of Women During the Industrial Revolution 1795–1820', mimeo.

—— and S. Shergold (1987). 'Human Capital and Irish Pre-Famine Emigration to England', *EEH*, 24: 158–77.

—— —— (1990). 'Irish Intercounty Mobility before 1840', *IESH*, 17: 22–43.

—— and R. Steckel (1991). 'Heights and Health of Workers during the Early Years of British Industrialisation', *JEH*, 51/4: 937–57.

Nicholson, Asenath (1851). *Annals of the Famine in Ireland in 1847, 1848, and 1849*, New York: E. French.

Nolan, William (1979). *Fassadinin: Land, Settlement and Society in South-East Ireland 1600–1850*, Dublin: Geography Publications.

Nowlan, K. B., and T. D. Williams (eds.) (1969). *Ireland in the War Years and After, 1939–51*, Dublin: Gill & Macmillan.

O'Brien, George (1918). *The Economic History of Ireland in the Eighteenth Century*, Dublin: Maunsell.

—— (1921). *The Economic History of Ireland from the Union to the Famine*, London: Longman.

—— (1927). 'The Last Years of the Irish Currency', *Economic History*, 1/2: 205–221.

—— (1936). 'Patrick Hogan, Minister for Agriculture, 1922–32', *Studies*, 25: 353–68.

O'Brien, Gerard (1986). 'Workhouse Management in Pre-famine Ireland', *PRIA*, 86C: 113–34.

O'Brien, John B. (1977). 'Agricultural Prices and Living Costs in Pre-Famine Cork', *JCHAS*, 82: 1–10.

—— (1977). 'Sadleir's Bank', *JCHAS*, 82: 33–8.

—— (1985). 'Glimpses of Entrepreneurial Life in Cork 1800–1870', *JCHAS*, 90: 150–7.

O'Brien, W. P. (1896). *The Great Famine in Ireland*, London: Downey.

O Broin, Leon (1982). *No Man's Man: A Biographical Memoir of Joseph Brennan*, Dublin: Institute of Public Administration.

—— (1986). *Just Like Yesterday*, Dublin: Gill & Macmillan.

O'Connell, Thomas (1992). 'Do Regions Naturally Converge or Diverge in an Economic and Monetary Union?', *Central Bank of Ireland Quarterly Bulletin*,

Spring, 51–66.

O'Connell Bianconi, M., and S. J. Watson (1962). *Charles Bianconi: King of the Irish Roads*, Dublin: Figgis.

Ó Curraoin, P. L. (1991). *Féara agus Bánta na hÉireann*, Dublin: An Gúm.

O'Dowd, Anne (1991). *Spalpeens and Tattie Hokers: History and Folklore of the Irish Migratory Agricultural Worker in Ireland and Britain*, Dublin: Irish Academic Press.

O'Flanagan, P., P. Ferguson, and K. Whelan (1987). *Rural Ireland: Modernisation and Change, 1600–1900*, Cork: Cork University Press.

Ó Gráda, Cormac (1973). 'Seasonal Migration and Demographic Adjustment in Post-Famine Ireland', *SH*, 13: 48–76.

—— (1974). 'Irish Head Rents, Pre-Famine and Post-Famine', *ESR*, 5: 149–65.

—— (1975). 'A Note on Nineteenth-Century Emigration Statistics', *PS*, 25: 143–9.

—— (1977a). 'The Beginnings of the Irish Creamery System 1880–1914', *EHR*, 30: 284–305.

—— (1977b). 'Some Aspects of Nineteenth-Century Irish Emigration', in Cullen and Smout (1978), 65–73.

—— (1984). 'Malthus and the Pre-Famine Economy', in Murphy (1984), 75–95.

—— (1985). 'Did Ulster Catholics Always Have Larger Families?', *IESH*, 11: 89–98.

—— (1988). *Ireland Before and After the Famine: Explorations in Economic History 1800–1930*, Manchester: Manchester University Press (revd. edn., 1993).

—— (1989a). 'Poverty, Population and Agriculture' and 'Industry and Communications', in Vaughan (1988), v. 108–57.

—— (1989b). *The Great Irish Famine*, London: Macmillan.

—— (1991a). 'Reassessing the Irish Pound Report of 1804', *Bulletin of Economic Research*, 43/1: 5–19.

—— (1991b). 'Dublin's Demography in the Early Nineteenth Century: Evidence from the Rotunda', *PS*, 45/1: 43–54.

—— (1991c). 'Irish Agriculture North and South Since 1900', in Campbell and Overton (eds.), *Land, Labour and Livestock: Historical Studies in European Agricultural Productivity*, Manchester: Manchester University Press, 439–56.

—— (1991d). 'New Evidence on the Fertility Transition in Ireland c.1900', *Demography*, 28/4: 535–48.

—— (1991e). 'The Heights of Clonmel Prisoners 1845–9: Some Dietary Implications', *IESH*, 19: 24–33.

—— (1991f). 'An Early Irish Reaction to Malthus', *History of Political Economy*, 23/1: 93–4.

—— (1991g). 'Literary Sources and Irish Economic History', *Studies*, 80/3 (1991), 290–9.

—— (1992a). '"Making History" in Ireland in the 1940s and 1950s: The Saga of The Great Famine', *Irish Review*, 12: 87–107.

—— (1992b). 'Slices of Irish Agricultural History', *Proceedings of the Agricultural Economics Society of Ireland*, forthcoming.

Ó Gráda, Cormac (1993). 'The Irish Paper Pound of 1797–1820: Some Clio-metrics of the Bullionist Debate', *OEP*, 45.

—— and N. Duffy (1990). 'Fertility Control Early in Marriage in Ireland *c.* 1900: Some Local Contrasts', TS.

—— —— (1994). 'Fertility Control in Ireland and Scotland *c.* 1880–1930: Some New Findings', in Connolly, Houston, and Morris.

Ó Gráda, Diarmuid (1982–3). 'The Rocky Road to Dublin: Transport Modes and Urban Growth in the Georgian Age', *SH*, 22–3: 128–48.

O'Keefe, P. J. (1980). 'Richard Griffith: Planner and Builder of Roads', in G. L. Herries Davies and R. C. Mollan (eds.), *Richard Griffith, 1784–1878: Papers Presented at the Centenary Symposium Organised by the Royal Dublin Society*, Dublin: RDS, 57–75.

O'Kelly, Eoin (1959). *The Old Private Banks of Munster*, Cork: Cork University Press.

Oldham, C. H. (1924). 'After the Fiscal Inquiry Report', *Studies*, 13: 1–13.

Ollerenshaw, Philip (1985). 'Industry 1820–1914', in Kennedy and Ollerenshaw (1985), 62–108.

—— (1985). *Banking in Nineteenth-Century Ireland: The Belfast Banks, 1825–1914*, Manchester: Manchester University Press.

—— (1989). 'Aspects of Bank Lending in Post-Famine Ireland', in Mitchison and Roebuck (1988), 222–32.

—— (1991*a*). 'Textiles and Regional Economic Decline: Northern Ireland 1914–70', in Colin Holmes and Alan Booth (eds.), *Economy and Society, European Industrialisation and Its Social Consequences: Essays Presented to Sidney Pollard*, Leicester: Leicester University Press, 58–83.

—— (1991*b*). 'The Business and Politics of Banking in Ireland 1900–1943', TS.

Ó Lúing, Seán (1975–6). 'Richard Griffith and the Roads of Kerry', *JKAHS*, 8: 89–113; 9, 92–124.

O'Mahony, Colman (1987). 'Copper-Mining at Allihies, Co. Cork', *JCHAS*, 92/251: 71–85.

—— (1989). 'Shipbuilding and Repairing in Nineteenth-Century Cork', *JCHAS*, 94/253: 74–87.

O'Malley, Eoin (1981). 'The Decline of Irish Industry in the Nineteenth Century', *ESR*, 13/1: 21–42.

—— (1989). *Industry and Economic Development: The Challenge for the Latecomer*, Dublin: Gill & Macmillan.

O'Neill, Kevin (1984). *Family and Farm in Pre-Famine Ireland: The Parish of Killeshandra*, Madison, Wis.: Wisconsin University Press.

—— (1985). 'A Demographer Looks at Cuirt an Mhean Oiche', *Eire-Ireland*, 19/2: 135–143.

O'Neill, Thomas P. (1950). 'The Society of Friends and the Great Famine', *Studies*, 39: 203–13.

O'Neill, Timothy P. (1973). 'Fever & Public Health in Pre-Famine Ireland', *RSAIJ*, 103: 1–34.

—— (1974). 'Clare and Irish Poverty', *SH*, 14: 7–28.

O'Rourke, John (1902, 1867). *History of the Great Irish Famine of 1847*, 3rd edn., Dublin: Duffy.

O'Rourke, Kevin (1991*a*). 'Did the Great Famine Matter?', *JEH*, 51: 1–22.

—— (1991*b*). 'The Causes of Depopulation in a Small Open Economy: Ireland 1856–1876', *EEH*, 28: 409–32.

—— (1991*c*). 'Burn Everything English but Their Coal: The Anglo-Irish Economic War of the 1930s', *JEH*, 51/2: 357–66.

—— (1991*d*). 'The Costs of International Economic Disintegration: Ireland in the 1930s', TS, Columbia University.

—— and Ben Polak (1992). 'Property Transactions in Ireland, 1708–1988: An Introduction', unpublished.

O'Sullivan, Charles J. (1987). *The Gasmakers: Historical Perspectives on the Irish Gas Industry*, Dublin: IGA/O'Brien.

O'Sullivan, William (1937). *The Economic History of Cork City from the Earliest Times to the Act of Union*, Cork: Cork University Press.

Owen, D. J. (1921). *History of Belfast*, Belfast: Baird.

Parnell, Henry (1804). *Observations upon the State of Currency in Ireland and upon the Course of Exchange between Dublin and London*, Dublin: Mahon.

Patterson, Sir R. Lloyd (1903). 'The Linen Industry', in Harold Cox (ed.), *British Industry under Free Trade*, London: Fisher Unwin, 39–64.

Prager, Jeffrey (1986). *Building Democracy in Ireland: Political Order and Cultural Integration in a Newly Independent Nation*, Cambridge: Cambridge University Press.

Pratschke, John (1969). 'The Establishing of the Irish Pound: A Backward Glance', *ESR*, 1/1: 51–76.

Proudfoot, Lindsay (1986). 'The Management of a Great Estate: Patronage, Income and Expenditure on the Duke of Devonshire's Irish Property, *c.*1816 to 1891', *IESH*, 23: 32–55.

—— (1992). 'The Estate System in Mid-Nineteenth-Century Waterford', in W. Nolan and T. Power (eds.), *Waterford, History and Society*, Dublin: Geography Publications.

Riordan, E. J. (1920). *Modern Irish Trade and Industry*, London: Methuen.

Robinson, Olive (1962). 'The London Companies as Progressive Landlords in Nineteenth-century Ireland', *EHR*, 11/1: 103–18.

—— (1970). 'The London Companies and Tenant Right in Nineteenth-Century Ireland', *AHR*, 18: 54–63.

Rooth, T. (1985). 'Trade Agreements and the Evolution of British Agricultural Policy in the 1930s', *AgHR*, 33: 173–90.

Ryan, W. J. L. (1948–9). 'Measurement of Tariff Levels for Ireland in 1931, 1936, 1938', *JSSISI*, 18: 109–33.

Scrope, George Poulett (1847). *Reply to a Speech of the Archbishop of Dublin*, London: Ridgeway.

Semple, Maurice (1981). *By the Corribside*, Galway: Maurice Semple.

Senior, Nassau W. (1868). *Journals, Essays and Conversations Relating to Ireland*, London: Longmans, Green.

Share, Bernard (ed.) (1979). *Root and Branch: Allied Irish Banks Yesterday, Today and Tomorrow*, Dublin: AIB.

Shaw Mason, William (1814–19). *Statistical Account or Parochial Survey of Ireland*, Dublin: Graisberry & Campbell.

Sheil, Richard Lalor (1855). *Sketches Legal and Political*, London: Henry Colburn.

Silverman, Marilyn, and P. H. Gulliver (1986). *In the Valley of the Nore: A Social History of Thomastown, County Kilkenny 1840–1983*, Dublin: Geography Publications.

Simpson, Noel (1975). *The Belfast Bank 1827–1970*, Belfast: Blackstaff.

Slattery, Sir M. (1972). 'The National Bank 1835–1970', *Three Banks Review*, nos. 93–6.

Smyth, W. J. (1983). 'Landholding Changes, Kinship Networks and Class Transformation in Rural Ireland: A Case-Study from County Tipperary', *IG*, 16: 16–35.

Solar, Peter M. (1979). 'The Agricultural Trade Statistics in the Irish Railway Commissioners' Report', *IESH*, 6: 24–40.

—— (1983). 'Agricultural Productivity and Economic Development in Ireland and Scotland in the Early Nineteenth Century', in Devine and Dickson (1983), 70–88.

—— (1984). 'Why Ireland Starved: A Critical Review of the Econometric Results', *IESH*, 10: 107–15.

—— (1988a). 'The Singularity of the Great Irish Famine', in E. M. Crawford (1989), 112–31.

—— (1988b). 'A Belgian View of the Ulster Linen Industry in the 1840s', *Ulster Folklife*, 34: 16–25.

—— (1989). 'Harvest Fluctuations in Pre-Famine Ireland: Evidence from Belfast and Waterford Newspapers', *AgHR*, 27/2: 157–65.

—— (1989–90). 'The Irish Butter Trade in the Nineteenth Century: New Estimates and their Implications', *SH*, 25: 134–61.

—— (1990). 'The Irish Linen Trade 1820–1852', *Textile History*, 21/1: 57–85.

—— and M. Goossens (1991). 'Belgian and Irish Agriculture in 1840–5', in Campbell and Overton, *Land, Labour and Livestock*, 364–84.

Solow, B. L. (1971). *The Land Question and the Irish Economy*, Cambridge, Mass.: Harvard University Press.

—— (1981). 'A New Look at the Irish Land Question', *ESR*, 12/4: 301–14.

Staehle, Hans (1950–1). 'Statistical Notes on the Economic History of Irish Agriculture, 1847–1913', *JSSISI*, 18: 444–71.

Tanner, J. M. (1981). *A History of the Study of Human Growth*, Cambridge: Cambridge University Press.

Teitelbaum, Michael (1986). *The British Fertility Decline*, Princeton, NJ: Princeton University Press.

Thomas, W. A. (1987a). *The Stock Exchanges of Ireland*, London: Francis Cairns.

—— (1987b). 'The Evolution of a Capital Market: The Case of Ireland', *JEEH*, 16/3: 527–60.

Turner, Michael (1991). 'Agricultural Output and Productivity in Post-Famine Ireland', in Campbell and Overton, 410–38.

Vann, Richard T., and David Eversley (1992). *Friends in Life and Death: The Births and Irish Quakers in the Demographic Transition*, Cambridge: Cambridge University Press.

Van Zanden, J. (1991). 'The First Green Revolution: the Growth of Production and Productivity in European Agriculture, 1870–1914', *EHR*, 44/2: 215–39.

Vaughan, W. E. (1977). 'Landlord Tenant Relations in Ireland 1850–1870', in Cullen and Smout (1978), 216–26.

—— (1982*a*). 'Agricultural Output, Rent and Wages in Ireland, 1850–1880', in Cullen and Furet (1982), 85–98.

—— (1982*b*). 'Farmer, Grazier and Gentleman: Edward Delany of Oldtown', *IESH*, 9: 53–72.

—— (1984). *Landlord and Tenant 1850–1904*, Dublin: Irish Economic and Social History Society.

—— (1988). *A New History of Ireland: Ireland under the Union 1801–70*, Oxford: Oxford University Press.

Wakefield, Edward (1812). *An Account of Ireland, Statistical and Political*, 2 vols. London: Longman.

Walsh, B. M. (1970). 'Marriage Rates and Population Pressure: Ireland, 1871 and 1911', *EHR*, 23: 148–62.

Warburton, J., J. Whitelaw, and R. Walsh (1818). *History of the City of Dublin*, 2 vols. London: Cadell & Davies.

Watkins, Susan C., and Jane Mencken (1985). 'Famines in Historical Perspective', *Population and Development Review*, 11: 647–75.

Weir, R. B. (1980). 'In and Out of Ireland: The Distillers Company Ltd. and the Irish Whiskey Trade 1900–1939', *IESH*, 7, 45–65.

Whelan, K. (1986–7). 'An Account of the Baronies of Forth and Bargy in 1814', *Journal of the Wexford Historical Society*, 11: 14–32.

—— (1990*a*). 'The Catholic Community in Eighteenth-Century Wexford', in T. P. Power and K. Whelan (eds.), *Endurance and Emergence: Catholics in Ireland in the Eighteenth Century*, Dublin: Irish Academic Press.

—— (1990*b*). 'Aithbhreithniú Staire', *Oghma* 2: 9–19.

—— (1991). 'Catholic Mobilization', in P. Bergeron and L. M. Cullen (eds.). *Culture et Pratiques Politiques en France et en Irlande XVIe-XVIIIe Siècles*, Paris: CRH, 235–58.

Whitelaw, James (1805). *An Essay on the Population of Dublin*, Dublin: Graisberry & Campbell.

Willis, Thomas (1845). *Facts Connected with the Social and Sanitary Condition of the Working Classes in the City of Dublin*, Dublin: O'Gorman.

Woodham-Smith, Cecil (1962). *The Great Hunger*, London: Hamilton.

Woods, C. J. (1987*a*). 'American Travellers in Ireland Before and During the Great Famine: A Case of Culture-Shock', in Wolfgang Zach and Heinz Kosok (eds.). *Literary Interrelations: Ireland, England and the New World*, Tübingen: Narr.

—— (1987*b*). 'Select Documents XLI: Johann Friedrich Hering's Description of Connacht, 1806–7', *IHS*, 15/99: 311–21.

Wrigley, A. E., and R. Schofield (1981). *The Population History of England 1541–1871: A Reconstruction*, London: Arnold.
Young, Arthur (1780). *A Tour in Ireland*, Dublin: Whitestone.

Unpublished Dissertations

Almquist, Eric (1977). 'Mayo and beyond: Land, Domestic Industry and Rural Transformation in the Irish West' (Ph.D., Boston University).
Bourke, P. M. A. (1965). 'The Potato, Blight, Weather and the Irish Famine' (Ph.D., NUI/UCC).
Boyle, Emily (1979). 'The Economic Development of the Irish Linen Industry, 1825–1913' (Ph.D., QUB).
Byrne, Michael (1980). 'The Development of Tullamore 1700–1921' (M.Litt., TCD).
Caskey, Alan (1983). 'Entrepreneurs and Industrial Development in Ulster 1850–1914: A Study in Business History' (M.Phil., UU).
Crawford, W. H. (1983). 'Economy and Society in Eighteenth-Century Ulster' (Ph.D., QUB).
Dickson, David (1977). 'The Economic History of the Cork Region in the Eighteenth Century' (Ph.D., TCD).
Duffy, Mark (1985). 'The Socioeconomic Composition of the Dublin Jewish Community 1880–1910' (MA, UCD).
Eiriksson, Andres (1992). 'Crime and Popular Protest in Co. Clare 1815–1852' (Ph.D., TCD).
Ferris, Thomas G. (1979). 'The Ulster Railway, 1835–48' (MA, QUB).
Fitzpatrick, Andre (1971). 'The Economic Effects of the French Revolutionary Wars in Ireland' (Ph.D., University of Manchester).
Fogarty, Margaret T. (1968). 'The Malcolmsons and the Economic Development of the Lower Suir Valley 1782–1877' (M.Sc., NUI/UCC).
Foley, Kieran (1987). 'The Killarney Poor Law Guardians and the Famine 1845–52' (MA, NUI/UCD).
Gamble, Norman (1978). 'The Business Community and Trade of Belfast 1767–1800' (Ph.D., QUB).
Grant, James (1986). 'The Great Famine in the Province of Ulster—The Mechanism of Relief' (Ph.D., QUB).
Gray, Peter H. (1992). 'British Politics and the Irish Land Question, 1843–1850' (Cambridge University).
Greeves, Oliver (1969). 'The Effects of the American Civil War on the Line, Woollen, and Worsted Industries of the United Kingdom' (Ph.D., University of Bristol).
Guinnane, Timothy (1987). 'Migration, Marriage, and Household Formation: The Irish at the Turn of the Century' (Ph.D., Stanford University).
Harrison, Richard (1988). 'Dublin Quakers in Business' (M.Litt., TCD).
Hickey, Patrick (1980). 'A Study of Four Peninsular Parishes in Cork, 1796–1855' (Ph.D., NUI/UCC).
Holt, Jon H. (1967). 'The Quakers in the Great Irish Famine' (M.Litt., TCD).

Hume, John (1964). 'Social and Economic Aspects of the Growth of Derry, 1825–1850' (M.A., NUI/Maynooth).

Huttman, James (1970). 'Institutional Factors in the Development of Irish Agriculture, 1850–1915' (Ph.D., University of London).

Kelly, James (1985). 'The Search for a "Commercial Arrangement": Anglo-Irish Politics in the 1780s' (Ph.D., NUI/UCD).

L'Amie, Aileen (1984). 'Chemicals in the Eighteenth-Century Irish Linen Industry' (Ph.D., QUB).

Lee, J. J. (1965). 'An Economic History of Irish Railways, 1836–1853' (MA, NUI/UCD).

McCabe, Desmond (1991). 'Law, Conflict and Social Change: County Mayo 1820–1845' (Ph.D., NUI/UCD).

McCarthy, R. B. (1982). 'The Estates of Trinity College, Dublin, in the Nineteenth Century' (Ph.D., TCD).

McCavery, Trevor Robert (1980). 'Finance and Politics in Ireland, 1801–17' (Ph.D., QUB).

McCorry, F. X. (1986). 'History of Lurgan' (Ph.D., QUB).

McCourt, Desmond (1950). 'The Rundale System in Ireland: A Study of its Geographical Distribution and Social Relations' (Ph.D., QUB).

McKeever, Gerald (1979). 'Economic Policy in the Irish Free State' (Ph.D., McGill University, Montreal).

Monahan, John (1940). 'A Social and Economic History of Belfast in the First Half of the Nineteenth Century' (Ph.D., QUB).

Montague, R. J. (1976). 'Relief and Reconstruction: Public Policy in Ireland 1845–9' (D.Phil., Oxford University).

O'Neill, Timothy P. (1965). 'The Famine of 1822' (MA, NUI/UCD).

—— (1971). 'The State, Poverty and Distress in Ireland 1815–45' (Ph.D., NUI/UCD).

O'Neill, Tomas P. (1946). 'The Organisation and Administration of Relief during the Great Famine' (MA, NUI/UCD).

O'Rourke, Kevin (1989). 'Agricultural Change and Rural Depopulation: Ireland 1845–1876' (Ph.D., Harvard University).

Pollock, Vivienne (1988). 'The Seafishing Industry of Co. Down, 1860–1939' (Ph.D., University of Ulster).

Robinson, Olive (1958). 'The Economic Significance of the London Companies as Landlords in Ireland during the Period 1800–1870' (Ph.D., QUB).

Ryan, W. J. L. (1949). 'The Nature and Effects of Protective Policy in Ireland, 1922–39' (Ph.D., TCD).

Solar, Peter M. (1987). 'Growth and Distribution in Irish Agriculture Before the Famine' (Ph.D., Stanford University).

Takei, Akihiro (1990). 'The Early Mechanization of the Irish Linen Industry 1800–1840' (M.Litt., TCD).

NOTES

Chapter 1

1. Anon. (T. R. Malthus), 'Newenham and Others on the State of Ireland', *Edinburgh Review*, July 1808, repr. in B. Semmel (ed.), *Occasional Papers of T. R. Malthus* (New York, 1963), 32–71.
2. H. Townsend, *Statistical Survey of the County of Cork* (Dublin, 1810), 704.
3. Quoted in J. M. Keynes, *Essays in Biography* (New York, 1933, 1963), 98.
4. Compare M. Flinn, *The European Demographic System, 1500–1820* (Baltimore, Md., 1981).
5. Thomas Newenham, *A Statistical and Historical Enquiry into the Progress and Magnitude of the Population of Ireland* (London, 1805), 131–2, put excess mortality at 40,000.
6. T. R. Malthus, *An Essay on the Principle of Population*, Everyman edn. (London, 1973), i. 277–8 (the passage is quoted in Patricia James, *Population Malthus* (London, 1979), 145–60); 'Newenham and Others on the State of Ireland' and 'Newenham on the State of Ireland', in Semmel, *Malthus*, 32–71. For modern sociological interpretations, Mary Douglas, 'Population Control in Primitive Groups', *British Journal of Sociology* 17 (1966), 263–73; Jacques Dupâquier, 'De l'animal à l'homme: le mécanisme autorégulateur des populations traditionnelles', *Revue de l'Institut de Sociologie* (1972), 177–211.

   Compare Caesar Otway's account of north Connemara: 'I also was informed that there was much ignorance and contented destitution of all that a better informed people would call comforts, so that a man when he became wealthy did not by any means exhibit it in his living, his house or his furniture' (*A Tour in Connaught* (Dublin, 1839), 252).
7. This issue of the time taken for the Malthusian equilibrium to establish itself is discussed in Walter Eltis, *The Classical Theory of Economic Growth* (London, 1983), 117–19, and Samuel Hollander, 'Malthus and the Post-Napoleonic Depression', *History of Political Economy*, i (1969), 306–35.
8. Quoted in Michael Drake, 'The Census 1801–1891', in E. A. Wrigley (ed.), *Nineteenth Century Society: Essays in the Use of the Quantitative Method for the Study of Social Data* (Cambridge, 1972), 21.
9. Lee, 'On the Accuracy of Prefamine Censuses', 46–7.
10. Daultrey, Dickson, and Ó Gráda, 'Eighteenth-Century Irish Population'; Dickson, Ó Gráda, and Daultrey, 'Hearth Tax, Household Size and Irish Population'; Lee, 'On the Accuracy'.
11. Dickson, Daultrey, and Ó Gráda, 'Hearth Tax', 155; Vaughan and Fitzpatrick, *Irish Historical Statistics*, 3, p. 16.
12. T. Crofton Croker, *Researches in the South of Ireland* (London, 1824), 235; Malthus,

evidence to Select Committee on Emigration from the UK, BPP 1826–7 (V), Qs. 3183–200.

13. This way of describing Malthus owes much to Mokyr, *Why Ireland Starved*, 42–4.
14. Solow, *The Land Question*, 196.
15. Connell, *Population of Ireland*, 59; 'JKL', *Letters on the State of Ireland* (Dublin, 1825), 110–12.
16. Peter Laslett, *The World We Have Lost* (London, 1965), 81.
17. For a different view of Merriman see Kevin O'Neill, 'A Demographer Looks at Cúirt an Mheán Oíche', *Eire-Ireland*, 19/2 (1985), 135–43. But see also Seán Ó Tuama, 'Cúirt an Mheánoiche', in his *Cúirt, Tuath agus Bruachbhailte: Aistí agus Dréachtaí Liteartha* (Dublin, 1991), 7–37; Ó Gráda, 'Literary Sources'. On the debate about pre-Famine illegitimacy and premarital sex see Akenson, *Small Differences*, 28–36.
18. Inglis, *Tour of Ireland*, i. 247; *1841 Census*, 202.
19. Morgan, 'The Church of Ireland Registers of St Patrick's Coleraine'; Morgan and Macafee, 'Irish Population in the Pre-Famine Period; Macafee, 'Killyman'; Ó Gráda, 'Pre-Famine Dublin Demography'; D. Griffin, 'An Inquiry into the Mortality Occurring among the Poor of the City of Limerick', *Journal of the Statistical Society of London*, 24 (1843); E. Walsh Kelly and R. Ffolliott, 'The 1821 Census Returns for the Parishes of Aglish and Portnaskully, Co. Kilkenny', *Irish Ancestor*, 8 (1976), 113–23; Kathleen Kelly, 'Extracts from the Census of the City of Waterford, 1821', *Irish Genealogist*, 4/1 (1968), 17–24; 4/2 (1969), 122–30; John Hajnal, 'European Marriage Patterns in Perspective', in D. V. Glass and D. E. C. Eversley (eds.), *Population in History* (Cambridge, 1965).
20. Connell, *Population of Ireland*, 52; George O'Brien (ed.), *Advertisements for Ireland* (Dublin, 1926), 43; Dickson, 'No Scythians Here'; Valerie Morgan, 'A Case Study of Population Change over Two Centuries: Blaris, Lisburn, 1661–1848', *IESH*, 3 (1976), 5–16.
21. Kevin O'Neill, 'Cúirt an Mheánoíche'.
22. Sean Connolly, 'Marriage in Pre-Famine Ireland', in A. Cosgrove (ed.), *Marriage in Ireland* (Dublin, 1985), 78–98; 'JKL', *Letters*, 110. Maighréad Ní Dhomhnaill's excellent *Gan Dhá Phingin Spré* (Gael-Linn, 1991) contains several songs on the 'dowry' theme.
23. John H. Andrews, 'Limits of Agricultural Settlement in Pre-Famine Ireland', in Cullen and Furet, *Irlande et France*, 47–58; id., 'Changes in the Rural Landscape of Late Eighteenth and Early Nineteenth-Century Ireland: An Example from County Waterford', paper presented at the conference of the Institute of British Geographers, Belfast, 1970; Smyth, 'Landholding Changes'.
24. 'JKL', *Letters*, 112.
25. For an elementary introduction, E. A. Wrigley, *Population and History* (London, 1969), 80–9.
26. See Ildiko Vasary, 'The Sin of Transdanubia: The One-Child System in Rural Hungary', *Continuity and Change*, 4/3 (1989), 429–68.

27. D. C. Eversley, 'The Demography of the Quakers', 67; Vann and Eversley, *Friends in Life and Death*, ch. 4.

28. Thus Peter Razzell's claims for inoculation's *leading* role in Ireland's demographic revolution goes too far. See P. E. Razzell, 'Population Growth and Economic Change in Eighteenth- and Nineteenth-Century England and Ireland' in E. L. Jones and G. E. Mingay (eds.), *Land, Labour and Population in the Industrial Revolution* (London, 1967), 260–81.

29. David Dickson, 'The Gap in Famines: A Useful Myth?', in F. M. Crawford, *Famine*, 107.

30. Ó Gráda, *Ireland*, 2–5; O'Neill, 'The Famine of 1822'. Compare Michael Turner's review of Roger Wells's, *Wretched Faces: Famine in Wartime England 1793–1801* in *Social History*, 15/3 (1990), 390–2.

31. The issue awaits research, but indicators include rises in the consumption of items such as tea, sugar, tobacco, printed works; the rise in the value of stock owned and rents; increased demand for middle-class housing; and the increasing political clout of Catholic professionals and farmers.

32. A. Young, *Tour in Ireland* (Dublin, 1780), ii. 34–5 (App.); Adam Smith, *An Inquiry into the Nature and Causes of the Wealth of Nations*, R. Campbell and A. Skinner (eds.), (Oxford, 1976), bk. 1, ch. 11; also John Carr, *The Stranger in Ireland* (Philadelphia, 1806), 156. Kevin Whelan reminds me that outsiders' diatribes against the quality of Irish housing may also be part culture-specific. Students of vernacular Irish architecture such as Estyn Evans and Caoimhín Ó Danachair have stressed its advantages.

33. *First Report of the General Board of Health for the City of Dublin* (Dublin, 1822). Despite the title, this report is mainly concerned with health and living conditions in the province of Munster.

34. Bourke, 'The Use of the Potato in Pre-Famine Ireland'; Mokyr, 'Irish History with the Potato'; Ontario Archives, Peter Robinson Papers, MS 12, reel 1 (Peter Robinson to Wilmot Horton). In Clare during the Famine of 1822 rice could not find a sale, even at knock-down prices, 'owing chiefly to the ignorance of the people' (Guildhall Library, MS 7472, Irish Relief Fund, report from Inchiquin).

35. Clarkson and Crawford, 'Dietary Directions'; E. M. Crawford, 'Subsistence Crises and Famines in Ireland: A Nutritionist's Views', in Crawford, *Famine*, 198–219; William Tighe, *Statistical Observations Relative to the County of Kilkenny* (Dublin, 1802), 479–80; Síle Ní Chinnéide, 'Coquebert de Montbret's Impressions of Galway City and County in the Year 1791', *Journal of the Galway Historical and Archeological Society*, 25/1 and 2 (1952), 10.

36. Townsend, *Cork*, 233–6, 301–2; Wakefield, *Ireland*, i. 395–6; Whitelaw, *Population of Dublin*.

37. Wakefield, *Ireland*, ii. 811; James Cropper, *Present State of Ireland* (Liverpool, 1825), 7.

38. Mokyr, 'Is There Still Life in the Pessimist Case? Consumption During the Industrial Revolution', *JEH*, 48/1 (1988), 69–92.

39. Solar, 'Growth and Distribution', Table 2.16; B. R. Mitchell and P. Deane, *British Historical Statistics* (Cambridge, 1962), 468–9.

40. D'Arcy, 'Wages of Labourers in the Dublin Building Industry'; H. Townsend, *A View of the Agricultural State of Ireland in 1815* (Cork, 1816), 47; NA, 1A-58–125–6 (records of Bryan Bolger, building measurer); Thomas Bolger, 'Papers of Bryan Bolger, 1792–1834', *DHR*, 3 (1940–1), 8–18.

41. W. H. Crawford, *Domestic Industry in Ireland*, 40–1.

42. R. W. Fogel, L. Engerman, R. Floud, G. Friedman, R. A. Margo, K. Sokoloff, R. H. Steckel, J. Trussell, G. Villaflor, and K. W. Wachter, 'Secular Changes in American and British Stature and Nutrition', in R. I. Rotberg and T. K. Rabb (eds.), *Hunger and History: The Impact of Changes in Food Production and Consumption Patterns on Scarcity* (Cambridge, 1986).

43. Malthus, *Essay*, 93–4. Earlier Samuel Johnson was moved by his observations in the inner Hebrides to note that 'in regions of barrenness and scarcity, the human race is hindered in its growth by the same causes as other animals' (S. Johnson, *A Journey to the Western Islands of Scotland*, i (Dublin, 1775), 190).

44. See e.g. Fogel *et al.*, 'Secular Changes'; Lars G. Sandberg and Richard H. Steckel, 'Overpopulation and Malnutrition Reconsidered: Hard Times in 19th-Century Sweden', *EEH*, 25 (1988), 1–19; John Komlos, *Nutrition and Economic Development in the Eighteenth-Century Hapsburg Monarchy: An Anthropometric History* (Princeton, NJ, 1989); Floud, Wachter, and Gregory, *Height, Health and History*.

45. N. Williams (ed.), *Pairlimint Chloinne Tomáis* (Dublin, 1981), 57.

46. James Kelly, 'Prosperous and Irish Industrialisation in the Late Eighteenth Century', *Journal of the Kildare Historical and Archaeological Society*, 16/5 (1985–6), 442–67. See also Ch. 12 below.

47. Mokyr and Ó Gráda, 'Heights of Irishmen and Englishmen in the Late Eighteenth Century'; Kenneth L. Sokoloff and Georgia Villaflor, 'The Early Achievement of Modern Stature in America', *Social Science History*, 6/4 (1982), 462.

48. Compare Mokyr and Ó Gráda, 'The Heights of the British and the Irish *c.*1800–1815: Evidence from Recruits to the East India Company's Army', and Floud, Wachter, and Gregory, *Height, Health and History*, 101.

49. Nicholas and Steckel, 'Heights and Living Standards of English Workers'; Nicholas and Oxley, 'The Living Standards of Women'. Ch. 4 returns to the issue of representativeness.

50. Mayo returned 47 centenarians, but Down and Antrim (with comparable populations in 1821) returned only 13 and 19, respectively. See also Ó Gráda *Ireland*, ch. 1.

51. C. Woods, 'Johan Friedrich Hering's Description of Connacht', *IHS*, 25 (1987), 318. See too Hilary Richardson (ed.), *Ordnance Survey Memoirs for the Parishes of Desertmartin and Kilcronaghan 1836–1837* (Ballinascreen, 1986), 21; Angelique Day and Patrick McWilliam (eds.), *Ordnance Survey Memoirs of Ireland*, vi (Belfast, 1990), 55; Samuel M'Skimin, *History and Antiquities of the . . . Carrickfergus*, new edn. (Belfast, 1909), 335; *Freeman's Journal*, 14 Apr. 1847; M. Livi-Bacci, *Population and Nutrition: An Essay on European Demographic History* (Cambridge, 1991), 9, 67–9. For a sceptical assessment of unsubstantiated claims of longevity see Jacques Dupâquier, *Introduction à*

la démographie historique (Paris, 1974), 29–31. On measuring Irish life expectancy, Boyle and Ó Gráda, 'Fertility Trends'.

52. Samuel Hayes, *Essays in Answer to All the Queries on the Culture of Potatoes* (Dublin, 1797), 11.

53. At least from the late eighteenth century on; according to Warburton *et al.* (*History of Dublin*, ii. 1344), Dublin medical men believed that 'contagious fever had not prevailed in Ireland till within these last twenty-five years'.

54. Bourke, 'The Use of the Potato'; also Mokyr, 'Irish History with the Potato'.

Chapter 2

1. C. H. Hull, *The Economic Writings of Sir William Petty* (London, 1899), i. 176.

2. PRONI, *An Anglo-Irish Dialogue: A Calender of the Correspondence Between John Foster and Lord Sheffield 1774–1821* (Belfast, 1976), 3. The closest Young got to Collon on that occasion was 'Glaston Hill' on the Slane–Dundalk road, from which he surveyed Foster's improvements. However, Young called on Foster later on and was unstinting in his praise for the Lord Chief Baron! The account of Collon in the *Tour* is among the most detailed and authoritative of Young's set-piece descriptions. See Young, *Tour*, Dublin edn., i. 41, 146–53.

3. Robert Fraser, *Statistical Survey of the County of Wexford* (Dublin, 1807), 56.

4. Allen and Ó Gráda, 'On the Road Again with Arthur Young'.

5. Ó Curraoin, *Féara agus Bánta*; Solar and Goosens, 'Belgian and Irish Agriculture'.

6. These passages and other relevant excerpts from each of the twenty-three completed surveys are reported in Ó Gráda, *Ireland*, ch. 2.

7. Fraser, *Wexford*, 54–5.

8. Townsend, 233–5.

9. Shaw Mason, *Statistical Account*, i. 66–7; iii. 140.

10. Solar, 'Growth and Distribution', 91–2; Davis, *Industrial Revolution and British Overseas Trade*, 110–11, 116–17.

11. Young, *Tour*, ii (suppl.), 11; Wakefield, *Ireland*, i. 305; Solar, 'Rent'.

12. Solar, 'Growth and Distribution', Table 2.14.

13. Cullen, *Emergence of Modern Ireland*, 253.

14. Crotty, *Irish Agricultural Production*; Solow, *The Land Question*; Mokyr, *Why Ireland Starved*.

15. Yet the same Kingston's reaction to Quaker James Cropper's investment schemes (see Ch. 12) was that there was 'no capital' to promote manufactures and mills in Ireland (Kingston to Peter Robinson, 19 Dec. 1824, in Ontario Archives, Peter Robinson papers, MS 12, reel 1).

16. Ian d'Alton, *Protestant Society and Politics in Cork 1812–1844* (Cork, 1980), 21, 26; Wakefield, *Ireland*, i. 308–9; PRONI, *Letters of a Great Irish Landlord: A Selection from the Estate Correspondence of the Third Marquess of Downshire, 1809–45* (Belfast, 1974), 62; Peter Roebuck, 'Landlord Indebtedness in Ulster in the Seventeenth and Eighteenth Centuries', in Goldstrom and Clarkson, *Population, Economy, and Society*, 135–54; A. P. W. Malcolmson, *The Pursuit of the Heiress: Aristocratic Marriage in Ireland 1750–1820* (Belfast,

1982), 10; Maguire, 'A Resident Landlord'; Townsend, Cork, 681–2 (on Lord Muskerry); Byrne, 'Tullamore', 144–6; Séamus Ó Maolchathaigh, *An Gleann agus a Raibh Ann* (Dublin, 1963), 21–2.

17. Wakefield, *Ireland*, i. 244; Dubourdieu, *Down*, 29; T. Jones-Hughes, 'The Large Farm in Nineteenth Century Ireland', in Alan Gailey and Daithí Ó hÓgáin (eds.), *The Gold Under the Furze* (Dublin, n.d.), 93–100; Kevin Whelan, 'Catholic Mobilisation, 1750–1850', in Bergeron and Cullen (eds.), *Culture et Pratiques Politiques en France et en Irlande*, 235–58; Nolan, *Fassadinin*, 198.

18. One curious example of the consequent undercapitalization is provided by the Duke of Devonshire's estate, where the middlemen's tenants were obliged to thresh their grain in the open air on town streets and highways, 'the bottom thereof being harder than grass ground'. Cited in John Barry, 'The Duke of Devonshire's Estate 1794–1797: Reports by Henry Bowman, Agent', *Annalecta Hibernica*, 22 (1966), 271–314.

19. Dickson, 'Middlemen'; Donnelly, 'The Kenmare Estates during the Nineteenth Century'; *Address to the Tenants on Small Farms on the Lands of Springfield, County Waterford* (Dublin, 1803). For a hostile assessment of the middleman, Wakefield, *Ireland*, i. 286–7.

20. On whom see Eoghan Ó Néill's *Gleann an Óir: Ar Thóir na Staire agus na Litríochta in Oirthear Mumhan agus i nDeisceart Laighean* (Dublin, 1988).

21. Whelan, 'Catholic Mobilisation'; Young, *Tour*, ii. 154–6; Nolan, *Fassadinin*, 130–1, 197–8; Jonathan Bell, 'The Improvement of Irish Farming Techniques since 1750: Theory and Practice', in O'Flanagan *et al.*, *Rural Ireland*, 24–41.

22. W. H. Crawford, 'Landlord-Tenant Relations'; also Raymond Gillespie, *Settlement and Survival on an Ulster Estate* (Belfast, 1988), xi–xxv; John Andrews, 'The Struggle for Ireland's Public Commons', in O'Flanagan *et al.*, *Rural Ireland*, 20.

23. Peter Roebuck, 'Landlord Indebtedness in Ulster in the Seventeenth and Eighteenth Centuries' in Goldstrom and Clarkson, *Irish Population*, 135–54; id., 'The Economic Function and Functions of Substantial Landowners, 1660–1815: Ulster and Lowland Scotland Compared', in Mitchison and Roebuck, *Economy and Society*, 81–92; W. A. Maguire, 'Lord Donegall and the Sale of Belfast: A Case History from the Encumbered Estates Court', *EHR*, 29/4, 570–84.

24. K. Whelan, 'Settlement and Society in Eighteenth-Century Ireland', in G. Dawe and J. W. Foster (eds.), *The Poet's Place: Ulster Literature and Society* (Belfast, 1991), 45–62.

25. The zone corresponds closely with Physiographic Division No. 24 in Royal Irish Academy, *Atlas of Ireland* (Dublin, 1979), 24–5.

26. Thompson, *Meath*, 78–9, 81; Young, *Tour*, i. 51–2, 309.

27. Whelan, 'An Account of the Baronies of Forth and Bargy in 1814', 23; id., 'The Catholic Community in Eighteenth-Century Wexford'.

28. Desmond McCourt, 'Infield and Outfield in Ireland', *EHR*, 7 (1955), 369–76;

Freeman, *Pre-Famine Ireland*, 119–200; Desmond McCabe, 'Law, Conflict and Social Order: County Mayo 1820–1845', ch. 2.

29. Whelan, 'The Catholic Community in Eighteenth-Century Wexford', 165.
30. 'Farmland' is defined as total area less the estimated extent of bog, wasteland, and water in 1854.
31. Hochberg and Miller, 'Varieties of Colonialism'.
32. Jones Hughes, 'The Large Farm'. For an excellent case-study, see Ó Néill, *Gleann an Óir*.
33. Lynch and Vaizey, *Guinness's Brewery*, 9.
34. 'He was good about the rent; he never minded waiting a month or two till the cow or the piece in the loom were sold.' See Nicholas Williams, *Riocard Bairéad: Amhráin* (Dublin, 1978), 70, 102–3.
35. Robert Bell, *The Conditions and Manners of the Peasantry of Ireland such as they were between the Years 1780 and 1790* (London, 1804), 10–12.
36. Lynch and Vaizey, *Guinness's Brewery*, 9–17; Mokyr, *Why Ireland Starved*, 23–4; Johnson, 'Seasonal Migration'; Dickson, *New Foundations*, 97, 112; Patrick O'Flanagan, 'Settlement, Development and Trading in Ireland 1600–1850', in Devine and Dickson, *Scotland and Ireland*, 146–50; *Thom's Irish Almanac 1845* (Dublin, 1845), 44–52; 'Select Committee on Agriculture', BPP [602] 1833 (V), evidence of R. Clendining Department of Extra-Mural Studies (QUB), *Ordnance Survey of the Parish of Donegore* (Belfast, 1974), 8; W. H. Crawford, 'Markets and Fairs in County Mayo', in R. Gillespie and G. P. Moran (eds.), *A Various Country: Essays in Mayo History 1500–1900* (Westport, 1987), 82–90; Charles Coote, *Armagh*, 221–3; P. O'Flanagan, 'Markets and Fairs in Ireland, 1600–1800: An Index of Economic Development and Regional Growth', *Journal of Historical Geography*, 11/4 (1985), 364–78.

Chapter 3

1. Cullen, *Anglo-Irish Trade*, 45–7.
2. Smith, *The Wealth of Nations*, ii. 944.
3. McCavery, 'Finance and Politics in Ireland', ch. 1.
4. Castlereagh cited in E. R. R. Green, 'Industrial Decline in the Nineteenth Century', in Cullen, *Formation of the Irish Economy*, 90; McCavery, 'Finance and Politics in Ireland', 35; G. C. Bolton, *The Passing of the Act of Union* (Oxford, 1966), 193–6, 220. The clauses of Art. 6 are cited *in extenso* in O'Brien, *Economic History of Ireland in the Eighteenth Century*, 417–21.
5. J. R. Hill, 'Artisans, Sectarianism and Politics in Dublin, 1829–48', *Saothar*, 7 (1981), 20–5.
6. Murray, *Commercial Relations*, 320–1; McCavery, 'Finance and Politics in Ireland', 29–31.
7. Murray, *Commercial Relations*, 372, 382; Kiernan, *History of the Financial Administration of Ireland*, ch. 12; Johnson and Kennedy, 'Nationalist Historiography', 18–19.
8. Patrick Fagan, 'The Population of Dublin in the Eighteenth Century with

Particular Reference to the Proportions of Protestants and Catholics', *Eighteenth-Century Ireland*, 6 (1991), 121-56.

9. Edwin Cannan, *The Paper Pound of 1797-1821: The Bullion Report* (London, 1919); George O'Brien, 'The Last Years of the Irish Currency'.

10. Hugh Boulter, *Letters Written by His Excellency Hugh Boulter DD* (Dublin, 1769), ii. 155-9; John Stevenson, *Two Centuries of Life in Down 1600-1800* (Belfast, 1990), 265-71.

11. Carr, *Stranger in Ireland*, 25.

12. Anon., *Considerations on the Silver Currency, Relative to both the General Evil as Affecting the Empire, and the Present Enormous Evil in Ireland* (Dublin, 1805), 30-3; Fetter, *Irish Pound*, 86.

13. On the real bills doctrine see Fetter, *British Monetary Orthodoxy*, 40-3.

14. See Ó Gráda, 'The Irish Paper Pound' and 'Some Cliometrics of the Bullionist Controversy'.

15. McCavery, 'Finance and Politics in Ireland, 1801-17'.

16. Cullen, 'Landlords, Bankers and Merchants', 42.

17. Fetter, *Irish Pound*, 73-4; John Foster, *An Essay on the Principle of Commercial Exchanges, and More Particularly the Exchange between Ireland and Great Britain* (London, 1804), 138-9.

18. Ibid., 137.

19. e.g. Dom Patrick Nolan, *The History and Mystery of Banking in Ireland and Elsewhere* (Bruges, 1923), ch. 19.

20. Lionel Pressnell, *Country Banking in the Industrial Revolution* (Oxford, 1956), 441; Fetter, *British Monetary Orthodoxy*, 48-54; N. Silberling, 'British Prices and Business Cycles', *Review of Economics and Statistics*, Oct. 1923.

21. Pressnell, *Country Banking*, 447-8, 538.

22. C. McC. Collins, *The Law and Practice of Banking* (Dublin, 1880), 77; O'Kelly, *Old Private Banks of Munster*, 24; 'Lords Select Committee on Promissory Notes', BPP (HL) 1826-7 (VI) [245], 47, 50; Carr, *Stranger in Ireland*, 218-19; see also, however, Barrow, 'Some Dublin Private Banks'.

23. Robert G. King, 'On the Economics of Private Money', *Journal of Monetary Economics*, 12 (1983), 127-583; Lawrence White, *Free Banking in Britain: Theory, Experience and Debate, 1800-1845* (Cambridge, 1984); Eugene N. White, 'Free Banking During the French Revolution', *EEH*, 27/3 (1990), 257-76; Charles Goodhart, *The Evolution of Central Banks* (Cambridge, Mass., 1988).

24. *Parliamentary Debates*, 21 Mar. 1804, 650-1. For the traditional view see O'Brien, *Economic History of Ireland in the Eighteenth Century*, ch. 28. O'Brien's account relies too heavily on an uncritical reading of Malcolm Dillon, *The History and Development of Banking in Ireland* (London and Dublin, 1889). Much more reliable is Barrow's 'Some Dublin Private Banks', 51-2.

25. Quoted in Pressnell, *Country Banking*, 208.

26. Among the collection of banknotes in NLI, MS 10,709, the notes of French's Tuam bank bear the promise, as do those of small-note issuers such as the Aughnacloy, Enniscorthy, and Leighlinbridge banks. See O'Kelly, *Old Private*

Banks of Munster, 28, 82, 93, 98a, for similar evidence on Maunsells' in Limerick, and Pike's, Roches', and Newenhams' in Cork.

27. King, *Thoughts on the Restriction of Payments in Specie at the Banks of England and Ireland*, 52–3.
28. 'Lords Select Committee on Promissory Notes', 44.
29. Hall, *Bank of Ireland*, 91.
30. Wakefield, *Ireland*, ii. 173, and 166–75 *passim*.
31. O'Kelly, *Old Private Banks of Munster*, 25; PRONI, MIC 338/11 (on the failure of the Newry Bank). John Anderson, the owner, blamed his 'unfortunate purchase of the Barrymore Estate and the extraordinary continuance of the annuities granted thereon', together with 'the late extraordinary change of times' (John Anderson to Robert Peel, 20 June 1816, cited in Brunicardi, *John Anderson Entrepreneur*, 106).
32. A. Rolnick and W. Weber, 'The Causes of Free Banking Failures: A Detailed Examination', *Journal of Monetary Economics*, 14 (1984), 290. As Vera Smith noted long ago (*The Rationale of Central Banking*, London, 1936, 44–6), banking in the USA was not completely 'free' in this period.
33. O'Kelly, *Old Private Banks*, 27; BofIA, Transactions of the Court of Directors, 1820.
34. Compare Pressnell, *Country Banks*, 445; Julian Hoppit, 'Financial Crises in Eighteenth-Century England', *EHR*, 39/1 (1986), 39–58. Strictly speaking, of course, the critical question is less the number of failures than how much the bank's depositors and other customers lost.
35. Barrow, 'Some Dublin Private Banks', 50–2; id., *Emergence*, 207, 212; *Address to the Creditors of the Late Firm of Ffrench & Co. by a Suffering Creditor* (n.p., 1818). Nevertheless, the bankruptcy laws were subject to abuse: see *Memorial and Suggestions of the Merchants of the City of Dublin . . . Relative to Bankruptcy* (Dublin, 1807).
36. *FJ*, 7 June 1820.
37. For an analysis of the 1972 strike, Antoin Murphy, 'Money in an Economy Without Banks: The Case of Ireland', *Manchester School of Economic Science*, 46/1 (1978), 41–50.
38. The outcome of a simple Granger–Simms 'causality' test confirms this. Let the dependent variable (*Fhouse*) be the number of bankers and allied trades reported in the *Dublin Gazette* each half-year between 1776:1 and 1823:2, *Lother* the logarithm of the number of other business failures reported in the same source, and T a time trend. Running *Fhouse* on its own past values and those of *Lother*, and T, the value of the F-statistic for a joint test of zero restrictions on the coefficients of $Fhouse(-i)$, $i = 1$ to 3 is 2.06, which is insignificant at the conventional levels. This result fails to support the hypothesis that bank failures 'caused' other bankruptcies. The returns for 1800 are incomplete since a complete series of the *Dublin Gazette* could not be obtained for that year in either Dublin or London. On British failures, Pressnell, *Country Banking*, 535–8.
39. A. D. Gayer, W. W. Rostow, and A. J. Schwartz, *The Growth and Fluctuation*

of the British Economy 1790–1850: An Historical, Statistical and Theoretical Study of the British Economy (Oxford, 1953), 634–5, 663.

40. Cited in Hall, *Bank of Ireland*, 123 n.
41. Goodhart, *Evolution of Central Banks*.
42. However, in Dec. 1800 the Bank refused to accommodate George Maunsell, of the Limerick banking family, for £2,000 on the basis that 'money will not be advanced but to a resident in Dublin'. But we are not told whether Maunsel sought this loan to support the Limerick Bank or for other reasons (BoIA, Transactions of the Court of Directors, December 1800).
43. Fetter, *Irish Pound*, 65; William Jebb, *An Inquiry into the Depreciation of Irish Bank-Paper, its Effects and Causes, and a Remedy Proposed* (Dublin, 1804), 14–15.
44. PRONI, D3439/3 (Belfast Discount Company archive), letters of 15 and 20 Feb. 1799.
45. Fetter, *Irish Pound*, 67; Parnell, *Observations*, 22, 48, 52–3.
46. 'Commons Select Committee on Promissory Notes', BPP [402] 1826 (III), 102–3; also ibid. 77–80.
47. Cullen, 'Landlords, Bankers and Merchants', 40–3; Noel Simpson, *The Belfast Bank* (Belfast, 1974), 6–7.
48. Fetter, *Irish Pound*, 67; Parnell, *Observations*, 24; Foster, *Essay*, 12 n, 123; O'Brien, 'Last Years of the Irish Currency', 254; Royal College of Physicians of Ireland, Kirkpatrick MS 94, letter from Thomas Mills to Michael Mills, 23 Aug. 1805.
49. Cited in Fetter, 'Legal Tender During the English and Irish Bank Restrictions', *JPE*, 58 (1950), 250; also André Fitzpatrick, 'The Economic Effects', 81; Ollerenshaw, *Banking*, 4–9.

Chapter 4

1. Boyle and Ó Gráda, 'Fertility Trends'.
2. Mokyr, *Why Ireland Starved*, ch. 2. I_g is defined as $B/\Sigma M_i H_i$, where B is the annual number of legitimate births, M_i the number of married women aged i, and h_i the Hutterite weight for age-group i. The latter refers to the average number of children per year born to a married woman member of the American Hutterite community. Anthropological work on the Hutterites early in this century revealed their extraordinarily high fertility. I_f is defined as $B/\Sigma W_i h_i$, where W_i is the number of women aged i, and I_f as $(I_m)(I_g)$. The history of these measures is outlined in Coale and Treadway, 'A Summary of the Changing Distribution of Overall Fertility, Marital Fertility, and the Proportions Married in the Provinces of Europe', in A. J. Coale and S. C. Watkins (eds.), *The Decline of Fertility in Europe* (Princeton, NJ, 1988), 153–62. The assumptions set out in Ó Gráda, *Ireland*, ch. 5 yield an I_g of 0.84 for Ireland in 1841.
3. Eversley, 'The Demography of the Irish Quakers'; Vann and Eversley, *Friends in Life and Death*, chs. 1 and 4. Hutterite fertility is routinely invoked as the highest on record (see e.g. Coale and Treadway, 'Summary of the Changing

Distribution', in Coale and Watkins, *The Decline of Fertility in Europe*, 34). On the status of the Irish Quaker community, Holt, 'The Quakers in the Great Irish Famine', ch. 1.

4. Cited in W. H. Crawford, *Domestic Industry in Ireland*, 64. Along the same lines is 'The Sprigger's Lament' (TCD broadsheet collection, OLS 189.t.2/ 192*b*).

5. Newenham, *Statistical and Historical Inquiry*, 10, 18−28, 276−82; *1841 Census*, 438−9, 486−7. Young (*Tour*, ii (suppl.), 86−7) also refers to the prevalence of marriage in Ireland relative to England. For Mokyr's overview and estimates of the birth-rate and marital fertility on the eve of the Famine, see *Why Ireland Starved*, ch. 2. The data for other European countries are taken from Ansley Coale and Roy Treadway, 'A Summary'.

6. Compare Wrigley and Schofield, *Population History of England*, 255; Mokyr, *Why Ireland Starved*, 35.

7. Morgan and Macafee, 'Irish Population in the Pre-Famine Period'; Macafee, 'Pre-Famine Population in Ulster'; Ó Gráda, 'Dublin's Demography'.

8. Malthus, in evidence to the Select Committee on Emigration, Q.3198; Eversley, 'The Demography', 74.

9. Ó Gráda, 'Malthus'; O'Neill, 'The Famine of 1822'; Guildhall Library, MSS 7440−94 (papers of 1822 Irish Relief Fund).

10. Ó Gráda, 'Dublin's Demography', 50−1. Further analysis of second- and third-parity mothers in 1845−7 suggests an improvement over the survival rates previously reported for 1824.

11. Young, *Tour*, ii (suppl.), 42.

12. Quoted in Leyburn, *The Scotch-Irish in America* (Chapel Hill, NC, 1962), 151. Since presumably only household heads were asked to sign, the true percentage of literate people must have been considerably lower. The main point still stands, however.

13. Farley Grubb, 'The Market for Indentured Immigrants: Evidence on the Efficiency of Forward-Labor Contracting in Philadelphia, 1745−1773', *JEH*, 45 (1985), 861−8.

14. Young, *Tour*, ii. 184−5.

15. John Mannion (ed.), *The Peopling of Newfoundland: Essays in Historical Geography* (St John's, 1977); John Mannion, 'Migration and Upward Mobility: The Meaghar Family in Ireland and Newfoundland, 1780−1830', *IESH* 15 (1988), 54−70. Also Kevin Whelan, 'Gaelic Survivals', *Irish Review* 7 (1989), 141; Eoghan Ó Néill, *Gleann an Óir* (Dublin, 1988).

16. Bruce S. Elliott, *Irish Migrants in the Canadas: A New Approach* (Kingston and Montreal, 1988); Cecil Houston and W. J. Smyth, *Irish Emigration and Canadian Settlement* (Belfast, 1990). For evidence from an earlier period of the tendency to cluster see J. Lemon, *The Best Poor Man's Country: A Geographical Study of Early Southeastern Pennsylvania* (Baltimore, Md., 1972), 83.

17. PRONI, T3506/1−13, 'Quarterly Return of Vagrants Passed by the Contractor at Colnebrook to Maidenhead'; Lees, *Exiles of Erin*; David Fitzpatrick, 'Emigration, 1801−70', in Vaughan, *NHI*, 5, pp. 571−3.

18. Cf. Brendan Walsh, 'Emigration: an economist's perspective' (UCD Centre for Economic Research Policy Paper 1989/3).
19. Mokyr and Ó Gráda, 'Emigration and Poverty'; Nicholas and Shergold, 'Human Capital and the Pre-Famine Irish Emigration to England'.
20. Mokyr and Ó Gráda, 'Emigration and Poverty'.
21. R. A. Berry and R. Soligo, 'Some Welfare Aspects of International Migration', *JPE*, 77/8 (1969), 778–94. For an argument in this spirit, less formally stated, see Lee, *Modernisation of Irish Society*, 12.
22. Though Irish was in *relative* decline as a vernacular in these decades, the number of Irish-speakers probably reached an all-time peak as recently as 1846.
23. Fernand Braudel, *La Méditerranée et le Monde Méditerranéen à l'époque de Philippe II*, 2nd edn. (Paris, 1966), 46; O'Dowd, *Spalpeens*. For comparative perspective, Pier Paolo Viazzo, *Upland Communities: Environment, Population and Society in the Alps since the Sixteenth Century* (Cambridge, 1989), 100–8; Abel Poitrineau, *Remues d'hommes: les migrations montagnardes en France 17e–18e siècles* (Paris, 1983).
24. *Poor Inquiry*, App. E, 2.
25. IFC, MS 1071/44 (spelling standardized). 'Pat Daly has a bag of meal; he has stuck two hundred potatoes into the fire; he is eating one and has another ready in his hand; and he'd swear on the book that he'd eat more of them.'
26. Cited in James Pope-Hennessy, *Anthony Trollope* (London, 1971), 72.
27. Mokyr, *Why Ireland Starved*, 12; Mokyr and Ó Gráda, 'Poor and Getting Poorer?'.
28. References to the eagerness for education abound: e.g. Asenath Nicholson, *The Bible in Ireland (Ireland's Welcome to the Stranger . . .)*, A. T. Sheppard, ed. (New York, 1927), 62; Royal College of Physicians of Ireland, Kirkpatrick MS 94, Letter from Thomas Mills MD to Michael Mills, Loughbrickland, Co. Down, 29 June 1803. On heights and literacy see Mokyr and Ó Gráda, 'The Heights of the British and the Irish'; Nicholas and Steckel, 'The Heights of Working Men'; Peter R. Moock and Joanne Leslie, 'Childhood Malnutrition and Schooling: the Terai Region of Nepal', *Journal of Development Economics*, 20 (1986), 33–52.
29. Mokyr and Ó Gráda, 'Poor and Getting Poorer?', 622; *1841 Census*, 438–9; Ó Gráda, *Ireland*, ch. 1. See also Mary Daly, 'The Development of the National School System, 1831–40', in Art Cosgrove and Donal McCartney (eds.), *Studies in Irish History Presented to R. Dudley Edwards* (Dublin, 1979). For a gloomier view, John Logan, 'Sufficient to Their Needs: Literacy and Elementary Schooling in the Nineteenth Century', in Daly and Dickson (eds.), *Language Change and Educational Development 1700–1920* (Dublin, 1990), 112–16.
30. D'Arcy, 'Wages of Labourers in the Dublin Building Industry', 28; O'Brien, 'Agricultural Prices and Living Costs'; Solar, 'Growth and Distribution', Table 2.16; NA, M7069 (Labour accounts of Ardgillan Castle, County Dublin, 1815–1847).

31. Compare, however, R. C. Allen, *Enclosure and the Yeoman: The Agricultural Development of the South Midlands 1450–1850* (Oxford, 1992), 297–300.

32. Mokyr and Ó Gráda, 'Poor and Getting Poorer?'. The caveats mentioned in the text are discussed in greater detail in this study. See also Mokyr, 'Is There Still Life in the Pessimist Case?', *JEH*, 48 (1988), 69–92.

33. W. Peter Ward and Patricia Ward, 'Infant Birth Weight and Nutrition in Industrializing Montreal', *American Historical Review*, 89 (1985), 324–45; Goldin and Margo, 'The Poor at Birth'.

34. 'Martin Doyle' (Revd. W. Hickey), *The Labouring Classes in Ireland: An Inquiry as to What Beneficial Changes May be Effected in their Condition* (Dublin, 1846), 62.

35. Mokyr, *Why Ireland Starved*, 8–9.

36. Solar, 'The Great Famine', 123–4; R. W. Fogel, 'Second Thoughts on the European Escape from Hunger: Famines, Price Elasticities, Entitlements, Chronic Malnutrition, and Mortality Rates', Working Paper Series on Historical Factors in Long-Run Growth, National Bureau of Economic Research, Working Paper No. 1 (May 1989); S. R. Osmani, 'Food Deprivation and Undernutrition in Modern Bangladesh', WIDER Working Paper No. 82 (Helsinki, 1990), 18. Compare Marcel Lachiver, *Les Années de misère: La Famine au temps du Grande Roi* (Paris, 1991), 41–2.

37. 'Appendix to the Sixth Report of the Poor Law Commissioners' BPP 1840 (XVII) [245], 397; Crawford, 'Dearth, Diet and Disease', 152–3.

38. Ibid.; id., 'Aspects of Irish Diet, 1839–1904' (unpublished Ph.D. thesis, University of London, 1985); id., 'Subsistence Crises and Famines in Ireland: A Nutritionist's View', in id., *Famine*, 198–219; Jennifer A. Woolfe, *The Potato in the Human Diet* (Cambridge, 1987), 31–2. The source for the 1839 diet is 'Appendix to the Sixth Annual Report of the Poor Law Commissioners', BPP 1840 (XVII) [245], 447.

39. Since the Irish intake excludes meat and dairy products, its distribution may well have been less egalitarian than those assumed.

40. Townsend, *Cork*, 89.

41. Bourke, 'The Potato, Weather', 113; Denis Knight (ed.), *Cobbett in Ireland: A Warning to England* (London, 1984), 94; Martin Doyle [William Hickey], *The Labouring Classes*, 62. The shift to a 'white, soft potato, which is productive and requires little manure' is noted in *First Report of the General Board of Health for the City of Dublin* (Dublin, 1822), 43. In 1832 a Kerry campaigner against tithes complained of *gan do bhiadh againn act lompers agus an nidh nach ar bfiudh leis na ministeirighe d'ithead* (our only food being lumpers and what the ministers would not eat) (S. P. Ó Mórdha, 'An Anti-Tithe Speech in Irish', *Éigse*, 9/4 (1960–1), 225.

42. Bourke 'Potato, Weather and the Blight', 56.

43. Jennifer N. Woolfe, *The Potato in the Human Diet* (Cambridge, 1987), 8–9.

44. Average of the weekly prices of cups and lumpers quoted in the *Farmers' Gazette* (120 observations); Killarney Board of Guardians minute-book, 2 Apr. 1845 (Kerry County Library (Tralee), BG 104/A/1).

45. Crawford, 'Dearth, Diet and Disease', 153.

46. Cited in Burton, *The Potato*, 3rd edn. (London, 1989), 599–601.

47. Bourke, 'The Potato, Weather, Blight, and the Irish Famine', 60–1; W. G. Andrews, 'An Essay on the Properties, Habits, and Nature of the Potato', in *Prize Essays on the Potato* (Dublin, 1835), 6–7, 12–16; Ora Smith, *Potatoes: Production, Storing, Processing* (Westview, Conn., 1977), 607.

48. Thomas P. McIntosh, *The Potato: Its History, Varieties, Culture and Diseases* (Edinburgh, 1927), 17, states that the Irish Lumpers (*sic*) still grown then could be taken 'with reasonable certainty to be identical with the varieties mentioned by Lawson under these names'. Messrs. Lawson published an *Agriculturalists' Manual* in 1836 listing 146 potato varieties cultivated at that date.

49. Dubourdieu, *Antrim*, i. 205.

50. e.g. E. R. R. Green, 'Agriculture', in Edwards and Williams, *Great Famine*, 103; Mokyr, *Why Ireland Starved*, 12. On testimony to the Lumper's sturdiness from Westmeath, *Prize Essays on the Potato* (Dublin, 1835), 62.

51. 'First Report of Inquiry into the Conditions of the Poorer Classes in Ireland', BPP 1836 (XXX) to (XXXIII) [henceforth *Poor Inquiry*], suppl. to App. D. On the Lumper vs. the Cup and the Apple see *Poor Inquiry*, App. E, *passim*. On the food value of the potato see Jennifer A. Woolfe, *The Potato in the Human Diet* (Cambridge, 1987), ch. 2; R. A. McCance and E. M. Wooson, *The Composition of Foods* (London, 1960); W. G. Burton, *The Potato*, 2nd edn. (Wageningen, 1966).

52. R. McHugh, 'The Famine in Irish Oral Tradition', in Edwards and Williams, *The Great Famine*, 393; IFC, vols. 1068–70. McHugh's study is based on the IFC archive material. In 1852 a waiter in Westport told Sir Francis Head how 'a gentleman had won a sovereign by betting with a party of jolly good Papists, with whom he was dining, "that he could prove there were at the table more *Protestants* than Catholics"'. He was referring to the potato variety called 'Protestants' (F. Head, *A Fortnight in Ireland* (London, 1852), 151).

53. M. G. Moyles and P. de Brún, 'Charles O'Brien's Agricultural Survey of Kerry, 1800', *JKAHS*, 1 (1969), 90; *Returns of Agricultural Produce in Ireland in the Year 1854* (Dublin, 1855), xxvii; Edward Carroll, 'Boiled Cabbage as Food for Milch Cows', *IF&GM*, 7 (June 1834), 391; David O'Kane (ed.), *Statistical Reports of Six Derry Parishes* (Ballinascreen, 1983), 94; Diarmuid Ó Doibhlín (ed.), *Ordnance Survey of the Parish of Artrea 1833–1836* (Ballinascreen, 1983), 56.

54. E. M. Crawford, 'Dearth, Diet and Disease', 152–3; Hayes, *Essays in Answer*, 9. Margaret Crawford has also suggested in correspondence the high biological value of potato protein.

55. E. Evans, *Irish Folk Ways* (London, 1957), 134; Charles Coote, *Statistical Survey of the County of Armagh* (Dublin, 1804), 192–3; Bell and Watson, *Irish Farming*, 57; E. J. T. Collins, *Sickle to Combine* (Reading, 1969), 9.

56. Mokyr, *Why Ireland Starved*, 215; K. M. D. Snell, *Annals of the Labouring Poor: Social Change and Agrarian England, 1660–1900* (Cambridge, 1985), ch.

1. Compare the estimate of the labour year in *Irish Farmers' Gazette*, 17 Aug. 1822 (cited in full in Ó Gráda, *Ireland*, ch. 1, n. 40) which puts the number of days 'idly and profanely spent' at 150.

57. *Poor Inquiry*, App. E, 16. For an extensive discussion of the 'meal months' see Bourke, 'The Potato, Weather, and the Blight', 73–7.

58. Rose E. Frisch, 'Population, Food Intake and Fertility', *Science*, 199 (1978), 22–30; John Bongaarts, 'Does Malnutrition Affect Fecundity? A Summary of the Evidence', *Science*, 208 (1980), 564–9; Henri Leridon, *Saisonalité des naissances* (Paris, 1973); E. A. Wrigley and R. Schofield, *The Population History of England 1539–1871: A Reconstruction* (London, 1981), 286–7. The data used here were collated under the supervision of the late Iognáid Ó Cléirigh. I am grateful to Kevin Whelan for a copy.

59. Compare Wrigley and Schofield, *Population History of England*, 286–7.

60. Livi-Bacci, *Population and Nutrition*, 16–17, 96.

61. See Anthony Y. C. Koo, 'An Economic Justification for Land Reformism', *Economic Development and Cultural Change*, 25 (1977), 523–38; R. Albert Berry and William R. Cline, *Agrarian Structure and Productivity in Developing Countries* (Baltimore, Md., 1979) and the works cited therein.

62. The proposals of Mill and Thornton were prompted by the Famine. See J. S. Mill, *Principles of Political Economy* (London, 1848), i. 381–400; W. T. Thornton, *A Plea for Peasant Proprietors with Outlines of a Plan for Their Establishment in Ireland* (London, 1848); Black, *Economic Thought*, 28–31.

63. Mokyr, *Why Ireland Starved*, 26; Young, *Tour*, ii. (suppl.), 38–9; Wakefield, *Ireland*, ii. 208–29. I am grateful to Joel Mokyr for his county data.

64. PRONI, T1536/4.

65. Mokyr, *Why Ireland Starved*, 10–1; Deane and Cole, *British Economic Growth*, 166.

66. Compare J. Bhagwati, 'Why are Services Cheaper in the Poor Countries?', *EJ*, 94 (1984), 279–86.

67. Mokyr, *Why Ireland Starved* (2nd edn.), 27; Deane and Cole, *British Economic Growth*, 166; N. F. R. Crafts, 'Gross National Product in Europe, 1879–1910: Some New Estimates', *EEH*, 20 (1983), 387–401.

68. Hall and Hall, *Ireland*, iii. 360 n.

69. David Dickson, 'In Search of the Old Irish Poor Law', in Mitchison and Roebuck, *Economy and Society*, 148–59; Timothy P. O'Neill, 'The State, Poverty and Distress in Ireland 1815–45'; id., 'Poverty and Public Health in Pre-Famine Ireland, *RSAIJ* (1974), 1–34 (with map of dispensaries and hospitals on p. 6); Warburton *et al.*, *History of the City of Dublin*, ii. 730–43, 1345–6; F. Barker and J. Cheyne, *An Account of the Rise, Progress, and Decline of the Fever Lately Epidemical in Ireland* (Dublin, 1821), ii. 166–71; Patrick Sharkey, *An Essay on the Causes, Progress, and Treatment of Typhus Fever as it Has Appeared in the City of Cork* (Cork, 1817); Eoin O'Brien, *Conscience and Conflict: A Biography of Sir Dominick Corrigan 1802–1880* (Dublin, 1983), 191–3.

70. O'Neill, 'Poverty and Public Health'; Oliver MacDonagh, 'Ideas and Institutions', in Vaughan, *NHI*, 209–11.

71. Angus McIntyre, *The Liberator: Daniel O'Connell and the Irish Party 1830–1847* (London, 1965), 211, 217–18.

72. *Abstracts of the Accounts of the South Dublin Union for the Half-Year ending 29th September 1840* (Dublin, 1841); *Thom's Irish Almanac 1845*, 180.

73. Hall and Hall, *Ireland*, iii. 339–60; Helen Burke, *The People and the Poor Law in Nineteenth Century Ireland*; Gerard O'Brien, 'The New Poor Law in Pre-Famine Ireland', *IESH*, 12 (1985), 33–49; id., 'The Establishment of Poor Law Unions in Ireland, 1838–43', *IHS*, 23 (1982–3), 97–120; id., 'Workhouse Management in Pre-Famine Ireland', *PRIA*, 86C (1986), 113–34; *Tenth Annual Report of the Poor Law Commissioners* (London, 1844), 4, 579. The numbers relieved per quarter in workhouses in England and Wales averaged 200,000 in the early 1840s, compared to 50,000 in Ireland. In England and Wales, in addition, over 1,000,000 received some form of outdoor relief.

74. Ibid., App. B, No. 17, 572–9.

75. Thackeray, *Irish Sketch Book*, 344–6. See too Kohl, *Ireland*, 278–82. The North Dublin Union had recently been the subject of a parliamentary investigation (*Inquiry into the Treatment and Mortality of Infant Children in the Workhouse of the North Dublin Union*, BPP 1842, (XXXVI) [370]; Thomas Willis, *Facts Connected with the Social and Sanitary Condition of the Working Classes in the City of Dublin* (Dublin, 1845), 7–9.

76. Thackeray would not have been surprised to hear that 'procuresses' from the city's brothels had infiltrated the Cork Union workhouse in 1841 (*The Constitution*, 26 Jan. 1841, cited in O'Brien, 'The New Poor Law', 44–5). For an analysis of admissions to the South Dublin Union see Burke, *The People and the Poor Law in Nineteenth Century Ireland*, 74. The number of widows aged 17–25 in the whole city in 1841 was 309. In the 26–35 age-group it was 1,931.

Thackeray's 'fallen women' are more clearly in evidence in the records of the Westmoreland Lock Hospital, which accommodated about 800 syphilitic female patients annually. The Famine had a marked impact on their composition, though (due to capacity constraints) not on their number. The share of women from counties other than Dublin, Kildare, Meath, and Wicklow rose from 8% in 1842–3 to 30% in 1847–8, and that of girls aged 17 years and less from 7 to 13.5% (RCPI, Lock Hospital admissions registry).

77. Mokyr, *Why Ireland Starved*, 6–9.

78. Komlos, *Nutrition and Economic Development*; Sandberg and Steckel, 'Overpopulation and Malnutrition Reconsidered'; Floud, Wachter, and Gregory, *Height, Health and History*, 205–6; Komlos, 'The Secular Trend in the Biological Standard of Living in the United Kingdom, 1730–1860', *EHR*, 26/1 (1993), 136.

79. Floud *et al.*, *Height*, 38–9.

80. East India Library, L/MIL/9/58.

81. Floud *et al.*, *Height*, 88–9.

82. Time-series comparisons are given in Komlos, *Nutrition and Economic Development*; Floud, Wachter, and Gregory, *Height, Health and History*; Lars Sandberg and Richard Steckel, 'Heights and Economic History: The Swedish Case', *Annals of Human Biology*, 14 (1987), 101–10.

83. Tim Hatton tells me that in shoemaking, a clicker is one who cuts out the leather, and in printing, an underforeman compositor who distributes work to others.

84. Madan Paul Singh, *Indian Army under the East India Company* (Delhi, 1976), 98; Edward M. Spiers, *The Army and Society 1815–1914* (London, 1980), 53.

85. Mokyr and Ó Gráda, 'Heights and Health, *c.*1780–1850', TS.

86. Ó Gráda, 'The Heights of Clonmel Prisoners'.

87. The Kilmainham convicts discussed below were much more likely to be recidivists and thus atypical in terms of socio-economic status at time of arrest, if not socio-economic background. The representativeness or otherwise of Australian transportees is a controversial issue for Australian economic historians. See the exchanges between Ralph Shlomowitz and Stephen Nicholas in *Australian Economic History Review*, 31 (1991).

88. Compare Roderick Floud, 'The Heights of Europeans Since 1750: A New Source for European Economic History', NBER Working Paper No. 1318 (1984). Since chi-square tests could not reject the hypothesis that the Clonmel prisoners' heights were normally distributed, there was no need in this case to apply the QBE technique.

89. I am very grateful to Mr Douglas MacDonald of the Agricultural and Fisheries Department, Edinburgh, and his staff for growing extra batches of the potatoes listed in 1991 and carrying out the experiments described here.

Chapter 5

1. Farr to Larcom, 28 Sept. 1849 (NLI, MS 7743/52). On Larcom see J. H. Andrews, 'Thomas Aiskew Larcom', *Geographas: Biobibliographical Studies*, 7 (1983), 171–4.

2. Solar, 'Growth and Distribution'; Ó Gráda, *Ireland*, ch. 2; Turner, 'Agricultural Output and Productivity'.

3. Discussed in more detail in my 'Slices of Irish Agricultural History'.

4. Peter Froggatt, 'The Census of Ireland 1813–15', *IHS*, 14 (1965), 227–35; Bourke, 'The Agricultural Statistics of the 1841'; Lee, 'On the Accuracy of Pre-Famine Censuses'; David Fitzpatrick, 'The Study of Nineteenth-Century Irish Population', unpublished, 1978; Walsh, 'Marriage Rates and Population Pressure'; Ó Gráda, 'Nineteenth-Century Emigration Statistics'.

5. 'The number who are recusant', he continued, 'are now reduced to two individuals in all Ireland! one a noble lord in a northern county who is not so admired as to make his example contagious, but the reverse'. The 'noble lord' was Lord Leitrim. This and the other evidence in this paragraph are taken from NLI, MSS 7743–4 (Thomas Larcom Papers).

6. 'Report of the S. C. Appointed to Inquire into the Best Mode of Obtaining Accurate Agricultural Statistics', BPP (HL) 1854–5 (VII) [501], Q. 395. See also Donnelly to Larcom, 25 June 1855 (NLI, MS 7744).

7. Allen and Ó Gráda, 'On the Road Again', 114.

8. M. Turner, 'Agricultural Productivity in England in the Eighteenth Century: Evidence from Crop Yields', *EHR*, 35/4 (1982), 489–510; J. D. Coppock,

'The Statistical Assessment of British Agriculture', *AgHR*, 4 (1956), 4–21 and 66–79.

9. Exports fell by 5% in 1847–53, while numbers enumerated rose by 31%. See *Agricultural Statistics*; Solar, 'Growth and Distribution'; Ó Gráda, 'Slices'.

10. e.g. Kane, *Industrial Resources*, ch. 2. See also Ch. 13.

11. The bogs were widely scattered, though some observers complained of resource depletion even before the Famine, e.g. Townsend, *Cork*, 255, 603.

12. *Poor Inquiry*, App. E ('Cottages and Cabins').

13. Hall and Hall, *Ireland*, ii. 261–8, and Anon. (1855) are good contemporary sources on the turf harvest. My thanks to Peter Solar for the second reference. Compare C. C. Ellison, 'Materials for the Dublin Society Agricultural Survey of County Louth', *Journal of the County Louth Historical and Archaeological Society* (1974), which contains several assessments of the cost of a family's fuel requirements in 1808.

14. Ó Gráda, *Ireland*; Solar, 'Growth and Distribution'; 'Report of the Select Committee on Agriculture', BPP 1833 (V) [612] evidence of Alexander Clendinning, Thomas Spencer Lindsay, More O'Ferrall, John McMahon; *LTD*, county entries; Mokyr, *Why Ireland Starved*, 130–1.

15. Ibid., 147–9; Solar, 'Growth and Distribution', 37–40; Solar, 'Rent in Ireland' (mimeo, 1990), 18.

16. Cited in Kevin Whelan, 'Settlement and Society in Eighteenth-Century Ireland', mimeo.

17. J. R. MacCulloch, *A Descriptive and Statistical Account of the British Empire* (London, 1854), i. 549–50; Deane and Cole, *British Economic Growth 1688–1959* (Cambridge, 1962), 166; F. M. L. Thompson, 'Rural Society and Agricultural Change in Nineteenth-Century Britain', in G. Grantham and C. Leonard (eds.), *Agrarian Organization in the Century of Industrialization: Europe, Russian and North America* (Greenwich, Conn. 1989), 191–2; Allen, 'Agriculture During the Industrial Revolution'; Solar, 'Agricultural Productivity', 73. For further discussion, Ó Gráda, *Ireland*, ch. 2.

18. Solar, 'Productivity in Scottish and Irish Agriculture'; Solar and Goosens, 'Agricultural Productivity in Belgium and Ireland'; Ó Gráda, *Ireland*, ch. 2.

19. For Ireland: Ó Gráda, 'Irish Head Rents'. For Britain: James Caird, *English Agriculture in 1850–1* (London, 1852), 480; Thompson, 'Rural Society and Agricultural Change', 191.

20. Young, *Tour* (Dublin, 1780), ii (suppl.), 6; id., *A Six Months Tour Through the North of England* (Dublin, 1770), iii, 320; Caird, *English Agriculture*, 474. Caird's 1770 estimate is an average of 26 county estimates produced by Young. Young's own estimate (*Six Month Tour*, 318, 321) is lower, but it is based on his Northern tour, biasing it downward.

21. McCulloch, *Statistical Account*, 514; Bell and Watson, *Irish Farming*. See the excerpts from the Dublin Society statistical surveys and *LTD* in Ó Gráda, *Ireland*, Apps. 2.2 and 2.3.

22. Davis, *Industrial Revolution and British Overseas Trade*; Peter Solar, 'Growth and Distribution', Tables 6.9 and 6.10.

23. Kevin O'Rourke, 'The Repeal of the Corn Laws and Irish Emigration', mimeo, Columbia University, Feb. 1991; NLI, MS 10127, Mathew O'Connor to Denis Mahon, 25 May 1841.

24. Ó Gráda, *The Great Irish Famine*, 24; Solar, 'The Great Famine was No Ordinary Subsistence Crisis', 114–18.

25. TCD MSS 9215–6.

26. Tomás Ó Néill, *Fiontán Ó Leathlobhair* (Dublin, 1962); D. N. Buckley, *James Fintan Lalor* (Cork, 1990).

27. 'Appendix to Minutes of Evidence taken before HM Commissioners of Inquiry into . . . Land in Ireland [henceforth, Devon Commission], pt. iv, BPP 1845 (XII), Apps. 101–4; RIA, Halliday Pamphlet no. 2024/10, *Cases of Tenant Eviction from 1840 to 1846, Extracted from the Public Journals*. The data appended to the Devon Commission report indicate that tens of thousands of people were evicted annually in the late 1830s and early 1840s. Comparing the number of ejectments and the estimated aggregate acreage in dispute (as given in App. 104) suggests that the average size of affected holdings was small.

28. Hely Dutton, *Statistical Survey of the County of Clare* (Dublin, 1808), 34.

29. Townsend, *Cork*, 543.

30. Almost by definition, surviving farm accounts exclude the laggard and the lazy farmer. Yet the competence and dynamism shown in accounts such as those of the Barringtons of Fassaroe or the Filgates of County Louth should not be overlooked. The Filgates, small-time landlords, in the mid-1830s travelled to fairs and markets at Jonesboro, Mullacrew, Dundalk, Newry, Ballinasloe, and Clermont, and exhibited at the Belfast and Dublin agricultural shows (RDS, Barrington accounts; NLI, MS 11,944).

31. Quoted in Olive Robinson, 307. See too 'Martin Doyle', *An Address to the Landlords of Ireland* (Dublin, 1831), 7–8; Proudfoot, 'The Management of a Great Estate'; id., 'The Estate System in Mid-Nineteenth Century Waterford' in Cowman, Nolan, and Power (eds.), *Waterford: History and Society*, forthcoming; Ó Gráda, 'The Investment Behavour of Irish Landlords 1850–1875', *AgHR*, 23/2 (1975), 139–55; T. Jones Hughes, 'The Estate System of Landholding in Nineteenth-Century Ireland', in W. Nolan *et al.* (eds.), *The Shaping of Ireland* (Dublin, 1985), 137–50; L. M. Cullen, *Irish Towns and Villages* (Dublin, 1979); L. J. Proudfoot and B. J. Graham, 'Landlords, Planning and Urban Growth in Eighteenth- and Early Nineteenth-Century Ireland', *Journal of Urban History*, 18/3 (1992), 308–29.

32. David Thompson and Moya McGusty (eds.), *The Irish Journals of Elizabeth Smith* (Oxford, 1980), 120–2.

33. W. A. Maguire, 'A Resident Landlord in His Local Setting: The Second Marquis of Donegall at Ormeau, 1807–1844', *PRIA*, Sect. C, 83 (15), 395.

34. Mokyr, *Why Ireland Starved*, 201–3; *Return of Owners of Land of One Acre and Upwards in Ireland* (Dublin, 1876); Robinson, 'The London Companies'. In the 1876 calculations, owners living outside the county, but near by, or in big towns in adjoining counties, e.g. Donegal landowners living in Derry or Kilkenny landowners living in Waterford, were not deemed absentees.

35. Robinson, 'The London Companies as Progressive Landlords'; A. P. W. Malcolmson, 'Absenteeism in Eighteenth-Century Ireland', *IESH*, 1 (1974).
36. Terence Reeves-Smith, talk to the Dublin Historical Settlement Group, University College, Dublin, 13 Mar. 1991; Proudfoot, 'The Estate System in Mid-Nineteenth Century Waterford'; id., 'Landscaped Demesnes in Pre-Famine Ireland: A Regional Case-Study', in J. Vervloet (ed.), *Proceedings of the Permanent European Conference for the Study of the Rural Landscape* (Baarn and Ghent, 1990).
37. McCarthy, 'The Estates of Trinity College, Dublin', 151; TCD, MUN V 79/19.
38. National Bank archive, D16/4/1 (statement of annual income . . . from the estates and property in mortgage from Daniel O'Connell Esq. to the National Bank of Ireland). O'Connell's mark-up on a smaller letting from the Earl of Cork was 50%. See also McCarthy, *Trinity College Estates*, 184–5.
39. James S. Donnelly, jun., 'The Journals of Sir John Benn-Walsh Relating to the Management of His Irish Estates, 1823–64', *JCHAS*, 81 (1975), 111.
40. Olive Robinson, 'The London Companies', 27, 246; Mokyr, *Why Ireland Starved*, ch. 4; Donnelly, *Cork*, 52–72; Townsend, *Cork*, 183–4; Dickson, 'Middlemen'.
41. Johnson and Kennedy, 'Nationalist Historiography', 28–30. These estimates are not adjusted for land quality, but such an adjustment would probably make the case for tenant right (given Ulster's relatively poor land endowment) only harder to answer.
42. Coulter, *The West of Ireland*, 319–20. For a more sophisticated version of this hypothesis see Guinnane and Miller, 'Bonds without Bondsmen'. On landlord views in Ulster see Robinson, 'The London Companies and Tenant Right'.
43. Mokyr, 'Uncertainty and Irish Agriculture', in Devine and Dickson, *Scotland and Ireland*, 89–101; Bourke, 'Potatoes, Weather and Blight', 120–4.
44. Senior, *Essays*, i. 276.
45. David Fitzpatrick, *Irish Emigration*; Nolan, *Fassadinin*, 204–9; Tom Devine, 'Why the Highlands Did Not Starve'.
46. NLI, MS 14816.
47. Solar and Goossens, 'Agricultural Productivity in Belgium and Ireland'.

Chapter 6

1. Maurice Lenihan, *Limerick: Its History and Antiquities* (Dublin, 1866), 477–8 n; O'Brien, *Eighteenth Century*, 359–60.
2. Wakefield, *Ireland*, i. 668; 'Sixth Report of the S. C. on the Road from London to Holyhead', BPP 1822 (VI) [513]; 'Report of the S. C. on the Post Communications with Ireland', BPP 1831–2 (XVII) [716]; Mokyr, *Why Ireland Starved*, 182–3; D. Ó Gráda, 'Rocky Road to Dublin'. Compare Derek H. Aldcroft, 'Aspects of Eighteenth Century Travelling Conditions', in *Der curieuse Passagier: Deutsche Englandreisende des achtzehnten Jahrhunderts* (Heidelberg, 1983), 27–45.
3. J. H. Andrews, 'Road Planning in Ireland Before the Railway Age'; id., 'The

Use of Half-Inch Ordnance Survey Maps in Irish Historical Geography with Special Reference to Road Patterns', *Geographical Viewpoint*, 5 (1976), 20–9; N. Brunicardi, *John Anderson Entrepreneur* (Fermoy, 1987), ch. 2; McCutcheon, *Industrial Archaeology*, 16–27; 'Late Arrivals' and Fines Book of the General Post Office 1819–21 (in private possession); Dubourdieu, *Antrim*, ii. 553; *Thom's Irish Almanac and Official Directory for the Year 1845*, 612.

4. Inglis, *Ireland in 1834*, i. 25; Thackeray, *Irish Sketchbook*, 104–8, 131–2; J. G. Kohl, *Ireland* (London, 1843).

5. Monaghan; 'Social and Economic History of Belfast', 363, 370; Ivor Herring, 'Ulster Roads on the Eve of the Railway Age, *c.*1800–40', *IHS*, 2 (1940–1), 160–88; McCall, *Industry*, 2nd edn., 514–15; M. O'C. Bianconi and S. J. Watson, *Bianconi, King of the Irish Roads* (Dublin, 1962), 109, 121; Augustus J. C. Hare (ed.), *The Life and Letters of Maria Edgeworth* (London, 1891), i. 582–3.

6. Constantia Maxwell, *The Stranger in Ireland* (London, 1954), 230; NA, M7092; John Conway, *Bianconi's Car and Coach Lists, &c.* (Dublin, 1842).

7. Monaghan, 1940, 381; Crawford, 'Economy and Society', 130; 'On Scotch Carts', *Munster Farmer's Magazine*, 5 (1812), 53–5; McCutcheon, *Industrial Archaeology*, 22–3.

8. *1841 Census*, 455, 457; *Returns of Agricultural Produce 1854*, xliii. According to F. M. L. Thompson, 'Horses and Hay in Britain, 1830–1918', in Thompson (ed.), *Horses in European Economic History, A Preliminary Canter* (Reading, 1983), 59, there were 350,000 town-horses in Britain in the 1830s.

9. Andrews, 'Road Planning in Ireland Before the Railway Age'.

10. R. Griffith, 'Report on the Roads Made at the Public Expense in the Southern District of Ireland', BPP 1831 (XII) [119]; Seán Ó Lúing, 'Richard Griffith and the Roads of Kerry'; Timothy O'Neill, 'The Poor Employment Act of 1817' (typescript, 1986); Peter J. O'Keefe, 'Richard Griffith: Planner and Builder of Roads', in G. L. H. Davies (ed.), *Richard Griffith* (Dublin, 1980), 57–75.

11. *LTD*, 1, p. 316.

12. Lee, 'Irish Railways', 173–89. Kennedy, 'Specialization', 186–93, sounds a more positive note.

13. Turf, building materials, and manure accounted for 63.3% of the Grand's total tonnage in 1801, 51.1% in 1844. Coal would become important later. See Delany, *Grand Canal*, 234–5. On the canals generally, Delany, *A Celebration of 250 Years of Ireland's Inland Waterways*; Delany and Delany, *Canals of the South of Ireland*.

14. McCutcheon, *Canals of the North of Ireland*; id., *Industrial Archaeology*, ch. 2.

15. Weld, *Roscommon*, 165–6, 174–5.

16. Railway Commission, Second Report, 15–16; Herring, 'Ulster Roads'; Joseph Lee, 'Irish Railways', 176; Wakefield, *Ireland*, i. 651; Ó Gráda, *Ireland* (1st edn.), 30; Green, *Lagan Valley*, 39; NA, I/5/11/2 (letter-book of the Board of Control); McCutcheon, *Industrial Archaeology*, 76–8; Delany, *A Celebration of*

250 Years of Ireland's Inland Waterways, 15 (citing Arthur Young), 58–60, 139, 150–3.

17. NLI, MS 8146/31; *FJ*, 8 Apr. 1825, 15 Apr. 1825; Alexander Nimmo, *Report on the Proposed Railway between Limerick and Waterford* (Dublin, 1825).

18. *Prospectus of the Dundalk Western Railway* (London, 1838), 9; Thomas, *The Stock Exchanges of Ireland*, ch. 6; H. G. Lewin, *Early British Railways* (London, 1925).

19. Hazel P. Smyth, *The B & I Line: A History of the British and Irish Steam Packet Company* (Dublin, 1984), chs. 1–2.

20. Oliver MacDonagh, 'The Victorian Bank, 1824–1914', in Lyons, *Bank of Ireland*, 32–3.

21. National Bank, Transactions of the Court of Directors, 1834–47 (esp. 11 July 1840, 12 Feb. 1844, and 17 July 1844); Oliver MacDonagh, *The Emancipist: Daniel O'Connell 1830–47* (London, 1989), 217. After O'Connell's death, four directors (including his son-in-law and his son Maurice) were dismissed for borrowing far smaller sums; see e.g. *Bankers' Magazine* 11 (1851), 58–60, 185–90.

22. Barrow, *Emergence*, 215–21.

23. *Bankers' Magazine*, 1 (1844), 129.

24. AIBA, Youghal Branch, John Baker to James Marshall, 29 Aug. 1831.

25. Ó Gráda, *Ireland* (1st edn.), 28–9; Ollerenshaw, *Banking*, 82. On the Royal, see Harrison, 'Dublin Quakers', 274–81.

26. *Banking*, ch. 3.

27. Charles Munn, 'Bank Credit for Industry in Scotland and Ireland' (typescript, 1981).

28. 'The Agricultural Bank of Ireland', *Bankers' Magazine* (1845), 65–70, 200–6, 280–7 (citation at 206).

29. Barrow, 'Justice for Thomas Mooney'; Ollerenshaw, *Banking*, 39–41. See too W. T. W., 'The Strange Story of an Irish Bank', *Irish Banking Magazine*, 14 (Sept. 1932), 52–4; Anon., *The Origins and Progress of the Agricultural and Commercial Bank of Ireland* (Dublin, 1835).

30. O'Connell to Mooney, 13 June 1834 (in M. O'Connell (ed.), *Correspondence of Daniel O'Connell* (Dublin, n.d.), v. 143); BofEA, Minutes of the Court of Directors, 24 Nov. 1836.

31. PRONI, D1720. See also Ollerenshaw, *Banking*, 5–6 and D1255/21 (business records of a firm of Downpatrick merchants and moneylenders).

32. UCDA, P12/5/125–146b.

33. Lawrence White, *Free Banking in Britain* (Cambridge, 1984); A. J. Rolnick and W. E. Weber, 'The Causes of Free Banking Failures', *Journal of Monetary Economics*, 14 (1984), 267–91; Howard Bodenhorn, 'Free Banking in Ireland' (unpublished, Rutgers University, 1989).

34. 'Report of the Select Committee on Joint Stock Banks', BPP 1838 (IV) {626}, Qs. 1174–83, evidence of Ignatius Callaghan.

35. Hall, *Bank of Ireland*, 399; Barrow, *Emergence*, 68, 74, 80–1, 130, 135; Edward Darley Hill, *The Northern Banking Company Limited: An Historical Sketch* (Belfast, 1925), 122–5.

36. Ollerenshaw, *Banking*, 51–2.

37. Barrow, *Emergence*, 142–3; 'Report from the Select Committee on Banks of Issue', BPP 1840 (IV), 114–15, 186; Howard Bodenhorn in Kevin Dowd (ed.), *The Experience of Free Banking* (London, 1992).

38. And reprimanded its agents in Sligo and Westport for having done so locally (BofIA, TCOD, 16 Nov. 1836).

39. Fetter, *Monetary Orthodoxy*, 195–7; Hall, *Bank of Ireland*, 207–12; National Bank of Ireland, Transactions of the Court of Directors, 23 Apr. 1845.

40. Wakefield, *Ireland*, ii. 33–137.

41. Ibid., ii. 102; James Kelly, 'William Burton Conyngham and the North West Fishery of the Eighteenth Century', *JRSAI*, 115 (1985), 64–85.

42. NA, 2D-57-113 (Fisheries' Board Letter Book), letters from Henry Townsend (on behalf of the Board), 6 Mar. 1824 and 8 May 1824.

43. Freeman, *Pre-Famine Ireland*, 92–4; Seventeenth Report of the Board of Works (1847–8), 24; Devon Commission, App. (report by the Earl of Glengall); Woodham-Smith, *Great Hunger*, 288–92. Wallop Brabazon, *The Deep Sea and Coast Fisheries of Ireland* (Dublin, 1848), ix claimed that a thousand herrings, worth £2. 10*s*. in Dublin salted, 'several times' fetched only 10*d*. on the coast of Donegal.

44. Hall and Hall, *Ireland*, i. 132 (also i. 275; ii. 150 n).

45. Freeman, *Pre-Famine Ireland*, 93; Mokyr, *Why Ireland Starved*, 172–3; *LTD*, ii. 356; Devon Commission, evidence of J. Burgoyne and W. T. Mulvany (on behalf of the Board of Works); NLI, MS 24,723 (copy of 'Instructions to Board of Works Agents at Curing Stations', 1847).

46. See, however, Vivienne Pollock's excellent dissertation, 'The Seafishing Industry of Co. Down, 1860–1939', and John de Courcy Ireland, *Ireland's Sea Fisheries: A History* (Dublin, 1981).

47. 'First Report of the Commissioners of Inquiry into the State of Irish Fisheries', BPP 1836 (XXII) [77], iv.

48. In 1911 nearly three-quarters of Scotland's full-time fishermen lived on that country's east coast. On Scottish fishing in the previous century see A. J. Youngson, *After the Forty-five* (Edinburgh, 1973), ch. 5; Jean Dunbar, *The British Fisheries Society* (Edinburgh, 1978).

49. NA, M3419 (minute-book of the Fisheries Company of Ireland 1818–1824); J. Good, *Trawling on the East Coast of Ireland* (Dublin, 1861); J. L. Hughes, 'The Dublin Fishery Company, 1818–1830', *DHR*, 12 (1951), 34–46.

50. 'First Report of the Commissioners . . .', 190; *FJ*, 25 Apr. 1825.

51. Thomas Edward Symonds, *Fisheries of Ireland, Having Reference More Particularly to the Operations of the London and West of Ireland Fishing Company* (London, 1855).

52. NLI MS 13629(1) (Statement of Baldoyle fishermen, 1833); Fraser, *Report on the County Surveys and the Best Means for the Further Encouragement of the Fisheries of Ireland* (London, 1818), 6; de Courcy Ireland, *Ireland's Sea Fisheries*, ch. 6. Also Townsend, *Cork*, 396; Wakefield, *Ireland*, ii. 100–3; Kenneth McNally, *The Sun-Fish Hunt* (Belfast, 1976).

53. 'First Report of the Commissioners . . .', 203; Solar, 'Growth and Distribution', App. 2.17.
54. Pollock, 'Seafishing', concentrates on the County Down fishery, but ch. 2 provides a general introduction.
55. Michael McCaughan, 'Dandys, Luggars, Herring and Mackerel: A Local Study in the Context of the Irish Sea Fisheries in the Nineteenth Century', in McCaughan and Appleby, *Irish Sea*, 121–33; Vivienne Pollock, 'The Installation of Engine Power in the County Down Sea Fisheries', *Ulster Folklife*, 37 (1991), 1–12; id., 'Co. Down Herring Girls and the Herring Curing Industry', *Folklife*, 29 (1990–1), 29–43; id., 'Change in the County Down Fisheries in the Twentieth Century', in McCaughan and Appleby, *Irish Sea*, 135–44; id., 'Seafishing', *passim*; Vaughan and Fitzpatrick, *Irish Historical Statistics*, 32–3; Riordan, *Modern Irish Trade and Industry*, 293, 295.
56. 'Minutes of Evidence Taken before the Commissioners on Sea Fisheries', BPP 1866 (XVIII) [3596-I], Qs. 37,288–37,308.
57. W. L. Micks, *History of the Congested Districts Board* (Dublin, 1925), 35–55; Commission of Inquiry into the Resources and Industries of Ireland, *Report on Sea Fisheries* (Dublin, 1921).

Chapter 7

1. I am grateful to P. J. Mulhall, who owns Morrissey's, for permission to consult and reproduce these data.
2. O'Rourke and Polak, 'Property Transactions in Ireland, 1708–1988'.
3. Ian Duffy, *Bankruptcy and Solvency during the Industrial Revolution* (New York, 1985).
4. Cited in David Kelly, 'The Conditions of Debtors and Insolvents in Eighteenth-century Dublin', in Dickson, *The Gorgeous Mask*, 103.
5. NA, OP 379/4.
6. *FJ*, 13 June 1820; O'Kelly, *The Old Private Banks*, 28; Barrow, *Emergence*, 20–1; 'S. C. on the Employment of the Poor', BPP 1823 (VI) [561, evidence of Robert Pauncefote].
7. Foster, *Modern Ireland*, 318. McCabe notes that the post-war depression 'stunned the livestock trade for over a decade and undercut the profits of cereal production' (see Desmond McCabe, 'Social Order and the Ghost of Moral Economy in Pre-Famine Mayo', in R. Gillespie and G. Moran (eds.), *A Various Country: Essays in Mayo History 1500–1900* (Westport, Conn., 1987), 100–1).
8. John D. Post, *The Last Great Subsistence Crisis of the Western World* (Baltimore, 1977); The Board of Agriculture, *The Agricultural State of the Kingdom, in February, March and April, 1816* (London, 1816 (1970)); Glenn Hueckel, 'Agriculture During Industrialisation', in Floud and McCloskey, *Economic History of Britain since 1700*, i. 192–3. Also Townsend, *A View of the Agricultural State of Ireland*, 46.
9. Clarkson, 'The Carrick-on-Suir Woollen Industry'.
10. Davis, *Industrial Revolution*, 89–93.
11. Solar, 'Growth and Distribution', 79, col. (4); Mitchell and Deane, *Abstract*, 331.

12. O'Brien, *Union to Famine*, 371−2.
13. Crotty, *Irish Agricultural Production*; Foster, *Modern Ireland*, 319; Solar, 'Growth and Distribution'.
14. Solar, 'Growth and Distribution', App. Table 2.15.
15. Ibid., 296.
16. Solar, 'Rent in Ireland, 1790−1830'; McCarthy, 'The Estates of Trinity College Dublin', 1982), 119; Donnelly, 'The Kenmare Estates'; A. P. W. Malcolmson, *The Pursuit of the Heiress: Aristocratic Marriage in Ireland 1750−1820* (Belfast, 1982), 3; NA, Business Records DON21/1/1−3. On the subset of townlands on the Stewart estate where data are available for 1812, 1815, and 1844, the totals were £1,040, £1,360, and £1,280.
17. Wakefield, *Ireland*, ii. 208−30; Townsend, *Cork*, 203; Devon Commission, Index, 69−78. Unless specified otherwise, I have assumed that Devon Commission quotations refer to Irish acres.
18. Solar, 'Growth and Distribution', 267.
19. Allen, 'Agriculture During the Industrial Revolution'; G. Clark, 'In Search of the Agricultural Revolution: Southern England, 1611−1850' (University of California, Davis, Calif., Dec. 1991).
20. Using Solar's indices of agricultural prices in 'Growth and Distribution', Tables 2.14 and 2.15.
21. 'Second Report of the S.C. on Agricultural Distress', BPP 1836 (VIII) [189], Q.6008 (evidence of Joseph Sanders).
22. Ollerenshaw, *Banking in Nineteenth-century Ireland*, 54; TCD, MS G/27/11 (William Jones to Donoughmore, 19 Jan. 1842); *Farmers' Gazette*, 16 Dec. 1843.
23. Barrow, *Emergence*, 226−7.
24. *Ireland*, ch. 2.
25. Allen, 'Agriculture During the Industrial Revolution'; Clark, 'In Search of the Agricultural Revolution', Table 13.

Chapter 8

1. Edwards and Williams, *The Great Famine*; Foster, *Modern Ireland*. The long gestation period of the Edwards−Williams volume and its ultimate form— an unco-ordinated series of studies rather than a comprehensive and definitive account—are symptomatic. See Ó Gráda, 'Making History in Ireland'.
2. For an *exposé* of the myth of Victoria's stinginess see Thomas P. O'Neill, 'The Queen and the Famine', *Threshold*, 1/2 (1957), 60−3. See also Jim Jackson, '*Famine Diary*: the Making of a Best Seller', *Irish Review*, 11 (1991−2), 1−8. Compare Rosalind Mitchison, 'The Highland Clearances', *Scottish Economic and Social History*, 1/1 (1981), 11.
3. *Irish Times*, 22 May 1989.
4. IFC, vol. 1070, 219 (South Kerry); vol. 1071, 92−3 (Knocknagree, Cork); vol. 1071, 133−4, 235, 276 (Enniskean, Cork); vol. 1070, 14−15 (Dún Chaoin, Kerry); Séamus Ó Catháin and Caitlín Uí Sheighin (eds.), *A Mhuintir Dhú Chaocháin Labhraigí Feasta* (Indreabhán, 1987), 148.

5. IFC, vol. 1075/19 (Stradbally, County Laois). The following account from the great Kerry *seanchaí* Peig Sayers, who lost an uncle in the Famine, conveys some sense of the horror and ensuing guilt: 'Micheal Garvey got the cholera, and he and the entire household succumbed. They died together. I think he died before his wife. He had a daughter, and had she survived, she would have been the finest girl in the parish of Dún Chaoin. Somebody went to their cottage door, and could see that they were all dead. All they did then was to set fire to the thatch on the cottage, burn it, and let the walls fall in on one another. I remember myself in autumn-time how we used to pick blackberries near that spot—because there were lots of bushes where the house used to be—my mother warning us to keep away from the place. 'Stay away from there', she used to say, 'or no good will come of you.'

6. Meanwhile see R. J. McHugh, 'The Famine in Irish Oral Tradition' in Edwards and Williams, *The Great Famine*, 391–436; Ó Catháin and Uí Sheighin, *A Mhuintir Dhú Chaocháin*, 153–6; S. Ó Duilearga (ed.), *Leabhar Stiofáin Uí Ealaoire* (Dublin, 1981), 309–10.

7. Indeed, their revisions have prompted a reaction, and critics suspect that aspects of the new historiography contain their own political message. B. Bradshaw, 'Nationalism and Historical Scholarship in Ireland', *IHS*, 26/104 (1989), 329–51; K. Whelan, 'Clio agus Caitlín Ní Uallacháin', *Oghma*, 2 (1990), 9–19; T. Dunne, 'New Histories: Beyond Revisionism,' *Irish Review*, 12 (1992), 1–12.

8. Woodham-Smith, *The Great Hunger*; Robert Kee, *Ireland: A History* (London, 1980), 77–101.

9. e.g. Tom Garvin, *The Evolution of Irish Nationalism* (Dublin, 1981), 54; Mary Daly, *The Economic History of Ireland* (Dublin, 1978), 20–1; Foster, *Modern Ireland*, 324. As noted below, recent estimates of the death-toll tend to support the traditional figure of one million.

10. *Poverty and Famines: An Essay on Entitlement and Deprivation* (Oxford, 1981).

11. Foster, *Modern Ireland*, ch. 14. This chapter on the Famine is surely the weakest in a long and excellent book.

12. Daly, *Famine*, 138; Roy Foster, 'We Are All Revisionists Now', *Irish Review*, 1 (1986), 3.

13. See Kevin O'Neill's remarks in *Irish Literary Supplement* (Spring, 1988), 41.

14. Crotty, *Irish Agricultural Production*; Foster, *Modern Ireland*.

15. Mokyr, *Why Ireland Starved*, 292; on Mitchel, compare Donnelly (in *NHI*, v. 330); id., 'The Famine: Its Interpreters Old & New', *History Ireland*, 3 (1993); Daly, *Famine*, 115; Foster, *Modern Ireland*, 314. Foster dubs Mitchel 'a well-known American slaver'.

16. See, however, Peter M. Solar, review of *Why Ireland Starved* in *IESH*, 11 (1984), 107–15, and Patrick McGregor, 'Demographic Pressure and the Irish Famine: Malthus after Mokyr', *Land Economics*, 65/3 (1989), 228–38.

17. See esp. James S. Donnelly's account in Vaughan, *NHI*, 5, 272–371.

18. For the wider scientific controversy sparked off by the blight, see P. M. A. Bourke, 'Potato Blight in Europe in 1845: the Scientific Controversy'.

19. Martha Deane Cox, Dunmanway, to Sophia H. Cox in America, 28 Apr. 1847 (I am grateful to Robert Evans of Washington, DC for permission to cite); Revd. Webb, Caheragh, cited in Hickey, 'Four Parishes', 453.

20. Quaker relief workers singled out some particularly cruel landlords (Jon H. Holt, 'The Quakers in the Great Irish Famine', 43, 148–9). Such proprietors were the target of James Tuke's A Visit to Connaught (London, 1847).

21. Mokyr, 'The Deadly Fungus: An Econometric Investigation into the Short-Term Demographic Consequences of the Irish Famine, 1846–51', Research in Population Economics, 2 (1980), 233–77; Boyle and Ó Gráda, 'Fertility Trends'. Local data are very scarce. See, however, Patrick Hickey, 'Mortality and Emigration in Five Parishes in the Union of Skibereen, 1846–7', in C. Buttimer, G. O'Brien, and P. O'Flanagan (eds.), Cork: History and Society (Cork, 1993).

22. Mokyr, 'Deadly Fungus', 240; Edwards and Williams, The Great Famine: Studies in Irish History (Dublin, 1956), vii, 126, 255, 312; Foster, Modern Ireland, 324.

23. Serbyn and Krawchenko, Famine in the Ukraine (Edmonton, 1986), 11, 38–40. See Alexander Cockburn's critique of the excess mortality estimates of Robert Conquest in the Nation, 7 Aug. 1988, 181–4. On China, Xizhe Peng, 'Demographic Consequences of the Great Leap Forward in China's Provinces', Population and Development Review, 13/4 (1987), 648–9.

24. Mokyr, 'The Deadly Fungus'; Mokyr, Why Ireland Starved, 34, 266; G. Jacquemyns, 'Histoire de la crise économique de Flandres', Académie Royale de Belgique, Mémoires, 26 (1929), 370.

25. Jacquemyns, 'Histoire de la crise économique', 11–472; M. Bergman, 'The Potato Blight in The Netherlands and its Social Consequences', International Review of Social History, 17/3 (1967), 391–431; Mokyr, 'The Deadly Fungus'; Robert Conquest, The Harvest of Sorrow: Soviet Collectivization and the Terror-Famine (London, 1986), 302–4.

26. Tom Devine, The Great Highland Famine (Edinburgh, 1988), 63. See too id., 'Why the Highlands Did Not Starve'.

27. Devine, The Great Highland Famine, 111–13; id., 'Why the Highlands Did Not Starve'. Compare Tim O'Neill, 'The Food Crisis of the 1890s', in E. M. Crawford, Famine, 178–97.

28. Boyle and Ó Gráda, 'Fertility Trends'. Compare Sen, Poverty and Famines, 210–14; Maksudov, 'Ukraine's Demographic Losses', 38; Jean Drèze and Amartya Sen, Hunger and Public Action (Oxford, 1989), 54–5.

29. 1851 Census, 'Tables of Death', ii. 660–3. Hickey, 'Mortality and Emigration' also reports higher male mortality in west Cork.

30. Conquest, The Harvest of Sorrow, 243, 262, suggests that mass mortality in the Ukraine was limited to the period from early March to late May in 1933. The impression that the proportion of excess deaths due to starvation rather than to dysentery or typhoid fever was higher in the Ukraine than in the other cases mentioned is consistent with this.

31. Sen, Poverty and Famines, 215. See too Tim Dyson, 'On the Demography of South Asian Famines', Population Studies, 45/1 and 45/2 (1991).

32. Ó Gráda, *Ireland*, ch. 3; O'Neill, 'The Organisation and Administration of Relief', 238–240.
33. Ó Gráda, *Ireland*, ch. 3.
34. McArthur in Edwards and Williams, *The Great Famine*; Yrjo Kaukiainen, 'Harvest Fluctuations and Mortality in Agrarian Finland, 1810–1870', in Tommy Bengtsson, Gunnar Fridlizius, and Rolf Ohlsson (eds.), *Pre-Industrial Population Change* (Stockholm, 1986), 241; John Lefgren, 'Famine in Finland', *Intermountain Economic Review*, 4/2 (1973); Jacquemyns, 'Histoire de la crise économique', ch. 4.
35. Eoin O'Brien, *Conscience and Conflict: A Biography of Sir Dominic Corrigan 1802–1880* (Dublin, 1983), 188–9.
36. MacArthur, 'Medical history', 286; *1851 Census*, 'Tables of Death', ii. 660–3; [W. Wilde], 'Reports upon the Recent Epidemic Fever in Ireland' *The Dublin Quarterly Journal of Medical Science*, 7 (1849), 64–126, 340–404; 8 (1849), 1–86. Margaret Crawford has noted that MacArthur drew heavily on Wilde's account.
37. O'Neill, 'The Organisation and Administration of Relief 1845–52', map on p. 243 (on which Fig. 8.1 is based); S. H. Cousens, 'Regional Death Rates in Ireland During the Great Famine from 1846 to 1851', *PS*, 14/1 (1960), 55–74; id., 'The Regional Variation in Mortality during the Great Irish Famine', *PRIA*, 63C (1963), 127–49; Mokyr, 'Deadly Fungus'; Ó Gráda, 'Some Aspects of Nineteenth-Century Irish Emigration', in Cullen and Smout, *Comparative Aspects*, 68–71.
38. Mokyr, 'Deadly Fungus', Tables 3 and 4.
39. Ibid., 248–9.
40. Cousens, 'Regional Death Rates'.
41. Ó Gráda, *Ireland*, ch. 3, presents an econometric analysis of the regional incidence of mortality.
42. Cullen, *Economic History*, 132.
43. e.g., Pier Paolo Viazzo (in *Upland Communities: Environment, Population and Society in the Alps since the Sixteenth Century* (Cambridge, 1989), 52–3). In the 1960s Wolf described the nearby Alpine villages of Tret (Ladin) and St Felix (German) as 'different cultural worlds'; see E. R. Wolf, 'Cultural Dissonance in the Italian Alps', *Comparative Studies in Society and History* 5 (1962), 1–14; J. W. Cole and E. R. Wolf, *The Hidden Frontier: Ecology and Ethnicity in an Italian Valley* (New York, 1974).
    For impressing on me the distinction between population density and settlement concentration I am grateful to Kevin Whelan. On the spread of nucleated settlements see D. McCourt, 'The Dynamic Quality of Irish Rural Settlement', in R. Buchanan, E. Jones, and D. McCourt (eds.), *Man and His Habitat: Essays Presented to Emyr Estyn Evans* (London, 1971).
44. O'Brien, *Sir Dominic Corrigan*, 188, 367–8.
45. Peter Froggatt, 'The Response of the Medical Profession to the Great Famine', in E. M. Crawford (ed.), *Famine*, 134–56. Also F. Barker and J. Cheyne, *An Account of the Rise, Progress, and Decline of the Fever Lately Epidemical in Ireland* (Dublin, 1821), i. 102; Patrick Sharkey, *An Essay on the*

Causes, Progress and Treatment of Typhus Fever particularly as it has Appeared in the City of Cork (Cork, 1817), 1.

46. Barker and Cheyne, *Fever*, i. 101, 135, 138, 422; Pakenham-Mahon papers (Strokestown House); Jon H. Holt, 'The Quakers in the Great Irish Famine', 30. On deaths of Catholic clergy, see the (probably incomplete) returns in the *Catholic Directory, Almanac and Registry*, 1844–8. The *Directory* reports many deaths of young priests in 1847 of 'fever' or 'typhus fever'. Forty members of the Church of Ireland are reported to have died of fever in 1847 (Daly, *The Famine*, 68).

47. Ó Gráda, 'Malthus'.

48. Mokyr, *Why Ireland Starved*, ch. 3; McGregor, 'Demographic Pressure and the Irish Famine: Malthus after Mokyr', *Land Economics*, 65/3 (1989); Kennedy, 'Irish Econometric History', *IHS*, 23 (1983).

49. Ó Gráda, 'Malthus'; Solar, 'The Great Famine'; id., 'Harvest Fluctuations'.

50. Mokyr, 'Uncertainty in Irish Agriculture'; Solar, 'The Great Famine'.

51. Ibid.

52. Hoffman and Mokyr, 'Peasants, Poverty and Potatoes'.

53. S. C. Watkins and Jane Menken, 'Famines in Historical Perspective', *Population and Development Review*, 11 (1985), 647–75.

54. Lefgren, 'Famine in Finland', 25; Mitchell, *European Historical Statistics*, 20, 85.

55. Senior, *Essays*, ii. 12.

56. Pim, *Condition of Ireland*; *The Nation*, 15 Nov. 1845 (cited in T. P. O'Neill, 'Food Problems during the Great Famine', *JRSAI*, 82 (1952), 108); Mokyr, *Why Ireland Starved*, 292; Donnelly, 'The Great Famine', 329; Norman Longmate, *The Hungry Mills* (London, 1978).

57. See, however, the feature by John Noble Wulford on Garrett Hardin, 'A tough-minded ecologist comes to the defence of Malthus: he believes that gifts of food to Ethiopia were harmful', *New York Times*, 30 June 1987. Hardin's ideas are also discussed in 'Feeding the World's Hungry only Makes the Hunger Worse', *Los Angeles Times*, 3 Nov. 1985. Nearer home, Richard West argued in the *Spectator* in 1983 that 'giving money to Liverpool is rather like sending food to Ethiopia . . . Unemployment in Liverpool, like famine in Africa, is almost entirely caused by human folly and wickedness' (quoted in Richard Loney, *The Politics of Greed* (Pluto Press, 1986)).

58. PRO (London), T64/369A/2, Trevelyan to Routh, 27 Dec. 1847; Senior, *Essays*, i. 264. Curiously Senior's article on the poor law, when first published in the Whig *Edinburgh Review*, was widely attributed to Lord Monteagle (British Library, Add. MSS 32624/292). For Malthus on the moral hazard implications of welfare, see his *Essay on the Principle of Population* (1st edn.), ch. 5.

59. Quoted in Grant, 'Famine in Ulster', 412; also John Prest, *Lord John Russell* (London, 1972), 240.

60. As cited in Montague, 'Relief and Reconstruction', 213.

61. Ibid. See too Peter Gray, 'Potatoes and Providence'.

62. Twistleton, quoted in Ó Gráda, *Ireland*, ch. 3; Scrope, *Reply to the Speech of the Archbishop of Dublin . . .* (Dublin, 1847), 40; Donald H. Akenson, *A Protestant in Purgatory: Richard Whately Archbishop of Dublin* (Hamden, Conn., 1981), 125-6. On the Established Church and evangelical attitudes, Boyd Hilton, *The Age of Atonement* (Cambridge, 1989), 108-14.

63. Ó Gráda, *Ireland*, ch. 3; *Tipperary Vindicator*, 4 Nov. 1846.

64. Bergman, 'The Potato Blight in The Netherlands', 417-19; G. Jacquemyns, 'Histoire de la crise économique', 406.

65. Black, *Economic Thought and the Irish Question*, ch. 8; Bergman, 'The Potato Blight in The Netherlands'.

66. IUP, vii. 576, Captain Fishbourne to Trevelyan, 6 Mar. 1847.

67. Senior, *Essays*, i. 218-19. Arguing the dire consequences of overgenerous poor relief from the example of Cholesbury, a hamlet of two families, is a famous example of 'Senior's vice'. See Brian Inglis, *Poverty and the Industrial Revolution* (London, 1971), 380-1, 400-1, and S. G. and O. Checkland (eds.), *The New Poor Law* (Harmondsworth, 1974), 141-4.

Senior's claims bear comparison with those of Commissariat official Dobree from Cahirciveen in late 1847 (PRO T64/369A/2; Dobree to Routh, 11 and 12 Dec. 1847): The farmers are making all along the coast the most extraordinary and indefatigable exertions in collecting sea weed for manure and preparing the ground for planting potatoes. The cliffs swarm with men women and children bringing it up on their backs to the high road whence it is carted to the fields—there is a vast supply for none was collected last year . . . [Potatoes] everywhere very good and as yet no appearance of disease. This has inspired the people with courage to resume the cultivation as in former years and nothing but extreme destitution will drive them from their little holdings.

68. See M. Ravallion, *Markets and Famines* (Oxford, 1987) for a discussion of the Bangladeshi famine of 1972.

69. On the public works see Mary Daly, *Famine*, 73-87; T. P. O'Neill, 'Organisation and Administration of Relief', in Edwards and Williams, 223-34; A. R. G. Griffiths, 'The Board of Works in the Famine Years', *Historical Journal*, 13/4.

70. Burgoyne to Trevelyan, 23 Feb. 1847, IUP, viii. 537; Jones to Trevelyan, 27 Feb. 1847, IUP, vii. 7, 192. Finally, from Sligo in the north-west: There is a population of 30,000; of these 24,000 are destitute; and, in the whole locality, the proprietors together do not afford employment of any kind to more than 100 to 110 men; and this is the position of a great portion of the country. There is also a great disinclination to work on the land, or rather, perhaps, to leave the Public Works. Here, at Sligo last week, the principal proprietor applied to the Board of Works for a number of men, to whom he would have given 1s. per day. These have nearly all returned to their 8d wages on the public roads; and Captain Gilbert tells me he is obliged to take them. (Deputy Commissary-General Dombree to Trevelyan, 1 March 1847.)

NOTES TO PP. 196–202

71. Roscommon, 3 Sept. 1846, IUP, vi. 74. See too Woodham-Smith, *Great Hunger*, 148–9.

72. IUP, 81; Seán Ó Ceallaigh (ed.), *Filíocht na gCallanán* (Dublin, 1967), 68. The poem again makes the point that the 8*d.* a day granted by *muintir Shasana* (the English) to an average family was less than a subsistence wage; on Sundays and wet days there was no pay.

73. IFC MS 1068/23 (south Tipperary); Aubrey de Vere, *English Misrule and Irish Misdeeds* (Dublin, 1848), 7–13.

74. Jean Drèze, 'Famine Prevention in India', WIDER Discussion Paper No. 45 (Helsinki, 1988), 92; also Jean Drèze and Amartya Sen, *Hunger and Public Action* (Oxford, 1989).

75. E. M. Crawford, 'Subsistence Crises and Famines in Ireland', in Crawford, *Famine*, 198–219; Woodham-Smith, *Great Hunger*, 178–9. On seasonality, Ó Gráda, *Ireland*, 85.

76. *Transactions of the Central Relief Committee of the Society of Friends during the Famine in Ireland in 1846 and 1847* (Dublin, 1852), 68–9, 453–4. On the Quakers' efforts, see Thomas P. O'Neill, 'The Society of Friends and the Great Famine', *Studies*, 40 (1951), 203–13; Holt, 'The Quakers in the Great Irish Famine'; Harrison, 'Dublin Quakers', 472–7.

In Ireland private donations to the Catholic relief agency, Trócaire, rose from £2.4 million in 1983 and £2.8 million in 1984 to £10.8 million in 1985, but fell off then to £4.0 million in 1986 and to £3.4 million in 1987. I am grateful to Mary Sutton of Trócaire for this information.

77. NLI, MS 10,102 (Denis Mahon, landlord, to John Ross Mahon, agent, 12 Aug. 1847). The gun did not save Denis Mahon, who was murdered a few months later.

78. Sen, *Poverty and Famines*, 96, 111; but also Bob Baulch, 'Entitlements and the Wollo Famine 1982–1985', *Disasters*, 11/3, 195–204.

79. Sen, *Poverty and Famines*, 54–5, 149; Kuakiainen, 'Harvest Fluctuations and Mortality', 238–40.

80. Sen, *Poverty and Famines*; Sen, 'Food, Economics and Entitlements', WIDER Working Paper No. 1 (Feb. 1986), 15 (citing Ricardo); Solar, 'Great Famine'; Ó Gráda, *Ireland*, ch. 3; id., *The Great Irish Famine*. Barbara Solow has taken Mokyr to task for not dealing with Sen's model. See her review of *Why Ireland Starved* in *JEH*, 44 (1984), 839–40.

81. P. M. A. Bourke, 'The Irish Grain Trade, 1840–50', *IHS* 20 (1970). Traffic on the Grand Canal during the 1840s also dramatically reflects the shift. See Delany, *The Grand Canal of Ireland*, 234–5.

82. Woodham-Smith, *The Great Hunger*, 324–5.

83. Mokyr, *Why Ireland Starved*, 92; Donnelly, *Land and People of Nineteenth-Century Cork*, 106–7.

84. James S. Donnelly, 'The Great Famine', in Vaughan, *NHI*, 5; James Grant, 'The Great Famine and Poor Law in Ulster: The Rate-in-Aid Issue of 1849', *IHS*, 27 (1989), 30–47.

85. Donnelly, 'A Famine in Irish Politics', in Vaughan, *NHI*, 5 p. 371.

86. Michael Davitt, *The Fall of Feudalism in Ireland* (London, 1906), 48; Kevin

Nowlan, 'The Political Background', 138; Jacquemyns, 'Histoire de la crise économique', 407, 422.

87. I am grateful to Dr Bill Vaughan for alerting me to this source.

88. Sir George Grey to Lord Clarendon, 5 Feb. 1849 (cited in Woodham-Smith, *Great Hunger*, 377); *Hansard*, 104 (1849), cols. 1109–10. Woodham-Smith also (p. 136) relates the extraordinary tale of thirty-four Mayomen in eleven currachs plundering a ship for food ten miles out to sea in late 1846. On crime during the Famine, Hoppen, *Elections, Politics and Society*, 366–8.

89. NA, Prison Records, V16-2-18 and V16-1-32.

90. The average age of 593 males sentenced to be transported in Dublin in 1843–4 was 26.3 years, and of 572 sentenced in 1847–9 26.8 years; 34% of the former and 37% of the latter were, or had been, married. These numbers are taken from NA, V16-6-19. See too James Haughton, 'On the Intimate Connexion between Ignorance, Intemperance, and Crime', paper read to the Dublin Statistical Society, 15 Dec. 1850. For further evidence that 'it was chiefly offences against property committed without violence that swelled the criminal calender of Ireland' during the Great Famine, see James Moncrieff Wilson, 'Statistics of Crime in Ireland, 1842 to 1856', *Journal of the Dublin Statistical Society*, 2/10, 91–122; J. Pim, 'Address', *JDSS*, 1/1 (1855), 18.

   On Clare see Sinéad Curley, 'Clare Convicts Before and After the Famine', in Bob Reece (ed.), *Irish Convicts: The Origins of Convicts Transported to Australia* (Dublin, 1989), 81–112.

91. M. Bergman, 'The Potato Blight in The Netherlands', 404–13.

92. O'Neill, 'Organisation and Administration of Relief', 245; Ó Gráda, *Ireland*, ch. 3.

93. Marx, *Capital*, i. (Harmondsworth, 1976), 854–70; J. S. Donnelly, 'The Irish Agricultural Depression of 1859–64', *IESH*, 3 (1976), 33–54.

94. Ibid.

95. Fitzpatrick, 'Disappearance of the Irish Agricultural Labourer'.

96. O'Rourke, 'Agricultural Change and Rural Depopulation: Ireland 1845–1876'; id., 'Did the Great Famine Matter?'; id., 'Rural Depopulation in a Small Open Economy: Ireland 1856–1876'; Crotty, *Irish Agricultural Production*, ch. 2.

97. On CGE modelling by economic historians see John James, 'The Use of General Equilibrium Models in Economic History', *EEH*, 21 (1984), 231–53; Mark Thomas, 'General Equilibrium Models and Research in Economic History', in Alexander Field (ed.), *The Future of Economic History* (Boston and Dordrecht, 1987), 121–83.

98. O'Rourke, 'Agricultural Change and Rural Depopulation', 41.

99. Ó Gráda, *Ireland*, 57; O'Rourke, 'Agricultural Change and Rural Depopulation', 78.

100. Ó Gráda, *The Great Irish Famine*; Solar, 'Great Famine'; *Irish Independent* (Farming suppl.), 'Potato Blight: Six-Page Guide to Growers' Nightmare', 17 July 1990.

101. e.g. J. Bradford De Long, 'Productivity Growth, Convergence and Welfare:

Comment', *American Economic Review*, 78/3 (1988), 1138–59; W. J. Baumol, S. A. Batey, and E. N. Wolff, *Productivity Growth: The Long View* (Cambridge, Mass., 1989).

Chapter 9

1. M. W. Flinn (ed.), *Scottish Population History* (Oxford, 1981), 304–5; Devine, *The Great Highland Famine*, 21–7.
2. Adding the adjoining boroughs of Pembroke (29,294) and Rathmines and Rathgar (37,840) fails to close the gap.
3. Calculated from Vaughan and Fitzpatrick, *Irish Historical Statistics: Population*, 27–41.
4. Fitzpatrick, 'Marriage in Ireland', 129–30.
5. Ó Gráda, *Ireland*, ch. 5.
6. T. Paul Schultz, *Population Economics* (Reading, Mass., 1981), ch. 2; R. D. Lee and R. S. Schofield, 'British Population in the Eighteenth Century', in Floud and McCloskey, *Economic History of Britain Since 1700*, i. 31–5.
7. Guinnane, 'Migration, Marriage, and Household Formation', 202. Also id., 'Re-thinking the Western European Marriage Pattern'; Connell, *Irish Peasant Society*. Guinnane's interpretations is broadly in line with that in Kennedy, *The Irish*, ch. 7.
8. Arensberg and Kimball, *Family and Community*, 215; B. M. Walsh, 'A Study of Irish County Marriage Rates, 1961–1966', *PS*, 29/2, 205–16.
9. Donnelly, *Land and People*, 242–50.
10. For corroboration, see Smyth, 'Landholding Changes, Kinship Networks and Class Transformation in Rural Ireland'.
11. This and the excerpt in the following paragraph are to be found in the L-G correspondence in the Marie Stopes archive, Wellcome Institute Library, London.
12. In Ó Gráda, *Ireland*, ch. 5.
13. J. Knodel, 'Demographic Transitions in German Villages', in Coale and Watkins, *The Fertility Decline in Europe*, 337–89; M. Lachiver, 'Fécondité légitime et contraception dans la région parisienne' in Société de Démographie Historique (ed.), *Sur la population française au XVIIe et XVIIIe siècles: hommage à Marcel Reinhard* (Paris, 1973).
14. Ireland's small Quaker community was exceptional in this, showing signs of marital fertility decline early in the nineteenth century (Vann and Eversley, *Friends in Life and Death*, ch. 4).
15. Michael Teitelbaum, *The British Fertility Decline* (Princeton, 1984); A. J. Coale and Roy Treadway, 'A Summary of the Changing Distribution of Overall Fertility, Marital Fertility, and the Proportion Married in the Provinces of Europe', in Coale and Watkins, *Decline in Fertility*, 40; F. van de Walle, 'Infant Mortality and the European fertility Transition', in Coale and Watkins, 220.
16. Ó Gráda, *Ireland*, App. 5.1. The estimates given there correct a computational error marring those given in 'New Evidence on the Fertility Transition

in Ireland'. In fairness to Teitelbaum, he noted the possibility of defective registration data; but the point is surely that he has been cited without such qualification by several others.

17. P. A. David and W. C. Sanderson, 'Measuring Marital Fertility Control with CPA', *Population Index*, 54/4; P. A. David, T. A. Mroz, W. C. Sanderson, K. W. Wachter, and D. R. Weir, 'Cohort Parity Analysis: Statistical Estimates of the Extent of Fertility Control', *Demography*, 25/2 (1988), 163–88.

18. Ó Gráda, *Ireland*, App. 5.2.

19. David Fitzpatrick, 'The Study of Irish Population, 1841–1921' (paper delivered to the conference of the Irish Economic and Social History Society, Cork, September 1977); Ó Gráda, 'Did Irish Catholics always Have Bigger Families?'.

20. e.g. Ian Paisley in 'This Week They Said', *IT*, 11 June 1988. For a stimulating discussion of Irish religious demography in the period under review see Akenson, *Small Differences*. See too Liam Kennedy, *Two Ulsters: A Case for Repartition* (Belfast, 1987); *Independent*, 1 Nov. 1992.

21. John Knodel, *The Decline of Fertility in Germany* (Princeton, 1974); Ron Lesthaege, *The Decline of Belgian Fertility, 1800–1970* (Princeton, 1977); Ó Gráda, *Ireland*, ch. 5; Ó Gráda and Duffy, 'The Fertility Transition in Ireland and Scotland c.1880–1930'.

22. Ó Gráda, 'New Evidence'; Ó Gráda and Duffy, 'The Fertility Transition in Ireland and Scotland'.

23. Ó Gráda and Duffy, 'Fertility Control Early in Marriage in Ireland c.1900: Some Local Contrasts', UCD Centre for Economic Research Working Paper 93/21, July 1993.

24. Coale and Treadway, 'A Summary', 88, 94, 120, 122.

25. Coale and Watkins, *The Decline of Fertility in Europe*, 120 and Map 2.4.

26. Lyon, 'Natality in Dublin'.

27. The 1936 Free State census provides the data to calculate I_g for the twenty-eight urban and rural districts in the three Ulster border counties. Religious affiliation explains hardly any of the variation in I_g; an urban dummy (set at unity for urban districts) does a little better. See too A. T. Park, 'An Analysis of Human Fertility in Northern Ireland', *JSSISI*, 21 (1962–3), 1–13; B. M. Walsh, *Religion and Demographic Behaviour in Ireland*, ESRI Paper No. 55 (Dublin, 1970).

28. Northern Ireland Census 1937, Belfast County Borough (Belfast, 1937), xxi.

29. Ó Gráda, 'A Note on Nineteenth Century Irish Emigration Statistics'; Dudley Baines, *Emigration from Europe 1815–1930* (London, 1991), 10.

30. Commission on Emigration, *Report* (Dublin, 1956), 20, 318. True emigration and natural increase rates in the early decades were probably higher than indicated here.

31. Joanna Bourke, 'Women and Poultry in Ireland, 1891–1914', *IHS*, 25 (1987), 310; J. Lee, 'Women and the Church since the Famine', in Margaret McCurtain and Donnchadh Ó Corráin (eds.), *Women in Irish History: The Historical Dimension* (Cork, 1979), 37–45. For the parallels with the develop-

ment literature see Mary E. Norris, 'The Impact of Development on Women: A Specific-factor Analysis', *Journal of Development Economics*, 38/1 (1992), 183–202, and the references cited there.

32. H. Diner, *Erin's Daughters in America* (Baltimore, Md., 1986); T. Guinnane, 'Coming of Age in Rural Ireland at the Turn of the Twentieth Century', *Continuity and Change*, 5/3 (1990), 449–51; US Immigration (Dillingham) Commission, *Report*, vi–xvi (Washington, DC, 1911).

33. Claudia Goldin and Kenneth Sokoloff, 'Women, Children, and Industrialization in the Early Republic: Evidence from the Manufacturing Censuses', *JEH*, 42/4 (1982); C. Goldin, *Understanding the Gender Gap: An Economic History of American Women* (Oxford, 1990), ch. 3.

34. Guinnane, 'Coming of Age in Rural Ireland at the Turn of the Twentieth Century'; id., 'Age at Leaving Home in Rural Ireland, 1901–11', *JEH*, 52/3; Ó Gráda, 'Across the Briny Ocean', in Devine and Dickson, *Ireland and Scotland*, 124; Commission on Emigration, *Report*, 122, 129.

35. Gary S. Becker, *A Treatise on the Family* (Cambridge, Mass., 1981), 225.

36. I owe this suggestion to Paul David.

37. Dudley Baines, *Emigration from Europe 1815–1930*, 37–42; Marjolein 't Hart, 'Irish Return Migration in the Nineteenth Century', *Tijdschrift voor Economische en Sociale Geografie*, 76/3 (1985), 223–31; US Immigration Commission, *Report*, xx (Washington, DC, 1911), Table 44.

38. Arnold Schrier, *Ireland and Irish Emigration to the New World* (Minneapolis, 1956); *Reports of the Immigration Commission: Immigrant Banks*, (xxxvii), Washington, DC, 1911, 273–6; J. F. Maguire, *The Irish in America* (London, 1868). Of course, the numbers do not reflect quite *that* well on the emigrants' generosity. The USA contained 1.6 million Irish-born emigrants in 1900, so the evidence is of an annual average of less than two pounds sterling per emigrant, or merely a few days' wages in America.

39. Samuel H. Preston and Michael R. Haines, *Fatal Years: Child Mortality in Late Nineteenth-Century America* (Princeton, NJ, 1991), 104, 180, 183.

40. Éamon de Valera in Maurice Moynihan (ed.), *Speeches and Statements by Éamon de Valera* (Dublin, 1980), 154.

41. Mokyr and Ó Gráda, 'Emigration and Poverty in Pre-Famine Ireland'.

42. C. H. Oldham, cited in Freeman, *Pre-Famine Ireland*, 38.

43. O'Rourke has produced a model which establishes a presumption that the 'shirkers' would stay at home: see his, 'Why Ireland Emigrated: A Positive Theory of Factor Flows', *OEP*, 44 (1992), 322–40; but also Commission on Emigration, *Report*, 139–40.

44. Cf. the results for present-day Sweden and Puerto Rico reported in R. B. Freeman, 'Immigration from Poor to Wealthy Countries: Experience of the United States', paper delivered at the European Economic Association Meetings, Dublin, Sept. 1992.

45. P. T. Geary and C. Ó Gráda, 'Immigration and the Real Wage: Time Series Evidence from the US 1820–1977', CEPR Working Paper No. 71 (1985); Tim Hatton and J. G. Williamson, 'After the Famine: Emigration from Ireland', *JEH*, 53 (1993), 575–600.

46. Arnold Schrier, *Ireland and the American Emigration, 1850–1900*, 7–9; Peter Lindert and J. G. Williamson, 'Workers' Living Standards During the Industrial Revolution: A New Look', *EHR*, 36 (1983), 1–25; but also Joel Mokyr, 'Is There Still Life in the Pessimist Case? Consumption During the Industrial Revolution', *JEH*, 48 (1988), 69–92.
47. Cf. J. G. Williamson, *Late Nineteenth Century American Development* (Cambridge, Mass., 1973), ch. 11.
48. O'Rourke, 'Agricultural Change and Rural Depopulation', 196–9.
49. Baines, *Emigration*, 32; S. Carlsson, 'Chronology and Composition of Swedish Emigration to North America' (cited in Baines, *Emigration*, 32); Ó Gráda, 'Some Aspects of Nineteenth-Century Emigration'; Ó Gráda and B. M. Walsh, 'Recent Irish Emigration: Patterns, Causes, and Effects' (TS, July 1992); Hatton and Williamson, 'After the Famine'.
50. This section follows Ó Gráda, 'Demographic Adjustment and Seasonal Migration in Nineteenth Century Ireland', in Cullen and Furet, *Irlande et France*, 181–94. See also an article which I previously overlooked, J. H. Johnston's excellent 'Harvest Migration from Nineteenth-Century Ireland', *Transactions of the Institute of British Geographers*, No. 41 (1967), 97–112; Armstrong, *Economic History of Agriculture in Northern Ireland*, 230–5; Ruth-Ann Harris, 'Seasonal Migration between Ireland and England prior to the Famine', in D. H. Akenson (ed.), *Canadian Papers in Rural History*, vii (Gananoque, Ontario, 1990), 363–86; O'Dowd, *Migrants and Tatie Hokers*. Eoghan Ó Domhnaill, *Scéal Hiúdaí Sheáinín* (Dublin, 1940), 73–100, and Pádraig Ua Cnáimhsí, *Róise Rua* (Dublin, 1988), 61–78, both contain astute, evocative accounts of the working conditions facing harvesters.
51. Migration also had the effect of imposing a degree of social control. Gerard Moran has argued that when shortage of work forced many migrants to stay at home during 1879 and 1880, they turned their energies to the Land League. See his 'A Passage to Britain: Seasonal Migration and Social Change in the West of Ireland', *Saothar*, 13 (1989), 22–31.
52. The Kirkintilloch incident prompted an interdepartmental committee of inquiry and an outspoken editorial from the *Irish Times* (24 Sept. 1937). See NA/SPO, S10191A.
53. Peadar O'Donnell, 'Migration is a Way of Keeping a Grip', The *Bell*, Nov. 1941.
54. *Report of the Interdepartmental Committee on Seasonal Migration to Great Britain, 1937–8*, P. No. 3403 (Dublin, 1938), 13–4 and Table V.
55. Trends in mortality and life expectancy are briefly discussed in Ch. 10.

Chapter 10

1. Cited in Kennedy *et al.*, *Economic Development of Ireland*, 27.
2. 'On a Saturday evening at dusk I saw a couple alone in their vegetable garden. The wife was going on and on about the tea, and her husband wished she'd stop' (from *Amhrán an tae*—The Tea Song—by Connemara song-writer, Colm

de Bhailís). The song refers to an era when whether a household in the west could afford tea was a contentious matter.

3. Compare Fitzpatrick, 'Disappearance of the Irish Agricultural Labourer' and E. H. Hunt, 'Industrialization and Regional Inequality: Wages in Britain 1760–1914', *JEH*, 46 (1986), 965–6. In Ireland the weekly wage in the 1890s and 1900s averaged somewhat less than 11*s*. (£0.55), in Britain in 1893 it was a little over 17*s*. (£0.85).

4. TCD, MS 9828 (memoirs of R. M. Hilliard, Killarney), 13–14.

5. Fitzpatrick, 'Disappearance of the Irish Agricultural Labourer', 82; O'Rourke, 'Agricultural Change', 179; D'Arcy, 'Wages of Labourers in the Dublin Building Industry', 28; Maura Cronin, 'Work and Workers in Cork 1800–1900', in Buttimer, O'Brien, and O'Flanagan, *Cork: History and Society*. No index of the cost of living in Ireland exists, but the Statist-Sauerbeck should reflect trends in Dublin during these decades. See Mitchell and Deane, *Abstract*, 474–5.

6. McCorry, 'Lurgan', 201.

7. Compare Paul Johnson, *Saving and Spending: The Working Class Economy in Britain 1870–1939* (Oxford, 1985), esp. 90–4.

8. 'Return by Counties. Showing for Each Post Office and Trustee Savings Bank the Number of Accounts . . .', BPP 1913 (LVII) [272].

9. Lee, *Modernisation*, 13; Cullen, *Eason & Son, A History*, 7–9, 68.

10. Compare Donnelly, *Land and People*, 242–50. A remark from north-west Mayo that *ní bhíodh seomra ar bith iontu ach i gcorrcheann bhíodh seomra amháin* (the houses had no rooms, except for the odd house with one room) explains why in parts of rural Ireland the dining-room is still called 'the room'. See Ó Catháin and Uí Sheighin, *A Mhuintir Dhú Chaocháin*, 152.

11. Nugent Robinson, 'The Condition of the Dwellings of the Poor in Dublin, with a Glance at the Model Lodging Houses', in *Transactions of the National Association for the Promotion of Social Science* (London, 1862), 517–18.

12. Daly, *Deposed Capital*, ch. 9; John V. O'Brien, *Dear, Dirty Dublin: A City in Distress 1899–1916* (Berkeley, 1982), 126–28; Paul-Dubois, *Contemporary Ireland*, 325; Cameron, *How the Poor Live*; Donal T. Flood, 'The Decay of Georgian Dublin', *DHR*, 27 (1973–4), 78–100; Aalen, 'Health and Housing in Dublin *c*.1850–1921'; Whitelaw, *Essay on the Population of Dublin* (Dublin, 1805); Henry McCormac, 'A Few Particulars Relative to Our Town-Poor, Especially the Irish Town-Poor', in George W. Hastings (ed.), *Transactions of the National Association for the Promotion of Social Science* (London, 1862), 613–18.

13. Lee, *Modernisation*, 35; Kennedy *et al.*, *Economic Development of Ireland*, ch. 1; Mokyr, *Why*, 10–11. The 1914 estimate is further discussed in Ch. 15.

14. Ó Gráda, *Ireland* (1st edn.), 161–2; O'Rourke, 'Agricultural Change', 179.

15. Boyle and Ó Gráda, 'Fertility Trends'; Commission on Emigration, *Report*, 106–7; Barry, 'Irish Regional Life Tables'.

16. Boyle and Ó Gráda, 'Fertility Trends'; Dan Usher, 'An Imputation to the Measure of Economic Growth for Changes in Life Expectancy', in M. Moss

(ed.), *The Measurement of Economic and Social Performance* (Chicago, 1973), 193–226; J. G. Williamson, 'British Mortality and the Value of Life, 1781–1931', *PS*, 38 (1984), 157–72. Compare too Giovanni Federico and Gianni Toniolo, 'Italy', in G. Toniolo and R. Sylla (eds.), *Patterns of European Industrialization* (London, 1991), esp. at 200–2.

17. NA, V16-6-6 (Kilmainham) and V16-1-10 and V16-1-12 (Castlebar).
18. Excluding men charged in connection with the 1916 Rising (who were taller).
19. The small size of our samples rules out hard generalizations, but both 1880s' datasets indicate that the male adolescent growth spurt occurred early, before the age of 16 years. For the Dublin teenagers the pattern was very similar to that recently reported for Christ's Hospital school, London, in the 1870s (in Floud *et al.*, *Height*, 182–3).

Age	14	15	16	17	18	19
Height	57.72 (18)	60.38 (20)	62.97 (19)	64.59 (56)	65.21 (71)	65.46 (68)
Growth (%)	+4.6	+4.2	+2.6	+1.0	+0.4	

Note: Height in inches, number of observations in parentheses

Many of the non-Catholic in Kilmainham were foreigners. This probably accounts for the negative coefficients on 'Religion' in Table 10.4.

20. R. W. Fogel, 'New Sources and New Techniques for the Study of Secular Trends in Nutritional Status, Health, Mortality, and the Process of Aging', NBER Series on Historical Factors in Long Run Growth, Working Paper No. 24 (May 1991).
21. Quoted in W. Peter Ward, 'Birth Weight and Standards of Living in Vienna, 1865–1930', *JIH*, 19/2 (1988), 204.
22. W. P. Ward and P. Ward, 'Infant Birth Weight and Nutrition in Industrializing Montreal' *American Historical Review*, 89 (1985), 324–45; W. P. Ward, 'Birth Weight and Standards of Living in Vienna'.
23. W. P. Ward, 'Weight and Length at birth in Dublin, 1869–1930' (unpublished). For some background on the hospital see Ó Gráda, 'Dublin's Demography'.
24. Ward, 'Weight at Birth in Vienna', 500.
25. Joseph Clarke, 'Observations on Some Causes of the Excess of the Mortality of Males over that of Females', *Philosophical Transactions of the Royal Society of London*, 76 (1786), 349–64; cited in Tanner, *The Worldwide Variation in Human Growth* (Cambridge, 1976), 257. For modern evidence on Irish birth weights, see Brian Nolan and Hugh Magee, 'Perinatal Mortality and Low Birthweight by Age, Parity and Socio-economic Background: Evidence for Ireland', ESRI Seminar Paper, 8 Oct. 1992.
26. C. Goldin and R. Margo, 'The Poor at Birth: Birth-weights and Infant Mortality at Philadelphia's Almshouse Hospital, 1848–73', *EEH*, 26/3 (1989), 360–79.
27. *1861 Census*, 44; *1911 Census*, 453. For more on status and marriage rates, Walsh, 'A Study of Irish County Marriage Rates'. For bleaker accounts of

women's status in post-Famine Ireland see J. Lee, 'Women and the Church Since the Famine', in M. McCurtain and D. Ó Corráin (eds.), *Women in Irish Society* (Dublin, 1978), 38–9; Bourke, 'The Best of All Home Rulers'.

28. *1926 Census*, Pt. X, 94–6.

29. PRO, T168/74; O'Rourke and Polak, 'Property Transactions in Ireland'.

30. Cited in Ollerenshaw, 'Aspects of Bank Lending', 227. The number of bankruptcies in Ireland, averaging less than a hundred in 1853–8, reached 260 in 1861 and 1862, BPP 1864 (XLVIII) [235], 543.

31. Donnelly, 'Agricultural Depression'; Fitzpatrick, 'Decline of the Irish Agricultural Labourer'; *Report of the Central Committee for the Relief of Distress in Ireland* (Dublin, 1864).

32. Burke, *People and Poor Law in Nineteenth Century Ireland*; NLI, MS 11221 (Report on the State of Ireland in 1867 by W. N. Hancock); Ian Levitt, 'Poor Law and Pauperism', in Langton and Morris, *Atlas*, 160–3.

33. Mansion House Relief Committee, *The Irish Crisis of 1879–80* (Dublin, 1881), App. IX; Donnelly, *Cork*, 259–64; PRONI, D627/293b (James Watt to H. de F. Montgomery, 13 Mar. 1880). Another letter from Watt to Montgomery, a local landlord, accused other landlords of doing 'next to nothing' for their tenants (D627/293c).

34. 'Relief was a word often on people's lips when I was young; relief roads, relief clothes, relief biscuits, and so on' (Ua Cnaimhsí, *Róise Rua* (Dublin, 1988), 1). See too Micheál Ó Conghaile, *Conamara agus Árainn 1880–1980: Gnéithe den Stair Shóisialta* (Béal an Daingin, 1988), chs. 9–10; Dublin Mansion House Relief Committee, *The Irish Crisis of 1879–80* (Dublin, 1881), 1 and 345–71 (list of subscriptions); Donnelly, *Cork*, 261–2; Paul-Dubois, *Contemporary Ireland*, 307.

35. Pádraig Ó Conaire, 'Páidín Mháire', in *Scothscéalta* (Dublin, 1956); Liam O'Flaherty, *The House of Gold* (London, 1929). See also Synge, *Wicklow, West Kerry and Connemara*, 174–180.

36. T. P. O'Neill, 'The Food Crisis of the 1890s' in Crawford, *Famine*, 176–97; Ó Conghaile, *Conamara agus Árainn 1880–1980*, 148–55; Ó Gráda, *Great Irish Famine*, 68.

Chapter 11

1. IFC, MS 404/234.

2. Bence Jones, *A Life's Work by a Landlord Who Tried to Do His Duty* (London, 1880), 37.

3. Compare the Bank of Ireland, which reminded the Irish in 1879 that if they devoted less time to politics and 'more to keeping a credit balance at their bankers, they would see things looking better all over the country' (cited in Ollerenshaw, *Banking*, 120).

4. Solow, *The Land Question*; Vaughan, *Landlord and Tenant*; Séamus MacPhilip, 'Profile of a Landlord in Folk Tradition and in Contemporary Accounts—the Third Earl of Leitrim', *Ulster Folklife*, 34 (1988), 26–40; W. E. Vaughan, *Sin, Sheep and Scotsmen: John George Adair and the Derryveagh Evictions* (Belfast, 1983); Geary, *The Plan of Campaign*, ch. 7.

5. Foster, *Modern Ireland*, 408; Murray, 'Agrarian Violence and Nationality in Nineteenth Century Ireland: The Myth of Ribbonism', *IESH*, 13 (1986), 72; Comerford in Vaughan, *NHI*, 5, p. 390.

6. Solow, *Land Question*, ch. 3; W. Bence Jones, *The Life's Work in Ireland*, 89. The following seems apposite: 'Thomastown [County Kilkenny] farmers who insisted that evictions were common were seldom able to give examples in the parish. When asked why, the reply was the evictions were "over by Graigue way" or "up the country". That is, they were said to have happened somewhere else, not too far away, although not actually in the parish' (Marilyn Silverman and P. H. Gulliver, *In the Valley of the Nore: A Social History of Thomastown, County Kilkenny 1840–1983* (Dublin, 1986), 123). But see too Lee, *Modernisation*, 101.

7. Liam Kennedy, 'The Rural Economy', in Kennedy and Ollerenshaw, *An Economic History of Ulster 1820–1939*, 43.

8. T. Jones Hughes, 'Landholding and Settlement in the Cooley Peninsula in County Louth', *IG*, 4/3 (1961), 149–74; Arnold Horner, 'The Scope and Limitations of the Landlord Contribution to Changes in the Irish Landscape, 1700–1850', in V. Hansen (ed.), *Collected Papers Presented at the Permanent European Conference for the Study of the Rural Landscape* (Copenhagen, 1981), 71–8; Smyth, 'Landholding Changes', 19.

9. e.g. Armstrong, *Economic History*, 174–7; Ó Gráda, *Ireland*, ch. 4.

10. Ó Gráda, 'The Beginnings of the Irish Creamery System'; Kennedy, 'Regional Specialisation in Irish Agriculture'.

11. Turner, 'Agricultural Output and Productivity in Post-Famine Ireland', in Campbell and Overton, *Land, Labour and Livestock*, 410–38; id., 'Output and Productivity in Irish Agriculture from the Famine to the Great War', *IESH*, 17 (1990), 62–78; W. E. Vaughan, 'Potatoes and Agricultural Output', *IESH*, 17 (1990), 79–92.

12. Solow, *The Land Question*, 199–201; Michael Turner, 'Output and Productivity in Irish Agriculture from the Famine to the Great War', *IESH*, 17 (1990), 62–78; Ó Gráda, *Ireland*, ch. 4.

13. *1901 Census*, 119, 126; *1926 Irish Free State Census*, 6; *1926 Northern Ireland Census*, 24; Lionel Smith-Gordon and Laurence C. Staples, *Rural Reconstruction in Ireland: A Record of Co-operative Organisation* (Dublin, 1917), 109–110; Joseph Hanly, *Mixed Farming: A Practical Text Book of Irish Agriculture* (Dublin, 1921), 410–15; Ó Gráda, 'Beginnings of the Irish Creamery System'.

14. Vaughan, 'Farmer, Grazier and Gentleman'; NLI, MSS 19,247–8. In Co. Meath as a whole the number of cattle almost doubled in the period studied.

15. R. M. Barrington, 'The Prices of Some Agricultural Produce and the Cost of Farm Labour for the Past Fifty Years', *JSSISI*, 9 (1886–7), 137–53. Unfortunately, the source gives no yield data.

16. For corroboration regarding 1883–5 see NLI MSS 19,546 (demesne farm, Clonbrock estate), and NLI, 23,833–6 (Dunmore farm, Ormonde estate). On the former the balance of receipts over outlays fell from an average of £1,008 in 1880–2 to £631 in 1883–6. On the latter receipts rose from an average of £1,347 in 1884–5 to £1,800 in 1886–8.

17. Barrington, 'The Prices of Some Agricultural Produce'; Royal Dublin Society, Barrington farm accounts. The introduction of new blight-resistant varieties and potato spraying were probably responsible for the rise in potato yields.

18. Staehle, 'Statistical Notes on the Economic History of Irish Agriculture' (includes comments by R. C. Geary); Kevin O'Rourke, 'Winners and Losers in the International Growth Stakes: Denmark and Ireland, 1870–1930' (TS, 1991); Van Zanden, 'The First Green Revolution'.

19. Most recently by Timothy Guinnane and Ronald Miller in 'The Limits to Land Reform: Land and Rural Credit in Nineteenth-Century Ireland' (mimeo, August 1992). See also Irish Banking Commission, *Second Interim Report* (Dublin, 1926).

20. 'Report of the Departmental Committee on Agricultural Credit in Ireland', BPP 1914 (XIV).

21. Banking Commission, *Second Interim Report* (Dublin, 1926); Commission of Inquiry into Banking Currency and Credit (CIBCC), *Reports* (Dublin, 1938), 262–3.

22. AIBA, book detailing 'securities on which advances have been made', Enniscorthy branch of the Munster & Leinster Bank, *c.*1913–60. The Wyndham Act expressly prohibited tenants from mortgaging their holdings for more than ten times the annual repayment without special permission (Moritz Bonn, *Modern Ireland and Her Agrarian Problem* (Dublin, 1906), 157–8).

23. CIBCC, *Reports*, 205–6.

24. W. Bence Jones, *A Life's Work in Ireland*, 216; John W. Boyle, 'The Agricultural Laborer: A Marginal Figure', in Clark and Donnelly, *Irish Peasants*, 311–38; Fitzpatrick, 'The Disappearance of the Irish Agricultural Labourer'.

25. David S. Jones, 'The Cleavage Between Graziers and Peasants in the Land Struggle, 1890–1910', in Clark and Donnelly, *Irish Peasants*, 374–417; Paul Bew, *Conflict and Conciliation in Ireland, 1890–1910: Parnellites and Radical Agrarians* (Oxford, 1987); Gearóid Ó Tuathaigh, 'The Land Question, Politics and Irish Society, 1922–1960', in P. J. Drudy (ed.), *Irish Studies 2 (Ireland: Land, Politics and People)* (Oxford, 1982), 167–90.

26. *1841 Census*, 170; W. M. Thackeray, *The Irish Sketch Book* in *Works*, xvii (London, 1888), 142. Note too the sketches on pp. 90, 114, 130. Thackeray's impressions are worth comparing to those of Henry Coulter, *The West of Ireland*, 30, 56. Coulter claims a great improvement in retail outlets after the Famine.

27. Charles Booth, 'The Economic Distribution of Population in Ireland', in *Ireland, Industrial and Agricultural*, 64–5; Paul-Dubois, *Contemporary Ireland*, 334.

28. Kennedy, 'Farmers, Traders, and Agricultural Politics in Pre-Independence Ireland', in Clark and Donnelly, *Irish Peasants*, 341–3; 1871 census, Summary Tables 18–19; 1911 census, Tables 19–20; J. Lee, 'The Golden Age of Irish Railways', in K. Nowlan (ed.), *Travel and Transport in Ireland* (Dublin, 1973), 110–19.

29. NA, Business Records, Mayo 10/1, Kilkenny 12/1–16; J. M. Synge, *Wick-*

low, West Kerry and Connemara, 225–31. Compare D. Alexander, *Retailing in England during the Industrial Revolution* (London, 1970); G. Shaw and M. T. Wild, 'Retail Patterns in the Victorian City', *Transactions of the Institute of British Geographers*, n.s. 4 (1979), 278–91.

30. PRONI, D2008/1/1 and D2008/1/6.

31. Kennedy, 'Regional Specialization'; *Returns of Agricultural Produce in Ireland ... 1854* (Dublin, 1855), 151; *Agricultural Statistics 1847–1926* (Dublin, 1930), 76; Ó Gráda, *Ireland*, ch. 4.

32. Smith, *Wealth of Nations*, Book I, ch. 9.

33. Coulter, *The West of Ireland*, 23–4.

34. Kennedy, 'Retail Markets'; Synge, *Wicklow*, 226–7.

35. Patrick Bolger, *The Irish Cooperative Movement: Its History and Development* (Dublin, 1977), ch. 12.

36. Congested Districts Board, *Reports on Congested Districts* (Dublin, 1892–7), 132.

37. CDB, *Reports*, 162; Ó Gráda, 'Soláthar Creidmheasa don Íseal-Aicme in Éirinn sa Naoú Aois Déag', *Central Bank of Ireland Quarterly Bulletin*, 3 (1974), 120–35; Conrad Arensberg and Solon Kimball, *Family and Community in Ireland*, 2nd edn. (Cambridge, Mass., 1968), 396–410.

38. W. N. Hancock, *Is the Competition between Large and Small Shops Injurious to the Community?* (Dublin, 1851); Anon., *The Origins and Progress of the Monster House Monopoly* (Dublin, 1851); P. Costello and T. Farmar, *The Very Heart of the City: The Story of Denis Guiney and Clerys* (Dublin, 1992).

39. The underlying data are discussed in Chs. 4–7. The export estimate reflects Solar's point that the Drummond Commission's figure of £16.7 million is too high.

40. Paul Krugman and A. J. Venables, 'Integration and the Competitiveness of Peripheral Industry', in C. Bliss and J. de Macedo (eds.), *Unity with Diversity in the European Economy: The Community's Southern Frontier* (Cambridge, 1990), 56–75; O'Connell, 'Do Regions Naturally Converge?'. Also see Kevin O'Rourke and J. G. Williamson, 'Were Heckscher and Ohlin Right? Putting History Back into the Factor-Price Equalization Theorem', UCD Centre for Economic Research, Working Paper 92/6.

41. Sidney Pollard, *Peaceful Conquest: The Industrialization of Europe 1760–1970* (Oxford, 1981), 77.

Chapter 12

1. John McEvoy, *Statistical Survey of the County of Tyrone* (Dublin, 1802), 135; Charles O'Hara, 'A Survey of the Economic Development of Sligo in the Eighteenth Century' (PRONI, T2812/19), entry for 23 Oct. 1766. I am grateful to W. H. Crawford for alerting me to these references.

2. Dickson, 'The Irish Cotton Industry', 110–15.

3. Bielenberg, *Cork*, 21–30, and 'The Growth and Decline of a Textile Town'; O'Sullivan, *Economic History of Cork City*, 191–2; George Bennett, *The History of Bandon* (Cork, 1862), 372–3.

504   NOTES TO PP. 276–81

4. Whitelaw, Warburton, and Walsh, *History of the City of Dublin* (London, 1818), ii. 973–5; Dickson, 'The Irish Cotton Industry'; id., 'An Economic History of the Cork Region in the Eighteenth Century', 596–600.

5. Dickson, 'The Irish Cotton Industry'; Dubourdieu, *Antrim*, 404–5; Geary, 'Rise and Fall', 30–8; Horner, *Linen Trade*, 132–3; Monaghan, 'The Rise and Fall of the Belfast Cotton Industry', *IHS* 3/9 (1942), 1–17; Gamble, 'The Business Community and Trade of Belfast 1767–1800', 372–4; Green, *Lagan Valley*, 95–103; Ó Gráda, *Ireland*, ch. 1; Mitchell and Deane, *Abstract*, 178–180; Mokyr, *Industrialization in the Low Countries 1795–1850*, 28–36. Strictly speaking (as Frank Geary has reminded me), the wool in Table 12.1 should be weighted at 0.89 rather than unity.

6. Dickson, 'The Irish Cotton Industry', 104–6; Wakefield, *Ireland*, i. 706.

7. *Dublin Gazette*, 1780–1820, *passim*.

8. NLI, MS 13629(7), 'Report on Cotton Manufacturers 1834'.

9. Frank Geary, 'The Belfast Cotton Industry Revisited'; Takei, 'Mechanization', *passim*; Ollerenshaw, 'Industry', 67–8; PRONI, D1725/18 (diary of James Black of Randalstown, failed cotton-spinner, late 1830s).

10. O'Brien, *Union to Famine*, 313; *1841 Census*, 440.

11. D. J. Owen, *History of Belfast* (Belfast, 1921), 300.

12. McCutcheon, *Industrial Archaeology*, 231–66.

13. Day and McWilliams, *OSMI: Antrim*, i (Carnmoney), 52.

14. R. L. Sheil, *Sketches Legal and Political*, i (London, 1855), 358.

15. Representative Church Body Library MS 173 (David Malcolmson to Richard Ussher, 18 Apr. 1825); Kenneth Charlton, 'The State of Ireland in the 1820s: James Cropper's Plan', *IHS*, 17 (1970–1), 320–39. Cropper was a Liverpool businessman and philanthropist.

16. NA, Business Records WAT 8/1.

17. Marmion, *Maritime Ports*, 559.

18. NA, 975/14/7 [1A.1.21] (Hardman, Winder and Stokes papers, Malcolmson bankruptcy proceedings: statement of Malcolmson Brothers' Assets and Liabilities, Apr. 1870).

19. NA, MS 975/14/6–7; PRONI, D1905/2/27 (records of Belfast solicitor acting on behalf of Malcolmsons' creditors in 1876–7).

20. The Morrill tariff of 1861 raised tariff levels on cotton back to where they have been in the 1830s, and they remained at over 40% until the First World War (J. R. T. Hughes, *Economic History of the US* 3rd edn. (New York, 1989), 383).

21. NA, MS 975/14-7-9.

22. P. Power, 'The Portlaw Cotton Factory', *Waterford and South Eastern Archaeological Society Journal*, 13 (1910), 59–64; Irish Countrywomen's Association (Portlaw Guild), *Portlaw: A Local History* (Waterford, 1985); Matthew Butler, series of articles on the Portlaw enterprise in the *Waterford Evening News* 12 July–20 Sept. 1935; David Dickson, 'Rise and Decline of the Irish Cotton Industry', 111; NLI Microfilm P6935, 'A Memoir of the Malcolmson Family'; Margaret T. Fogarty, 'The Malcolmsons and the Economic Development of

the Lower Suir Valley'; Marmion, *Maritime Ports of Ireland*, 559; Emmet O'Connor, *A Labour History of Waterford* (Waterford, 1989), 67–8.

23. Horner, *Linen Trade of Europe*, 15–75; Mairéad Dunlevy, *Dress in Ireland* (London, 1989), chs. 4–6; Warburton *et al.*, *History of the City of Dublin*, ii. 965–7, 980–3.

24. Horner, *Linen Trade of Europe*, chs. 2–8; Gill, *Linen Industry*, 342–3; H. Gribbon, 'The Irish Linen Board, 1711–1828', in Cullen and Smout, *Comparative Aspects*, 77–87; W. H. Crawford, *Domestic Industry in Ireland*, 1–6; id., 'Economy and Society'.

25. Dickson, *New Foundations*, 126–7; W. H. Crawford, *Domestic Industry in Ireland*; Horner, *Linen Trade*, 125–7 (citing the report of Linen Board inspector Peter Besnard); Eric Almquist, 'Mayo and Beyond'.

26. Horner, *Linen Trade*, 202–3. The share of Dublin and Cork in total plain linen exports dropped from 49% in 1802–3 to 34% in 1809–10 and 27% in 1814–15. Belfast's linen exports rose while the Belfast region was developing its cotton industry.

27. L'Amie, 'Chemicals in the Eighteenth-Century Irish Linen Industry'; Cohen, 'Tullylish', 426.

28. Cited in W. H. Crawford, 'The Evolution of the Linen Trade in Ulster', 51.

29. Horner, *Linen Trade*, 129. I am reminded by W. H. Crawford that since much of Mayo's trade was in tow-yarn shirts for local consumption, this implies a considerable trade in linen yarn with the weaving counties.

30. Thompson, *Meath*, 390; Liam Kennedy, 'The Rural Economy', in Kennedy and Ollerenshaw, *Economic History of Ulster*, 5–6; *LTD*, i. 500; ii. 255, 524, 566; Ballinascreen Historical Society, *Statistical Report of the Parishes of Ballinascreen, Kilcronaghan . . . in the County of Londonderry by John McCloskey* (n.p., (c.1823) 1983), 97; Otway, in BPP 1840 (XXIII), 627, 650; Desmond McCabe, 'Law, Conflict and Social Order: County Mayo 1820–1845', 11; Marmion, *Maritime Ports of Ireland*, 459; Horner, *Linen Trade*, 114. Marmion (*Maritime Ports*, 428) also notes the importance formerly of the linen trade for the port of Sligo.

31. Market sales cannot be relied on too much after *c.*1825 since marketing arrangements changed as a result of the new process, with fewer independent weavers and more putting-out. In the outlying districts dealers went round buying up linens and taking them for sale in the better markets. Cf. Crawford, 'The Evolution of the Linen Trade'.

32. Crawford, *Domestic Industry*, 78–80; Handloom Weavers' Report, BPP 1840 (XXIII), 711.

33. Gill, *Linen Industry*, 342–3; Solar, 'The Irish Linen Trade, 1820–1852'; Mitchell and Deane, *Abstract*, 182–3.

34. Alan McCutcheon, *Wheel and Spindle: Aspects of Irish Industrial History* (Belfast, 1977), 63–5; Takei, 'Mechanization', 100–2; Green, 'James Murland'; Hall and Hall, *Ireland*, iii. 92. Takei effectively demolishes Green's case for Murland being the pioneer.

35. Lord Sheffield, quoted in Portlock, *Londonderry* (Dublin, 1837), 271.

36. Marmion, *Maritime Ports of Ireland* 3rd edn., 648–9; L'Amie, 'Chemicals', 18.
37. Alastair Durie and Peter Solar, 'Linen', in Mitchison and Roebuck, *Economy and Society*, 219.
38. Davis, *Industrial Revolution*, 118–19; 1835 Railways Commission Report, App. B, no. 10; Solar, 'The Agricultural Trade Statistics in the Irish Railway Commissioners' Report'; id., 'The Irish Linen Trade 1820–1852'. The numbers given in the 1835 report are £3.7 million and £16.7 million; the fraction of one-quarter allows for Peter Solar's point that the report exaggerated agricultural exports, though the linen exports in the Report are also inflated in the sense that 1835 was the best year in half a century.
39. Davis, *Industrial Revolution*, 98–9, 118–19.
40. Deane and Coale, *British Economic Growth*, 188, 212.
41. A. Bielenberg, 'An Estimate of Irish Industrial Output (1841–7) . . .' (unpublished, 1991). The estimate of Irish national income is that in Mokyr, *Why Ireland Starved* (rev. edn.), 10–11.
42. Greeves, 'The Effects of the American Civil War', 180.
43. On the growth of the industry generally see Boyle, 'The Economic Development of the Irish Linen Industry'; Gill, *Irish Linen Industry*; Solar, 'Irish Linen Trade'. On relative prices, Boyle, 'Linen', 544 (citing *Belfast Linen Trade Circular*, 6 Aug. 1852). On the similarities and differences between cotton and linen, John Bray, *All About Dress* (London, n.d.), 7–8; Moore, *Linen*, 102–3; Boyle, 'Linen', 106–8.
44. W. R. McMurray, 'Hand-loom Linen, Cambric and Damask Weaving', in *Irish Life and Industry* (issued in Connection with the Home Industries Section, Irish International Exhibition) (Dublin, 1907), 162–7; Moore, *Linen*, 82–4. Compare Hall and Hall, *Ireland*, iii. 96 n.
45. Riordan, *Modern Irish Trade and Industry*, 116; Gribbon, *Water Power*, 98–102; Moore, *Linen*; Sir Graham Larmor, 'Mechanisation and Productivity in the Linen Industry', *JSSISI*, 19 (1954–5), 31–5. On the technology McCutcheon's *Industrial Archaeology*, ch. 5, is unrivalled.
46. Alfred S. Moore, *Linen from the Raw Material to the Finished Product* (London, 1914), 71.
47. 'Final Report of the First Census of Industrial Production of the United Kingdom 1907', BPP 1912–13 (CIX) [6320]; Riordan, *Irish Trade and Industry*, 110–11.
48. Emily Boyle, 'Linenopolis: the Rise of the Textile Industry', in J. C. Beckett et al., *Belfast: The Making of a City* (Belfast, 1983), 48; *The Industries of Ireland, 1: Belfast and Towns of the North* (London, 1891), 26 (on the York Street Flax Spinning and Weaving Company); Gill, *Rise of the Irish Linen Industry*, 330–1; Patterson, 'The Linen Industry'; Moore, *Linen, from the Raw Material to the Finished Product*, 62; 'SC on Industries (Ireland)', BPP 1884–5 (IX), Qs. 11731–2, 11752 (evidence of R. H. Reade).
49. *The Industries of Ireland, 1: Belfast and Towns of the North* (London, 1891), 165–6. Compare Peter Temin, 'Product Quality and Vertical Integration in the Early Cotton Industry', *JEH*, 48 (1988), 891–907.

50. Green, *Industrial Archaeology*, 9–10; Collins, 'Sewing and Social Structure'; id., 'Sewing Outwork'; *OSMI*, Donaghadee, 48.

51. CDB, *Reports on Congested Districts*, 155, 174; 'Royal Commission on Congestion, Minutes of Evidence', II, BPP 1907 (XXXV) [3319]; Riordan, *Irish Trade and Industry*, 122–3; 'The Londonderry Shirt-making Industry', in Coyne, *Ireland Industrial and Agricultural*, 417–19; 'Shirt Making in Counties Londonderry and Donegal', in *Irish Rural Life and Industry*, 169; Ollerenshaw, 'Industry', 84–6.

52. O'Sullivan, *Economic History of Cork City*, 194–6.

53. Wakefield, *Ireland*, i. 718.

54. Horner, *Linen Trade of Europe*, 15–25; Cullen, *Anglo-Irish Trade 1660–1800*, 59–60; Tighe, *Kilkenny*, 539, 543–8; Clarkson, 'The Carrick-on-Suir Woollen Industry'; Dickson, 'Inland City: Reflections on Eighteenth-Century Kilkenny', in Nolan and Whelan (eds.), *Kilkenny* (Dublin, 1989), 342; Bielenberg, *Cork's Industrial Revolution*, 31–40.

55. William Cronin, 'How a Small Woollen Factory Could Succeed', in *Irish Rural Life and Industry*, 158–61.

56. Comerford, in Vaughan, *NHI*, 5, p. 380; Bielenberg, *Cork's Industrial Revolution*, ch. 4; *Dublin, Cork and South of Ireland* (London, 1892), 198–9.

57. T. W. Rolleston, 'The Woollen Industry in Ireland', in Coyne (ed.), *Ireland Industrial and Agricultural*, 396.

58. Ua Cnáimhsí *Róise Rua*, 49–51. See too Áine Ní Dhíoraí, *Na Cruacha, Scéalta agus Seanchas* (Dublin, 1985), 177.

59. 'Homespun Manufacture in the West of Ireland, Mayo and Kerry', in *Irish Rural Life and Industry*, 150–2.

60. Robin Sweetnam, 'The Development of Belfast Harbour', in McCaughan and Appleby, *The Irish Sea*, 101–9; Sidney Pollard and Paul Robertson, *The British Shipbuilding Industry 1870–1914* (Cambridge, Mass., 1979), 66.

61. O'Mahony, 'Shipbuilding and Repairing in Nineteenth-Century Cork'; Bielenberg, *Cork*, 103–13.

62. Harland & Wolff would have grown even faster but for Pirrie's expensive tastes in mansions and yachts (see Caskey, 'Entrepreneurs', 158).

63. Riordan, *Modern Irish Trade and Industry*, 97–101; Michael Moss and John R. Hume, *Shipbuilders to the World: 125 Years of Harland & Wolff 1861–1986* (Belfast, 1986); Owen, *History of Belfast*, 302–5; F. Geary and W. Johnson, 'Shipbuilding in Belfast, 1861–1986', *IESH* 16 (1989), 42–64; Ollerenshaw, 'Industry', in Kennedy and Ollerenshaw, *Ulster*, 87–96; *Industries of Ireland, 1: Belfast and the Towns of the North* (London, 1891; repr. Belfast, 1986), Introduction (by W. H. Crawford) and 62–3. On shipbuilding in Cork, Bielenberg, *Cork*, 103–13.

64. John Smellie, *Shipbuilding and Repairing in Dublin* (Glasgow, n.d.). Smellie ran the Dublin Dockyard Company.

65. Our focus here will be on the legal trade. On illegal distillation see Connell, *Irish Peasant Society*, ch. 1.

66. Cited in R. B. Weir, 'The Patent Still Distillers and the Role of Competition',

in Cullen and Smout, *Comparative Aspects*, 136. On the early history of blending E. B. McGuire, *Irish Whiskey: A History of Distilling in Ireland* (Dublin, 73), 316–23. On Coffey, Mollan *et al.*, *Some People and Places*, 22–3.

67. J. Jameson *et al.*, *Truths about Whisky* (Dublin, 1878). Ron Weir informs me that this was written in response to competition from Scotch whisky on the London market. In the same vein is Cork Chamber of Commerce, *Cork: Its Trade and Commerce* (Cork, 1919), 154–5.

68. The prospectus of the Dublin & Chapelizod put the valuation of premises, plant, water and power at over £80,000. Dargan had fitted his mill with 'two extensive weirs, two mill races (taking the whole water and water-power of the river Liffey at Chapelizod), stone piers, and foundations of most solid and costly character, two steam engines by Fairbairn, two tubular and one circular boilers, lifting and pumping machinery, water tank, two powerful water wheels by Fairbairn (reputed among the finest in Ireland)' (from *Wine Trade Review*, Oct. 1873). I owe this reference to Ron Weir.

69. Riordan, *Modern Irish Trade and Industry*, 160–4; Department of Agricultural and Technical Instruction for Ireland, *List of Irish Exporting Manufacturers* (Dublin, 1911), 8; Alfred Barnard, *The Whisky Distilleries of the United Kingdom* (London, 1887); J. B. McGuire, *Irish Whiskey: A History of Distilling in Ireland* (Dublin, 1973); R. B. Weir, 'In and Out of Ireland; Bielenberg, *Cork*, 61–76; Bielenberg, *Locke's Distillery* (Dublin, 1993); Daly, *Dublin*, 26–30.

70. 'R. C. on Whiskey and Other Potable Spirits', App. Q, BPP 1909 (XLIX) [4876], 225. The survey ignored the age of the Whiskeys.

71. NLI, MSS 20020–2 (daybooks of Locke's Brusna Distillery, Kilbeggan).

72. Derived from sales analysis books, CDC archives (deposited in Cork Archives Institute). The 1870 and 1901 books refer to sales on Tuesdays, Thursdays, and Saturdays, that for 1890 to sales on Mondays, Wednesdays, and Fridays.

73. Lynch and Vaizey, *Guinness's Brewery*; Daly, *Dublin*, 23–6; Bielenberg, *Cork*, ch. 6.

74. Hall and Hall, *Ireland*, i. 404–7; Sheil, *Sketches Legal and Political*, i. 358; Cullen, 'Eighteenth-Century Flour Milling in Ireland'.

75. Ó Gráda, 'Industry and Communications', 146.

76. 'S. C. on Industries (Ireland)', BPP 1884–5 (IX) [288], 401–2; Bielenberg, *Cork*, ch. 5; 'The Irish Milling Industry', in Coyne, *Ireland Industrial and Agricultural*, 402–7; Riordan, *Modern Irish Trade and Industry*, 88–92; Green, 'The Belfast Grain Trade'; W. M. Scott, *A Hundred Years A-Milling* (Omagh, 1956).

77. Bielenberg, *Cork*, 79 (citing D. Clark, 'Printing in Ireland', *An Leabharlann* (Dublin, 1954), 7); Riordan, *Modern Irish Trade and Industry*, 171–5; Cullen, *Eason & Son*, 1–8; Mary Pollard, *Dublin's Trade in Books 1550–1800* (Oxford, 1989).

78. Riordan, *Modern Irish Trade and Industry*, 166–7; M. S. D. Westropp, *Irish Glass: A History of Glass-Making in Ireland* (Dublin, 1978); Johnson and Kennedy, 'Nationalist Historiography', 26.

79. Referring to the Cork Exhibition organized by J. F. Maguire in 1852.

80. For Smith's belief that Ireland should be given unfettered access to British markets, E. C. Mossner and I. S. Ross (eds.), *The Correspondence of Adam Smith* (Oxford, 1977), 240−6.

81. Murray, *Commercial Relations between England and Ireland*, 247−8; Black, 'Theory & Policy in Anglo-Irish Trade Relations'; Kelly, 'The Search for a "Commercial Arrangement"'; Cullen, *Anglo-Irish Trade*, 206; McCavery, 'Finance and Politics in Ireland', 33−41.

82. Davis, *Industrial Revolution*, 88−93.

83. Cullen, 'Irish Economic History: Fact and Myth' in id., *The Formation of the Irish Economy*, 113−15; Johnson and Kennedy, 'Nationalist Historiography', 21−8.

84. Compare Johnson and Kennedy, 'Nationalist Historiography', 27. It is also worth noting that in 1821 the percentages of the population deemed 'occupied' and in 'trades, manufactures, or handicraft' were highly correlated. A plausible implication is that the wives of men engaged in agriculture were often excluded. For more on employment shifts before 1845, see Ó Gráda, *Ireland*, ch. 1.

85. See Frank Geary, 'The Act of Union, British-Irish Trade, and Pre-Famine Industrialisation in Ireland'. I am grateful to Frank Geary for letting me see a preliminary version of his paper.

86. John Sproule (ed.), *The Irish Industrial Exhibition of 1853: A Detailed Catalogue of its Contents* (Dublin, 1854); Alan Davies, 'Ireland's Crystal Palace, 1853', in Goldstrom and Clarkson, *Irish Population*, 249−70. On the agricultural exhibits, see Sproule, *Irish Industrial Exhibition*, 224.

87. John Kanefsky, 'Motive Power in British Industry: the Accuracy of the 1870 Factory Return', *EHR*, 32 (1979), 360−75.

88. Andy Bielenberg is currently completing a Ph.D. thesis which will address this question.

Chapter 13

1. Cullen, *Anglo-Irish Trade*, ch. 11; Mokyr, *Why Ireland Starved*, 211−13; Johnson and Kennedy, 'Nationalist Historiography', 14−28.

2. Bielenberg, *Cork*, 125.

3. According to George O'Brien, 'the true secret of the industrial success of Ulster was the prevalence of the Ulster custom of land tenure' (*Union to the Famine*, 442).

4. PRONI, 'Robert Stevenson's View of Co. Armagh 1795', D562/1270; Lee, *Modernisation*, 16. See also Connolly, 'Religion'.

5. Arthur Griffith (ed.), *Thomas Davis: The Thinker and Teacher* (Dublin, 1916), 182.

6. Nick von Tunzelmann, 'Coal and Steam Power', in Langton and Morris, *Atlas*, 72; Lawrence Adamson, *A Letter to the Right Hon. the Lord Mayor of the City of Dublin on the Abuses in the Coal Trade* (Dublin, 1827).

7. Mokyr, *Why Ireland Starved*, 154−5; Ollerenshaw, 'Industry', in Kennedy

and Ollerenshaw, 63; Geary, 'The Belfast Cotton Industry Revisited'; Coe, *Engineering Industry*, 169. Cf. M. Altman, 'Resource Endowments and Location Theory in Economic History: A Case Study of Ontario and Quebec at the Turn of the Twentieth Century', *JEH*, 46/4 (1988), 999–1010, for an application of Kane's point to Canada.

8. PRONI, D2966/40; Caskey, 'Entrepreneurs', 183–5; Coe, *Engineering Industry*, 168–9. I owe the first reference to Peter Solar.

9. (Anon.), *Statement on Behalf of the Manufacturers of Ireland Shewing that the Existence of the Present Rate of Duty on the Importation of Coal into Ireland is a Violation of the Treaty of the Union* . . . (Dublin, 1830), 2.

10. On England, essays by Nick von Tunzelmann and Philip Riden in J. Langton and R. Morris (eds.), *Atlas of Industrializing Britain* (London, 1986), 73–7, 128. On the Low Countries, A. E. Wrigley, *Industrial Growth and Population Change* (Cambridge, 1962). Mokyr, *Industrialization in the Low Countries 1895–1850*, 204–5, demurs.

11. Von Tunzelmann, 'Coal and Steam Power', 72–4; Kane, *Industrial Resources*, 351; Lee, 'Irish Railways', 175–8; H. O'Hara, *Report on the Supply of Fuel in Ireland* (Dublin, 1866), 16; Coe, *Engineering Industry*, 168; Johnson and Kennedy, 'Nationalist Historiography', 26.

12. Ibid. 26.

13. McCutcheon, *Industrial Archaeology*, 325–42; Caskey, 'Entrepreneurship', 25.

14. Weld, *Roscommon*, 681–2 and App. B; Freeman, *Pre-Famine Ireland*, 97. Weld's reference is to the giant Carron ironworks near Glasgow.

15. Kane, *Industrial Resources*, 11; Freeman, *Pre-Famine Ireland*, 94–8; Hall and Hall, *Ireland*, ii. 39–40; Riordan, *Modern Irish Trade and Industry*, 146; Mitchell and Deane, *Abstract*, 115–16.

16. Kane, *Industrial Resources*, ch. 5. Even more enthusiastic about Irish mineral endowments was T. Crofton Croker, *Researches in the South of Ireland* (London, 1824), 310–24. See also Fraser, *Wicklow*, 15.

17. *First Half-Yearly Report of the Mining Company of Ireland* (Dublin, 1825).

18. NLI, MSS 16,309, 16,326 (Minutes and sales of the Associated Irish Mining Company); Kane, *Industrial Resources*, 181–204.

19. Ibid. 196; O'Mahony, 'Copper-Mining at Allihies'.

20. Hall and Hall, *Ireland*, i. 141; Kane, *Industrial Resources*, 192; Thomas A. Reilly, 'Richard Griffith and the Cappagh Mine Fraud', in Davies, *Richard Griffith*, 197–210.

21. Grenville A. J. Coale, 'Irish Minerals and Building Stones', in Coyne, *Ireland Industrial and Agricultural*, 19–21; Freeman, *Pre-Famine Ireland*, 98–106; Kane, *Industrial Resources*, 203–4. On the working conditions faced by the copper miners see Des Cowman, 'Life and Labour in Three Irish Mining Communities circa 1840', *Saothar*, 9 (1983), 10–19.

22. Cole, *Memoirs*, 90; NLI, MS. 20,916 (Reports on prospecting for lead at Glengola, County Galway, 1851).

23. McCracken, 'A Mid-Victorian Irish Iron-ore Mine'.

24. On these fields, McCutcheon, *Industrial Archaeology*, ch. 6; Nolan, *Fassadinin*, 142–8, 216–18.

25. Richard Griffith, *Report on the Metallic Mines of the Province of Leinster in Ireland* (Dublin, 1828), 8.

26. Cole, *Memoirs*. Seventy years earlier Richard Griffith's *Catalogue of the Several Localities in Ireland Where Mines or Metalliferous Indications have hitherto been Discovered Up to June 1854* (Dublin, 1854 (1884)) listed 155 post-towns, many of which contained several sites. The shortest chapter in George O'Brien's *Union to Famine*, less than five pages, is that on mining. Inevitably, O'Brien blamed the failure of mining on deficient land legislation and English speculators (*Union to Famine*, 283–7).

27. D. W. Bishopp, 'A Short Review of Irish Mineral Resources', in Department of Industry and Commerce, *Geological Survey Emergency Period: 1* (Dublin, 1943); id., 'Mineral Resources', in Royal Dublin Society, *Sir Robert Kane's 'Industrial Resources of Ireland'* (Dublin, 1845), 55–61.

28. Those investing in one small concern, the Arigna Mining Company, incorporated in 1921 and dissolved some years later, seem typical of industry as a whole. Mostly Irish, they included baronets, spinsters, widows, clergymen, esquires, attorneys, an engineer and a Dublin surgeon (Oliver St John Gogarty) [NA, V/8a/1249].

29. 'If only we had potatoes and turf, life would be rosy.'

30. Kane, *Industrial Resources*, 38–44; Wakefield, *Ireland*, i. 609; R. Dennis, *Industrial Ireland* (Dublin, 1887), 93; Department of Scientific and Industrial Research, *The Winning, Preparation and Use of Peat in Ireland: Reports and Other Documents* (London, 1921). See also, Irish Amelioration Society, *Prospectus* (Dublin, 184?); R. Kane, 'Chemical Products of Peat', *Chemist*, ii (1850), 552; R. M. Alloway, 'Peat and Its Profitable Utilization', *Journal of the Royal Dublin Society*, v (1870), 281; W. F. Bailey, *The Woods, Forests, Turf-Bogs and Foreshores of Ireland* (Dublin, 1890); Hugh Ryan, *Reports upon the Irish Peat Industries, I and II* (Dublin, 1907–8); T. Johnson, 'The Irish Peat Question', *Economic Proceedings of the Royal Dublin Society*, i (1899), 1–72; C. S. Andrews, 'Some Precursors of Bord na Móna', *JSSISI*, 20 (1953–4), 132–51.

31. Henry O'Hara, *Report on the Supply of Fuel in Ireland* (Dublin, 1866), 16, 20.

32. 'Observations on the Cost of Cutting Turf in Ireland', *Journal of Industrial Progress*, (Feb. 1855), 68. I owe this reference to Peter Solar.

33. Sproule, *Cork Exhibition Guide* (Dublin, 1854), 185.

34. PRO, DSIR/8/18–19 ('The Utilisation of Irish Peat Deposits').

35. Compare Andrews, 'Limits of Agricultural Settlement', 49–50.

36. Lee, *Modernisation*, 12, 19; Pim, *Conditions and Prospects of Ireland*, 153. For a modern, more sceptical assessment of nineteenth-century Ulster businessmen, Alan Caskey, 'Entrepreneurs and Industrial Development in Ulster'.

37. Cf. Floud and McCloskey, *Economic History*, ii, 1st edn., esp. the chapters by Sandberg and Floud, and B. Elbaum and W. Lazonick (eds.), *The Decline of the British Economy* (Oxford, 1985).

38. Caskey, 'Entrepreneurs', 144, 154.

39. Cullen, *Economic History*, 145; Riordan, *Modern Irish Trade and Industry*, 176–8; W. K. Sullivan, 'Leather, Including Furs and Saddlery and Harness',

in John Sproule, *The Irish Industrial Exhibition of 1853* (Dublin), 304–5; O'Brien, 'Glimpses of Entrepreneurial Life'.

40. Lee, 'The Provision of Capital'.

41. O'Sullivan, *The Gasmakers*, 35–8.

42. Lee, *Modernisation*, 19, and Mokyr, *Why Ireland Starved*, 212, make the point. See also E. R. R. Green, 'Business Organization and the Business Class', in T. W. Moody and J. C. Beckett (eds.), *Ulster since 1800: A Social Survey* (2nd series) (Belfast, 1957), 110–18.

43. Green, *Industrial Archaeology*, 26.

44. McCracken, 'A Mid-Victorian Irish Iron-Ore Mine', 61.

45. Dickson, 'The Irish Cotton Industry', 105–6, 102, 109; Gill, *Irish Linen Industry*, 229, 232, 233; Dubourdieu, cited in Geary, 'The Decline of the Belfast Cotton Industry', 262; Green, *Lagan Valley*, 98–9; id., 'Thomas Barbour and the American Linen-Thread Industry', in Goldstrom and Clarkson, *Irish Population*, 213; Ollerenshaw, 'Ulster Industry', 68; Marmion, *Maritime Ports*, 262; Thompson, *Meath*, 391; *Pictorial World*, 14 Feb. 1889.

46. Brunicardi, *John Anderson, Entrepreneur*. On Robert Gordon, Townsend, *Cork*, 678–81.

47. Ollerenshaw, 'Ulster Industry', 92.

48. *1926 Census*, x. 53. There was entrepreneurial mobility within Ireland too. David Malcolmson, who made his fortune in Clonmel and in Portlaw, was a native of Lurgan; John Grattan, who established the Belfast Mineral Water Company, was a Dubliner; J. Brennan, who in 1834 introduced the provisions trade to Ballina and for a time cured 10,000 pigs annually for export, was from Belfast (Marmion, *Maritime History*, 437); the railway engineer William Dargan was a Carlowman; John Locke, who moved from Monasterevan via Tullamore to found the Brusna Distillery at Kilbeggan in 1843, was from Kilkenny.

49. Eoin O'Malley, *Industry and Economic Development*, 51; Lee, *Modernisation*, 12.

50. e.g. John Foster, *Class Struggle and the Industrial Revolution* (London, 1974), 12–13, 25–7, 177–82; Alexander Gerschenkron, *Europe in the Russian Mirror* (Cambridge, 1980), 9–61.

51. Louis Hyman, *The Jews in Ireland from Earliest Times to the Year 1910* (Dublin, 1972), 160–6; Duffy, 'Dublin's Jewish Community'. By 1914 the UK contained 0.3 million Jews and the USA about 4,000,000, most of them recent immigrants and their families.

52. Harrison, 'Quakers in Dublin'; Holt, 'Quakers in the Famine', ch. 1; Vann and Eversley, *Friends in Life and Death*, 52–65; Petty, *Collected Economic Writings*, 264 (cited approvingly by Gerschenkron, *Europe*, 46).

53. See Micheál Ó Cíosáin, *Cnoc an Fhómhair* (Maynooth, 1988), 137–52, for a useful account of the clerical campaign against the Whiteboys in north-west Kerry.

54. Connolly, 'Religion'; Crawford, *Domestic Industry*, 34; Wakefield, *Ireland*, ii. 739–40; John Hind, cited in Takei, 'Mechanization', 184; Dickson, 'Catholics and Trade'. On the role of the Catholic Church, Fergus D'Arcy, 'The

Decline and Fall of Donnybrook Fair: Moral Reform and Social Control in Nineteenth-Century Dublin', *Saothar*, 13 (1989), 7−21; Colm Kerrigan, 'The Social Impact of the Irish Temperance Movement', *IESH*, 14 (1987), 20−38; Elizabeth Malcolm, *Ireland Sober, Ireland Free: Drink and Temperance in Nineteenth-Century Ireland* (Dublin, 1986).

55. On religion and literacy see the excellent essays by Graeme Kirkham and Linda Lunney, in Daly and Dickson, *The Origins of Popular Literacy*, 73−111.

56. e.g. Lars Sandberg, 'Ignorance, Poverty and Backwardness in the Early Stages of European Industrialization', *Journal of European Economic History*, 11/3 (1982), 675−97.

57. Emmet Larkin, *The Historical Dimensions of Irish Catholicism* (Washington, DC, 1984), 4−5; L. Kennedy, 'The Roman Catholic Church and Economic Growth in Nineteenth Century Ireland', *ESR*, 10 (1978), 45−59.

58. James Cropper, *Present State of Ireland* (Liverpool, 1825), 14.

59. Wakefield, *Ireland*, i. 666; Asenath Nicholson, *The Bible in Ireland* (Alfred T. Sheppard, ed.), (New York, 1927), 148−9. Christopher Woods tells me that his content-analysis of several hundred eighteenth- and nineteenth-century travellers' accounts showed up few, if any, examples of his subjects being attacked or 'mugged'.

60. George Cornewall Lewis, cited in O'Brien, *Union to Famine*, 572; S. J. Connolly, *Priests and People in Pre-Famine Ireland 1780−1845* (Dublin, 1982), 219; M. O'Connell Bianconi and S. J. Watson, *Bianconi, King of the Irish Roads* (Dublin, 1962), 169; Blacker to W. C. Kyle, 30 Mar. 1846 (PRONI, D1606/5/1); G. Broeker, *Rural Disorder and Police Reform in Ireland 1812−36*, 239; Akenson, *A Protestant in Purgatory*, 126. See also Senior, *Journals*, i. 31, 38, 41; 'Martin Doyle', *Address to Landlords*, 10; R. M. Martin, *Ireland Before and After the Union*, 3rd edn. (London, 1848), 85; Boylan and Foley, *Political Economy and Colonial Ireland*, 85−6, and compare John A. Davis, *Conflict and Control: Law & Order in Nineteenth-Century Italy* (London, 1988), pt. 1.

61. e.g. Nolan, *Fassadinin*, 145; Delany, *Grand Canal*, 80−96.

62. Ó Gráda, 'Poverty, Population, and Agriculture', 130−1; McCabe, 'Law, Conflict, and Social Order, 55−6; Hoppen, *Ireland since 1800*, 52−3.

63. e.g. J. R. MacCulloch, *Statistical Account*, 542; Senior, *Journals*, i. 31−43; Thomas Campbell Foster, *Letters on the Condition of the People of Ireland* (London, 1847).

64. Guildhall Library, London, MS 11,937.

65. McCabe, 'Law, Conflict and Social Order', ch. 5; Mokyr, *Why Ireland Starved*, 137−8.

66. Lee, 'Patterns of Rural Unrest', 155; Hoppen, *Elections, Politics and Society*, 376−8; Clark and Donnelly, *Irish Peasants*; Eiriksson, 'Crime and Popular Protest'.

67. 'A return of the number and nature of offences reported to the government as having taken place in the County of Clare in the Years 1831 and 1832', BPP 1833 (XXIX) [79]; 'Petition of Clare Magistrates', PRO, HO 100/237; James S. Donnelly, 'The Terry Alt Movement of 1829−31' (mimeo); Ó Gráda, 'The

Owenite Commune at Ralahine 1831–3: A Reassessment', *IESH*, 1 (1974), 36–48.

68. 'Second Report, Workmen's Combinations', BPP 1837–8 (VIII). Robert Stephenson's classic commentary on the linen industry in 1755 was highly critical of the role of trade unions in Dublin (Horner, *Linen Trade of Europe*, 47–8).

69. e.g. Cropper, *Present State of Ireland*, 33; Pim, *Conditions and Prospects*, 154; Kane, *Industrial Resources*, 400.

70. E. H. Hunt, *British Labour History 1815–1914* (London, 1981), 194–6; S. G. Checkland, *The Gladstones: A Family Biography 1764–1851* (Cambridge, 1971), 151–4; Kane, *Industrial Resources*, 384–6.

71. Donnelly, 'The Social Composition of Agrarian Rebellions in Early Nineteenth-Century Ireland: The Case of the Carders and Caravats, 1813–16', in P. J. Corish (ed.), *Radicals, Rebels and Establishments: Historical Studies XV* (Belfast, 1985), 151–69; Eiricksson, 'Crime and Popular Protest'; IFC, MS 1457/310; Cullen, *Economic History*, 114; Foster, *Modern Ireland*, 333.

72. Tom Devine, 'Unrest and Stability in Rural Ireland and Scotland, 1760–1840', in Mitchison and Roebuck, *Economy and Society*, 126–39.

73. David Fitzpatrick, 'Emigration, 1801–70', in Vaughan, *NHI*, 5, pp. 588–9; id., *Irish Emigration*, 17–20; Wendy Cameron, 'Selecting Peter Robinson's Emigrants', *Social History/Histoire Sociale*, 9 (1976), 29–46; PRO, CO/384/12–3.

74. Mokyr, *Industrialization in the Low Countries 1800–1850* (New Haven, Conn., 1976); E. H. Hunt, 'Industrialisation and Regional Inequality: Wages in Britain 1760–1914', *JEH*, 46/4 (1987), 935–66.

75. Mokyr, 'Dear Labour, Cheap Labour'; Young, *Tour* (1892 edn.), ii. 278, 306; Black, 'Theory and Policy', 318; Kane, *Industrial Resources*, 397–400.

76. Gregory Clark, 'Productivity Growth without Technical Change in European Agriculture: A Reply to Komlos', *JEH*, 49 (1989), 979–91; id., 'Labour Productivity in English Agriculture 1300–1860', in Campbell and Overton, *Land, Labour and Livestock*, 211–35.

77. According to Tighe (*Kilkenny*, 213), 'six men can reap . . . an acre of wheat in the day: it may sometimes be done by fewer hands'. The implied ratio (assuming Tighe means Irish acres) is 0.27 acres per day.

78. Lee, 'An Economic History of Irish Railways 1830–1853', 101–3.

79. Wakefield, *Ireland*, ii. 759, 779; Weld, *Roscommon*, 660; RIA, OSM/Dungiven.

80. Tighe, *Kilkenny*, 495 (converted to statute measure and English currency).

81. Thompson, *Meath*, 349–51. The British data are taken from the following county surveys (all published in London); J. Wilson, *Renfrewshire* (1810); Walter Davies, *North Wales* (1810); G. S. Mackenzie, *Ross and Cromarty* (1810); W. Pitt, *Leicester* (1813); Joseph Plymley, *Shropshire* (1803); Richard Parkinson, *Rutland*; Thomas Davis, *Wiltshire* (1811); John Bailey, *Durham* (1810); Henry Holland, *Cheshire* (1808); Arthur Young, *Norfolk* (1813); J. Barley and G. Culley, *Northumberland* (1793); W. Gooch, *Cambridge* (1811).

82. Alfred Marshall, *Principles of Economics*, 8th edn. (London, 1920), 267–77, 284–6; id., *Industry and Trade* (London, 1920), 167, 244–7, 487–92; McCutcheon, *Industrial Archaeology*, 302 (citing *Belfast Naturalists' Field Club: Guide to Belfast and the Adjacent Counties* (Belfast, 1874), 291–2).

83. W. B. Arthur, 'Competing Technologies, Increasing Returns, and Lock-in by Historical Events', *EJ*, 99 (1989), 116–31; id., 'Positive Feedback in the Economy' *Scientific American*, 262/2 (1990), 80–5; P. A. David, 'Clio and the Economics of QWERTY', *American Economic Review Proceedings*, 75 (1985), 332–7; id., 'Factor Market Externalities and the Dynamics of Industrial Location', *Journal of Urban Economics*, 28/3 (1990), 349–70. On the localization of the Lancashire cotton industry see Paul Laxton, 'Textiles', in Lawton and Morris, *Atlas*, 106, and D. A. Farnie, *The English Cotton Industry and the World Market* (Oxford, 1979), ch. 2.

84. Paul R. Krugman and A. J. Venables, 'Integration and Competitiveness of Peripheral Industry', in C. Bliss and J. de Macedo (eds.), *Unity with Diversity in the European Economy* (Cambridge, 1990), 56–9; Krugman, 'Increasing Returns and Economic Geography', *JPE*, 99/3 (1991), 483–99.

85. Dickson, 'The Irish Cotton Industry', 111; O'Malley, *Industry and Economic Development*, esp. 50–2; Kennedy, 'Rural Economy', 1–16; Ollerenshaw, 'Industry', 72–3; McCutcheon, *Industrial Archaeology*, 299–301; Durie and Solar, 'The Scottish and Irish Linen Industries Compared', in Mitchison and Roebuck, *Economy and Society*, 211–21.

The regional concentration or localization that made Ulster the 'workshop' of Ireland echoed patterns of industrialization equally found in places such as southern Lancashire and Massachusetts in the nineteenth century. Compare Sidney Pollard, *Peaceful Conquest: The Industrialization of Europe 1760–1970* (Oxford, 1981), 117–23; John Hekman, 'The Product Cycle and New England Textiles', *Quarterly Journal of Economics*, 94 (1980), 697–717; D. A. Farnie, *The English Cotton Industry and World Markets* (Oxford, 1979), 45–77.

86. Thomas H. Mason, 'Dublin Opticians and Instrument Makers' *Dublin Historical Record*, 6 (1944), 158–9, as cited in Burnett and Morrison-Low, *Vulgar and Mechanick*, 45–6. But see also Mokyr, *Why Ireland Starved*, 196.

87. James McMillan, *The Dunlop Story* (London, 1989), 9–13.

88. Monaghan, 'The Rise and Fall of the Belfast Cotton Industry', *IHS*, 3/9 (1942), 1–17.

89. Coe, *The Engineering Industry of Northern Ireland*, 63; *The Industries of Ireland, I: Belfast and the Towns of the North* (London, 1891), 95, 127; McCutcheon, *Industrial Archaeology*, 299–302; Emily Boyle, 'Linen', 191, citing J. H. Dickson, *A Series of Letters* (London, 1846).

90. A. Gerschenkron, *Economic Backwardness in Historical Perspective* (Cambridge, Mass., 1962).

91. Crafts, *British Economic Growth*, 84. See, however, the studies by Allen and by Clark cited in Ch. 5, where much lower estimates of agricultural productivity growth are proposed.

92. N. F. R. Crafts, 'British Industrialization in an International Context', *Journal of Interdisciplinary History*, 19 (1989), 415–28.

Chapter 14

1. *Economic Thought and the Irish Question*, 134.
2. Geary, 'The Rise and Fall of the Belfast Cotton Industry'. Geary attributes the decline of the Ulster cotton industry not to lack of capital, but to the Belfast region's comparative advantage in linen from the 1820s on.
3. Bielenberg, *Cork*, 132; Black, *Economic Thought*, 152.
4. Thomas, 'The Evolution of a Capital Market'.
5. The distribution of Provincial Bank stock is derived from *Report of the Directors of the Provincial Bank of Ireland . . .* (London, 1838). On the railways and the other banks see Thomas, *Stock Exchanges*, 108–10, 140–2.
6. 'SC on Irish Industries, Minutes of Evidence', BPP 1884–5 (IX) [288], Qs. 13,352–7.
7. e.g. L. Paul-Dubois, *Contemporary Ireland* (Dublin, 1911), 327–8.
8. The ratio refers to all advances. Borrowers outside Ireland absorbed an unknown fraction.
9. Figures cited in Daly, 'Government Finance for Industry', 91.
10. J. A. Bermingham, *The Rise and Decline of Irish Industries* (Dublin, 1884), 38–9.
11. Sidney Pollard, 'Fixed Capital in the Industrial Revolution in Britain', *JEH*, 24 (1964), 299–314; S. D. Chapman, 'Financial Constraints on the Growth of Firms in the Cotton Industry 1790–1850', *EHR*, 32/1 (1979), 50–69.
12. Ollerenshaw, *Banking*, 188–202; id., 'Aspects of Bank Lending in Post-Famine Ireland', in Mitchison and Roebuck, *Economy and Society*, 222–32. Also Caskey, 'Entrepreneurship', 106–13.
13. Ollerenshaw, 'Aspects', 224, 228–9; id., *Banking in Nineteenth-Century Ireland*, 175; Greeves, 'American Civil War', 424–5; Michael Byrne, 'The Distilling Industry in Offaly', in Harman Murtagh, *Irish Midland Studies* (Athlone, 1980), 224–5; Cullen, 'Germination and Growth', in Share, *Root and Branch*, 54; Moss and Hume, *Shipbuilders*, 44; PRONI, T3068 (Ulster Bank, Maghera branch); Boyle, 'Linen', 185.
14. Ollerenshaw, 'The Business and Politics of Banking in Ireland 1900–1943'.
15. The useful reports on local conditions prepared by branch managers—some of which survive in the archive of Allied Irish banks—are a different matter.
16. *Bankers' Magazine* (1886), 20; Hall, *Bank of Ireland*, 279–94; Cullen, 'Germination and Growth', 36–7, 43; AIB Archive (letters dated 12 June 1918 and 20 Oct. 1919).
17. Oliver MacDonagh, 'The Victorian Bank', in Lyons, *Bank of Ireland 1783–1983*, 36–40; Hall, *Bank of Ireland*, 396–7.
18. Compare Sidney Checkland, *Scottish Banking, A History 1695–1973* (Glasgow, 1975), 535; Forrest Capie, 'Structure and Performance in British Banking 1870–1939', in P. Cottrell and D. Moggridge (eds.), *Money and Power* (Cheltenham, 1988).
19. Representatives of the two banks pleaded their case together before the 'SC on Banks of Issue', BPP 1875 (IX) [351], 135–48.

20. Hall, *Bank of Ireland*, 241–43, 299–300; Ollerenshaw, 'Aspects of Bank Lending', 238–9; id., *Banking in Nineteenth-Century Ireland*, 20–1, 32, 51, 135, 153; Simpson, *The Belfast Bank*, 148, 151–2. Ollerenshaw (*Banking*, 110) notes the hefty dividends paid by the northern banks in the late 1860s and early 1870s. On the degree of inter-bank competition in England and Scotland compare E. T. Nevin and E. W. Davis, *The London Clearing Banks* (London, 1970), 77–8; Michael Collins, *Money and Banking in the UK A History* (London, 1988), chs. 7–8; Checkland, *Scottish Banking*, 486.

21. Hall, *Bank of Ireland*, 224–31, 246–9; John O'Brien, 'Sadleir's Bank', 33–8. O'Brien's study is built round an interesting eye-witness account of the failure, as reflected through events at the Tipperary town branch in February 1856.

22. NBA, 'Suggestions for Improvement in its Administration and Management in Ireland, Signed on Behalf of a Large Deputation of Proprietors of the National Bank'; George Madder, *To the Shareholders of the National Bank* (shareholder's broadsheet) (Cork, 1867); *Sir Joseph Neale McKenna's Statement to the Shareholders of the National Bank* (London, 1869); Edward O'Loughlin, *The National Bank, its Wrongs, its Rights, and its Remedies* (Dublin, 1869); Hall, *Bank of Ireland*, 224–31, 279–94.

23. However, McKenna's support of Parnell did not prevent his landed estate near Youghal from becoming a target of the Plan of Campaign in 1885–6. McKenna capitulated to his tenants in 1887 (Donnelly, *Nineteenth-Century Cork*, 317–18, 348).

24. *Irish Banker*, Aug. 1876, Feb. 1877, Aug. 1878, Mar. 1879.

25. 'The Late Run Upon the Bank of Ireland', *Bankers' Magazine* (1885), 954–6; Simpson, *The Belfast Bank 1827–1970*, 151–2, 224–5.

26. Hall, *Bank of Ireland*, 288–9; *Hansard*, 299 (1885), col. 1407.

27. *Cork Examiner*, 30 July 1885.

28. *Bankers' Magazine* (1904), 750–3, 851–2; *Hansard*, 134 (1904), 746, 774; 135 (1904), 931–2.

29. PRONI, T1107/35 (Merchant Banking Company v. William Spotten and others). Also Ollerenshaw, *Banking*, 110, 113.

30. Hall, *Bank of Ireland*, 319.

31. Cited in Milne (who did not identify the Hibernian), *Royal Bank*, 83–4. The Ulster Bank had already opened a branch in Blessington in 1918.

32. The Dublin Chamber of Commerce frequently complained about bank charges during the 1920s and 1930s. See Proceedings of the Council of the Dublin Chamber of Commerce (NA, 1064/3/19–20), passim.

33. G. Crowther, 'Report on the Irish Banking and Currency System' (unpublished, 1932; copy in IBSCA). As regards complaints about rates, e.g. IBSC minutes, 15 Dec. 1926, 19 Oct. 1927, 19 Jan. 1928, 23 Jan. 1928, 23 Sept. 1931, 28 Sept. 1931.

34. BofEA, G1/341 (minute by Niemeyer, 1 Nov. 1927).

35. Sir John Keane, a Governor of the Central Bank, gave evidence, but only on what he deemed to be the follies of Fianna Fáil fiscal policy.

36. *Reports*, 194–5.

37. For evidence that suspicion of bankers' monopolies was not confined to cranks in the interwar period, see Plumptre, *Central Banking*, 165–70; R. S. Sayers, *The Bank of England 1891–1944*, i (Cambridge, 1976), 236–7.

38. Michael Collins, *Banks and Industrial Finance in Britain 1800–1939* (London, 1991), 70–3.

39. CIBCC, *Reports*, 99, 199.

40. IBSCA, IBSC minutes, 18 Oct. 1933; BofEA, OV81/1 (Jacobsson to Glenavy and Sweetman, 11 Aug. 1938). See too Milne, *The Royal Bank of Ireland*, 85–6. For an analogous argument see William Lazonick, 'Industrial Relations and Technical Change: The Case of the Self-Acting Mule', *Cambridge Journal of Economics*, 3 (1979).

41. UCDA, P35b/20 (minute by R. C. Ferguson); Banking Commission, *Third Interim Report* (Dublin, 1926), 32.

42. The following paragraphs are based in part on material culled from the Transactions of the Court of Directors of the Bank of Ireland. I am grateful to Mr Terry Forsyth, the Bank's secretary, for allowing me to consult and quote from this source. For an astute analysis of the Bank's adjustment to the Irish Free State, see Fanning, 'The Impact of Independence'.

43. Andrew Jameson, for example, became a member of the Free State senate. By March 1927 he was having Kevin O'Higgins and his wife round to lunch in Howth, 'to walk round and see the Spring flowers and not to talk over affairs' (BofEA, OV19/19 [Jameson to Montagu Norman, 27 Mar. 1927]).

44. Bank of Ireland Governor Captain Nutting asked Montagu Norman for the names of individuals who 'could lay claim to some Irish ancestry'. Norman, fearing the appointment of Brennan (because 'he doesn't carry the guns for this position'), made two suggestions, but the Commission opted for Brennan. In thanking Norman for his trouble Nutting noted that 'many and varied considerations had to be taken into account which I feel sure you will appreciate' (BofEA, OV9/19; Nutting to Norman 10 Sept. 1927; Norman to Nutting, 17 Sept. 1927; Nutting to Norman, 20 Sept. 1927).

45. BofEA, ADM22/17 (Lord Glenavy to Henry Clay, 16 Feb. and 5 Apr. 1934); OV9/19 (Norman to Jameson, 25 Mar. 1927); OV81/8 (memo by L. Leveaux, 13 Mar. 1933).

46. BofIA, Transactions of the Court of Directors, 31 Aug. 1939. Also cited (in part) in Fanning, 'The Impact of Independence', 88. On the confidential assurances received by Dublin, see too the loaded hint in James Meenan, 'The Irish Economy During the War', in Kevin Nowlan and T. D. Williams (eds.), *Ireland in the War Years and After 1939–51* (Dublin, 1969), 29–30.

47. C. Wye Williams, letter to the *Albion*, 31 Mar. 1834; NA, D5925 ('Deed of Settlement of the City of Dublin Steam Packet Company').

48. Thomas, *Stock Exchanges of Ireland*, 138–40; E. A. French, 'The Origin of General Limited Liability in the United Kingdom', *Accounting and Business Research*, 21/18 (1990), 15–34.

49. *Statist*, 3 June 1893, 604–5; as cited in Thomas, *Stock Exchanges*, 154.

50. Ibid. 142–60.

Chapter 15

1. *PDDE*, 12 May 1932, 1673. Lemass became Minister of Industry and Commerce in 1932.

2. Quoted in Meenan, *George O'Brien*, 129.

3. Suppose e.g. the output elasticity of labour was 0.5% in 1914. Then a population of 8.5 million in 1914—the pre-Famine level—would have produced an average income one-half of Britain's.

4. The GNP estimate is due to L. M. Cullen, 'Income, Foreign Trade, and Economic Development: Ireland as a Case Study' (TS *c.*1976). It forms the basis for Lee's comparison with some other European countries *c.*1914 (in Lee, *Ireland 1918–1985: Politics and Society*, 512–14). Lee's (and Cullen's) numbers have been lampooned by Tom Garvin as 'far too high, perhaps by a factor of two' in his review of Lee in *IHS*, 27/105, p. 87. See also N. F. R. Crafts, 'European Nineteenth-Century Growth in Comparative Perspective', *OEP*, 36 (1984), 440; Kennedy *et al.*, *Economic Development of Ireland*, ch. 1; Angus Maddison, *Dynamic Forces in Capitalist Development: A Long-Run Comparative View* (Oxford, 1991), 6–7.

5. O'Connor and Guiomard, 'Irish Agricultural Output', Table 1, put 26-county consumption of feedstuffs, fertilizers, and seeds at £7.1m. in 1912.

6. Andy Bielenberg, 'The 1907 Census of Production and the 1911 Census of Population' (TS), and personal communication, 30 June 1992.

7. Calculated from data in Feinstein, *Statistical Tables of National Income*, Tables 9 and 59, and Kevin O'Rourke, 'The Costs of International Economic Disintegration: Ireland in the 1930s' (mimeo), data appendix.

8. *Report on the Trade in Imports and Exports at Irish Ports*, 1905–13; Thom's *Directory*. Note also (from Table 12.13 above) that the estimated value of beer and malt produced in the 26 Counties in 1912 exceeded that of the whole island in 1907. The volume, though not the value, of exports rose impressively over the same period.

9. The comparison assumes that average British incomes almost trebled over the same period. See also David Johnson, 'The Economic Performance of the Independent Irish State', *IESH*, 18 (1991), 48–53.

10. K. A. Kennedy *et al.*, *Economic Development*, ch. 1; N. F. R. Crafts, *British Economic Growth* (Oxford, 1985), ch. 3; Angus Maddison, 'A Comparison of the Levels of GDP Per Capita in Developed and Developing Countries 1700–1980', *JEH*, 43/1 (1983), 27–42.

11. T. J. Kiernan, 'The National Income of the Irish Free State in 1926', *EJ*, 43 (1933), 74–87; 'The National Expenditure of the Irish Free State in 1926', *JSSISI*, 15/91 (1932–3); Duncan, 'The Social Income of the Irish Free State, 1926–38'; id., 'The National Income of the Irish Free State', in CIBCC, *Reports*, (Dublin, 1938), App. 7.

12. Kiernan, 'The National Income of the Irish Free State in 1926', *JSSISI*, 43 (1933), 74–87; Kennedy *et al.*, *Economic Development*, 26; O'Rourke, 'Trade Destruction'.

13. G. A. Duncan, 'The Social Income of the Irish Free State, 1926–38', *JSSISI*,

16 (1939–40); id., 'The Social Income of Eire, 1938–40', *JSSISI*, 16 (1940–1); Kennedy *et al.*, *Economic Development*, 53–4 n. *The Economist*'s correspondent (13 Aug. 1938) thought Duncan's totals too low.

14. PDDÉ, *Reports*, 188–92; Mitchell and Deane, *Abstract*, 448. During the 1930s, the Irish capital market raised about £10 million for joint-stock companies, and the national debt also grew. The availability of such alternative outlets for saving *may* account, in part at least, for the stagnation in bank deposits. See too *JIBI*, 39 (1938), 79.

15. PDDÉ, *Reports*, 192; *JIBI*, (1938), 95; Thomas, *Stock Exchanges*, 182–9; Colbert, 'The Irish Free State', *Lloyds Bank Review*, 9/95 (1938), 3–18.

16. Daly, 'Government Finance for Industry'. The 'gap' was Ireland's version of the famous 'Macmillan Gap', blamed for holding back British industry in the 1920s.

17. Defining Class III (B–E) in the trade statistics (e.g. *Statistical Abstract 1939*, 92) as capital goods.

18. *JIBI* (1939), 87.

19. Kennedy *et al.*, Table 6.2.

20. C. H. Oldham, 'After the Fiscal Inquiry Report', *Studies* 13 (1924), 1–13. Also Meenan, *George O'Brien*, 128–9.

21. T. K. Daniel, 'Arthur Griffith on his Noble Head', *IESH*, 3 (1976), 56–65.

22. Maurice Manning and Moore McDowell, *Electricity Supply in Ireland: The History of the ESB* (Dublin, 1985), 17–53.

23. Compare R. B. Weir, 'Structural Change and Diversification in Ireland and Scotland', in Mitchison and Roebuck, *Economy and Society*, 297–307.

24. A recent analysis of the political context is Jeffrey Prager, *Building Democracy in Ireland* (Cambridge, 1986). See also Ronan Fanning, *The Four-leaved Shamrock* (Dublin, 1983).

25. James Meenan, 'Derating as a Means of Agricultural Relief', *Studies*, 26 (1937); Cullen, *An Economic History of Ireland*, 173–81. For the attitudes of academic economists, see Ronan Fanning, 'Economists and Governments: Ireland 1922–52', in Murphy, *Economists and the Irish Economy*, 138–56.

26. Walsh, who later resigned from the government, sought to influence the composition of the Tariff Commission 'in view of certain pledges he made at a recent Party meeting' (NA, S4594, 24 July 1926). His foreword to a pamphlet by a supporter saw the choice facing the state as one between 'ranching plus emigration on the one hand, or a growing prosperity based on intensive agricultural and industrial development on the other' (in John Sweetman, *Protection: Some Letters to the Press* (Dublin, 1926)).

27. *The Economist*, 26 Nov. 1927; Parliamentary Debates Dáil Éireann, 36 (1930), 109; Brian Girvin, *Between Two Worlds: Politics and Economy in Independent Ireland* (Dublin, 1989), 70–3; Ronan Fanning, *Department of Finance*, 205–6.

28. George O'Brien, 'Patrick Hogan', *Studies*, 25 (1936), 360–1. In the circumstances, Horace Plunkett's praise for Hogan as 'the best minister for agriculture in Europe' may seem excessive. See Stephen Gwynn, 'Ireland Since the Treaty', *Foreign Affairs*, 12 (1934), 321.

29. League of Nations, *World Economic Survey* (Geneva, 1939), 189. For average tariff rates, compare W. L. Ryan, 'Measurement of Tariff Levels for 1931, 1936, and 1938', *JSSISI*, 18 (1948–9), 109–33, and Friedman, *Trade Destruction* (Florida, 1974), Table 23. Despite the pitfalls involved in invoking the ratio of customs revenue to imports as a measure of protection (cf. League of Nations, *International Economic Conference: Tariff Level Indices* (Geneva, 1927)), the following results are also worth noting:

Customs Receipts as a Percentage of Imports in Several European Economies

Period	UK	Ireland	Denmark	France	Germany	Belgium	Norway	Finland
1925–9	9.1	11.4	5.3	7.7	7.8	3.3	10.3	18.9
1932–6	23.1	24.6	7.7	24.1	27.2	8.9	14.3	28.9

Sources: Mitchell and Deane, *Abstract*; B. R. Mitchell, *Abstract of European Historical Statistics* (London, 1975).

30. Official emigration data are poor, but age-cohort analysis tells the story. Of those who were aged 15–19 years in 1911 only about 63% were still living in Ireland (North and South) in 1926. However, 74% of the 15–24-year-old Southern cohort of 1926 were still living in the South in 1936. Emigration had been relatively higher in the South since the Great Famine. See too Eoin Mac Neill, 'Developments since Independence', *Foreign Affairs* 10 (1932), 235–49.

31. Fanning, 'Economists and Governments: Ireland 1922–52'; Keynes, 'National Self-Sufficiency'. Keynes began by outlining his own change of outlook from 'unshakeable Free Trade convictions'. Yet while 'finding much to attract [him] in the economic outlook of your present Irish government towards greater self-sufficiency', he questioned whether Ireland was large enough for more than 'a very modest measure of self-sufficiency'. Kennedy *et al.*, *Economic Development*, ch. 2, show more sympathy than most for the difficulties facing policy-makers in the 1930s and 1940s.

32. *Report of the Scottish Commission of Agriculture to Ireland* (Edinburgh, 1906), 34.

33. The claim is Patrick Kavanagh's, *The Green Fool* (Harmondsworth, 1964), 113.

34. NLI, MSS 19,546 and 23,833–6.

35. NLI, MS 19,546. Further deficits were to follow in 1931–4. The accounts of the Dunmore farm, part of the Ormonde estate in Kilkenny, show it barely breaking even in 1920–1 and making a huge loss in 1921–2, after five years of record-high profits (NLI MSS 23,833–6).

36. McKeever, 'Economic Policy in the Irish Free State', 84; D. Hoctor, *The Department's Story* (Dublin, 1971), 164; Kennedy *et al.*, *Economic Development*, 37 8.

37. McKeever, 'Economic Policy', 76–9.

38. Department of Agriculture and Technical Instruction, *Agricultural Output of Ireland, 1908* (Dublin, 1912).

39. Johnston, *Irish Agriculture in Transition* (Dublin, 1951); id., 'Aspects of the Agricultural Crisis at Home and Abroad', *JSSISI*, 15 (1935–6), 80. In a contribution in Seanad Éireann, Johnston asserted that were it not for the policies of the 1930s, national income would have been £20 million higher (*Seanad Éireann Parliamentary Debates*, 26 (1942), 2126).

40. Gillmor, 'The Political Factor in Agricultural History'. The index increased further to 27.9 in 1960, and then dropped back to 13.4 by 1985. For a rather similar analysis of industry North and South see D. McAleese, 'Do Tariffs Matter? Trade and Specialization in a Small Open Economy', *OEP* (1977), 117–27, and Ó Gráda, 'Do Tariffs Matter That Much? Ireland Since the 1920s', CEPR Discussion Paper No. 242 (1985).

41. Johnston, 'Price Ratios and Irish Agriculture', *EJ*, 47 (1937), 685; see also Johnston, *The Nemesis of Economic Nationalism* (Dublin, 1934). According to one critic, the ensuing slaughter of cattle turned James Ryan, the Minister for Agriculture, into 'a bovine Herod' (*Round Table*, 1933–4, 584).

42. O'Brien, *Eighteenth Century*, 417.

43. Horace Plunkett, 'Ireland's Economic Outlook', *Foreign Affairs*, 5 (1926–7), 205–18.

44. G. Fitzgerald, 'Mr Whitaker and Industry', *Studies*, 58 (1959), 146–7; M. Daly, 'The Employment Gains from Industrial Protection in the Irish Free State during the 1930s: a Note', *IESH*, 15 (1987), 71–5; Neary and Ó Gráda, 'Protection, Economic War and Structural Change'; Lee, *Ireland*, 193–4.

45. Thomas, *The Stock Exchanges of Ireland*, 184–9.

46. I am grateful to Mary Daly for this example. See also Jon Press, *The Footwear Industry in Ireland 1922–1973* (Dublin, 1989), 33, 46.

47. Ibid., 57–8; TCD, MS 9828, 205 ff (memoirs of R. M. Hilliard, Killarney merchant and boot manufacturer).

48. Mary Daly, 'Industrial Policy in Ireland and Scotland in the Interwar Years', in Mitchison and Roebuck, *Economy and Society*, 294; NA, S.11987B, 'Information Relating to Industries Established in 1932 and Onwards'. These data were prepared 'in connection with the Taoiseach's pre-election tour' of Jan.–Feb. 1948.

49. Gerschenkron, *Economic Backwardness in Historical Perspective*.

50. An analysis of the 70 biggest towns and cities (excluding Dublin and Dún Laoghaire) containing 2,000 or more people *c*.1914 produced a coefficient of variation of 0.69 in 1871, 0.66 in 1891, 0.63 in 1926, 0.59 in 1936, and 0.61 in 1946.

51. Compare Albert O. Hirschman, 'The Political Economy of Import-Substituting Industrialisation in Latin America', *Quarterly Journal of Economics*, 72/1 (1968), 1–32, cited in Girvin, *Between Two Worlds*, 204–5.

52. Kennedy, *Productivity and Industrial Growth: The Irish Experience* (Oxford, 1971), 43; Matthews, Feinstein, and Odling-Smee, *Economic Growth* Table 8.3. Kennedy also showed that the statistical association called Verdoorn's Law applied to inter-war Irish manufacturing, though with far less force than

elsewhere. The 'law', which claims that there is a close relation between the growth of output in manufacturing and the growth of productivity, is best seen as a loose affirmation of the presence of increasing returns to scale. Estimating the elasticity of output per worker with respect to output in cross-section across twenty sectors, Kennedy found that in inter-war Ireland it was about 0.2, instead of the 0.4–0.5 repeatedly reported in other studies.

53. Kennedy, *Productivity and Industrial Growth*, ch. 2.
54. K. S. Isles and Norman Cuthbert, *Economic Survey of Northern Ireland* (Belfast, 1957), 572, 578.
55. David Johnson, *The Interwar Economy in Ireland* (Dundalk, 1985), 31–2; Moss and Hume, *Shipbuilders to the World*, chs. 7–9; Geary and Johnson, 'Shipbuilding in Belfast', 52–8.
56. P. Ollerenshaw, 'Textile and Regional Economic Decline: Northern Ireland 1914–70', in Colin Holmes and Alan Booth (eds.), *Economy and Society: European Industrialisation and Its Social Consequences* (Leicester, 1991), 64–5; W. Black, 'Cyclical Variations in the Linen Industry', in Isles and Cuthbert, *Economic Survey*, 556–8.
57. Ollerenshaw, 'Textiles and Regional Economic Decline'; Johnson, 'The Northern Ireland Economy', in Kennedy and Ollerenshaw, *Economic History*, 194–7.
58. *Ulster Year Book 1950* (Belfast, 1950), xxxvii–ix.

Chapter 16

1. Cited in K. Whitaker, 'From Protection to Free Trade: the Irish Experience', *Administration*, Winter 1973, 40.
2. *Statistical Year-Book of the League of Nations 1939/40* (Geneva, 1940), 189. The decline in the United Kingdom's trade was 57%. Cf. A. Coppé, 'International Consequences of the Great Crisis', in H. van der Wee (ed.), *The Great Depression Revisited* (The Hague, 1972); P. Friedman, *The Impact of Trade Destruction on National Incomes* (Gainesville, Fla., 1974); Sven Grassman, 'Long-Term Trends in Openness of National Economies', *OEP*, 32/1 (1980), 123–33.
3. Fiscal Inquiry Committee, *Final Report* (Dublin, 1924), 47.
4. e.g. Fitzgerald, 'Mr Whitaker and Irish Industry'.
5. See Daly, 'An Irish-Ireland for Business'. For a more theoretical analysis of the issues see Neary and Ó Gráda, 'Protection, Economic War and Structural Change'.
6. Ryan, 'Measurement of Tariff Levels for Ireland'. Ryan's results are often invoked. See also D. McAleese, *Effective Tariffs and the Structure of Industrial Protection in Ireland* (Dublin, 1971).
7. Ryan used his estimates to compute 'the excess cost of protection', or the difference between the cost of producing protected goods in Ireland in the mid-1930s and their cost under free trade. Thus defined, the 'excess cost' was

substantial, but it did not represent the economist's standard measure of the loss from protection. Quite apart from the inflated estimates of protection, the net loss to Ireland was less, since the Government received the proceeds of the tariffs (presumably in lieu of alternative tax revenue). The connection between 'the excess cost of protection' and slow output growth is thus not clear, though Ryan's case might be seen as implicitly one about 'Harberger triangle' welfare losses. These are discussed further below. Meanwhile, for a textbook introduction to such welfare losses see D. N. McCloskey, *The Applied Theory of Price* (New York, 1982), ch. 10.

8. See e.g. League of Nations, *World Economics Survey 1938−9* (Geneva, 1939), 84.

9. NA, TID/207/5 (31 Jan. 1939), emphases in the original.

10. Isaac Butt, *Protection to Home Industry: Some Cases of its Advantages Considered* (Dublin, 1846), 44−5.

11. Proceedings of the Council of the Dublin Chamber of Commerce (National Archives, 1064/3). The Council passed another motion in the same vein in July 1932.

12. *PDDÉ*, 59, 850.

13. Canning, *British Policy Towards Ireland* (Cambridge, 1985), 127−30.

14. For details see Johnson, 'Cattle Smuggling', 44.

15. NA, S. 59 ('Memorandunm on Past Effects and Probable Future Consequences of the Financial Dispute with Great Britain', 13−14); *The Economist*, 23 Dec. 1933; 2 June 1934. On commerical tensions between the UK and Australia in the 1930s see John B. O'Brien, 'The British Civil Service and Australia between the Wars', in F. B. Smith (ed.), *Ireland, England and Australia: Essays in Honour of Oliver MacDonagh* (Cork and Canberra, 1990), 146−58.

16. *New Statesman and Nation*, 20 July 1932. Also Canning, *British Policy towards Ireland*, 149−53; Henry Harrison, *The Anglo-Irish Economic War of 1932−1934* (London, 1934).

17. Neary and Ó Gráda, 'Protection, Economic War and Structural Change', 260.

18. D. Nunan, 'Price Trends for Agricultural Land in Ireland 1901−86', *Journal of Irish Agricultural Economics and Rural Sociology*, 12 (1987), 69; NA, S.59 ('Memorandum on Past Effects and Probable Future Consequences', 17). According to the Finance memo, dairy producers were least affected, those specializing in young cattle, pigs, and poultry, worst hit.

19. A small point: the calculation takes no account of the consumer surplus accruing to Irish meat-consumers.

20. O'Rourke, 'Burn Everything English but their Coal'.

21. McMahon, *Republicans and Imperialists*; Jeffrey Frankel, 'The Embargo of 1807−1809', *JEH*, 42 (1982); *New Statesman and Nation*, Aug. 20 1938.

22. Johnson, 'Cattle Smuggling', 47−9.

23. *The Economist*, Oct. 26 1935. The 'special duty' on fat cattle was £6 per head.

24. *Belfast Newsletter*, 25 May 1933, quoted in Johnson, 'Cattle Smuggling', 46.

25. Jagdish Bhagwati and Bent Hansen, 'A Theoretical Analysis of Smuggling', *QJE*, 87 (1973), 172−87; D. A. G. Norton, 'On the Economic Theory of Smuggling', *Economica*, 55 (1988), 107−18.

Chapter 17

1. UCDA, P67/125.
2. UCDA, P67/121 [1937], also P67/125 [1938].
3. CIBCC, *Reports*, 304–6.
4. See also John P. Colbert, 'The Banking Commission in General', *Irish Monthly*, Sept. 1939, 603–23; id., 'The Irish Free State', *Lloyds Bank Review*, 9/95 (1938), 3–18. Colbert, chairman of the Industrial Credit Company and a somewhat reluctant signatory of Commission's Majority Report, noted that the 'prudent' economies singled out by the Commission for emulation 'had small debts because they have not been able to raise much debt', and that 'one might as well hold up a starved man as a model for the obese'.
5. *Statistical Abstract 1939*, 154–7, 173; Mitchell and Deane, *Abstract*, 459; Banking Commission, *Reports*, 198. T. E. Gregory, in the course of questioning John Leydon before the Banking Commission, claimed that the high rates offered on some preference shares implied a shortage of industrial capital, while conceding that government credit was sound (*Memoranda and Minutes of Evidence*, 1376–7).
6. Nevin, *Capital Stock*, 17–22. See also CIBCC, *Memoranda and Minutes of Evidence*, QQ. 2914–16.
7. The UK series is taken from the *Stock Exchange Weekly Official Intelligencer*. The Irish series are based on the official Dublin quotations for Wednesdays, as reported in the *Irish Times*.
8. This interpretation is confirmed by a co-integration analysis of the Irish and British series (see App. 17.1). This shows that movements in the two Irish series were co-integrated, but either Irish series and the British were not.
9. Keynes, 'National Self-Sufficiency', 187; James Meenan, *George O'Brien*, 170–1.
10. In *Seanad Éireann Parliamentary Debates*, 26 (1942), 2126.
11. Pratschke, 'The Establishing of the Irish Pound', 74; E. Nevin, *Textbook of Economic Analysis*-Irish Edition (London, 1963), 291 (as quoted in John Hein, *Institutional Aspects of Commercial and Central Banking in Ireland* ESRI Paper No. 36 (Dublin, 1967), 1).
12. Compare the case-studies in Harold James, Hakan Lindgren, and Alice Teichova (eds.), *The Role of Banks in the Interwar Economy* (Cambridge, 1991), and the long list of interwar banking crises in Ben Bernanke and Harold James, 'The Gold Standard, Deflation, and Financial Crisis in the Great Depression: An International Comparison', in Glenn Hubbard (ed.), *Financial Markets and Financial Crises* (Chicago, 1990), 51–3.
13. The banks were firmly opposed (e.g. *IT*, 26 Jan. 1933).
14. NA, S5185, minute of 29 Jan. 1926; IBSCA, IBSC minutes, 22 Dec. 1925.
15. On the wariness of bankers in other similarly circumstanced economies towards central banking, see A. F. W. Plumptre, *Central Banking in the British Dominions* (Toronto, 1940), 178–9.
16. Ibid. 4.

17. Ibid. 187; CIBCC, *Reports*, 224; Erin E. Jacobsson, *A Life for Sound Money: Per Jacobsson, a Biography* (Oxford, 1979), 131.

18. The Commission made the point, and de Valera conceded it later, during the protracted debate about the Central Bank Bill. See *PDDE*, 87, pp. 29, 119.

19. Curiously a very similar institution had been mooted in a Bank of Ireland memorandum prepared for the meeting with Montagu Norman in January 1922. This scheme for a Central Reserve Bank of the Irish Free State envisaged seven directors (including three from the banks and two from the business community), and one hundred percent backing in gold, notes and approved securities for note issue. See IBSCA, file X(iii), Jan. 1922.

20. UCDA, P67/173.

21. e.g. *Statement of Accounts of the Currency Commission for the Year Ended 31st March 1936*, P. 2306 (Dublin, 1936), 3.

22. Moynihan, *Currency*, 512.

23. Thomas, *Stock Exchanges of Ireland*, 164–71; CIBCC, *Memoranda and Minutes of Evidence*, 395–426 (evidence of G. L. Kennedy and J. F. Stokes of the Dublin Stock Exchange); BofIA, Court of Governors Transactions, 1923–39, *passim*.

24. Colbert, 'The Irish Free State', 14–18; Industrial Credit Company, *Twenty-One Years of Industrial Financing 1933 to 1954* (Dublin, n.d.); Daly, 'Government Finance for Industry'.

25. e.g. Steven Broadberry, 'The North European Depression of the 1920s', *Scandinavian Economic History Review*, 32 (1984), 159–67.

26. BofEA, OV81/9, memoranda by Leveaux and Niemeyer, 11 and 23 Sept. 1931.

27. BofEA, C43/466.

28. UCDA, P67/139, 'Memorandum on certain financial and economic aspects of the annual payments by Saorstát Éireann to Great Britain' (4 Oct. 1932); Fanning, *Department of Finance*, 207–8; Currency Commission, *Report for the Year Ending 31 March 1932*, P. No 729 (Dublin, 1932), 5; Moritz Bonn, *Wandering Scholar* (London, 1949), 318–19.

29. UCDA, P67/105(3), P67/105(2) (letters from MacEntee to De Valera, 23 Feb. 1933 and 31 Jan. 1934).

30. BofEA, OV81/1 (Ernest Harvey to Joseph Brennan, 30 July 1934).

31. See n. 9 above. O'Brien was a trusted friend of the banks. Asked by the IBSC in June 1932 for advice 'as to the case which can be made by them in the event of the appointment of a Banking Commission', he felt unable to comply, but got them Geoffrey Crowther (future editor of *The Economist*) instead.

32. NA, S2235A (letter from Hugh V. Flinn to É. De Valera, 13 Apr. 1935). See too Lee, *Ireland*, 199–200.

33. BofEA, OV81/1 (Jacobsson to Otto Niemeyer, 20 Dec. 1937).

34. As early as Apr. 1935 Hugh Flinn, parliamentary secretary to McEntee, predicted the eventual split into majority and minority camps very well in an amusing letter to De Valera. He was wrong about Seán Ó Muimhneacháin and Robert Barton (both government supporters), however; they signed the Majority Report. See NA, S2235A, 13 Apr. 1935.

35. CIBCC, *Reports*, 122–3.

36. Moynihan, *Currency and Central Banking*, 209, 211, 216. Lord Glenavy, the Bank of Ireland's man on the Commission, was handsomely rewarded by the Bank for his services (Bank of Ireland Court Transactions, 22 July 1937). Like other bank representatives on the Commission (though not other members), he was allowed to send a substitute to meetings. George O'Brien sat on the Commission at the behest of Lord Glenavy (Meenan, *George O'Brien*, 136–8).

37. *The Economist*, quoted in Moynihan, *Currency and Central Banking*, 224. *The Economist*'s correspondent was George O'Brien!

38. Hein, *Institutional Aspects*, 13.

39. Seán O Faoláin, *De Valera: A New Biography* (Harmondsworth, 1939), 140; UCDA, P80/1116(1) (draft of a memorandum on the Irish Question by Desmond FitzGerald).

40. Barry Eichengreen and Jeffrey Sachs, 'Exchange Rates and Economic Recovery in the 1930s', *JEH*, 45 (1985), 925–46; Ben Bernanke and Harold James, 'The Gold Standard, Deflation, and Financial Crisis in the Great Depression: An International Comparison', in R. G. Hubbard (ed.), *Financial Markets* (Chicago, 1991).

41. *International Labour Review*, 15 (1927), 128; 26 (1932), 108; 39 (1939), 391.

42. *Fiscal Inquiry Committee Reports*, App. A. The data reveal that both skilled and unskilled male workers had the edge in Ireland in 1923, and that Irishwomen had almost caught up with British women. The war eroded skill differentials in Ireland substantially; in 1914 skilled industrial workers earned more than twice as much as unskilled workers, in 1923 less than half more. See also O'Rourke, 'International Migration and Wage Rates in Twentieth Century Ireland'.

43. Compare Daly, 'The Dublin Working Class, 1871–1911', 127–8.

44. CIBCC, *Reports* (Minority Report III by Peter O'Loughlin), 640; NA, F88/6/33. Jacobsson is cited in Erin E. Jucker-Fleetwood, 'Many Thanks, Mr. Chairman: The Irish Banking Commission 1934–8 as seen by Per Jacobsson', *Central Bank of Ireland Quarterly Bulletin* (Dec. 1972), 81 n. The 1942 Statistical Abstract (p. 92) put the higher increase in female unemployment since 1930 down to 'the industries which have been created or which have developed most since that year [being] those in which normally the majority of employees are females.'

45. Johnson, *Interwar Economy*, 40–2.

46. Deeny and Booker, 'Male Linen Weavers'; Deeny, 'Poverty as a Cause of Ill-health'. While neither study is based on a random sample, Deeny sought expert advice in his efforts at making the subjects 'typical'. Only able-bodied males were considered, and women suffering from chronic ailments or who were pregnant at the time of the survey were excluded. I calculated the BMIs from data in Deeny's study. Deeny (*To Cure and to Care*, 40–7) also identified some cases of pellagra, an acute dietary-deficiency condition, in the Lurgan area in 1941.

47. Social conditions in the Dublin's tenement slums had attracted a lot of attention in the 1900s and 1910s. See e.g. 'Report of the Departmental

Committee Appointed by the Local Government Board for Ireland to Inquire into the Housing Conditions of the Working Classes in the City of Dublin', BPP (7273) 1914, XIX, 61; Charles Cameron, *How the Poor Live* (Dublin, 1908); Daly, *Deposed Capital*, esp. ch. 9; Lee, *Ireland*, 193; Horner, 'From City to City-region'. For an evocative account of the move from the inner city to one of the new housing estates, see Kathleen Behan, *Mother of All the Behans* (London, 1984), chs. 4—5.

48. *Report of the Rotunda Hospital, Dublin for the Year Ended 31st December, 1938* (Dublin, 1938), 56—7. Inner-city apartment complexes such as those on Usher's Quay and Townsend Street were also constructed in the 1930s.

49. Cited in Tim O'Neill, 'Poverty and Administrative Reform in Ireland 1815—1845' (lecture to Irish Historical Society, 11 Oct. 1983).

50. Lee, *Modern Ireland*, 195; Ronan Fanning, *The Four-leaved Shamrock: Electoral Politics and the National Imagination in Independent Ireland* (Dublin, 1983). Fianna Fail's share of the vote south of the Liffey rose from 35.4% in September 1927 to 55.8% in 1938, and on the north side from 25.3 to 46.4%. Its nation-wide share rose from 35.6 to 51.9%.

INDEX